The Evolution of the
American Economy

THE EVOLUTION OF THE AMERICAN ECONOMY

ECONOMY

Growth, Welfare, and

Decision Making

SIDNEY RATNER

JAMES H. SOLTOW

RICHARD SYLLA

Basic Books, Inc., Publishers   *New York*

Library of Congress Cataloging in Publication Data

Ratner, Sidney, 1908–
  The evolution of the American economy.

  Includes bibliographies and index.
    1. United States—Economic conditions. 2. United
States—Economic policy. I. Soltow, James H., joint
author. II. Sylla, Richard Eugene, joint author.
III. Title.
HC103.R34   330.973   78–13838
ISBN: 0–465–02127–1

CONTENTS

———

PART I

From Colonialism to National Independence
(1492–1790)

PART II

The Agricultural Era and Emerging Industrialism
(1790–1860)

PART III

The Transformation of the American Economy
(1860–1914)

PART IV

The Superindustrial Economy
(1914–1979)

ACKNOWLEDGMENTS

This volume embodies the knowledge and insights that each of us has gained from specialized research; we are, however, acutely conscious of our great debt to the research and analyses of many other economists and historians. We feel a special obligation to those who have framed and tested theories about the major developments and factors in American economic growth, welfare, and decision making. The range of our indebtedness to "old" and "new" economic historians is indicated by the works cited in the text and by the suggested readings at the end of each chapter.

In this joint venture, James Soltow, of Michigan State University, wrote the chapters on the colonial and early national periods and on American industry, 1860–1914. Richard Sylla, of North Carolina State University, contributed the chapters on the period 1790–1860; on money, banking, and public finance, 1860–1913, 1914–1979; and on transportation and communications, 1860–1913. Sidney Ratner, of Rutgers University, wrote the introduction and the majority of the chapters dealing with the period 1860–1913 and the period 1914–1979. He conceived the original plan for this book and, as senior author, had the responsibility of coordinating it.

Professor Stanley Engerman, of the University of Rochester, read portions of the manuscript and made valuable suggestions. Professor Louise Rosenblatt, of New York University, gave much-appreciated stylistic advice. We are grateful to Martin Kessler, president and co-publisher of Basic Books, for his constructive criticism and wholehearted support. Maureen Bischoff, editorial manager of Basic Books, brought exceptional interest and expertise to the production of the book. Helpful secretarial assistance was given by Geraldine DiCicco, Carolyn Kappes, Betty Kaminski, and Karen Praul in Princeton, New Jersey, and by Ruth Ann Struble, Glenda Fulmer, and Ann Cooke in Raleigh, North Carolina.

During the writing of this book, Sidney Ratner received a sabbatical leave from Rutgers University, and James Soltow received an All-University Research Fund grant from Michigan State University.

We wish also to express our indebtedness to our students. Over the years, the stimulating interchange of ideas with them in courses in American economic history has contributed much both to the substance and form of this book.

The Evolution of the
American Economy

INTRODUCTION

━━

The Study of Economic Growth, Welfare, and Decision Making

In this volume we attempt to carve out a fresh perspective on the history of the American economy from the abundant new source materials, novel techniques, and challenging interpretations that have emerged in recent years. The old economic history is now considered obsolete. A new American economic history is being energetically created on both a quantitative and a qualitative level. Traditional assumptions about the structure, the efficiency, and the equity of the American economy are being reexamined. New questions have been raised about the customary methods of explaining the genesis and development of American institutions—economic, social, and political. The champions of the new economic history have called for enlarging the scope of quantitative measurement and the consideration of alternative ways in which different sectors of the economy might have evolved—for example, transportation without railroads. This is called counterfactual history. Radical economists have urged paying more attention to the welfare of disadvantaged or oppressed groups. Concurrently some scholars have stressed the importance of entrepreneurs in introducing creative innovations into the economic system, while others have underlined the expanded role of government in dealing with the critical problems of depression, recovery, economic growth, and war.

These new winds of economic and historical thought have quickened interest in American economic history. In this volume we shall explore the development of the economy of the United States, from its roots in the primitive economy of the North American Indians and in the mercantile capitalism of Elizabethan England and Renaissance-Reformation western Europe to the position that the United States holds in the twentieth century as the greatest industrial country in the world, with the highest standard of living of any large country in the world. Our book is addressed to college and university students in economics and history who wish not only to learn the important facts about the development of the American economy, but also to see the complex factors involved in economic change through the prism of the best-tested theories advanced to explain it.

Three themes will be emphasized: economic growth, economic welfare, and decision making. Many American economic histories in the past have been predominantly narrative. Some that have stressed economic analysis have done so by focusing on the special characteristics and growth patterns of different sectors of the economy. A few that have dared to present a general theory of American economic growth have tended to overstress certain factors or to advance an oversimplified stage theory of development. By contrast, this work will combine an analytical narrative of economic growth with an evaluation of economic welfare in four major economic periods. In addition we focus on the important role decisions by different social groups and their leaders have played in shaping and changing the structure of the economy.

The conditions of economic progress will be analyzed so as to throw light on the changes in the structure and the efficiency of the American economy as an increasingly large percentage of the working population first shifted from agriculture to manufacturing and then to the service industries. Attention will also be given to subjects that often have not received adequate treatment in past textbooks, such as the relative distribution of wealth and income at different periods among different social groups, the role of government and of private enterprise, and the economic skills and contributions of various cultural groups.

Because we cannot treat all phases of American economic development with equal thoroughness, our work will center on the main phases, the turning points, and the trends in American economic history. The epic sweep and increasingly complex processes of American economic growth, we believe, can best be understood when studied in four periods: (1) From colonialism to national independence, 1607–1790; (2) the agricultural era and emerging industrialism, 1790–1860; (3) the transformation of the American economy, 1860–1914; and (4) the superindustrial economy, 1914–1979.

Economics and Economic History

THE SCOPE OF ECONOMICS

If we are to comprehend the scope of economic history, we have to have some grasp of economics as an independent discipline and as a storehouse of tools for use by the economic historian. Economics has been characterized by noted economists in at least three different ways. Alfred Marshall, the great Victorian economist, stressed the quest for material welfare and defined economics as the study of the production, exchange, distribution, and consumption of goods and services needed to satisfy individual and group wants. A complementary approach to Marshall's is that of institutional economists like John R. Commons, who view economics as the study of relationships among different property-owning groups—landowners, merchants, and industrialists—and between these groups and their workers. This second approach has been used to reveal the social status and the economic power position of different social groups within the same hierarchy.

A third approach, made famous by the English economist, Lionel Robbins, defines economics, in his words, as the "science which studies human behavior as a relationship between ends and scarce means which have alternative uses." * This definition has become accepted by nearly all contemporary economists. It has wide implications for the general public. All of us have to establish priorities or scales of preference among the things we want, and we have to allocate our limited time, energy, money, and materials in order to get as many of the desired things as possible. We often have to sacrifice certain things we want because getting them would require giving up other things we want more. Economics seeks to help us use our scarce resources to achieve our goals. It aids us in understanding how far the substitution of one thing or service for another can be used to satisfy some of our wants.

But important as this third (Robbins) definition of economics has become, it supplements, rather than supplants or contradicts, the two prior definitions. In practice most economists use all three approaches, depending on the kind of problem they are dealing with and the emphasis they wish to give to one approach as against the others. This situation inspired Jacob Viner, a distinguished American economist, to say, "Economics is what economists do." * His statement implies that any narrow definition is arbitrary and that economics is not a rigidly closed discipline but is as broad as the various issues economists explore.

A list of the major subjects studied by economists and by economic historians from both a theoretical and an empirical point of view embraces a study of (1) the factors of production—land and other natural resources, capital, labor, and management; (2) problems of supply and demand in markets ranging from pure competition to monopoly; (3) the allocation of scarce resources in agriculture, manufacturing, and the serv-

* Lionel Robbins, *The Nature and Significance of Economic Science*, 2nd ed. (London: Macmillan Co., 1937), p. 16.
* Alan A. Brown et al., eds., *Perspectives in Economics* (New York: McGraw-Hill, 1971), p. 3.

ice industries under different forms of business and government organization; (4) the distribution of wealth and income; (5) the role of domestic
and foreign trade; (6) the functions of money, banking, credit, and the
price system; (7) the importance of taxes and government spending; (8)
the rate of economic growth; and (9) the overall levels of local, state,
and national income.

Another way of viewing what economists do is to divide their field
of activity into microeconomics and macroeconomics. Microeconomics is
centered like a microscope on the study of individual decision units—individuals or households as consumers or as producers—and the process
whereby their interrelated decisions determine the relative prices of goods
and the factors of production. By contrast, macroeconomics is focused on
broad aggregates of individuals and commodities for the whole economy,
or for major subdivisions of the entire economy, such as national income,
total consumption, investment, government spending, the quantity of
money, and the balance of payments. Hence, this division of economics
is primarily concerned with the problems of depression and inflation,
unemployment and high-level employment, and the rate of economic
growth.

THE RANGE OF ECONOMIC HISTORY

Economic historians work on the same empirical subjects as economists do, but from a long-term perspective. Although the variety of topics
economic historians explore can be staggering, in recent decades two subjects have acted as magnets. One is the economic growth of nations over
long periods of time and the causes or determinants of that growth. That
subject is one of the major themes of our book. Another is the economic
welfare of groups within a society, especially as measured by the concentration or distribution of wealth, income, and other forms of economic
power—for example, control divorced from ownership of property. This is
another of our central themes.

DECISION MAKING IN ECONOMIC HISTORY

Most history books present a narrative of past conditions and events
as if the events occurred as inevitably as in classical Greek drama, with
the sequence of actions undertaken by individuals seen only from the
standpoint of the present. The author and the reader look back upon a
past that seems dead, finished, without the possibility of ever having
developed in a different way. This dogma of inevitability leads to a
frozen–block universe in which men are forced to do precisely what they
do, and there is only one course for the march of events.

This retrospective view of a closed, rigidly determined universe is
opposed to a history based upon modern science, which presents an

open universe where men help to determine the course of events by making choices among several possible policies and risking in certain cases their lives, their careers, or their fortunes. The character and intelligence displayed by men and women in their decisions are crucial elements in the determination of their success or failure. This kind of history is written from the prospective point of view and presents history in the making. The focus is on decisions such as those that led to the shaping of the colonial economy within the British world empire, the formation of the Constitution, the expansion of the frontier, the rise of the factory system, and the development of a unique mass-production/mass-consumption economy.

American economic history becomes most useful and alive when scholars and students explore the problems confronted by various decision makers—statesmen, farmers, industrialists, merchants, bankers, workers—at various turning points in their personal careers and in American history. Insight into historic decision-making processes will be gained by examining (1) the various objectives desired; (2) the resources that were considered available; (3) the various courses of action that might have been taken; (4) the gravity and extent of the risks that were taken; and (5) the consequences of the adopted policies for the decision makers and for those affected by their decisions. By so doing, we understand better the significance of the choices made by the historical decision makers from their own points of view. Then we come to see more clearly how their wise or unwise decisions made their future, which we have inherited from them as our past. History becomes a laboratory in which we can reconstruct the experiments in living performed by the millions of diverse human beings who have inhabited this country and have made it what it is today. We, in turn, will have to make our decisions on varied economic issues such as inflation, unemployment, the energy crisis—and, by so doing, make our country's future and become part of the history that our children will explore. The important thing for most of us is that we can benefit from the experience of others and that we can make our own decisions with some sense of historical perspective. Thereby, we link the past with the present and with our vision of the future.

SUGGESTED READINGS

Some lively discussions on the nature of economics and economic history can be found in Alan A. Brown et al., eds., *Perspectives in Economics* (New York: McGraw-Hill, 1971); Nancy D. Ruggles, ed., *Economics* (Englewood Cliffs, N.J.: Prentice-Hall, 1970); and Douglass C. North, "Economic History," *International Encyclopedia of the Social Sciences*, vol. VI (New York: Free Press, 1968), pp. 468–473. The most

PART I

FROM COLONIALISM TO NATIONAL INDEPENDENCE

(1492-1790)

INTRODUCTION

The colonial period, covering almost one half of the total American experience, began in 1607 with the effort by an English trading company to plant a small settlement of only a few more than one hundred men and boys in what is now Virginia. By 1790, America was not only an independent nation of almost four million people but, more important, possessed a well-developed market economy, a relatively high level of wealth, and the economic institutions and entrepreneurial leadership to embark upon the course of industrialization that was just getting under way in England. The theme of part one is how transplanted Europeans and their descendants, in exploiting the abundant resources of the North American continent, created a rapidly growing market economy and moved toward a considerable amount of autonomy in economic decision making even before they had won political independence.

Settlement of America began at a time when middle-class or entrepreneurial values as well as market institutions were growing in importance in Europe. Through a process of selective migration, the colonies that England established attracted not a cross section of society but an unusually large proportion of people who had come to believe in the virtue of individual achievement and in the acquisition of material goods as a goal in life. In short, these men and women were willing to invest themselves and whatever capital they possessed in the process of colonization because they believed that hard work, frugality, and diligence paid off more handsomely in America than in Europe. In contrast to many other colonial societies, where the labor of the indigenous population was harnessed to the purpose of Europeans, English colonizers replaced the native people with members of their own race and with black slaves from Africa.

In the economy that evolved in the seventeenth and eighteenth centuries, staple commodities produced for export became the engine of growth, as settlers capitalized on the abundance of resources and especially on the fertility of the soil. However, as economist Watkins points out in elaborating a staple theory of economic growth, what is important is "the impact of export activity on domestic economy and society." *

---

* Melville H. Watkins, "A Staple Theory of Economic Growth," *Canadian Journal of Economic and Political Science*, vol. 29 (1963), p. 144.

The southern mainland colonies, along with the West Indies, produced tropical and semitropical commodities for the European market and remained dependent upon England for commercial services and most manufactured goods; they thereby fulfilled the economic role of a colony and perpetuated a pattern of dependence, leading eventually to a "staple trap," or inability to change when their staples no longer served as an engine of growth. On the other hand, the northern colonies became integrated into the European economy in a distinctive way, with the unplanned result that more autonomy in decision making developed in this region than one would normally expect in a colony. From new centers of entrepreneurial initiative in this broad region came direction for the basic transformation of American economic life that occurred in the nineteenth century.

British regulation did not impose a serious economic burden on the colonies in terms of growth or welfare, and having ties with the strong British economy proved beneficial. Nevertheless, British mercantilism and British rule in general came to be viewed as obstacles to the attainment of greater autonomy in the northern colonies and as the cause of the continuing economic dependence of the southern provinces. Political independence made possible continued evolution toward economic independence, with businessmen, the principal economic decision makers, taking advantage of new opportunities created by the sweeping away of legal restrictions on enterprise. When the "crisis of legitimacy" of the new nation was resolved by the adoption of the Constitution, America was a leading nation in world commerce and was ready to take economic advantage of the sweeping technological changes occurring in European industry.

CHAPTER 1

———

America and the Developing World Economy

America had its beginnings as a part of the economic expansion of Europe. Starting in the fifteenth century, western Europeans moved to organize close and continuous economic relations with large parts of Africa, Asia, and the Western Hemisphere, trading with some regions and settling in others. This was a European-centered world economy, as the imperialists expected to derive most of the benefits to be gained from the economic ties that they established with other continents. In the process elements of the western European economy were transferred to new environments.

In this chapter we will examine first the European economic concepts and institutions that furnished the means and much of the motivation for overseas expansion. Not always had Europe possessed the ability to dominate so much of the world. It was from the expansion of their economy over many centuries that Europeans gained the power to widen their economic horizons. The second section of the chapter will focus on the overseas expansion of Portugal, Spain, Holland, and France, the four nations that together with England supplied leadership in the creation of a world economy. As we shall see, not all national states practiced imperialism in precisely the same manner, nor did all attain the same measure of long-run success. The third section reviews the economic developments in England that enabled that nation eventually to achieve leadership among European imperialist nations. We shall emphasize the train of events leading to England's planting of the settlements in North America in the early seventeenth century which much later became the nucleus of the United States.

Commercial Revolutions in Europe

Europeans were unable to take advantage of their first discovery of America, made by the Vikings around the year 1000. At that time, Europe was characterized by low levels of population, production, and consumption. Most people were engaged in subsistence agriculture and lived in small, largely self-sufficient communities where activities were carried out in traditional ways—a system called manorialism. For the ordinary person this organization of economic and social life held a basic security; in an era of political turmoil, a warrior class of lords of the manor provided protection for the inhabitants of the village, who in return gave their labor. But there existed few other opportunities and little mobility for the ordinary individual who, in effect, was tied to the land he worked.

However, Europe was on the eve of a commercial revolution, which extended over the next several centuries. Production, population, settled areas, and towns grew significantly, along with an increased emphasis on market-oriented economic activity carried on for profit. Businessmen acquired more power in economic decision making, a function previously performed almost exclusively by landowners.

BUSINESS AND INTERNATIONAL TRADE

The basis of the commercial revolution of medieval Europe was the large-scale growth of international trade, particularly between the eastern Mediterranean and western Europe. From Asia, Europeans imported a variety of luxury goods, spices being the most important. To the East they exported raw materials like copper, tin, and lumber, and an assortment of manufactured goods, principally woolen and linen cloth. Italy was the pivot of this trade. Merchants of Venice, Genoa, and other cities, who controlled much of the commerce around the Mediterranean basin, established colonies, or trading posts, at strategic locations in the Levant. There they purchased goods that had been carried by Arab middlemen along sea and land routes from the East Indies, India, and China, and then distributed them throughout western Europe. The Crusades helped to stimulate the expansion of this trade, as merchants increased the capital at their disposal with the profits earned outfitting and transporting expeditions of crusaders to the Holy Land. A second area of economic strength appeared in Flanders, centering around the manufacture of woolen cloth for export to Italy and to other parts of Europe. Hand in hand with the growth of international commerce went an increase in regional and local trade as more and more people were incorporated into the evolving market economy of Europe.

The pioneer in developing new patterns of trade through western and central Europe was the traveling merchant, who personally accompanied his goods to market. For example, Flemish merchants carried cloth south to the Italian marts, while Venetian traders moved with spices north across the Alpine passes to Germany and the Low Countries. They met other merchants in towns, where they disposed of their merchandise and acquired a new set of wares for the journey home. Over time the traveling merchant as a dominant figure in international trade yielded to the sedentary merchant, who concentrated on planning and directing his affairs from his countinghouse instead of spending much of his time in travel.

More sophisticated business practices were developed to carry on the increasingly larger volume of long distance trade. The sedentary merchant often relied upon agents who transacted his business in faraway places for a commission; he might perform the same function for businessmen who lived in other parts of Europe. New forms of partnership were worked out, sometimes for a single venture and sometimes for a stipulated term of years. The invention of double-entry bookkeeping made it possible for each businessman to know more precisely the state of his business, which was particularly important if he worked with or through a number of other individuals. Business correspondence carried by couriers supplied a network of information on which to base decisions about projected ventures. Merchants assumed leadership in forming a body of international commercial law, including procedures to enforce contracts. To spread the risks involved in shipping, the ownership of a vessel was divided into shares held by several or many owners.

Perhaps the single most important innovation made by medieval businessmen was banking, which evolved from their money-changing activity. Merchants accepted deposits of funds for safekeeping, settled the affairs of clients by making transfers in their account books, and made loans. To settle balances arising from transactions at distant places without incurring the risk of shipping precious metals, merchant-bankers devised the bill of exchange, an instrument that resembles our modern check. The bill of exchange became a credit device; interest was charged but concealed in the rate of exchange to evade medieval regulations against usury.

A second commercial revolution occurred in the latter part of the fifteenth and through the sixteenth centuries and was characterized by a further expansion of a market economy. Techniques that had been earlier developed in Italy for the rational conduct of business were now diffused through much of the rest of Europe, as the invention of printing facilitated the spread of information in published manuals about deposit banking, bills of exchange, and double-entry bookkeeping. There was a significant expansion of selling on credit. Innovations in marketing, such as using samples to sell commodities traded in large volume, contributed to an improvement in economic efficiency. This period was marked by the shift of economic leadership from Italy and the Mediterranean to northwestern Europe and the Atlantic, with the overall balance of economic strength within Europe influenced by Portugal's development of a new route to Asia, Spain's discovery and exploitation of the treasures of the Western Hemisphere, and the vigorous commercial growth of England and Holland—themes to which we shall return later.

As opportunities in international trade expanded, businessmen developed a new form of association, the chartered company, to combine enterprise and capital in the conduct of commerce with distant areas. Such ventures usually required a relatively large amount of capital, carried a high degree of risk, and involved the conduct of business in an alien environment. A charter granted by the government of a national state conferred upon a company special privileges, such as a monopoly of a branch of commerce and politico-judicial rights in its trading area abroad. One type of chartered company—the regulated company—evolved out of the medieval guild system. With only professional merchants eligible to join, each member traded on his own account, earning profits from his own enterprise, but each had to accept the rules imposed by the company. Businessmen were encouraged to invest capital in new forms of trade, since participation in a cartellike organization protected them from competition by nonmembers. Slowly growing out of the regulated company was the joint stock company, which more nearly resembled today's corporation. The joint stock company also received a charter from the government, conveying economic and politico-judicial privileges, but it traded as a company, using pooled financial resources. Membership, which was not limited to merchants, was attained by the purchase of shares, which in time came to be traded on organized exchanges. The joint stock company served to mobilize large amounts of capital for risky ventures, since its shares could be readily converted to cash and held by anyone with capital to invest, and its special privileges conferred the potential of monopoly profits. The chartered company contributed to the organization of European economic relationships with other continents and played an important role in colony building.

MERCANTILISM

While the expansion of the market had the overall effect of widening the scope of individual decision making, there existed a consensus among leaders in sixteenth and seventeenth-century Europe that the economy should be regulated by government for the purpose of increasing the power of the national state—an approach to economic policy that later came to be called mercantilism. As costs of government rose with the growth of bureaucratic administration and the escalation of military operations, rulers of national states seeking to enlarge their political authority became ever more aware of the relationship between the amount of revenues that could be raised and the wealth of the population, or at least of its richest members. Thus, the government of each national state held a vital interest in economic expansion. At the same time various business groups searched for ways to advance their own welfare through specific measures or policies of government, particularly where they could argue that their own interests paralleled those of the state.

Mercantilists put emphasis on achieving the economic self-sufficiency of the nation, an understandable objective in an era of almost constant warfare among European nations. Special attention was directed to the importance of a favorable balance of trade: exports should equal imports plus specie. Some economic advocates known as bullionists stressed the need for the nation to build up a store of gold and silver in order to be able to purchase military and other supplies when needed. But mercantilism embraced a broader sphere than trade balances and supplies of precious metals. Policy makers recognized the importance of manufactures; they put into effect tariff protection, grants of monopoly, and subsidies to encourage the establishment and growth of industries deemed essential to the national welfare. Authorities imposed maximum wage rates to keep labor costs low, but they also regulated the price of foodstuffs to reduce popular pressure for higher wages. Since a merchant marine and a strong business community brought to the nation earnings from carrying freight and performing commercial services, each national government imposed regulations and discriminatory taxes and duties to encourage its own shippers and traders at the expense of foreigners. Finally, colonies could contribute to the economic self-sufficiency of the nation by providing supplies of wanted goods not produced in the European national state, including not only tropical commodities like sugar but also defense materials such as naval stores and timber for shipbuilding and ship repair.

A MARKET ECONOMY

By the sixteenth and seventeenth centuries the influence of the market extended more widely and penetrated more deeply than ever before. Agriculture still predominated in Europe in terms of the labor force and the total product; the clergy and the nobility continued to occupy top positions in the social structure. But a speculative spirit of gain had spread through large segments of European society. Business values, particularly a belief in the legitimacy of profit taking, were becoming more respectable, a contrast to the almost universally held assumption of an earlier era that subsistence was the appropriate goal of economic activity. Modern economic concepts were beginning to be reflected in writings that recognized the link between prices and supply and demand as well as a relationship between risk and interest in moneylending. Entrepreneurial values did not totally replace traditional doctrines even among members of the business class, as merchants of these centuries often headed their ledgers: "In the name of God and profit." As a result of the commercial revolutions, a true market economy operated through much of Europe, which generated the enterprise and the capital invested by Europeans in the creation of economic bonds with Asia, Africa, and the Americas. The interest of political leaders in the expansion of the economic power of the national state, expressed through mercantilistic policies, gave encouragement to business leaders seeking profits through overseas ventures.

Imperial Leaders

Many motives led Europeans to take part in the overseas expansion of the fifteenth, the sixteenth, and the seventeenth centuries. Some men were guided by religious considerations, a desire to strike down or to convert the heathen. Others hoped to advance the glory of their national state. Some were stimulated by an intellectual curiosity to determine the shape and nature of the earth. Still others looked for adventure as a way to escape from a humdrum life. But most included in their calculations a hope to gain personal wealth.

The immediate impetus to the Age of the Discoveries was the search for a passage to the Far East, the source of spices and other luxury goods. Venice, by its control of access to these goods in eastern Mediterranean markets, maintained a monopoly of their distribution in western Europe. The goal of the national states along the Atlantic—Portugal, Spain, Holland, France, and England—was to outflank the Venetian position by finding another route to Asia. With the discovery of the Western Hemisphere, bullion became for a time the principal attraction to Europeans. But sooner or later, as the growing wealth of European society generated demand for a wide range of products, the New World came to be seen as a source of bulk supplies of agricultural produce and other raw materials.

If a variety of motivations impelled Europeans to participate in overseas expansion, it was the technological progress of the fifteenth and the sixteenth centuries that enabled them to undertake voyages of exploration to distant places and to extend their control over large areas of the world. Improvement in the rigging and hull design of sailing vessels resulted in ships capable of carrying more cargo, with smaller crews, for long voyages. Advances in navigational techniques—the astrolabe to determine latitude, the compass to determine direction, and maps and charts to show geographical data—were essential. The development of nautical gunnery —particularly innovations in gun mounting which made possible the use of larger pieces—gave European ships a marked superiority in weaponry over non-European ships. When small bands of Europeans confronted large native forces in battle on land, the decisive factors for achieving victory were the former's military skill and discipline acquired in the constant warfare of Europe, the superiority of metal over stone weapons, and the diplomatic talent of encouraging divisions among rival political groups and leaders.

Major imperial rivals were Portugal, Spain, Holland, France, and England. Initially Europeans did not wish to settle in the overseas areas. Rather, they thought in terms of trade, to tap into an existing system of production and internal marketing already organized by the native population. To them a colony was what it had been in the Middle Ages—a community of traders located in the midst of an alien population. Ultimately Europeans came to perceive the economic advantages to be gained by organizing production. In contributing to the creation of a European-centered world economy, each power came into contact with other areas possessing a unique mix of human and natural resources, which influenced the specific pattern of colonialism it imposed. In addition, while western Europe was evolving along some common lines, each nation possessed its own economic and social characteristics that governed its ability to perceive and to act upon colonial opportunities.

PORTUGAL

The Portuguese, like other western Europeans, had a strong ambition to replace Venice in the spice trade. But geographical position helps to explain why this small country on the edge of Europe made the initial thrust in overseas expansion: It was in the best location from which to carry out a flanking operation to bypass the Venetians. Moreover, the Portuguese had assumed an early leadership in maritime technology, due primarily to the efforts organized by Prince Henry the Navigator, a member of the royal family. Then, too, Portugal as the most unified national state in fifteenth-century Europe could throw the full strength of governmental machinery into expansion even before businessmen developed institutions to carry on large-scale commercial activity in distant places. In the absence of internal warfare there existed individuals with military skills whose interest in battle could be directed abroad. Not only might they gain wealth, but they might also undermine the power of Islam, now expelled from Portugal itself, by continuing the struggle against the Moors beyond European shores.

Through the fifteenth century Portuguese expeditions explored farther and farther along the west coast of Africa, gaining valuable geographical knowledge and, significantly, developing a profitable trade in gold, slaves, and other African commodities. Their objective was not to acquire territory, or even to produce goods, but rather to plug into existing systems of trade. They established fortified factories, or trading posts, at strategic points along the coast, to which they diverted trade that previously had

moved across the Sahara. However, the Portuguese did settle in the unin-
habited Azores and Madeira Islands, where they established sugar plantations that were worked by slaves transported from Africa.

Portugal's long search for a passage to the Far East around Africa was
ended when Bartholomeu Dias rounded the Cape of Good Hope in 1488
and Vasco da Gama reached India in 1498. The Portuguese moved quickly
to establish by naval force a widely dispersed seaborne empire in Asia.
Through the sixteenth century they dominated the maritime trade of the
Indian Ocean from a series of forts and factories linked by sea power
superior to that of any native state in the region. Not only did the Portuguese organize regular shipments of spices and other Far Eastern products
to Europe, but they also carried on an extensive trade within Asian waters
as far as China and Japan. As in Africa, the Portuguese did little to
impinge on domestic production and trade in the Far East but, to provide
cargoes for their ships, they relied upon the existing commercial network
operated by Muslim merchants.

However profitable its commercial empire may have been, Portugal
lacked the resources to maintain and defend it. The country's small population was insufficient to provide the manpower needed to staff naval
forces and forts in the Far East. Neither could it build a fleet of ships
large enough to exploit fully the opportunity that it had created. Finally,
the Portuguese never completely closed the old route through the Red
Sea to Levant markets; this pattern of trade, under the direction of
Venice revived significantly by the middle of the sixteenth century, undermining Portugal's monopoly of the growing market for spices and other
luxury products in western Europe. When more powerful European states
—Holland and England—challenged its supremacy in Asia in the seventeenth century, Portugal lost its Far Eastern empire almost as quickly as it
had gained it.

The Portuguese were also present in the Western Hemisphere, claiming a vast area of eastern South America. However, Portugal initially displayed less interest in Brazil than in Africa and the Far East, because in
Brazil there were no trading systems already organized to bring valuable
cargoes to the coast for sale and shipment. Brazil's major asset was an
abundance of fertile land, but it was obvious that agricultural production
would have to be organized under European direction if the region was
to be integrated into the world economy. Since the government of Portugal, already engaged in building its seaborne empire, lacked the ability to
finance and organize colonization, it delegated much of the responsibility
to private individuals, using the *donatario* system which had been employed earlier to colonize Madeira and the Azores. The king made large
grants of land to individuals on condition that they launch the settlement
process; the *donatarios* also received political and judicial powers. The
Portuguese already knew how to cultivate sugar and recognized the growing European demand for that commodity. The major obstacle was labor.

The ordinary people who migrated, whatever their social circumstances in the old country, had little intention of doing hard work in the new. Settlers first sought to organize the natives into a labor force, but they eventually imported slaves from Portuguese Africa. Sugar quickly became the base of the Brazilian economy. By the end of the sixteenth century a leading planter boasted "that the sugar of Brazil was more profitable to the Iberian monarchy than all the pepper, spices, jewels, and luxury goods imported in the Indiamen from 'Golden' Goa." * Sugar remained the leading product of Brazil through the colonial period, although new economic booms resulted from the discovery of gold in the late seventeenth century and of diamonds in the early eighteenth, stimulating an increase in immigration from Portugal and slave importations from Africa. Cattle ranching and stock raising also became important activities in several areas. But in the middle of the eighteenth century the sugar-producing regions of the colony still accounted for more than one-half of Brazil's population of around one and one-half million.

Portugal was a pioneer in the expansion of Europe; but the profits of imperialism did not contribute to its own economic strength. From the beginnings of overseas activity the Portuguese had to use most of the earnings derived from trade with other areas of the world to pay for manufactured goods imported for home consumption as well as for export. Portugal, a tiny country with a huge colony, literally lived on its colony's productive energies. While the economic weakness of Portugal resulted in part from its small resource base and the drain of some of its most vigorous people to the colonies, a major factor was the lack of a strong business community. It was principally Genoese, then Dutch, and finally English merchants who supplied the essential entrepreneurial services to Portugal. By the eighteenth century England, not Portugal, was the major beneficiary of the colonial economy of Brazil. Indeed, Portugal itself had become an economic colony of England.

SPAIN

While the Portuguese were carrying out voyages of exploration along the west coast of Africa, seeking a route to the Far East, the Spanish were absorbed in creating a national state and completing the recovery (*Reconquista*) of their lands from the Moors; the latter task they accomplished in 1492. When the Spanish did turn to overseas expansion, they had to take into account Portuguese achievements. Under existing concepts of international law, recognized by treaties between the two Iberian nations and confirmed by papal bulls, Portugal held a monopoly of the southeast passage to the Far East. Thus Spain, in authorizing and backing the voyages of Christopher Columbus, concentrated on find-

---

* C. R. Boxer, *The Portuguese Seaborne Empire, 1415–1805* (London: Pelican, 1973), p. 107.

ing another route to Asia—a southwest passage. Belief in the feasibility of Columbus' proposition was encouraged by the notion that Asia lay not too far distant to the west, since existing geographical knowledge greatly underestimated the circumference of the earth. Instead of reaching the Far East, the Spanish discovered and laid claim to a vast new continent, whose extent they only slowly came to realize.

From the beginning gold was the lure for the military adventurers who organized expeditions, first to Hispaniola and Cuba and then to the mainland. Frontiers of plunder were opened to Spaniards with the conquest of Mexico and Peru, accomplished by the middle of the sixteenth century. But even the highly developed societies of the Aztecs and the Incas produced little that was in demand in European markets. Thus, after they had seized the treasures accumulated by the Indians, the Spaniards had to create an economic system to tap the great wealth of natural and human resources in the Western Hemisphere.

It was spectacular silver discoveries in the 1540s, in Peru and Mexico, that opened up great new economic opportunities for the Spanish in America. For a century and a half mining dominated the economies of these two provinces. Agriculture was organized to provide food supplies for the mining regions and for the large urban communities that developed at Mexico City and Lima to administer the political, economic, and religious affairs of the viceroyalties. Mining suffered a temporary decline in the middle of the seventeenth century, but it recovered and reached new heights of production by the latter part of the eighteenth. Now, however, silver no longer occupied the dominant position in the economic life of Spanish America. Both Mexico and Peru achieved a broader economic base; the expansion of industrial and agricultural production and the growth of intercolonial trade created a greater measure of self-sufficiency than had been characteristic of early years. In addition, the Spanish undertook in the eighteenth century the development of peripheral areas that had previously been neglected. Colonies in and along the Caribbean—notably Cuba, Puerto Rico, Venezuela, and Colombia—became major producers of sugar, cocoa, and other tropical commodities for export to Europe. Ranching developed as the economic base of present-day Argentina and Paraguay, while production of wheat, wine, and fruit expanded in Chile.

In Mexico, Peru, and several other areas, the Spaniards encountered a native population with a highly organized society and economy in which the heavy work of agriculture was an accepted aspect of life for the ordinary person. The Spanish inserted themselves at the top level of society, replacing the Indian upper class, and encouraged a reorientation of production to meet their own needs. The masses of the Indian population supplied the labor, willingly or unwillingly. Since the Spanish government prohibited enslavement of the native peoples of America, settlers devised other forms of forced labor. In the early decades of colonization, the encomienda, a semifeudal institution developed in Spain during the *Reconquista*, was employed to harness the labor of Indians to European purposes. The encomendero was authorized to collect tribute in the form of labor from Indian villages. When the encomienda system was abolished by the Spanish government on the grounds that it posed a political threat to the crown, it was succeeded by peonage, or debt bondage, by which large numbers of Indians, nominally free wage earners, were effectively tied to the haciendas, or large estates, on which they worked. Another system of forced labor—the *mita*, or a draft of Indian workers— was employed in Peruvian mining.

For the native populations, however, the most disastrous result of the Spanish conquest and occupation was demographic. Within a little more than a half-century after Columbus' first voyage, the Amerindian people of the Caribbean region were virtually annihilated, a result of European diseases and the unaccustomed pattern of disciplined labor imposed by the Spanish. To replace native workers Spaniards quickly initiated the import of slaves from Africa, where climatic conditions were similar to those in the West Indies. Slavery of blacks became the prevalent form of labor in this region.

In the highland areas of Spanish America, demographic disaster was almost as severe. An estimated pre-Conquest population of twenty-five million in central Mexico dropped to perhaps slightly over one million by the end of the sixteenth century. In the central Andes the early sixteenth-century population of somewhere between three million five hundred thousand and six million may have declined to as few as six hundred thousand in the middle of the eighteenth century. The initial drop in population was caused by epidemics of European diseases to which the Indians lacked immunity. The hardships of forced labor and cultural shock then contributed to the continuing decline of population, as Spanish colonists attempted to adjust to a reduction of their labor supply by a more intensive exploitation of the survivors. Then at various times in the seventeenth and the eighteenth centuries in various regions the population stabilized and resumed growth.

Spain had created a vast empire that produced great wealth, but it proved to be a failure at the business of imperialism, unable to derive lasting benefits from the treasures of the New World. By 1700, Spain was clearly an economic backwater of Europe. Much of the wealth that had been acquired from the New World was consumed by the aristocracy, the bureaucracy, the church, and the military. Businessmen never gained positions of influence, power, or prestige in Spanish society. The result was that American silver paid for the import of goods that Spain's economy was unable to produce, so that her imperial rivals were the ultimate beneficiaries of the integration of the Western Hemisphere into the European-centered world economy. Trade was closely controlled, but from the beginning this failed to prevent foreigners from participating in colonial commerce; Genoese and Dutch merchants found ways to work through the formal regulatory machinery created by the Spanish government. By the eighteenth century Spain's inability to meet many of the economic needs of its colonies made it increasingly difficult to defend them against the commercial penetration of its empire by the strong nations of Europe. The economic expansion of Spanish America in the eighteenth century served only to increase the attractiveness of that market to French and English business.

HOLLAND

The first to take advantage of the growing weakness of the Iberian powers was Holland, a province of Spain until its war of independence in the latter part of the sixteenth century. The Dutch held a position of leadership in the trade of northern Europe, based on their efficiency in commerce, shipping, and shipbuilding and on their central geographical location. They carried bulky commodities from the Baltic region to the Low Countries and much of the rest of western Europe, returning salt, fish, wine, woolen textiles, and increasing amounts of Asian and American goods purchased in Lisbon and Seville. By the early years of the seventeenth century Amsterdam had established itself as the business metropolis of Europe—the principal commodity market, a major shipping point, and the most important banking center.

When continued warfare with Spain disrupted the trade of Holland with the Iberian countries, the Dutch realized that they would have to develop their own trade with the New Worlds in order to maintain distribution of Asian and American goods in western Europe. After initial efforts to find a northeast passage around Russia proved unsuccessful, the Dutch government chartered the United East India Company to challenge the Portuguese directly in the Far East and along their southeast passage via the Cape of Good Hope. With a monopoly of trade between Holland and Asia, this joint stock company's large supply of permanent capital facilitated long-term investment in ships, warehouses, trading posts, and other commercial facilities as well as in large amounts of trading goods for voyages that lasted as long as five years. The company also possessed the naval power to oust the Portuguese from the Indonesian islands, where its principal interests lay. Not only did the Dutch expand significantly the volume of trade beyond levels attained by Portugal, but by the end of the seventeenth century they were conducting commerce involving a far more diversified range of goods. The company also developed an important source of earnings by extensive participation in the inter-Asiatic trade, holding a monopoly of Japan's trade for two centuries.

While the East India Company was expanding Dutch commercial interests in Asia, the West India Company, chartered in 1621, was conceived as an instrument to undermine the power of Holland's archenemy

Spain in the Western Hemisphere, with the government subscribing almost one-seventh of its original capital. However, merchant-directors concentrated the activities of the West India Company mainly against Portuguese possessions, which were considered softer militarily than the wealthy but heavily fortified Spanish provinces of Mexico and Peru. An exception was the capture of the entire Mexican silver fleet in 1628. The company's major effort was the conquest of Portuguese Brazil, an area with which it was familiar since Dutch shippers already controlled much of the transatlantic sugar trade. For a time in the 1630s and 1640s the Dutch occupied at least one-half of the sugar-producing regions of Brazil; they also seized Portuguese strongholds in West Africa, gaining control of the slave trade. When the Dutch were forced out of most of Brazil, they continued to dominate for at least another decade the trade in slaves to the Western Hemisphere.

By comparison with its concerns in South America and Africa, New Netherlands in North America was of slight importance to the West India Company. The prospects of a supplementary income from the fur trade, already established by Dutchmen in the Hudson Valley, induced the company to make a small investment in colonization. But for some time directors of the company were unable to evolve a consistent policy for development of the colony. Maximization of profits from the fur trade required enforcement of the company's monopoly of that trade; this in turn involved discouragement of agricultural settlement, since each colonist represented a potential smuggler. On the other hand, Dutch claims to this territory could be better enforced if the colony had a larger population engaged in farming. In order to minimize commitment of its own resources in this area peripheral to its activities, the company in the late 1620s introduced the patroonship system, a way of delegating to private individuals much of the responsibility for organizing agricultural settlements. Using a semifeudal form for a modern purpose of capitalistic economic development, the company made large grants of land to patroons on condition that they settle at least fifty families within four years. With the failure of this system, the directors appealed directly to individuals and families to migrate to improve their economic opportunity. Not only did the company provide grants of land to new settlers, but it now opened up the fur trade to all residents of the colony. Company earnings would be derived from shipping, from taxes imposed on exports and imports, and from the sale of slaves. Although the company did not succeed in recruiting many settlers from Holland or other northern European countries, Dutch policy did serve to attract groups of migrants from New England, who formed new settlements in various parts of the colony. Although a majority of the population of about ten thousand in the early 1660s engaged in farming, the fur trade continued as the economic mainstay of New Netherlands. From New Amsterdam the Dutch by the middle of the century had organized a large part of the carrying trade of the English colonies in the Chesapeake and the Caribbean. This was one factor contributing to England's decision in 1664 to take over the Dutch holdings in the Hudson Valley, as well as those along the Delaware which the Dutch had seized from the Swedes in the 1650s. From the vast efforts undertaken by the West India Company, only Guiana in South America and a few Caribbean islands remained in Dutch control. Clearly Holland was far less successful as an imperialist in the Western Hemisphere than it was in the Far East.

In the middle of the seventeenth century Holland was the greatest trading nation of the world, with commercial outposts in Asia, Africa, and the Americas as well as throughout Europe, all focused on a sophisticated system of exchange at Amsterdam. The nation had a productive agriculture and a diversified industry in addition to its highly efficient commercial sector. Economic energy and enterprise found a hospitable environment in Holland; in no other country did businessmen exercise more power, influence, and prestige. Indeed, the directors of the East India Company could write to the governing body of the Dutch Republic: "The colonies of the East Indies are not acquisitions made by the state, but by private traders who may sell them if they wish, even to the king of Spain or to any other enemy of the United Provinces." *

By the eighteenth century Holland was no longer the economic leader of Europe. Competitive advantages in shipping, shipbuilding, and commerce held by the Dutch were reduced as other maritime nations copied their methods. Holland as a small country was unable to deal effectively with the economic threat to its position posed by English and French mercantilistic measures. Equally serious was the military and naval strength that far larger countries deployed against the Dutch in a series of wars between 1650 and 1680. Warfare undermined Amsterdam's entrepôt position and gave its maritime competitors a chance to take over a portion of what had been Dutch carrying trade. Underlying these developments was the fact that Holland's population and resource base was too small to support a worldwide imperialism on a competitive basis once larger national states developed ways to mobilize their own resources.

FRANCE

With the decline of the Iberian powers and the inability of Holland to maintain its commercial supremacy, France and England came to be the principal contenders in the struggle for imperial leadership. The interest of France in North America began in the sixteenth century, when the French king promoted several voyages of exploration to seek a northwest passage to the Far East. On the basis of these and other expeditions in the

* E. E. Rich and C. H. Wilson, eds., "The Economy of Expanding Europe in the Sixteenth and Seventeenth Centuries," in *Cambridge Economic History of Europe*, vol. 4 (Cambridge: Cambridge University Press, 1967), p. 249.

seventeenth century, France established claims to a large part of the North American continent—the St. Lawrence Valley, the Great Lakes region, and the Mississippi Valley.

The initial economic activity of the French in North America was in the fisheries of Newfoundland and the Banks. This led to the discovery of an even more lucrative resource of the North American continent—furs; the demand for them grew rapidly as beaver hats came into style in western Europe. Like Europeans elsewhere, French fur traders for some decades dealt not with the producers, the Indian hunters, but with intervening native traders who took European goods inland and brought furs down to trading posts like Quebec, which was founded in 1608. However, after the 1670s the fur trade underwent a major reorganization as the locus of hunting moved westward into the Great Lakes area and even farther. The French no longer depended entirely upon Indian middlemen. They now organized their own transport and distribution systems, making direct contact with the western tribes, the sources of furs.

It was clear that only through permanent settlement of a significant population could this territory be held against foreign encroachment. Protection of the fur trade was important not only for its own sake as a profitable business enterprise, but also because policy makers in France came to regard it as a key to the control of the interior of the continent. During a period of over a century and a half, France tried various methods to stimulate settlement. In 1627 the government chartered the Company of One Hundred Associates, to which it delegated much of the responsibility of organizing colonization. The company was to receive title to a large grant of land (the entire North American continent!) on condition that it settle four thousand people within fifteen years.

After the failure of this company and others chartered for similar purposes, the government, beginning in the 1660s, developed plans along new lines to stimulate population growth and to promote diversification of economic activity. Royal authorities would sponsor immigration, provide subsidies to large families, and encourage soldiers to settle in the colony after their terms of service. But the government would again delegate much of the responsibility for colony building, this time to private individuals rather than to chartered companies. Under a system of modified feudalism to be established in New France, men with capital and enterprise would become seigneurs, or nobles, by undertaking to settle farmers on tracts of land they had been granted. However, the system did not achieve the success anticipated by its planners. French peasants did not perceive enough of a material advantage to induce them to migrate in large numbers. Yet an attempt to lure settlers by reducing their feudal obligations appeared to reduce the profit potential of the seigneurial system, thereby diminishing the incentive to the seigneur to invest in the development of the colony. Under any system the harsh climate and the limited amount of arable land along the St. Lawrence would have discouraged the expansion of farming. And the fur trade was an ever-present attraction to labor and capital, offering the freedom of the wilderness and the possibility of getting rich. New France had attained a population of about fifty-five thousand by the middle of the eighteenth century—no more than 5 percent of the total of the English mainland colonies at that time. The colony had become barely self-sufficient in its food supply. Some industry, chiefly centered around shipyards and ironworks, had developed. But fur remained the only important export. Because of its narrow economic base, New France did not become an important market for French manufactured goods, except those that entered the fur trade.

Louisiana, France's other large province in North America, was even less developed; it had a population of about four thousand in the 1740s. Exports of indigo, tobacco, and naval stores supported a small trade with France. New Orleans, founded in 1718, served intermittently as a base for an interloping trade with nearby Spanish colonies. In short, Canada and Louisiana represented in the words of Lawrence Gipson, "enormous parasites clinging to, and nourished by, the royal treasury," as both provinces required increasing subsidization from the French government.

France's major imperial success in the Western Hemisphere was in the Caribbean. Guadeloupe, Martinique, and Saint-Domingue were among the wealthiest of the West Indian colonies, and produced coffee, chocolate, and cotton as well as sugar. A flourishing slave trade furnished a supply of labor from French posts on the Guinea Coast of Africa. Colonial trade contributed to the growth of Bordeaux, Nantes, and other Atlantic ports in France. But this expansion of commodity imports was not matched by a growth of exports of manufactured goods. Paradoxically, the expansion of the French West Indies served as an engine of growth for the English mainland colonies, which furnished them with foodstuffs. France's inability to develop agriculture in Canada to supply her tropical possessions thus encouraged migration to the colonies of her archenemy, which helped to create the population pressure that eventually crushed New France.

France, the largest national state of western Europe, was unable to create a viable overseas empire. As a continental power France was heavily involved in land warfare and the struggle for territory in Europe, using resources that might otherwise have been invested in colonial development and in a larger navy to protect its lines of communication and supply with its overseas possessions. Significantly, the peculiar process by which the French national state was formed gave extensive economic power to government and limited the influence of business, as compared with England and Holland. Regulation of almost every aspect of industry and commerce in the seventeenth and the eighteenth centuries restricted the mobility of labor and capital and stifled initiative and innovation. Merchants of the Atlantic ports were aware of the potential for expanding foreign and colonial trade; but they found that chartered companies dominated by government officials held monopolies of the French trade with much of Asia, Africa, and the Western Hemisphere and thus reduced the attractiveness of overseas investment by business. The basic problem for France was the inability of business and government to find a close identity of interest in promoting the nation's colonial expansion.

TOWARD A WORLD ECONOMY

Each of these four nations contributed to the creation of a world economy centered on Europe. Portugal, the early leader, demonstrated the profitability of establishing direct commercial relations with Africa and Asia. In Brazil the Portuguese pioneered in the development of plantation export agriculture, using slave labor from Africa, to incorporate a distant region into the European economy. The Spanish discovered the greatest treasures of any European imperialist and spurred adventures of other nations to seek sources of precious metals in other parts of the Western Hemisphere. While the wealth of America did not serve to strengthen Spain's economy, the large increase in specie did help to stimulate economic expansion in other areas of Europe in the sixteenth century; this in turn further expanded demand for the products of the New World. For Latin America, the "success" of export-oriented mining and agriculture, using forced labor, encouraged a pattern of economic colonialism, or dependence, that was difficult to change even after the achievement of political independence in the nineteenth century. In view of the economic backwardness of the Iberian colonies' mother countries, it is not surprising that Brazil and Spanish America did not develop vigorous business communities.

Holland held the center of the imperial stage for a short time. In the Far East the Dutch developed patterns of intensive exploitation of their colonial relationship with non-Europeans. In the Western Hemisphere Holland's commercial activity tied several parts of North America closely into the European economy. France attained some measure of success in developing staple commodities for the European market—fur in Canada and tropical commodities in the West Indies. However, the North American empires of both Holland and France rested on narrow economic and demographic bases. The developmental efforts made by these two powers ultimately benefitted England, which took over most of the colonies established by the Dutch and French. How the English prepared themselves to become the most successful European colonizers forms the subject of the next section.

Expansion of England

Several factors contributed to England's rise to economic prominence. The nation's insular position conferred an initial advantage, enabling it to avoid heavy involvement in European wars and to concentrate on building the sea power essential to maintaining overseas possessions. Its small size facilitated the early development of a national state and thus a national market, but at the same time, its resource base was broad enough to support a wide range of economic activity. Significantly, in no other country (except Holland) did businessmen attain the extent of power, influence, and market freedom, or ability to make and carry out decisions on the basis of anticipated profits. While the French government was expanding controls over industry and commerce, England was creating an institutional framework that enabled entrepreneurs to exploit economic opportunities with a minimum of restraint.

Over the course of the sixteenth century the English economy changed at a fast rate. Manufacturing expanded and became more diversified. Woolen textiles, the leading export industry in the Middle Ages, grew in volume and in the variety of cloths produced. Shipbuilding and metal working increased in importance, while the development of coal as a low-cost energy source led to expansion of soap making, brewing, and dyeing.

In agriculture, the enclosure movement represented an acceleration of a trend away from subsistence farming toward production for the market. This required a reorganization of property rights that took decision-making power away from members of the village community, who held land under various forms of tenure, and put it in the hands of profit-oriented entrepreneurs; they then could adjust land use to the demands of the market. In the sixteenth century, opportunity lay in producing wool for the growing textile industry; the landlord who could find a way to turn tenants with small holdings off the land could then shift the land from cultivation to sheep pasture. In English society land was increasingly perceived as not just a means of subsistence for the community but as a form of capital investment. The modern institution of private property, including the concept of autonomy of individual decision makers, was what most English settlers carried to America. Private property had increasingly replaced the variety of legal relationships to the land that had characterized the medieval open-field system and its communal organization of decision making.

FOREIGN TRADE AND OVERSEAS EXPANSION

England's first contact with the Western Hemisphere came in 1497 as a result of the voyage of John Cabot, who had been authorized by the king to search for a northwest passage to the spice markets of Asia. The most important immediate result of Cabot's explorations was to draw attention to the treasure of the sea, the cod fisheries of Newfoundland, in which England developed a substantial interest.

During the first half of the sixteenth century the buoyant European markets for woolen cloth, which could be reached through the exchange facilities at nearby Antwerp, drew the attention of English exporters. The Merchant Adventurers, a regulated company, held a monopoly of the trade, sending fleets across the Channel twice a year and maintaining an English House staffed by young men who could take advantage of the opportunity to learn about the most sophisticated ways of doing business then known in Europe. When the European boom tapered off, and Antwerp's position as an entrepôt was undermined, English merchants were stimulated to search for markets outside of the traditional pattern of trade with the Low Countries inherited from the Middle Ages.

The chartered company proved to be the most useful device to develop new markets and trade routes. Pooling capital and enterprise in a joint stock company and securing a monopoly from the crown were of great advantage in carrying on commerce that involved long voyages, heavy expenses to initiate business, lack of immediate profits, overhead costs of operating warehouses and other facilities, and perhaps diplomatic negotiations with foreign rulers. Beginning in the 1550s a series of chartered companies worked to open up new areas to English trade. The Eastland Company conducted most of the direct trade between England and the Baltic, not only a valuable market for woolen cloth but, more important, a source of naval stores for England's shipbuilding industry. One objective of the Muscovy Company was to find a northeast passage to Asia, but it was more successful in developing a fur trade with Russia. In the last quarter of the sixteenth century, the Levant Company captured from the Venetians the commerce to England in spices and other Asian commodities that still flowed through the long-established markets of the eastern Mediterranean. Then, with the chartering of the East India Company in 1600, England made a direct challenge to Portugal's monopoly of the southeast passage around Africa.

At the same time that England was expanding its trade to the Baltic, the Mediterranean, and other parts of Europe, business and political leaders were looking for ways to gain access to the wealth of Spain's empire in America. When Spanish officials prevented the establishment of regular trade, the English turned to smuggling and then to privateering. Each year in the last decade of the sixteenth century as many as two hundred English ships sailed to the Caribbean to extract what wealth they could from the Spanish Main.

However profitable privateering was for the sea dogs and their financial backers in England, some policy makers were urging the establishment of permanent settlements in the areas of North America not occupied by the Spanish. The first English attempt at colonization grew out of the revival of interest in finding a northeast passage, with Sir Humphrey Gilbert's venture in the 1580s to found a settlement in New-foundland. A few years later Sir Walter Raleigh organized an effort to plant a colony on Roanoke Island (in what is now North Carolina), de-signed primarily as a support base for English privateers operating in the Caribbean. These unsuccessful ventures were small forerunners of the much greater effort toward creating settlements in North America that England mounted in the seventeenth century.

ESSENTIAL ELEMENTS OF COLONIZATION

When England began to organize settlements in North America in the early seventeenth century, there was little precedent to follow. Coloni-zation had been undertaken in Ireland, but it had not been entirely suc-cessful. The experience of Spain did not furnish a useful model, since the Spanish had attained their greatest profits in areas where they found a combination of silver mines and a native population that could be uti-lized as a labor force. It was not certain that the English would find such a combination of resources and labor in the regions of the Western Hemi-sphere that they claimed. However, England was able to furnish the neces-sary elements of colonization: organizational methods and funds of capital, people to migrate, a favorable governmental policy, and a flow of infor-mation about opportunities.

1. Trade was the keystone of colonization: Profits from trade fur-nished much of the capital, while prospects of expanded commerce created an incentive for investment in overseas expansion. Many of the same businessmen who had led the way in opening commercial relations with Russia, the eastern Mediterranean, and the Baltic, were searching by 1600 for new investment opportunities in the Western Hemisphere. They applied the organizational method they had earlier used—the char-tered company—to develop new markets and trade routes. While mer-chants served as the dynamic force in organizing and arranging the financ-ing of early colonial ventures, wealthy landowners also made substantial investments. Drawing upon profits derived from market-oriented agricul-tural enterprise, nobles and gentry perceived their participation in large-scale trading and colonizing companies as a means to advance national goals as well as a source of personal gain.

2. Several developments resulted in situations that encouraged more migration from England—individuals, families, and groups—than from any other national state. One development was an intensification of middle-class values and a growing emphasis on individual achievement, material success, and upward mobility. To some Englishmen who felt blocked by the high price of the land they needed to expand their farming operations,

and to others who experienced difficulty in gaining a foothold in the established business community, America did indeed seem a land of opportunity. A second development involved the Reformation settlement in England which left two dissatisfied groups: Roman Catholics and Puritans (Calvinists). These minorities were too large and too tenacious to be suppressed, but in an era of close association of church and state, governmental authorities regarded religious freedom as dangerous. Political leaders looked with increasing favor upon colonization as a way to relieve them of the necessity of dealing with minority problems at home; the prospect was particularly attractive because many members of both religious groups had sufficient funds to finance their own migration. A third development, the enclosure movement in agriculture, in combination with other changes of the sixteenth century, contributed to demographic dislocation and a belief that the nation was overpopulated. Colonization was seen as a way to relieve the nation of its surplus manpower at home and at the same time to resolve what seemed to be a shortage of labor in the colonies. A system of indentured servitude was organized to allow people who lacked funds to pay for passage to America with their own labor.

3. Colonization of English America was accomplished in the main by individuals and groups in the private sector, but each project required a charter or grant from the monarch, conferring not only a wide range of economic rights (land titles and trading monopolies) but also extensive political and judicial authority. The government lacked ability to organize and finance settlements overseas, but it did have the power to influence the course of colonization through the distribution of privileges. Organizers of each colonizing venture bargained with the crown over the specific mix of privileges to be conveyed in the charter. However, the set of rights granted to private individuals or groups had to be justified in broad social, economic, and political terms. It was mercantilism that provided a rationale for the extensive exercise of power by private individuals and groups. Thus, projectors of colonies had to show how their ventures would contribute to an increase in the economic strength of the nation.

4. Decisions about investment of money and human capital in colonization rested upon the information (or often misinformation) available about potential opportunities, circulated at the time through the printed word. In the late sixteenth and the early seventeenth centuries, proponents of English expansion like the Richard Hakluyts (cousins) collected and published accounts of explorations and settlements to excite broad interest. They then added arguments that they thought would make colonization attractive to potential investors, traders, migrants, and government policy makers. Appeals were made along several lines: business profits, national glory and prestige, religion, and the ability of individuals to improve their social and economic position. In addition to the general litera-

ture promoting colonization, the founders of colonies, anxious to attract recruits, issued pamphlets extolling the virtues of their own particular settlements.

Summary

The creation of a world economy within which English colonization took place can best be viewed as an outgrowth of a long-run expansion of the European economy, highlighted by a shift in emphasis from subsistence as a goal to market orientation and profit making. Business played a central role in the development of institutions, practices, and concepts of fundamental importance in the European conquest of large parts of the non-European world. These institutions, practices, and concepts were carried to America by settlers, and became part of the colonies' basic outlook on economic affairs. The leading national states at first emphasized the establishment by their own traders of links with existing commercial systems as the means by which non-European areas would be integrated into the European economy. Early in the history of imperialism, however, decision makers recognized the importance of organization by Europeans of production systems specifically oriented to furnish supplies of raw materials for the European market, which would in turn involve the creation of overseas settlements of Europeans. To become a leader in overseas expansion, England proved to be better able than any other national state to supply organization, capital, and manpower for colony building.

SUGGESTED READINGS

Robert S. Lopez, *The Commercial Revolution of the Middle Ages, 950–1350* (Englewood Cliffs, N.J.: Prentice-Hall, 1971); and Harry A. Miskimin, *The Economy of Early Renaissance Europe, 1300–1460* (Englewood Cliffs, N.J.: Prentice-Hall, 1960) contain readable and fresh accounts, while Carolo M. Cipolla, ed., *The Fontana Economic History of Europe* vol. I, *The Middle Ages* (London: Collins-Fontana Books, 1972) presents a comprehensive survey. Students who wish to pursue specific topics dealing with the economic history of medieval Europe will find discussions by specialists in M. M. Postan and E. E. Rich, eds., "Trade and Industry in the Middle Ages," in *Cambridge Economic History of Europe*, vol. 2 (Cambridge: Cambridge University Press, 1952) and M. M. Postan, E. E. Rich, and Edward Miller, eds. "Economic Organization and Policies in the Middle Ages," in *Cambridge Economic History of Europe*, vol. 3 (Cambridge: Cambridge University Press, 1963); Douglass C. North and Robert

P. Thomas, *The Rise of the Western World: A New Economic History* (Cambridge: Cambridge University Press, 1973); and Immanuel Wallerstein, *The Modern World-System: Capitalist Agriculture and the Origins of the European World-Economy in the Sixteenth Century* (New York: Academic Press, 1974) offer challenging but very different explanations of European economic history useful for their perspectives on expansion. D. C. Coleman, ed., *Revisions in Mercantilism* (London: Methuen & Co., 1969); and W. E. Minchinton, ed., *Mercantilism: System or Expediency?* (Lexington, Mass.: D. C. Heath & Co., 1969) contain essays presenting the full range of interpretations of this subject.

Ralph Davis, *The Rise of the Atlantic Economies* (London: Weidenfeld and Nicolson, 1973); K. G. Davies, *The North Atlantic World in the Seventeenth Century* (Minneapolis: University of Minnesota Press, 1974); and Max Savelle, *Empires to Nations: Expansion in America, 1713–1824* (Minneapolis: University of Minnesota Press, 1974) are all notable for their comparative approach to the development of colonial empires. Chapters in E. E. Rich and C. H. Wilson, eds., "The Economy of Expanding Europe in the Sixteenth and Seventeenth Centuries," *Cambridge Economic History of Europe*, vol. IV (Cambridge: Cambridge University Press, 1967) furnish information on specialized subjects.

Ruth Pike, *Enterprise and Adventure: The Genoese in Seville and the Opening of the New World* (Ithaca, N.Y.: Cornell University Press, 1966) examines the role of non-Spanish businessmen and firms in the establishment of the Spanish overseas empire, while Stanley Stein and Barbara H. Stein, *The Colonial Heritage of Latin America: Essays on Economic Dependence in Perspective* (New York: Oxford University Press, 1970) discusses the significance of the colonial experience for Latin America's later economic fate. Van Cleaf Bachman, *Peltries or Plantations: The Economic Policies of the Dutch West India Company in New Netherland, 1623–1639* (Baltimore: Johns Hopkins University Press, 1969) focuses on decision making by the Dutch West India Company. Harold A. Innis, *The Fur Trade in Canada*, rev. ed. (New Haven, Conn.: Yale University Press, 1962) analyzes the influence of this staple commodity on Canadian history in a classic work. Sigmund Diamond, "An Experiment in 'Feudalism': French Canada in the Seventeenth Century," *William and Mary Quarterly*, 3d ser., 18 (1961); and John G. Clark, *New Orleans, 1718–1812: An Economic History* (Baton Rouge: Louisiana State University Press, 1970) explore French efforts to organize economic activity in the St. Lawrence Valley and the lower Mississippi Valley, respectively. W. T. Easterbrook and H. G. J. Aitken, *Canadian Economic History* (Macmillan: Toronto, 1956) contains a useful summary of the colonial era.

On the economic expansion of England, essays in W. E. Minchinton, ed., *The Growth of English Overseas Trade in the 17th and 18th Centuries* (London: Methuen, 1969) explore various aspects of foreign commerce, while Ralph Davis, *English Overseas Trade, 1500–1700* (London: Macmillan, 1973) presents a brief overview of the subject. Theodore K. Rabb, *Enterprise & Empire: Merchant and Gentry Investment in the Expansion of England, 1575–1630* (Cambridge, Mass.: Harvard University Press, 1967) supplies a quantitative study of investment in English trading and colonizing companies. David B. Quinn, *England and the Discovery of America, 1481–1620* (New York: Alfred A. Knopf, 1974) traces England's changing interest in North America. Joyce Appleby, "Modernization Theory and the Formation of Modern Social Theories in England and America," *Comparative Studies in Society and History*, 20 (1978) contains an analysis of economic concepts formed in sixteenth and seventeenth century England.

CHAPTER 2

——

Regional Patterns of

Colonial Development

By the middle of the eighteenth century Britain had established a worldwide empire, including a number of colonies along the eastern coast of North America and on islands in the Caribbean. Early English efforts to establish a foothold in the Western Hemisphere had been inspired by the hope of finding precious metals or of expanding the volume of the nation's foreign trade. But England's major discovery was an abundance of natural resources, particularly a seemingly unlimited supply of fertile land, and a growing realization of what could be gained by exploiting that base for the production of staple commodities for the European segment of the world economy. At first joint stock companies, and later individuals or groups of individuals known as proprietors, arranged the essential planning, management, and financing of colonial ventures. Settlers, who came from a society with a strong commercial orientation, organized productive efforts in each colony; they directed them not only toward their own subsistence but also toward the development of an export base resting on one or more staple commodities. Integration of the North American settlements into a commercial empire then required creation of channels of transatlantic commerce to handle the export of colonial commodities and the import of the wide range of goods to the colonies.

The settlements throughout British America were a classic model of economic colonialism—a strong orientation toward extractive industry and dependence upon a more advanced economy for commercial services and manufactured goods. However, efforts of the colonies to find suitable staples led to the emergence by the middle of the eighteenth century of distinctive regional patterns of development. The West Indian and the southern mainland provinces found success in plantation capitalism—a system that produced staple commodities for the European segment of the world economy. At the same time, the New England and Middle colonies were evolving, not entirely by choice, a system of merchant capitalism —a more complex economy that enabled economic decision makers in that region to assume leadership in the long process that transformed America into a leading industrial nation.

Planting the English Colonies

JOINT STOCK COMPANIES

England's first permanent settlement in America was initially planned and undertaken as a business enterprise. London merchants who had assumed leadership in organizing large-scale trading companies to Russia and the eastern Mediterranean secured a charter for the Virginia Company in 1606, authorizing them to plant a settlement and to hold a monopoly of its trade. From the colony initiated at Jamestown in 1607, they planned to explore for a northwest passage to the Far East, to look for precious metals, to trade with the natives, and to organize a base from which to support continued economic penetration of Spanish America. On the basis of their projections of profitable activity, the promoters sold shares of the Virginia Company to a wide range of investors, including nobles and gentry as well as merchants. Indeed, the company, with nearly seventeen hundred members, was the most popular venture for those attracted by the potential profits in overseas enterprise.

However, the Virginia Company soon learned that the establishment of a profitable economic base required long-run economic development, which in turn involved investment of far larger amounts of capital than was originally anticipated. But the inability of the company to produce a profit quickly resulted in a sharp decline of interest on the part of investors. Subscribers, receiving no dividends, refused to make further payments on installments due on their purchases of shares. After the first great hopes for profits were unfulfilled, a lottery run by the company provided the "real and substantial food" to maintain the Jamestown colony, supplying almost one-third of the total funds raised by the company during its eighteen years of operation.

No less perplexing than the problem of raising money was that of determining what could be profitably produced for export. Hopes centered at various times on a wide variety of products: wine, silk, iron, glass, and oranges and pineapples. On an interim basis furs and lumber provided some return. It was tobacco that proved to be the most satisfactory staple to support the Jamestown colony. A market in Europe already existed for the commodity; it had been satisfied largely by imports from the Spanish West Indies. Now a variety of tobacco suitable for European tastes could be cultivated in Virginia.

Intertwined with the problems of securing adequate financial support and of finding an export staple was the need to organize productive effort in Jamestown. Since the company lacked funds to pay the "planters" (settlers) whom it sent to the colony at its expense to work on its projects and property, it promised each settler a share in the enterprise's profits and a tract of land after seven years. However, this carrot did not work, as the company earned no profit, nor did the stick of paramilitary organization employed to impose strict discipline. In 1618 the company developed a new policy of turning over to individual planters a major share of the responsibility for managing production in the colony. Each settler who came at his own expense received fifty acres of land, and was given a like amount for each additional person he brought. This marked the beginning of the headright system of land distribution in Virginia, which continued even after the company's charter was revoked in 1624. Individuals and groups who transported their own work forces were authorized to organize new plantations or new settlements. Only after a decade of effort did the promoters realize that land hunger would provide the motive to develop Virginia. But it was not merely the fact of land ownership that attracted settlers. Rather it was the lure of profits to be made from tobacco, as Jamestown in the 1620s acquired the characteristics of a boom town.

The joint stock company was used in several other efforts to establish colonies, without success for investors. However, in one case a religious group used this form of business organization as a device to facilitate their own migration from England to America. The Puritan promoters of the Massachusetts Bay Company, chartered in 1629, planned to establish in the New World a community organized according to Calvinist socioreligious principles. Their experience was a decided contrast to that of the Jamestown colonists. By taking the government of the company with them to America, settlers in Massachusetts Bay assured themselves of considerable autonomy in making decisions about their religious, political, and social affairs. Since their English business backers made minimal economic demands, the Puritans did not feel the pressure to export that had existed in Virginia.

Financing settlement in the Massachusetts Bay Colony was not the difficult problem that it had been in Virginia. Most settlers financed their own migration and that of their families, using proceeds from the sale of their property in England. Immigrants came from many occupational backgrounds, but most became farmers, an occupation that met the economic need of a pioneer country. Since the Puritans constituted a tightly knit group whose settlement in Massachusetts was motivated largely by religious considerations, they attempted to recreate in the colony the old style open-field system that still survived in parts of England. Inhabitants resided in houses along the streets of a village rather than on scattered farms. Land was distributed in large open fields, and members of the community possessed strips or parcels; this method of farming required common decisions by the group to determine what would be produced. Land was granted by the provincial authorities to the town founders, who, in turn, distributed tracts to individuals. Of basic economic significance right from the start, however, was private land ownership. The ability to buy, sell, and trade land made possible accumulation by individuals, and this undermined the communal system of farm operations.

Other colonies were established in the New England region as offshoots of Massachusetts Bay. Corporate bodies of religious dissenters created communities in the wilderness in what became Rhode Island, Connecticut, New Hampshire, and Maine; they organized them according to their own particular variety of Calvinist principles. The emphasis of the Puritans on orthodoxy in the seventeenth century had the unplanned economic result of stimulating settlement over a wider area of New England than was anticipated by the original founders of the Bay Colony.

PROPRIETORS

After colonization companies lost favor as a way to finance and organize settlement in North America, government policy came to rely upon wealthy individuals or groups of individuals to develop colonies. With a charter conferred by the king, a proprietor or proprietors received title to a large tract of land as well as extensive political authority. Some proprietors had a particular objective, such as enabling members of a religious minority to establish their own community. Most planned to create in the New World an orderly society to strengthen some of the older, hierarchical values that were diminishing in influence in England. However, proprietors also had a more modern economic purpose in projecting colonies, a hope to increase their own fortunes. The proprietors of seventeenth-century colonies were the first great real estate developers in American history. Maryland, Carolina, the Jerseys, and several West Indian colonies were among the ventures undertaken by individuals or groups. The experience of William Penn illustrates the methods used by seventeenth-century proprietors to establish colonies.

A charter granted in 1681 enabled Penn to undertake his plan to establish in America a Holy Experiment, a community satisfying to Quakers (members of the Society of Friends), who were being persecuted in England. He initially contemplated an orderly kind of settlement in Pennsylvania where people would live in agricultural villages built around their meeting houses.

But Penn was also a realistic colony builder. Like other proprietors, he knew that he could not provide all of the capital by himself, although he was prepared to make a substantial investment. Thus he sold large tracts of land to "first purchasers," mostly wealthy Quakers in England; some of them later migrated and undertook development of their estates in Pennsylvania. He chartered a Free Society of Traders, composed of some two-hundred British investors who subscribed a total of ten thousand pounds. This forerunner of a modern development corporation received a grant of twenty thousand acres of land, extensive trading privileges (including Indian trade as well as supplying the settlers), and authority to organize a glass works, a saw mill, a tannery, a fishery, and other facilities.

Penn also appealed to an extensive group of ordinary people, issuing tracts explaining the advantages of settlement in Pennsylvania and distributing them widely among Quakers and other groups throughout the British Isles and on the continent. Significantly, he offered a variety of terms that appeared attractive to a broad range of prospective settlers. The moderately well to do could buy land at the rate of one hundred pounds for five thousand acres. For those without command of much capital, Penn agreed to rent land at a low rate. Even those unable to pay rent could seek an assignment of land and a stake of tools, seed, and the right to work the tract for seven years, at which time they had an option to buy. To encourage the migration of those unable to pay the cost of passage, Penn made a grant of fifty acres to the person financing the transportation and another fifty acres to the servant upon expiration of his term. Large blocks were promised to religious or other groups of people migrating to the colony. As in the other proprietary colonies, Penn received a return on his investment of capital and entrepeneurial activity by collecting an annual quitrent on land that he sold or granted. The proprietor also set aside for his own manors as much as one-tenth of the land in each area to be held against future increases in value.

Instead of following Penn's plan of settlement in agriculture villages, the first settlers turned the Holy Experiment into a major real estate speculation. Penn's liberal land policies, plus the Quaker toleration of other religious faiths and ethnic groups, appealed not only to large numbers of Englishmen but, from the early years of the eighteenth century, to other Europeans as well, particularly to Germans and Scotch-Irish. Those who came to farm wanted to adopt the most up-to-date kind of agricultural organization existing in England rather than outmoded communal farming. They wanted to live on their own farms, in line with the growing emphasis on individual achievement. This encouraged a dispersion of rural settlement, the exact opposite of the founder's hope for compactness.

Proprietors, like joint stock companies, received small financial rewards for their developmental efforts in British North America. Of all of the proprietors involved in colonization, only the Penns and the Calverts (of Maryland) retained ownership until the American Revolution. Even the Penn family, the most successful of colonizing proprietors, earned a return on investment in Pennsylvania probably no higher than what they would have received from a similar investment in government bonds.

SETTLERS AND TRADERS

The major contribution of joint stock companies and proprietors was the creation of a framework within which the initial settlement of an area could be organized, including a method of establishing title to the land. However, it was the productive effort of settlers and the commercial enterprise of traders that made growth of these settlements possible within the orbit of the European-centered world economy.

What distinguished English colony building from that of other national states was the readiness of large numbers of men and women to invest themselves and whatever funds they possessed in the development of overseas colonies. About one-half of those who migrated in the seventeenth century appear to have been of middle-class status in England; they had sufficient capital for their own transportation and for the establishment of a plantation, farm, or other productive enterprise in the New World. They hoped to produce a surplus beyond their subsistence needs for sale to the market. If they were at all successful, expansion of their operations required the labor of others; but with an abundance of land and its low cost few individuals were willing to work for wages. Thus, almost from the beginning, much of the colonial labor force consisted of indentured servants, men and women who agreed to work for a term of four to seven years in return for their passage. These servants, whose indentures, or contracts, were purchased by planters and farmers through English agents or ship captains, comprised the other half of the migrants. Attracted by the possibility of land ownership after their service, most of these people came of their free choice. But the others—criminals, prostitutes, paupers, and beggars who were regarded as the dregs of English society—came involuntarily; their servitude in the colonies was regarded by English authorities as a low-cost alternative to maintaining jails and poorhouses. The shipment of indentured servants became a highly organized business, with local officials cooperating with ship captains to furnish a supply when needed.

Merchants organized the export of staple commodities produced by the settlers as well as the import of goods for their consumption. However, these merchants were not the elite businessmen who had initiated the settlement process by their formation of joint stock companies in the early years of the seventeenth century. When the American colonization efforts failed to produce quick profits through trade or discovery of precious metals, these merchants had concentrated their efforts on other large-scale ventures, like the East India Company. The opportunities that arose with the growth of the American colonial population and of production were developed by English entrepreneurs from the middle and lower ranks of the business community. These were men willing to make the innovations required for success in the Atlantic trade.

Other Americans

The economic concepts and practices brought to America by the English settlers were predominant in the American colonies. But other peoples also played a role in the creation of the economy including both the native population and the unwilling migrants brought from Africa.

AMERICAN INDIANS

Historians once conveyed the impression that the North America discovered by Europeans was a forested wilderness inhabited by only a few nomads. Actually many parts of the continent had relatively dense population. (For example, there was a native population of five thousand within sixty miles of Jamestown at the time of its founding.) Indians in the coastal areas inhabited semipermanent villages, supplementing hunting and fishing with agriculture, notably the cultivation of maize (Indian corn). But the native culture lacked some of the basic elements of European culture, such as writing, the wheel, the plow, livestock, iron implements, and firearms. From the time of their first contacts with European traders, Indians became increasingly dependent upon them for iron goods, textiles, liquor, and especially guns and ammunition. Furs were the only surplus commodity that the Indian economy could offer in exchange. Thus trade tended to disrupt their traditional economic life and to encourage intertribal warfare as the Indians sought to expand their production of furs by devoting more time to trapping and by moving into hunting grounds claimed by other Indians.

The interest of the traders was in preserving the Indian economic system, which furnished a valuable export commodity and provided a profitable market for imported goods. But the settlers, who wanted to engage in European-style agriculture, had an entirely different attitude. Unlike the Spanish in Mexico and Peru, English colonists could find no way to turn the native peoples into an effective labor force. Indians were enslaved everywhere; in South Carolina an extensive Indian slave trade developed late in the seventeenth century. But the culture shock associated with the uprooting from their traditional way of life, as well as harsh unaccustomed discipline, made them unsatisfactory workers. Thus, everywhere that the English settled the Indians came to be regarded as an obstacle to be removed so that their land could be taken. In the early stages of settlement, English colonists managed to maintain a truce with the more numerous Indians in the vicinity of their settlements, principally by taking advantage of intertribal tensions. The settlers sometimes obtained essential supplies of food from the Indians, by purchase or by theft. And the Indians taught the settlers some useful lessons about the cultivation of crops. As in other parts of the Western Hemisphere, contact with European diseases like smallpox resulted in demographic catastrophe for the native population. While the Indians were declining in number, the English base was growing. Disagreements and friction between the two peoples over land use, which usually revolved around different concepts of property rights, and other problems led to open and bloody war. The English settlers, including rival groups, united long enough to triumph over an enemy that was never able to develop a pan-Indian resistance. Many survivors among the defeated retreated to the West; those who stayed sought to eke out a living on the margin of the white economy.

SLAVES AND THE SLAVE TRADE

The demand for slaves stemmed from the desire of agricultural entrepreneurs in America to expand their production of low-cost staple commodities for the growing European market. With land abundant and labor scarce, settlers had early turned to forced labor in the form of indentured servants. But slaves represented a real economy in comparison with white indentured servants. When slavery was becoming important in the Chesapeake colonies after the middle of the seventeenth century, the purchase price of a slave was eighteen pounds to twenty pounds, compared with ten pounds to fifteen pounds for the indenture of a servant with a four-year term. For the higher initial cost of a slave the planter purchased the slave's labor for life as well as the ownership of any offspring of female slaves. If it was more difficult to train the African to perform in European-organized agriculture, the cost could be apportioned over a longer period of time. In addition, black women could be assigned to work in the fields, an activity that white women servants were not generally expected to perform. Planters were in a position to impose lower living standards on Africans than on European servants, representing lower maintenance costs. Finally, use of black slaves rather than white servants avoided the threat to social stability sometimes created by dissatisfied freedmen, especially those who gained release from service during a depression.

One problem for the colonists was to create legal status for slavery, which did not exist in English law. At first, the blacks in Virginia, who had begun to arrive in small numbers as early as 1619, were regarded as servants, some of whom served for life and whose children inherited the same obligation. By the 1670s and 1680s the colonies had worked out a legal code creating the status of slavery for blacks; it embraced total deprivation of their personal rights and liberty as well as their treatment as chattel property. At the same time ethnocentric assumptions about differences in people helped to enforce notions held by whites about the supposed inferiority of black people and thus to justify their enslavement. Control was facilitated by racial differentiation, since the black could be easily marked off from the European population. The blacks' lack of familiarity with America discouraged them from trying to escape into the wilderness; such escapes were easy for the Indians and were a factor that had made it almost impossible to enslave them.

Effective demand for slave labor in the Americas resulted in a significant expansion of activity by private merchants and government authorities in Africa, a rational response to economic opportunity. An estimated nine million five hundred thousand blacks were transported from Africa to the Western Hemisphere colonies of Portugal, Spain, Holland, France, and England in the period from 1450 to 1870, two-thirds of them in the eighteenth century. Since most slaves were purchased by Europeans from African traders, an efficient system of middlemen developed in Africa not only to gather slaves in the interior and deliver them to the coast but also to distribute European imported goods—firearms, liquor, textiles, and a variety of metal products. In the eighteenth century available evidence indicates that about one-half of the slaves produced by the middlemen were prisoners of war and about one-quarter were enslaved in small-scale operations of slave raiders. It is likely that the demand for slaves induced Africans to alter their military strategy so as to maximize the number of prisoners taken in battle without actually increasing the incidence of warfare. But to some extent wars in Africa may have been stimulated by the opportunities of the slave trade.

Since slave trading in the British Empire was open to any citizen of the empire, except for a short time late in the seventeenth century when it was a monopoly of the Royal African Company, many colonial and English merchants participated in some aspect of that commerce. In addition, slavers from many other nations of western Europe participated in this trade, seeking supplies of labor for their own colonies. At the same time a substantial number of Africans organized the sale of slaves to Europeans. Thus, the existence of many European buyers and many African sellers contributed to a highly competitive market for slaves, whose prices reflected conditions of supply and demand rather than monopoly power.

The slave trade was a highly speculative business as well as a competitive one. Some ventures were extremely profitable, but others returned only losses to the traders. If bad weather lengthened the time of passage from Africa to America, profits could disappear as a result of a high death rate among the slaves. In addition to unpredictable weather, economic factors might have a depressing effect on profits. If the trader had purchased his cargo in a tight market in Africa, paying high prices, and sold in a weak market in America, he saw his profit margin squeezed or eliminated. Slave traders who knew the odds usually spread their risk by investing in shares in several different voyages.

Slavery and the slave trade supplied what seemed like a never-ending stream of labor to produce staple commodities in tropical and semi-tropical regions of the Western Hemisphere. Expansion of production inevitably drove down the prices of these commodities, creating in Europe a mass market for what had once been luxuries. But this was accomplished at a high cost in human life and dignity for the forced immigrants from Africa who composed the labor force.

Plantation Capitalism

The simplest way for early Americans to satisfy their desire to consume goods that they could not themselves produce was to exchange the products of their own agricultural economy for those made in England. This is essentially what happened for colonists in the West Indies and southern mainland colonies, where efficient application of enterprise, capital, and labor to the resource base (soil and climate) resulted in a system of plantation capitalism—the organization of production of staple commodities like sugar, tobacco, and rice, usually on a large unit known as a plantation, using slave labor. This broad region was integrated into the European economy as a supply area for tropical and semitropical products. As the following survey of the West Indies, the Chesapeake, and the lower South shows, production of staple commodities for export to Europe generated growth of wealth and population in these provinces, but it did not have an entirely beneficial impact on long-run development.

THE WEST INDIES

Of all their American possessions, the English regarded their West Indian provinces most highly. Jamaica, Barbados, and several smaller islands occupied a land area no larger than New Jersey and contained midway in the eighteenth century a white population of a little more than one-tenth the size of the population of European origin in Britain's colonies on the mainland. Yet the value of the commerce of the Sugar Islands (so termed after their principal product) with the mother country was actually greater than the combined trade carried on by all thirteen of the mainland colonies.

In the early years of English settlement in the West Indies, tobacco was the chief cash crop, produced mainly by small farmers using their own labor and occasionally that of a few indentured servants. A sharp drop in tobacco prices just before the middle of the seventeenth century stimulated a shift to sugar, a commodity for which the tropical climate of the Caribbean was well suited. A Golden Age was ushered in, first for Barbados and later for the other West Indian islands, based on a combination of low cost, high yield, and good prices for sugar. Although prices declined from the peak experienced at the beginning of the sugar boom, the drop was moderate and served to broaden the market.

With the change to sugar, slaves became the principal element in the labor force. The same reasons that made the forced migrant from Africa a desirable source of labor in other plantation colonies were apparent to decision makers in the Caribbean: cost and discipline. In contrast to the mainland, where the slave population grew by natural increase as well as by importations, in the West Indies, at least in the eighteenth century, underfeeding and overworking resulted in a natural decrease—an excess of deaths over births—so that the slave supply had to be constantly replenished by imports. Demographic data reflect the close relationship between sugar and slavery. As early as 1660 the number of blacks surpassed the number of whites on Barbados. By the mid-eighteenth century slaves accounted for 80 to 90 percent of the total population of England's Caribbean colonies.

The sugar revolution created opportunities for aggressive entrepreneurs with command of capital to increase considerably their economic distance from those with slender financial resources. Not only did the purchase of slaves require a larger investment in labor than had been the case with indentured servants, but also sugar processing involved the use of expensive equipment, with a competitive advantage held by the planter who owned his own machinery. In Barbados in 1680 just 175 planters (comprising 7 percent of all property holders) owned 54 percent of the slave labor force. The situation was similar elsewhere in the Caribbean where sugar was dominant. A large sugar plantation was a complex agro-industrial operation, "a factory set in a field," as Richard Pares has put it,* with the greatest financial rewards going not to the famed absentee planters living in London but rather to the owner-managers who paid the most diligent attention to business. Despite the system of large estates there continued to be opportunities for enterprising newcomers to enter sugar production by purchasing a plantation with capital accumulated through practicing a commercial or professional activity. Unlike the mainland colonies, where production of a staple for export was combined with the tillage of food crops, the high returns from sugar and the limited amount of arable land encouraged the West Indies to rely upon imports from England, Ireland, and mainland North America to provide much of the food for both

---

* Richard Pares, "Merchants and Planters," *Economic History Review*, supplement 4 (1960), p. 23.

planters and slaves. Some small producers gained success in minor tropical commodities like ginger, coffee, cocoa, and cotton.

In the late seventeenth and the early eighteenth centuries, much of the sugar shipped to England was re-exported to continental Europe. But by the 1730s the home market had expanded to absorb almost the entire production of the British West Indies, except what was exported to Britain's colonies in North America. Insulation of the British market by tariff protection served to maintain sugar prices at a higher level than on the continent. Most planters consigned their sugar to merchants in London, who arranged its sale and then purchased goods to order. The consignment merchant also performed an essential financial function, selling goods on credit and making long-term loans secured by mortgages.

From England's point of view the West Indies constituted an almost perfect colony—it supplied tropical commodities and used English commercial services and manufactured goods. Its highly commercial agriculture was a profitable activity in the sense that the commodities exported from the West Indies sold for more than they cost to produce. Satisfying the sweet tooth of Europeans, however, took a toll of both human and natural resources—the lives and freedom of slaves and soil exhaustion. Despite the presence of vigorous and aggressive entrepreneurs among the planter-businessmen in these colonies, developmental activity took place almost entirely within the limits of staple production for export, with crucial control of foreign trade remaining in the hands of British business. With sugar apparently so profitable, there was little encouragement for development along lines that might have resulted in greater economic diversity. In short, these provinces remained economic colonies dependent upon Britain's more highly developed economy. Historians have long argued about the role of West Indian sugar profits in financing Britain's Industrial Revolution. But what is most significant is that no such basic economic transformation occurred in the Caribbean.

THE CHESAPEAKE TOBACCO COAST

On the eve of Independence, Virginia and Maryland together contained nearly one-third of the total population of the mainland colonies, and they accounted for 60 percent of the value of exports to Britain from the thirteen provinces. Here was a colonial area literally built upon smoke, as the economic health of these two provinces rested upon one great staple export, tobacco.

Economic leadership in the early years was assumed by aggressive planters; their principal talent was the application of brute force and shrewd manipulation to produce as much tobacco as possible. When expanding tobacco exports, from the Caribbean as well as from the Chesapeake, caused a glut in the English market in the 1640s, Virginia and Maryland producers, unlike the West Indian planters who faced the same situation, did not change their basic staple crop. While some of the older planters thought that the way to deal with low prices was to restrict production, younger planters were devising ways to expand their activities, sensing that the lower price of tobacco would broaden the market. Indeed, a smoking craze swept across Europe in the last half of the seventeenth century, stimulating a twentyfold increase by 1700 in the tobacco exports of Virginia and Maryland.

The way to wealth that ambitious entrepreneurs discovered was to combine merchandising, shipping, moneylending, and land speculation with volume production of tobacco. Moreover, they took the lead in solving the persisting problem of a labor shortage by shifting from indentured servitude to slavery. Robert "King" Carter, a leader among leaders, serves as the prototype of the Chesapeake planter-tycoon at the turn of the eighteenth century. The youngest son of a middling Virginia planter, Carter recognized early in life the importance of application and drive to stay on top in the highly competitive system based upon low and fluctuating tobacco prices. He amassed a family empire of three hundred thousand acres, obtaining much of it while serving as an agent for English proprietors of the Northern Neck of Virginia. Using his political position in the province, he resisted the efforts of the royal government to prevent the creation of large landed estates in the colony. By the time of his death in 1732 he operated forty-four plantations in twelve counties, owned over one thousand slaves, ran a store system that bought tobacco and sold goods to small planters, and lent money like a banking firm.

Slavery, by making possible the employment of gangs of many workers, was a major force in widening the gap between large and small producers of tobacco. It was easier for a planter with enough capital to buy even a few slaves to expand his volume and earn enough to purchase several more slaves than it was for a man working in the field by himself to save enough to acquire his first slave. However, tobacco culture did not provide economies of scale (or decreasing unit costs with rising output), so the older structure dominated by yeomen farmers survived alongside the large plantations worked by slaves. At the end of the colonial period whites still formed a majority of the total population of the tobacco colonies, despite the importation of substantial numbers of slaves.

During the Golden Age of the Chesapeake, the half century before the American Revolution, exports of tobacco more than tripled, as production expanded to meet the growing demand. As early as the 1660s, the Netherlands and Germany consumed over one-half of the tobacco exported from Virginia and Maryland; then, in the 1720s, France emerged as a major market. A labor bottleneck had been broken with the establishment of slavery. Faced with soil exhaustion in the older tidewater area, large planters and small farmers alike took up fresh lands in the Piedmont region west of the fall line.

British law required that all tobacco be exported to Britain, regardless of where it was to be ultimately shipped. British business dominated the trade. Some colonial planters, usually the larger ones, consigned their tobacco to an English merchant; he sold it at the best market price and received a commission for his services. The consignment merchant also purchased goods ordered and attended to other needs of the consigning planter, including the extension of credit. Smaller planters and farmers normally sold their tobacco outright in their own communities at stores run by agents or employees of British firms. There they also bought imported goods, usually on credit. Several Scottish houses operated chains of stores; in the 1770s one Glasgow firm owned seven stores in Maryland and fourteen in Virginia.

Urban development in the Chesapeake was limited. Since the tributaries of the Chesapeake were accessible for long distances to ocean-going vessels, exports could be shipped directly from many points rather than channeled through a single port serving a large region, as in other colonies. Then, too, tobacco required little processing, so that there was nothing to stimulate the growth of towns around an industrial base. Jefferson's assertion that Virginia had "no ports but our rivers and creeks" * may have been applicable in the seventeenth century when English ships did indeed load tobacco and discharge imported goods at the wharves of individual planters. But by the mid-eighteenth century small urban centers in all parts of Virginia and Maryland performed most of the business of their immediate localities. The provincial capitals, Williamsburg and Annapolis, took on special significance in certain kinds of business, such as the buying and selling of foreign exchange and the retail and service trades. Norfolk and Baltimore were beginning to assume importance as entrepôts in the years just prior to the Revolution. But most parts of the Chesapeake maintained direct economic communications with Britain.

After 1750 the Chesapeake experienced greater success than in earlier years. There is considerable evidence that grain production was increasing faster than tobacco growing in the last decades of the colonial era, and that it provided a surplus for export as well as meeting the region's own food needs. But on the eve of the Revolution the "stinking weed" still accounted for three-quarters of the value of the exports of Virginia and Maryland.

In spite of the promising trend toward diversification and the resulting expansion of opportunities for independent business, the economy of the Chesapeake evolved through the colonial period within the framework created in the early phases of its development. Recent research has done much to dispel older notions of the tobacco planters as agrarian gentlemen who frowned upon engagement in business. Even though they often talked like agrarians, they did indeed act as aggressive entrepreneurs. But the result of their activities in economic development was to strengthen

* Thomas Jefferson, *Notes on the State of Virginia*, ed. William Peden (Chapel Hill: University of North Carolina Press, 1955), Query III.

rather than to challenge the basic pattern of staple production for the European market, with foreign trade controlled by British business.

THE LOWER SOUTH

The third region of British North America characterized by plantation capitalism—South Carolina and Georgia—contained less than a quarter of the population of the Chesapeake colonies. Yet on the eve of the Revolution, these two provinces exported almost half as much in value as did Virginia and Maryland. The author of *American Husbandry*, first published in 1775, remarked, "How valuable the climate is to produce so largely in exportable staples." * Two commodities—rice and indigo—accounted for over three-quarters of the value of the Lower South's exports.

Slavery was introduced into Carolina even before the colony's staple commodities were discovered. Settlers in Charleston, which was founded in 1670, made slow economic progress for several decades by producing foodstuffs for export to the West Indies. Then, in the late years of the century, they found a variety of rice suitable to the physical conditions of the area. Black slaves played an essential role in the establishment of rice as a major staple, supplying from their African experience a knowledge of its cultivation and processing as well as a low-cost labor force. With the natural advantages of a subtropical climate and inland swamps fed by fresh-water streams, rice production expanded rapidly, with exports advancing from a scant three hundred ninety-four thousand pounds in 1700 to over eighteen million in 1730, twenty-seven million in 1750, and over seventy-five million on the eve of the Revolution. Indigo, the region's second staple, was successfully introduced in the 1740s, with exports growing tenfold from 1750 to 1775. Needing better drainage than rice and soil of a different composition, indigo was produced on lands up the rivers and streams from the rice fields.

In contrast to the Chesapeake where tobacco was tilled by small farmers as well as by plantation slaves, in the Lower South white workers would not willingly endure the hard and disagreeable labor involved in the production of rice and indigo. The arduous nature of work on swampy ground under adverse climatic conditions led to the assumption that these staples could be cultivated only by slaves. Although slaves had constituted one-fourth to one-third of the population of South Carolina almost from its beginnings, during the two decades following 1695 when rice cultivation took permanent hold, the black population drew equal to and then surpassed the white. By 1730 blacks comprised two-thirds of the total population of the province, a majority that they continued to hold in the lowland area of South Carolina and attained in Georgia after slavery was established there.

* Harry J. Carman, ed., *American Husbandry* (New York: Columbia University Press, 1939), p. 314.

British law required that rice be exported to the mother country, although an exemption was made after 1730 for shipments to southern Europe. However, almost all of the rice shipped to British ports was re-exported to the European continent. Growing demand for indigo stemmed from the expansion of the textile industry in Britain. A bounty was paid by the British government to encourage colonial production, and even though Carolina indigo was deemed inferior in quality to that of the French West Indies, a high tariff on foreign indigo served to protect the market for American planters.

Some planters shipped their rice and indigo to British merchants on consignment, while others sold their crops to merchants in Charleston, a port through which flowed much of the foreign trade of the region. However, even the larger firms in Charleston were in effect branches of houses in London or in some other British port. As in the Chesapeake, there were aggressive planter-entrepreneurs who saw that large profits were to be made from developmental activities—slave dealing, land speculation, and moneylending. But dominance by British business of the export of rice and indigo was just as complete as its control of the tobacco trade to the north. While Charleston was a busy port, it was not a real commercial center. London actually performed much of the entrepôt function for the Carolina-Georgia staple economy. In the words of Jacob Price: "Entrepreneurial decisions were made in Britain, capital was raised there, ships were built or chartered there and outfitted there, insurance was made there—all for the South Carolina trade." *

Beginning in the 1730s a back-country sector grew vigorously in South Carolina and Georgia (as well as in neighboring North Carolina) where settlers engaged in mixed farming: the raising of cattle and hogs, hunting and fishing, and lumbering. Most holdings were small and were worked by family members; to a considerable degree they were self-sufficient, but once transportation and marketing channels were available, it was usual for farmers to sell some portion of their output. In small urban centers throughout this back country, storekeepers sold imported goods and purchased local produce for shipment to Charleston by either inland waterways or wagon roads.

The rise of a back-country sector had the effect of shifting the overall balance of the Lower South's economy away from the plantation capitalism of rice and indigo. The export of wheat, corn, meat, and other foodstuffs provided business for independent merchants and gave a new dimension to Charleston's role as the region's principal commercial outlet. It also altered the racial composition of the population, since few slaves were employed in general farming. But with the discovery in the nineteenth century that the soil and climate of the uplands could be exploited in the cultivation of cotton, plantation capitalism—production of

* Jacob Price, "Economic Function and the Growth of American Port Towns in the Eighteenth Century," *Perspectives in American History*, 8 (1974), p. 163.

staple commodities for export, using slave labor—became relevant to the back country.

Merchant Capitalism

While the West Indies and southern mainland colonies developed staple crops suited to the European market, settlers in the colonies with a more temperate climate in the area from Pennsylvania north to New Hampshire found that the commodities that they could produce most efficiently largely duplicated rather than supplemented those of the mother country. Only by seeking outlets for their surplus outside of the normal, or bilateral, pattern of trade between a European country and its dependencies could the New England and Middle colonies obtain the means to pay for desired imports. Significantly, in contrast to the experience of the plantation colonies, where British merchants and their agents maintained control of foreign commerce, trade outside of the ordinary colonial pattern created opportunities for American businessmen to manage a large portion of the export trade of their provinces. In the process of integrating their regions into the world economy in a novel way, American merchants in the Middle and New England colonies assumed many of the business functions that were usually performed for colonial areas by the merchants of the mother country. This led to a development unusual in the history of colonialism: the growth within a colonial area of strong centers of entrepreneurial decision making, creating the basic conditions necessary for the evolution of a diversified economy less dependent upon the export of staple commodities.

NEW ENGLAND

Throughout the colonial period farming supported a large majority of the New England population. However, the mediocre soil and harsh climate produced low yields, and the spread of a parasitic fungus growth, which first appeared around 1660, led to the abandonment of wheat growing in many parts of the region. A few areas of New England were able to find a profitable form of specialization, such as horses and cattle in Rhode Island, flax in southwest Connecticut, and tobacco in the Connecticut River Valley. But most farmers who grew maize and rye earned only a frugal living, which was made somewhat more comfortable when they were able to supplement their income by other activities, such as operation of a sawmill or gristmill, tavern keeping, small-scale retailing, or simply hiring out for wages. During the early decades of the eighteenth century,

Boston and other towns became dependent upon imports of foodstuffs from the Chesapeake and the Middle colonies, as the farm production of the region could not be expanded to feed the growing urban population.

When agriculture did not provide a way to wealth, as it did in most other colonies, English settlers in New England had to look elsewhere: to the sea. Fishermen—from Boston and from the smaller ports along the Massachusetts coast and then from New Hampshire—worked the shores of New England and by the 1660s went as far north as Nova Scotia and Newfoundland.

However, this treasure of the sea, unlike the sugar of the Caribbean, the tobacco of the Chesapeake, and the rice and indigo of the Lower South, did not provide the basis of a bilateral trading system with England, the typical colonial relationship. English markets were served by England's own fishing fleets. New Englanders had to find other outlets for their fish in order to pay for imports from England. This they did by selling the better grades of fish to Spain and Portugal and their island possessions in the Atlantic. The poorer grades of fish went to feed the slaves in the expanding sugar economy of the West Indies. In both markets, fish was exchanged for cash, for credits, or for commodities that could be sold in England, such as Caribbean sugar products or Iberian wine and salt.

The business that New England merchants began to organize in the mid-seventeenth century was much more than merely collecting a staple commodity and then shipping it to the best markets. The fisheries led to the development of a more general commerce and to the emergence of Boston as one of the major commercial centers of the Atlantic world. Boston traders reached out to collect a variety of commodities from nearly all of England's scattered settlements along the Atlantic coast: lumber from New Hampshire, fish from Newfoundland, wheat and various kinds of provisions from Connecticut and Rhode Island and from the Middle colonies of New York, New Jersey, and Pennsylvania, tobacco from Maryland and Virginia, rice and naval stores from the Carolinas, and sugar and other tropical products from the West Indies. The New Englanders sold fish to all of these colonies and served as distributors of European goods shipped from England to Boston, and, to the mainland provinces, as distributors of the tropical products of the Caribbean. In short, Boston became the hub of a complex system of exchange of cargoes of goods, credits, and cash; and in all of this trading, fish was a central element. The fisheries and shipping also fostered a shipbuilding industry, which first constructed the small vessels used for fishing and the coastwise trade and eventually made large ships for the transatlantic traffic.

Before the middle of the eighteenth century Boston lost its position as a major trade center for all of British America. Merchants in Philadelphia and New York took advantage of the growth of population and economic activity in the Middle colonies to create their own domains. But

Boston remained the most important factor in the commercial life of New England. A number of smaller ports in the region participated in the West Indian trade. Aside from Boston, only Newport, Rhode Island, conducted a direct trade with England; and because of geographical factors it drew upon a limited hinterland.

THE MIDDLE COLONIES

Diversified farming was characteristic of the area south of New England and north of the Chesapeake, where climate and soil made possible a bountiful agriculture. Wheat was the most important crop grown in Pennsylvania, New York, and New Jersey (the Bread Colonies), but most farms also raised corn, flax, hemp, fruit, vegetables, cattle, hogs, and poultry. The typical unit of production in this region was the family farm, where the labor of members of the family was sometimes supplemented by that of an indentured servant or two. In spite of the tendency of farmers to make inefficient, extensive use of their land, they produced enough to feed their families well and a surplus for sale. While the extent of a farmer's participation in the market varied according to such factors as distance from the market, one scholar has estimated that farmers in a settled rural area like Chester County, Pennsylvania, sold as much as 40 percent of their output.*

The farmers of the Middle colonies grew a surplus of agricultural commodities beyond the needs of the population of the region; yet their production largely paralleled that of western Europe. Unlike the staples of the southern mainland colonies and the West Indies, wheat and other foodstuffs from the Middle colonies were not in demand in northern Europe until near the end of the colonial era. Thus, the commodities produced most efficiently in this region had to find markets outside of the usual colonial pattern of bilateral trade ties to the mother country. Merchants in Philadelphia and New York, the ports through which flowed most of the trade of the Middle colonies, developed a growing market for food in England's West Indian colonies, where planters concentrated their efforts on the production of sugar. Because of France's failure to develop export agriculture in the St. Lawrence Valley, the English mainland colonies became the principal suppliers of foodstuffs to the French West Indies as well as to the British sugar colonies. Beginning in the 1730s commerce with southern Europe, especially with Spain and Portugal, assumed growing significance. Trade with these areas supplied colonial consumers with sugar products and wine and, more important, earned cash and credits to pay for manufactured goods imported from Britain.

* James T. Lemon, "Household Consumption in Eighteenth-Century America and its Relationship to Production and Trade: the Situation Among Farmers in Southeastern Pennsylvania," *Agricultural History*, 41 (1967), p. 60.

METROPOLITAN ECONOMY

Boston, New York, and Philadelphia were busy shipping points and the three most populous cities of British America. Merchants in each city created a system of exchange to organize the business of a metropolitan economy that consisted of mutually dependent communities within a large region. In a real sense each city was a metropolis—a center through which producers and consumers from a wide area maintained economic relations with the outside world.

Unlike the colonies characterized by plantation capitalism, where foreign commerce was dominated by British business, the export trade of the Middle colonies and of New England was organized by American merchants. British trading houses were accustomed to thinking in terms of recognized staples with European markets, but exports from the northern colonies involved a variety of commodities which were shipped to widely scattered markets, many of them relatively small. The American merchant was in a strategic position to make many specific decisions about the selection of commodities, the destination (or destinations) of the voyage, terms of sale, and disposition of the proceeds—whether in cash, in credits, in another cargo, or in some combination of all three. Each merchant relied on a network of agents who had to be given considerable discretion in doing business in distant places. Sometimes it was the ship captain or the supercargo (a business agent who accompanied the shipment) who had responsibility for selling the cargo and investing the proceeds. More often, the cargo was consigned to a resident merchant, who transacted business for a commission. Kinship formed an important element in creating a network of correspondents, as a number of family business groups spread through the Atlantic world in the seventeenth and the eighteenth centuries. The merchant in Boston, New York, or Philadelphia derived an element of confidence from doing business at a distance with relatives or close friends whom he knew personally, especially when their interests were identified in some way with his own.

No less important than the establishment of market relations overseas was the growth of a network of marketplace communities for the collection of commodities and the distribution of goods in the hinterlands. In each colony there emerged a complex of urban places, varying in size and importance from small cities like Lancaster, which prided itself on being a little Philadelphia, to hamlets built around flour mills and taverns. Storekeepers in these places sold goods to farmers in the neighborhood and purchased local produce, usually serving as agents for merchants in the metropolis. Much of the inland trade moved by natural waterways, transported on small open boats that could carry as much as thirty-five tons while drawing only four or five feet of water. Overland transport was also important, though more expensive than water travel, with wagons moving over road systems that had Philadelphia, Boston, or New York as their hubs.

In the eighteenth century the leading businessmen of the three metropolitan centers were more than exporters and importers; as unspecialized merchants they carried out many business functions that in the nineteenth century became the province of specialized branches of business. Merchants were owners, often in partnership with other merchants, of the vessels that carried their cargoes to and from the West Indies, Southern Europe, and, to a lesser extent, the British Isles. By the 1770s, for example, Philadelphia businessmen had accumulated an investment of five hundred thousand pounds in ocean-going ships. In the conduct of their business, merchants performed many financial functions; they dealt in foreign exchange, borrowed from British exporters and extended credit to inland traders and retailers (who then extended credit to consumers), and arranged for insurance of ships and cargoes. In the absence of an adequate supply of currency in the colonies, they helped to clear payments for transactions through bookkeeping techniques. Merchants promoted and financed a wide range of manufacturing activities, many of them ancillary to foreign commerce and shipping: shipyards (with ships becoming an important export), rope walks, cooperage establishments, sail lofts, flour mills (usually located in the countryside at water-power sites), bakeries (for ship biscuits), rum distilleries, and iron furnaces (hardware for ships constituted one of the most important end products of iron).

Entrepreneurs in Philadelphia, New York, and Boston succeeded in organizing the economic activity of their regions within, but partially autonomous from, the British commercial system. The three great port cities provided services for their hinterlands of a kind supplied directly by British business to the plantation colonies. Historian Bernard Bailyn's description of Boston applies equally well to Philadelphia and New York: The meeting place of the merchants in the townhouse, to which they were summoned by bell each working day, "was in every way, except geographically, closer to the 'New–England walke' on the London Exchange than to the market places of most inland towns." * The extensive and complex commercial life of these regional centers mirrored London but on a smaller scale.

---

* Bernard Bailyn, "Communication and Trade: The Atlantic in the Seventeenth Century," *Journal of Economic History*, 13 (Fall 1953), p. 383.

Summary

The economy of the Atlantic world in the seventeenth and the eighteenth centuries contained many challenges and opportunities for business-minded men who possessed energy, vision, and access to capital. Whether they went to the Chesapeake or to the Caribbean, to Boston or to Philadelphia, entrepreneurs who organized the economics of their colonies possessed enormous ambition as well as an ability to find the "way to wealth" that was most appropriate for the economic environment in which they operated. For some, it centered around producing sugar, tobacco, rice, or indigo with slave labor; for others, it was organizing a trade in fish; for still others, it was merchandising foodstuffs to producers of tropical commodities.

However, when viewed from the perspective of long-term development, the colonies that were characterized by plantation capitalism played an adaptive and passive role, as their economies evolved within the limits of the structure created in the initial phases of colony building. Business centers from outside the region continued to dominate the trade in export staples. The basic pattern of the relationship of such regions with the outside world would change but little in the nineteenth century, even with the development, within the area that became a part of the United States, of a new staple (cotton) and the growth of new centers of initiative to which plantation capitalism responded (New York and Boston).

Where merchant capitalism prevailed, new centers of entrepreneurial initiative were emerging to modify the pattern of economic colonialism. With increasing ability to challenge the dominance of London and other British centers, Americans became better able to achieve a measure of economic autonomy, even before political independence was gained. Merchant capitalism was building in the Middle colonies and in New England what W. T. Easterbrook has called a transformation area, where responses to the technological and economic changes of the nineteenth century would result in a basic change in the structure of economic life. In short, this region was moving toward greater economic autonomy, an accomplishment achieved by few colonies.

SUGGESTED READINGS

D. A. Farnie, "The Commercial Empire of the Atlantic, 1607–1783," *Economic History Review*, 2d ser., 15 (1962), as well as the books by Davis, Davies, and Savelle cited at the end of chapter 1, place the economic development of England's North

American colonies in a broad context. Melville H. Watkins, "A Staple Theory of Economic Growth," *Canadian Journal of Economics and Political Science*, 29 (1963), provides a useful theoretical orientation.

Among the many case studies of the formation of English settlements in North America are Sigmund Diamond, "From Origin to Society: Virginia in the 17th Century," *American Journal of Sociology*, vol. 63 (1958); Sumner C. Powell, *Puritan Village: The Formation of a New England Town* (Middletown, Connecticut: Wesleyan University Press, 1963); and Darrett B. Rutman, *Winthrop, Boston: Portrait of a Puritan Town* (Chapel Hill, North Carolina: University of North Carolina Press, 1965). Abbot E. Smith, *Colonists in Bondage: White Servitude and Convict Labor in America, 1607–1776* (Chapel Hill, North Carolina: University of North Carolina Press, 1947) is a readable account which may be supplemented by David Galenson's article "British Servitude and the Colonial Indenture System in the 18th Century," *Journal of Southern History*, vol. 44, (1978). A summary of the experiences of the American native population during the colonial era is contained in T. J. C. Brasser, "The Coastal Algonkians: People of the First Frontier," in Eleanor V. Leacock and Nang O. Lurie *North American Indians: An Historical Perspective* (New York: Random House, 1971). W. T. Easterbrook, "The Entreprenural Function in Relation to Technology and Economic Change," in Bert F. Hoselitz, ed., *Industrialization and Society* (Paris: UNESCO, 1963) points to a way to analyze contrasting patterns of colonial regional development.

Lewis C. Gray, *History of Agriculture in the Southern United States to 1860*, vol. I, reprinted, (Gloucester, Mass.: Peter Smith, 1958) is still the standard account of the agricultural sector in the southern mainland colonies. Out of a large literature dealing with the evolution of plantation capitalism in the Chesapeake, the following afford several useful perspectives: Jacob M. Price, *France and the Chesapeake: A History of the French Tobacco Monopoly, 1674–1791, and of its Relationship to the British and American Tobacco Trades*, 2 vols. (Ann Arbor: University of Michigan Press, 1973), on the development and organization of a major European market for this leading colonial staple; J. H. Soltow, "Scottish Traders in Virginia, 1750–1776," *Economic History Review*, 2d ser., 20 (1959), on the marketing channels created by one group of British merchants; Aubrey C. Land, "Economic Behavior in a Planting Society: The Eighteenth-Century Chesapeake," *Journal of Southern History*, 33 (1967) on the developmental role of leading planter-merchants in these colonies; and Carville Earle and Ronald Hoffman, "Urban Development in the Eighteenth-Century South," *Perspectives in American History*, 10 (1976), on the relationship between the South's pattern of urban development and the characteristics of the region's leading export staples. Aubrey C. Land, ed., *Basis of the Plantation Society* (New York: Harper & Row, 1969) is a compilation of documents illustrating various aspects of plantation capitalism. The most useful discussions of slavery in the Chesapeakes are Edmund S. Morgan, *American Slavery, American Freedom: The Ordeal of Colonial Virginia* (New York: W. W. Norton, 1975), and Gerald W. Mullin, *Flight and Rebellion: Slave Resistance in Eighteenth-Century Virginia* (New York: Oxford University Press, 1972). For the Lower South, Peter H. Wood, *Black Majority: Negroes in Colonial South Carolina From 1670 Through the Stono Rebellion* (New York: Knopf, 1974) stands out. The West Indies has received much recent attention from scholars. Richard B. Sheridan, *Sugar and Slavery: An Economic History of the British West Indies, 1623–1775* (Baltimore: Johns Hopkins Press, 1974) furnishes a comprehensive account of the history of sugar production and trade, but it may be usefully supplemented with Richard S. Dunn, *Sugar and Slaves: The Rise of the Planter Class in The English West Indies, 1624–1713* (Chapel Hill: University of North Carolina Press, 1972), which places the economic development of the region in a broad social context. The starting point for the study of the slave trade is Philip D. Curtin, *The Atlantic Slave Trade: A Census* (Madison: University of Wisconsin Press, 1969). Henry A. Gemery and Jan S. Hogendorn, "The African Slave Trade: A Tentative Model," *Journal of African History*, 15 (1974) examines the mechanism of slave supply in Africa, while Robert P. Thomas and Richard N. Bean, "The Fishers of Men: The Profits of the Slave Trade," *Journal of Economic History*, 34 (1974) analyzes the profitability of the slave trade.

Percy W. Bidwell and John I. Falconer, *History of Agriculture in the Northern United States, 1620–1860*, reprinted (Gloucester, Mass.: Peter Smith, 1941) is outdated but not yet replaced. Bernard Bailyn, *The New England Merchants in the Seventeenth Century* (Cambridge: Harvard University Press, 1955) is a classic account of the role of business in organizing the region's commercial relationships with other parts of the Atlantic world. Douglas R. McManis, *Colonial New England: A Historical Geography* (New York: Oxford University Press, 1975) is a brief survey of the principal economic activities of these colonies. Harold A. Innis, *The Cod Fisheries: The History of an International Economy* (New Haven: Yale University Press, 1940) is still essential reading on New England's staple export. James T. Lemon, *The Best Poor Man's Country: A Geographical Study of Early Southeastern Pennsylvania* (Baltimore: Johns Hopkins Press, 1972) and Sung Bok Kim, *Landlord and Tenant in Colonial New York: Manorial Society, 1664–1775* (Chapel Hill: University of North Carolina Press, 1978) focus on different aspects of the development of the two most important Middle colonies. Jacob M. Price, "Economic Function and the Growth of American Port Towns in the Eighteenth Century," *Perspectives in American History*, 8 (1974) emphasizes the entrepreneurial decision-making functions of the major colonial business centers. Special aspects of the history of merchant capitalism in the eighteenth century are discussed in Richard Pares, *Yankees and Creoles: The Trade Between North America and the West Indies Before the American Revolution* (London: Longmans, Green, 1956); Arthur L. Jensen, *The Maritime Commerce of Colonial Philadelphia* (Madison: State Historical Society of Wisconsin, 1963); and James B. Hedges, *The Browns of Providence Plantations: The Colonial Years* (Cambridge: Harvard University Press, 1952). Stuart Bruchey, *A Colonial Merchant: Sources and Readings* (New York: Harcourt, Brace and World, 1968) contains documents showing seventeenth- and eighteenth-century businessmen at work.

CHAPTER 3

Growth and Welfare

in the Colonies

Agriculture was the basic industry of colonial America, with much of the market-oriented activity of the colonists connected with the production of agricultural commodities for export. In looking at this agrarian world, some observers have been most impressed with its simple character compared to the highly developed industrial economy of the United States in the late twentieth century. Yet, at the time of Independence, Americans lived and worked in a dynamic economy, one which was not backward when viewed in the perspective of the Western World of that day. One reflection of its dynamic character was the rapid growth of population and production in the colonies. An abundance of natural resources encouraged the colonists to concentrate on the production of raw materials, an activity in which they held a comparative advantage. At the same time regulations imposed by Britain were intended to channel the economic evolution of its political dependencies along lines that would perpetuate dependence upon the mother country for manufactured goods and commercial services. Nevertheless, a striking development in eighteenth-century America was the expansion of the nonagricultural sector—commerce and manufacturing. Furthermore, in this rapidly growing market-oriented economy, colonials exercised considerable ingenuity in adapting and devising financial instruments to use in making transactions. Finally, as to colonial welfare issues, while a marked increase in economic inequality is often associated with the industrialization process of the nineteenth century, a considerable portion of the total wealth of society was in fact already concentrated in the hands of the wealthiest people in 1776.

Aspects of Growth

DEMOGRAPHIC TRENDS

Since there exists no general census of the American people for the period before 1790, our knowledge of the colonial population must be based on estimates prepared by historical demographers from data in tax lists, militia rolls, and other surviving records. From these sources, it is clear that the population of the colonies grew rapidly by European standards. Between 1650 and 1700 the number of inhabitants in the mainland colonies grew more than fivefold to a total of nearly two hundred seventy-five thousand people. Then in the three-quarters of a century before the American Revolution, the colonies added almost two and one-quarter million people; this represented a near doubling of the population every twenty-five years.

In the seventeenth century, the population of the colonies as a whole grew as a result of both immigration and natural increase; slave importation became numerically important only toward the end of the century. However, there were striking differences in the demographic experience of the settlements with the greatest concentrations of population. In the Chesapeake a high mortality rate persisted. Malaria took a particularly heavy toll among new arrivals and left many of the survivors in poor health, easy victims of respiratory disease and other infections. Thus until late in the century the growth of population in Virginia and Maryland depended not on natural increase but entirely on immigration. On the other hand, seventeenth-century New England was relatively healthy, with a lower death rate than in England itself. Since religious exclusiveness minimized the region's appeal to prospective immigrants, particularly after the middle of the seventeenth century, natural increase was the principal factor in the growth of the New England population.

In the eighteenth century natural increase, immigration, and slave importation all contributed to the growth of colonial population. Attracted by economic opportunity in America, or repelled by social and economic circumstances in their homeland, three hundred thousand, or more, Europeans crossed the Atlantic; most came from the British Isles with a large minority from Germany. Over two hundred fifty thousand Africans were unwilling migrants; most went to the southern plantation colonies.

The dynamic force in demographic growth in eighteenth-century

America was the high rate of natural increase. America experienced a high birth rate, one that was somewhat higher than that of Europe. Greater opportunity for young people to assume economic responsibility encouraged a slightly earlier age of marriage for women in America. Colonial families did not deliberately limit their size, so that most women spent a considerably longer portion of their lives bearing and rearing children than did women in the twentieth century. The major demographic contrast with Europe was a reduced death rate, particularly lower levels of infant mortality. An adequate supply of food contributed to the good health of most Americans, especially women of childbearing age whose children were better able to survive the hazards of infancy and early childhood.

THE PUZZLE OF GROWTH RATES

In the absence of calculations of national product for the colonial period, it is not surprising that historians have offered widely varying estimates of trends in real product per capita. Goldsmith * has argued that anything approaching a modern growth rate of 1.6 percent per annum for long periods before 1840 would be highly questionable, implying that economic growth did not occur in America in the seventeenth and eighteenth centuries. Contrarily, Taylor † has concluded on the basis of his assessment of trends that "the average level of living about doubled in the sixty-five years before the Revolution," working out to "an average rate of increase of slightly more than 1 percent per annum" from about 1710 to 1775. Finally, Gallman ‡ has estimated that the average real product per capita increased by 50 percent at most in the six and a half decades prior to 1775—a maximum rate of growth of 0.5 percent per year—only one-half that of Taylor's figure but allowing for the possibility of more growth than assumed by Goldsmith. A further possibility is that Americans were already well off by 1700, suggested by Anderson's § calculation of an average annual increase of 1.6 percent in real wealth per capita for New England in the second half of the seventeenth century and Menard's ‖ calculations for Maryland.

---

* Raymond W. Goldsmith, "Employment, Growth, and Price Levels," Hearings Before the Joint Economic Committee, 86th Congress, First Session, Part 2, Historical and Comparative Rates of Production, Productivity and Prices; April 7, 1959 (Washington, D.C.: Government Printing Office, 1959), pp. 230–279.

† George Rogers Taylor, "American Economic Growth Before 1840: An Exploratory Essay," Journal of Economic History, 24 (December 1964), 427–444.

‡ Robert E. Gallman, "The Pace and Pattern of American Economic Growth," in Lance E. Davis et al., American Economic Growth: An Economist's History of the United States (New York: Harper & Row, 1972).

§ Terry L. Anderson, "Wealth Estimates for the New England Colonies, 1650–1709," Explorations in Economic History, 12 (April 1975), 151–176.

‖ Russell R. Menard, "Comment on Paper by Ball and Walton," Journal of Economic History, 36 (March 1976), 118–125.

Perhaps what is most important is the point, made by Egnal, that a colonial growth rate, however accurate it may be, represents an average of the widely divergent experiences of different regions at different times. Thus his estimate of an annual increase of 0.5 percent in per capita income from 1720 to 1775, based on trends in foreign trade, includes rates of growth as high as 5 percent in the Lower South from 1720 to 1735 and in the northern colonies from 1745–60, but actual declines in per capita income in both these regions from 1735–45.[*]

In spite of the difficulty of developing widely accepted estimates of rates of growth, it is clear that free white Americans of the revolutionary generation were well off by eighteenth-century standards. On the basis of an extensive analysis of the wealth held by a large sample of the colonial population, Alice Hanson Jones has estimated the average net worth of a free American on the eve of the Revolution to be seventy-four pounds sterling, equivalent to about $3,800 at 1978 prices, providing "evidence that a rather high level of living was reached in the American colonies at the close of over 150 years of economic development . . . high as compared with likely wealth in Europe at that time and in some developing countries today." [†]

SOURCES OF GROWTH

While historians cannot state with precision the overall rate of growth in colonial times, they have pointed to several conditions that served to lend strength to the American economy. Shepherd and Walton have argued that a significant decline in distribution costs occurred in the colonial era. The reduction of piracy and privateering contributed to an improvement in the productivity of ocean shipping, indirectly as well as directly, since merchant ships could sail unarmed and therefore could have smaller crews and carry more cargo. Greater security of trade also meant lower insurance costs. Improvements in commercial organization reduced the turn around time of ships in port (thus increasing the number of sailings each ship could make during a season) and enabled buyers and sellers to find markets and make transactions more quickly and economically.

It is possible, as Egnal has suggested, that an improvement in the terms of trade occurred—that is, the prices of American export commodities rose relative to prices of imported manufactured goods. Certainly

---

[*] Marc Egnal, "The Economic Development of the Thirteen Continental Colonies, 1720 to 1775," *William and Mary Quarterly*, 32 (1975), 191–222.

[†] Alice Hanson Jones, "Wealth Estimates for the New England Colonies about 1770," *Journal of Economic History*, 32 (March 1972), 98, 105. A summary of Jones' analysis of colonial wealthholding appears in "Components of Private Wealth Per Free Capita for the Thirteen Colonies, by Region: 1774," in *Historical Statistics of the United States: Colonial Times to 1970* (Washington, D.C.: United States Government Printing Office, 1975), Ser. 2 169–191, p. 1175. For a discussion of the underlying data and methodology see Alice Hanson Jones, *American Colonial Wealth: Documents and Methods*, 3 vols., 2nd ed. (New York: Arno Press, 1977).

Americans benefited from strong European demand for many of the raw materials of the Western Hemisphere. The sensory stimulus provided by luxury products like tobacco and sugar led to their incorporation into the consumption patterns of more and more middle-class households in England, France, and other countries over the course of the eighteenth century. Growing European demand for sugar and other tropical products was transmitted into expanding demand in the British and the French West Indies for foodstuffs imported from New England and the Middle colonies. (The West Indies took over one-fourth of the colonies' total exports in the 1760s and 1770s.) As southern Europe sought to develop new sources of supply of basic foods in the 1720s, Carolina rice producers were the first to profit. Then in the 1760s Spain, Portugal, and Italy began to import substantial amounts of American wheat and other food products. (Southern Europe took nearly one-fifth of the exports of the colonies on the eve of the Revolution.)

While the domestic market did not become the major interest of American business until the nineteenth century, the expansion of inter-colonial trade in the decades prior to the Revolution foreshadowed that development. Figures on ship clearances provide dramatic evidence of the growth of domestic trade. For example, in 1772 nearly one-third of the tonnage shipped from New York was destined for ports in the mainland colonies, compared to less than one-fifth a half century earlier. In 1768–72 the value of commodities involved in the coastal trade represented an estimated 20 percent of that in overseas commerce. Bread and flour alone constituted nearly one-fifth of this trade, reflecting to a considerable extent New England's dependence on the Middle colonies and the Upper South for its food supply. The evidence suggests that a large proportion of commodities shipped from one province to another was destined for consumption in the colonies rather than for reshipment overseas, a significant reflection of increasing specialization of production by region.

While colonial agriculture experienced very limited technological change, it was undergoing a progressive capitalization. A recent study of one county in Pennsylvania estimates a near doubling of the average real value of agricultural equipment per farm from the early eighteenth century to the Revolution.* Individual farmers in settled communities usually owned their plows, hoes, rakes, sickles, wagons, and other capital equipment, in contrast to their need to share the use of implements in the initial phase of settlement. Throughout the colonial period increased use was made of horse power, even though assuring an adequate supply of fuel (hay) was sometimes and in some places a problem. Control of the flow of water was achieved by the construction of dikes and irrigation

---

* D. E. Ball and G. M. Walton, "Agricultural Productivity Change in Eighteenth-Century Pennsylvania," *Journal of Economic History*, 36 (March 1976), 109.

ditches. Greater capital intensity contributed to greater productivity of the land and the labor employed in agriculture.

British Mercantilism and American Economic Growth

Starting in the middle of the seventeenth century, England passed Navigation Acts and other statutes designed to promote its own economic welfare at the expense of its European rivals. What effect did the resulting pattern of mercantilistic regulation have upon economic growth in America? Granted that government regulation, whatever its purpose, imposed some distortions upon the pattern of economic activity and thereby encouraged inefficient use of resources, how serious was the effect of these distortions? Mercantilism applied a set of specific rules to the economic life of the colonies that can be summarized and evaluated for the nature and level of their impact.

1. The Navigation Acts restricted the carrying trade of the colonies to English-built, English-owned, and English-manned ships. Since this legislation accorded to shipbuilders and shipowners in the colonies the same legal rights as possessed by their counterparts in England, colonial businessmen participated in an empire-wide monopoly. Indeed, evidence points to the ability of colonial shipowners to increase their share of the shipping business of the British Empire in the eighteenth century. On the eve of the Revolution, sales of shipping services and invisible export of the colonies generated "earnings larger than the value of any commodity with the one exception of tobacco," according to the findings of Shepherd and Walton.* As we shall see in the next section, shipbuilding became an important industry in the colonies and ships became an important export.

2. British regulation required that certain commodities, which were enumerated, could be exported only to England; the most important were sugar, tobacco, rice, indigo, and naval stores. Where large amounts of such commodities as tobacco and rice were re-exported from Britain to continental Europe, indirect routing imposed extra costs such as port charges, middlemen's commissions, and customs duties; this has led some historians to argue that American producers would have earned more with direct routing. However, it cannot be assumed that distribution costs would have been substantially lower if the Navigation Acts had not existed. In the case of tobacco, for example, British business provided marketing

---

* James F. Shepherd and Gary M. Walton, *Shipping, Maritime Trade, and the Economic Development of Colonial North America* (Cambridge: Cambridge University Press, 1972), p. 116.

services and developed commercial connections with the purchasers who bought in large volume for the French tobacco monopoly and with the many importers and wholesalers who handled distribution in Holland and Germany. Within the framework of enumeration, British business introduced significant economies into the marketing system in the mid-eighteenth century, some of which were passed along to planters because of vigorous competition among buyers.

3. Another provision of the Navigation Acts stipulated that all goods of European origin destined for the colonies had to be shipped through England, with the exception of certain products of southern Europe. This was intended to encourage the colonials to purchase British manufactured goods, since foreign wares would be more expensive because of transshipment costs. Yet it is likely that Britain would in any event have been the principal supplier of manufactured goods for the colonies, due to her industrial lead over France and other potential European rivals. As François Crouzet, a leading French historian, has concluded, "British superiority [over France] in the eighteenth century was in the manufacture of good quality products suitable for middle-class consumption," * the kind of goods most suitable for the colonial market.

4. The British government extended subsidies and tariff protection in the British market to encourage increased production of certain colonial commodities such as naval stores (tar, pitch, and turpentine) essential to shipbuilding and ship repair, and indigo, a raw material used by the textile industry. However rewarding such governmental favors might have been to individual producers, they did not represent a clear gain to the colonies, since, as Thomas has noted, "part of the bounty was a payment for the inefficient allocation of colonial resources." Yet it is impossible to measure exactly the extent to which resources were diverted "from more efficient uses into industries where they were employed less efficiently." † For example, the production of naval stores provided part-time employment for farmers. And indigo was grown mainly in areas of South Carolina containing soil not suitable for rice cultivation or other uses.

5. In order to preserve the provincial market for the products of British industry, Parliament imposed various kinds of restrictions on manufacturing in the colonies. No kind of manufacturing was ever forbidden. Rather, expansion of colonial industry was discouraged through statutes restricting the size of the market (for woolen goods and hats), prohibiting the erection of new facilities (for making finished iron goods), or levying a prohibitive duty on raw material (molasses used in distilling rum). (This last regulation was intended to protect the sugar planters of the

* F. Crouzet, "England and France in the Eighteenth Century: A Comparative Analysis of Two Economic Growths," The Causes of the Industrial Revolution in England, ed. R. M. Hartwell (London: Methuen & Co., 1967), p. 165.

† Robert Paul Thomas, "A Quantitative Approach to the Study of the Effects of British Imperial Policy upon Colonial Welfare: Some Preliminary Findings," Journal of Economic History, 25 (December 1965), 627.

British West Indies.) In no case did the restrictive legislation have much practical significance, since little attempt was made to enforce these laws. This is not to say that British policy was purposely benign. If the policy makers in London had possessed more accurate information about the extent of manufacturing in the colonies, they perhaps would have created effective regulations to restrict industrial growth.

It should be emphasized that the colonials were in no way opposed to the basic assumption of mercantilism that government should be actively used to shape economic development toward desired goals. Provincial governments enacted a variety of measures to achieve economic purposes. They created inspection systems for their major exports, usually to promote these exports by improving their reputation for quality in foreign markets. For example, Pennsylvania officials inspected flour, meat, and lumber products destined for export, while Virginia and Maryland required the tobacco they shipped out to be of a minimum quality. To encourage production of certain commodities, most colonies provided bounties. The items most commonly subsidized were hemp and flax, but Virginia and South Carolina also tried to promote shipbuilding by granting bounties. Some colonies experimented with tonnage duties as a device to favor local shippers.

Thus a century of British mercantilistic regulation did little to alter the pattern of development of the colonial economy, a pattern of providing raw materials to an economically more advanced area and, in turn, using that area's manufactured goods and commercial services. For many decades colonials were unable to provide a full range of goods and services for their own use. The Navigation Acts meant that most of the goods and services which the colonials could efficiently provide for themselves were supplied by British businessmen and that businessmen of other European powers were excluded. Within the framework of regulation, Americans organized legal trade outside of the normal patterns of economic relationships between colony and imperial power—particularly commerce with the West Indies and with southern Europe.

British governmental regulation imposed only a light economic burden upon the colonials. Thomas has calculated the annual net cost to America of membership in the British Empire for the decade following 1763 at twenty-six cents per capita. (This takes into account the value of defense provided by the British armed forces.) * Even Harper, who estimated the burden to have been somewhat heavier, concluded that "judged by contemporary standards, the colonies might have fared much worse." † However, as we shall see in the next chapter, new regulations

---

* Thomas, "A Quantitative Approach to the Study of the Effects of British Imperial Policy," p. 637.

† Lawrence A. Harper, "The Effect of the Navigation Acts on the Thirteen Colonies," *The Era of the American Revolution*, ed. Richard B. Morris (New York: Columbia University Press, 1939), p. 39.

and new perceptions of the impact of British mercantilism upon American economic life contributed to the revolutionary crisis of the 1760s and 1770s.

The Industrial Sector

Although agriculture was paramount, colonial Americans supplied a substantial portion of their industrial goods. In rural areas farm families with limited cash engaged in household manufactures, the production of a wide range of goods by members of the family for their own use— prepared foods, clothing, furniture, and many other items consumed in day-to-day living. But the finished products of household manufactures, made with very limited skills, were necessarily rather crude. An increasing ability to acquire commercially produced goods through exchange constituted encouragement for farmers to expand their production of agricultural commodities for the market so that they could take advantage of the opportunity to improve the quality of their consumption. By the end of the colonial era commercial manufacturing had developed to meet many of the needs of American consumers and even to export certain kinds of industrial products.

As in contemporary Europe, the typical manufacturer of colonial America was a craftsman whose industrial activity rested upon his own skill in the use of hand tools, and who principally served a local market, often producing individual items to the orders of specific customers. Every town and village had its complement of artisans to provide basic services for the community—carpenter, blacksmith, tanner, shoemaker, wheelwright, and stoneman. In rural areas itinerant craftsmen travelled from farmhouse to farmhouse to perform skilled work that farmers themselves were unable to do. In the southern colonies slaves were trained to perform many kinds of skilled work.

But it was in the cities, where the largest population and the greatest amount of wealth were concentrated, that craftsmanship flourished. Philadelphia, New York, and Boston were industrial centers as well as port towns. They contained almost all the kinds of handicraft manufacturers to be found in European cities, and supplied not only the basic needs of the population but a variety of luxury goods as well. In Philadelphia, for example, craftsmen accounted for slightly over one-half of the tax-assessed population in 1774, and included 713 people engaged in making clothing, 532 in construction trades and furniture manufacture, 361 producing transportation equipment, 246 in food processing and preparation, and 103 in metal work, ranging from guns to silverware.

The handicraft manufacturer was a small businessman. The family was the unit of labor, with the master craftsman assisted by his wife and children and perhaps an apprentice or two; his workshop and home were usually contained in the same building. The craftsman normally financed his entry into independent business with savings earned during a relatively short period of work as a journeyman. But the ease of entry into most crafts, due to the small investment required, limited the ability of craft manufacturers to expand their operations by hiring journeymen to work in their shops. The failure of guilds to control industry as they did in Europe and the ability of relatively large numbers of individuals to acquire skills through apprenticeship made competition intense. Individual craftsmen attempted through advertising to establish product differentiation based on their reputation for workmanship and originality of design. Immigrant craftsmen continually introduced new techniques that had been developed in Europe, and the force of competition encouraged members of the trade to adopt these new ways. Thus over a period of time the productivity of many crafts must have risen by at least a small amount, although we have no specific data.

While the European tradition of industry was transmitted principally through the activity of independent craftsmen-entrepreneurs, there also existed in America a variety of "mill and furnace industries," * to use Victor S. Clark's term; they often operated on a somewhat larger scale and sometimes utilized machinery and water power. Most of these industries involved the processing of natural resources: flour milling, lumbering, leather tanning, or the making of tar and turpentine. Other industries, like rum distilling, converted imported materials into consumer goods.

Shipbuilding and iron manufacture were two important industries of the eighteenth century which applied industrial skills to capitalize on America's comparative advantage in raw materials. Ships were constructed in the early settlements to meet the needs of colonists for local transport; some builders soon turned to the production of vessels for the coastal and the West Indian trades. Later, American yards made some of the large ships employed in the transatlantic trade. America's competitive advantage in shipbuilding lay in the cost of raw material—wood—which outweighed the higher wages paid to colonial workers. Shipyards were located in all of the mainland colonies, but output was concentrated in New England, which accounted for nearly two thirds of the tonnage built in the early 1770s. By the eve of the American Revolution the estimated annual value of shipbuilding in the thirteen colonies was three hundred thousand pounds, of which nearly one-half was sold abroad. Thus ships had become an important export product of American industry. Although ships do not appear in the customs records, they were perhaps the fourth most valuable export of the colonies.

* Victor S. Clark, *History of Manufactures in the United States*, reprinted New York: Peter Smith, 1949 (Washington, D.C.: Carnegie Institution of Washington, 1929), vol. I, pp. 164–181.

With the advantage of cheap fuel—charcoal from the forests—and ores available close to the surface, the colonial iron industry expanded in the half century prior to the Revolution to meet the needs of the growing American economy. By 1775 the colonies had more blast furnaces and forges than did England and Wales, and they produced nearly one-seventh of the world output of iron, a relative position not again gained by America until the 1860s. Ironworks were located in every colony except Georgia, with Pennsylvania the leader in this activity from the 1750s. In contrast to urban handicraft industry, iron plantations were established in rural areas at sites of water power and adjacent to supplies of ore and of wood for charcoal. Because ironmaking required technical skill and a large amount of capital as well, most firms consisted of a partnership between a merchant, who supplied funds and developed marketing channels, and an ironmaster, who organized production. Most of the pig iron and bar iron produced on colonial iron plantations was used to manufacture tools, or other implements, metal wares, a branch of production still in the handicraft stage. The British government, in order to assure a supply of material for its own manufacturers, offered in the Iron Act of 1750 tariff preference to encourage the colonies to export semifinished iron to the mother country. But neither this provision nor one that prohibited the erection in the colonies of new mills to make finished iron goods was effective. Some iron was shipped to England by colonial producers, but as long as skilled artisans were available in the colonies, it seemed to make little economic sense to send iron to Britain to be returned in the form of finished goods.

Despite the high cost of labor and capital in a country with an abundance of land, and despite British efforts to discourage manufacturers, industrial development in America did not lag far behind that of Europe in the eighteenth century. As Victor Clark has commented, the industrial history of colonial America embodied "the total experience of European industry." * Household manufactures were widespread in the colonies, but it should be noted that this form of production also continued to supply a significant share of consumer goods in rural areas in England even in the nineteenth century. In activities in which the colonies held an advantage in raw materials, they attained a degree of development in manufacturing equivalent to that of the mother country. Indeed, flour millers in the colonies early gained a reputation for using water power more extensively than was common in Europe.

In both Europe and America in the eighteenth century much of the increase in industrial production was preindustrial in the sense that it resulted from an expansion of traditionally organized handicrafts, dependent upon manual dexterity and knowledge rather than upon machinery and power. But this preindustrial development contributed to a

---

* Clark, *History of Manufactures in the United States*, vol. I, p. 7.

widespread diffusion of industrial knowledge, and business skills since most colonial artisans were self-employed and had to use rudimentary business methods. As the market for the products of local handicraft industry expanded with the growth of population, various crafts began to diversify and specialize, so that artisans became familiar with the economy division of labor. Although the modern factory system was just being created in England toward the end of the American colonial period, elements of that method of industrial organization were already employed in the colonies. In some lines of manufacture, like gun making, a number of hand operations were brought together in one establishment, thereby "knitting them into a continuous and reciprocally adjusted process." * Other entrepreneurs were organizing textile "manufactories," or workshops, where they assembled implements and gathered a number of workers in one building. The societies that operated these establishments, organized for philanthropic and patriotic reasons as often as for commercial purposes, foreshadowed the later manufacturing corporation. And adoption of labor-saving machinery, which would become a widely recognized characteristic of American manufacturing industry by the middle of the nineteenth century, was a tradition already established in the colonies in industries like flour milling. Merchants, the most important economic decision makers in colonial America, had already turned their attention to manufacturing, which often complemented their commercial activities. Some, like the Browns of Rhode Island, were beginning to think of themselves primarily as industrialists, as they increasingly conducted their foreign and domestic trade to meet the needs of their candle-making and iron-manufacturing businesses.

The Financial Sector

As participants in a market-oriented economy, colonials recognized the inherent efficiency of money in the exchange process. The problem, in their eyes, was that there was not enough money with which to do their business. They meant that there was an insufficient amount of specie —gold and silver—which they regarded as the only "real" money. The scarcity of specie was due basically to an adverse balance of trade. Since the colonists consumed imported goods having greater value than the commodities they exported, a considerable portion of the specie that they gained in trade with areas like the West Indies was drained out to pay for imports. Americans then devised a variety of expedients, using both the

* Clark, *History of Manufactures in the United States*, vol. I, p. 193.

public and the private sectors, to settle transactions with the use of a minimum of real money: overvalued foreign coins, monetized commodities, paper currency, commercial instruments like bills of exchange, and mercantile bookkeeping devices. One result was a separation of two of the principal functions of money: As a *standard of value*, all colonies used a variant of the English monetary system of pounds, shillings, and pence. But they employed as a *medium of exchange* several different kinds of money, principally non-English, and nonmoney, or as some called it in the eighteenth century, "imaginary money."

PUBLIC SECTOR RESPONSES

Due largely to a shortage of hard money in England itself, English law prohibited the export of English coins to the colonies, although some coins were in fact carried by travellers. Since provincial governments were forbidden to mint their own coins, Spanish and Portuguese gold and silver coins, obtained through trade with the West Indies, provided most of the real money in circulation in the colonies. These pieces of eight (or milled dollars), johannes, and coins of other denominations were valued in terms of the English monetary system. For example, the Spanish piece of eight, on the basis of its silver content, was equivalent to 4 shillings 6 pence in sterling. However, each colony, in order to discourage a drain on its supply of coins because of the adverse balance of trade with England, overvalued these coins by raising their value as legal tender in terms of the colony's own provincial currency. Although the British government put a stop to this practice in the early eighteenth century, at least five different valuations of pounds, shillings, and pence prevailed among the mainland colonies. The value of a piece of eight ranged from four shillings eight pence in South Carolina to eight shillings in New York. This colonial action did not alter the sterling value of gold and silver coins. What it did mean was that a given number of pounds in colonial currency purchased fewer pounds in English currency; for example, £156 in New York currency was equivalent to £100 sterling.

Commodity money provided a second kind of currency for the colonies. The use of commodities, ranging from tobacco and sugar to wheat and lumber, as money differed from simple barter. A provincial legislature would decree that a certain product of that province would be accepted, at a stipulated rate, in payment of taxes and other public debts. In other words, the commodity was denominated in terms of pounds, shillings, and pence, and carried an element of legal tender. However, commodity money posed several serious problems: transporting and storing bulky goods, assessing the quality of the commodities tendered, and fluctuations in price. The Chesapeake colonies developed in the eighteenth century a variant of commodity money which dealt with the first two of these deficiencies. After inspection systems were organized in Virginia (1730) and in Maryland (1747), tobacco notes, which were receipts issued to owners of tobacco deposited in public warehouses, were accepted in payment of provincial taxes and thus became a form of money. But fluctuations in the price of tobacco continued to create difficulties; a currency increasing in value worked hardships on debtors, as did a depreciating currency on creditors.

Paper money, issued by all of the colonies in varying amounts, served not only to supplement the currency supply but also to meet the fiscal needs of government and to provide credit to stimulate agricultural expansion. To finance military operations, provincial governments issued bills of credit, or treasury notes, with the understanding that they would be retired out of future tax receipts—a process called currency finance. Since these bills or notes were accepted in payment of taxes and other government obligations, they were used in private transactions as well and thus became part of the currency. A second form of paper money consisted of notes issued by the land banks, agencies created by the provincial governments to lend at low interest rates on the security of real estate. These notes too could be used to pay taxes, were accepted in private transactions, and formed part of the money supply.

When some of the colonies issued large amounts of paper currency, creating inflation which undermined the value of debts owed to creditors (in America as well as in Britain), the British government attempted to develop a control mechanism. After efforts to limit the volume of paper money by administrative means failed, Parliament passed the Currency Act of 1751, which prohibited the issue of paper money in the New England colonies, the place where the most serious inflation had occurred. The Currency Act of 1764 extended this prohibition to the rest of the mainland colonies. Some easing of these restrictions was contained in the Currency Act of 1773, which permitted colonies to make paper money legal tender in payments to provincial governments but not in private transactions. At the same time serious consideration was given to the establishment of a continental land bank with a branch office in each province, to be centrally managed from London. But by the 1770s monetary problems had become too much entangled in the conflict over taxes and trade regulation to be considered as a separate issue.

BUSINESS AND THE MONEY PROBLEM

An expansion of the use of financial instruments allowed businessmen to carry on an enlarged trade without a proportionate increase of their money holdings. These devices, generated in the course of private business, served as a functional equivalent of money in providing a medium of exchange.

The financial instrument most familiar to colonial merchants was the bill of exchange, which had originated in medieval Europe as a means of settling international transactions. An American importer making payment for goods that he had purchased from a British exporter normally used a bill of exchange rather than shipping specie. When he found another American businessman who held credits on the books of a British firm, usually representing the proceeds from the sale of a shipment, he might purchase from his colonial colleague an order directing the British firm to pay a specified sum of money to him. He used his colonial currency when he bought the bill, which he then endorsed and sent to his creditor in Britain; the latter presented it for payment in British currency. In this simplified exchange transaction, the seller of the bill had in effect transferred funds from Britain to America; the buyer had transferred funds from America to Britain.

A bill of exchange was negotiable when it was endorsed by the person to whose order it was drawn. Bills could be endorsed as many times as desired, and thus could be used as a form of payment among businessmen either in the colonies or in England. In eighteenth-century London specialized business firms discounted bills of exchange, not only those which had their origin in transatlantic trade but also inland bills arising out of transactions between London and the provinces. In the colonies the market for bills developed in a less formal manner. In the large port towns merchants met daily in a designated place where they could make known their wishes to buy or sell bills on London, the most useful form of sterling exchange. In a colony like Virginia, where no one urban center dominated trade, merchants and planters bought and sold bills of exchange in the provincial capital at periodic meetings, which coincided with the orderly sessions of the courts.

In conducting business within a colony, urban merchants and country storekeepers used a variety of techniques to buy and sell without actually using money. Even though no cash might change hands, all transactions were calculated in money values. The most sophisticated of several methods was the triangular transfer of credit, a method by which bookkeeping entries made it possible to settle debts among several parties. If an individual had neither cash nor goods on hand to pay a sum owed to another, he might direct a merchant or storekeeper on whose books he had a cash balance to transfer funds from his own account to the account of his creditor. If the order was written, it could be made "to order," endorsed by the payee, and then circulated as a form of money until presented for payment. It resembled a modern bank check in that it could be endorsed and transferred from party to party.

ADEQUACY OF THE MONETARY SYSTEM

The expedients devised by decision makers in both the public and the private sectors have to be judged an overall success in providing a supply of money for a rapidly expanding market-oriented economy. At least the colonies did not experience the long-run deflation, or the decline in the price level, that would have been associated with an insufficient supply of money. The record of various colonies, however, was uneven with respect to controlling inflation, or a rise in the price level. In Pennsylvania, where the paper money supply was well managed, prices rose by 57 percent from 1720 to 1774, an annual rate of 0.8 percent. On the other hand large volumes of paper currency were issued by the New England colonies, particularly Massachusetts and Rhode Island. It is not surprising that Boston prices rose four and one-half times higher than did those of Philadelphia in the half century prior to the Revolution.

That the colonial monetary systems "worked" does not imply the absence of several serious inadequacies. In the first place, supplying a medium of exchange was often only a secondary function of issues of paper money. War finance was usually the occasion for the emission of bills of credit, with provision for retirement when peace returned. Thus an important component of the money supply expanded and contracted not with the changing level of economic activity but in response to the fiscal needs of provincial government. Even the paper money issues made by land banks in connection with agricultural developments were not managed with a view to keeping a specified amount of currency in circulation. In Pennsylvania, for example, year to year fluctuations of 10 to 67 percent in the stock of paper money outstanding were not uncommon.

The second weakness was related to the significant role in the financial mechanism of the colonies played by trade credit, an inherently unstable element. The ability of British merchants to extend credit to Americans depended on the working of the financial system in Britain. When problems in the London money market caused contraction by bankers there, British merchants had to reduce the amount of credit outstanding in the colonies by collecting old debts and refusing new credit. A credit crunch in Britain meant a serious decline in colonial purchasing power, a product of the withdrawal of trade credit, a drain of available hard money to settle balances, and a reduction in the amount of sterling bills of exchange available. This had severe effects on the well-being of all Americans who participated in the market economy. In this setting of adversity, colonials might have sought to offset decreases in certain kinds of money with increases in local paper currency. But they were blocked by British restrictions on the issue of paper money—these restrictions that were designed primarily to protect British investments in America. Perhaps the nub of the currency problem was the inadequacy of the imperial system to resolve conflicts between British and American interests. American businessmen could view lack of effective control of their own monetary policy as a serious impediment to the achievement of economic autonomy.

Issues of Economic Welfare: Wealth and Poverty

Only in recent years have historians directed serious attention to the study of wealth distribution in colonial society. Now, however, research into hitherto little used tax records and probated wills provides the basis for some tentative generalizations about the broad patterns of wealth holding before the American Revolution.

One point is clear: Colonial America was not a land of equality, or near equality, of property ownership. According to estimates by Alice Hanson Jones, on the eve of the Revolution the richest 10 percent of the free population owned 60 to 65 percent of the personal wealth in the colonies. We can speak with less certainty about the trends in the overall profile of wealth holding. Some historians have argued that the concentration of wealth increased steadily during the half century before the American Revolution, and that the rate of increase may even have accelerated. Yet there is more support for the conclusion of Lindert and Williamson that "stability in wealth distribution seems to characterize the century prior to 1776." * In other words, broad patterns of wealth distribution were established fairly early in the history of the colonies, and there were no strong trends toward either greater or lesser equality in the century before 1776.

Concentration of wealth tended to be greatest in commercial centers and in areas with staple production that used slave labor. Rewards were large for those who successfully assumed leadership in integrating the economy of their regions into the British commercial empire—the merchants of the port towns and the planter-entrepreneurs of the southern colonies. However, the wealthy did not constitute a closed circle, since a growing population and a growing economy provided room at the top for newcomers. The need for a relatively large amount of capital to carry on foreign trade or to operate a plantation with slave labor meant that there were few rags-to-riches dramas. But there existed the strong possibility for families to achieve significant upward mobility over several generations.

In spite of the prominent position of a small wealthy class, what was most distinctive about the society of colonial America, viewed in the perspective of the eighteenth-century Western World, was its large proportion of middle-class property owners, estimated by Jackson Turner Main to comprise "well over half of the white population" in the 1770s.† The growth of cities and towns furnished opportunities for artisans, shopkeep-

* Peter H. Lindert and Jeffrey G. Williamson, "Three Centuries of American Inequality," *Research in Economic History*, 1 (1976), 98.
† Jackson Turner Main, *The Social Structure of Revolutionary America* (Princeton, N.J.: Princeton University Press, 1965), pp. 65–67.

ers, tavern operators, and other small-scale entrepreneurs. There were few guild regulations to restrict entry or activity, and municipalities levied only a small license fee. For most kinds of business only a small amount of initial capital was required, and the necessary technical and business skills could be readily acquired by most young people through a relatively short apprenticeship to a master craftsman or a merchant. As Cochran has noted, "Ease of entry into small business was the most important difference between the Old World and the New." *

Much more numerous among the middle class were landowning farmers. In contrast to European peasants, most American farmers viewed their land as an economic asset that could be sold as readily as it had been acquired, a perception reflected in the legal system of property rights. Of the various forms of tenure in real property used in England, the settlers instituted only ownership of land in fee simple; by thus giving real estate owners control of their property, including the right to will, lease, or sell it, subject only to the payment of taxes, land became a marketable commodity. The declining importance of the extended kinship group reduced the significance of family influence and tradition on the reaching of decisions, and encouraged mobility and individual initiative in making rational responses to economic opportunity.

Few communities had to suffer a decline of living standards due to pressure of population on the land. Typically, early settlers in an area acquired more land than they required for their immediate needs. Average acreage per farm then tended to decline over the ensuing decades as each generation divided the land among its sons, until a minimum size was reached. Younger sons who wanted to continue a career in farming migrated to the frontier, sometimes going to land purchased by their fathers. Other "surplus" members of a farm community elected to move to the city to become apprentices to artisans or shopkeepers. Sometimes it was not necessary to leave the community to find an opportunity outside agriculture. A growing population of farm families made up a market for many kinds of goods and services—things that the farmers had provided for themselves in the early stage of settlement but now sought to buy from specialized producers: millers, blacksmiths, carpenters, tanners, and distillers. A rise in the nonagricultural sector of the labor force was an alternative to outmigration for a community no longer able to support all of its members in farming.

THE PARADOX OF POVERTY

In spite of the relatively high average of wealth in colonial America, poverty existed. Since the poor were regarded as part of the order of things, each colony early in its history enacted legislation assigning to local

* Thomas C. Cochran, *Business in American Life: A History* (New York: McGraw-Hill, 1972), p. 26.

governments responsibility for the care of those unable to support themselves. County or town officials were required to levy taxes upon residents
to provide a minimum level of living for those entitled to seek relief by
virtue of their birthright or their residence in the community for a stipulated period. Poor Laws not only fixed but also limited responsibility,
as nonresidents could be "warned out" out of the community. Much of
the assistance consisted of outdoor relief—funds allocated by overseers of
the poor to provide for a particular need of an individual, such as an item
of clothing or a pair of shoes, a specified amount of firewood, funeral
expenses, or medical care. By the 1730s the large towns had built alms-
houses where the poor were housed and required to perform useful work
for the community. In addition to the Poor Laws, efforts were made in
the private sector to deal with the problems of poverty. Churches mobilized support for their less fortunate members as did societies formed by
immigrant groups and organizations created by artisans.

Evidence indicates that the amount expended for relief of the poor
by public bodies and by voluntary organizations was increasing in the
half century prior to the American Revolution. But we cannot determine
whether rising outlays resulted from an increase in the number of poor
or reflected growing humanitarian concern. Moreover, the increasing size
and complexity of communities may have encouraged a rationalization of
poor relief, as society decided to dispense a greater proportion of its help
to the poor through formal institutions rather than through individual giving, whether to neighbors or to beggars.

Who were "the Proper Objects of Publick Charity?" Unfortunately,
the records do not permit us to classify the sources of poverty, since
colonial Americans tended to define the poor by their needs, not by a
process. However, it is clear that the largest group of needy consisted
of the "unfortunates": women and children left widowed and orphaned
as a result of loss of the head of the household—at sea, by epidemic,
from an accident, or as a casualty of war; the sick and injured suffering
a long-term disability; the physically and mentally handicapped; and the
aged. Individuals or families sometimes experienced temporary misfor-
tune from which they had to be rescued through the poor-relief machinery: victims of fire or other disasters to their property, war refugees from
frontier areas, and newly arrived immigrants who were too ill to work or
to proceed to rural areas because of the atrocious conditions they had experienced on shipboard. Few colonials would have denied at least a
minimum amount of support to these unfortunates. At the other end of
the spectrum were the vagabonds and drifters, often English convicts released after their terms of service in the colonies. These people probably
received more attention than their actual numbers warranted, since they
were also held responsible for much of the crime in city and countryside.
Support was provided for these people more grudgingly. It is likely that
Benjamin Franklin had them in mind when he argued that the "best

way of doing good to the poor is not making them easy *in* poverty, but leading or driving them *out* of it." What is more difficult to determine is the extent to which "industrious," able-bodied persons, who were ordinarily self-supporting, needed to seek public assistance as a result of their unemployment during a depression or during one of the trade stoppages which were employed by colonial leaders as a strategy in their political controversy with Britain. We know even less about the extent and sources of poverty among those who did not receive public support because they were just above the poverty line as it was then perceived.

Whatever conclusions future historical research may support regarding the extent and sources of poverty in colonial America, it is significant that this provincial society developed a set of standards for making decisions about the care of its economically less fortunate members—standards that were operative for several generations. In an age when the wealth of society was still low by modern standards, and so its ability effectively to "abolish" poverty, colonials accepted the inevitability of poverty and determined that the most extreme forms of economic deprivation were intolerable. Borrowing both from tradition and from continuing development in the mother country, Americans developed a set of attitudes and institutions, in the public and the private sectors, to carry out the responsibilities that had been defined for the relief of the poor. These attitudes and institutions survived until the twentieth century when larger amounts of wealth generated by the Industrial Revolution made possible new approaches to deal with poverty—approaches now regarded as more realistic.

Summary

The American population nearly doubled every twenty-five years after 1700, the result of immigration, slave importations, and, most significantly, a high rate of natural increase compared to the Old World. While widely accepted estimates of trends in per capita product for the colonial era do not exist, free white Americans were relatively well off on the eve of the Revolution. Sources of growth in the eighteenth-century economy included productivity increases in the distribution sector, possibly improvements in the terms of trade resulting from strong European demand for American commodities, expansion of domestic trade with its encouragement of regional specialization, and a progressive capitalization of agriculture within a framework of slow technological change. British mercantilism, till 1763, tended to reinforce the pattern of colonial economic development that most likely would have occurred anyway without regulation—

exploitation of the resource base through specialization on production of staple commodities for export. But regulation did not prevent the growth of commerce outside of the British Empire nor the expansion of a manufacturing sector. Although colonials experienced what they perceived to be a shortage of money (specie), they developed substitutes, most notably, government-issued currency, with which to carry on their business. On the eve of the Revolution wealth was highly concentrated in the hands of the wealthiest segments of the population; however, the large proportion of middle-class farmers, artisans, and traders, compared to Europe, reflected the numerous opportunities for ordinary people in a growing economy.

SUGGESTED READINGS

Aspects of economic growth and its sources in the colonial era are discussed in Stuart Bruchey, *The Roots of American Economic Growth, 1607–1861: An Essay in Social Causation* (New York: Harper & Row, 1965); George Rogers Taylor, "American Economic Growth before 1840: An Exploratory Essay," *Journal of Economic History*, 24 (1964); Robert E. Gallman, "The Pace and Pattern of American Economic Growth," in Lance E. Davis et al., *American Economic Growth: An Economist's History of the United States* (New York: Harper & Row, 1972); Marc Egnal, "The Economic Development of the Thirteen Continental Colonies, 1720 to 1775," *William and Mary Quarterly*, 3d ser., 32 (1975); Gary M. Walton and James F. Shepherd, *The Economic Rise of Early America* (Cambridge: Cambridge University Press, 1979); James A. Henretta, *The Evolution of American Society, 1700–1815: An Interdisciplinary Analysis* (Lexington, Mass.: D. C. Heath, 1973). Terry L. Anderson, "Wealth Estimates for the New England Colonies, 1650–1709," *Explorations in Economic History*, 12 (1975); Terry L. Anderson and Robert P. Thomas, "Economic Growth in the Seventeenth-Century Chesapeake," *Explorations in Economic History*, 15 (1978); and D. E. Ball and G. M. Walton, "Agricultural Productivity Changes in Eighteenth-Century Pennsylvania," *Journal of Economic History*, 36 (1976). Developments in overseas and intercolonial trade, as they relate to the growth of the colonial economy, are covered in James F. Shepherd and Gary M. Walton, *Shipping, Maritime Trade, and the Economic Development of Colonial North America* (Cambridge: Cambridge University Press, 1972), and James F. Shepherd and Samuel H. Williamson, "The Coastal Trade of the British North American Colonies, 1768–1772," *Journal of Economic History*, 32 (1972). Gary M. Walton, "The New Economic History and the Burdens of the Navigation Act," *Economic History Review*, 2d ser., 24 (1971) reviews the controversy about the impact of British mercantilism upon American economic life. Sources of information about demographic change include J. Potter, "The Growth of Population in America, 1700–1860," in D. V. Glass and D. E. C. Eversely, eds., *Population in History: Essays in Historical Demography* (Chicago: Aldine, 1965), Robert V. Wells, *The Population of the British Colonies in America before 1776* (Princeton: Princeton University Press, 1975); David Scott Smith, "The Demographic History of Colonial New England," *Journal of Economic History*, vol. 32, 1972; and Daniel Blake-Smith, "Mortality and Family in the Colonial Chesapeake," *Journal of Interdisciplinary History*, vol. 8, 1978.

Victor S. Clark, *History of Manufactures in the United States, Volume I, 1607–1860*, reprinted (New York: Peter Smith, 1949) is still the only general history of manufacturing in the colonial period although it may be usefully supplemented by Carl Bridenbaugh, *The Colonial Craftsman* (New York: New York University Press,

1950), and Arthur C. Bining, *British Regulation of the Colonial Iron Industry* (Philadelphia: University of Pennsylvania Press, 1933).

A good introduction to the study of the financial sector is Curtis P. Nettels, *The Money Supply of the American Colonies before 1720* (Madison: University of Wisconsin, 1934); a valuable supplement is Leslie V. Brock, *The Currency of the American Colonies, 1700–1764* (New York: Arno Press, 1975). Joseph A. Ernst, *Money and Politics in America, 1755–1775* (Chapel Hill: University of North Carolina Press, 1973) analyzes American responses to British regulation of the issue of paper currency by provincial governments, while W. T. Baxter, *The House of Hancock: Business in Boston: 1724–1775* (Cambridge: Harvard University Press, 1945) illustrates the use of monetary expedients devised by the private sector. John J. McCusker, *Money and Exchange in Europe and America, 1600–1775: A Handbook* (Chapel Hill: University of North Carolina Press, 1977) extends our understanding of the role of foreign exchange in the colonial financial system.

Alice Hanson Jones, *American Colonial Wealth: Documents and Methods*, 3 vols. (New York: Arno Press, 1977) supplies basic data for study of living standards and property ownership at the end of the colonial period. A starting point for reading on trends in wealth distribution is Peter H. Lindert and Jeffrey G. Williamson, "Three Centuries of American Inequality," *Research in Economic History*, 1 (1976), which contains a summary statement and an extensive bibliography. Several studies of colonial wealth distribution are included in Gary B. Nash, ed.. *Class and Society in Early America* (Englewood Cliffs, N.J.: Prentice-Hall, 1970), but see also Gloria L. Main, "Inequality in Early America: The Evidence from Probate Records of Massachusetts and Maryland," *Journal of Interdisciplinary History*, 7 (1977). Gary B. Nash, "Urban Wealth and Poverty in Pre-Revolutionary America," *Journal of Interdisciplinary History*, 6 (1976), marshals data about the extent of poverty, but Jacob M. Price, "Quantifying Colonial America: A Comment on Nash and Warden," *Journal of Interdisciplinary History*, 6 (1976) sounds a note of caution on the use of statistical evidence in the study of colonial economic and social issues.

CHAPTER 4

━━━

Foundations of Economic

Independence

Although Americans had fared well within the London-centered commercial empire of the Atlantic, economic and political developments after 1763 brought to the fore the basic problem of colonial status—the colonies' lack of control over the decision-making system that influenced many aspects of their affairs. When political means failed to change British policy, Americans mobilized their economic resources to support a prolonged military operation. Attainment of independence released their entrepreneurial energies into new channels and made possible the use of government policy to stimulate economic development. However, independence, coincided with a period of difficult economic readjustment, and confronted the new nation's leaders with the problem of establishing the authority to cope with it through a new national government. The Constitution that they adopted both provided the political stability necessary for economic growth and furnished the legal framework for the establishment of a nationwide market economy.

Breakdown of the Imperial-Colonial Structure

In 1763 the British government needed more revenue in order to retire the large debt it had incurred during the Seven Years' War as well as to finance future defense efforts. The British government was also concerned with inadequate enforcement of commercial regulations in the colonies; even while England was fighting France, some American colonials had persisted in trade with the enemy. To secure a source of revenue in the colonies, the British government attempted in the decade after 1763 to impose a tax on newspapers and legal documents and to levy import duties upon a series of items. To improve the customs service—its efficiency was at such a low level that the amount it collected was only one-fourth of the cost of administration—the British government tried to impose stricter discipline on appointed officials in America and to tighten the enforcement of the regulations. More colonial commodities were placed on the enumerated list, and Americans were prohibited from exporting nonenumerated items to northern Europe. The Tea Act of 1773, which authorized the East India Company to set up a system of direct distribution of tea in the colonies, showed that British business could use political means to penetrate colonial markets. Under the Tea Act the East India Company could undersell American merchants, whether they imported tea legally from Britain or smuggled it from Holland.

As a result of the broadened scope and closer enforcement of trade regulation and the efforts to collect taxes in the colonies to support the royal government, it seemed to Americans that American economic interests would always be subordinated to those of British business. Americans organized political opposition and formed nonimportation agreements to apply pressure on British merchants and on the British government. The experience of the 1760s and 1770s raised questions concerning the ability of Americans to control their own economic affairs. As we indicated earlier, the growth of strong merchant communities and metropolitan economies in Philadelphia, Boston, and New York meant that the New England and Middle colonies had achieved more autonomy in economic decision making than was typical of a colony—it was an autonomy that they wanted to maintain. Although production of staple commodities for export stimulated the growth of the southern colonies, some planters were becoming concerned about such problems as indebtedness which they perceived to be the result of dependence upon British business. Mercantilistic regulation may have imposed only a light economic burden on Americans; but in the 1760s and 1770s it appeared to interfere with their goal of managing their own economic destiny.

ECONOMICS OF WAR: MANPOWER AND MATERIAL

The outbreak of armed conflict in the spring of 1775 required the Continental Congress, occupied up to this time with political strategy, to organize a major military effort for a period of eight years—the longest war in American history until Vietnam. Its economic task was to provide manpower, materials, money, and management to support military operations against one of the most powerful nations in Europe.

The size of the Continental Army was never large by modern standards. The peak number of soldiers serving under Washington's command at any one time was sixteen to eighteen thousand; more often the commander-in-chief had a force of five to ten thousand troops. Manpower for the armed forces was recruited by voluntary enlistment at first and then by conscription. As in other wars the well-to-do could avoid military service by hiring a substitute. In the last years of the struggle the military burden fell heavily on the low-income segment of the community, fulfilling John Adams' prediction that a shift from a one-year to a three-year term of service would result in only "the meanest, idlest, most intemperate and worthless" men serving in the Army.* Although eighteenth-century military technology did not require a large-scale shift of manpower from civilian to war industry, the government provided exemption from military service for workers in manufacturing establishments serving the war effort and sometimes assigned prisoners of war to alleviate labor shortages.

To provide material for the armed forces, Congress and several states established armories for the manufacture of rifles and muskets and also offered subsidies to encourage producers of war supplies to expand their facilities. In most cases the profits to be made from military material were all the incentive that was needed to cause businessmen to invest in the equipment and to take on the production problems involved in converting to munitions manufacture. Their experience in establishing textile "manufactories" prior to the war proved useful in organizing the production of cloth to meet the wartime needs of civilians and the military. Perhaps the most ambitious effort was the founding in 1775 of the United Company of Philadelphia for Promoting Manufactures, which purchased spinning jennies and looms and employed as many as five hundred workers in making woolen, cotton, and linen cloth. The merchants who bought the cloth organized a network of cottage industry composed of makers of homespun; for many workers this represented a first step in the transition from household industry to commercial manufacturing.

While the Americans manufactured a wide range of goods in 1775, they were not yet able to produce enough military supplies for the Continental armies and the militias, and foreign aid was indispensable. Over the course of the war 60 percent of all the gunpowder used by the revolutionary forces came from Europe. France was the most important foreign supplier, providing not only material for American troops but also (after 1778) military and naval support. Other aid was secured from Spain and Holland. The enemy also became an important, although unwilling, supplier, when American forces captured British arms and equipment.

A continuing problem was to fashion an adequate administrative

* Quoted in Robert A. Gross, *The Minutemen and Their World* (New York: Hill and Wang, 1976), p. 150.

structure for the war effort. Congress supervised the operation of the Continental Army through subcommittees and designated a commissary general of stores and purchases as well as a quartermaster general to secure the necessary food, feed, equipment, and services. Their lack of experience in managing such a large effort caused frequent breakdowns; these led to frequent administrative reorganizations, changes in leadership, and experimentation with new procedures of collecting supplies and distributing them to the men in the field. But whatever the political leaders tried, certain problems of procurement continued to plague the war effort: rivalry between purchasing agents of Congress and the states (each state had a committee to purchase supplies for its own militia), lack of cooperation between the commissary and the quartermaster, inaccurate bookkeeping leading to overcharges, graft, and corruption among minor employees, and delivery of goods of inferior quality.

What made the system work at all was the development of a "military mercantile complex," an informal network of businessmen. While various structural reorganizations and shuffles in top-level positions went on, merchants continued to staff key positions in the procurement services. These men continued in their private businesses while they performed their public functions, and dealt with their fellow traders on both public and private accounts simultaneously. While they sometimes financed their own private businesses with funds advanced by the government, they also advanced their own money for public purposes when necessary. Although Congress eventually created an imposing bureaucratic structure, with almost three thousand employees in the quartermaster department alone, merchants had a better knowledge of the commercial world to carry out the business of supply.

ECONOMICS OF WAR: MONEY

Inflation was a more serious problem during the Revolution than in any other war in American history. The government of the United States had no power to tax. Congress determined each year the overall revenue needs of the nation and then levied a requisition upon the states, which held the power to tax, each for its share. Unfortunately, they usually failed to provide the funds needed; requisitions from states accounted for only a bit more than 6 percent of the total revenues of the United States government during the war years. Congress had to finance the war effort by borrowing—seeking voluntary loans from foreign and domestic holders of funds and obtaining involuntary loans throught the issue of fiat money.

Loans and subsidies furnished by France, Spain, and Holland were used primarily to finance American purchase of weapons, gunpowder, and other supplies in Europe. Only a promise of a high rate of interest to be paid in scarce specie enticed United States citizens to make voluntary loans to the new government. Foreign and domestic loans together accounted for less than one-fifth of the revenues of the United States government during the war.

Congress began in the summer of 1775 to issue noninterest-bearing notes to pay troops and military suppliers. With little alternative means to meet the enormous expense of the war, Congress authorized emissions of over two hundred twenty-five million dollars by the end of 1779. States and sometimes even counties issued their own paper money. Quartermaster and commissary certificates also served as money when they were used by military purchasing agents for impressment—a process that forced owners of goods to sell below the market level, at prices stipulated by government buyers.

By issuing a large volume of paper currency, Congress created a substantial amount of purchasing power. The result was predictable—severe inflation accompanied by depreciation of bills of credit. According to an index of wholesale prices of key commodities on the Philadelphia market, the average more than doubled in 1776, in 1777, and in 1778, and then advanced almost tenfold from the spring of 1779 to the spring of 1781. To describe the impact of inflation in another way, the one hundred pounds that in 1776 bought over 14,000 pounds of flour or 5,000 pounds of beef commanded considerably less than 100 pounds of either commodity in 1781. An individual with one hundred sixty-seven pounds in paper money held the purchasing power of only one pound in specie at the latter date.

It is clear that monetary factors were the dominant influence in the dramatic price rise, although shortages of specific goods, which developed at different times, contributed to the problem. For example, sugar and other West Indian staples led the increase in the price level in 1776, as a result of a scarcity of shipping, while domestic staples exceeded the average rise in 1778, because a poor harvest meant meager supplies for which military and civilian purchasers competed. But inflation had built-in generative powers. Buyers sought to assure a supply for themselves by offering ever higher prices; holding commodities was considered preferable to holding cash.

When depreciation of the currency seriously threatened to undermine the war effort in the late 1770s, some national and state political leaders called for price controls, arguing that "speculators" and "monopolists" were to blame for inflation. Some states enacted price-fixing laws and placed embargoes on the export of key commodities; they then attempted to formulate regional agreements to regulate economic transactions. State restrictions proved ineffective in holding down prices. Farmers refused to sell in the regulated markets, and merchants found ways to evade the rules. Some critics argued that regulation contributed to price increases; one Philadelphian reported that "many articles, though not scarce, are not to be bought at the regulated price without taking along with it some other article which from its great plenty will not bring the price limited." Even if eighteenth-century governments had possessed the capacity to administer effective price controls, such regulation would not have dealt with the source of inflation, the large increase in purchasing power resulting from the issue of paper money as a way of financing the war. At best, controls would have only postponed a rise in prices until after the conflict, as happened, for example, after World War II.

Congress also attempted monetary reform with the hope of stabilizing the currency. In early 1780 the government of the United States in effect repudiated a substantial portion of the debt it had incurred by revaluing outstanding Continental notes at one-fortieth of their face value. When paper money continued to depreciate, lending further support to the expression "not worth a continental," Congress determined to put government finances on a more secure foundation. Robert Morris, a leading Philadelphia businessman and member of Congress, was appointed superintendent of finance in 1781; he imposed budgetary controls, attempted to maximize the flow of revenue from requisitions upon the states, and called for a central bank to serve as the government's fiscal agent. The Bank of North America, chartered by Congress in 1781, was the nation's first commercial bank. In connection with its loans to the government and to private businessmen, the bank issued notes that became a part of the country's circulating currency. However, Morris' principal objective—to secure taxing power for the national government—was a victim of politics, when the issue of taxation became enmeshed in a struggle for power between "centralists" and "localists." And with the winding down of military operations after Yorktown, financial reform appeared less pressing.

Inflation as a way to pay for the war effort imposed a heavy tax upon the American people; in addition, it had potentially serious disruptive effects upon the operation of the economy. However, when money no longer served as a reasonable standard of value, private individuals and groups arranged among themselves to carry out transactions at prewar price and wage levels—"the rate they used to be"—and to make payments in kind when possible. As Anne Bezanson has pointed out in her study of prices in Pennsylvania, throughout the war period all groups "searched for means of shifting part of the impact of inflation" from themselves.* Despite inefficiencies in making transactions, which arose from monetary practices, America's ability to mobilize its resources for a long war demonstrated the productive strength of the economy and the sophistication of the business structure that kept channels open for the flow of goods and materials from abroad and within and country.

---

* Anne Bezanson et al., *Prices and Inflation During the American Revolution: Pennsylvania, 1770–1790* (Philadelphia: University of Pennsylvania Press, 1951), pp. 312, 316.

Impact of the War and Independence on the Economy

Although the political results of the American Revolution—independence—were highly visible, the economic effects were not so obvious. The American economy still displayed an important characteristic of colonialism: emphasis on production of raw materials for export. The country still operated within the orbit of London's business and financial system. Yet the war and the new political status of the United States accelerated the trend toward greater autonomy for economic decision makers in America.

TRENDS IN THE ECONOMY

The war brought to a temporary halt the growth that had characterized the economy of the colonies during much of the previous half century. Although there are no firm statistical data, it is likely that gross national product actually declined during the years of hostilities. In the last years of the war, plantations and farms in many parts of the southern states suffered extensive damage at the hands of British troops. Production was further curtailed when the British carried away large numbers of slaves from Virginia and South Carolina. Normal trade was disrupted by a British blockade and by the enemy occupation for varying lengths of time of major business centers—New York, Philadelphia, Newport, and Charleston. Curtailment of immigration contributed to labor shortages, and in some areas the mobilization of farmers into the armed forces may have reduced the acreage that was planted. Many farm producers experienced prosperity from sales to the military, and various kinds of industry expanded to meet the demand for equipment. But the technology of warfare did not then involve the large-scale commitment of economic resources that we associate with total war in the twentieth century.

The adverse effect of the war on economic output was not serious enough to prevent a rapid recovery of production after the close of hostilities. By 1790 total production was at least as large as it had been prior to the war. However, the population had grown by over 50 percent, so that per capita output probably had not recovered completely to the level of the early 1770s.

Various regions had strikingly different experiences. Exports of flour, wheat, and meat, long the specialties of the Middle states, rose dramatically from prewar levels, with continued expansion of sales to the West Indies and southern Europe. On the other hand, the traditional southern staples did not fare so well. Tobacco exports stood at an all-time high in the early 1790s, but this level was only moderately above that set before the war. Rice and indigo did even less well. Without a British subsidy and tariff protection, production of indigo ceased. There was little evidence that plantation capitalism in the Lower South was on the threshold of enormous expansion to be based on cotton and slave labor.

NEW LINES OF ENTERPRISE

Attainment of political sovereignty made possible the expansion of American business along new lines. As indicated in chapter 2, even before Independence merchants in the major commercial centers performed functions of a kind that British businessmen carried out for the plantation colonies. During the war merchants from Philadelphia, New York, Boston, and a few smaller centers—people not always from the top level of the prewar business community—attained wealth and prestige by organizing military supply and taking advantage of other war-related opportunities. They then played key roles in developing a new world-wide commerce legalized by the Revolution. During and after the war, American businessmen found commercial outlets in France and Holland and in Germany, Sweden, and Russia as well. Trade with the West Indies and southern Europe resumed its expansion. Although the ships of United States traders were legally excluded from the British West Indies and faced restrictions in the Caribbean colonies of other powers, European colonial officials were unable to prevent large-scale smuggling by Americans. The slave trade was renewed, although commerce with Africa accounted for only a minute percentage of total American foreign trade. The most striking new direction of trade was the opening of commercial relations with the Far East, which had been a monopolistic preserve of the British East India Company before the war. Initiated by a voyage from New York to Canton in 1784, within half a decade this unusually profitable branch of trade was a complex one involving not only China but also India and the East Indies.

Britain remained the single most important trading partner of the United States. Immediately after the war, it seemed that American economic ties to the former mother country would become stronger than ever. British exporters, offering generous credit terms, earnestly solicited orders from importers in the United States. But the adjustments in commercial patterns made by American merchants resulted in significant overall reduction in American dependence upon the British market and the British marketing system. By the early 1790s, Great Britain was the destination of fewer American exports than before the war and accounted for less than one-third of the total, compared to nearly 60 percent when Britain was the mother country.

Significant developments of the 1780s foreshadowed the Business Revolution of the nineteenth century. Its principal elements were the creation of new mechanisms to facilitate investment, the development of greater specialization of business units by function, and improvements in transportation and communication. The use of the corporation was a major organizational innovation by which government delegated much of the responsibility for economic development to private business groups. The corporate form gave greater flexibility than did a partnership owned by many individuals; it ensured continuity of the firm apart from the biological lives of its members; and it sometimes limited the financial liability of owners. Thus the corporation facilitated the mobilization of larger amounts of capital from a greater number of investors than could the private firm. Only a few corporations had been chartered in the colonial period, and those were chartered for activities that met a strict definition of "general welfare." By the end of the eighteenth century, state governments had conferred corporate charters upon over three hundred enterprises, in comparison to no more than a score of business corporations in either England or France. The principal difference between the United States and Europe on this score was that Americans, as one historian has put it, "expanded the definition of general welfare to include practically all local economic growth." * The most frequent use of the corporation before 1800 was in transportation, banking, and insurance.

Removal of British restrictions made possible new institutional developments in the financial sector. We have already recounted the founding of the Bank of North America as a part of Robert Morris' program to revive government finance. After the war the bank concentrated on developing a commercial banking business to serve Philadelphia merchants. Similar institutions were chartered in Boston and New York in 1784. Each bank accepted deposits, usually from wealthy mercantile customers. But a more important activity was discounting—making short-term loans to finance commercial transactions. As N. S. B. Gras has written of the bank formed in Boston: "Discounting was to the Massachusetts Bank what teaching is to a college, playing to an orchestra, and moving to a train. It was not everything but it was the chief function." † For the bank as a business enterprise, lending was the principal way to make profits. The founders of many banks were merchants and one of their major motivations was to secure a source of loans to finance their own commercial operations. In connection with their lending operations these banks issued notes redeemable in specie; these notes became an increasingly important part of the nation's money supply as more banks were organized in ensuing decades. From the beginning bank organizers launched their enterprises as corporations, securing a charter from the state in which they operated. Accepting deposits, making loans, and issuing private paper that circulated as money were not new in American business life. But these functions, once the province of unspecialized merchants, were per-

---

* Thomas C. Cochran, 200 *Years of American Business* (New York: Basic Books, 1977), p. 16.
† N. S. B. Gras, *The Massachusetts First National Bank of Boston 1784–1934* (Cambridge: Harvard University Press, 1937), p. 45.

formed increasingly by specialized business units contributing to mobilization of credit resources. By organizing credit more effectively, commercial banking lessened American economic dependence upon Britain.

When the war was over, Americans turned their attention to transportation—to the improvement of turnpikes and other roads, canals, and toll bridges. Seventeen corporations were chartered for this purpose before 1790. The corporate form was used for the same reason that it had been found useful in banking—greater ease in collecting large amounts of capital. But many smaller projects were organized and financed by individual entrepreneurs. The flow of communication was as important to business operation as was the movement of goods and materials. The Continental Congress determined to improve the postal service, which, because of its high cost, was used mainly by businessmen. In 1786 the postmaster general negotiated contracts for thrice-weekly transportation of mail along the main route between Portsmouth, New Hampshire, and Savannah, Georgia, and in the following year expanded service in the interior of the country, setting up regular routes as far west as Pittsburgh. (Postal contracts provided encouragement to private carriers to build and improve roads in the areas where they carried the mail.) The most important function of newspapers was to supply business information, in the form of commercial news and advertising. The number of newspapers increased from thirty-seven on the eve of the Revolution (none appeared more than once a week) to ninety-two in 1790 (including eight dailies).

Through the 1780s industrial development continued. Manufacturing in the colonies had not lagged far behind Europe and the war had stimulated the expansion of such industries as metal products and cloth. Manufactures were still carried on in America, as in Europe, under several forms of industrial organization: household industry in rural areas, handicraft manufacturers producing a wide variety of goods, usually to the order of individual customers, and mill and furnace industries, some of which utilized water power and relatively sophisticated machinery.

Americans were alert in the postwar era to the economic potential of the inventions being introduced into English industry, particularly into textiles; some manufacturers in the United States, like Oliver Evans in flour milling, were developing new machinery and devising ways to adapt steam power to industrial use. Societies were organized in several cities to promote "useful manufactures"; they employed fairly sizeable work forces in manufactories to make cloth. Expansion of manufacturing generally was encouraged by a patriotic urge—the desire to achieve economic as well as political independence from Britain. Necessity was also a factor since a trade depression required a reduction in imports. The depression also induced several states to pass tariff laws designed to protect domestic industry from foreign competition. The greatest incentive to expand the nation's industry was the belief of entrepreneurs and investors that it would be profitable.

In the words of Victor S. Clark, the historian of American manufactures from the 1760s to 1790, "The industrial progress of the country had been hardly less remarkable than its political advance." In varied circumstances before the Revolution, during the war, and after independence, a number of industries "had encountered nearly every adverse technical and commercial condition that such political vicissitudes afforded, and their survival was due to natural advantages of which they were not likely to be deprived." *

LAND POLICIES: SPECULATION AND SETTLEMENT

Land had always been a major interest of most Americans, and mobility, in the form of migration to new areas, was one of their leading characteristics. Businessmen often participated in the organization of settlements, seeking profits through land speculation and through other enterprises associated with the development of a new region. From the middle of the eighteenth century increasing numbers of potential settlers and speculators looked to the territory west of the Appalachian Mountains, an area where there were few Europeans, most of whom were engaged in the fur trade. Rival business groups attempted to secure grants of land and developed plans for settlement and agricultural development of large parts of the West. But the British government blocked expansion into the area by issuing the Proclamation of 1763, which prohibited colonization west of the mountains.

Independence ended British control of land disposal policy in America. State governments, by confiscation and by forced purchase, took over title to lands formerly held by the king and by various proprietors, such as the descendants of William Penn and Lord Baltimore. States also seized the estates of loyalists. At the same time the last vestiges of feudalism, like quit rent, were eliminated from the land system.

As states ceded to the federal government their land claims based on colonial charters, the United States found itself in the 1780s the owner of vast tracts of western land. The concept of public domain was firmly held, but it was not envisioned that land was to be held in common forever. The assumption was that the land would be privately owned rather than used for government-operated activity. The government's revenue from the public domain would derive from the proceeds of land sales and from taxes generated by private use of the land for economic pursuits.

The major problem for political decision makers, therefore, was to determine how to transfer the land from government to private ownership. Congress contributed to a solution through two major statutes. The Land Ordinance of 1785 created a mechanism for the survey and orderly dis-

---

* Victor S. Clark, *History of Manufactures in the United States*, 3 vols. (Washington, D.C.: Carnegie Institution of Washington, 1929), reprint ed., vol. 1 (New York: Peter Smith, 1949), p. 232.

posal of land to which the United States government held title. Tiers of townships of six square miles were opened to settlement; sales were to be made, by auction, of tracts of not less than 640 acres at a minimum price of one dollar per acre. Two years later, the Northwest Ordinance provided that new areas, as they became settled, would be admitted into the Union as states in full partnership with the existing states. This represented a replay of the actions of the English founders of the colonies, who encouraged settlement by granting political rights to the colonists.

Turning to the economic dimension of land disposal, Congress looked to land companies to play an important role in managing the settlement of the West; this was not unlike the earlier reliance of the English government upon joint stock companies and proprietors as agents of colonization. This policy enabled Congress to make sales in large tracts, and relieved it of the responsibility of dealing directly with many small buyers. Also, middlemen could provide the credit needed by many settlers. Thus in 1787 Congress granted one million acres of land in what is now southern Ohio to the Ohio Company, a land company which was originally formed by army veterans planning to migrate west but came to involve leading eastern business interests as well. The tract was paid for in depreciated government paper, making the effective price eight or nine cents an acre. A smaller grant was made on similar terms to the Miami Reserved Land Associates, which was also backed by eastern investors. These ventures developed as part of a surge of speculative interest in land promotion in the postwar period. Unincorporated joint stock companies, partnerships, and individuals negotiated with the states as well as with Congress to gain control over large tracts of land. However, few speculative ventures yielded the high profits anticipated by the original promoters, and many suffered losses. It soon became apparent that migrants, many of them operating in "the Daniel Boone manner," would assume major responsibility for settlement. Individuals, families, and small groups migrated to the West in increasing numbers; many of the men had become acquainted with the potential of the new areas while serving in the military. Some purchased land from speculators. Others acquired their land directly from the government. But many disregarded the legalities to "squat" on the land; some moved in even before Indian titles had been legally extinguished. By the end of the 1780s over one hundred thousand people of European origin had settled in the area between the Appalachians and the Mississippi River.

SOCIAL STRUCTURE

The American Revolution resulted in little change in the overall shape of American society. Studies of wealth distribution are by no means in agreement regarding the precise effects of the war and independence. On one hand, analyses of property ownership in one large city (Boston) and in a settled agricultural area (Chester County, Pennsylvania), based upon tax records, suggest a drift toward greater concentration of wealth in the hands of the wealthiest property holders of these communities.* On the other hand, Jackson Turner Main has concluded, after an examination of six thousand estate inventories in five states, that "the share of the nation's wealth owned by the richest tenth of the population probably declined slightly between 1770 and 1788" † In any event, the ideals of the American Revolution did not include equality of wealth.

The 1780s marked the beginning of a change in the legal status of slavery in the northern states. In two states—Massachusetts and New Hampshire—slavery was ended; in three other states—Pennsylvania, Connecticut, and Rhode Island—laws were enacted providing for the emancipation of the children of slaves. But in New York and New Jersey even gradual emancipation did not commence until the turn of the century. We should emphasize the extremely limited impact of the abolitionist movement of the Revolutionary period. For one thing, it affected rather small numbers. States with immediate and gradual emancipation combined contained only 3½ percent of the nation's black population. Furthermore, freedom did not carry with it political rights, nor did it mean improvement in social and economic standing. The black, whether slave or free, remained for all intents and purposes an outcast of American society.

While chattel slavery continued for a large majority of the black population, white bound labor tended to disappear in the decades following the Revolution. The war put a halt to traffic in indentured servants, which when it resumed in the 1780s was in reduced numbers. Independence meant a stop to the shipping of convicts, who had constituted one source of supply; the British government further discouraged the migration of individuals under indenture by prohibiting the use of English ships for it.

The Revolution did not bring revolutionary results to American society. Anthony Trollope later commented: "This new people, when they had it in their power to change all their laws, to throw themselves upon any Utopian theory that the folly of a wild philanthropy could devise . . . did not do so." ‡ American ideology continued to emphasize opportunity and mobility. The war contributed to the creation of a group of *nouveaux riches*, entrepreneurs who to some extent displaced older merchants at the top level in large urban communities. For middle-class

---

* Allen Kulikoff, "The Progress of Inequality in Revolutionary Boston," *William and Mary Quarterly*, 28 (July 1971), 375–412. James T. Lemon and Gary B. Nash, "The Distribution of Wealth in Eighteenth Century America: A Century of Change in Chester County, Pennsylvania, 1693–1802," *Journal of Social History*, 2 (Fall 1968), 1–24.
   † Jackson Turner Main, *The Sovereign States 1775–1783* (New York: New Viewpoints, 1973), p. 347.
   ‡ Quoted in Samuel Mencher, *Poor Law to Poverty Program* (Pittsburgh: University of Pittsburgh Press, 1967), p. 147.

Americans, the majority of whom were farmers, the resumption of the westward movement meant cheap land and the possibility of economic advancement. New directions in industry and commerce provided opportunities for the middle-class Americans who were craftsmen and traders.

Economic Forces and the Constitution

Political leaders of the new nation fashioned a highly decentralized governmental structure with effective decision-making power at the state level. However, it was clear that the new United States, like most new nations, faced what Seymour Lipset has termed a "crisis of legitimacy." * The old order had been abolished, but the new government was not able to secure widespread support. As Seymour Lipset has argued, "A basic condition for acquiring legitimacy in a new state is effectiveness, particularly in the economic sphere." † After surveying the new nation's economic and political problems, a meeting of delegates of the thirteen states in the summer of 1787 determined to strengthen the central government; they soon realized that their objective could be attained only by replacing the Articles of Confederation with an entirely new structure of government.

A majority of the delegates to the Constitutional Convention were strong nationalists, who through war service had acquired a continental as opposed to a provincial perception of political problems. Some were concerned about the inability of the government to deal effectively with encroachments upon the nation's sovereignty: the United States apparently could neither remove British troops from the Northwest forts nor counter Spanish opposition to American frontier expansion into the Southwest. Others were alarmed about the threat posed by local insurrections such as Shays's Rebellion in Massachusetts in 1786, when a band of armed farmers had closed the courts to prevent foreclosures on farms and imprisonment of debtors and had even appeared to threaten a federal arsenal.

Nationalists emphasized the importance of a strong economic base for the development of a powerful nation. Most obvious was the power to tax, essential to the ability of the government of the United States to meet external and internal challenges to its independence and unity. Honoring the nation's debt was crucial to establishing a credit standing that would enable the country to meet future financial emergencies.

---

* Seymour Martin Lipset, *The First New Nation: The United States in Historical and Comparative Perspective* (New York: Basic Books, 1963), p. 16.

† Lipset, *The First New Nation*, p. 60.

This required payment of interest and eventual redemption of securities. While advocates of a strong government recognized that "windfall" profits would be gained by some investors who had purchased bonds at discounted prices, they regarded this as a small price to be paid to attain more authority for the central government. Nationalists went on to argue that government should actively promote the economic growth essential to an increase of national power. As early as 1782, Robert Morris had advocated a protective tariff to promote domestic manufacturing as well as government construction of transportation improvements, needed to encourage rapid development of the West. Significantly, the nationalists assumed that the successful operation of the kind of government they were seeking would require the attachment to that government of the business community, the principal economic decision makers in America.

Assessments of the effectiveness of government under the Articles of Confederation were taking place in the context of a serious economic depression. After the termination of hostilities, a decline in government expenditures had created deflationary pressures. Furthermore, the economic benefits that America might gain from political sovereignty could not be realized immediately.

In response to widespread expectations of action to improve economic conditions, states pursued a variety of antidepression policies: tariffs to protect local industries, navigation acts to penalize British shippers (whose own Navigation Acts now discriminated against American shippers), and issues of paper money to provide a circulating medium and to ease deflationary pressures. However, these state government actions to combat the depression seemed inadequate to many. Manufacturers quickly saw the limited effectiveness of the tariff laws passed by industrial states; they did not afford protection against cheap English imports in the agricultural states where tariffs were not enacted. Shippers found fault with the navigation laws of the states because of their lack of uniformity and the possibility that such legislation would be used as a weapon against the shipping of rival states. Above all, serious depreciation of paper money, which occurred in Rhode Island and North Carolina, revived memories of the recent wartime inflation. Paper money was particularly upsetting to creditors, since state laws often required its acceptance at face value in settlement of debts. Compounding the problem of dealing with the depression was the apparent failure of the national government in its efforts to expand foreign markets for American goods and commercial services. Negotiations with Britain and with Spain failed to gain any substantial trade concessions.

Even though the government, with all of its political defects, had not produced the economic difficulties, nor could it reasonably be expected to remove them, people blamed the Confederation for hard times and for the failure of depression remedies to work. To put this another way, the depression had raised the level of dissatisfaction with the political system, and tended to create a favorable climate for making changes in the constitution. Steady improvement of American trade relations with the rest of the world, achieved in large part independently of government action, provided the basis for the return of more prosperous times even before the establishment of a new government. In looking at the relation between economic conditions and politics in the 1780s, Guy S. Callender observed many years ago, "Just as hard times had brought failure to the old confederation, so prosperity, if it did not actually cause the success of the new government, greatly simplified the problem of its establishment." *

ECONOMIC PROVISIONS OF THE CONSTITUTION

While the Constitution apparently had little immediate economic impact, the new system of government would have important long-range effects on the nation's economy. The federal system furnished a framework for the containment of the political controversy between centralism and localism, and created the stability essential to economic growth. Beyond this, specific provisions of the Constitution provided a set of basic rules for many aspects of economic life.

With its authorization to levy import duties, the national government for the first time acquired a basic attribute of sovereignty, the power to tax. This assured to the government a source of financial support; in addition the tariff could be used to protect domestic industry. Congress was empowered to assume and redeem the debt incurred by the old national government and by the states and also to borrow money in the future. Government securities would play a key role in the development of a capital market. In order to assure a single national monetary system, Congress was given exclusive power to coin money and issue paper currency. (However, states retained the right to charter banks which issued bank notes, which circulated as money.) The national government had sole authority over foreign affairs. With the power to adjust import duties, the hand of the United States was strengthened in negotiating commercial treaties. This source of revenue also enabled the national government to develop military forces to reinforce its diplomatic efforts. Shipping was encouraged by the passage of navigation acts. Using its constitutional powers to make regulations regarding territory in the West and to regulate Indian affairs and employing its ability to field an army against the native population, Congress could accelerate the pace of settlement in the West.

The Constitution also furnished the legal underpinnings for a national market. It gave Congress exclusive power to regulate interstate commerce, and thus to minimize legal barriers to trade within the country's boundaries. Congress was also empowered to maintain a postal sys-

* Guy Stevens Callender, ed., *Selections from the Economic History of the United States, 1765–1860* (Boston: Ginn and Co., 1909), p. 182.

tem, basic to the flow of communication; to pass patent and copyright laws to promote invention; "to establish an uniform Rule of Naturalization" of foreign immigrants; and to create bankruptcy laws that would be applied uniformly throughout the states. States were prohibited from enacting laws impairing the obligation of contracts, with this provision to be enforced in federal courts. As the legal historian, James Willard Hurst, has remarked: "Federal protection would embrace all the conditions important to the existence of broad markets." * Specifically, "The federal Constitution sanctioned and protected the play of supply and demand in sectional or national markets, including the free movement of labor and investment money wherever they might find profitable employment." † In short, a legal framework of contracts and property rights established by the Constitution contributed to the creation of the market system through which entrepreneurs in nineteenth-century America would make and carry out the decisions that transformed an economy. Americans of the Revolutionary generation did not discover for the first time the concept of the market. Indeed, Americans almost from the beginning of colonization had looked to the market as a guide for deciding how to use and allocate resources. But the existence of a large body of law concerning property and contract, resting upon basic rules contained in the supreme law of the land, in the words of Hurst "in itself encouraged men to think of market processes as the normal mode of ordering the economy." ‡

Summary

The colonies determined on a course of strategy leading to Independence when they perceived that the policies of the British government after 1763 imposed limitations upon their economic and political autonomy. Despite shortcomings in the arrangements made to supply the troops and to finance the war, the new United States achieved victory in a military struggle against the imperial leader of Europe. Once political sovereignty was achieved, Americans moved toward expansion of their economic autonomy. Development of new commercial contacts reduced American economic dependence upon the former mother country, while use of the corporation, the organization of commercial banks, and improvements in transportation and communication gave growth potential to the

---

* James Willard Hurst, *Law and the Conditions of Freedom in the Nineteenth-Century United States* (Madison: University of Wisconsin Press, 1956), p. 45.
† James Willard Hurst, *Law and Economic Growth: The Legal History of the Lumber Industry in Wisconsin, 1836–1915* (Cambridge: Harvard University Press, 1964), p. 53.
‡ Hurst, *Law and Economic Growth*, p. 52.

economy. The "crisis of legitimacy" of the new nation led to the adoption of the Constitution, which not only provided the political stability necessary for economic growth but also furnished the legal underpinnings for a market economy operating on a national scale.

SUGGESTED READINGS

Marc Egnal and Joseph A. Ernst, "An Economic Interpretation of the American Revolution," *William and Mary Quarterly*, 3d ser. 29 (1972) emphasizes economic sovereignty as a major objective of the Revolutionary movement. Still useful for its account of the responses of American business to British legislation after 1763 is Arthur M. Schlesinger, *The Colonial Merchants and the American Revolution, 1763–1776* (New York: Columbia University Press, 1918). Joseph D. Reid, Jr., "Economic Burden: Spark to the American Revolution?" *Journal of Economic History*, 38 (1978) suggests directions that economic analysis of Revolutionary political activity might follow.

Curtis P. Nettels, *The Emergence of a National Economy, 1775–1815* (New York: Holt, Rinehart and Winston, 1962), a volume in the *Economic History of the United States* series, furnishes an overview of the principal economic events. Military supply forms the subject of Victor L. Johnson, *The Administration of the American Commissariat During the Revolutionary War* (Philadelphia: University of Pennsylvania Press, 1941) and R. Arthur Bowler, *Logistics and the Failure of the British Army in America, 1775–1783* (Princeton, N.J.: Princeton University Press, 1975). E. James Ferguson, *The Power of the Purse: A History of American Public Finance, 1776–1790* (Chapel Hill: University of North Carolina Press, 1961) covers well the subject of war finance, while Clarence L. Ver Steeg, *Robert Morris, Revolutionary Financier* (Philadelphia: University of Pennsylvania Press, 1954) focuses on the financial role played by a leading businessman-politician. Anne Bezanson et al., *Prices and Inflation During the American Revolution: Pennsylvania, 1770–1790* (Philadelphia: University of Pennsylvania Press, 1951) is the most valuable study that we have of the course of wartime inflation. The social and economic effects of the larger events of the period are seen from the vantage point of the ordinary people of a New England community in Robert A. Gross, *The Minutemen and Their World* (New York: Hill & Wang, 1976).

Robert A. East, *Business Enterprise in the American Revolutionary Era* (New York: Columbia University Press, 1938) traces the emergence of new business leadership during and after the war, while James B. Hedges, *The Browns of Providence Plantations: The Colonial Years* (Cambridge: Harvard University Press, 1952) and Robert F. Jones, "William Duer and the Business of Government in the Era of the American Revolution," *William and Mary Quarterly*, 3rd ser., 32 (July 1975) furnish case studies of different kinds of business behavior in this period. James F. Shepherd and Gary M. Walton, "Economic Change After the American Revolution: Pre- and Post-War Comparisons of Maritime Shipping and Trade," *Explorations in Economic History*, 8 (October 1976) analyzes changes in patterns of American foreign trade that took place after the Revolution; Gordon C. Bjork, "The Weaning of the American Economy: Independence, Market Changes, and Economic Development," *Journal of Economic History*, 24 (December 1964) sets forth a tentative assessment of the economy in the 1780s. On the emergence of the corporation as an important form of business organization, see Joseph S. Davis, *Essays in the Earlier History of American Corporations*, 2 vols. (Cambridge: Harvard University Press, 1917) and James Willard Hurst, *The Legitimacy of the Business Corporation in the Law of the United States, 1780–1970* (Charlottesville: University Press of Virginia, 1970), and on the early development of commercial banking, Fritz Redlich, *The Molding of American Banking: Men and Ideas* (New York:

Johnson Reprint Corporation, 1968) and N. S. B. Gras, *The Massachusetts First National Bank of Boston, 1784–1934* (Cambridge: Harvard University Press, 1937). Jackson Turner Main, *The Social Structure of Revolutionary America* (Princeton, N.J.: Princeton University Press, 1965) and the same author's *The Sovereign States, 1775–1783* (New York: Franklin Watts, 1973) contain analyses of social changes of the Revolutionary era, while Allan Kulikoff, "The Progress of Inequality in Revolutionary Boston," *William and Mary Quarterly*, 3d ser., 28 (1971) focuses on developments in one major city.

The publication of Charles A. Beard, *An Economic Interpretation of the Constitution of the United States* (New York: Macmillan, 1913) touched off a continuing controversy among historians about the precise nature of the relationship between economic factors and the political movement to strengthen the central government in the 1780s. Robert E. Brown, *Charles Beard and the Constitution: A Critical Analysis of "An Economic Interpretation of the Constitution"* (Princeton, N.J.: Princeton University Press, 1956) assesses Beard's use of historical evidence. Also useful on this subject, in different ways, are Forrest McDonald, *We the People: The Economic Origins of the Constitution* (Chicago: University of Chicago Press, 1958) and Seymour M. Lipset, *The First New Nation: The United States in Historical and Comparative Perspective* (New York: Basic Books, 1963). For the role that the Constitution would play in furnishing a legal framework for a market economy, the works of James Willard Hurst are indispensable; see *Law and the Conditions of Freedom in the Nineteenth-Century United States* (Madison: University of Wisconsin Press, 1967).

PART II

THE AGRICULTURAL ERA AND EMERGING INDUSTRIALISM

(1790-1860)

INTRODUCTION

——

Industrialization and sustained increases in real production and income per capita were the key economic developments of long-term importance in the United States during the seven decades from 1790 to 1860. These developments marked the beginning of a process of modernization that before the end of the nineteenth century propelled the American economy to the first rank. The theme of Part II is economic modernization. The process, of course, involved much more than industrialization and higher rates of economic growth. Modernization's important antecedents and accompaniments included a revolution in internal transportation and communication, transcontinental territorial expansion, the transfer of huge amounts of land from public to private ownership, the dynamic expansion of commercial agriculture, the mushroomlike growth of banks, and increasingly specialized commerce in both foreign and domestic markets. In the long run, however, it was industrialization that sustained economic growth at the high rate that differentiates the modern from the premodern economy. And it was industrialization that transformed America from the simple agrarian economy of colonial times to the complex, highly specialized, and interdependent economy and society of today.

As the process of economic modernization took hold, the territorial and human resources of the United States were greatly enlarged. By 1860 the geographical area of the nation was more than three times larger than it had been in 1790; the republic stretched from sea to sea.

The growth of human resources was both a cause and a result of economic modernization. Between 1790 and 1860 the population of the United States increased at a very high rate by historical standards. The rate was 3 percent per year and was fairly uniform across the seven decades; the population doubled every twenty-three years, and in the seven decades increased eightfold, rising from 3.9 million in 1790 to 31.5 million in 1860.

Although immigrants contributed much to the drama of American history, they were not the major source of population growth; a high rate of natural increase was—both before and after the Civil War. Annual birth rates of about fifty per thousand combined with death rates of about twenty per thousand to produce a rate of natural increase of roughly 3 percent, a rate that prevailed from colonial times up to about 1830. Before the 1830s the contribution of immigrants to population growth averaged only about 3 or 4 percent of the total increase. In the next decades immigration became more important. During the 1820s, the number of immigrants averaged about 13,000 per year, rising to 54,000 per year in the 1830s, to 143,000 in the 1840s, and to 281,000 in the 1850s. The arrival of greater numbers of immigrants offset a declining rate of natural increase and helped to maintain a 3 percent rate of population growth up to the Civil War. But even in the 1850s, more than two-thirds of the population growth derived from natural increase.

The economic significance of the immigrants in both antebellum and later decades was disproportionate to their numbers. Immigrants were more concentrated in the fifteen-to-forty age group than was the population as a whole. This meant that the labor force grew faster than did the population. The elasticity that immigrants gave to the labor force very likely made an important contribution to the expansion of economic activity.

From the point of view of the American economy, immigrants were something of a gift of human capital. American resources were not expended on their early upbringing and training; instead these costs of creating an enlarged labor force were borne by others. It is also possible that many of the immigrants were especially energetic and talented. Whether the main incentive was, as some argue, the attraction of economic opportunity in America or, as others hold, that of escape from unfavorable economic, political, and social conditions in the country of origin, a certain boldness was required to undergo the hardships of migration and the uncertainties surrounding life and work in a new land. American life in all of its dimensions was enriched by the flow of human resources from overseas.

CHAPTER 5

———

The Revolution in

Transportation and

Communication

Reliable, low-cost transportation and a rapid flow of information are crucial factors in economic development. Economic history offers no better illustration of this principle than the experience of the United States during the seven decades from 1790 to 1860. In 1790, after nearly two centuries of colonization and settlement, most of the 3.9 million Americans still lived within a hundred miles or so of the Atlantic coast. The high cost of internal transportation was chiefly responsible for this situation. The young nation was extremely well-endowed with land and other natural resources but high internal transport costs, particularly for products of the land that were bulky in relation to their value, constituted a great barrier to turning these endowments of nature into economic resources. Americans of 1790 therefore tended to live and work in proximity to navigable waters which provided them with a means of reaching larger domestic and overseas markets.

The lure of untapped resources farther inland was nonetheless strong for a people whose numbers continued to grow at a rapid rate. By 1790 there were 109,000 settlers in Kentucky and Tennessee, with perhaps an equal number west of the mountains in Pennsylvania and Virginia. It is estimated that at the outbreak of the War of 1812, just over two decades later, at least 1.5 million people out of a total population of around 8 million had moved westward across the Appalachians. Many of these pioneers could find only local markets for their resource-intensive products; other markets were virtually non-existent because of high transportation costs. What the pioneers needed was an improved means of internal transportation and communication to help them get their products to the markets in the East and overseas.

Then a revolution in transportation and communication began. In short order, the improvement of roads, canal projects, the introduction of steam railroads and steam navigation on rivers provided a solution to the age-old problem of high inland transport costs. At the same time, information gathering and communications—two essential ingredients for effective decision making—improved significantly with advances in newspaper publishing and in the postal service, and with the introduction of the electromagnetic telegraph. By 1860, Americans, with the help of these revolutionary developments, had settled half a continent. In the process the vastly enlarged *economic* resources of the United States were turned toward specialized, market-oriented production.

Transportation Costs and Economic Development

Why is costly transportation a barrier to economic development? Improvements in transportation were so critical to America's economic progress in the early decades of the nation's history that it is worth devoting attention to some theoretical aspects of this question. In his classic work, *The Wealth of Nations* (1776), the Scottish economist Adam Smith wrote, "The division of labor is limited by the extent of the market." * A progressing division of labor and specialization of economic activity were the keys to increasing productivity. The essence of Adam Smith's insight is that increased specialization will lead to economies of larger scale production, or in other words, that as the size of a producing unit grows, output produced will grow more rapidly than the productive inputs of labor, land, and capital. In the early nineteenth century another great economist, the Englishman David Ricardo, amplified and extended Smith's argument with his theory of comparative advantage, which suggested that nations, regions, and even individuals could increase their standards of material well-being by specializing in the kind of economic activity in which they had the greatest capabilities, natural and acquired.

To reap the great advantages of specialization, as analyzed by Smith and Ricardo, it is necessary to have markets that are large enough to ab-

* Adam Smith, *An Inquiry into the Nature & Causes of the Wealth of Nations* (New York: Modern Library, 1937), p. 17.

sorb the increased production derived from specialization. This is where the cost of transportation becomes important. If high transportation costs double or triple the price of a commodity when it is sold more than a few miles away from where it is produced, most of that commodity will be sold locally. But a group of people in a given location will demand a variety of goods and services. High transportation costs will therefore dictate that most of the items demanded be produced in that local area. This limits the extent of the market, and, in consequence, the possibilities for greater specialization and the exploitation of comparative advantages in production.

Many aspects of economic life in the United States before the transportation revolution of the early 1800s are illuminated by the foregoing analysis. Food, fuel, and construction materials for cities and towns on or near the Atlantic seaboard were obtained either from nearby agricultural areas or from more distant areas within reach of navigable water; the freight rates over water were much lower than those over land. Most of the manufactured articles of that era were simple and were produced locally, many of them at home. The first settlers of fertile western lands marketed their products outside their own locales to a limited extent; they converted their bulky crops into livestock, which often could walk to distant markets, or turned crops into whiskey and other products that had greater value in relation to their bulk than the crops from which they were made. Decisions to produce and market in these ways reflected the economic realities of high-cost transportation.

The people who moved west in the decades after the Revolution were more disturbed than other Americans by the implications for market development of high transportation costs. Congressman P. B. Porter from western New York State, spoke for them in 1810:

> The great evil, and it is a serious one indeed, under which the inhabitants of the western country labor, arises from the want of a market. There is no place where the great staple articles for the use of civilized life can be produced in greater abundance or with greater ease, and yet as respects most of the luxuries and many of the conveniences of life the people are poor. They have no vent for their produce at home, and, being all agriculturalists, they produce alike all the same article with the same facility; and such is the present difficulty and expense of transporting their produce to an Atlantic port that little benefit is realized from that quarter. The single circumstance of want of a market is already beginning to produce the most disastrous effect, not only on the industry, but on the morals of the inhabitants. Such is the fertility of their land that one-half their time spent in labor is sufficient to produce every article which their farms are capable of yielding, in sufficient quantities for their own consumption, and there is nothing to incite them to produce more. They are, therefore, naturally led to spend the other part of their time in idleness and dissipation.*

* As quoted by G. S. Callender, "The Early Transportation and Banking Enterprises of the States in Relation to the Growth of Corporations," *Quarterly Journal of Economics*, vol. 27 (1902), p. 123.

Very soon, however, the "great evil" described by Congressman Porter was itself being dissipated by revolutionary changes in American internal transportation.

Gallatin's Report on Roads and Canals (1808)

In April of 1808, Treasury Secretary Albert Gallatin delivered to Congress a voluminous report on roads and canals.* The report contained a sophisticated discussion of the benefits to be derived from improved transportation, a consideration of the difficulties that stood in the way of improving transportation, and a comprehensive ten-year plan for a governmental solution to America's transportation problems.

In the United States, Gallatin argued, a "great demand for capital" and the "extent of territory compared with population," had prevented improvements or had rendered them unprofitable. The prosperity of foreign trade from 1793 to 1807, which was induced by wars in Europe, had caused the demand for capital to grow rapidly in the United States. High interest rates militated against internal transportation improvements "which offer only the prospect of remote and moderate profit." Also, the low density of the American population did not, "except in the vicinity of seaports, admit that extensive commercial intercourse within short distances, which, in England and some other countries, forms the principal support of artificial roads and canals." From his observations Gallatin drew a sweeping conclusion. "The General Government can alone remove these obstacles."

Gallatin's program called for a ten-year expenditure of $20 million, either in the form of federal construction of internal transportation improvements or of federal aid through stock subscriptions or loans to specially chartered private corporations. His project proposals included (1) canals and a turnpike road along the Atlantic coast, (2) canals, roads, and river improvements from the east across the Appalachians to the Mississippi Valley, and (3) canals and river improvements to connect the Atlantic coast with the Great Lakes and the St. Lawrence River. Of the $20 million projected expenditures, $16.6 million was to be allocated to Gallatin's specified projects and $3.4 million to unspecified local improvements designed to fit in with the overall system.

Gallatin's farsighted proposals for a federally sponsored transportation system were not carried out in a way that even remotely corresponded

* Albert Gallatin, "Report on Roads and Canals," Document No. 250, 10th Congress, 1st Session, in the *New American State Papers—Transportation*, vol. 1 (Wilmington, Del.: Scholarly Resources, 1972).

to his plan. Only a section of the previously planned National Road from Cumberland, Maryland, to Wheeling on the Ohio River, was completed by 1818. There were a number of reasons for this early failure of federal decision making on transportation. Fiscal problems were the immediate source of difficulty. Federal revenues came mostly from duties levied on imports, and these fell as a result of the Jeffersonian embargo and nonintercourse policies (1807–09), and the trade derangements resulting from the War of 1812. Also, in 1808 and in later years domestic political debates impeded federal action. President Jefferson had strong misgivings about the constitutionality of federally aided improvements and felt that a constitutional amendment was necessary before such a program as that suggested by Gallatin could be undertaken. This strict-constructionist view of the constitutional powers of the federal government led to vetoes of internal improvement bills by Presidents Madison, Monroe, and Jackson in 1817, 1822, and 1830, respectively. Finally, the local and sectional interests and jealousies Gallatin had foreseen in 1808 proved difficult to harmonize on the national level. The South in particular grew increasingly hostile to the tariffs which provided the federal revenues that might have been used to finance transportation improvements on the comprehensive scale of Gallatin's plan; indeed the South opposed any extension of federal powers that might set precedents for federal interference with its slave labor system.

In consequence, before 1860 the federal government's role in internal transportation improvement remained largely passive. The national road was extended to Illinois by the 1850s, and some further aid was given in the form of Congressional appropriations of revenues from land sales, subscriptions to the stock of corporations constructing improvements, and land grants to states for improvements. But the bold and imaginative federal programs suggested by Gallatin, and later by John C. Calhoun, Henry Clay, and John Quincy Adams, did not come to fruition.

While this failure of federal transportation policy probably delayed the economic development of the United States, it was not crippling. Private enterprise and state and local governments, sometimes working separately but more often in close cooperation, moved in to fill the void left by the federal failure. At the time Gallatin wrote his report the country was in the midst of a road improvement boom, and soon there were other developments: the application of steam power to water transportation, a canal building era, and the railroad age. By the time of the Civil War the objective of improved transportation was largely realized, but it had come about through decentralized decision making rather than through the central government planning Albert Gallatin had thought necessary.

Turnpike and Other Roads

The United States in its early days, in addition to having rivers and coastal waters as avenues of transportation, was served—but not well served—by a lengthy network of local country and post roads. Most of them were little more than widened dirt paths over which horses and horse- or ox-drawn wagons and carriages could travel, weather permitting. Constructing and maintaining the roads was a community responsibility in settled areas. The roads were financed largely by taxes in kind, that is, by required labor services exacted during the slack season for agricultural work; as a result the roads were poorly designed and poorly maintained. Local interest did not call for great expenditures of effort or funds to ease the way for nonlocal users. The road engineers of ancient Rome would not have been impressed by eighteenth-century American roads, nor would they have noticed much change in techniques of road building and repair from that in Europe in the Middle Ages.

Americans were aware of the British use of turnpike roads, which at the time of the American Revolution had, for example, cut the time of travel between Edinburgh and London, a distance of 400 miles, from about two weeks to three days. Americans seized upon the concept and the result was a boom in turnpike construction that lasted from the 1790s to the 1820s. Turnpike roads were built primarily to connect the larger towns to the settled rural areas in the New England and the Middle Atlantic States; a few turnpikes, such as the federally constructed national road, provided routes to the trans-Appalachian West. Of the more than 11,000 miles of turnpikes in existence by 1830, most had been planned and largely built in the two decades from 1800 to 1820. Four states—New York, Pennsylvania, Connecticut, and Massachusetts—contained 80 percent of the mileage, with New York accounting for nearly 40 percent of the national total.

The typical turnpike road was built and operated by a corporation that had received from the state legislature a special charter outlining its rights and obligations. Important aspects of the turnpike movement may be seen in the history of the first, and one of the more successful, turnpikes—Pennsylvania's Philadelphia and Lancaster, which connected those two urban places separated by sixty-two miles. An ordinary road between Philadelphia and Lancaster had been laid out in 1733, but like other colonial roads it was not very good. The president and managers of the Philadelphia and Lancaster Turnpike Road, as the company was called, were incorporated in April 1792. The charter called for the issuance of 1,000 shares of stock at three hundred dollars per share; the issue was sold immediately. Construction began in the fall of 1792; the road was completed two years later at a cost of $465,000, or $7,500 per mile. Construction costs were well in excess of the projected $300,000, a common fate of later turnpikes as well. Paved with stone overlaid with gravel and well drained, the Lancaster Pike was built to last, which it did as a corporate entity until late into the nineteenth century, long after most of the early nineteenth century turnpikes had been abandoned or turned over to the states. The tolls did not produce large dividends for the Lancaster Pike's stockholders; Gallatin's report of 1808 quoted a rate of 2.5 percent. Primarily responsible for the low return were unexpectedly large costs of construction, maintenance, and operation, coupled with smaller gains in efficiency than those resulting from subsequent transportation technologies.

Despite low returns, the turnpike movement flourished in the first two decades of the century, in part because the stockholders were often interested in other businesses; the returns from these businesses were increased by the greater volume of economic activity arising from road improvements. Early American decision makers were well aware of the modern economic distinction between private and social returns on investment, and in the turnpike movement they showed that government planning and finance of transportation improvements were not necessary to bring about an adequate level of investment.

By 1820 private enterprise, acting through the medium of turnpike companies, had furnished the settled areas of the northeastern United States with a network of improved roads.

The Canal Era, 1817–1844

In the era of canal building, after the War of 1812, the role of state governments in planning, building, and financing was much greater than for turnpikes. What motivated canal building? And why did governmental decisions play the major role in it? The answer to the first question again involves England as a model. The success of canals had clearly been demonstrated there in the last half of the eighteenth century. Americans began trying to emulate England's canals in the 1790s but had little success until 1815; only some 100 miles of canals were constructed in that quarter century. Again America's orientation toward foreign commerce delayed progress in internal economic development. Another reason for America's turning to canals was that turnpikes were still a costly means of transportation. Moving goods over water, the ancient method of city and commercial development, involved much less friction than movement over roads and required much lower inputs of energy.

Government involvement on a major scale in canal building came about because of the high cost of such undertakings and the important role canals played in opening up and developing new areas and resources. This role was quite different from providing an improved means of transport between places already settled and engaged in production for markets. While turnpike construction costs could be measured in the thousands or at most hundreds of thousands of dollars, the major canals cost in the millions. Yet wealth accumulations in the new nation were limited and its capital markets were primitive; the decision calling for publicly sponsored investment, as Albert Gallatin had argued, was obvious.

Of course not all American canal building was aimed at opening up newly settled, or unsettled, areas to market development. The major projects of the period before the War of 1812—the Middlesex in Massachusetts, the Santee and Cooper in South Carolina, and the Dismal Swamp between Norfolk, Virginia, and North Carolina's Albemarle Sound—provided more efficient connections between developed trading areas. Many later canals, such as the Delaware and Raritan connecting Philadelphia and New York City, were also of this nature. Such canals—relatively short and oriented toward existing trade—could be built by private enterprise and usually were. So were the several canals that helped to develop the anthracite coal area of eastern Pennsylvania.

The more noteworthy American canal projects were of a different magnitude. Two significant patterns emerged. The first is represented by New York's Erie, Pennsylvania's Mainline, the Chesapeake and Ohio, and Virginia's James River and Kanawha. All of these canals joined the Atlantic tidewater with the eastern upcountry and the growing settlements of the trans-Appalachian West. The second pattern of canal building on a grand scale was stimulated by the first and is represented by the efforts of Ohio, Indiana, and Illinois to connect the Ohio and Mississippi River Valleys with the Great Lakes, thereby providing direct water routes to eastern population centers.

The earliest and most successful of the great canals was the Erie, built between the Hudson River above Albany and Buffalo on Lake Erie between 1817 and 1825. Although the idea of a canal project across New York State had been in the air since the 1790s, the immediate stimulus for the building of the Erie arose from the fear of New Yorkers that the federal government's National Road and Pennsylvania's east-west turnpike, which was developed under private auspices, would deny New York a proper share of the developing western trade. New York's decision to compete for this trade paid off handsomely. The Erie, forty feet wide and four feet deep with 84 locks covering the rise of some 650 feet between the Hudson and Buffalo, was built at a cost of some 7.1 million dollars. Even before its completion nearly a million dollars of toll revenue was collected. Between 1826 and 1835, when some three thousand canal boats were operating on it, the Erie and its sister canal, which connected the Hudson with Lake Champlain, earned a rate of return of nearly 8 percent on cost.

With the success of the Erie Canal, New York had outflanked its com-
merical rivals to the north and south. They attempted to remain competitive by imitating the Erie, but their endeavors largely met with failure.
Between 1826 and 1834 Pennsylvania completed its Mainline between
Philadelphia and Pittsburgh. It was a conglomeration of canal and railroad with 174 locks, a rise over the mountains much higher than the
Erie, and, as a result, transshipment problems. The Mainline also had
advantages over the Erie in the form of a longer operating season and a
direct connection with the Ohio River Valley. But its deficiencies were
sufficient to overcome its advantages. More costly to construct than the
Erie, it earned a far lower return than its New York competitor.

Farther south, the Chesapeake and Ohio Canal Company in 1828
began construction of a canal along the Potomac from the District of
Columbia westward toward Cumberland, Maryland, with the goal of
reaching the Ohio River. Despite generous financial support from Maryland, Virginia, Washington city, and the federal government, construction
costs far exceeded estimates, and construction proceeded slowly; Cumberland was not reached until 1850. This disappointing experience combined with the emerging competition of the Baltimore and Ohio Railroad
resulted in the shelving of the plan to extend the canal farther. In a like
fashion, the James River and Kanawha Canal, extending west from Rich-
mond, never reached its goal of the Kanawha River across the Appalachians in western Virginia.

The artificial waterways built in imitation of the Erie Canal largely
failed in their purpose of opening up various regions to the trans-
Appalachian West. The fact that they were started later than the Erie, just
as the railroad was proving itself a potential competitor, may have been
partially responsible. But more important were the improvements in western river transportation, which before the railroad era provided an effective river and sea alternative to waterway trade over the mountains. And
it must be recognized that the terrain where the Erie was built was vastly
better suited for a canal than were any of the other sites.

For all of its early success, even the Erie did not immediately accomplish a revolution in interregional trade. Until 1830 most of its west-east
shipments originated in western New York, and only small amounts of
grain came to it from northern Ohio via Lake Erie, while the products of
the more densely settled Ohio Valley moved down river toward New Orleans. Nevertheless, the potential for development in Ohio resulting from
the Erie Canal was recognized very early. While the Erie was still in the
planning stage, Thomas Worthington, governor of Ohio from 1814 to
1818, urged the state legislature to contribute financial support to the New
York project. It was not forthcoming, but before the Erie was completed
Ohio had embarked on a program that resulted in the construction of two
great north-south canals which joined the Ohio River Valley with Lake
Erie. The first canal, the Ohio and Erie (completed in 1833) between

Cleveland and Portsmouth, traversed the central and eastern parts of the state. Farther west, the Miami and Erie Canal moved north from Cincinnati and reached Dayton in 1832; but not until 1845 was the through route to Toledo on Lake Erie opened.

Ohio's canal system, consisting of over eight hundred miles of canal and slack-water navigation, never returned to the state toll revenues sufficient to pay back its sixteen million dollar cost. This does not mean that the decision to build was unwise. While even in its best years the more successful eastern branch did not yield an annual direct return on the state's investment of more than 4 percent, it has been estimated that the social rate of return, which included rising land values and increased production due to lower costs of transportation, ranged from 6 percent to over 12 percent between 1836 and 1853. Recognition of such social returns helps to explain the American enthusiasm for canals, but it may have been carried too far, producing excessive construction of short feeder canals. Although they were built in virtually all the major canal-building states, the feeders seldom carried enough traffic to prove economical and they served to reduce substantially the direct return on the states' investments.

Just as the Erie found imitators in the East, Indiana and Illinois followed Ohio's lead in the West. Both states had received federal land grants in 1827 to aid canal building. Construction of Indiana's Wabash and Erie Canal, joining Lake Erie in Ohio to Evansville, Illinois, on the Ohio River, was begun in 1832 but not completed until 1853. It was America's longest single canal, and also one of its least successful. A good part of the canal's revenue came from land sales rather than tolls, and total revenue was only a fraction of total cost; soon the railroads rendered the canal obsolete. Illinois began its Illinois and Michigan Canal connecting Chicago with the Illinois River, a tributary of the Mississippi, in 1836. As happened in Indiana, the nationwide financial and economic gyrations of the late 1830s and early 1840s increased construction costs and delayed completion until 1848. As a consequence, its direct financial success was limited. And whatever social returns it created for Chicago and north central Illinois were dwarfed by benefits from the railroads which were soon built in that area.

Table 5-1 summarizes some important features of antebellum canal construction. It shows that canal building was neither a steady activity nor a wholly unpatterned one. Instead, there were three identifiable cycles; the first two, spanning the years from 1815 to 1844, were of special significance in terms of mileage completed, resources expended, and the relative role of public investment. The third cycle, from 1844 to 1860, was less significant on all three counts and also in its economic impact. To a large extent the third cycle was marked by the carrying out or completion of canal projects planned earlier; by this time almost all the canals were facing the competitive pressure of the railroads.

TABLE 5-1
Cycles of Canal Construction, 1815-1860

	Peak Year	Completed Mileage	Investment over Cycle ($ millions)	Public Investment as Percentage of Total Investment
First cycle, 1815-34	1828	2,188	58.6	70.3
Second cycle, 1834-44	1840	1,172	72.2	79.4
Third cycle, 1844-60	1855	894	57.4	66.3
Total for all cycles		4,254	188.2	73.4

SOURCE: Harvey H. Segal, "Cycles of Canal Construction," in Carter Goodrich, ed., Canals and American Economic Development, (New York: Columbia University Press, 1961), pp. 172, 215.

Nearly three quarters of the total investment in canals during the three cycles came from public agencies, although most of these funds were borrowed from private investors rather than being derived from taxation. A significant fraction, about one-third, of the loans came from foreign countries, chiefly Great Britain. In this respect, state governments were acting in effect as financial intermediaries by substituting their superior credit, based primarily on the power to tax, for that of the less well-known and less trusted private intermediaries; they might have financed canals but could have done so only at greater capital costs.

The Steamboat

As the turnpike era was giving way to the canal building era in the eastern part of the United States, an equally significant transportation event—the development of the steamboat—was taking place in the West. The significance of the steamboat was threefold. First, it represented the earliest large-scale application to transportation of steam power, a prime feature of the emerging industrial age. Turnpikes and canals, in contrast, relied on the ancient animate converters of energy, primarily horses, for their motive power. Second, the steamboat vastly increased the transportation capacity of the great river system of the American heartland, which stretched from the Appalachians to the Rockies and from Canada to the Gulf of Mexico. The earliest and greatest development of this system occurred along the Mississippi and its great eastern tributary, the Ohio. But numerous other tributaries were also opened up to regional, interregional, and international trade by the steamboat. Finally, steamboating from all indications was a competitive business par excellence; as such it proved extremely flexible and responsive in meeting the growing and changing transportation needs of the western areas it served.

The successful commercial application of steam power to water transportation did not originate on western rivers, but rather on the Hudson where Robert Fulton's *Clermont* made its historic voyage from New York to Albany in 1807. Fulton and his partner, Robert Livingston, secured a monopoly right to steam navigation in New York waters from the state legislature, a tactic that they attempted, without great success, to extend to other areas of the country including the lower Mississippi. A landmark Supreme Court decision in 1824, *Gibbons* v. *Ogden*, ruled against the monopoly insofar as it attempted to control interstate steam transportation; the grounds were that the Constitution granted Congress, not state legislatures, the right to oversee interstate commerce. Thus, the new technology was opened up to competitive enterprise. In eastern and coastal waters, as well as on the Great Lakes, steamboats became important supplements to sailing vessels, particularly in carrying passenger traffic. They also proved complementary with canals; as we have seen, they were used as tows for canal boats on the Hudson between Albany and New York.

Far more important to American development because of the lack of a viable alternative, particularly in upriver navigation, was the application of steam power on the western rivers. On these waters flatboats and keelboats, relying primarily on river current and manpower, had provided a slow but moderately effective means of moving products downstream. Keelboats furnished a slow, strenuous, and therefore costly means of moving merchandise upstream. The first steamboat, built at Pittsburgh in 1811, made the down river trip to New Orleans in about two and a half months. It continued to operate on the lower Mississippi for several years, but not until 1815 did a steamboat make a round trip between Louisiana and Pennsylvania. From then to the Civil War the western steamboat business expanded rapidly, as is indicated by the boat number and tonnage (a measure of capacity by volume rather than weight) figures of Table 5–2. The greatest economic impact of the steamboat was in the reduction of upriver freight rates; it caused a rapid decline in the keelboat business during the 1820s. Flatboats, however, continued to operate throughout the antebellum era for two reasons: The volume of bulky agricultural produce moving down river was greater than that of the merchandise carried upstream and the steamboat provided an efficient means of transporting the flatboatmen back upstream.

The significance of the competitive nature of steamboating can be seen in part in Table 5–2's statistics on the industry's rapid expansion and growth in productivity. Profits generated by the quantum jump in transport efficiency generated a competitive expansion that quickly reduced freight rates. The cost of constructing a steamboat was not large; hence, most were owned and operated by one man or by a few partners. The

TABLE 5-2
Western River Steamboat Progress, 1815-60

Year	Number of Boats Operating	Operating Tonnage (in thousands)	Productivity Index (1815 = 100)
1815	7	1.5	100
1820	69	14.2	180
1825	80	12.5	203
1830	151	24.6	290
1835	324	50.1	441
1840	494	82.6	514
1845	538	96.2	710
1850	638	134.6	722
1855	696	172.7	732
1860	817	195.0	655

SOURCES: Boats and tonnage from Erik Haites and James Mak, "The Decline of Steamboating on the Ante-bellum Western Rivers: Some New Evidence and An Alternative Hypothesis," Explorations in Economic History, 11 (Fall 1973) 35-36; productivity index, calculated from Louisville-New Orleans route, is adapted from James Mak and Gary Walton, "Steamboats and the Great Productivity Surge in River Transportation," Journal of Economic History, 32 (September 1972), p. 639.

decentralized nature of ownership and decision making led to considerable experimentation and innovation in boat design and operation. The long, narrow, and prominently keeled design of eastern steamboats soon gave way to the wider, relatively flat-bottomed, and ornately superstructured vessel so admirably suited to the natural and social realities of river life, as Mark Twain showed in his *Life on the Mississippi*. Boat size increased, particularly on the major routes, and the ratio of carrying capacity to measured tonnage increased by a factor of three to four between 1820 and the 1840s. Speeds also were increased, as was the navigation season, while more efficient operations in the river ports reduced cargo collection time. Between 1820 and 1860, a roughly fourfold increase in productivity applied to a thirteenfold increase of measured tonnage in operation yielded a greater than fiftyfold increase in the amount of transport capacity supplied by western steamboats.

Virtually all of the improvement in productivity in river steamboating occurred before 1845. While tonnage doubled in the next fifteen years, a rather full exploitation of possible means of increasing productivity plus the imminent appearance of rail competition boded ill for the western river steamboat. Its colorful era did not last much beyond the Civil War, but during the period of its ascendancy the steamboat had made a crucial contribution to western and, perforce, to American economic development. Indeed, there are indications that the lower Mississippi Valley

with its great port at New Orleans, the focal point of steamboat navigation, was the most prosperous region of the entire United States on the
eve of the Civil War.

The Early Railroad Age, 1828–60

Just as American canal building and steamboating developments were
getting into high gear, a new transportation technology, the railroad, arrived to present a challenge. Ultimately the railroad prevailed. In a way
the railroad was a combination of the basic principles of earlier technologies. From the steamboat it inherited the idea of steam as the motive
power for a carrier of passengers and freight, while the canal furnished a
compelling example of the benefits of a low-friction, artificially constructed route of commerce. The railroad's inherent advantage over canal
and steamboat lay partly in its greater speed and regularity of operation,
but more importantly in the flexibility that allowed it to serve areas away
from natural waterways or where high costs made canal building
prohibitive.

The railroad's advantages over other means of conveyance were not
obvious at first. Its first application to public transportation in the late
1820s occurred almost simultaneously in England and the United States.
This meant that Americans did not have with the railroad, as they did
with canals, successful and long-existing precedents from abroad on which
to base their own planning. Given this context, it is easier to understand
why, for example, Pennsylvanians debated vigorously the merits of canals
and railroads and chose a curious and rather unsuccessful amalgam of
both in the state's Mainline. The merits of the nation's dedication to decentralized decision making are evident, however, in the rapid progress of
the railroad in the 1830s. By 1840 when the railroad was barely a decade
old, American railroad mileage virtually equalled that of its canals. By
1860 some thirty thousand miles of track had been put into operation,
and railroad mileage was over seven times canal mileage.

Why was the steam railroad—an unproven concept—seized upon so
boldly by American decision makers? The initial impetus can be found
in the old but rapidly changing commercial rivalries among eastern seaport
cities for trade with the interior. When the first general-purpose American
railroad, the Baltimore and Ohio, was chartered in 1828, Baltimore businessmen feared that the projected Chesapeake and Ohio Canal, which ran
roughly parallel, would divert inland trade to Virginia ports. In South
Carolina, similarly, the business interests of Charleston hoped to cut into
Savannah's trade by building a railroad inland to Hamburg on the Sa-

vannah River. When completed in 1833 the railroad was 136 miles long, the longest railroad anywhere in the world. In other states along the Atlantic seaboard these examples were soon imitated, and the railroad quickly proved itself an effective competitor to other modes of transportation, especially in the carrying of people.

From the beginning most American railroads were organized as corporations chartered by state governments. They followed the pattern used by the turnpike companies and by a few short canals, not the one employed by the major canals and by the steamboat enterprises. It is interesting to inquire why these differing forms of organization were chosen. The customary answer emphasizes the advantages of the corporate form of organization in raising large amounts of capital. Since steamboats could be built for relatively small sums, individual enterprises and small partnerships were feasible forms of organization. Turnpikes, in contrast, were rather costly to construct by the standards of the day, but unlike the great canals they were not near to being statewide in length. Moreover, local interests along the roadway received enough indirect benefits from them to induce private stock subscriptions sufficient to finance construction even when the direct return from tolls was not as high as the return from other investments. The relatively small turnpike corporation thus provided an efficient middle ground between individual or partnership organization, which was unfeasible, and state planning and ownership, which was unnecessary since inland economic activity was still local rather than statewide.

More perplexing for the capital-requirements argument is the comparison of railroads with the great canals. Both were devourers of capital as compared with turnpikes and steamboats. Why, therefore, were corporations dominant in railroads and state ownership in canals? Timing provides part of the answer, although it is perhaps too much emphasized. The railroad era began somewhat later than the canal era, and wealth no doubt had increased to such an extent that private financing was more easily forthcoming for railroads. Also, many of the earliest railroads were more like turnpikes in length than like the statewide canals. Another factor less often emphasized, however, may well have been more important. Of all the transport innovations of the early nineteenth century, the railroads alone found it most efficient both to build the fixed facilities to carry goods and people and to operate the means of conveyance themselves. In the cases of turnpikes, canals, and steamboats these two functions were organized separately. The sheer complexity of the problems of when, where, and how to build the roadway coupled with those of acquiring and operating locomotives and rolling stock was of a nature that lent itself to private, decentralized decision making in an age when limited government was both a fact and an ideal.

Although early railroads were usually organized as private corporations, they received significant financial and other help from all levels of government. State charters granted them rights of eminent domain and in some cases tax exemptions, banking privileges, and even monopoly rights. In the South and West when enough private capital and entrepreneurship were not forthcoming to match the desires of the people, railroads were sometimes built and operated by state governments. Eventually—in some cases, rather quickly—most such railroads were transferred to private ownership and operation. Usually state and local governments provided financial assistance to railroad corporations, often in the form of loans but sometimes with stock subscriptions and guarantees of railroad securities. State aid was greatest in the South. In the less developed West, where substantial state aid might also have been expected, it was in fact less important. The timing of regional railway development provides a clue to this conundrum. By the 1850s, the decade of greatest antebellum railway expansion, eastern and foreign sources of private capital became available to the West and the South where, in fact, most of the expansion took place. Also, under long pressure from the West to aid railroad development, the federal government in 1850 granted several million acres of land to the states of Illinois, Alabama, and Mississippi to aid in the construction of a north-south railroad from Illinois to the Gulf of Mexico. These lands were turned over to the Illinois Central Railroad Company, which then mortgaged or sold the lands and used the money they obtained to build the railroad. It was completed in 1856. This federal action set a precedent for the massive land grants made directly to railroads later in the century.

Despite the large amount of governmental assistance, however, private capital supplied about three-fourths of the over one billion dollars invested in American railroads from 1828 to 1860. In contrast, only about one-fourth of the $188 million cost of antebellum canals came directly from private sources, the rest from public investment. The comparison is somewhat biased in that locomotives and rolling stock are included in the railroad figure while canal boats and horses are excluded from canal costs; nonetheless it emphasizes the differing magnitudes and natures of railway and canal investment before the Civil War. Even in its infancy in 1860 the railroad demonstrated a much wider range of application. Its triumph over other means of internal transportation was a tribute to the railroad's greater flexibility and efficiency.

The Decline of Transport Costs

Our survey of the early nineteenth century's transportation innovations thus far has emphasized technological and organizational characteristics. From it one learns something of the ways in which Americans of the early national period approached their problems of economic development. During the first decades of the new nation's history the artificial stimulus of European wars served to focus much of the country's attention on foreign commerce rather than on internal market development. There were constitutional debates and the emergence of clashing sectional interests on the subject of transportation improvements. These trends pointed up some drawbacks of a federal system of government and caused some questioning of Albert Gallatin's view that only the central government could mount an effective attack on the nation's transport problems. Out of this milieu there developed a more decentralized approach to transportation problems, one which promoted progress through a pragmatic pursuit of local and regional interests instead of allowing these interests to stand in its way. Thus pragmatism appeared in the varied roles assumed by government and by private enterprise in turnpike, canal, steamboat, and railroad development. Ideologies of laissez-faire and of government intervention had little or no influence on the organization of the rapidly expanding transportation sector. The mix of public and private decision making was determined by the technical characteristics of each innovation and by economic conditions in the state or region involved.

While the technologies and organizational forms of American transportation innovations were varied, their effects on transportation costs were similar and usually quite dramatic. This is evident in Figure 5–1, which is based on the thoughtful researches of Professor Douglass C. North. Over the course of the nineteenth century inland freight rates fell, in rough terms, to less than one-fiftieth of their level in the late eighteenth century. Costs fell because of the widespread application of new technologies and the competition that arose among, as well as between, sellers of the major categories of transport services. For example, wagon freight rates fell before the introduction of steamboats and canals because of the competition of wagon haulers on improved turnpike roads; they fell even further when the water alternatives came along.

The greatest reduction in inland freight rates, Figure 5–1 indicates, occurred between 1815 and the 1850s and was due primarily to steamboats and canals. The fall in upstream river rates is especially noteworthy both for its rapidity and for the fact that it was virtually complete before 1830. Freight rates on the earliest railroads were five to ten times those on rivers and canals. It is not surprising that in their first two decades of development the railroads earned more than half of their revenue in the passenger business, the place where their advantage over alternative carriers was greatest. By the 1850s, however, the growth and improvement of rail transport led to its effective, and sometimes devastating, competition for freight with water carriers even though railroad rates, on a ton-mile basis, remained well above water rates. Rail transport was faster and more direct than shipping by water, and railroads, unlike canals and steam-

boats, operated throughout the year and went places where water transport was unavailable.

It is not an exaggeration to term these developments a transportation revolution. The internal markets of the United States at the start of the nineteenth century were for the most part scattered and local affairs. By the 1850s, and in many cases as early as the 1820s, this was no longer the case. The products of the farm, the forest, the mine, and the factory—and people themselves—were moving more quickly and at greatly reduced costs in regional and interregional trade. In consequence producers received higher real prices for their goods and services and saw the value of their resources increased, while consumers witnessed declines in the prices they paid for goods and services. Greater specialization in production based on individual, local, and regional comparative advantage was encouraged and even demanded by the increased competition of distant producers as markets were extended by improved transportation. The Constitution had created the possibility of a great common market throughout the United States. The transportation revolution made it a reality.

Information and Communications

Improved transportation in antebellum America also facilitated an increased flow of information and its faster dissemination. In comparison with the exchange of commodities, the exchange of information has received relatively little attention from economic historians. This is unfortunate. In an economy based on decentralized decision making and coordination of economic activity through prices and markets, information is a fundamental factor of production. It is said with good reason that a man's decisions are no better than his information.

Information reduces the boundaries of uncertainty faced by decision makers. It plays a key role in the efficient allocation of scarce resources. Suppose, for example, a commodity is being produced and sold in two different places at prices that differ by more than the cost of transporting the commodity between them. In such a case scarce resources are being allocated in an inefficient manner. Someone who had price information from both markets could profit by buying low and selling high. This commercial activity, in addition to being profitable, serves the social function of improving resource allocation because it tends to equalize prices in the two markets. The orders placed in the low-price market draw more resources into producing the commodity where it can be made more efficiently. Shipments to the high-price market then release resources from producing the commodity and they now can be used in more productive activities. Once again this illustrates the relationship of specialization and comparative advantage.

In the antebellum era the single greatest innovation in the technology of information transmission was the electromagnetic telegraph. It came relatively late in the period; its first practical demonstration took place in 1844. In the pretelegraph age the volume and speed of the flow of information depended heavily on the means of moving people and goods from place to place. In other words, before the telegraph, communications and transportation improvements went hand in hand. But the story of improved communication before the telegraph was introduced involves more than roads, canals, steamboats, and railroads. It also includes improvements in ocean transport, the growth of newspapers and postal services, and the development of commercial practices.*

An idea of the slowness of pretelegraphic information flows and of the extent to which the time involved was reduced may be illustrated by specific examples. In 1799 it took a week for the news of George Washington's death to travel from Alexandria, Virginia, to New York City. By 1831, in contrast, relay expresses traveling over improved roads carried the news of President Jackson's State of the Union address from Washington, D.C. (near Alexandria) to New York in fifteen and a half hours. Again, the Battle of New Orleans on 8 January 1815, took place some two weeks after the peace treaty "ending" the second war with Britain had been signed in Europe. New York City did not receive news of the battle until 6 February, twenty-eight days later, or of the treaty until 11 February 1815, or forty-nine days after its signing. By 1841, however, news traveled between New York and New Orleans in nine days, three times faster than in 1815. By the late 1830s steamships had begun to cross the Atlantic in two to three weeks. Finally, while in the 1790s it had taken some twenty days for information to move between New York and distant cities such as Cincinnati, Detroit, and Charleston, by 1840 the time had been reduced to about five days, even less when express mail was used. By modern standards all of these pretelegraphic communication times seem slow, but that should not obscure the substantial improvement that occurred in the period, particularly between 1815 and 1840.

Communication is, of course, much more complicated than the mere transmission of information. It also involves gathering and processing information as well as making decisions about what information to gather, process, and transmit. Insight into these activities may be gained by examining the development of three institutions: newspapers, postal services, and common carriers.

The American newspaper business developed rapidly from 1790 to

* The discussion that follows is indebted to a recent and thoughtful book by the geographer, Alan R. Pred, *Urban Growth and the Circulation of Information: The United States System of Cities 1790–1840* (Cambridge: Harvard University Press, 1973).

1840. Its growth in quantitative terms is shown in Table 5-3. Over this half century, the annual circulation of newspapers increased by a factor of 37, whereas per capita newspaper consumption grew by a factor of almost 9. These data represent compounded annual rates of increase of 7.2 percent and 4.3 percent, respectively, rates that were well in excess of those of population and per capita income. Why were newspapers, like other types of information enterprises, growth industries in the early United States? Among the many reasons one would have to include relatively high levels of literacy, growing urban populations, and the great interest of Americans in both international and domestic politics. But newspapers also served important economic functions. They published advertising, shipping intelligence, current price lists, and other commercial information. In a period when markets were expanding geographically, this type of information was important for producers, consumers, and, perhaps most of all, for the various middlemen of commerce. Their day-to-day decisions depended on their having the best information available, and newspapers often provided that information.

TABLE 5-3
Growth of U.S. Newspaper Publishing, 1790-1840

	1790	1800	1810	1820	1828	1835	1840
Newspapers published	92	235	371	512	861	1,258	1,404
Annual Circulation (in millions)	4.0	12-13	24.6	50.0	68.1	90.4	147.5
Annual Newspaper copies per capita	1.0	2.4	3.4	5.2	5.6	6.0	8.6

SOURCE: Adapted from Pred, Urban Growth and the Circulation of Information, p. 21.

Newspapers flourished in the commercially oriented cities, especially in New York, and from these papers many other city and town papers cribbed their news. The frontier was also served, largely through the agency of postal services. Writing during his visit to America in 1831-32, the Frenchman Alexis de Tocqueville noted of Kentucky and Tennessee:

> There is an astonishing circulation of letters and newspapers among these savage woods. We travelled with the mail. From time to time we stopped at what is called the post office; almost always it was an isolated house in the depths of a wood. There we dropped a large parcel from which no doubt each inhabitant of the neighborhood came to take his share. I do not think that in the most enlightened rural districts of France there is an intellectual movement either so rapid or on such a scale as in this wilderness.*

* Alexis de Tocqueville, *Journey to America*, J. P. Mayer, ed. (New York: Doubleday and Company, 1971), p. 283.

Tocqueville observed a similar attentiveness to information and communications throughout the United States.

As Tocqueville's comments imply, a major agency for the diffusion of
newspaper information was the United States Post Office. The postal
service also transmitted information in the form of business and personal
correspondence. Table 5–4 presents data on this agency's growth from
1790 to 1860. The number of post offices increased greatly in these years.
Aggregate postal revenues and revenues per capita expanded at compound
annual rates of 9.6 percent and 6.6 percent, respectively, between 1790
and 1840, a period when postage charges did not change appreciably.
From 1840 to 1860, rates of growth of total and per capita revenues fell,
but this was due more to a dramatic reduction in postage charges in
1845 than to a slower growth in the volume of mail carried.

TABLE 5-4
Growth of U.S. Postal Services, 1790-1860

	1790	1800	1810	1820	1830	1840	1850	1860
Post Offices	75	903	2,300	4,500	8,450	13,468	18,417	28,498
Population per Post Office (in thousands)	52.4	5.9	3.1	2.1	1.5	1.3	1.3	1.1
Postage Revenues (in $ thousands)	38	281	552	1,112	1,185	4,543	5,500	8,518
Postage Revenue per capita (in $)	.01	.05	.08	.12	.14	.27	.30	.27

SOURCES: 1790-1840, adapted from Pred, Urban Growth and the Circulation of Information, p. 80;
1850 and 1860, U.S. Bureau of Census, Historical Statistics of the United States (Washington, D.C.:
United States Government Printing Office, 1960), pp. 7, 497.

The Post Office improved the quality of its services over the antebellum period. Easier access to post offices, implied by the sharp decline
in population per post office, is one aspect of improved quality. There
were others. In the 1830s, express mails and the use of railroads as mail
carriers speeded up deliveries and made them more regular and reliable.
The introduction of postage stamps in 1847 allowed people to mail letters
at times when local post offices were closed. And throughout the period,
federal policy resulted in an extension of service that kept up with the
westward movement of population.

The 1845 Postal Act's large reductions in charges for transmitting
correspondence marked acceptance of the policy decision, long debated
in government circles, that the Post Office did not have to make a profit,
or even cover all of its costs; the idea was that even if the Post Office

lost money the social benefit to the nation from more extensive information flows could easily outweigh the loss of federal revenue.

Another development aiding the flow of information, particularly before the telegraph, was an improvement in common-carrier passenger transportation. This facilitated the spread of information from one place to another by word of mouth. In the early days of the republic, passenger travel over land by stagecoach was slow, costly, and exceedingly uncomfortable. Travelers had to add to their stagecoach fare the cost of meals and lodging at the inns that dotted the landscape. As roads were improved and as steam was applied to the movement of people over water and land, both fares and journey times fell sharply. Total cost of travel was therefore greatly reduced by the antebellum transportation revolution.

The chief result of reduced travel costs was an increased intensity of travel, particularly between growing urban centers. Consequently the flow of information via the movement of people became more intense. Regularly scheduled passenger services were expanded and improved. Who were the travelers? They were predominantly businessmen. Retailers from all over the country made seasonal or annual trips to eastern cities to place orders for their stores. This was especially common in the earlier decades when the spatial dispersion of retail markets made it too expensive for middlemen to seek out the retailers. As transportation improved in the 1820s and 1830s, inland cities began to develop into wholesale markets, and wholesale merchants and the selling agents of manufacturers swelled the ranks of business travelers.

The preceding discussion indicates that in the developing economy of the antebellum decades there was a growing demand for faster and more reliable means of transmitting information and economic intelligence. There was also a variety of supply responses in which both public and private parties participated, often as competitors. But before the 1840s information transmission did not come close to the ideal of nearly instantaneous communication. The invention and application of the telegraph represented a solution to this problem. Therein lay its greatest economic and social significance.

Samuel F. B. Morse, the telegraph's inventor, developed the idea and made limited experiments with it in the 1830s. However, as is often the case with original ideas, a convincing demonstration of the invention's utility required substantial financial backing. It was not forthcoming from private sources. Morse therefore sought the aid of the federal government, and in 1843 Congress appropriated thirty thousand dollars for the construction of a telegraph line between Washington, D.C. and Baltimore. This pilot project, completed in 1844, was a technical success, and private investors soon became interested in the innovation. A number of telegraph companies were formed, and the mileage of telegraph line in operation grew rapidly, from forty miles in 1846, to two thousand in 1848, to twelve thousand in 1850, and to twenty-three thousand in 1852. By that time the major cities of the Northeast and Middle West were connected by telegraph. Competition led to rate wars which bankrupted some of the companies and caused others to merge or consolidate their operations. On the eve of the Civil War only three companies were left, and they operated some fifty thousand miles of telegraph line. Also, an undersea cable for transmitting messages across the Atlantic was completed in 1858; however, it ran into technical problems that were not solved until after the War.

The Western Union Company was by far the most successful of the early telegraph firms. Its organizers and managers were skilled businessmen whose acumen produced the profits that soon allowed the company to absorb many of its weaker competitors and to tap the capital markets for more funds for expansion. Western Union's patents and its demonstrated abilities also were instrumental in gaining governmental subsidies to construct an east-west transcontinental line; the company completed it in 1861. Another key reason for Western Union's success was that it was the first company to convince the railroads that the telegraph could be complementary to railroad operations. Western Union then could cut its construction and operating costs by utilizing railroad right of ways and by teaching railroad workers to operate and maintain telegraph equipment. In return railroads gained access to a means of transmitting information that allowed them to coordinate and follow their traffic movements more effectively.

Conclusion

The transportation and communications revolutions of early United States economic history are keys to an understanding of developments that unfolded in other sectors of the economy then and later. Without the revolutionary improvements, vast acreages of land would not have been settled and turned toward specialized, commercial agriculture at anything like the rate that actually occurred. Nor would commerce and industry have enjoyed the expanding markets that promoted specialization, economies of scale, and the incentive to develop and use new technologies. Nor would demands for money, bank credit, and an integrated financial system have expanded as they did. One does not have to imagine a world without rapid, low-cost transportation and communication in order to appreciate the difference these factors made. Reflecting on the slower pace of seventeenth- and eighteenth-century American economic development in all sectors helps one realize that transportation and communications improvements were basic to economic modernization in the United States.

SUGGESTED READINGS

For a general survey of the development of the antebellum economy with an appropriate emphasis on transportation, see George R. Taylor, *The Transportation Revolution, 1815–1860* (New York: Holt, Rinehart & Winston, 1961). Chapter 13 of Lance Davis et al., *American Economic Growth: An Economist's History of the United States* (New York: Harper & Row, 1972) on "Internal Transportation" is a masterly treatment of the subject in its command both of the historical facts and their meaning in terms of economic analysis. A basic source of data on the remarkable decline of transport costs is Douglass C. North, "The Role of Transportation in the Economic Development of North America," *Les grandes voies maritimes dans le monde XV–XIX Siecles* (Paris: Sevpen, 1965). The revolutionary character of nineteenth-century transportation improvements is reaffirmed in a recent article that surveys much of the technical work done by economic historians in this area during the past two decades; see Robert W. Fogel, "Notes on the Social Saving Controversy," *Journal of Economic History*, 39 (March 1979).

Studies of specific transportation technologies and facilities are numerous. On turnpikes, one may consult Joseph A. Durrenberger, *Turnpikes: A Study of the Toll Road Movement in the Middle Atlantic States and Maryland* (Cos Cob, Conn.: John E. Edwards, Publisher, 1968). The canal era is surveyed and analyzed in Carter Goodrich, ed., *Canals and American Economic Development* (New York: Columbia University Press, 1961). For case studies see Ronald E. Shaw, *Erie Water West: A History of the Erie Canal, 1792–1854* (Lexington: University of Kentucky Press, 1966) and Harry Scheiber, *Ohio Canal Era: A Case Study of Government and the Economy, 1820–1861* (Athens: Ohio University Press, 1969). Economic issues pertaining to the contributions of canals are in Roger L. Ransom, "Social Returns from Public Transport Investment: A Case Study of the Ohio Canal," *Journal of Political Economy*, 78 (September/October 1970), 1041–1059, and Ronald W. Filante, "A Note on the Economic Viability of the Erie Canal," *Business History Review*, 48 (Spring 1974), 95–102.

The classic study of steamboating is Louis C. Hunter, *Steamboats on the Western Rivers* (Cambridge, Mass.: Harvard University Press, 1949), but the economic analysis of the contribution of this technology is well set out in the more recent book by Eric F. Haites, James Mak, and Gary M. Walton, *Western River Transportation: The Era of Early Internal Development, 1810–1860* (Baltimore: Johns Hopkins Press, 1975).

The economic impact of early railroads is analyzed in considerable detail by Albert Fishlow in his *American Railroads and the Transformation of the Antebellum Economy* (Cambridge, Mass.: Harvard University Press, 1965). For both more general questions and an emphasis on the path breaking influence of railroads on business organization and management, see two works of Alfred D. Chandler, Jr., *The Railroads: The Nation's First Big Business* (New York: Harcourt, Brace & World, 1965) and *The Visible Hand* (Cambridge, Mass.: Harvard University Press, 1977).

Governmental concerns with and activities in early transportation improvements are an important part of the story. One can still gain a valuable perspective on the dimensions of America's transportation problems circa 1808 by reading the recently reprinted work of Albert Gallatin, "Report on Roads and Canals," Document No. 250, 10th Congress, 1st Session, in *The New American State Papers—Transportation*, vol. 1 (Wilmington, Del.: Scholarly Resources, 1972). Another classic discussing forms of governmental aid is Guy S. Callender, "The Early Transportation and Banking Enterprises of the States in Relation to the Growth of Corporations," *Quarterly Journal of Economics*, 27 (November 1902), 111–162. For more recent discussions, see two studies by Carter Goodrich, *Government Promotion of American Canals and Railroads, 1800–1890* (New York: Columbia University Press, 1960) and "Internal Improvements Reconsidered," *Journal of Economic History*, 30 (June 1970).

Information and communications improvements, as noted in the text, have received much less study by economic historians than has transportation. Two valuable studies relating to the antebellum years are Alan R. Pred, *Urban Growth and the Circulation of Information: The United States System of Cities, 1790–1840* (Cambridge, Mass.: Harvard University Press, 1973) and Robert L. Thompson, *Wiring a Continent, The History of the Telegraph Industry in the United States, 1832–1866* (Princeton, N.J.: Princeton University Press, 1947).

CHAPTER 6

———

Land Policy and

Agricultural Expansion

———

The most abundant resource of the young United States was land, and the primary use of land was as an input into agricultural production. Yet at the close of the War of Independence most of the new nation's land resources were not economic resources. The lands extending westward from the Appalachians to the Mississippi were scarcely used at all except occasionally by Indian and non-Indian hunters and trappers. Although it was unclear who controlled or owned these lands, the interest of Americans in the ownership and utilization of this resource was great; they perceived a need for making fundamental decisions about the unsettled land. Who owned the land? Who should own it? Under what terms and conditions could it best be converted from a natural to an economic resource? What public and private aspirations could be achieved by various land policy options? These were momentous questions. Some of them were definitively answered by policy decisions of the 1780s, while the answers to other land questions evolved and changed as the nation grew. In general, the result was a transfer of vast acreages of public lands through market mechanisms to the hands of numerous private owners who for the most part were farmers.

United States Land Policies Before the Civil War

In 1783, as a result of the Treaty of Paris which formally ended the American Revolution, the original territory of the United States consisted of some 889,000 square miles of land. This territory extended from the

Atlantic coast westward to the Mississippi River, and from the Great Lakes and Maine in the north to a rough line stretching westward from the southern boundary of Georgia in the south. During the half century from 1803 to 1853 the territory of the United States expanded to more than three times its original size and covered slightly more than three million square miles—all the land now occupied by the forty-eight contiguous states.

The territorial acquisitions of 1803–53 emphasized in bold strokes the acquisitive and expansionist goals of the young republic. President Thomas Jefferson had hoped in 1803 to secure American control of the mouth of the Mississippi, but when Napoleon offered not only to fulfill that limited objective but also to give Jefferson a chance to double the size of the U.S. with one move, Jefferson quickly set aside his fondness for constitutional procedures and accepted. Four decades later, under President James K. Polk, territories larger in their aggregate than the Louisiana Purchase were added.

EARLY LAND POLICY, 1781–1802

The early land policy of the United States was directed toward acquiring a national public domain, setting the conditions under which it would be utilized economically, and determining the political position of the new territories. The problem of acquisition was complicated by the claims of several of the original states, dating from their colonial charters, to lands lying beyond their borders. States without such claims wanted the landed states to be stripped of their holdings which would then pass into the national domain. However, the alliance of states under the Articles of Confederation was fragile, and delicate political maneuvering was needed to persuade the claimant states to cede their western lands to the federal government. New York began the process in 1781. By 1790, Virginia, Massachusetts, Connecticut and the Carolinas had relinquished most of their western claims, and in 1802 Georgia ceded to the United States its western lands that covered most of what is now Alabama and Mississippi. The pre–Louisiana Purchase national domain then consisted of this southern area and the lands north and west of the Ohio River.

In the earliest stages of the national domain's formation, the basic pattern for transferring its land to private ownership and utilization was established by the Land Ordinance of 20 May 1785, which was patterned in part after an earlier plan of Thomas Jefferson's. Systematic land division into townships followed the orderly pattern of colonial New England rather than the haphazard method of locating practiced in much of the South. Rectangular surveys established the boundaries of each township, 6 miles on a side, and divided it into 36 sections, each measuring one square mile, or 640 acres. The lots thus surveyed were to be sold for cash but for not less than $1 per acre. Hence, a minimum of $640 was required initially to purchase a tract of the minimum size set by the United States. In each township four sections were retained by the United States, and an additional section was reserved to support public schools.

The first surveys, which were made in southeastern Ohio, commenced in 1785. But little land was sold by the United States in the early years. The original states still possessed land within and without their borders, and they could offer better financial terms and more immediate economic opportunity. The states, in fact, were much more innovative and flexible in land policy than was the national government. They took the lead in abolishing the feudal obligations attached to land use which had migrated to the American colonies from Europe and instead they sold or granted land on the basis of freehold tenure. Although the widespread practice among the states of paying or rewarding soldiers with land grants was feudal in origin, it might best be viewed as an intelligent decision based on economic reality: the states' economies were underdeveloped and land was by far their greatest disposable resource. The states, particularly in the South, also pioneered in the practice of granting pre-emptive rights to land to those who had settled upon it in advance of survey and sale. These state policies, often developed during the colonial era, provided a wealth of experience for the United States government to draw on, but it did so rather slowly.

With national land sales going slowly, and with the federal government pressed for funds, the United States in 1786 and 1788 sold million-acre tracts of Ohio lands to two eastern groups, the Ohio Company and John Symmes and his associates. This was an attempt to decentralize the sale of national lands in order to raise revenue and encourage more rapid settlement. However, the plan was not very successful on either count. The companies were permitted to tender depreciated government debt certificates and soldiers' warrants rather than cash for the lands, but even with this concession, which amounted to a price reduction, they were not able to make full payment. The companies faced the same problem that plagued the central government: land at better locations was still available in large quantities from the states.

While national land sales remained modest for a decade under the Ordinance of 1785, a significant piece of related legislation came in 1787: the Northwest Ordinance; it provided for the political organization of the Northwest Territory. In addition to forbidding the extension of slavery, it granted specific rights to inhabitants of the territory and established the steps to be taken for the territory to become a state (or states) with powers and privileges equal to those of existing states. In rejecting the mercantilist idea of metropolis–colony relationships—the idea against which the American colonies had rebelled—the Northwest Ordinance marked a far-reaching decision about the basic pattern that the constituent units of the United States were to follow in their political development.

The Land Act of 1796, the first under the new federal government, reaffirmed the rectangular survey principle of the 1785 Ordinance. The minimum price was doubled to $2 per acre, where it remained until 1820, while the minimum tract was kept at 640 acres. Congress had several motives in setting the higher price. It was meant to discourage the large, speculative purchases that had caused both the federal and state governments embarrassment in preceding years. (It actually discouraged all other potential purchasers as well.) Some members of the dominant Federalist party were opposed to cheap land and believed that high-priced land would encourage commerce and manufacturing. Finally, the existing states and other land sellers desired to keep the price of federal land noncompetitive with their own properties. Two features of the act, however, worked to stimulate sales, not in themselves so much as because they set a precedent that was followed and liberalized up till 1820. One provision of the act allowed land to be bought on credit, with a small down payment, half the purchase price in thirty days, and the remainder within one year. Another provision established auction sales at specific locations, initially in the east.

Federal land sales continued to be sluggish until 1800 when, at the behest of William Henry Harrison, a future president but then a delegate from the Northwest Territory, the land laws were modified in three ways to encourage sales and settlement. The minimum purchasable tract was reduced to 320 acres, credit terms were liberalized to provide for installment payments spread over four years, and land offices were located more conveniently in the vicinity of the lands offered for sale. Thereafter federal land sales picked up speed.

PUBLIC POLICY AND THE LAND MARKET, 1800–60

The federal land acts of the late eighteenth century established the essential principles and mechanics of land sale in later years without actually selling much land. After 1800 and until the Civil War, the annual rate of disposal of the public domain, as the accompanying Figure 6–1 indicates, was typically in the hundreds of thousands of acres up to the 1830s and in the millions of acres thereafter. Three periods of rapidly rising and ultimately frenzied sales occurred during the years 1814–19, 1833–36, and 1854–55. The rising trend of federal land sales reflects a growing population, transportation improvements that extended the markets for the products of the land, and increasingly liberal disposal policies. The periods of peak sales, often attributed to irrational speculation, were in actuality a rather rational response to generally rising price levels and relative price increases for products of the land. Such price movements increased the value of land at a time when federal policies held its price relatively constant. Predictably, sales of land soared.

The increasingly liberal character of antebellum public land policy

was evident in the reduction of prices and of the minimum acreage that could be purchased, in the recognition of squatters' rights to pre-emption, in the adoption of graduated price reductions for offered but unsold lands, and in the growing use of grants of land to promote public purposes. Minimum acreage offered for sale, set at 320 acres in 1800, was reduced to 160 acres in 1804, to 80 in 1820, and to 40 in 1832. Throughout the period from 1796 to 1820 the federal government financed sales by granting credit to buyers at the set price of $2 per acre. Although a discount to $1.64 per acre was offered for cash sales in 1804, a great many private purchasers availed themselves of federal credit, especially during the boom sales period of 1814–19. This was not surprising, for the interest charge of only 6 percent was generally well below what private credit institutions, insofar as they existed at all in frontier areas, were charging. Before 1820, however, the limited extent of western markets plus the time involved in bringing virgin land into production made it difficult for the settlers to pay their debts to the government when they fell due. In response to the settlers' plight numerous relief and credit extension acts were passed, but even with this aid, over a third of the lands sold between 1787 and 1820 had reverted to the federal government by 1820. Faced with this problem and with an outstanding amount of over $20 million due on land sales, the federal government in 1820 abolished the credit system and reduced the minimum price of land to $1.25 per acre, payable in cash only. Cash sales of newly offered land at the $1.25 price remained in effect until the Homestead Act of 1862 belatedly fulfilled the fond hope of many people by providing for free land. Most sales after 1820 were also financed by credit, but from private sources rather than from the federal government. The federal government's abandonment of credit sales marked a recognition that it had discharged an early developmental function that from then on could be handled by private credit-granting enterprises.

Throughout the antebellum era federal land policy operated to keep the supply of land extremely elastic at the minimum price. The pace of surveying and offering land for sale continually outpaced demand, with the result that average prices received were, with few exceptions, close to the minimum price asked. Nonetheless, a good many people settled and improved western lands in advance of government sale. These squatters constituted a potent political force in favor of the granting of liberal pre-emption rights. Before 1830 a number of special acts recognized their claims, and in 1830 the first general pre-emption act was passed. It provided that settlers who were living on public land which they had improved as of 1829 had the right to purchase it, up to a maximum of 160 acres, at the minimum price of $1.25 per acre. This policy was renewed periodically in the 1830s, but the pre-emption rights remained retrospective rather than prospective. Finally in 1841 the right of prospective pre-emption was enacted into law; from then until the Homestead Law achieved the goal of free land, anyone could go out and settle on unsold public land and gain the right to buy it later at the minimum price.

Since parcels of land vary greatly in their physical and economic attributes, the federal government, before 1854, exhibited inflexibility in setting a single minimum price for all land. Substantial acreages of public land remained unsold behind the westward moving frontier. As early as 1824, Senator Thomas Hart Benton of Missouri called for graduated price reduction for unsold land. Congress did not act positively until three decades later. The Graduation Act of 1854 reduced prices to $1 per acre for land offered but not sold for ten years. The price fell to 12.5 cents per acre for land unsold for thirty years. Graduated prices proved very successful in promoting sales. Until repealed in 1862, the 1854 Act resulted in over 70 million acres being sold at the reduced prices.

The use of land grants was another significant aspect of federal policy of the antebellum era. The major beneficiaries were veterans of military campaigns and the states; the major purposes were to reward veterans for their service to the nation and to promote useful public functions by the states, chiefly education, internal improvements in transportation, and land reclamation. Granting land warrants to veterans dated back to the Revolution and was based on colonial, even ancient, precedents. From the earliest years the ex-soldiers often disposed of these beneficences without ever claiming or setting foot on them, a practice that became officially sanctioned in the 1850s when an active market in warrants developed. Warrants selling at prices below $1.25 per acre became an important land-office currency. In some years the acreage purchased with warrants actually exceeded the amount of land bought for cash.

The practice of granting federal lands for educational purposes originated with the ordinances of 1785 and 1787; grants for improvements began with the 1802 act enabling Ohio to become a state. Five percent of the proceeds of federal land sales in Ohio were set aside for road building under both state and federal auspices. This precedent was followed in other states, culminating before the Civil War in grants to states to aid railroad construction. The Illinois Central railroad was the most prominent example. Other large grants, but less specific in purpose, were donations of swamp lands to states in the 1850s. The states were to sell these inferior lands and use the proceeds for reclamation.

Thus before the Civil War the federal government gave away some sixty-eight million acres of the public domain for military support purposes and twice that quantity to the states. These grants added up to an area larger than the state of Texas; yet the most significant aspect of federal land policy was the creation and nurturing of a great land market through which the public domain passed into private ownership and utilization. Both publicly and privately, Americans looked upon their vast land endowment as a resource to be applied toward material ends. The quickest way to realize this goal was to turn the resource over to widespread private ownership and decentralized decision making. The evolution of American land policy is best understood by recognizing the pervasiveness of these attitudes over the course of the nineteenth century.

SECTIONAL POLITICS AND LAND ECONOMICS

The increasingly liberal terms on which the federal government disposed of the public domain between the 1780s and the 1860s reflect both economic rationality and the rising political power of the western states and territories. A basic principle of economics is that increased use of productive resources will give rise to greater production. In the American context more land also contributed to rising levels of per capita output and to material welfare. This occurred for two reasons: First, the ratio of land per worker increased, promoting a rise in output per worker. Second, the western lands settled and brought into production before the Civil War were more productive than the lands east of the Appalachians which had been settled earlier. These two factors along with the growth of markets go a long way toward explaining the magnetic attractiveness of the West to nineteenth-century Americans.

Indeed, these economic arguments are sufficiently compelling to cause one to ask why the decision to have a liberal land disposal policy was adopted only gradually and not at the very beginning of the period. The underdeveloped state of early transportation no doubt mitigated the appeal of the economic argument, but it is also important to recognize that politico-economic factors of a sectional nature operated to protract the movement toward a more liberal land policy. Many advocates of manufacturing feared that the availability of cheap land in the West would raise the wages of industrial labor by drawing actual and potential workers into western agriculture. The advocates of manufacturing therefore favored a policy of high land prices. But they also favored protection to manufacturers through tariffs. Since customs duties and land sales were alternative sources of government revenue, policies calling for both high land prices and high tariffs might have furnished more revenue than the federal government required to carry out its functions. In the earlier decades reducing the national debt provided a convenient outlet for surplus revenues. As the debt shrank, the manufacturing interests found a way out of their dilemma by advocating that further surplus revenues be turned over to the states for financing internal improvements.

The farming interests of the South were very much opposed to high tariffs on manufactures because they were primarily consumers rather than producers of manufactured goods. Also, since they relied on export markets for selling their agricultural products they opposed restrictions on international trade. Relatively well-endowed with natural routes of water transportation, the southerners took a dim view of internal improvements financed by federal tariff revenues. The South's views on land policy were initially ambiguous. Cheap and more productive land in the Southwest would undercut land values in the older South Atlantic states, but opening up the southwestern lands to plantation agriculture might also serve to increase the value of slave labor. Because planters and their slaves were quite mobile and because the dominant slave-owning interests felt a political need to extend their slave system as it became subject of growing opposition both within and outside the South, southerners tended over time to favor cheap land policies. Their perceived interests were therefore diametrically opposed to those of the manufactures in the North, but not to many farmers or their sons in that region.

Westerners desired expansion of both their political and economic power through low land prices. Less wealthy than the South and not as well-endowed with natural navigable waterways, they were less opposed to tariffs which could provide federal revenues for internal improvements. As the West grew in population in both its northern and southern sections and developed economically, a shift in the sectional balance of power in the country operated to reinforce the economic argument for greater exploitation of the nation's land resources, and federal land policy became increasingly liberal. Tariffs on manufactures were not, however, eliminated.

The clashing and shifting of sectional interests over land policy undeniably contributed to the pattern of policy evolution in the antebellum years. But we should not conclude that sectional interests as perceived at the time were necessarily correct. Alexander Hamilton, architect of many of the new nation's economic policies and an ardent advocate of tariffs and subsidies to aid manufacturers, saw no opposition of manufacturing and agricultural development. Hamilton in fact recommended, in 1790, that federal lands be sold to the public at the low price of thirty cents per acre. He foresaw what was later to become fact, namely, that a prosperous and growing agriculture would be both a source of abundant food and raw materials for the manufacturing sector and a great market for manufactured products. For example, much of the benefit to the United States of increasing cotton production on new lands in the South was reaped by northeastern manufacturers in the form of lower raw cotton prices. And the farmers and their families engaged in the more specialized agriculture that was emerging in the South and the West soon furnished an important component of the demand for factory-produced cloth.

What is to be made of the fear of manufacturers that cheap land would harm manufacturing by raising wages? It was largely ungrounded for two reasons. In the first place, tariff protection was granted and remained in effect at varying levels from 1789 on. By allowing American manufacturers to charge higher prices, the tariff provided a cushion against wage pressures. Second, labor supplies available to manufacturers increased sufficiently to prevent wages from becoming high enough to be a drawback

to manufacturing growth. Indeed, agricultural expansion was partially responsible for the increased labor supply, for as the West developed on
better and more abundant land, farms in the Northeast were abandoned,
and many farm workers took jobs in manufacturing. Also, while the free
flow of manufactured goods to America from abroad was interfered with
by tariff policies, the flow of immigrant labor was encouraged by America's liberal immigration policies. Immigrant workers swelled the supply
of industrial labor. Thus, in conjunction with federal tariff and immigration policies, Hamilton's broad view of the national interest in cheap
land was vindicated in the notable antebellum progress made by both
agriculture and manufacturing.

Agricultural Development with Abundant Land
and Growing Markets

Although America's increasingly liberal land policies were controversial in many respects, there is little reason for doubting that these policies
favored the growth of agriculture. As with most of the world's people two
centuries ago, the experience and skills of Americans were overwhelmingly
those of the farmer. The availability of land on progressively easier terms
would have been expected to draw an ever-increasing number of Americans into agriculture as a traditional and appealing way of life. With the
coming of the industrial and transportation revolutions, however, agriculture began to become less a highly individualistic and independent
way of life and more an increasingly specialized and market-oriented
business.

Agriculture was far and away the dominant economic activity in the
United States before the Civil War, and in absolute terms the expansion of
agriculture was remarkable. The number of farms and total farm output
are estimated to have increased sixfold between 1800 and 1860. During
these same decades the agricultural labor force quadrupled. On the eve
of the Civil War agriculture accounted for about three-fifths of the nation's total production of commodities. In terms of value added (the
measure of a sector's contribution to the national product), the agricultural sector was nearly twice as large as the manufacturing sector in 1859.

Equally significant for our understanding of the nature of antebellum
economic development, however, is agriculture's relative decline. At the
beginning of the nineteenth century approximately five out of every six
American workers labored in agriculture. By 1860 this proportion had
fallen to just over one out of two. And while the value added by

agricultural commodity production in 1859 was still nearly twice that of manufacturing, just two decades earlier it had been about three times larger.

Operating within these two trends of absolute expansion and relative decline, American farmers made a great contribution to the nation's early economic development. They provided increasing supplies of food and raw material to themselves and, more important, to the nation's growing nonagricultural sectors and its foreign customers. Agricultural expansion also provided a major source of demand for the products of other sectors, notably transportation services and manufactured goods. Last, but by no means least, increases in the productivity of agriculture meant that an expanding proportion of the nation's labor force could be released from agricultural pursuits to find employment in nonagricultural activities. The antebellum release of labor from agriculture (in relative terms) was particularly pronounced during the three decades from 1820 to 1850, when agriculture's share of the nation's labor force declined from 79 to 55 percent. This momentous shift toward economic diversification reflects the youthful vigor of an economy entering upon modernization.

AGRICULTURE IN THE 1790S

In the last decade of the eighteenth century American agriculture was similar to what it had been in colonial times. In the South tobacco continued as the major cash crop, while in the Middle Atlantic states and New England general grain and livestock farming predominated. As noted earlier, most Americans were farmers, and to a great extent agricultural production was destined for on-farm consumption or for sale in local markets. Production for larger markets was confined to areas in the vicinity of coastal port cities and to the export-oriented, staple-producing areas of the South. The latter included the Chesapeake Bay area which produced exportable surpluses of tobacco and grain, and the Atlantic coastal area from southern North Carolina to the Sea Islands of Georgia, where rice and long-staple cotton were the important cash crops.

Already in the 1790s, however, two forces were at work which would soon alter the pattern of American agriculture. One was Eli Whitney's invention of the cotton gin in 1793; it overcame a technical barrier to extensive and specialized production of short-staple upland cotton. Whitney's invention laid the foundation for the cotton kingdom of the antebellum South. The other impetus for agricultural change in the 1790s involved the New England and Middle Atlantic regions where large numbers of people began to move out to the settlements on the western and northern frontiers of the original states and to the territories beyond. A combination of factors contributed to this movement: population growth in the settled eastern areas, the availability of cheap and fertile land on the frontier, and a striving for the cherished independence of family farming.

These factors along with the cotton gin and improved transportation were the proximate causes of the great northern and southern migrations to the West which shaped the development of American agriculture in the next decades.

THE COTTON ECONOMY OF THE SOUTH, 1793–1860

When Eli Whitney solved the problem of removing the seeds from short-staple cotton bolls, virtually all the conditions were present in the American South for one of the great expansions of specialized agriculture in recorded history. In the three decades from 1763 to 1793 a series of remarkable English inventions for the spinning of cotton yarn by means of power-driven machinery in centralized factories created the first great industry of the Industrial Revolution. At that time much of the world's production and consumption of cotton took place in Asia, particularly in India. The expansion of English cotton mills created a new demand for raw cotton and resulted in sharply rising cotton prices. Until Whitney's invention American participation in the growing international cotton market was limited to production of the high-quality, long-staple cotton that could be grown along the coasts of Georgia and South Carolina. It was not difficult to remove the smooth seeds from this variety of cotton, but the area in which it could be produced was small. Short-staple cotton, however, could be grown in a much larger area extending from southern Virginia through the Carolinas, Georgia, Tennessee, Alabama, Mississippi, and into the later acquisitions, Louisiana, Arkansas and Texas, as well.

In addition to an expanding market for cotton, the South was favored with numerous navigable rivers which, although not ideal avenues of transportation, were more than adequate for moving cotton, a crop that had a relatively high value in relation to its bulk. The situation with regard to the traditional economic factors of production—land, labor, and capital —was equally propitious. Cotton could be grown over an extensive area— land that was still largely unsettled at the end of the eighteenth century. A slave labor force easily adaptable to cotton culture was already present in the South, and the declining attractiveness of tobacco, rice, and indigo culture made the use of the slaves in cotton cultivation both feasible and profitable. Finally, the fact that cotton was a major cash crop meant that its growers would be able to accumulate the capital and to have access to the credit that they would need to carry on an expanding agricultural operation.

The cotton kingdom of the South expanded by leaps and bounds. In 1793, the year Whitney unveiled his gin, American cotton production was about five million pounds, mostly of the long-staple or Sea Island variety, and amounted to less than one percent of the world's production. By the first years of the nineteenth century, it had increased to over forty million pounds, about half of which was exported, mainly to Great Britain. Thereafter, production approximately doubled each decade up to 1860, reaching some two billion pounds by the close of the antebellum era. By 1830 the southern United States produced about one-half of the world's supply of cotton; by the 1850s this fraction had risen to two-thirds. After the War of 1812 exports typically absorbed at least 75 percent of the crop, and cotton became the dominant export of the nation. Often it accounted for over half the value of all American exports.

The growing world-wide demand for cotton along with the seemingly limitless supply of land on which it could be grown contributed to a pattern of intensive land use by continuous cropping and, as soil fertility declined in the older states, to a westward shift of production. Antebellum writers as well as latter-day historians often comment unfavorably on this pattern of land use, but given the abundance of land and the mobility of the southern population, it very likely was a wise decision at the time. Thomas Jefferson, a paragon of rational thinking, remarked that it was usually cheaper and more efficient to buy new land than to restore depleted soils with fertilizer.* His fellow southerners generally followed his advice, as can be seen in the westward movement of the cotton kingdom. South Carolina was the leading producer into the 1820s; then Georgia assumed the mantle. By the 1830s, Alabama and Mississippi were the leading producers, a position they kept until the Civil War. Tennessee had been one of the four leading producers in the 1820s, but it gave way to Louisiana in subsequent decades. Although the center of production gradually moved west, the antebellum cotton kingdom essentially consisted of the five states of South Carolina, Georgia, Alabama, Mississippi, and Louisiana. Throughout the period these five states accounted for over three-fourths of total American cotton production.

THE DIVERSITY OF SOUTHERN AGRICULTURE

Although cotton was the leading cash crop of the lower South and at times an important source of income in some areas of the upper South, the southern agricultural economy was far larger, more complex, and more diversified than is implied by the phrase, "cotton economy." There were two broad aspects of the South's agricultural diversity. First, a number of cash crops besides cotton were produced in sufficient quantity to make foreign markets and domestic markets outside of the South important to southern farmers. Second, the South produced large quantities of products such as corn, wheat, livestock, vegetables, and fruits for home consumption on the farm or for sale at local markets within the South. In recent years, accumulating evidence and research findings have tended to demon-

---

* Paul W. Gates, *The Farmer's Age: 1815–1860* (New York: Holt, 1960), p. 101.

strate that, contrary to earlier assumptions, the antebellum South was largely self-sufficient in food production despite its emphasis on producing cash crops for sale in distant markets.

Southern cash crops, in addition to cotton, included tobacco, rice, sugar, hemp, flax, and even wheat until the 1840s and 1850s when the center of wheat production shifted to the states of the old northwest. Unlike cotton, which could be grown over a large area of the South and which was planted in millions of acres, the other cash crops were grown in limited areas, in the places where climate and soil made their culture feasible. Tobacco, along with rice a major market crop of the colonial era, originally had been cultivated intensively in the tidewater area of the Chesapeake Bay in Virginia and Maryland. However, it had taken a heavy toll from the soil, and this led to a shift of tobacco production into the Piedmont region of Virginia and North Carolina. The development of a mild, bright leaf variety of tobacco and of the process of flue curing in the late antebellum years helped to revive a tobacco culture that had been stagnating since the American Revolution. Across the Appalachians, Kentucky and Tennessee also became leading tobacco producers before the Civil War.

From colonial times through the antebellum period, rice production was concentrated in a small area within a few miles of the Atlantic coast in South Carolina and Georgia. It was grown on large plantations that made intensive use of slave labor. Much of the American rice crop was exported to West Indian and European markets.

After the American Revolution, French settlers in Louisiana developed economical processes for making sugar from the sugar cane plant which grew well along the Mississippi River near New Orleans. The Louisiana Purchase in 1803 created a favored American market. There ensued a rapid growth of sugar production in southern Louisiana. Because expensive equipment was required for refining sugar, large plantations using slave labor tended to dominate the business, but many smaller planters also participated. Most of the sugar produced found its way into the domestic American market. This domestic-market orientation, along with the large capital investment needed to produce sugar, perhaps explains why sugar was one of the few agricultural products favored with tariff protection. (Wool, produced chiefly in the North for domestic consumption, was another.)

Wheat, not usually thought of as a southern cash crop, was actually important to the states of the upper South right up to the Civil War. Virginia, for example, was the nation's fourth largest producer in 1839, following Ohio, Pennsylvania, and New York. By 1859, Virginia had even passed New York and Pennsylvania in wheat output, although in that year the western states of Illinois, Indiana, and Wisconsin had assumed leadership. The emergence of wheat as a major crop in Virginia, Maryland, and, to some extent, in North Carolina, was in part a response to problems with tobacco: soil exhaustion and stagnant demand. Wheat represented a move toward diversification and mixed farming. Major markets for southern wheat were in the northeast. Small amounts were sent to the lower South, although it appears that these areas, so clearly identified with cotton specialization, were able to meet a large part of their own needs for wheat and flour. Kentucky and Tennessee also produced wheat surpluses, and it is likely that this wheat, rather than wheat from the northwest, satisfied the remaining needs of the cotton and sugar areas of the lower Southwest.

Even more important to the diversified nature of antebellum southern agriculture was corn production. Corn was grown nearly everywhere —North and South—and in 1849, for example, a southern corn planting of some eighteen million acres was far in excess of the five million acres planted to cotton. In some antebellum years, moreover, the value of the southern corn crop exceeded the combined values of the South's cotton, tobacco, sugar, and rice crops! Unlike these crops, corn was not often sold for cash or shipped in large quantities to distant markets. Rather, it was a principal food for slaves and livestock and was largely consumed where it was produced.

Until recent years economic historians had often argued that specialization on staple crops for export led to the South becoming a food deficit area, and that the newer states of the northwest developed agriculturally and commercially in order to supply the South's food requirements. This view no longer is tenable. The South's plantations and farms largely met their own needs and supplied food to the southern non-agricultural population as well.

Do these recent findings imply that the South's degree of agricultural specialization was not as complete or efficient as it might have been? Probably not. The nature of agricultural production in the South made food self-sufficiency a rational choice. The South's cash crops required relatively great amounts of labor at concentrated times in the production cycle, usually at the harvest. During other times of the year labor, whether that of free farmers or slaves, would have been underemployed if it had not been engaged in growing corn and other foods or in tending livestock. It would have been wasteful for the South not to have grown its own food supplies.

SLAVERY

No single aspect of American economic history has given rise to more controversy, often and understandably quite emotional, than the antebellum South's "peculiar institution" of black slavery. And none has been more altered in its interpretation by recent scholarship. Older interpretations of the southern slave economy often emphasized its inefficiency and economic irrationality. Planters' investments in slaves were thought to be unprofitable or, if profitable, only within the context of a stagnant southern economy which could barely overcome the poor work incentives of slaves by treating them in a harsh and degrading manner. However, accumulating evidence gathered and analyzed by many scholars now makes it appear that these past contentions are subject to reasonable doubt. The southern economy was far from stagnant in the antebellum years, and its slave labor system, however deplorable on other grounds, apparently contributed to the South's economic prosperity.

In thinking about southern slavery it is important to recognize that until about two centuries ago slavery was not much thought of as an abnormal or illegitimate institution. Its roots were ancient and it had existed over wide areas of the world. Europeans introduced African slaves into the new world at the beginning of the sixteenth century, primarily to work on sugar plantations. The relative insignificance of sugar production in the North American colonies and in the United States in its early years explains why this area received only a small fraction, about one in sixteen, of the millions of Africans brought to the New World in the three and one-half centuries after 1500. Before the 1790s most of the slaves in North America were concentrated near the tidewater from Maryland to Georgia and worked on plantations where tobacco, rice, and indigo were the major cash crops. In the first years of the United States markets for these crops were not expanding, and southern planters on the whole showed no great and irrevocable attachment to the institution of slavery. At the Constitutional Convention of 1787, slavery was an issue open to compromise.

Then came the cotton gin. The rapidly expanding market for American cotton which it helped to create injected new vigor into the institution of slavery. Thus, in the same era that ideas of political liberty and individual freedom were translated into action through great revolutions and the beginnings of the slave emancipation movement, slavery was becoming more entrenched in the American South. Through the constitutional compromise of 1787, the import of slaves into the United States could be—and was by later legislation—made illegal after 1807. Nonetheless, the American slave population grew and grew, mostly through natural increase, from about a million in 1800, to two million by 1830, and to nearly four million in 1860. Planters and their slaves moved west in these years in response to the expanding demand for cotton and the availability of cotton land.

The nearly four million slaves of 1860 were owned by fewer than four hundred thousand persons. Less than one-third of southern families, in fact, held slaves. The slaveholders were greatly outnumbered by small, nonslaveholding planters and yeoman farmers, but slaveholders nevertheless played a dominant role in the economic, political, and social life of the South and, to a lesser extent, in that of the whole country. In part this resulted from their inherited wealth and social position, but recent findings suggest that it may also have been due to the differential efficiency of slave agriculture over free agriculture in both the South and the North.

Slave agriculture appears to have been more efficient than free agriculture in the sense that slave farms on the average produced more output (in value terms) with given inputs of land, labor, and capital than did free farms. What was the secret of this efficiency? A clue is provided in the finding that the most efficient of all American farms were the larger plantations utilizing great numbers of slaves. In short, there were significant economies of large-scale production in southern agriculture; they resulted from the high degree of specialization that large-scale production facilitated, and from the superior management practices that coordinated it. In the economy of the plantations, slaves specialized in a great variety of agricultural tasks (for example, plowing, hoeing, seeding, ginning) and nonagricultural jobs (for example, carpentry, blacksmithing, cooking, child care). Field labor was performed by groups of specialized gangs, particularly in planting and cultivating operations, which worked with a rhythm and intensity that made them highly interdependent. This specialization and intensity of work, along with its careful coordination, apparently accounts for the efficiency of slave agriculture.

The efficiency of large-scale slave agriculture raises the important question of why free farmers did not strive for similar efficiency by organizing their production in the same way. The answer appears to be that the gain in efficiency was not sufficient to compensate free men for the drudgery and intensity of effort required to achieve it. Slaves, in contrast, had no real choice but to do what their owners required of them. This does not necessarily mean that the material conditions of life for slaves were exceptionally harsh or cruel. Indeed, some scholars contend that the food, clothing, and shelter accorded slaves, while lacking the variety free people chose, did not much differ in terms of basic necessities, for example, nutrition, from that of free workers of the same era. These findings do not seem especially surprising. Slaveowners had a substantial portion of their capital invested in slaves, and it was very much to their economic advantage to see that this capital was well maintained. Exceptions to such rational behavior can, of course, be documented. But the weight of recently analyzed evidence is that they were just that—exceptions. Such findings, however, remain controversial.

Who benefited from the efficiency gains created by the denial of freedom to the black population of the South? The planter slaveowners reaped some of the gains but apparently not the major part of them. Agricultural production was a highly competitive business, and competition in both slave and product markets appears to have led to competitive returns of about 10 percent throughout the South on slave investments. Those who owned slaves in the period before the slaves increased greatly in value due to restricted supplies and a growing cotton demand did better since they reaped additional capital gains on their slave assets. The

major beneficiaries of slave exploitation were American and foreign consumers of the products produced by slave labor. The greater efficiency and
larger output of slave plantations increased supplies and reduced prices
for products such as cotton to less than what they would have been without slavery. However, as indicated by our discussion of why free farmers
did not organize themselves as on large-scale plantations, what the slaveowners and consumers of slave-produced products gained was more than
offset by what the slaves lost in not having freedom to choose their own
working conditions.

While slavery was therefore efficient in a narrow, economic productivity sense, it was far less than optimal from the point of view of overall
economic welfare. Free men could always produce more material goods
by working under unpleasant conditions, but they chose not to. Slaves
did not have that choice. In this sense slavery represented a violation of
the nation's professed ideals of individual liberty and equality of opportunity and was, therefore, fundamentally immoral. Thus, both economic
and moral arguments provided a rationale for the ending of slavery. Unfortunately for the United States, the valid economic arguments against
slavery were not well understood in 1860, and in any case would not
have appealed to those who deemed slavery to be a legitimate institution.
Consequently, the issue of slavery was resolved in civil warfare which
set back for two decades the prosperous agrarian economy of the South
while ending its immoral labor system.

NORTHERN AGRICULTURAL DEVELOPMENT TO 1860

In the early decades of the American nation agricultural progress in
the northern states was more gradual and less dramatic than in the southern cotton economy. The reasons for the contrast follow from our earlier
discussion of the South's extremely fortunate situation following the invention of the cotton gin in 1793. No invention of similar economic
impact was brought forward to release the latent productivity of northern
soils. Also, northern inland transportation facilities, particularly for bulky,
low-value agricultural commodities, were slow to develop in the early
years of the republic. Largely as a result of inadequate transportation,
markets for northern farm products were rather limited in comparison
with the international markets enjoyed by southern staples. Indeed, a high
degree of self-sufficiency and lack of specialization rather than an orientation to market production characterized northern farming.

The contrast with the South should not, however, be overdone. As
in the South, abundant virgin land lay both within the borders of the
original states and just beyond them. The North, even more than the
South, possessed a population of energetic and individualistic agricultural-
ists who were willing to undertake the arduous task of pioneering settlement on this western land. And, perhaps because of necessity in the face

of greater natural and economic obstacles, the North developed a greater sense of community will in tackling, for example, its problems of transportation.

The earliest pioneering in the northern area of the new nation occurred in northern New England and in western Pennsylvania and New York. After 1800 the turnpike movement encouraged this process of settlement by providing improved facilities for moving settlers west and their surplus commodities east. A more significant impact of turnpikes, however, was in encouraging greater agricultural specialization and production for market in the settled eastern areas.

The overriding importance of transportation facilities in stimulating western agricultural development is clearly evident in the early settlement of the Ohio River Valley, which occurred while substantial acreages of unsettled land still remained in northwestern Pennsylvania and western New York. The reason lies in the advantage of water over land transportation. Even with primitive flatboat and keelboat technologies, the advantage of water was so great that it was more efficient to move most western agricultural products to eastern markets over several thousand miles of water than over a few hundred miles of land. The relative efficiency of waterway transport was very much on the minds of proponents of steamboating and canal building.

The gradual development of transportation and markets for northern farmers led to an equally gradual movement toward greater specialization. For much of the antebellum period agricultural production on many northern farms in both the east and the west was nonspecialized. Individual farmers grew several different crops and raised a number of varieties of animals. While this diversification perhaps reduced risks and was attuned to the farm family's manifold needs, it did not promote productivity by economizing on the range of knowledge needed to farm efficiently. The process of becoming a farmer was in many ways more complicated in the North than in the South. A young man would often work for a time as a farm laborer, perhaps on his parents' farm, and accumulate as best he could the range of knowledge and the funds required to obtain his own farm. Then he would face the choice of buying a developed farm in the East, a partially developed farm near the frontier, or virgin land on the frontier. Growing numbers of farmers chose one of the latter alternatives; among the reasons: the soil improved and the land costs fell as one moved west.

After 1820 eighty acres of land in the West could be purchased for as little as one hundred dollars from the federal government. The estimated total cost of establishing a farm was from five to ten times the cost of acquiring the land. A good part of this cost, especially in the forested areas east of the Illinois prairie, represented the value of a settler's own labor employed in clearing and fencing the land and erecting buildings on it. This direct labor investment economized on cash outlays in an era when credit facilities were underdeveloped, but it also meant that several years passed before as much land was cleared as could profitably be tilled. Prairie farming required more cash for breaking the tougher soils and purchasing fencing materials; developed at a later time, it gained feasibility from the establishment of better-organized product and credit markets. The railroad, which penetrated the prairies in the 1850s, played a large role in this development.

The influence of transportation improvements on northern agriculture between 1790 and 1860 is evident in the changing location of production centers and in greater specialization. Wheat, the leading breadstuff and chief cash crop of the northern states, was produced nearly everywhere in the earliest decades, mostly for farm consumption and local marketing. Improved roads and, especially, the completion of the Erie Canal, caused wheat production to become concentrated in the western sections of New York and Pennsylvania and in Ohio during the 1820s and 1830s. In 1839 these three states produced about one-half of the nation's wheat crop of eighty-five million bushels. Two decades later the extension of railroads into the West led to a second major shift. In 1859 the wheat crop was over twice as large as in 1839. Illinois, Indiana, and Wisconsin were the leading producers, accounting together for a third of the total national production. The combined share of Ohio, Pennsylvania, and New York fell to 22 percent. This decline was not merely relative; each of these three states produced fewer bushels in 1859 than it had in 1839.

While wheat in the North and cotton in the South were the nation's leading market crops, corn was actually the nation's greatest crop and was raised practically everywhere. In 1859 the corn crop in bushels was nearly five times that of wheat. Used mostly as animal feed, corn was also an important part of the diet of farmers, both slave and free. The pattern of shifting corn production was somewhat different from that of wheat, but the direction was the same. The first reliable data, for 1839, reveal that the leading corn-producing states were not in the North but rather in the upper tier of the South—Tennessee, Kentucky, and Virginia. Ten years later Ohio assumed leadership, and by 1860 the center of production had shifted to Illinois.

The ubiquity of corn production as well as the production of grasses and other forage materials meant that livestock raising was feasible in nearly all agricultural areas. Nonetheless, specialized producing areas developed quite early. Cattle and hogs raised in the Ohio Valley were driven overland to eastern seaboard cities well before the canal era. In this period Cincinnati emerged as a leading center of pork packing, with the meat products moving to market down the Ohio and Mississippi rivers. Under the pervading influence of transportation improvements, a gradual westward shift of livestock production followed. Chicago, on the basis of its growing rail connections, developed into a leading shipping point for livestock and meat products in the 1850s. The greatest gains in western livestock production and meat packing, however, occurred after the Civil War under the influence of further railroad extensions and the invention of the refrigerated freight car. In the antebellum years most of the meat consumed in a given region was also produced in that region.

Recognition that livestock and meat production did not shift westward as rapidly as grain production, or with quite the force, provides insight into how the older farming areas in the northeast responded to western agricultural growth. Their loss of comparative advantage in grain did not entail a corresponding loss in the raising of cattle and hogs for consumers of fresh meat. As the grain belt moved farther west, sheep raising, mainly for wool but also for meat, provided another outlet for the farmers left behind, particularly in the hilly areas of New England and New York but also in Ohio. Eastern dairy farming also expanded in response to lost grain markets. Initially butter and cheese were the main marketable products, with fresh milk and the by-products of butter and cheese making consumed by the farm family and its hogs. The spreading network of eastern railroads in the 1830s and 1840s, however, created the possibility of shipping fresh milk from farms to cities located some distance away and resulted in a substantial boost to dairy farming. Growing fresh fruits and vegetables for urban markets was also stimulated by rail transportation. A diversified and market-oriented agriculture thus developed in the older states to help solve the problems created by the agricultural progress of the West. This mixed farming was a creative response to changing market conditions.

AGRICULTURAL TECHNOLOGY AND PRODUCTIVITY

Between 1790 and 1860 improvements in transportation and the consequent growth of markets wrought a revolution in American agriculture. Farming changed from a way of life for most of the American people to an increasingly specialized business for about half of them. The sheer magnitude and diversity of the nation's agricultural enterprise along with its highly decentralized organizational structure make the task of generalizing about technological progress and agricultural productivity both difficult and important. The overall impression one gains is that of substantial progress in output, techniques, and productivity as markets grew. Because of the highly competitive nature and rapid expansion of agricultural production in these decades, the major beneficiaries of agricultural progress may very well have been not the farmers but rather the growing numbers of nonfarm people who obtained cheap food and raw materials from the farms and sold back to them much of their output of nonagricultural goods and services.

The antebellum era is often viewed by agricultural historians as one that set the stage for an agricultural revolution marked by the widespread application of horse-powered machinery in the two or three decades after 1850. There is validity in this view, but it has had the unfortunate effect of leading many to disregard or play down the significant technological progress made in earlier decades. In a few cases this progress was dramatic. The cotton gin revolutionized southern agriculture as early as the 1790s. Steam power was introduced on the plantation sugar mills of Louisiana in the 1820s, and in short order most of the cane crop was processed with the aid of steam engines. The horse-drawn reaper for harvesting wheat and small grain crops was applied on a large scale during the 1850s. In each of these cases an existing or rapidly emerging market played a crucial role in the widespread adoption of an impressive new technique.

The more gradual widening of markets for other agricultural products was marked by less dramatic but nonetheless effective technical advances. For much of the antebellum period hand tools—hoes, forks, rakes, scythes, and axes are examples—were major implements, and they were continually improved through better design and the use of new materials. The nation's abundance of land, however, exerted a powerful influence on the development of animal-powered implements and machines which would allow relatively less abundant labor to till more acres per person. In preharvest operations—soil preparation, seeding, and cultivating—significant inventive and innovative progress was made. Plows were transformed from crude, multipurpose tools to specialized implements for different types of plowing and varied soil conditions. Wooden plows with a few iron parts gave way to cast-iron plows and then to steel plows by the late 1830s; they allowed more land to be plowed with less effort. Horse-drawn cultivators and seeding machines were developed, although not widely applied, before 1840.

In harvesting operations similar sequences emerged. Grain cradles supplanted sickles and scythes, and in turn gave way to the horse-powered rakes in hay making. In the earlier decades, limited markets and the availability to farmers of free time during the winter months made threshing with simple flails and corn shelling by hand feasible postharvest activities, but from the 1830s onward machines of varying complexity began to take over these tasks.

While the greatest development of organized science and education in the service of agriculture came later, the antebellum years witnessed a growth of technical and economic informational channels commensurate with the importance of agriculture in the economy. The ubiquitous general newspaper often devoted space to agricultural topics and market conditions. From the 1820s on this role was more and more fulfilled by specialized agricultural periodicals. Their combined circulation is estimated to have reached three hundred fifty thousand by 1860. Agricultural societies and fairs also spread information and encouraged improved farming practices. Starting in the 1830s, the federal Patent Office began to collect and distribute both seeds and general agricultural information. By the 1850s its annual reports on agriculture received wide distribution.

Improved transportation and wider markets encouraged westward movement onto more fertile lands; this along with better techniques and information flows led to increased agricultural specialization and to growth in productivity. Significant progress was made before 1840, even though mechanization and the widespread use of animal power were still in their infancy. A study of labor productivity in the major crops—wheat, corn, and cotton—indicates steady gains between 1800 and 1840, even under the assumption that crop yields per acre did not improve during these four decades. In wheat production, man-hours of labor per 100 bushels are estimated to have fallen from 373 in 1800 to 233 in 1840, an improvement of 38 percent. Much of the gain was due to improvement in harvesting, where man-hours per acre fell from 40 to 23. Over the same four decades man-hours per 100 bushels of corn declined from 344 to 276, a 20 percent gain in labor productivity. Man-hours per bale of cotton declined from 601 to 439; most of this 27 percent productivity gain was the result of a drop from 135 to 90 man-hours per acre in preharvest labor, that is, plowing, planting, and cultivating.

With land and capital inputs expanding faster than the farm labor force, one would normally expect such increases in agricultural labor productivity. However, a recent study of *total* factor productivity, a measure of output per weighted unit of all three inputs, also demonstrates notable efficiency gains before 1840.* The average rates of total productivity growth for the 1820s and 1830s were estimated at over one percent per year. These rates are at best only suggestive because of measurement problems and the lack of adjustment for relatively good or poor crops in the decade years surveyed, but they do indicate that improvements in agricultural efficiency between 1820 and 1840 compare favorably with those for other decades of the century. Coming largely before the advent of widespread mechanization, these gains are testimony to the substantial effects of transport improvements and market growth in bringing about a more intensive application and efficient allocation of resources in agriculture.

Early gains in agricultural efficiency were instrumental in promoting the increasingly diversified nature of economic activity in antebellum America, and in bringing about sustained increases in incomes and material welfare. In these years agriculture was the nation's biggest business, its major supplier of food and raw materials, and the chief market for a wide range of nonagricultural goods and services. Agriculture's absolute expansion increased greatly these sources of both supply and demand. If agriculture had merely expanded without becoming more efficient, how-

* Robert E. Gallman, "Changes in Total U.S. Agricultural Factor Productivity in the Nineteenth Century," *Agricultural History*, vol. 46 (January 1972), Table 8, p. 208.

ever, it seems clear that economic development would have proceeded much more slowly than it actually did. Gains in agricultural efficiency were among the major forces allowing forty-five out of one hundred American workers to labor outside of agriculture in 1850, whereas just three decades earlier, in 1820, only twenty-one out of one hundred workers were in nonagricultural employments.

Conclusion

In the land policies and agricultural development of the young United States, different levels of decision making neatly complemented one another. Decisions to acquire a public domain and to set the terms for disposing of it in order to encourage its use as an economic resource were centralized at the national governmental level. One sees in these fundamental decisions a preference for uniform national policies in regard to the nation's most abundant resource. After these basic decisions were made at the center, however, decisions on who was to own land and how it was to be used were left to competitive markets and the decentralized decisions of individuals. Because of the centralized decisions, Americans were not plagued by such problems as differing concepts of ownership and land tenure, nor by uncertainties about the terms under which land might be acquired and used. And because of the scope of decentralized decision making, the specialized knowledge of time and place possessed by individuals generally guided the nation's land resources into economically efficient uses. With these decision-making approaches, the United States avoided many of the disincentives that hindered agricultural development in much of the rest of the world.

SUGGESTED READINGS

On land policy, two general works are Benjamin H. Hibbard, A History of the Public Land Policies (New York: Macmillan, 1924) and Roy M. Robbins, Our Landed Heritage: The Public Domain, 1776–1936 (Princeton, N.J.: Princeton University Press, 1942). An incisive shorter treatment of the major issues may be found in Lance Davis et al., "The Land, Minerals, Water and Forests," in American Economic Growth: An Economist's History of the United States (New York: Harper & Row, 1972), chap. 4; chapter 11 of this work, "Agriculture," is also useful for amplification of some themes of our chapter. More specialized studies on land include Vernon Carstensen, ed., The

Public Lands: Studies in the History of the Public Domain (Madison: University of Wisconsin Press, 1963) and Malcolm J. Rohrbough, *The Land Office Business: The Settlement and Administration of American Public Lands, 1789–1837* (New York: Oxford University Press, 1968). For formal economic analyses of the impacts of abundant land on the antebellum economy, see the articles by Peter Passell, "The Impact of Cotton Land Distribution on the Antebellum Economy," *Journal of Economic History*, 21 (December 1971), 917–937, by Passell and Maria Schmundt, "Pre-Civil War Land Policy and the Growth of Manufacturing," *Explorations in Economic History*, 9 (Fall 1971), 35–48, and by Passell and Gavin Wright, "The Effects of Pre-Civil War Territorial Expansion on the Price of Slaves," *Journal of Political Economy*, 80 (November/December 1972), 1188–1202.

A valuable survey of antebellum agricultural developments is Paul W. Gates, *The Farmer's Age: Agriculture, 1815–1860* (New York: Holt, Rinehart, & Winston, 1960). See also Darwin P. Kelsey, ed., *Farming in the New Nation: Interpreting American Agriculture* (Washington, D.C.: Agricultural History Society, 1972). On northern agriculture in these decades see Clarence H. Danhof, *Change in Agriculture: The Northern United States, 1820–1870* (Cambridge: Harvard University Press, 1969) and James W. Whitaker, ed., *Farming in the Midwest, 1840–1900* (Washington, D.C.: Agricultural History Society, 1974).

Antebellum southern agriculture and slavery have exercised a powerful attraction for generations of economic historians. A comprehensive classic is Lewis C. Gray, *History of Agriculture in the Southern United States to 1860*, 2 vols. (Washington, D.C.: Carnegie Institution, 1933). More recent works include Stuart Bruchey, *Cotton and the Growth of the American Economy* (New York: Harcourt, Brace & World, 1967) and William N. Parker, ed., *The Structure of the Cotton Economy of the Antebellum South* (Washington, D.C.: Agricultural History Society, 1970). An important and still controversial work on slavery is Robert W. Fogel and Stanley L. Engerman, *Time on the Cross: The Economics of American Negro Slavery* (Boston: Little, Brown, 1974); to see why it is controversial, see Paul A. David et al., *Reckoning with Slavery* (New York: Oxford University Press, 1976). Still another thoughtful and provocative analysis is Gavin Wright, *The Political Economy of the Cotton South* (New York: W. W. Norton, 1978).

On agricultural technology and productivity, in addition to a number of the above-cited works, one may consult with profit Paul A. David, "The Mechanization of Reaping in the Ante-Bellum Midwest," in Henry Rosovsky, ed., *Industrialization in Two Systems: Essays in Honor of Alexander Gerschenkron* (New York: John Wiley, 1966), pp. 3–39; Robert E. Gallman, "Changes in Total U.S. Agricultural Factor Productivity in the Nineteenth Century," *Agricultural History*, 46 (January 1972), 191–210; and U.S. Department of Agriculture, *Progress of Farm Mechanization*, Miscellaneous Publication No. 630 (October 1947).

CHAPTER 7

——

Critical Changes in

the Financial System

Of all the politico-economic decisions that had to be taken in order to create a truly independent United States, none were more crucial than those regarding the nation's public finances and debts, its monetary system, and the role of government in the new and controversial activity of banking. Few areas of modern economic organization are more closely interrelated than these, and in no other ones are the effects of governmental decisions on private economic activities more apparent and critical. Early American leaders, most notably Alexander Hamilton, understood these points; they proceeded to build a remarkably solid, though far from perfect, financial underpinning for the new nation. As problems arose in subsequent years, the interdependencies were less appreciated, and the United States proceeded in money, banking, and finance more by trial and error than by comprehensive reasoning and action. Fortunately for the nation, later experiments were predicated upon the firm financial foundation laid during the first federal administration of 1789–93. The debates and decisions of this creative period set the tone of American political economy for decades to come, till the Civil War and beyond.

Federalist and Republican Financial Policies to 1816

The initial business of the First Congress which met in the spring of 1789 was to implement its constitutional power "to lay and collect taxes, duties, imports, and excises to pay the debts and provide for the common defense and general welfare of the United States." After three months of deliberation the Tariff Act of 1789 was passed and signed into law by President Washington on July 4th. Significantly, its stated objectives were not only to support the government and help pay its debts, but also to encourage and protect manufactures. The Tariff Act also favored American shipping interests with a reduction of duties on goods imported on American vessels. The Tonnage Act, passed in the same month, extended this concept by calling for differentially high fees on foreign ships entering American ports. In effect, this act reserved the fishing business and coastal trade of the United States to American seamen.

The decision to make import duties the primary source of federal revenue initiated a policy that remained in effect for well over a century. Running counter to the powerful argument advanced by Adam Smith in 1776 that tariffs interfere with specialization and the division of labor, the tariff of 1789, even though its protectionist features were modest, opened up a veritable Pandora's box of politico-economic problems; they preoccupied Americans for decades. Nonetheless, at the time the choice made sense. Internal taxes were politically unpopular and would in any case have been difficult to collect because the country was so large and thinly populated, and because a market economy with widespread money transactions had not yet developed in most places within it. Tariffs, in contrast, were directed toward market transactions and could be collected at a relatively small number of seaports. And they had the advantage of appearing to be taxes on foreign producers, although in reality they also were taxes on Americans consumers.

With a revenue provided for, the First Congress turned next to establishing a treasury department. A bill was drafted by Alexander Hamilton who then became the first and most dynamic secretary of the treasury. Hamilton's first act as secretary was to report on and see through to enactment provisions for the support of the public credit of the United States. His celebrated *Report on the Public Credit* of January 1790, estimated the nominal value of the national debt, including arrears of interest, at $54.1 million, and of state debts at $25 million. Hamilton proposed that all of these obligations, incurred largely to finance the Revolution, be funded into long-term federal bonds with principal and interest guaranteed in specie—that is, metallic money. To do this, Hamilton argued, would make the federal government's credit so secure that money could easily be raised in case of future national emergencies. And it would have the immediate effect of augmenting the nation's purchasing power with debt instruments that would be close substitutes for money.

After much debate, Hamilton's proposals were adopted in the Funding Act of August 1790. The federal government's proposed assumption of state debts was a particularly knotty issue in the debate. Some states had already discharged large portions of their Revolutionary War obligations and felt it unfair to be asked to pay, indirectly through federal revenues, the debts of others. To gain their assent, Hamilton struck a famous bargain with Thomas Jefferson and other southern leaders who, in return for delivering votes needed to enact the funding proposals, gained the concession that the nation's permanent capital would be located in the South, on the banks of the Potomac River. More important in the short run, assumption relieved the states of heavy financial burdens and led to a wide diffusion of federal bonds, thereby strengthening the union. However, it also required more revenue to pay interest than had been provided for in the Tariff Act. Hamilton's persuasiveness again prevailed. In his *Report on the Public Credit* he recommended that additional revenue be raised by excise taxes on distilled spirits. His proposals were embodied in the Excise Act of March 1791, the first internal tax of the new government.

Hamilton's first *Report on the Public Credit* hinted he would soon recommend that Congress establish a national bank. His report on that subject came in December 1790. At the time there were only four state-chartered commercial banks in the United States. The bank proposed by Hamilton would be empowered to engage in the same lines of business as the other banks—discounting the bills of exchange and promissory notes of merchants, accepting deposits, and issuing bank notes that would serve as paper currency. But it was to be much larger than other banks and obligated to serve the federal government, which would own part of its capital stock. Hamilton stressed the bank's public functions: it would augment the nation's money supply by issuing several dollars of bank notes for each dollar of specie it held; it would be a source of short-term loans to the government; it would receive deposits of government funds and transfer them to places where they were to be expended; and it would support the public credit by increasing the value of the government's newly funded debt since in Hamilton's comprehensive plan, these securities could be used by private investors to subscribe for a large part of the bank's stock.

A bill embodying Hamilton's proposals was passed by Congress in February 1791. The Bank of the United States was to be chartered for twenty years with a capital of ten million dollars, more than twice the combined capital of the several existing banks. The federal government would subscribe one-fifth of the capital, and the eight million dollars of private capital could be subscribed one-fourth in specie and three-fourths in government bonds. Passage of the bill did not, however, imply enactment. In the congressional debate serious questions as to the constitutionality of Hamilton's bank were raised. When President Washington asked the secretary of state, Jefferson, and the attorney general, Edmund Randolph, for their advice, both were of the opinion that the bank was unconstitutional. In defense of the bank, Hamilton summoned all of his resourcefulness. His opinion, upholding the bank's constitutionality, developed the doctrine of implied powers that held that the federal government could do anything not specifically forbidden by the Constitution in pursuance of that document's explicit objectives. Jefferson, in contrast, had held that the government could not do anything unless it was specifically authorized by the Constitution. Washington was persuaded by Hamilton's argument and signed the bank bill into law.

In the midst of congressional debate on the bank, the tireless Hamilton submitted a *Report on the Establishment of a Mint* which, when embodied in the Coinage Act of 1792, defined the basic monetary unit of the United States and made provision for its supply. This was the least original of Hamilton's proposals in that it was based to a large extent on Jefferson's earlier recommendations adopted by the Confederation government. These had specified the dollar, a coin similar to the Spanish silver dollars widely circulating in America, as the unit of account, and had called for a decimal coinage including a ten dollar gold piece and small coins (cents and half cents) of copper. The 1792 Coinage Act defined the dollar as 371.25 grains of pure silver, and it also specified a ten dollar gold coin, termed an eagle, containing 247.50 grains of pure gold. Smaller silver and gold coins as well as copper cents and half cents were defined. The act established a mint that would coin gold and silver presented to it without charge and in unlimited quantities. Following provisions of the Constitution, gold and silver coins were made the only legal tender for all debts in the United States. The mint, located in Philadelphia, commenced operations in 1794.

The bimetallic coinage system thus adopted was to create many difficulties for the United States during the next century. Hamilton personally favored a monometallic system based on gold but, perhaps because of the Jeffersonian precedent and his own desire to increase the American money supply, he recommended bimetallism. The coinage ratio adopted by the United States implied that a dollar contained fifteen times as much silver as gold, which was very close to the market price ratio in the early 1790s. Had this parity of mint and market price ratios continued, bimetallism would have worked. But it was most unlikely to continue. Indeed, the price of silver in terms of gold soon fell, making it profitable for individuals to sell gold on world markets instead of bringing it to the U.S. mint. Few gold coins were in fact minted. Moreover, another tactical error made the U.S. silver dollar slightly lighter than the Spanish dollar. This caused many of the newly minted American dollars to be exported and exchanged for Spanish dollars which were then reminted into *more* American dollars, from whence this profitable operation could begin anew. Not wishing to supply everyone but Americans with U.S. silver dollars, President Jefferson in 1806 suspended their coinage. Americans rather paradoxically were forced to rely on foreign coins and bank notes for their money transactions as a result of their coinage laws.

The later history of American coinage is replete with attempts to cope with the nagging problems of bimetallism. In 1834 and 1837 the gold content of a dollar was reduced from one-fifteenth to about one-sixteenth of its silver content in an attempt to have both metals circulate in coined form. As the market ratio was in between these mint ratios, however, silver coins now became undervalued at the mint and silver coins soon began to disappear from the money market. A de facto gold standard replaced the de facto silver standard of 1792–1834. This shift of policy had negative effects because the shortage of silver coins created real problems in small retail transactions. In 1853, Congress finally solved the problem by reducing the silver content of coins under one dollar, thereby creating a subsidiary or token coinage, that is, a coinage worth less intrinsically than the value stamped on it by the government. The Act of 1853 effectively abolished bimetallism in the United States by withdrawing the right of citizens to unlimited coinage of silver and by limiting the legal tender of subsidiary silver coins to debts not exceeding five dollars. Foreign coins, which had possessed legal tender status from the earliest days of the republic, lost this status in 1857.

While Hamilton and his contemporaries thus failed to provide an efficient and lasting solution to coinage problems, in most other respects Federalist policies were very successful. The tariff, although modified on numerous occasions—most importantly by a temporary doubling of rates during the War of 1812—remained essentially a revenue measure until 1816. Its moderate rates together with the remarkable growth of the nation's foreign commerce between 1793 and 1808 supplied the greater part of early federal revenue requirements. The funded debt appeared to have the immediate effect, predicted by Hamilton, of raising prices and stimulating commercial activity. And well it might, for it increased current wealth by creating credible drafts on the future. The Bank of the United States, with its home office in Philadelphia and branches in four, and later eight, major cities, proved very useful to the government and the country. Besides performing fiscal functions for the Treasury, it supplied the country with a large quantity of paper currency and acted to strengthen the nation's other banks and their note issues in a manner that had some aspects of modern central banking. Internal taxes—the excise on distilled liquors was supplemented by additional excise, documentary, and direct taxes in 1794, 1796, and 1798, respectively—remained unpopular but they helped to avoid complete reliance on tariffs in a period when land sales produced little revenue. Their passage indicates that a people with growing commercial interests did not desire to impede this growth with higher tariffs.

Perhaps the greatest tribute to the wisdom of the Federalist financial policies came from the Jeffersonian Republicans who had vigorously opposed them when they were first introduced. This political party, formed during the period of opposition, gained the presidency in 1801 and held it for a quarter century. In office the Republicans either continued Hamiltonian and Federalist policies or when they did not, came to regret it. The claims of public creditors were honored, and in consequence Jefferson's government found it easy to borrow the money necessary to purchase the Louisiana territory in 1803. Trade prosperity swelled the Treasury coffers and allowed Secretary Albert Gallatin to reduce the debt from eighty-six million to forty-five million dollars between 1803 and 1812, thus accomplishing an objective held out by Hamilton.

Soaring customs duties allowed President Jefferson to fulfill his campaign promise to eliminate all internal taxes. This was to prove a mistake, however, for the taxes had to be reinstated during the War of 1812, at which time their effectiveness was greatly reduced by the necessity of rebuilding the machinery of collection. A similar error was the failure to recharter the federal bank when its original charter ran out in 1811. President Madison and Secretary Gallatin had come to realize the usefulness of the Bank to the government and they supported its rechartering. But some Republicans revived the issue of its constitutionality, and others resented the competition and control it created for state-chartered banks. This coalition of principle and interest defeated the recharter bill. The Bank was sorely missed in the war emergency which soon followed, and creating a similar but larger institution became one of the first tasks of postwar legislation. As for the tariff, the postwar Jeffersonian Republicans, for good or ill, became as enamored of the protective concept as Hamilton himself had ever been.

Specie Money and Bank Money

We began this chapter by emphasizing the importance of interrelationships between money, banking, and public finance. The comprehensive financial program of Alexander Hamilton well illustrated this point. The history of money, banks, and public finance up to the Civil War, to which we now turn our attention, is replete with further illustrations of the interaction of private and public decision making.

In examining this history, it will help to develop some basic theoretical ideas on the nature of the monetary system of the United States. Throughout its history two essentially different types of money have made up the money supply of the United States. One type of money is defined, and often created and managed, by the federal government for public or social purposes. Providing for an adequate supply of money is an important function of government. Money transactions are far more efficient than barter transactions, and money as a unit of account aids economic decision making at all levels by minimizing the costs of acquiring information about relative values of goods, services, and factors of production.

Up until the Civil War, with few and temporary exceptions, this governmental type of money consisted of metallic coins in multiples and fractions of the basic monetary unit, the dollar. Gold and silver coins and their equivalent in bullion thus made up the governmentally sanctioned monetary base of the antebellum American money supply. Furthermore, only gold and silver coins were recognized in American law as legal tender for all private and public debts.

The other type of money in the American money supply, bank money, was and is a product created by private banking institutions for profit-making purposes. Before the Civil War this bank money consisted of paper bank notes and bank deposits. Bank notes and deposits were created in the process of carrying out the ordinary banking functions of making loans and discounting the promissory notes and bills of exchange of bank customers. To illustrate the process of bank money creation suppose, for example, that an antebellum storekeeper in Ohio wanted to stock pots and pans which he would sell to his retail customers over the following six months. To buy the pans from a wholesaler he might give his note promising to pay $500 six months hence to his local banker. If the interest rate or discount rate were 6 percent per annum (equivalent to 3 percent for six months), the banker would take the note and hand the storekeeper $485 in bank notes. The storekeeper would use the bank notes to buy his pots and pans. As they were sold to retail customers in the following months the storekeeper would accumulate enough funds to pay the banker $500 plus, he normally expected, a surplus as a reward for his own mercantile effort. Less commonly in antebellum times, except in larger cities, the storekeeper would take his loan as a bank deposit on which he could write a check to pay for the pots and pans.

Once the paper bank notes were used to buy the storekeeper's stock of pots and pans, they would begin to circulate as money. The wholesaler would use them to pay himself, his workers, and his suppliers, and they would in turn respend them for other goods and services. Why was the bank necessary at all? Why could not the storekeeper have given the wholesaler his own notes? The answer to these questions hinges on the division of labor and growing specialization encountered so often in economic history. The bank was a specialized institution for supplying credit. By specializing on credit and developing modes of behavior consistent with performing its business efficiently, the bank developed a standing that made its notes more widely acceptable to sellers of goods and services than the notes of nonbank institutions and individuals would have been. This is what made the bank's paper notes and checks a generally acceptable means of exchange or, in short, money.

Recalling that only the gold and silver money specified by the federal government was legal tender, we can easily deduce what modes of behavior were consistent with performing individual banking functions effectively. The key to having its notes and checks accepted as money was the bank's willingness and ability to pay the gold and silver base money whenever the holder of a note or check of the bank presented it for payment. Maintaining the convertibility of notes and deposits into specie was, therefore, basic to effective bank operations.

To maintain convertibility a bank did not require a dollar of metallic specie money for every dollar of bank-note or deposit money. In a given period of days or weeks payments of specie by the bank in exchange for its own notes or checks would be balanced by receipts of specie. Banks were, among other things, storehouses and safe depositories for specie. The public usually preferred to use paper bank notes and checks to make payments since they were easier than specie to carry around and to transport from place to place in more distant transactions. Consequently, banks could normally issue several dollars of notes and deposits subject to check for each dollar of specie they held. This is the principle of fractional reserve banking. It was of great private advantage to the banks because they could make more loans and discounts, and thus earn more interest income, than would have been possible with 100 percent rather than fractional specie reserves. And it had a social advantage as well. In addition to being more convenient for the public, paper money was far less costly to create than specie money which had to be mined, refined, assayed, and minted.

Before the Civil War, then, the American money supply consisted of two types of money: a base of specie money as defined by the government in terms of gold and silver coins, and bank money—bank notes and deposits—created in the process of ordinary banking operations and normally convertible into specie. Specie in banks thus served as bank reserves. Banking and monetary data are notably sketchy and rather incomplete for the antebellum years, but a few scholars have attempted to cull from them estimates of the money supply and its components. One set of estimates, covering the period 1820–58, is shown in Figure 7–1; it probably reflects trends adequately. The overall trend is strongly upward at a rate of 5 percent per year for the whole period. This largely reflects the real growth of the country because price levels in the late 1850s were not very different from those of the early 1820s. The only major exception to the money supply's strong upward trend came in the period from the late 1830s to the early 1840s, which is one of the few periods in all of American history when the money supply trended downward for a period of several years.

Trends in the specie stock, the monetary base of the United States in these years, are also shown in Figure 7–1. Largely in the form of gold and silver coins, specie served as hand-to-hand currency and as reserves

FIGURE 7-1
U.S. Money Supply and Specie Stock, 1820-1858
(in millions of dollars, invato scale)

Money Supply

Specie Stock

SOURCE: Peter Temin, <u>The Jacksonian Economy</u>, (New York: W. W. Norton, 1969), pp. 71, 159.

for bank notes and deposits. In fulfilling these monetary functions, the specie stock was the primary determinant of the money supply. Indeed, the broad correspondence of the two series is evident in Figure 7–1. Specie, like the money supply, grew at approximately 5 percent per year over the period 1820–58. The only major divergence of the two series is in the decade 1822–32 when the stock of specie was relatively unchanged while the money supply nearly doubled. This departure is of special interest because in these years the second Bank of the United States was exercising a powerful influence in the nation's monetary and financial affairs. Its activities appear to have increased the public's confidence in banks, allowing bank money to become a much greater part of the total money supply.

Money and Prices

The expansion of the money supply and of bank money just described was a part of the real growth of the American economy in the antebellum decades. Although some Americans living in those decades, and many later writers on the period as well, thought that the process of creating bank money by monetizing private debts, that is, issuing bank notes and deposits in return for promises to repay the loans later, was highly inflationary, there is little evidence to support that view. Looking at the behavior of the general price level as shown in Figure 7–2, it is apparent that from the mid 1790s until the eve of the Civil War the overall trend was downward. This implies that over the whole period the money supply did not increase fast enough to maintain a stable price level. The supply of goods and services exchanged for money, to put it another way, grew faster than did the supply of money.

It is also clear from the price-level chart that there were a number of departures from the trend of falling prices. Were these departures the result of excessive monetization of private debt by banks, as has often been argued? The answer in general is negative, as can be inferred from an examination of four major upward movements in the price level occurring, respectively, in the mid-1790s, in the War of 1812, in the mid-1830s, and in the early 1850s. In each of these inflationary periods the chief impetus for rising prices did not come from overissues of bank money by reckless bankers responding to the loan demands of speculators and entrepreneurs, but rather from increases in the base of specie money or, in one instance, from paper money issued by the federal government.

For the 1790s period monetary and banking data are too limited to give a very precise answer to the question of why prices rose. However,

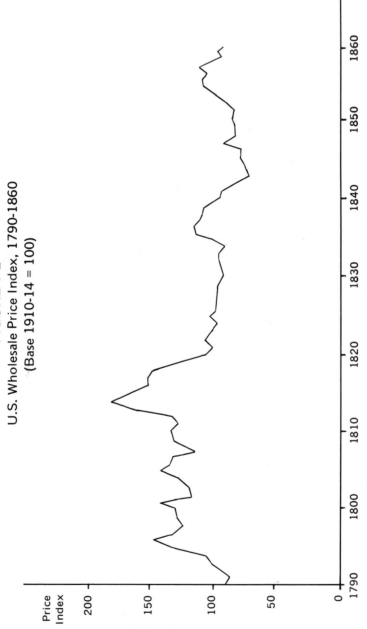

FIGURE 7-2

U.S. Wholesale Price Index, 1790-1860

(Base 1910-14 = 100)

SOURCE: U.S. Bureau of Census, Historical Statistics of the United States, Colonial Times to 1957 (Washington, D.C.: 1960), pp. 115-116.

there were only a few banks operating in these years and most of them were just getting organized. The major cause of rising prices, it seems clear, was the great foreign demand for American exports, American re-exports of West Indian products, and American shipping services as a result of wars between England and France. The wars interfered with both the production and commerce of those two countries, and the United States stood ready to take up the slack. Sales of American goods and services to foreigners generated an inflow of specie and foreign capital to the United States, and prices rose. After the initial rise peaked in 1796, American prices fluctuated up and down for the next fifteen years with the ebb and flow of European warfare. If there was a trend in these years, it appears to have been slightly downward despite the growth of American banks whose numbers increased from three in 1790 to about thirty in 1800 and about one hundred in 1810.

The explanation of the inflationary periods of the 1830s and the 1850s is much the same. In the 1830s imports of silver, primarily from Mexico, swelled the specie base of the American money supply and caused it to expand rapidly. Ordinarily, the rise of American prices would have led to exports of specie as foreigners stopped buying more expensive American products and Americans themselves sought cheaper imports. In the mid-1830s, however, the United States accomplished the rare historical feat of paying off its entire national debt, and this caused foreigners to have such extreme faith in the credit of Americans that they were willing to finance rising American imports by lending rather than demanding specie. This granting of loans by foreigners to Americans allowed the specie imported from Mexico to remain in the American money supply. An increased use of foreign bills of exchange to finance imports had the same effect. Americans earned these bills of exchange when they exported commodities such as cotton.

In the 1850s, the chief cause of rising prices was the expansion of specie money resulting from the discovery of gold in California. Much of this gold was exported, but enough remained in the United States to increase the specie base from $120 million to $260 million between 1848 and 1856. The fraction of bank money in the total money supply was roughly constant during this period of inflation.

The sharpest inflation of the whole antebellum period came during the War of 1812. In this case government borrowing to finance the war rather than a growth in specie was the major cause. The federal debt rose from $45 million to $127 million from 1812 to 1816. Part of this increase was in the form of short-term Treasury notes which were for all practical purposes a paper money issue. Though bearing interest and redeemable in one year, Treasury notes were receivable in payment of all duties, taxes, and debts of the federal government until redeemed. In all some $37 million of Treasury notes were issued during the war, with about $17 million as the maximum outstanding at one time. This was a substantial addition to the American money supply. Some small denominations circulated as hand-to-hand currency. However, most Treasury notes were in $100 denominations which, given their legal-tender status in government transactions and their short maturity, made them an ideal form of bank reserves. Aided by these paper reserves, bank credit expanded, largely to accommodate the government. The money supply increased and prices rose. Late in the war, the government's voracious demands for credit and the resulting swollen credit structure forced the banks, except in New England, to suspend specie payments. The suspension of convertibility between bank money and specie happened after, not before, the worst of the inflation.

This survey of major antebellum price trends may serve as a useful antidote to the all-too-common view that reckless, inflationary, wildcat banking practices were endemic to the early history of the United States. In the 1790s there were few banks, and in the 1850s perceptive observers realized that increases in monetary gold, not bank money, were the source of rising prices. However, it has often been said that the main causes of the price-level inflations that occurred during the War of 1812 and again in the 1830s were the large increases in the number of banks and the amount of bank-created money. This was not the case. Increases in the monetary base of specie (and in the War of 1812 government paper money) rather than sharp changes in banking practices or wildcat banking were at the heart of the inflations.

Banks and Politics

Lack of historical foundation for the long-accepted view that early American banks were engines of inflation does not imply that their numerous critics were unjustified in all of their charges. The business of banking was new to Americans, in part because the British had not looked with favor on attempts of their colonists in North America to engage in it. When in 1784 some merchants of Boston obtained a charter from the Massachusetts legislature to form the second incorporated bank in the newly independent country, they wrote to the first, the Bank of North America founded at Philadelphia in 1781, requesting advice on how to proceed. Thomas Willing, president of the Philadelphia bank and later president of the Bank of the United States, responded:

> When the bank first opened here, the business was as much a novelty to us . . . as it can possibly be to you. It was a pathless wilderness, ground but little known to this side of the Atlantic. No book then spoke of the in-

terior arrangements or rules observed in Europe—accident alone threw in our way even the form of an English bank bill. All was to us a mystery.*

In such circumstances, it is not surprising that banks sometimes made mistakes.

In addition to lack of experience and formal guides concerning bank management, early American bankers were hampered by the system under which they operated. Two related aspects of that system were problem areas until the early twentieth century, namely, the absence of a central bank and the metallic monetary standard. Under fractional reserve banking, in normal times a bank could issue bank-note and deposit liabilities in amounts several times greater than its reserves of specie into which these liabilities were supposed to be convertible. Unfortunately, not all times were normal. An abnormal time might well be defined as one in which holders of notes and deposits attempted to convert them into specie on such a scale that there was not enough specie to go around. No matter how well managed a bank might have been, if it could not borrow specie at such a time of panic it would be forced to suspend convertibility. Typically the problem would not be that of just an individual bank but of a great many banks all at once. Thus, it happened that in 1814, and again in 1837 and 1857, large numbers of American banks temporarily suspended convertibility of their liabilities into specie. This smacked of dishonesty to many, but in the particular circumstances it was a wise decision. When the banks did not have to redeem their own liabilities in specie, they could be more lenient in demanding it from their borrowers. This leniency prevented business failures that might otherwise have occurred and therefore hastened recovery from financial panics.

One of the functions of a central bank in the modern economy is to act as a lender of last resort to temporarily illiquid banks. This was not a recognized function in nineteenth-century America, although on a few occasions the banks of the United States and the United States Treasury did aid the commercial banks. A central bank would have held large reserves of the base money—specie before the Civil War—which it could have lent to banks under pressure to redeem in specie large amounts of their note and deposit liabilities. Had such an institution been present and the lender-of-last-resort function been recognized, the probability of temporary panics involving individual banks or the whole system of banks would have been reduced substantially. The problem of panics and widespread suspensions of convertibility, therefore, was one of institutional organization, not one of poorly managed banks.

The metallic monetary standard was another institutional factor that presented problems for price level and banking stability. For one thing,

---

* As quoted by Bray Hammond, *Banks and Politics in America, from the Revolution to the Civil War* (Princeton, N.J.: Princeton University Press, 1957), p. 66.

even if a central bank had been present, its own reserves of specie might have been severely strained in a major convertibility panic. Today's central bank, the Federal Reserve System, does not labor under such a disadvantage since it can create bank reserves and paper currency with, as is sometimes said, a stroke of its pen. The United States is no longer on a metallic monetary standard. But when it was, banking and price stability depended on the flow of specie into and out of the economy. Such specie flows arose from imports and exports of existing stocks, from discoveries of gold and silver deposits in the earth, and from improved technologies for extracting the monetary metals from their ores. In some cases such flows could be price stabilizing, but often they were not. The inflations of the 1830s and 1850s furnish examples of the latter. Inflows of specie stimulated rising prices that then were built into the expectations of borrowers and lenders. When prices failed to continue their rise because specie inflows tapered off or turned into outflows, these inflationary expectations were jolted and financial panic resulted. In principle, if not so clearly in practice, the managed paper monetary standard of today is more capable of promoting price level stability than its metallic predecessors.

Thus, both absence of experience and an imperfect institutional environment created problems for early American bankers. The same was true for many other businesses in the developing American economy. However, because the bankers' stock in trade, their bank notes and deposits, were owned by other people and circulated as part of the nation's money supply, it was natural that attempts to regulate bank behavior arose. Monetization of debt through creating note and deposit liabilities several times larger than specie reserves was a profitable activity and carried with it a temptation to excess, particularly since a bank itself would bear only a part of the costs of the failure that might result, with holders of its liabilities bearing the remainder. State legislatures and Congress, in chartering the earliest banks, attempted to face this problem by specifying the amount of equity capital to be paid into a bank before operations could commence and by limiting bank note issues to some stated multiple of capital. Though sketchy and often misdirected, such regulations furnished guidelines to inexperienced bankers and reminded them of their public responsibilities.

Continuing restraint on the temptation of bankers to overissue their monetary liabilities was accomplished by some large banks. The first and second Banks of the United States, operating under federal charters from 1791–1811 and 1816–36, respectively, were notable examples of nationwide regulation in this respect. These large and prestigious institutions with branches in the leading cities of the country received payments due the government and generally followed conservative lending policies. Therefore, they tended to accumulate net balances of notes and checks issued by other banks. By promptly returning these liabilities to the issuing banks for conversion into specie, the Banks of the United States could and sometimes did restrain the expansion of money and credit by the state-chartered banks.

Such credit restraining activities by the Banks of the United States were unpopular both with bankers and with entrepreneurs who desired more and cheaper credit. Still other factions were against banking and paper money in general, but most of all against the gigantic federal banks which were widely viewed as bastions of privilege with dubious constitutionality. As we saw earlier, these groups coalesced in 1811 to defeat the attempt in Congress to recharter the first Bank of the United States. The second federal bank, chartered for twenty years in 1816, ran into similar political difficulties in the early 1830s. Its friends in Congress succeeded in passing a recharter bill in 1832, but President Andrew Jackson's veto of the measure was sustained. The contest, or Bank War as it came to be known, pitted the strong-willed, antibank Jackson against an able but rather arrogant Philadelphian, Nicholas Biddle, president of the bank. Jackson was victorious when further attempts to recharter the bank ended in failure.

The immediate results of the Bank War were that the federal government, beginning in 1833, transferred its banking business to state banks while the Bank of the United States redeemed its stock held by the federal government and was reorganized as a Pennsylvania corporation. These new arrangements were short-lived, however. The reorganized bank failed in 1841, after ill-timed speculations in the international cotton market. And the federal government, growing increasingly wary of its new relations with state banks, moved to isolate its fiscal affairs from the nation's banking system by creating the so-called Independent Treasury. Instituted for a year in 1840–41 and then reestablished in 1846, the Independent Treasury accepted payments due the government only in specie or Treasury notes. Government funds were held in subtreasuries scattered throughout the nation rather than in banks.

In New England during the four decades before the Civil War the Suffolk Bank of Boston exerted control over money and credit on a regional basis in much the same way as the two Banks of the United States had done nationally during their years of existence. Cooperating with other Boston banks, which in the normal course of trade received net balances of New England country bank notes, the Suffolk Bank pressured the country banks into maintaining with it deposits for note redemption. If they did not, the Suffolk threatened to embarrass the smaller banks by suddenly presenting large amounts of their notes for redemption. In the face of this threat the country banks agreed to the Suffolk's terms, and the New England states, under this private regulatory scheme, enjoyed a stable paper currency with bank notes exchanging at par throughout the region for much of the antebellum period.

Outside of New England, bank notes commonly were received at a discount from par whenever they were presented away from the locale of the issuing bank. This discount, which varied with the distance from the issuing bank, was not, as is sometimes supposed, a sign of excessive note issue by banks. Rather, it reflected the real costs of returning notes for redemption in an era of slow communication. Only when the issuing banks refused to convert their liabilities into specie were the discounts more than a few percent.

The note redemption operations of the Banks of the United States and the Suffolk Bank, along with similar efforts on the part of numerous note and exchange brokers, represented the activities of private institutions pursuing essentially private ends while at the same time promoting the public goal of a more reliable money supply. Direct regulation by governmental agencies was slower in coming. When it did the state of New York was in the forefront. In 1829, the New York legislature instituted the Safety-Fund System, a scheme for insuring the note issues of its member banks. New York banks chartered by the legislature were required to contribute a small percentage of their capital to a safety fund and to submit to periodic inspection by state-appointed bank examiners. If a member bank of the system failed, the holders of its outstanding notes were reimbursed from the Safety Fund. The New York Safety Fund foreshadowed bank deposit insurance, one of the most significant innovations of twentieth century American banking.

New York State was also in the forefront of the movement to free the business of banking from the vagaries of politics. From their beginnings in the 1780s, American banks had been incorporated by special charters of legislative bodies. Banking was a new and often very profitable business. When the privilege of entering into it with corporate privileges was in the hands of politicians on a case-by-case basis, bribery and corruption inevitably resulted. Moreover, deposits of public funds could be used by politicians to assist friendly banks and to punish those less friendly. Lest one gain the impression that such attitudes were in the minds of only small men and political hacks, it may be pointed out that no less a statesman than President Jefferson wrote in 1803 to his treasury secretary, Albert Gallatin, that "I am decidedly in favor of making all the banks Republican, by sharing deposits among them in proportion to the dispositions they show." * Three decades later President Jackson followed in his illustrious predecessor's footsteps when he authorized the funds of the United States to be deposited in so-called pet banks, that is, banks friendly to the Jacksonians.

New York's solution to the problems created by too close a nesting of banks and politics was the Free Banking Act of 1838. This act made

* Jefferson to Gallatin, *Writings of Albert Gallatin*, ed. Henry Adams, 3 vols. (Philadelphia: 1879), vol. 1, p. 129.

the granting of corporate charters to engage in banking a function of an administrative office of state government instead of special acts of the legislature. Banking was made free in the sense that anyone or any group of associates could obtain a bank charter by complying with conditions and regulations specified in the act. As such, the act reflected the ascendant idea that free competition in banking as well as in other businesses was the best guarantee of effective economic performance.

In addition to reflecting the growing laissez-faire trend in American economic thinking, the New York Free Banking Act instituted a notable innovation in banking, namely, a bank-note currency backed by specified types of bonds and mortgages. These included state and federal bonds and mortgages on New York land. A free bank would purchase the allowable securities and deposit them with an agency of the state government, which would then issue to the bank notes equal to the amount of pledged bonds or to half the amount of pledged real-estate mortgages. Like the Safety Fund, this was an attempt to provide insurance to holders of bank notes. If a bank failed outright, or failed to redeem its notes when they were presented, the comptroller could liquidate the securities pledged by the bank and use the proceeds to redeem its notes. This system worked fairly well in New York. Between its adoption there in 1838 and the Civil War it gradually spread throughout the United States, and in 1863 it became the model for the National Banking System. However, the system was not foolproof. Events in other states demonstrated its drawbacks when securities of dubious value were allowed to serve as backing for bank notes. The desire of state governments to expand the market for their own bonds was often as much a motive for free banking legislation as was the desire to make bank notes safer.

As free banking spread to more and more states in the 1840s and 1850s, it helped to reduce the deleterious consequences of politics for banking development. The struggle for free banking was not an easy one, however, and its widespread institution came only after other possibilities were tried. A few states owned and operated their own banks, sometimes as monopolies and sometimes in competition with privately owned banks. Some of these state operations were among the best of antebellum banks, and others were among the worst. Other states, disgusted with their own bank experiences or with those that cropped up elsewhere, experimented with the extreme policy of a complete prohibition of incorporated banking within their borders. Such a policy merely served to encourage banks in other states to send their notes to the "bankless" states, and it was usually abandoned in favor of free banking.

In reality few states were ever bankless even when they tried to be. European and English common law traditions recognized the legal right of anyone to engage in banking operations without having to obtain the permission of the government. These traditions migrated to the United

States in the form of private, unincorporated banks that often grew out of, or were carried on along with, other types of business. Hundreds of these private banks were in business during the late antebellum years, but except for a few of the larger and more famous ones, very little is known about the nature and scope of their operations. Nonetheless, two patterns of private banking are discernible. In larger cities private banks often specialized in domestic and foreign exchange operations, and in marketing securities for both governmental bodies and private firms. The latter activity foreshadowed specialized investment banking. Private banks also operated in many smaller cities and towns, especially in the newer areas of settlement. Here they served as substitutes for incorporated banks which were slow to develop or were prohibited by law. Generally, private banks were forbidden by law from circulating their own bank notes, but they could accept deposits and extend credit in other ways.

The heterogeneous American banking system of the antebellum decades had a number of bad features, but it also had some good ones for an expanding and developing economy. A more uniform national currency of the type promoted but not altogether achieved by the Banks of the United States would have constituted a better medium of exchange and store of value than the thousands of varieties of bank notes that actually circulated. The diversity of bank notes—some of failed banks and some counterfeit—undoubtedly hindered smooth and efficient transactions, and it caused resources to be expended on the flourishing business of producing and distributing bank note reporters and counterfeit detectors. Such costs could have been avoided with better institutional arrangements. However, if such "better" arrangements had been accompanied by more centralized and restrictive controls over bank operations and money creation, it is not clear that the overall result would have been preferable to the dynamic and variegated bank-financed economic development of the period.

It should be remembered that in these years the American economy was expanding over a great geographical area and bringing previously dormant resources into use. Communication and transportation, although advancing with the westward movement, were nonetheless rather primitive during most of the antebellum period. Wealth that had accumulated in Europe and in the older, settled eastern states exhibited a reluctance to migrate to the newer areas of settlement even though there is evidence that it could have earned higher returns there. In these circumstances entrepreneurs, on the scene and hence more aware than others of the productive potential of the nation's expanding resources, turned to local banks for the supplies of money and credit needed to realize this potential. Had the spread of such local banking been restricted or disallowed by uninformed prejudice against banks, the United States might very well have advanced more slowly, both in settlement and in economic growth, before 1860.

Government Economic Activities and Their Finance

Measured in terms of dollar amounts or in relation to the national income, government economic activities between 1790 and 1860 appear rather limited by modern day standards. Total federal expenditures over these seven decades amounted to about two billion dollars, an amount equivalent to what the federal government now spends in two or three days. The United States, of course, is much larger in population and income today, and the purchasing power of the dollar in terms of comparable goods and services is much less than it was in antebellum years. Nonetheless, these factors account for only a part of the historical difference. Federal spending before the Civil War typically was only 1 to 2 percent of the national income of that period, or less than a tenth of its percentage share in today's economy. The spending of state and local governments was also small by later standards. A rough estimate for the states is about three billion dollars over the seventy years. On the whole, government spending on all levels probably amounted to 5 to 10 percent of the nation's income, with the former figure likely closer to the actual level in most years.

Absolute and relative levels of government spending, however, provide a misleading indication of the role of government in antebellum economic development. While Americans in general tended to agree with Adam Smith's view that government activity ought properly to be limited to such matters as defense, justice, and a few "public" works, they gave it a broad construction consistent with the expansion of a relatively undeveloped economy. Directly and indirectly, government decisions attempted, with substantial success, to augment the nation's resources of land, capital, and labor, as well as their efficient combination in the production of material wealth and welfare.

Federal Revenues and Expenditures

Before the Civil War, the federal government's revenue came essentially from three sources—customs duties, land sales, and internal taxes. Internal taxes were the least important of the three main revenue sources, accounting for about 2 percent of total receipts. They were levied in only sixteen years, the last time in 1817. Land sales provided about 10 percent of federal revenues over the whole seven-decade period. With the exception of the land boom of the mid–1830s, their contribution seldom rose much above this percentage. Moreover, if account were taken of all costs of acquiring, surveying, and marketing the public lands, the net federal revenue from land sales would be much less. Customs duties provided the best source of federal revenue, comprising some seven-eighths of the total.

The original Tariff Act of 1789 stated that import duties were "necessary for the support of government, for the discharge of the debts of the United States, and the encouragement and protection of manufactures." In varying degrees these three aims provided the rationale for all later measures. Revenue was the dominant purpose from 1789 to 1816. Duties averaged less than 10 percent of the value of imports except when they were temporarily doubled for revenue purposes during the War of 1812. The Tariff Act of 1816, although reducing average duties slightly from their temporarily high wartime levels, made protection of domestic producers the primary object of American tariff policy. This was a response to the wave of nationalism that swept through the country as a result of the war, and to special pleading by the manufacturing interests that had grown up under hothouse conditions of restricted foreign trade after 1808. Duties moved upward, reaching average levels of about 50 percent in the 1828 Tariff of Abominations. Thereafter, the rates were reduced periodically up to the Civil War, except for a brief revival of protectionist spirit in 1842.

Protective tariff policies undoubtedly led to greater production and higher profits in the industries protected, but it is far from clear that the nation as a whole benefited from the differential protection accorded to some producers. Protection may have allowed some producers to reap economies of scale and to engage in the process of learning how to employ the developing technologies of large-scale factory manufacturing. But protection often continued long after these benefits were reaped. It thus constituted more a means of transferring income to the protected industries from the users of their products than one of creating wholly new productive activities. To the extent that protected industries engaged in the production of consumer goods such as textiles, these continuing income transfers may well have led to higher levels of capital formation as profits were reinvested. But producer goods such as iron were also protected; in such cases the higher profits of some manufacturers were obtained at the expense of raising costs to other producers.

Considered as a whole, however, the tariff policies of the United States very likely did increase the overall rate of capital formation. To see why, it is necessary to examine how the federal government used the revenues it derived almost entirely from customs duties. A major use of tariff revenues throughout the nineteenth century was to pay interest on, and the principal of, the public debt of the United States. The time path of the federal debt in the antebellum decades is shown in Figure 7–3. In the first decade, the 1790s, the debt was more or less constant, but already

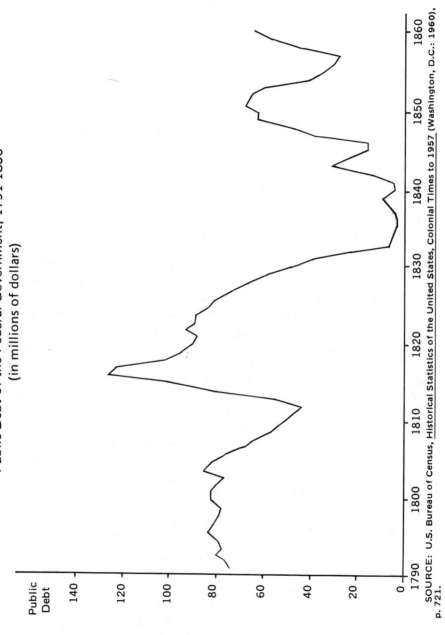

FIGURE 7-3

Public Debt of the Federal Government, 1791-1860

(in millions of dollars)

SOURCE: U.S. Bureau of Census, Historical Statistics of the United States, Colonial Times to 1957 (Washington, D.C.: 1960), p. 721.

at that time its value represented a huge capital gain to investors because Alexander Hamilton's funding scheme had raised the credit of the United States and consequently the value of government bonds. From 1800 to 1812 the conservative fiscal policies of Albert Gallatin reduced the debt in every year save one, 1803, when funds were borrowed for the Louisiana Purchase. During the War of 1812 the debt rose sharply to its antebellum peak as the government borrowed heavily to prosecute the War at highly inflated prices. Then in the two decades after 1816 the debt was virtually extinguished by payments that were made in dollars far more valuable than the ones that had been borrowed earlier. The debt rose again on three occasions before the Civil War—in the two depressions that followed financial panics during the late 1830s and 1850s, when lower imports combined with reduced tariff rates led to a falling off of federal revenues, and in the late 1840s as a result of increased spending for the Mexican War. From 1843 to 1846, and again from 1851 to 1857, the debt was substantially reduced.

The federal government, in short, borrowed when it had to but viewed the normal condition as one in which surplus revenues were desirable in order to reduce the public debt. This policy favored capital formation in two ways. First, the direct transfer of funds from import taxes to public creditors on balance taxed consumers to provide funds for investors. The dollar amount of such transfers actually understates the actual transfer of purchasing power because the government generally borrowed cheaper dollars (e.g., during wartime inflations) than it paid back (in peacetime years). Secondly, government debt retirement reduced the supply of bonds, thereby raising bond prices and reducing interest yields. To the extent that government bonds were viewed by investors as substitutes for other public and private investments, this tended to reduce the interest costs of other borrowers. Federal debt policy thus increased the availability, and reduced the supply price, of capital funds to private investors. In the decades after the Civil War, federal debt policies continued to promote private capital formation but on an even greater scale (see chapter 15).

Tariff and debt policies were only a part of economically significant federal activities. Expenditures on general government—the legislative, executive, and judicial branches—implemented a framework of law that protected individual and property rights, and carried out the Constitution's mandate for a nationwide free-trade area. That area was extended by expenditures for the acquisition, protection, and distribution of new territories; much of the spending on defense and Indian affairs, as well as on land management and aids to internal transportation, was for these purposes. Foreign commerce was promoted by favored treatment to American shipping interests and by expenditures on navigation improvements and the navy, which helped to suppress piracy. Subsidies to the Post Office and to the first telegraph line represented a recognition of the social nature and utility of information and communications. The federal government limited the scope of its operations, but most of what it did had strong economic motivation and significance.

State and Local Government Activity

For at least a quarter century after 1790 state and local financial activities were rather unimportant. Hamilton's funding scheme freed the states of most of their debts. An aversion to taxes and fondness for limited government led many to obtain the bulk of their revenues from land sales and interest on federal securities that they had received as a part of Hamilton's program. One economically significant state policy in this early period was the incorporation, and in some cases partial financing, of banking and transportation companies. Dividends, especially on bank stock, were a good source of revenue and allowed state taxes to be kept low.

After the War of 1812 wider appreciation of the need for transportation improvements coupled with federal reluctance to assume a major role in providing them led to a much more active economic role for the states. The great success of federal credit policies and a continuing aversion to taxes were important in determining how state activities were financed. Chief reliance was placed on borrowing, and many states actually hoped to pay the interest and principal of their bonded debts with earnings from their investments in banking and transportation facilities instead of from taxes. The early and great success of the Erie Canal showed that this might indeed be possible. Eventually, however, many of the states were to be frustrated in their attempts to operate as business enterprises rather than as governments. During the 1830s all sorts of enterprises were launched with funds borrowed, often from foreigners, on state credit. But the earnings of many of these ventures proved disappointing and when credit tightened in the late 1830s, many of the states were in trouble. In the ensuing depression some defaulted on their debt obligations, and a few actually repudiated their debts. State interest in improvement projects declined thereafter, and greater reliance was placed on taxation rather than on borrowing. This reorganization of state finances led to a sounder expansion of state borrowing in the 1850s, and on the eve of the Civil War the gross debt of the states was more than four times that of the federal government.

Local government economic activity was less innovative than that of the states but after 1820, under the stimulus of growing urbanization, it increased rapidly. Most of the public services of modern urban entities were introduced or expanded in this period. These included water and sewer systems, improved and lighted streets and sidewalks, police and fire protection, health services, and public education. Municipalities also aided transportation companies. Property taxes and license fees financed much of the public activity, but borrowing was utilized for extensive capital outlays. Municipal indebtedness increased from twenty-seven million dollars in 1843 to two hundred million dollars by 1860, when it was some three times the federal debt.

Conclusion

By 1860, after some seven decades of experimentation, the financial system of the United States had reached a high level of development. The most durable achievement, and also the oldest, was the establishment of public credit. With Alexander Hamilton as the architect, Federalist policies in the 1790s put the credit of American governments on such a high level that even debacles like the repudiation of some state debts in the 1840s were discounted by most American and overseas lenders as temporary deviations from normal practices. In the monetary area, by 1860 the United States had achieved a gold-based currency and was able to dispense with the assorted foreign coins and tokens that for many years had had to be used by Americans because of defects in their own coinage arrangements. And on the eve of the Civil War the utility of banks was no longer a highly charged issue in political economy; by then American banks numbering in the thousands were furnishing a low-cost medium of exchange as well as loans for commercial, agricultural, and industrial development. When one considers that in the 1780s the national government was virtually bankrupt, that currency systems varied from state to state, and that only three recently founded banks plied their trade in isolation not only from most Americans but also from one another, the financial progress of the next seven decades is obvious.

Yet problems remained. Federal revenue continued to place too heavy a reliance on customs duties. The metallic base of the monetary system was capricious, expanding with new ore discoveries and being abandoned when crises of confidence arose, and varying with changes in international trade and capital movements. The paper bank note currency, with thousands of varieties of notes, lacked a uniformity that would have minimized the information and transactions costs of exchanging goods and services. The banking system, moreover, lacked the central leadership that to some extent had been given by the abandoned Banks of the United States. And the federal government with its Independent

Treasury had isolated itself as far as possible from the rest of the financial system in a marked departure from the vision of Hamilton.

The next generation of financial decision makers would deal with most of these problems. As it turned out, events impending in 1860 did not allow them much time to prepare for the task. The coming of the Civil War created massive financial stresses that led to fundamental changes in the system (see chapter 15).

SUGGESTED READINGS

Federalist and Republican financial policies are set forth in some detail by Curtis P. Nettels, *The Emergence of a National Economy, 1775–1815* (New York: Holt, Rinehart and Winston, 1962), and interpreted by Stuart Bruchey, *The Roots of American Economic Growth, 1607–1861* (New York and Evanston: Harper Torchbooks, 1968). Also valuable on these and other financial policies is Paul Studenski and Herman E. Krooss, *Financial History of the United States* (New York: McGraw-Hill, 1963).

For longer term analyses of government revenue, spending, and debts, see Sidney Ratner, *The Tariff in American History* (New York: Van Nostrand, 1972); Ratner's *Taxation and Democracy in America* (New York: Wiley Science Editions, 1967); Paul B. Trescott, "The United States Government and National Income, 1790–1860," in National Bureau of Economic Research, *Trends in the American Economy in the Nineteenth century*, Studies in Income and Wealth, vol. 24 (Princeton, N.J.: Princeton University Press, 1960), pp. 337–361; Lance Davis and John Legler, "The Government in the American Economy: A Quantitative Study," *Journal of Economic History*, 26 (December 1966), 514–555; and B. U. Ratchford, *American State Debts* (Durham: Duke University Press, 1941).

The development and diversity of banking institutions are the subjects of Fritz Redlich, *The Molding of American Banking: Men and Ideas* (New York: Johnson Reprint Corp., 1968); J. Van Fenstermaker, *The Development of American Commercial Banking, 1782–1837* (Kent, Ohio: Kent State University Press, 1965); and two articles by Richard Sylla, "American Banking and Growth in the Nineteenth Century: A Partial View of the Terrain," *Explorations in Economic History*, 9 (Winter 1971–72), 197–228; and "Forgotten Men of Money: Private Bankers in Early U.S. History," *The Journal of Economic History*, 36 (March 1976), 173–188. The origins of the dollar as the American monetary unit are traced by Arthur Nussbaum, *A History of the Dollar* (New York: Columbia University Press, 1957), whereas issues in control of the money supply and banks are the subjects of Bray Hammond, *Banks and Politics in America from the Revolution to the Civil War* (Princeton, N.J.: Princeton University Press, 1957); Hugh Rockoff, *The Free Banking Era: A Re-Examination* (New York: Arno Press, 1975); Walter B. Smith, *Economic Aspects of the Second Bank of the United States* (Cambridge: Harvard University Press, 1953); Peter Temin, *The Jacksonian Economy* (New York: W. W. Norton, 1969); and Richard H. Timberlake, Jr., *The Origins of Central Banking in the United States* (Cambridge: Harvard University Press, 1978).

CHAPTER 8

———

Beginnings of

the Industrial Revolution

in America

Industrialization is the great watershed of modern economic history. Dating from the eighteenth century, this system of production so reduced the real cost (the cost in terms of labor and natural resources) of producing goods and services that the resulting levels of material welfare for the average person vastly exceeded the levels reached by premodern and nonindustrial economies. In the United States the process of industrialization began at the end of the eighteenth century and became firmly established in the early decades of the nineteenth century. By the late nineteenth century, the United States had become the leader among nations in industrial production, a position it has enjoyed up to the present day.

That the United States would become one of the first nations to embark on industrialization was far from obvious at the end of the eighteenth century. Favoring such an outcome were America's close ties with Great Britain (home of the first Industrial Revolution) and the vicissitudes of the Napoleonic War era, which both stimulated economic activity in the United States and at times interfered with the flow of manufactured goods from Britain and Europe. Obstacles standing in the way of industrialization appeared to be much greater. A population smaller than Britain's was scattered over a massive geographical area, and internal transportation costs were high. Together these factors limited the markets for mass-produced industrial goods. Accumulation of capital and facilities for mobilizing funds for investment were also limited. But the greatest obstacle, somewhat paradoxically, was the abundance of land and natural resources. This abundance meant that the return to labor applied in directions such as farming, forest products, and maritime activities was high enough to work against the formation of a concentrated labor force and the highly interdependent urban way of living typical of modern industrial economies. Later generations would view Thomas Jefferson's urgings that Americans follow an independent, uncomplicated existence in a simple, agrarian republic as a bit quaint and old-fashioned. In truth, there was economic logic in the great Virginian's views at the time he formulated them. Soon, however, the machine appeared in the garden.

Industrialization in the American context therefore meant a number of things. It meant that cost-reducing manufacturing technologies, when borrowed from overseas pioneers, had to be modified in many cases to fit in with America's different circumstances, and, for similar reasons, that new technologies developed by Americans emphasized principles different from those of foreign technologies. It meant that internal markets had to be opened up to absorb the enlarged flow of manufactured goods produced at new centers of production. Because of the attractions of agriculture, it meant that American manufacturing depended in a crucial way on agricultural raw materials and the farmers' needs for nonfarm products. The effects of abundant land on labor returns also meant that American manufacturers had to experiment in forming reliable industrial labor forces, and that they favored tariff protection for their products but desired a free flow of labor and capital from overseas. And industrialization meant that American workers searched for methods of protecting and advancing their interests in new situations of increased economic interdependence.

"Manufacturing" in the Early United States

Manufacturing today connotes the mass production of goods from raw materials in factories owned by large enterprises that employ wage laborers and salaried managerial staffs and that use large inputs of power-driven machinery embodying sophisticated technologies. Yet the etymology of the term "manufacture"—its Latin roots—has the rather simpler connotation of making things by hand. In the United States the years from 1790 to 1860 marked the transition from the original and simple meaning of "manufacture" to the new and more complex one. This shift in connotation reflected dramatic changes in the progress of economic development.

What manufacturing meant to Americans around 1790 can be seen in the contemporary account of Lancaster, Pennsylvania, by Tench Coxe, an advocate of American manufacturing in the early days of the republic:

> In the midland counties of Pennsylvania, many precious manufactures have resulted from *a flourishing agriculture*, and immediately on their birth, have contributed to the prosperity of the cultivators. The borough of Lancaster, which is the largest inland town in the United States, is sixty-six miles from a seaport, and ten from any practiced boat navigation. The number of families was in 1786, about 700, of whom 234 were manufacturers. The following is a list of them. Fourteen hatters, thirty-six shoemakers, four tanners, seventeen saddlers, twenty-five tailors, twenty-five weavers of woolen, linen, and cotton cloth, three stocking weavers, twenty-five white and black smiths, six wheel wrights, eleven coopers, six clock and watchmakers, six tobacco and snuff manufacturers, four dyers, seven gun smiths, five rope makers, four tinners, two brass founders, three skin dressers, one brush maker, seven turners, seven nail makers, five silver smiths, three potters, three brewers, three copper smiths, and two printers in English and German. There were in 1786 also, within thirty-nine miles of the town, seventeen furnaces, forges, rolling mills and slitting mills, and within ten miles of it, eighteen grain mills, sixteen saw mills, one fulling mill, four oil mills, five hemp mills, two boreing and grinding mills for gun barrels, and eight tanneries. . . . It may be safely affirmed, that the counties of Lancaster (in which the borough is), York and Berks are among the most vigorous in Pennsylvania, perhaps in the union, and that there are none in the state in which there are more manufactures, is beyond all question. They are all fifty miles or more, from the nearest seaport.*

Coxe's sketch of a progressive manufacturing area depicts the chief manufacturing unit as the family, not the specialized shop or factory. A good many of the manufacturing families were probably also farm families who engaged in the production of simple manufactures during slack agricultural times and seasons. Markets, although apparently competitive on the evidence of the number of manufacturers in each category, were highly localized. The primitive state of transportation was a boon to small-scale manufacturing, not a drawback; it acted like a high tariff on imported articles. Thus comparatively rural areas such as Lancaster were centers of manufacturing, while the larger seaport cities specialized in trade and imported most of their manufactured articles from overseas. American manufacturing was in and for local markets situated away from the seaports.

Two decades after Tench Coxe published his *A View of the United States of America*, he was employed by the federal government to compile a *Digest of Manufactures* of the United States based on returns

---

* Tench Coxe, *A View of the United States of America* (Philadelphia: 1794), pp. 312–313.

gathered under government instructions by the marshals of the 1810 Census. Coxe's *Digest* was the first extensive and tolerably systematic study of American manufacturing. It reported the value of manufactured products specifically enumerated as $127.7 million. Coxe added $45.1 million to this total to make up for undercounting, and also reported $25.9 million of items he termed of a "doubtful or agricultural" nature, covering such activities as flour and grist milling, saw milling, and brick making. The estimated gross value of American manufactures in 1810 was thus just under $200 million. Since the country's population was about 7.25 million, per capita production of manufactured goods was approximately $27–28 in 1810 values.

The leading manufactures specifically enumerated in the $127.7 million total for 1810 were textiles ($41.5 million), hides and skins ($17.9 million), distilled and fermented liquors ($16.5 million), iron (14.4 million), machinery ($6.1 million), wood products ($5.6 million), and cables and cordage ($4.2 million). The widespread businesses of grain milling and lumber production were excluded from these totals as being more agricultural than manufacturing activities. Most of the manufactured products of 1810 were produced in much the same way as they had been produced in Lancaster County, Pennsylvania, in the 1780s. For example, the Census returns showed that over 90 percent of textile products, the leading industry, were made in homes, not in shops or factories. In other industries two slightly more specialized types of productive organization were more common. These were the artisan shops where craftsmen labored with journeymen and apprentices, and the merchant-employer or putting-out system in which a merchant supplied raw materials to a craftsman who produced the product in his home and later turned it over to the merchant for sale. This type of manufacturing organization was more common in 1810 than in 1790, and became still more widespread in later decades as production for distant markets expanded under the influence of improved transport and communications. However, household, shop, and merchant-employer manufacturing represented the old order of making things by hand that had persisted for centuries.

The Industrial Revolution

The late eighteenth-century world witnessed a political revolution in America that gave rise to an independent United States. Great Britain opposed this revolution but was, at the same time, in the midst of revolutionary changes of a different nature—in manufacturing. Unlike political revolutions the Industrial Revolution did not have exact beginning and end points. Indeed, it is not over yet. The persistent nature of the Industrial Revolution as well as the difficulty of determining just when it began has led some scholars to question whether it was a revolution at all. It seems clear, in any case, that the way of life and standard of material welfare of the average Englishman or American two hundred years ago were very different from what they are today for the average person in any of a number of industrially developed countries. Whether revolutionary or evolutionary, modern industry has greatly advanced the productivity, and hence the value, of human labor in what, on the scale of man's history, has been a fairly brief period of time. Enormous economic, political, and social changes resulted from sustained industrial progress. It began in eighteenth-century England and has since spread in greater or lesser degrees throughout much of the world. The United States was one of the first countries to follow England's lead in developing a modern industrial sector.

What was the early Industrial Revolution of the eighteenth and nineteenth centuries? This is a complex question, but scholars today generally agree that it consisted of several major changes in the way goods were produced. Each change was first introduced in a particular line of production. Later, as their efficacy became clear, the principles involved were applied to more and more lines until virtually all manufacturing fell under their sway. One such change was the substitution of power-driven machines for human labor; the clearest illustration from the English Industrial Revolution came in cotton textile manufacturing. A second change was the substitution of inanimate for animate converters of energy; here the classic example from eighteenth-century England was the steam engine which converted the heat energy of fuels into mechanical power. A third major change characteristic of the Industrial Revolution lay in the large-scale substitution of new raw materials and fuels, chiefly minerals found in the earth, for vegetable and animal materials grown on the earth; iron and coal were leading examples from eighteenth-century England.

Each of the major innovations of the English Industrial Revolution interacted with the others. Steam engines were built of iron and burned coal; an early use was to pump mines so that more coal could be produced. Later steam engines came to be a primary source of power for a wide range of transportation and manufacturing technologies, including those of textile and iron production. Iron was used in textile machines as well as in steam engines; soon iron and its derivative products found so many uses that they became the chief raw materials and symbols of the new industrial age. These interactions were multiplied indefinitely as the principles involved in the core innovations of the Industrial Revolution were extended to more and more lines of economic activity. The result was a rather steady expansion of the output of manufactured goods at rates substantially in excess of population growth.

The Early Cotton Textile Industry in America

The first great factory industry of the English Industrial Revolution was cotton textiles. Cotton cloth imported from India became popular with English consumers in the early eighteenth century, but it was understandably less popular with the large numbers of English producers of wool and woolen cloth. The wool interests succeeded in obtaining restrictions on imports of Indian cotton goods. Nonetheless, the existence of a wide market for cotton textiles had been demonstrated; what remained for the English was to find ways of meeting it from their own production. From the 1740s to the 1780s, English inventors created a remarkable series of textile machines which greatly increased the productivity of labor in textile production. The chief inventions in yarn spinning and, somewhat later, cloth weaving were large machines requiring water power. As a result, textile production shifted out of homes and small shops and into factories located at sites where water power was available.

Americans in the 1780s were aware of the English inventions and desired to imitate the English success. However, they did not know how to build the new machines. The English, desirous of reserving the inventions for their own use, passed laws forbidding the export of the new machines and even made it illegal for persons knowledgeable in the modern technology to leave England. Nonetheless, one such person, Samuel Slater, migrated to America in 1789. One year later, in partnership with the Rhode Island merchants Almy and Brown, Slater established a cotton factory on the Blackstone River at Pawtucket, Rhode Island. The partners utilized the water-frame spinning machine developed by the English inventor Arkwright. Their business prospered and in the next quarter century, particularly after 1807 when Jefferson's embargo cut off imports from England, a number of similar ventures were founded with production centering in southern New England.

The major product of these new American cotton factories was yarn, the output of the spinning machines. The new yarn factories made great strides in supplanting household spinning, but cloth, the product of weaving, continued for the most part to be produced in households and shops on handlooms. As noted above, Tench Coxe's *Digest of Manufactures* indicated that in 1810 over 90 percent of American "products of the loom" were produced in homes.

Credit for initiating the complete transfer of cotton cloth production into factories goes to a Boston merchant, Francis Cabot Lowell. Lowell went to England from 1810 to 1812 to learn the secrets, still jealously guarded by the English, of constructing and operating power-driven looms. In this he was successful, but Lowell's contributions to American industrial development went well beyond the transfer of new technologies to the United States. More than other manufacturers of the time, Lowell realized that the improved technology was a complex and roundabout method of production requiring time and money to implement. One of his first steps upon returning from England was to persuade a group of Boston merchants to invest $100,000 in the stock of a corporation, the Boston Manufacturing Company, which would finance the development and implementation of the new techniques. The company was founded in 1813, and late in the following year Lowell and his coworker, skilled mechanic Paul Moody, constructed their first power loom.

The Boston Manufacturing Company built the first vertically integrated textile factory in the United States on the Charles River at Waltham, Massachusetts, near Boston. In the Waltham factory all of the steps in making textiles, from processing raw cotton to the production of finished cloth, were carried out in one place under a single management. The new techniques and organizational methods were quickly imitated, and large, integrated cotton factories were established along a number of rivers in New England, New York, and Pennsylvania. In the 1820s Lowell, Massachusetts, on the Merrimack River north of Boston, rapidly became the leading center of the new industry. Named for Francis Cabot Lowell, it was the first American urban place that was founded around an industry.

Cotton textile production in American factories increased at an extremely rapid pace in the two decades following the introduction of the power loom. Between 1815 and 1833 output of all cotton goods grew at a compound rate of over 16 percent per year. Over the same period cloth output alone grew at 29 percent per year as production shifted out of homes and into the factories. Prices of cotton cloth declined because the new technology was vastly more efficient in its use of resources than the handicraft methods of earlier years. Nonetheless, the supply factors of improved manufacturing techniques and falling raw cotton prices accounted for only part of the expansion of textile output. On the demand side, population and income were expanding and would have led to larger output even if prices had not declined. Transportation improvements helped further to widen the market for cloth mass-produced at centralized places. Tariffs on textile imports after 1816 also aided the new factories. All in all, the expansion of demand for American factory cloth may have outweighed the contribution of improved technology in this first great expansion of industrial output in the United States.

One reason why demand was so important in the early expansion of the cotton textile industry is that it took time to learn to build and operate the new machines on an extended scale. The people who knew how to do this were a scarce factor of production in the earliest years of the Industrial Age, and they earned substantial profits or, more properly, rents because the supply of their talents was limited. Only after machine-making and managerial skills became more widely diffused throughout the industry did textile prices fall to near the cost of production, as is the tendency of prices in a competitive market economy. In the interim the leaders of the new industry reaped substantial fortunes.

The Spread of Antebellum Manufacturing

Cotton textile manufacturing with water-powered machinery and a large labor force centralized in factories was the first truly modern industry to develop in the United States. In 1832, the *McLane Report*, a U.S. Treasury survey of American manufacturing, showed that 88 of 106 manufacturing enterprises with invested capital of $100,000 or more were textile companies. Most of these were producers of cotton cloth. The report also showed that 31 of 36 enterprises employing 250 or more workers were textile producers. The leading role of cotton manufacturing continued up to the eve of the Civil War. According to the Census of 1860, the cotton industry led all others in terms of value added—value of products less cost of raw materials—which is a measure of an industry's contribution to the total national product for any given year. Moreover, in terms of the factory organization of production, textile making far outdistanced other major industries. The average cotton factory in 1860 employed 143 wage laborers. Woolen goods production, which came next, was far behind with an average of 33 workers per establishment.

Leading American industries of 1860, ranked by value added, are shown in Table 8–1. The Census information is quite instructive as to the dual nature of American manufacturing in 1860. In the earliest decades of the republic most manufacturing, as noted earlier, was carried on in homes or in small shops, and the products were destined for consumption primarily in nearby markets. Specialization had increased substantially by 1860, but even then a number of the leading industries were still organized for the most part in small-scale producing units. Lumber, boots and shoes, flour and meal, and leather production fall into this category. Lumber and flour were used throughout the country, the former as a construction material and the latter as a basic element of nearly everyone's diet. Because both products were derived from the ubiquitous forests and farms and were rather bulky in relation to their value, it was still an efficient decision in 1860 to produce them near where they were to be consumed. Leather and its related products, boots and shoes, were more valuable in relation to their bulk, and thus could bear the cost of shipping from more centralized producing areas. The boot and shoe industry, for example, was concentrated to a great extent in New England; but up to

TABLE 8-1
Manufacturing in 1860: Leading Industries

		Value Added ($ millions)	Number of Establishments (thousands)	Hands Employed (thousands)	Number of Hands per Establishment
1.	Cotton goods	55	.8	115	143
2.	Lumber	54	20.2	76	4
3.	Boots and Shoes	49	12.5	123	10
4.	Iron	46	2.3	68	30
5.	Clothing	41	4.2	121	29
6.	Flour and Meal	40	13.9	28	2
7.	Machinery	33	1.4	41	30
8.	Leather	26	5.2	26	5
9.	Woolen Goods	25	1.2	41	33
	All Manufactures*	854	140.4	1,311	9

*Includes some mining activities.
SOURCE: Calculated from Eighth Census of the United States, 1860, vol. 3, Manufactures, (Washington, D.C.: United States Government Printing Office, 1865), pp. 733-742.

the Civil War production in relatively small shops continued to predominate over factory production.

In contrast, the factory by 1860 had made greater inroads, judging by employees per establishment, in the other leading industries. These fall into two related groups: textiles and clothing, and iron and machinery. Cotton and woolen cloth produced in factories supplanted home textile production in the decades after 1815. Since a major use of cloth was to make garments, a logical next step was the development of specialized clothing manufacturers. The invention of the sewing machine in the 1840s hastened this development. Production of ready-made clothing, however, was not based on technological improvements as dramatic as those in textile production. Consequently, even though clothing had become a leading industry by 1860, a great deal of clothing, especially women's clothing, continued to be made in the home or in small shops rather than in factories.

Iron, iron products, and machinery are widely and properly considered basic heavy industries in industrial economies. It is somewhat surprising, therefore, that as late as 1860, the average employment in individual iron-producing enterprises was far smaller than that in cotton textiles and on a par with woolen goods and clothing manufactures (see Table 8-1). To some extent the figure of thirty employees per establishment in 1860 is misleading because the category "Iron" lumps together a number of lines of manufacture. The two subcategories of pig iron production, and forged, rolled, and wrought iron products, for example, employed fifty-six and fifty-five persons per establishment, whereas in the production of castings the average was nineteen persons per establishment. Even so, much progress toward a larger scale of iron production in the individual firm was made in the last decade before the Civil War. Data from the 1850 Census indicate that there were about two and a half times as many iron enterprises in 1850 as there were in 1860, and the average employment in these firms was only ten people, as contrasted with thirty in 1860. Capital invested in the average iron enterprise nearly quadrupled in the 1850s, although in 1860 it still amounted to less than one-third of the capital invested in the average cotton mill.

The late antebellum transformation of the American iron industry to larger-scale production by individual firms is interesting because it contrasts rather sharply with the experience of the British iron industry in the first Industrial Revolution. The American cotton industry generally followed the pattern of its English predecessor, but American iron making had a different and somewhat slower development both in total production and in the scale of productive organization. What explains this?

Factors related to the fuels used in iron processing account for much of the difference in the early histories of the British and American iron industries. Before the industrial revolution pig iron was produced by smelting iron ore in charcoal-fueled furnaces, and charcoal was also widely used in refining pig iron into wrought iron, a more malleable form suited to making many iron products. In the seventeenth and eighteenth centuries wood for making charcoal became scarce in England, and in response to rising fuel costs British inventors laid the basis, during the eighteenth century, for the modern iron industry by perfecting methods of making iron and iron products with coal, which was abundant, as the primary fuel. Two English innovations were the use of coke derived from coal as the fuel for smelting ore in blast furnaces to make pig iron and the puddling process for refining pig iron into wrought iron. Both innovations allowed iron production to be concentrated in larger units.

In the United States, on the other hand, charcoal continued to be the major fuel used in iron production in the early decades of the nineteenth century. Wood was widely available in the forested eastern United States, and small iron deposits were numerous. The result was scattered, small-scale iron production by many firms which, because of their rural locations, were often called plantations rather than factories or mills. Bituminous coal for coking was available west of the Appalachian Mountains, particularly in western Pennsylvania, but the earliest deposits exploited contained impurities that resulted in low-grade iron. In addition, these coal deposits were located far from the major markets for iron in the East. By the 1850s, however, the American population had shifted westward and better grades of bituminous coking coal were discovered. This was part of the reason for the growing scale of iron-producing units in the 1850s. After the Civil War, these western coals and ores became the basis for a tremendous expansion of the American iron and steel industry along the lines pioneered by the British.

More significant for antebellum industrial development, in iron as well as a broad range of other industries, was the exploitation of the hard anthracite coal found on the eastern slope of the Alleghenies, again primarily in Pennsylvania. Though geographically closer to potential markets, the anthracite fields were in fact quite isolated in an economic sense until canals reached them during the 1820s and 1830s. There shortly followed the adoption of anthracite in all of the several stages of eastern iron production, from reheating wrought iron bars in order to fashion products, to refining pig iron into wrought iron, and finally to producing pig iron from ore in blast furnaces. In making pig iron the required technique for using anthracite—the hot blast method—was patented by an Englishman only in 1828, more than a century after the discovery of the bituminous coke-smelting process.

Anthracite coal production was insignificant in the early 1820s, but it rose to a million tons per year in the late 1830s, and to nearly four million tons by the end of the 1840s. Anthracite provided the first cheap source of mineral fuel for eastern manufacturers and urban dwellers. Makers of cast and wrought iron products were the major beneficiaries of anthracite development but other industries requiring substantial inputs of heat in their production processes were also aided. Anthracite became an important fuel for eastern steam engines, with far-reaching effects. Up until about 1840 factory production in the United States, except in textiles, was rather limited and was often carried on at water-power sites some distance from the major cities. From 1840 on the new mineral fuels allowed heat and power to be brought to population centers and thus made a major contribution both to factory organization across a wide range of industries and to the industrialization of American cities.

American manufacturing in 1860 was heavily concentrated in the northeastern part of the country. The three leading states by virtually all measures were New York, Pennsylvania, and Massachusetts. Containing about one fourth of the 1860 population, these three states accounted for approximately one half of the value added by all manufacturing. The leading positions of Massachusetts and Pennsylvania were tied to their dominant places in major industries—textiles, and boots and shoes in the former; iron and machinery in the latter. New York possessed a more diversified industrial base but was the dominant producer in the expanding ready-made clothing industry.

After the three leaders came Ohio, Connecticut, and New Jersey. The total value added by manufacturing in these states, however, barely exceeded that of Massachusetts alone and was less than that of either New York or Pennsylvania. The six leaders were contiguous states, and it is evident that antebellum America had a manufacturing belt every bit as real as the cotton belt across the deep South and the corn belt growing up in the Middle West. All three of these belts have shifted to the west since 1860, but they are still features of the economic landscape of the United States.

How significant was manufacturing in the economy of 1860? Earlier historians often viewed the antebellum years as an agrarian period with industrialization taking hold after, and in the view of some because of, the Civil War. It is true that as late as 1860—and even in 1880—more than half of the American labor force was engaged in agricultural pursuits. Yet the decline in the percentage of agricultural workers in the total labor force was rapid in earlier decades. From 1810 to 1850, the percentage fell from 84 to 55. Over the same period estimates of the percentage of American workers engaged in manufacturing on a relatively full-time basis rose from 3 to 15 percent. Thus a good fraction—something on the order of two fifths—of the decline in agriculture's share of the labor force can be viewed as a shift of workers into full-time manufacturing pursuits. The antebellum shift of workers into manufacturing pursuits was robust by later standards as well. The share of American workers in manufacturing increased to a peak of 27 percent in 1920, and declined thereafter. Clearly something more than mere modest beginnings were made in manufacturing before the Civil War.

The contribution of manufacturing to the total national product was even greater than its share of the country's labor force. It can be measured by the value added to raw materials by manufacturing processes, while the national product itself is the sum of value added by every sector of the economy. Value added by manufacturing was about 20 percent of the national product in both 1850 and 1860.

Comparison of manufacturing's share of the labor force with its contribution to national product provides a simple but significant insight into why the manufacturing sector grew so rapidly in the antebellum years. A worker in manufacturing produced, on the average, products having a greater value than he or she could produce in nonmanufacturing sectors. Well before 1860 the relatively greater productivity of manufacturing labor, as reflected in prices, wages, and profits, favored American industrial development by encouraging increasing numbers of entrepreneurs and workers to enter upon manufacturing pursuits.

Antebellum Technological Developments

The great technological advances of the nineteenth century were centered on the development of machinery, power, and the use of new materials, especially metals and mineral fuels. England's Industrial Revolution forcefully demonstrated the substantial advantages of new techniques of production in textiles, iron, and power. Americans were among the first of many peoples to benefit from borrowing the English techniques. There were also, however, some notably original contributions by ante-bellum Americans to modern technology. These led, even before the Civil War, to a reverse flow of productive knowledge across the Atlantic.

The borrowing phase of American technical development has already been touched upon at numerous points. In textile manufacturing, it was clearly epitomized in the late eighteenth century "borrowing" of the English mechanic, Samuel Slater, with his knowledge of new English spinning techniques, and in Bostonian F. C. Lowell's transfer of English power weaving methods to America in the second decade of the nineteenth century. James Watt's steam engine also migrated early to the New World. Robert Fulton's *Clermont,* the first steamboat introduced on the Hudson in 1807, was powered by an English low-pressure steam engine constructed by the firm of Boulton and Watt. Americans, however, pioneered in the development and application of high-pressure steam engines which, because of their comparatively light weight, were more suitable than the low-pressure engines for river steamboats. They also required more fuel than Watt's engine, but fuel—especially wood fuel—was abundant in the United States. An important point is illustrated: when a technology is transferred from one set of economic circumstances to another it often requires modifications for maximum economic efficiency. Early American technologists appear to have been particularly sensitive to this point and rather good at giving it effect.

Steam found its greatest American application in transportation. An 1838 report of the federal government on the scope of steam engine use in the United States indicated that 60 percent of steam power was devoted to propelling steamboats, and at that time the railroad was just beginning to exert its demand for steam as a source of tractive power. Yet stationary industrial uses were also evident. Steam engines, which were introduced into textile-making by Samuel Slater in 1828, furnished the power for an estimated 15 percent of textile production a decade later. Steam power was also employed extensively in iron making and in sugar and lumber mills in the late 1830s. Thereafter the greater availability of anthracite coal, along with a rather full exploitation of the best water power sites, encouraged rapid growth in the use of steam power in northeastern manufacturing. Water, nonetheless, remained the chief source of industrial power up to the Civil War.

Only in the smelting of iron did American producers lag well behind their British counterparts. As we have already seen, American smelters relied almost completely on charcoal before 1840 because of the nature and location of demand in relation to the nature and location of supplies of coking coal. The American iron industry much earlier had adopted the

British techniques of puddling and rolling at the refining and shaping stages of iron manufacture.

America's early and original contributions to technology came not in the great industries based on the core innovations of the English industrial revolution but rather in a group of smaller and lighter industries, and in methods of material handling having very general application. The industries affected were primarily those concerned with light metal products and woodworking. Gun making—where the important technical principle of interchangeable parts was introduced—was one of the earliest. Connecticut gun makers, including Eli Whitney, took the first steps in the earliest years of the nineteenth century by striving, generally with hand methods, to make uniform parts for the weapons they produced. The great advantage of standardization was that the finished product could be assembled by relatively unskilled labor instead of being fitted together on an individual piece basis by a skilled craftsman or gunsmith. After the gun was sold and in use, if a part wore out or became defective, it could easily be replaced with another one of the same specifications. The following decades witnessed the development of sophisticated machinery for parts making. This machinery operated with greater precision than was possible with handworking, and it could be run by nonhuman power sources, which greatly extended the scope and efficiency of machine operations. Machine operations were applied to both the metal and the wooden parts of the gun, including even the irregularly shaped gunstock which came to be made almost entirely by machine around 1820.

The principle of manufacturing goods with interchangeable parts made by sophisticated, power-driven machinery spread from gun making to a number of other industries. Among the most important in the antebellum era were watches and clocks, locks, simple fasteners such as nails, screws, nuts, and bolts, as well as sewing machines and agricultural implements. By midcentury Americans were showing their wares at European exhibitions and making such an impression that committees were formed to cross the Atlantic and visit the workshops of America. This led to orders from Europe for American goods and, more important, for the highly specialized machines that made them.

American ingenuity in making complex machinery and the sophisticated tools and machines that were used to make other machines was a critical input to the implementation of the principle of interchangeability. The antebellum decades saw specialized machine and machine-tool makers develop out of earlier, more general operations. The textile industry played an important role. During the early phases of the industry's expansion, textile companies established their own machine shops to build and repair both textile machines and the power apparatus. As the demand for textile machinery increased, some of these shops separated from their mills and joined other machine shops to form an industry of specialized machine makers. The machine shops also branched out into making nontextile equipment including not only machine tools but steam engines and railway locomotives as well. The growth of markets led to further economies as still more specialized firms emerged in each of these lines of activity. Thus machine making, which started as an adjunct of other industrial operations in the early nineteenth century, emerged as a separate industry before the Civil War, and in the twentieth century went on to become the leading American industry.

Another antebellum technical development had to do with the handling of materials. The origins of the concept of the assembly line where the product move through stages of manufacture and assembly while the workers remain relatively stationary can be found in an automated flour mill constructed by Oliver Evans, a Philadelphia inventor, in the 1780s. Grain entered the mill at one end, went through milling processes, and emerged as flour at the other end without the direct use of any labor in the intervening stages. Evans's mill does not appear to have enjoyed much success, possibly because at that early date ingenuity and capital, the chief factors in such an operation, were scarcer than labor. The idea of moving products automatically through processing stages reemerged, however, in the pork packing plants of Cincinnati some two to three decades before the Civil War. Hog carcasses were suspended from an overhead rail and moved at a steady rate past workers, each of whom performed one small specialized task in the packing process. The assembly line and interchangeable parts, early American contributions to technology, were later combined with dramatic effect in twentieth century industries such as automobile manufacturing.

What explains the success of early Americans both in adopting technologies invented by the British and in perfecting potent and original techniques on their own? Because technological change and its diffusion have played a major role in shaping the modern world and America's role in it, this question has long fascinated scholars. Some emphasize economic factors while others place more stress on social and even political characteristics of early American society. In practice, of course, it is difficult to separate such influences. Standardization of products and their mass production, for example, could be effective when a population had fairly homogeneous tastes but might also have worked because of the substantially lower product prices generated by cost economies and market competition.

Recognizing the interpretative problem, it is still fair to say that a few broad characteristics of antebellum America exerted powerful influences on the direction, if not the level, of technological change. Foremost among these characteristics was the nation's great endowment of natural resources in relation to the size of its population and of its accumulated savings. Contemporary Europeans viewed American production methods in agriculture and manufacturing as terribly wasteful of land, wood, and mineral resources. Today it is more widely recognized that such methods were a rational response to relative resource endowments. Cheap natural resources were rationally substituted for more expensive capital and labor. American techniques often reflected capital scarcity as much as labor scarcity. Early American textile machines were flimsily constructed and were made with much more wood and much less metal than were their English counterparts. Within the United States there were regional variations on the same theme. Stationary steam engines were relatively more important than water power in the West, in part because the rivers and streams there fell less rapidly than New England's, but also because steam was a more labor-intensive, less capital-using form of power than falling water, and capital was scarcer in the West than in New England.

Antebellum Americans were thus sensitive in their tinkering to the relative prices of productive factors. But the explanation of why they were that way transcends purely economic analysis. Large areas of the world have at one time or another in the last two centuries been in very much the same position with respect to factor endowments as was the United States in 1790, but have produced fewer advances in technological and economic development. Economic analysis illuminates the choices of techniques in the United States, but it cannot fully explain the level and the nature of the nation's technological achievements.

Government Assistance to Manufacturing

In the early United States direct governmental aid in the form of investment in manufacturing facilities or in the training of labor was uncommon although perhaps not altogether insignificant. The federal government underwrote part of the early development of gun making, a pioneering industry in the application of the principle of interchangeable parts. Later the government operated arsenals that manufactured weapons on that principle. Such policies were limited in scope, however, and not confined to the manufacturing sector. A few direct investments were made in transportation enterprises, and federal funds financed the first successful telegraph line in the 1840s. In transportation, communication, and banking, the direct role of state governments was much more extensive than the federal role. State and local participation in manufacturing, however, was negligible. Most of the benefits obtained from government by the manufacturing sector were therefore indirect: governments promoted institutions and activities that, while apart from manufacturing, were very useful to it.

In one area, however, government policy seemed directly attuned to the aspirations of manufacturers. That was the protective tariff. Alexander Hamilton's classic *Report on Manufactures* (1791) proposed to Congress an extensive program—the tariff was only one aspect of it—of aid to the development of manufacturing. One rationale for protection to manufactures—not clearly formulated by Hamilton although consistent with the tone of his report—is the so-called infant industry argument. An infant industry, the argument contends, needs protection if it is to exist and develop in a world where industries in other countries have already perfected modern techniques of manufacturing, management, raw material supply, and so on. Without protection, competition from the more mature industries of other countries such as Great Britain would stifle and perhaps destroy the native infant industry. When the infant eventually matures enough to compete on its own, presumably protection could be withdrawn.

American tariff policy became purposely protective in 1816, at a time when British manufacturers, who had backlogs of goods built up during the years when war interrupted their foreign trade, were underselling many of the products of domestic manufacturers. The tariff of 1816 and its successors undoubtedly alleviated some of the problems of American manufacturers, both by giving them a greater share of the domestic market and by acting to raise the prices they received. That much seems clear.

It is less than clear, however, that the actual existence of the protected industries depended on the tariff. An infant industry as vigorous as cotton textiles, which expanded its output from 1815 to 1833 at a compound rate of 16 percent per year, was unlikely to have needed the tariff for its survival. Indeed, painstaking analysts of its early growth have concluded that the tariff made almost no difference. Long ago Frank Taussig, a leading student of American tariff history, reasoned that by 1824 the textile industry was well able to stand on its own feet. More recent research by Paul David demonstrates that while productive efficiency in textiles increased over time through a process of learning by doing, the tariff on imported textiles nonetheless played a largely redundant role because the important learning effects had to do with perfecting the new technology. Once this was done—and it could have been accomplished by a free-trade policy accompanied by subsidies to a few pilot plants— the technology could have been transferred to other producers. Such a decision on the part of the federal government was far from unthinkable. By 1816 the government had already subsidized gun making and it was later to aid initial development of the telegraph. In both cases technologies perfected in subsidized pilot projects were quickly adopted by other producers.

In the case of pig iron production, on the other hand, there are indications that reductions in tariff rates beginning in 1846, from the high levels of the 1842 tariff, did in fact reduce American output significantly by stimulating increased imports. However, although many of the old charcoal smelters ceased operations, the newer anthracite smelters were much less harmed by the lower duties. These results were inconsistent with the infant industry argument for protection. They were accounted for by changes in the composition of American iron demand, more specifically by an increased demand for rails made from lower-grade iron smelted with coal and a stagnant demand for the more refined iron products that used charcoal-smelted pig iron as a raw material.

In two major industries, then, protective tariffs were far from critical in allowing the infants to mature to the point where they could survive in competition with foreign producers. Nor do tariffs appear to have served an infant-saving function in most other industries. This, of course, does not imply that tariffs had no effect on industrial growth. Tariffs increased the prices of protected goods as well as the market shares of domestic producers. Producers' profits were thus raised, which stimulated greater savings and capital formation in the protected industries. This, however, was income redistribution from consumers to producers. One would need also to know how the savings and capital-forming activities of those who bought the higher-priced protected products were affected before reaching a conclusion regarding the tariff's impact on aggregate capital formation.

Rudimentary Labor Organization

On the eve of the Civil War over half of the American labor force was engaged in farming, and many of the remaining workers were self-employed. Perhaps 70 percent of all workers worked for themselves rather than as employees of others. At the beginning of the nineteenth century the percentage of self-employed workers was even greater, probably around nine in ten. The antebellum economy was thus very different from that of later decades when a far greater percentage of the labor force came to be in the employee category.

The preponderance of self-employment in an essentially competitive economy of numerous small-scale producers meant that problems of labor organization were both less significant in an aggregate sense and of a different character than in later decades. Nonetheless, as the American economy became more diversified and as production became increasingly specialized, the labor problems of particular sectors demanded innovative solutions. The emergence of the factory system of manufacturing in textiles furnished perhaps the clearest example.

The great advantage of textile-making in factories lay in the use of sophisticated machinery that allowed labor to produce substantially greater quantities of yarn and cloth in a given time than was possible with older handicraft methods. But factories required power to run their machinery. For much of the antebellum period water was the primary power source. This restricted factory locations to sites where water power was available. The rivers of New England provided many such sites. Labor, however, was more of a constraint. Urbanization was rather limited in the United States and, in any case, many of the water power sites were in rural areas where the population was spread out and engaged in farming. For these reasons early American manufacturers faced labor supply problems of a more serious nature than those of manufacturers in more densely populated Europe.

Textile manufacturers came up with two solutions to their labor-supply problems. In southern New England and the middle states a system in which a whole family was hired to work in a textile factory grew out of the early use of child labor. When Samuel Slater opened his first cotton spinning mill in 1790, he followed the practice, familiar to him from experience in his native England, of employing children from the surrounding Rhode Island villages and countryside to operate the new machinery. Adult overseers were employed to supervise the children in the relatively simple tasks of tending the power-driven machinery. From their farm backgrounds, the new industrial workers were used to long hours of work for low renumeration and were probably easier to manage than their parents would have been. As the number of textile factories in southern New England grew, however, there were not enough children in nearby areas to man them. Slater and other mill owners therefore turned to hiring whole families and induced them to relocate in the burgeoning mill towns.

Farther north, Francis Cabot Lowell and other early textile manufacturers faced much the same labor supply problem as the southern New England firms had encountered but, having an aversion to replicating English industrial conditions, they hit upon a different solution: to hire young women, primarily farm girls, to work in the mills. The girls were induced to accept the offer of mill employment—and their parents were persuaded to allow it—by the promise of cash wages and the assurances that their living conditions away from home would be pleasant and instructive, and that their behavior would be carefully supervised both by mature factory overseers and by upright boardinghouse "mothers" in the mill towns. Most of the young women viewed the opportunity as a temporary one allowing them to get away from home and earn some money prior to settling down into married life.

By 1820 both the family and the boardinghouse systems of factory labor recruitment were well-established in America's first modern industry. Both worked well and were widely regarded as much more advanced and humane than European factory labor systems. From a modern perspective, however, they may be viewed as temporary solutions to industrial labor recruitment resulting from the unique circumstances of the early United States. By the late 1830s the extremely buoyant conditions of initial industrial development in textiles settled down to a more normal pattern of gradual expansion. Then the innovative labor systems of earlier years rather quickly evolved into something more nearly resembling European conditions. Since a fairly permanent labor force had been created, mill owners were able to abandon much of their earlier concern for the social conditions of their workers and to concentrate instead on increasing productive efficiency. Workers longed for the good old days of a slower paced and more humane industrial life, but their efforts to return to earlier practices and conditions were largely unsuccessful.

In addition to a slowdown in the growth of the market for factory textiles after the end of home production, two competitive developments in the industrial labor market undercut the earlier, more favorable position of factory workers. The growth of regional and interregional trade in agricultural products coupled with the opening up of new and fertile lands in the West subjected farmers in the older settled areas of New England and the middle states to increased competition. One option in responding to this new factor was to take up farming in the West. But a less costly decision was to abandon full-time farming and move into manufacturing employment. A second factor increasing the supply of industrial labor was the growth of immigration after the third decade of the century. Large numbers of antebellum immigrants, most of them of Irish, German, and British origin, arrived in the northeastern states and stayed there to swell the pool of industrial workers.

Increased competition for factory jobs militated against the development of an organized labor movement for industrial workers. Also, most of the jobs available required relatively little skill and many of them were filled by women and children. In 1860 cotton textiles, the nation's leading and most factory-organized industry, employed seventy-two thousand female hands and forty-three thousand male hands; many of them were children. Women were also the dominant employee group in clothing manufacturing, and they supplied a significant part of the labor used in footwear and woolen manufacturing. The importance of women and children in these leading industries, which either were already or were rapidly becoming organized along factory lines, helped to explain why industrial workers' organizations made little progress before the Civil War and indeed for many years after it. Women and children tended to view their jobs as temporary and less critical to family welfare than did male heads of families. They had less incentive to attempt to gain better working conditions and wages through organization.

The failure of labor organizations to develop among the largely unskilled or low-skilled factory workers contrasts with the emergence of such forces at earlier dates in the traditional craft trades carried out in small shops. In these lines of activity skills learned over long periods of apprenticeship and journeyman status represented a larger and more specific investment in human capital than the simpler knowledge necessary for factory employment. In the early days of the United States, these trades —a number are mentioned in the passage by Tench Coxe cited at the beginning of this chapter—were carried on for local markets. As the economy grew and markets widened, craft production became less personalized and custom work gave way to more standardized production for distant markets. The result, of course, was increased competition and less certain income and employment; craft workers responded in time-honored fashion by attempting through organized efforts to restrict production and to limit employment to members of their labor organizations.

Legal tradition frowned on such worker efforts to restrict competition, and in point of fact employers in the first decades of the United States were often successful in having labor unions declared to be unlawful conspiracies per se or illegal combinations against the public interest. Court hostility to craft workers' unions continued into the 1820s and 1830s, with special emphasis on preventing craftsmen from enforcing, by strikes or other means, their goal of a closed shop—a shop that would hire only union members. During the same period, however, the political power of laboring groups was extended by the relaxation of property requirements for voting in the chief manufacturing states. Juries, moreover, began to return verdicts of not guilty in a few labor conspiracy cases. In 1842, a Massachusetts court decision in a precedent-setting case, *Commonwealth v. Hunt*, declared that workers had the right to organize trade unions, and that unions were no longer to be regarded as illegal per se.

Craft labor organizations of the 1820s and 1830s pursued both direct economic objectives and indirect political objectives. They were less successful in the former than in the latter. In addition to the closed shop, economic objectives included higher wages, apprenticeship regulations, and shorter working hours. The hostility of the courts and the general public's aversion to strikes were among the reasons that craft unions were less than successful. But it is easy to exaggerate the importance of these factors. It is more likely that growing competition in product and labor markets played a greater role in undermining the direct economic efforts of unions, just as it had earlier given rise to the movement. The early craft union movement was largely confined to cities, mostly in the East, at a time when trade was becoming less and less local. If members of a craft union in one city went on strike for one or more objectives, goods could be brought in from another place. Recognizing this competitive threat, some craft unions attempted in the mid-1830s to develop wider regional or national organizations, but without much success. Depressed economic conditions in the late 1830s and early 1840s put an end to such efforts and even undermined the effectiveness of local unions; many of them simply disappeared.

After the depression of 1839–43 the trade union movement revived during periods of prosperity before the Civil War, only to decline when panic and depressed economic conditions returned. Craft workers, who had formed the earliest labor organizations, were becoming a smaller part of the labor force. Industrial labor, in factories, in mills, and in the scattered workshops of the putting-out system, became much more important in terms of numbers. The two groups of workers were very different in their ways of work and in organization, but they were partially successful in achieving one common economic objective, reduction in hours of work. The more organized craft unions led the way by negotiating or striking for a ten-hour workday in many places before 1860. The federal government provided an important fillip to the movement for reduced hours in 1840, when President Van Buren put into effect the ten-hour day for federal employees. In the late 1840s and early 1850s some states passed ten-hour laws applying to industrial labor, although all contained loopholes. Nonetheless, hours were gradually reduced from the sunrise-to-sunset system of earlier years, and by 1860 an eleven-hour workday was in effect at many factories. Interestingly, workers sometimes willingly accepted wage reductions in order to gain shorter hours, an early illustration of the pervasive, long-term tendency of labor to value increments of leisure more highly than increments of goods as incomes rise in a growing economy.

In politics the early labor movement enjoyed more success even though relatively few labor candidates were elected to important offices. Rather, success came when workers added their organized voices to those of reform-minded groups who sought to implement or extend free public education, to abolish imprisonment for failure to pay debts punctually, to protect workers against employers who defaulted on wages due, and to find solutions to other problems having a particular incidence on the laboring classes. Of these reform movements the one to increase educational opportunities is most interesting from the point of view of progress in wealth and welfare.

Education and Human Capital

Studies of modern economic growth undertaken during the past two decades have shown that substantial fractions of the growth over time in total national product cannot be wholly accounted for by growth in conventionally measured inputs of the traditional productive factors—labor, capital, and land. That is, the growth of man-hours or man-years of labor, of real capital stocks, and of acres of land used in production, when analyzed in the context of the economic theory of production, do not explain all of the growth of total output. The unexplained residual in measured economic growth, sometimes referred to as "productivity" or "technical progress," is in part the result of growing specialization and efficiency of economic organization, as improvements in transportation, communication, and information extend markets and make them more competitive. But the growth in productivity also derives from improvements in the *quality* of the productive factors, as labor forces gain more knowledge and as capital equipment increasingly embodies the most up-to-date advances in technology.

Since labor is an economy's most important factor of production—returns to labor typically make up two thirds to three fourths of an economy's total income—special attention is often given to the conditions that make labor more productive. One of these is the quantity and quality of the tools, or capital equipment, with which labor works. A major reason why workers in developed economies are more productive than their counterparts in underdeveloped economies is that the former have more and better tools. It is also apparent, however, that the quality of an economy's tools as well as the efficiency with which those tools are employed in productive processes depend in an important way on the quality of the labor force itself.

We are aware today that the skills and educational attainments of the American labor force are high in comparison with those of most other countries. Was this an old and distinguishing characteristic of labor in the American economy? Most indications point to an affirmative answer. In terms of both literacy and school enrollment rates—the fraction of student-age people actually attending school—the United States ranked close to the top of all nations surveyed during the years before the American Civil War. And this was true despite the institutional barrier of slavery which kept most black children from enjoying the benefits of formal schooling. Concentrating on the white population alone usually raises the United States to the first rank among nations in terms of literacy and schooling. The Census of 1850, for example, showed that only 10 percent of the white population of the United States was illiterate and that over half of the white population of school age attended school. Only Germany and Denmark were at approximately the same levels of literacy and school enrollment. In contrast, Britain and France, two of the most highly developed of the world's economies in the middle of the nineteenth century, lagged well behind the United States in terms of educational opportunities for the masses.

These findings should, of course, be amplified and placed in perspective. The provision of education varied substantially between various sections of the United States. In terms of enrollment rates New England was far and away the leader in the antebellum years with 75 to 80 percent of its student-age population attending school from 1840 to 1860. Next came the middle states, although by 1860 the states of the North Central region had caught up with the Middle Atlantic section. The southern section lagged behind, even when the slave population was excluded, but nonetheless exhibited large increases in enrollment rates in the last two antebellum decades.

The evidence that well before the Civil War, in the words of economist Albert Fishlow, "the United States probably was the most literate and education conscious country in the world," * should not, however, blind us to the fact that by modern standards the level of educational attainment was rather low. At the close of the antebellum era in the country as a whole the average annual number of days of school attendance per white person of school age was only forty. This figure is less than a third of modern-day levels. Yet it represented substantial progress in the antebellum era, particularly in the last decades. In 1840 the standard was twenty days, or only half of the 1861 level, while around 1800 it was only fourteen days.

As the American economy became more complex and lost its early overwhelmingly agricultural orientation, the need for a more highly educated populace made itself felt. The northeastern states, the first to industrialize, were foremost in extending general educational opportunity. As English observers sent in the 1850's to study American technology noted:

> The compulsory educational clauses adopted in the laws of most of the States, and especially those of New England, by which some three months of every year must be spent at school by the young operative under 14 or 15 years of age, secure every child from the cupidity of the parent, or the neglect of the manufacturer. . . . This lays the foundation for that wide-spread intelligence which prevails amongst the factory operatives of the United States. . . . The skill of hand which comes of experience is, notwithstanding present defects, rapidly following the perceptive power so keenly awakened by early intellectual training.†

Education to an increasing extent became a public concern and, at the lower levels, compulsory. By 1860 over one half of expenditures on formal education were public. The public stake in education reflected a recognition that its benefits extended beyond those reaped by the individual student. In an economic, as well as in a political and a social, sense the return to society from investment in education exceeded the private return to individuals. Hence, the decision was made for greater public involvement in providing formal schooling. Manufacturers, mindful of the industrial economy's need for adaptable and reliable workers, were often at the forefront of the movement for public education. To its credit, the early

---

* Albert Fishlow, "The American Common School Revival: Fact or Fancy?" in Henry Rosovsky, ed., *Industrialization in Two Systems* (New York: John Wiley, 1966), p. 49.

† As quoted by Stuart Bruchey, *The Roots of American Economic Growth 1607–1861* (New York: Harper & Row, 1968), p. 179.

labor movement in the United States also was an important force in giving expression and political backing to this important contributor to economic and social life in the age of industry.

Conclusion

The beginnings of industrialization in the United States in the early nineteenth century altered the pattern of American economic development that had prevailed during the first two centuries of European settlement. Foreign commerce, including trade in the products of commercial agriculture, gave way to factory industry as the driving force of economic development. Mechanical, chemical, and power-driven techniques began to turn out an ever-growing flow of manufactured products at declining real cost. Urban manufacturing centers emerged and began to sprawl, as both employers and workers realized the advantages of locating near other firms and industries. The new urban-industrial way of life led to institutional innovations that helped to sustain it. Of these, mass public education was perhaps the most important. In the short run it inculcated basic skills and served to socialize future workers, both native and foreign-born, to industrial society; in the long run it laid the groundwork for continuing advances in science, technology, and organization as applied to production. By 1860 industrialization was well established in the United States. Its greatest progress, however, was yet to come.

SUGGESTED READINGS

The most comprehensive discussion of American manufacturing before the Civil War is given by Victor S. Clark, *History of Manufactures in the United States 1607–1860* (Washington, D.C.: Carnegie Institution, 1916). Insights into premodern manufacturing can be gained from Rolla M. Tryon, *Household Manufactures in the United States, 1640–1860* (Chicago: University of Chicago Press, 1917); and Tench Coxe, "Digest of Manufactures," 13th Congress, 2nd Session (January 1814), in *The New American State Papers—Manufactures*, vol. 1 (Wilmington, Del.: Scholarly Resources, 1972), pp. 160–410. Cotton textiles, iron, and steam engineering are often termed the core industries of the industrial revolution. For early American developments in cotton manufacturing, see Caroline F. Ware, *The Early New England Cotton Manufacture* (Boston: Houghton Mifflin, 1931) and, for more economic analysis, Robert Brooke Zevin, "The Growth of Cotton Textile Production After 1815," in Robert William Fogel and Stanley L. Engerman, eds., *The Reinterpretation of American Economic*

History (New York: Harper and Row, 1971), chap. 10. On iron, see Peter Temin, *Iron and Steel in Nineteenth-Century America: An Economic Inquiry* (Cambridge, Mass.: M.I.T. Press, 1964), and Robert W. Fogel and Stanley L. Engerman, "A Model for the Explanation of Industrial Expansion during the Nineteenth Century: With an Application to the American Iron Industry," *Journal of Political Economy*, 77 (May/June 1969), 306–328. On steam power, see Peter Temin, "Steam and Waterpower in the Early 19th Century," *Journal of Economic History*, 26 (June 1966), 187–205. The paper by Alfred D. Chandler, Jr., "Anthracite Coal and the Beginnings of the Industrial Revolution in the United States," *Business History Review*, 46 (Summer 1972), 141–181, provides a valuable analysis of the impact of a new energy source on manufacturing. Locational aspects of manufacturing development are treated by the geographer Allen R. Pred, *The Spatial Dynamics of United States Urban-Industrial Growth, 1800–1914: Interpretive and Theoretical Essays* (Cambridge, Mass.: M.I.T. Press, 1966). Finally, for an excellent short survey of developments in cotton, iron, and manufacturing in general, see the chapter "Manufacturing," in Lance Davis, et al., *American Economic Growth: An Economist's History of the United States* (New York: Harper & Row, 1972), chap. 12.

A valuable and readable introduction to the role of technology is Nathan Rosenberg's *Technology and American Economic Growth* (New York: Harper & Row, 1972). More advanced analytical studies, including evaluations of the effects of tariffs on manufacturing development, may be found in Paul David, *Technical Choice, Innovation and Economic Growth: Essays on American and British Experience in the Nineteenth Century* (Cambridge, Eng.: Cambridge University Press, 1975).

The recent book by Merritt Roe Smith, *Harpers Ferry Armory and the New Technology* (Ithaca: Cornell University Press, 1978) offers interesting insights into both economic and social aspects of the introduction of new techniques. F. W. Taussig's *The Tariff History of the United States*, 8th ed. (New York: G. P. Putnam's Sons, 1931) remains a valuable study of a particular form of government aid to manufacturing.

On the role of education in improving the quality of the American labor force see Douglass C. North, "Capital Formation in the United States During the Early Period of Industrialization: A Reexamination of the Issues," in Robert William Fogel and Stanley L. Engerman, eds., *The Reinterpretation of American Economic History* (New York: Harper & Row, 1971), chap. 21, and two papers by Albert Fishlow, "The Common School Revival: Fact or Fancy," in Henry Rosovsky, ed., *Industrialization in Two Systems: Essays in Honor of Alexander Gerschenkron* (New York: John Wiley, 1966), pp. 40–67, and "Levels of Nineteenth-Century American Investment in Education," *Journal of Economic History*, 26 (December 1966), 418–436. Findings on the early motives behind mass public education are given by Alexander J. Field, "Educational Reform and Manufacturing Development in Mid-Nineteenth-Century Massachusetts," *The Journal of Economic History*, 36 (March 1976), 263–266.

CHAPTER 9

—

New Markets and Methods in Domestic and Foreign Commerce

For the young United States of 1790–1860 the transportation revolution and increased specialization in agriculture, finance, and manufacturing were part and parcel of a great economic historical theme—the growth of markets. These developments bear witness to the simple but profound truth of Adam Smith's dictum that the division of labor is limited by the extent of the market. In this chapter we turn to a closer examination of markets themselves. How did commercial activity in the United States evolve over the first seven decades of government under the Constitution? What were the major types of goods in trade? How were they marketed? And what did commerce contribute to economic growth during these decades?

Foreign trade was the dynamic factor in the economy of the colonial era and it continued in this role for nearly two decades after 1790. After the embargo and nonintercourse policies during the War of 1812 crippled foreign commerce, this element of the nation's economic activity revived and resumed expansion, with some interruptions, up to the Civil War. But after the return of peace to America and Europe in 1815 the dynamic economic role earlier played by foreign trade increasingly shifted toward domestic commerce. Barriers to domestic trade were progressively overcome, domestic markets for all types of American products were widened and deepened, and trade itself became more specialized. One must look at this process of extending domestic markets and trade specialization to find the origins of modern economic growth in the United States.

Foreign Commerce

COMPARATIVE ADVANTAGES OF THE UNITED STATES

Virtually all trade—whether between individuals, regions, or nations—is based on the principle of comparative advantage or relative cost. If individual or nation A can produce and market a good (or service) X at a lower relative cost than individual or nation B, then it is to B's advantage to cease producing X and to buy it from A. Since the principle is based on relative cost, there must be some good (or service) Y that B can produce and market at a lower cost than A. If A desires to have some Y, it is to A's advantage to buy it from B. These circumstances establish the basis for trade between A and B, and with trade each can specialize in making and selling the good for which it has the lower relative cost. The economic theory of markets and trade shows that both A and B will be better off with trade than without it.

What determines whether A or B has the lower relative cost of producing and marketing a particular good? In general, relative cost is based on a combination of innate and acquired characteristics of the respective producers. In the case of individuals it is well-established that both heredity and environment (for example, upbringing, formal education, and experience from on-the-job training) lead to differences in qualitative and quantitative production capabilities. Nations do not differ much from individuals in this respect. They are endowed with different combinations of economic resources, and they make decisions on how to allocate these resources. Resource endowments of nations in this sense are similar to the hereditary characteristics of individuals, while allocative decisions in historical time correspond to the individual's response to his environment. For both individuals and nations it is a difficult task to disentangle the hereditary and the environmental factors, and to attribute to each a certain share of whatever success, economic or other, they enjoy. But tentative generalizations are possible.

In the case of the early United States, with a European-skilled population, endowment played a major role in shaping the nation's trade with other countries. In terms of the classical economic resources—land, labor and capital—the United States was well-endowed with the first resource and relatively much less well endowed with the latter two. Consequently the United States had low costs, relative to its foreign trading partners, in the making and the selling of products that were intense in their use of natural resources. These included, as we have seen, the great staple crops of agriculture, and also the products of the forest and the ocean. In an era of wooden sailing ships when the seas were primary avenues of commerce, this happy conjunction of farm, forest, and ocean resources made the United States one of the world's great maritime nations.

The important insights that an understanding of American resource endowments can bring to the study of the foreign trade of the early U.S. cannot, however, explain all of the features of commercial evolution. In spite of favorable natural resource endowments the United States around 1790 was in the doldrums with respect to foreign commerce. Then a protracted period of trading prosperity set in and carried the nation to undreamed of heights of economic well-being in the first decade of the nineteenth century. To understand this sequence of events one must look at changes in the environment of the young nation rather than at its resource endowments.

TRADE AND PROSPERITY, 1793–1807

After the Revolution an independent United States lost the trading advantages enjoyed in colonial times. Great Britain was the chief buyer of American products but the annual value of United States exports to Britain was lower throughout the 1780s and early 1790s than it had been prior to the Revolution. British bounties and trade preferences, the pleasant features of colonial commerce, had disappeared, and the restrictive navigation policies of the colonial era, which continued after the Revolution, were found to be even less pleasant when one was no longer a member of the British Empire. Moreover, other European nations followed the British lead in limiting American access to their markets both at home and in their colonies. Independent Americans thus found that political decisions over which they had little control restricted the new nation's ability to pursue its comparative economic advantages in producing land-intensive commodities and in carrying the trade of other nations in American ships.

The dim economic prospects facing Americans during President Washington's first administration were altered in 1793 by two important events, one foreign and the other domestic. In Europe war broke out between Great Britain and revolutionary France, and in the United States Eli Whitney invented the cotton gin. Warfare between the two great powers of Europe lasted, with brief interludes, for more than two decades. It involved most of the countries of Europe and ultimately the United States itself. But between 1793 and the embargo year of 1808 the European wars created a great demand for traditional goods and services in international commerce that the United States, as a neutral country, was in a unique position to supply. The cotton gin came at a time when the demand for cotton, as a result of England's Industrial Revolution, was growing by leaps and bounds. Again, the United States, with its great southern territory suitable for growing cotton, was in an excellent position to meet the demand.

These sudden and favorable changes in the economic prospects of the United States are reflected in data on the quantity, value, and composition of American exports of goods and services. The total value of all exports of goods from the United States increased from about $20 million in the early 1790s to $108 million in the peak year of 1807. On the average exports grew at a rate of about 10 percent per year in value terms. The gain derived from both increased quantities and rising prices.

Rapid growth in the demand for U.S. exports should be placed in the perspective of the size of the American economy at the time. Estimates of the economy's gross product during the two decades from 1790 to 1810 are rather rough. However, if one accepts them, exports were in the range of 10 to 15 percent of gross national product. Such a level may not seem of especially great economic importance, but there are at least two reasons for suspecting that it was. In the first place, when better data on American national product in other periods are available —beginning in the late 1830s—they imply that exports were a significantly smaller fraction, some 6 to 7 percent, of total national product. Second, the most numerous contributors to the national product in the 1790–1810 period were self-subsisting farmers who seldom engaged in monetary transactions. Therefore, in relation to the part of national product passing through markets, exports bulked much larger than 10 to 15 percent.

What goods did the United States export in this period when foreign commerce played the dynamic role in the economy? Goods produced in the United States were of somewhat less importance than goods gathered in other places and re-exported from the United States. Re-exports grew from an inconsequential three-tenths of a million dollars in 1790 to nearly sixty million dollars in 1807. The re-export trade loomed so large because the ships of warring European nations, save for Britain, were removed from foreign commerce. By first carrying goods from all over the world to the United States and then re-exporting them, American merchants and seamen turned these products into exports of a neutral country which thus were less liable to seizure on the high seas by European belligerents.

Exports of products produced within the United States grew from twenty million dollars in 1790 to forty-nine million dollars in 1807. Only half of the increase consisted in exports of the traditional products of American farms and forests: foodstuffs, tobacco, lumber, and naval stores. The other half, cotton, was new. In 1790 the U.S. exported only 189 thousand pounds of cotton; in 1807, cotton exports of 66 million pounds were valued at more than fourteen million dollars.

Prosperity generated by the booming export sector led Americans to increase their imports of foreign goods dramatically. The value of imports destined for American consumption (rather than for re-export) rose from twenty-four million dollars in 1790 to eighty-two million dollars in 1807. Imported goods consisted largely of the same products imported in colonial times, namely manufactured goods from Europe and tropical and subtropical foodstuffs and beverages. Innovative Yankee traders also opened up a lucrative trade with the Far East in these years. In each of these cases the United States was consuming foreign products that it could not produce at all or could produce only at substantially greater costs than those of foreign sellers.

If one glances at the figures on the value of domestically produced exports and on imports destined for domestic consumption in 1790 and 1807, it is apparent that the balance of merchandise trade was, in mercantilist terms, unfavorable to the United States. In other words, the value of imports consumed by Americans exceeded the value of exports produced by Americans. Indeed, an unfavorable balance of merchandise trade was typical in these years, as it had been in colonial times and would continue to be for much of the nineteenth century.

There are a number of ways that such an unfavorable merchandise balance can be financed. An important way used in the years 1790 to 1807 was the net income of Americans from providing shipping services to their compatriots and to foreigners. From 1800 to 1812 American shipping earnings net of freight charges paid by foreign shippers ranged from eighteen to forty-two million dollars per year, with the peak coming in 1807. Such levels of net shipping earnings were not characteristic of earlier years (in 1790 net shipping earnings were less than six million dollars), and they were seldom seen again until the Civil War, despite further growth in the nation's foreign trade. The high level of shipping earnings reflected in part an increase in shipping capacity: the total tonnage of American ships engaged in foreign trade increased from 346 thousand in 1790 to 981 thousand in 1810. Also important were rises in ocean freight rates and a more intense utilization of existing tonnage. Earnings from shipping allowed Americans to import and consume substantially more goods, in value terms, than they themselves produced and exported.

American merchants led the way in the commercial expansion of 1793–1807, and they were its prime beneficiaries. These merchants, located mainly in the great port cities of Boston, New York, Philadelphia, and Baltimore, were much less specialized than were later merchants. This was perhaps an advantage in that it gave merchants the experience and flexibility to adapt to the rapid changes in the environment of foreign and domestic commerce. In addition to dealing in both exports and imports and handling both wholesale and retail trade, many of these diversified merchants engaged in commercial credit and insurance activities as well as shipping and ship-owning. The port-city merchants, strategically located at the centers of commercial activity, were the chief decision makers and risk takers of the early American economy. Their ingenuity, together with the boom in foreign trade between 1793 and 1807, allowed many of them to accumulate great wealth.

AMERICAN MERCHANT SHIPPING

Americans today tend to forget that in decades before the Civil War the United States was a leading maritime nation of the world. The nation's prominent position on the seas resulted from its comparative advantage in building and operating wooden sailing ships and from the rapid growth of its domestic and foreign commerce. Around the time of the Civil War, however, American merchant shipping began to decline both absolutely (in terms of tonnage) and relatively with respect to other nations, especially Great Britain. From 1800 to 1840 between 80 and 90 percent of the United States exports and imports were carried by American ships. By 1860 this proportion had declined to less than 70 percent.

There were two basic reasons for the turn of American maritime fortunes. In the first place, the British developed a technological superiority and comparative advantage in building and operating both sailing and steam-powered ships made of iron and steel. These new ships were more efficient economically than the old wooden ships and began in rapid fashion to replace them on the seas. Second, within the United States domestic commerce had grown rapidly relative to foreign trade, and a newer and far more adaptable means of moving goods and people, the railroad, eroded the former superiority of water transportation on ocean, river, and canal.

Some trends in the structure of the American merchant fleet in its heyday before the Civil War are shown in Table 9–1. Total tonnage and tonnage of vessels engaged in foreign trade increased at annual rates of 5 to 6 percent between 1790 and 1810 under the stimulus of booming foreign trade. Then a period of moderate decline in total tonnage set in for two decades. The reason for this decline is apparent in the drop of foreign-trade tonnage from 1810 to 1820. Carrying capacity built up before 1810 was underutilized during the embargo and war years from 1807 to 1815. After the war freight rates fell sharply, discouraging shipbuilding. By 1830 freight rates were only about one third of their level fifteen years earlier. Declining freight rates resulted primarily from greater competition as the ships of European maritime nations returned to the seas after peace was restored in 1815.

Within the United States tonnage of vessels engaged in coastwise and internal trade increased right on through the troubled decade 1810–20, and in both 1820 and 1830 domestic tonnage was on a par with that engaged in foreign trade. From 1830 on coastwise and internal tonnage (excluding the tonnage in fishing and whaling) surpassed foreign-trade

TABLE 9-1
Merchant Fleet of the United States, 1790-1860
(in thousands of tons)

| Year | Total Tonnage | Major Classes | | Trade in Which Engaged | | |
		Steam	Sailing	Foreign	Coastwise and Internal	Fisheries
1790	478	—	478	346	104	28
1800	972	—	972	667	272	32
1810	1,425	1	1,424	981	405	39
1820	1,280	22	1,258	584	588	108
1830	1,192	64	1,127	538	517	138
1840	2,181	202	1,978	763	1,177	241
1850	3,535	526	3,010	1,440	1,798	298
1860	5,354	868	4,486	2,379	2,645	330

SOURCE: U.S. Bureau of Census, Historical Statistics of the United States, Colonial Times to 1957 (Washington, D.C.: 1960), p. 445.

tonnage. The tonnage data thus reflect rather clearly the rising relative importance of domestic trade in the commercial activity of the country.

In 1860, despite the inroads of steam, the total sailing-ship tonnage of the American fleet was still over five times the steam tonnage. Most American vessels, whether sail or steam-powered, used wood as their primary construction material. The iron horse and the iron ship dealt this great American merchant fleet of wood and sail a devastating blow in subsequent decades.

Tonnage data by themselves do not adequately describe the capacity of a fleet. The productivity of the antebellum merchant fleet grew much more rapidly than its tonnage for a number of reasons. Suppression of piracy reduced both gunnery and manpower requirements on existing ships and thus increased cargo-carrying capacity. Through better hull and rigging design, ships increased in both size and speed. A famous example of improved design in this period is the clipper ship, the fastest large sailing vessel ever built. Between the 1830s and 1860s clippers dominated shipping on long-haul routes where time was of the essence—for example, in the China trade and in the California trade during the gold rush.

Also important in improving shipping productivity were growing markets and trade. Larger markets meant that ships spent less time gathering and unloading cargoes in ports. They therefore could make more voyages per year. Growing volume of trade also led to better load factors for ships, as did increases in immigration to the United States. In earlier days of smaller markets and low immigration, ships carrying the bulky primary products of the New World to the Old often returned largely in ballast.

Ocean trade before 1815 was not sufficiently great or settled in its patterns to encourage the development of regularly scheduled sailings by specialized shippers; instead merchant-owned and tramp ships moved irregularly in whatever directions seemed to promise the greatest trading profits. After 1815 shipping lines were formed to offer regularly scheduled sailings on major routes. Wooden packet ships dominated this business for some two decades, but then began to give way to more efficient steamships.

The most important result of shipping productivity gains was a drop in freight rates. As already noted, increased competition in shipping after 1815 reduced freight rates to about one third of their 1815 levels by 1830. Freight rates on U.S. exports continued to fall after 1830. Because of its great economic importance to the United States, cotton furnishes a good example of the effect of falling freight rates. During the 1820s some 10 percent of the delivered price of American cotton in England was a freight charge; by the 1850s this freight factor was reduced to less than 3 percent. Falling ocean freight rates thus increased market efficiency and stimulated greater production by making the prices that consumers paid more nearly equal to prices that producers received. While not as dramatic as the drop in freight rates over land in this period, the drop in ocean rates was nonetheless substantial.

EXPORTS, IMPORTS, AND THE BALANCE OF PAYMENTS

The year 1815 marked the end of a quarter century during which external political conditions first created a boom for American trade and shipping and then a depression. From 1815 until 1860 the foreign trade of the United States was carried on in a more peaceful atmosphere where economic rather than geopolitical factors exerted the major influence. Re-export trade declined substantially from the lofty levels reached in the years before 1808. American traders increasingly concentrated on exporting products of U.S. origin and importing products destined for consumption in the United States. What American products did foreigners buy in these years? Who were the chief customers? And what were the origins and nature of imports from abroad?

The comparative advantage of the young United States in agricultural products is clear from data on exports. Cotton was far and away the leading export commodity. It accounted for 39 percent of the value of commodity exports as early as the years 1816–20. After rising to 63 percent in 1836–40, cotton's share fell to 54 percent during 1856–60. If for these same five-year periods one adds to King Cotton's export share the combined shares of tobacco, wheat and flour, corn and cornmeal, rice, and beef and pork products, the total export share of these predominantly agricultural products was 78 percent in 1816–20, 81 percent in 1836–40, and 80 percent in 1856–60. Exports of domestic manufacturers, in contrast, were only 7, 9, and 12 percent, respectively, of total merchandise exports in the three periods. Throughout the antebellum years, then, agriculture was by far the economy's largest source of exports.

The nation's chief foreign customers from 1815 to 1860 were Britain and France. Britain alone, with its great cotton textile industry exerting the major demand, absorbed about one half of all American exports, and France took about one seventh. The West Indies and South America were important customers, especially in the earlier part of the period when they bought about a quarter of U.S. exports. By the 1850s, however, the share of these lands was much reduced. Exports to Canada and to European countries other than England and France rose to offset most of the relative decline in demand from Latin America.

The geographical pattern, although not the content, of American imports was rather similar to that of exports. From 1815 to 1860 Britain and France together supplied over one half of U.S. imports. The West Indies and Brazil on an average supplied another 20 percent. From the Europeans the United States obtained a variety of manufactured goods; textiles alone (cotton, wool, linen, and silk goods) represented a significant portion of products imported from Europe and also, in a smaller amount of trade, from the Orient. Sugar and coffee were the chief imports from Latin America. It is apparent that the import emphasis of antebellum Americans was on consumer goods.

Americans' tastes for imported merchandise outran their ability to pay for these imports by exporting American products in most of the years between 1790 and 1860. The exceptions occurred primarily during periods of domestic economic depression when falling American incomes reduced import demand sharply while commodity exports remained relatively stable. The relationship between exports and imports of merchandise, given in Figure 9–1, indicates the prevailing unfavorable balance of trade.

How were these trade deficits financed? Special circumstances were important in some periods. Before 1815, as we have seen, political conditions in Europe threw much of the world's carrying trade into the ships of American merchants and seamen. Shipping earnings were so great in the early years of the republic that they allowed the United States not only to cover its merchandise trade deficit, but also to pay interest on the country's debts to foreigners and even to reduce these debts moderately. Another such special factor became important during the 1850s. Exports of California gold in that decade by themselves covered over three fourths of the merchandise trade deficit.

In a majority of the years from 1790 to 1860 earnings from shipping and from exports of gold and silver were not sufficient to offset the American *payments* deficits with respect to the rest of the world. In addition

FIGURE 9-1

Merchandise Exports and Imports of the U.S., 1790-1860

(in millions of dollars)

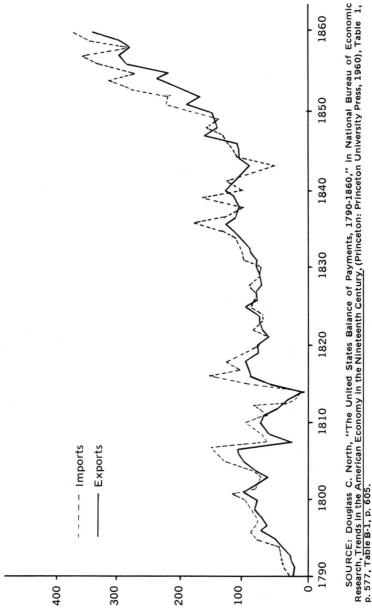

SOURCE: Douglass C. North, "The United States Balance of Payments, 1790-1860," in National Bureau of Economic Research, Trends in the American Economy in the Nineteenth Century, (Princeton: Princeton University Press, 1960), Table 1, p. 577, Table B-1, p. 605.

to importing more merchandise than they exported, Americans owed money to foreigners for other reasons. Expenditures of Americans traveling abroad often exceeded those of foreigners who came to the United States, either temporarily or to stay. And in every year of these seven decades Americans were committed to paying net amounts of interest and dividends to foreigners who had invested in American enterprises and governments. The resulting payments deficits with respect to the rest of the world were made up by a flow of capital from abroad to the United States. This important aspect of the nation's early economic history merits separate treatment.

Between 1790 and 1860 net foreign capital invested in the United States grew from about $70 million to over $380 million. Such an amount is rather trivial when compared with the investments Americans made in their own country during these decades. But the flow of foreign capital to the United States was not uniform over time. In some periods the flow was small or even negative, while in others it played an important role in underwriting both geographic and economic expansion. The motives of foreign investors were diverse, but for the most part they were responding to the higher investment return that could be offered by a young and developing nation deficient in capital resources.

British investors were by far the most important foreign creditors of the United States. There were two basic reasons for their interest in America. First, as we have already seen, Britain throughout the antebellum era was the pre-eminent trading partner of the United States. With trade goes finance. In the earliest days of the American republic domestic financial institutions were relatively undeveloped; American merchants dealing in exports and imports relied to a great extent on British merchants and bankers to finance their trade. Of the seventy million dollars estimated indebtedness of Americans to foreigners in 1790, probably the greatest part took the form of these mercantile credits. Mercantile credit supplied by the British to American importers and exporters continued to play an important role in the foreign trade of the United States even as the young nation developed its own banking and financial system.

The second reason for British interest in American investments has more to do with Britain's own economic history. The industrial and agricultural revolutions which swept across the British landscape in the late eighteenth and early nineteenth centuries created a tremendous amount of private wealth. Capital accumulation in Britain drove down domestic investment returns and spurred Britishers of property to search for higher returns abroad. The United States in the nineteenth century was just one among many foreign lands to benefit from their quest. British investors sought both steady incomes and capital gains from long-term securities or portfolio investments. Mercantile credit, in contrast, was short-term in nature and designed to facilitate trade.

While American merchants were the primary beneficiaries of foreign short-term credits in the antebellum decades, the focus of foreign long-term investments varied. In the first decades issues of the federal government attracted most of the foreign funds. Alexander Hamilton's provision for funding the national debt impressed foreign investors, and U.S. bonds began to move overseas. Dutch bankers played a leading role in floating the government's debt in 1791 and also in 1803, when funds were raised to purchase the Louisiana Territory from France. But these federal securities together with much of the stock of the Bank of the United States soon found their way to Britain. By 1805 the famed British banking house of Baring by itself handled the payment of interest and dividends on some twenty-eight million dollars of federal securities and bank stock. Most of these payments were to English investors. At the time they represented the return on about one third of all the indebtedness of Americans to foreigners. Other estimates for the years 1803 and 1807 show foreigners owning over one half of the entire debt of the federal government.

Aggregate indebtedness of Americans to foreigners declined in the years just prior to the War of 1812, but rose from sixty-three to one hundred million dollars in the postwar trade boom of 1815 to 1819. Much of the increase was in mercantile credit. Foreign capitalists also invested heavily in the stock of the second Bank of the United States and in New York State bonds issued to build the Erie Canal. But federal securities continued to remain the favorites of foreign investors. In 1828 British and other continental investors held some nineteen million dollars of federal bonds, about one third of the fifty-eight million dollars outstanding at the end of that year.

The success of both the Erie Canal and the federal government's efforts to retire the national debt conjoined in the 1830s to produce an unparalleled episode in the annals of foreign investment in the United States. The Erie demonstrated to foreigners the favorable economic prospects of the country, while the unprecedented act of paying off the national debt created euphoria over American creditworthiness—and cash to be reinvested as well. In this propitious environment foreign investment in the United States grew from seventy-five million dollars in 1830 to almost three hundred million dollars in 1839. Much of this capital inflow from abroad went into transportation improvements and banking enterprises sponsored by state governments. But the newer canals were much less successful as investments than the Erie, and several state governments were fiscally less responsible than the federal government. When the bubble burst, first in 1837 and then again in 1839, foreign investors began to take a ferocious beating. In 1841 and 1842 nine American states ceased paying interest on their debts, large amounts of which were foreign-held.

Three of these—Florida, Mississippi, and Michigan—even repudiated some or all of their debts. Moreover, the Bank of the United States, reconstituted under a Pennsylvania charter after 1836, failed in 1841, at a time when nearly twenty million dollars of its thirty-five million dollars of stock were in the hands of European investors. The image of America was tarnished. During the 1840s the nation's foreign indebtedness fell from $297 million to $193 million. Loans were not renewed and American securities were sent back across the Atlantic to be liquidated.

Then in the 1850s the inflow of capital began again. A number of factors renewed the earlier confidence of foreign investors. Discovery of gold in California was one. It stimulated a great interest in America's natural wealth. In addition, the railroads, with their voracious appetite for capital, had begun to demonstrate their worth as investments. English ironmasters exported great quantities of rails to America in the 1850s and often accepted railway securities as payment. Increasing urbanization created a further demand for investment in capital improvements and corresponding supplies of municipal bonds. And as gold flowed into the money stocks of the United States and other nations, prices rose and trade expanded, creating further demands for mercantile credits. With so many factors turning favorable, it is scarcely surprising that foreign capital flowed again to the United States in large amounts. Overall, America's net overseas indebtedness doubled from $193 million in 1849 to $387 million in 1859.

The flow of foreign capital to the United States in the antebellum years was of great significance to the growth of the economy. In the earliest years confidence in the new nation exhibited by foreign investors helped to place its public credit on a firm footing. In later decades loans from abroad allowed Americans to live beyond their current means while at the same time providing funds for enlarging those means in the future. Transportation improvements—first canals and later railroads—benefited disproportionately from the investment decisions of foreign wealth holders. These improvements were major instruments for extending the markets and trade of the United States. Complementing the facilities constructed with foreign funds were the flows of information, techniques, and ideas that accompanied them. Foreigners, especially the British, had much to teach American merchants, financiers, managers, and engineers. These lessons were important by-products of the flow of foreign capital.

Domestic Commerce

Although commercial intercourse between Americans and foreigners continued to be an important element of economic life in the decades before 1860, the truly significant development of this period was the growth of economic exchange between Americans. It has been said that in these years Americans turned their backs on European and other overseas markets in order to concentrate on the settlement and economic development of their own country, a country that had taken on the dimensions of a continent. This is an exaggeration because, as a glance back at Figure 9–1 will confirm, foreign commerce in the 1840s and 1850s was increasing about as rapidly as it did in any period of comparable length after 1790. Nonetheless, the early nineteenth century marks the beginning of a long-term trend toward the expansion of domestic relative to foreign commerce. Even as this trend was established, foreign trade was far from neglected; indeed, in our own time the United States is the largest foreign trading nation in the world economy. What the trend that began about a century and a half ago ultimately meant is that even though the United States is today the leading nation in international trade, the foreign trading sector of the American economy is relatively small when compared to the foreign trading sectors of most other advanced economies.

There were a number of reasons for the absolute and relative expansion of American domestic commerce after 1800. Fundamental was the economic principle of comparative advantage or relative cost, encountered earlier in this chapter. Just as in the world economy the young United States specialized in making resource-intensive products because, given its resource endowments, the relative cost of these products was lower than in other countries, so too within the United States, regions and cities specialized in those commodities that gave them comparative cost advantages over other regions and cities. But comparative cost advantages in production, although fundamental in determining the location of various economic activities, depend for the degree of their exploitation on the costs of transporting and marketing commodities to their users. Hence, a second major reason for the great expansion of domestic American commerce during the early decades of the nineteenth century was the dramatic decline in internal transportation costs, which we analyzed in chapter 6. Although both internal and overseas transport costs fell, by far the greatest impact of the transportation revolution was on the former. Thus, the transportation revolution did not lead Americans to turn their backs on foreigners so much as it led them—in an economic sense—to discover each other.

A third reason for the expansion of domestic relative to foreign commerce was the relative absence of artificial restrictions on trade within the United States. In trading with foreigners Americans of necessity had to conform to the taxes, the tariffs, and the other, often restrictive, commercial regulations of sovereign nations. Within the United States, on the other hand, the transportation revolution, in conjunction with judicial interpretations of the Constitution, was creating a massive area open to unrestricted trade.

These, then, were the broad facts that brought about an increased emphasis by Americans on domestic markets. Along with this change in commercial emphasis came an even more basic change. Reasonably accurate estimates of the United States's national product are now available for the two decades before the Civil War (see chapter 10). They indicate that the American economy was then expanding at the high and sustained rates of per capita product growth that characterize modern economies. It appears likely that these growth characteristics emerged in the quarter century before 1840, and that they were predicated upon the expansion of domestic markets. Just how did the expansion of domestic markets lead to modern economic growth? This has been a controversial issue among economic historians in recent times.

MARKETS AND ECONOMIC DEVELOPMENT

A traditional explanation of the expansion of domestic markets and the emergence of modern economic growth might succinctly be termed the cotton thesis. From the first to the seventh decades of this century, a number of scholars argued that the dynamic factor in the economy of the United States in its earliest years, but especially after 1815, was the growing world demand for American cotton. From a negligible share of world cotton output in 1790, U.S. cotton production rose to 9 percent by 1801, 16 percent by 1811, about 50 percent by 1831, and 66 percent by 1860. American cotton production grew at an average rate of almost 7 percent per year in the first three decades of the nineteenth century, and at 5 percent per year during the next three. The rate was close to 8 percent per year between 1811 and 1831. These rates of growth in output, sustained over such lengthy periods, are impressive by both historical and modern standards. Clearly the American South's antebellum cotton kingdom was a potent and dynamic economic entity.

Proponents of the cotton thesis have argued that extreme specialization in cotton production led the South to spend its growing income from cotton sales in other sections of the United States. Southern expenditures in the Northeast stimulated the growth of northern manufacturing, commerce, and finance. Southern expenditures in the West stimulated the growth of specialized grain and meat production in that region. Moreover, as the West specialized in production of agricultural goods, it in turn demanded manufactured goods and commercial services from the Northeast and supplied it with foodstuffs. The direct and indirect disposition of the South's growing cotton income was thus seen as the force that expanded American domestic markets and promoted continuing gains from specialization and intersectional trade.

Based on the powerful facts of cotton production and the appealing implications of intersectional trade—at least some of it could be documented—the cotton thesis offered an understandable and attractive model of how sustained economic growth began in the United States after 1815.

But in recent years a great deal of new evidence pertinent to the cotton thesis has appeared and much of it casts doubt on its intersectional trade emphasis. Consider first the West-South link. A basic tenet of the cotton thesis was that food products moved from the West to the South to supply specialized cotton plantations. But analysis of products traveling down the Mississippi indicates that most of these products were shipped out of the South, either to the Northeast or to foreign markets. Moreover, the notion that substantial quantities of Western foodstuffs moved to the South over other river routes or by wagon and rail has also been deflated. But most damaging of all to the cotton thesis are studies which show that southern cotton growers were largely self-sufficient in food and that southern agriculture was even capable of producing food surpluses for sale outside of the South (see chap. 6, pp. 143–145).

Consider next the Northeast-South link. The cotton thesis envisioned the Northeast supplying the South with a variety of goods and services, but emphasized the effect of southern demand on northern manufacturing. Most of the trade from the Northeast to the South was carried in ships engaged in the coastal trade. A recent study of this trade shows that it did in fact grow at fairly rapid rates between 1824 and 1839, but that even at the latter date less than one sixth of Northern manufacturing output moved to the South.[*] And since cotton income was but one eighth of the value of all southern production in that year, only a tiny fraction of northern manufacturing output could be said to have been directly stimulated by the demand of cotton growers for manufactures.

Finally, what may be said of the trade between the Northeast and the West? Some western foodstuffs undoubtedly reached the Northeast via the Mississippi River and coastal trades between 1815 and 1840, just as imported and domestic manufactured goods returned by these routes. This water route to the West was, however, circuitous and costly. And in terms of both population and per-capita income, it is now known that the West lagged behind the South in 1840. The West was unlikely, therefore, to have furnished the Northeast with a better market for manufactures than did the South. Analysis of Erie Canal toll revenues bears out this contention. The Erie, completed in 1825, is often thought to have stimulated agricultural development and population growth in the West, and it undoubtedly did. But when? From 1829 to 1835 toll revenues from western shipments over the Erie were but 7 percent of total revenues, while shipments from tidewater to the West were only 10 percent. Most of the revenues generated by the Erie in these years were derived from shipments within New York State, from its interior to tidewater and vice versa. Indeed, not until 1846 did toll revenue from western shipments over the Erie surpass revenue from shipments from the interior

---

[*] Lawrence A. Herbst, "Interregional Commodity Trade from the North to the South and American Economic Development in the Antebellum Period" *Journal of Economic History* 35 (March 1975), pp. 264–270.

of New York to tidewater. Thus, before the 1840s the West was neither a major supplier of food to the Northeast nor a major consumer of northeastern manufactures.

If growing trade between the three great sections of the United States between 1815 and 1840 cannot account for the expansion of domestic markets and the beginnings of sustained growth in these years, then what can? An emerging alternative to the cotton thesis contends that the initial stimulus to growth came from a widening and deepening of markets *within* sections of country, especially within the Northeast. If one thinks about it for a time, this explanation seems more sensible than does the cotton thesis. It is unlikely that Americans in the Northeast would begin to specialize in trading their manufactured goods over great distances in return for food before they began to trade these goods among themselves. Great quantities of food and raw materials were in fact produced within the Northeast, and most of the inhabitants were still farmers in 1815.

The already cited evidence from Erie Canal toll revenues supports the new view that *intra*sectional rather than *inter*sectional trade was the initiating force for greater specialization in the domestic economy. In the years from 1829 to 1835 shipments from the interior of New York State to tidewater accounted for almost one half of the Erie Canal's revenues, while shipments from tidewater to the state's interior made up nearly 30 percent. When local shipments along the Erie Canal are added in, the result is that over 80 percent of the total revenue was derived from New Yorkers trading with New Yorkers.

A recent and careful study of Philadelphia's economic development and trade between 1815 and 1840 makes much the same point.* In this quarter century Philadelphia changed from a major port city of the country's foreign commerce to a leading center of domestic manufacturing. Much of the impetus for this shift came from the demand for manufactured goods within the city's own hinterland and coastal trading areas in the states of Pennsylvania, New Jersey, Delaware, and Maryland. Trade in manufactures outside of this area—with other regions of the Northeast, with the South and the West, and with foreigners—was of comparatively much less significance. In earlier years Philadelphia's merchants thrived on importing both European manufactures and tropical goods for distribution within the Philadelphia region and to southern and western markets. From the 1820s on, however, New York City gained a progressively greater share of the American import trade. Philadelphia declined as a foreign trade center and turned to manufacturing. The city continued to receive and to ship out agricultural commodities and extractive products (notably anthracite coal) gathered from its hinterland, but the major markets for these shipments were in the Northeast—in growing cities such as New York, Boston, and Baltimore—rather than in

* Diane Lindstrom, *Economic Development in the Philadelphia Region, 1810–1850* (New York: Columbia University Press, 1978).

the South and West. Hinterland incomes derived from these northeastern shipments of farm products and coal, and from Philadelphia's own consumption of these goods, created an expanding market for Philadelphia's manufactures. Thus, trade within the Philadelphia region and with other emerging urban regions of the Northeast was the strongest stimulus to the city's market growth and increased specialization before 1840.

Much the same can be said for other regions of the Northeast. Increased specialization was promoted not so much by extraregional demand as by a growing volume of trade between urban areas and their hinterlands. Gradually interregional and intersectional demands became more important, but this largely happened after 1840. In the West a similar story, albeit on a lesser scale, unfolded. Active trade developed first within city–hinterland areas and then spread throughout the western section. The importance of intersectional and international trade came later. Thus the river-connected cities of Pittsburgh, Cincinnati, Louisville, and St. Louis grew first through trade with their hinterlands and with each other. Detroit, Cleveland, and Buffalo on the Great Lakes also traded extensively among themselves.

Only the South failed to develop an active internal trade between city and countryside. The South's lag in urbanization and trade stemmed from its great comparative advantage in specialized agriculture and its orientation toward international markets. These features of its economy led the South to rely heavily on outsiders for commercial and financial services, and on foreigners for many manufactured goods.

The new view of the beginnings of modern economic growth in the quarter century before 1840, with its emphasis on trade and specialization within regions and sections, particularly in the Northeast, is consistent with our knowledge of urbanization and income trends for the period. The fraction of Americans living in urban places (defined as two thousand five hundred or more in population) rose from 5.1 to 7.2 percent between 1790 and 1820. Then speed of urbanization picked up momentum, with the percentage living in cities rising to 8.8 and 10.8, respectively, in 1830 and 1840, and to 19.8 percent in 1860.

In 1840 almost a half of the urban population lived in just five cities: New York, Philadelphia, Boston, and Baltimore in the Northeast, and New Orleans in the South. Personal incomes on a per capita basis were highest in the regions containing these cities: estimates of this measure for 1840 show the Northeast to be 35 percent above the national average, and the West South Central region containing New Orleans 44 percent above the national average. Other regions of the South and the West were below the national average. Economic specialization reached its highest levels in cities, and through its effects on incomes it drew greater numbers of people to them.

The appearance of New Orleans on the list of largest cities and highest income areas in 1840 reinforces the point that internal commerce perhaps more than industrialization was the important factor in the emergence of modern economic growth in the United States. New Orleans was not a manufacturing center, but it served as the focal point of the great hinterland of the Mississippi Valley with its increasingly specialized agriculture. Commercial activity also outweighed manufacturing activity in the major Northeastern cities before 1840. Goods manufactured in smaller cities and towns of that section were distributed through the great commercial cities. In the Northeast domestic commerce increasingly assumed the form of trade of manufactured goods for agricultural products and the exchange of some manufactures for others. Home production of cloth, for example, fell precipitously in the 1820s and 1830s as rural producers turned to specialized farming and to buying their cloth from distributors of the factory-manufactured product.

Finally, the new view of the origins of modern economic growth in the United States should bring about a re-evaluation of the role of transportation improvements and communications after 1815. The initial significance of these improvements was not so much in opening up intersectional trade as in extending the hinterland markets and producing areas of cities within these sections. As the city-hinterland markets grew they began to overlap, and trade became interregional within each of the great sections of the country. Ultimately this same process brought intersectional trade into prominence and caused readjustments toward a greater degree of specialization within the Northeast, the South, and the West. The process was gradual, however, and had not been completed by the time of the Civil War.

SPECIALIZATION IN MARKETING AND COMMERCIAL INFORMATION

Before a nation made up overwhelmingly of farmers could obtain the income necessary to promote progressively greater economic diversification and specialization, ways had to be found to market more efficiently both agricultural commodities and manufactured goods. This called for greater specialization in marketing and for improved transportation facilities. Since marketing and transportation were so intimately related before 1860, it should come as no surprise that merchants often were the prime movers and key decision makers in the transportation revolution. Transportation improvements extended marketing areas, and in consequence marketing itself became more specialized.

Cotton, antebellum America's pre-eminent cash crop, provides one example of the trend toward specialized marketing. In the earliest years of the rise of cotton, planters often marketed the crop themselves by hauling it over land or water to southern coastal ports and selling it to port merchants and shippers. This was unspecialized marketing. It became less and less feasible as the cotton kingdom moved farther inland, and marketing specialists then appeared in the South. Most of them were so-called cotton factors—brokers who received shipments from farmers and planters and supervised their sale to buyers in Europe or the Northeast in return for a commission. Factors located themselves in southern port cities and in the inland towns that grew up in the cotton belt. They acted as agents for cotton growers and dealt with the buying agents of distant merchants and manufacturers. They relieved the grower of the burden of marketing his crop. The cotton factor had a comparative advantage in marketing while the cotton grower had a comparative advantage in production.

But the cotton factor was not completely specialized. In addition to arranging for the storing, selling, insuring, and forwarding of the crop, the factor often acted as a purchasing agent and banker for the grower. The grower then relied on the factor both for credit and for supplies of products imported into the South from abroad or from the Northeast—or both, since most foreign imported goods came first to northeastern port merchants for distribution to the rest of the country. The southern factor was not totally specialized in part because the southern planter was an extremely specialized agriculturalist. In the South agricultural specialization and an orientation toward export markets rather than toward local or regional sales worked against the tide of urbanization prevalent elsewhere in the United States. Cotton had a high value in relation to its weight and could be harvested, ginned, baled, and shipped efficiently from large plantations. Moreover, it did not have to be further processed until it arrived at faraway textile mills. Bulky grain and perishable livestock were another matter. Flour milling and meat processing facilities were developed near the places of grain and livestock production as a means of making savings in transport costs. Much of the notable antebellum differences in town development between the Northeast and West, on the one hand, and the South, on the other, can be attributed to these agricultural product differences. Because the South developed fewer towns per unit of area, southern growers usually relied for supplies and credit on their factors rather than on local merchants and bankers.

Agricultural marketing in the West began much as it had in the South —with the farmer performing much of his own marketing. As western populations grew and as towns sprang up to act as processing centers for grain and meat, local merchants assumed a larger role in agricultural marketing. The local merchant traded his stocks of manufactured goods for crops and then acted as an intermediary for selling the aggregated surpluses of a number of farmers to more distant buyers. In earlier years this sometimes required shipping the products all the way to New Orleans, but as the cities of the Ohio and Mississippi valleys emerged, specialized brokers and forwarding agents appeared to add a second layer of marketing intermediation. Thus, the West, and even earlier the Northeast, developed a higher degree of agricultural marketing specialization than did the South.

Product and market differences also go a long way toward explaining the evolution of decisions on how to market manufactured as well as agricultural goods between 1790 and 1860. Manufacturers had even more incentives than agriculturists for specialization because of the greater variety of products and because markets for manufactured goods grew more rapidly than did markets for most agricultural commodities. Before 1815 marketing of most goods was handled by the great merchants of the nation's leading port cities. The activities of these merchants—including exporting and importing, wholesaling and retailing, shipping and shipowning, and also commercial intelligence, insurance, and finance—were relatively unspecialized because the merchants dealt in numerous small and widely dispersed markets.

The growth of domestic commerce after 1815 led to progressively greater specialization in marketing. Larger markets for manufactured goods, of foreign and domestic origin, created opportunities for merchants to specialize both by function (for example, exporting or importing, wholesaling or retailing) and by product line (for example, textiles or dry goods, hardware, drugs). The marketing of textiles, America's first modern, factory-manufactured product furnishes a good example of growing specialization in commerce. Before 1815 early spinning mills sold small lots to nearby weavers and storekeepers. But production soon exceeded local demand, and yarn began to be marketed through more distant outlets, often on consignment. Under this arrangement the producer retained ownership and received payment for the goods once they had been sold by the consignee. After 1815, with the introduction of mechanized weaving followed by an extended period of remarkable growth in textile production, there appeared two new and still more specialized marketing agencies: the commission wholesaler of the large city, who purchased products from a number of mills, and the selling house, a wholesaling unit that handled the initial distribution of a given mill's entire production. These marketing specialists handled product distribution and furnished information to manufacturers about which goods were most in demand. They also provided the manufacturers with credit on goods produced but not yet sold to consumers. Freed from these credit and marketing concerns, manufacturers of textiles were able to specialize in producing more efficiently.

Commission wholesalers and textile selling houses dealt in volume sales. Located in large cities, they sold some of their stocks of goods to urban retailers. But the spatial expansion of the domestic market called forth still another type of specialized wholesaler—the jobber—who dealt in smaller lots with scattered retailers around the country. In textiles the jobber's main function was to purchase fairly large stocks of yarn and cloth products from commission wholesalers and selling houses, and then to break these up into smaller and more variegated lots for the nation's retailers. Jobbers played an important role in the auction system of distribution that was common, especially for imported goods, before the

1830s. Ships carrying imported textiles could not possibly wait for the goods to be sold to retailers far inland, and so they turned their cargoes over to port-city auctioneers. The jobber was a frequent auction buyer. Later, as goods of domestic manufacture increased in volume and as auction sales declined, the jobber turned to larger wholesalers and selling houses for his stocks. The big-city jobber was an important agent in the flow of economic information and credit. Retailers from around the nation visited him periodically to place their orders. The jobber's access to bank credit allowed him to provide these out-of-town retailers with credit and to gather information on consumer preferences around the country.

The patterns of marketing change and specialization that prevailed in textiles extended to many other products in the years after 1815. The importance of specialized marketing went beyond increased efficiency of distribution. Marketing specialists often played a dominant role in manufacturing development as well. This was due primarily to the fact that established merchants had better access than new manufacturers to a major requirement of modern industrial development: capital. Trade credit and commercial banking long antedated the appearance of factory industry in both Europe and the United States. These institutions developed initially to finance the movement of goods from small-scale producers to scattered consumers rather than to meet the working capital and long-term investment needs of modern industry. But they could be turned easily to the developing problems of industrial finance. As a result, the merchant's access to capital, in the form of bank credit and as part of his personal accumulation of wealth from trading activity, often became instrumental in financing early industrial enterprises. Many manufacturing firms in the antebellum U.S. were either founded by merchants or closely allied with them. In either case merchants' access to capital put them in a position to exert substantial control over manufacturing enterprises.

Even before the Civil War, however, the dominance of the merchant over the manufacturer was on the wane in some industries. Railroad equipment is a good example. In the 1830s the first railroads were small enterprises relative to what they were to become, and their worth as investments was largely untested. The railroad-equipment industry was also new and consisted of a number of relatively small and capital-hungry firms. In these circumstances independent wholesalers who had both more knowledge of the conditions of railroads and more capital than the equipment manufacturers became middlemen between manufacturers and their railroad customers. But railroad equipment was technically more sophisticated than most consumer and producer goods. Moreover, by the 1840s many railroads had proven themselves as viable economic entities, and the equipment industry itself had become more concentrated into larger-scale producing units. Hence, equipment manufacturers and railroads found it convenient to deal with each other directly rather than to go through merchant middlemen. This marked the beginning of a long-term trend toward a reduced role for the merchant in American economic development.

The beginnings of erosion in the dominance of the merchant over the manufacturer in some industries did not, however, mark the end of increasing specialization in commercial activity. Indeed, the nationwide market that was emerging for many products during the last antebellum decades stimulated still more specialization. Two examples from the area of information, the key ingredient to decision making, illustrate the continuing progress of specialization in commerce. Wholesale merchants had been so important to domestic economic development after 1815 in part because they took on the role, and assumed much of the risk, of providing credit to both retailers and manufacturers. The merchants were in a good position to undertake these functions because their day-to-day dealings generated the information that was necessary in making credit decisions. However, as the number of retail customers and suppliers grew, and as trade became much less personal than in earlier years, it became difficult for individual wholesalers to gather all the credit information they needed. And expanding their information bases would have involved much duplication of effort. A solution was found in 1841 when Lewis Tappan, a New York dry goods wholesaler, established the Mercantile Agency, a firm that specialized in gathering commercial credit information from all over the country and disseminating it to subscribing clients. Its business grew rapidly. Branches of the Mercantile Agency were organized in Boston (1843), Philadelphia (1845), Baltimore (1846), Cincinnati (1849), New Orleans (1851), and eleven other cities by 1858. Tappan's Mercantile Agency is the lineal ancestor of Dun & Bradstreet, a leading commercial information firm of today.

A second example of commercial specialization is the bank note reporter. Hundreds of independent commercial banks, each issuing its own handsomely engraved notes that served as a part of the nation's paper currency, emerged in the antebellum decades. Not all of the banks were well managed. In addition, the great number of differing bank notes encouraged counterfeiting. As domestic trade expanded and spread over greater and greater distances, these notes increasingly came to be presented to merchants far away from their place of origin. How was a merchant to know whether or not the notes presented were worth the nominal values printed on them? The answers were provided by bank-note reporters and counterfeit detectors. These publications presented information on the conditions of the banks and the prices at which their notes were being traded in major money markets. Bank note reporters were popular from the 1820s to the end of the Civil War, reaching their peak of importance during the 1840s and 1850s. In 1855, the most prominent publication, *Thompson's Bank Note and Commercial Reporter*, had one hundred thousand subscribers all over the country. The note reporters ceased publication after the Civil War as a result of federal banking legislation that finally gave the U.S. a uniform paper currency. But their earlier and widespread success, like that of the Mercantile Agency, served as an important indication that a nationwide market for many goods and services had developed well before the War.

Conclusion

Improvements in internal transportation and communications were the basic ingredients of the expansion of domestic commerce in the United States after 1800. These improvements allowed the interior resources of America to be exploited along lines of comparative cost advantage, just as the availability of cheap ocean transportation had promoted specialized production for overseas markets in the New England, Middle, and South Atlantic regions during the colonial era. An absence of artificial barriers to trade within and between regions also favored trade expansion as markets widened under the influence of ever-lower transport costs.

The expansion of domestic commerce created conditions favorable to still further expansion. The growth of domestic markets prompted an increasing division of labor and specialization in commercial activity and marketing organization. Transactions costs—the cost of moving products from producer to consumer—were reduced further by the more specialized and efficient middlemen of nineteenth-century commerce. Thus, the expansion of domestic markets became self-sustaining. The United States entered the era of modern economic growth with its continued increases in productivity per capita.

SUGGESTED READINGS

Although somewhat dated, the most comprehensive work on the subject matter of this chapter is still Emory R. Johnson et al., *History of Domestic and Foreign Commerce of the United States*, 2 vols. (Washington, D.C.: Carnegie Institution, 1915). A concise yet broad view of foreign commerce in American history is given in Chapter 14, "Foreign Trade," by Robert E. Lipsey in Lance Davis et al., eds., *American Economic Growth: An Economist's History of the United States* (New York: Harper & Row, 1972). The standard quantitative reference for this period on exports, imports, and the balance of payments is Douglass C. North, "The United States Balance of Payments, 1790–1860," in National Bureau of Economic Research, *Trends in the American Econ-*

omy in the Nineteenth Century, Studies in Income and Wealth, vol. 24 (Princeton: Princeton University Press, 1960), pp. 573–627. North has also provided a sophisticated analysis of the forces making for reduced transport costs in ocean shipping in his paper, "Sources of Productivity Change in Ocean Shipping, 1600–1850," Journal of Political Economy, 76 (September/October 1968), 953–970. Aspects of the American shipping industry in its antebellum golden age are illuminated in two works of the noted maritime historian, Robert G. Albion, The Rise of the Port of New York, 1815–1860 (New York: Charles Scribner's Sons, 1939); and Square Riggers on Schedule: The New York Sailing Packets to England, France and the Cotton Ports (Princeton: Princeton University Press, 1938).

On the organization and finance of foreign trade, see Norman Sydney Buck, The Development of the Organization of Anglo-American Trade, 1800–1850 (New Haven: Yale University Press, 1925); Ralph Hidy, The House of Baring in American Trade and Finance (Cambridge: Harvard University Press, 1949); and Edwin J. Perkins, Financing Anglo-American Trade: The House of Brown, 1800–1880 (Cambridge: Harvard University Press, 1975). Some specific aspects of foreign investment in the United States are given by Leland H. Jenks, The Migration of British Capital to 1875 (New York: Alfred A. Knopf, 1927).

The rise of internal commerce in the antebellum years is a subject of much interest because of its relation to the origins of modern economic growth. For the recent scholarship on the question, see Albert Fishlow, "Antebellum Interregional Trade Reconsidered," American Economic Review, 59 (May 1964) 352–364; Lawrence A. Herbst, "Interregional Commodity Trade from the North to the South and American Economic Development in the Antebellum Period," Journal of Economic History, 35 (March 1975), 264–270; Diane Lindstrom, Economic Development in the Philadelphia Region, 1810–1850 (New York: Columbia University Press, 1978); and Diane Lindstrom, "American Economic Growth Before 1840: New Evidence and New Directions," The Journal of Economic History, 39 (March 1979).

For insights into the changing nature of antebellum commerce and marketing organization, the following are valuable: Lewis E. Atherton, The Frontier Merchant in Mid-America (Columbia: University of Missouri Press, 1971); Stuart Bruchey, "The Business Economy of Marketing Change, 1790–1840, A Study of Sources of Efficiency," Agricultural History, 46 (January 1972), 211–226; Glenn Porter and Harold C. Livesay, Merchants and Manufacturers: Studies in the Changing Structure of Nineteenth-Century Marketing (Baltimore: Johns Hopkins Press, 1971); and Harold D. Woodman, King Cotton and His Retainers (Lexington: University of Kentucky Press, 1968). On the emergence of specialized commercial information services that accompanied the expansion of long-distance trade, see William H. Dillistin, Bank Note Reporters and Counterfeit Detectors, 1826–1866 (New York: American Numismatic Society, 1949); James H. Madison, "The Evolution of Commercial Credit Reporting Agencies in Nineteenth-Century America," Business History Review, 48 (Summer 1974), 164–186, and James D. Norris, R. G. Dun & Co., 1841–1900: The Development of Credit-Reporting in the Nineteenth Century (Westport, Conn.: Greenwood Press, 1978).

CHAPTER 10

————

Economic Growth and

Social Welfare in the

Early Republic

During the seven decades from 1790 to 1860 the economy of the United States was transformed from a premodern to a modern condition. Considerable self-sufficiency and slow rates of economic change gave way to a new order in which individuals, enterprises, and governments were specialized and interdependent, and change seemed to be built into the system. The preceding chapters of Part II have described and analyzed the key changes and the critical decisions that brought about this epochal transformation. The shift from handicraft manufacturing to mechanized, factory industry was of the greatest long-term significance because it embodied the forces that propelled later economic development. During the transformation itself, however, other changes—territorial and population growth, the transportation and communications revolutions, the rise of the cotton kingdom, and the emergence of specialized commercial institutions such as banks—appeared to be just as significant as industrialization in its narrow, mechanized-factory sense. Together, the key economic changes of 1790–1860 were a dominating fact of great historical significance, for they laid the foundation for the United States's later role of leadership in the international economy and in world politics.

After a brief summary of the striking economic changes of the ante-bellum era, this chapter takes up the important questions of what the transformation meant in terms of trends in economic growth and welfare. When did the rate of economic growth change from a premodern to a modern level? Were increases in aggregate income and wealth widely shared? Or were there increasingly large gaps between the haves and the have nots? The base of evidence for answering such questions has been greatly extended by the recent work of quantitative economic historians. Nonetheless, problems of interpretation remain.

The Economic Transformation in Perspective

Expansion in the resources of the American economy between 1790 and 1860 is very evident in terms of territory and population. The nation's land area more than tripled during the seven decades and reached its present-day continental proportions. Land resources actually utilized for economic purposes increased even more rapidly as a result of population expansion and redistribution. In 1790 the United States population of 3.9 million was about 40 percent of Great Britain's estimated 10 million. In 1860, it was 31.5 million, a figure nearly 40 percent greater than Britain's 23 million. Over the seven decades the United States population thus grew at the high rate of 3 percent per year.* And while doing so, it spread out from its initial concentration in a relatively narrow strip along the Atlantic seaboard to rather full settlement of the eastern half of the nation's continental territory and in thriving pockets of settlement from there to the Pacific.

Territorial and population expansion say little, however, about the movement toward economic modernity that took place between the administrations of George Washington and Abraham Lincoln. The contrasts between 1790 and 1860 have been addressed in previous chapters. In 1790 there were few good roads, no canals, no steamboats, no steamships, and no railroads. By 1860 relatively few Americans were without access to one or more improved facility for transporting goods and people. In 1790 communication and information flows, even between major cities along the Atlantic coast, were limited and very slow. By 1860 some fifty thousand miles of telegraph line furnished nearly instantaneous communication between widely separated points throughout the nation. In agri-

---

* In addition to the comparison with Britain, some hypothetical arithmetic will also show why 3 percent is a "high" rate by historical standards. Had the United States population continued to expand at 3 percent from 1860 to the present, it would reach one billion in 1980.

culture the dramatic change was the rise of cotton. From negligible production in 1790, the United States steadily increased its output to an estimated two thirds of the entire world's production of the fiber in 1860. But progress in other dimensions of the nation's agricultural enterprise was also great. Perhaps the most significant changes between 1790 and 1860 were in agricultural technology. By 1860 the age-old hand tools and simple implements of former years were giving way to sophisticated machinery and nonhuman power sources, animate and inanimate.

In commerce and manufacturing the contrasts were even more striking. For example, there were in 1790 only four commercial banks in the United States, one each in Philadelphia, New York, Boston, and Baltimore. None had existed a decade before. By 1860 there were one thousand six hundred state-chartered commercial banks, and hundreds more unincorporated merchants, bankers, and brokers who performed banking functions. These banking institutions ranged over the entire nation. The transformation was similar in manufacturing industry. In 1790 few Americans would have listed their major occupations or employments as being in manufacturing. Most Americans—approximately nine in ten—were farmers, and the nation's manufacturing in 1790 was more often than not a simple handicraft adjunct to farming and rural life. By 1860, in contrast, some 15 percent of the nation's workers were employed in manufacturing on a relatively full-time basis. A manufacturing labor force had been formed. Large-scale factory production was present in a number of industries and dominant in a few of them. Technological change was beginning to become institutionalized. Urbanization and manufacturing were reinforcing each other and breaking the path toward more complex forms of social and economic organization.

The common characteristic of these and other transformations of American economic life was the emergence, expansion, and intensification of internal market activity. Around 1790 the important markets of the United States were abroad, and a relatively small proportion of the American people was involved with them. Internally, the great majority of Americans were independent and self-sufficient farmers, although they sometimes traded agricultural products and handicrafted items with their neighbors. By 1860, in contrast, Americans in all lines of economic activity increasingly sold their products to distant consumers whom they never saw or knew about, and purchased their own consumption and capital goods in equally impersonal markets. The great advantage of this impersonalization of economic life was, of course, specialization and the increased efficiency, wealth, and welfare that specialization promoted. What made specialization possible and gave it coordination was the extension of both markets and the information that markets provide to economic decision makers. The growth of markets in the antebellum era fundamentally altered the context of decision making from one of independence to one of interdependence.

Remote and protracted as it may seem to one living in the late twentieth century, the great transformation of American economic life between 1790 and 1860 took place during the lifetime—even the adult lifetime—of many individuals. One such individual was Roger Brooke Taney, who was born in 1777 during the American Revolution, and who died in 1864 during the American Civil War, and whose life reflected something of the "life" of the young American nation before 1860.

Taney, the son of slaveholding planters, was born and grew up on a tobacco plantation in southern Maryland. After graduating from Dickinson College in 1795, he studied law and then entered upon a legal and political career. A Federalist, he was elected to the Maryland legislature in 1799, but was defeated for reelection in the Republican electoral tide of 1800. For the next three decades Taney practiced law, first in Frederick and later in Baltimore, but he continued to remain active in politics. Unlike many Federalists he strongly supported the United States government during the War of 1812. From 1816 to 1820 he was a state senator, and in 1827 he became attorney general of Maryland.

Two of Roger Taney's major concerns in his early private and public life were better currency and banking arrangements and improvement in the position and rights of blacks, both slave and free, in American society. A director of two Maryland banks at various times between 1810 and 1823, Taney became conversant with bank operations; during the 1820s he began to develop misgivings about the power and dominance that the second Bank of the United States exerted over other American banks. Taney deemed slavery an evil institution, one that had been saddled on Americans during their colonial dependency. It could and should be ended, he felt, but only gradually because of the problems a long-deprived black minority would face in a predominantly white society. Taney freed his own slaves around 1820, after ensuring that they would be able to cope on their own. On another occasion he lent a talented young slave the money to purchase his freedom from his owner. The great issues of banking and slavery were later to stamp Taney's name indelibly in the annals of American history.

Roger Taney's rise to national prominence commenced in 1824 when, with the disappearance of the Federalist party, he became an active and avid supporter of Andrew Jackson for the presidency. Jackson lost in 1824, but he and his supporters were successful in 1828. Jackson appointed Taney attorney general of the United States in 1831 and secretary of the treasury in 1833. In both of these roles Taney was a key figure and ally of the President during Jackson's "war" with the Bank of the United States over the recharter of that institution. Taney advised Jackson to veto the Congressional bill to recharter the Bank of the United States, and after the presidential veto was sustained he supervised the transfer of federal monies from it to state-chartered banks. Taney advocated free competition in banking, a policy toward which America was fitfully moving at the time.

In 1836 Jackson appointed Roger Taney to succeed John Marshall as Chief Justice of the U.S. Supreme Court. Taney served as Chief Justice until his death twenty-eight years later. On the Supreme Court he was an exponent of the principal of divided sovereignty between the states and the federal government. The states were not to hinder the execution of federal powers, but the federal government itself was not to prevent the states from interfering with the rights of property or from regulating private activities within their borders so long as the public interest was served and the Constitution not violated. A number of opinions of the Taney Court effectively promoted the competitive development of corporate enterprise and thus generalized the Chief Justice's views on banking.

Taney's most noted opinion, however, came in the case of *Dred Scott* v. *Sanford*. Scott, a black slave, sued his owner, claiming freedom and United States citizenship on the ground that he had been taken into "free" territory as defined in the Missouri Compromise of 1820. Taney's majority opinion in 1857 held that Congress had no Constitutional power to exclude slavery from United States territories and that Dred Scott remained a slave and had no right to sue in a federal court. The opinion caused a bitter reaction among opponents of slavery and thereby contributed to the hostile climate that soon led to the Civil War.

Roger B. Taney's long life thus illustrates the economic progress and problems, both resolved and unresolved, of the United States between 1790 and 1860. Economic development led men of agrarian origins to concern themselves with the emerging problems of law, of banking, of corporate rights and responsibilities, and of the framework of enterprise that best promoted increased wealth and welfare. Their solutions to these problems were on the whole effective. But they did not solve the vexing problem of slavery which divided the nation, just as it divided the conscience of individuals like Taney.

MODERN ECONOMIC GROWTH EMERGES

Quantitative knowledge of economic growth in pre-Civil War America has increased substantially since the 1950s. Scholars working with information from such sources as the decennial census of the United States and employing insights from economic theory and the modern concepts of national income accounting have constructed measures of national income and product for the antebellum era. The results of these careful labors, even when tentative and conjectural, have brought a freshness to our understanding of the overall performance of the early United States economy.

Attempts to measure antebellum economic growth are not all equally well-grounded in a firm base of quantitative evidence. The census material, for example, allows one to measure the national product, using the techniques of a modern economic statistician, only for the years after the late 1830s. Some results of the measurements of economic growth are presented in Table 10–1. In prices current at the dates shown in Table 10–1, GNP (Gross National Product) increased from $1.54 billion in the 1839 census year to $4.17 billion in 1859. Measured in prices of 1860, the economy's real gross product expanded a little less rapidly because prices in general rose somewhat over the two decades.

TABLE 10-1
Measures of Economic Growth, 1839-59

	GNP Current Prices (billion dollars) (1)	GNP 1860 Prices (billion dollars) (2)	Real GNP per Capita* (dollars) (3)
1839	1.54	1.62	95
1844	1.80	1.97	98
1849	2.32	2.43	104
1854	3.53	3.37	123
1859	4.17	4.10	130

*Col. 2, divided by population.
SOURCES: Cols. 1 and 2: Robert E. Gallman, "Gross National Product in the United States, 1834-1909," in National Bureau of Economic Research, Output, Employment, and Productivity in the United States after 1800, Studies in Income and Wealth, vol. 30 (New York: National Bureau of Economic Research, 1966), Table A-1, p. 26. Col. 3: Calculated from Col. 2 and population data from U.S. Bureau of Census, Historical Statistics of the United States (Washington, D.C.: United States Government Printing Office, 1960), p. 7.

Real GNP per capita, a good measure of economic growth because it adjusts for changes in both general price levels and population, is shown in column three of Table 10–1. It rises from $95 in 1839 to $130 in 1859, both measured in prices of 1860. Increases in real GNP per capita were greater, both relatively and absolutely, during the 1850s than during the 1840s. But not too much should be made of this, for the nation's business was relatively prosperous in 1839, and then suffered one of the most severe depressions in United States history in the several years thereafter.

Several historically important questions may be addressed to such data. What rates of economic growth do they indicate? How do these rates compare with subsequent American experience? And where did the United States stand economically in the world community at the time? The answer to the first question is that the indicated rate of growth of real GNP from 1839 to 1859 is approximately 4.6 percent per year, while that of GNP per capita is about 1.6 percent per year. The difference between the two rates, 3 percent, is of course the approximate rate by which population grew over these two decades.

The second question—How do these rates compare with subsequent experience?—may be answered by noting that the long-term trend for the growth rate of real GNP per capita has been roughly 1.6 percent per year from the late 1830s to the present day. In other words, during the two decades prior to the Civil War, the period for which reasonably detailed and comprehensive estimates of national product first become possible, the United States economy was already expanding in terms of per capita GNP at a rate characteristic of modern economic growth. This is a significant finding because it challenges the views of earlier historians who emphasized either the post-Civil War decades or the period from 1843 to 1861 as marking the beginning of economic modernization in the United States. Rather than beginning in the 1840s, the growth of the American economy was already at a high, modern level.

The third question—Where did the U.S. stand relative to other countries in, for example, 1840?—has a somewhat surprising answer. By almost any contemporary reckoning, Great Britain, "the workshop of the world," and France were considered to have the most successful economies. They had been the leading political powers in colonial North America, and their long national histories of institutional, social, and industrial development had established them as economic powers. The United States, on the other hand, was a new nation, and one with a still predominantly agricultural economy. Nonetheless, such international comparisons of national products as can be made indicate that the size of the American economy around 1840 was not very different from that of the two leading European nations. Various techniques of comparison show that the national product of the United States ranged from two thirds to three fourths of the national product of Britain and of France (their national products were roughly equal). But in 1840 Britain's population was somewhat greater, and France's substantially greater, than that of the United States. Hence, the U.S. national product per capita approached that of Great Britain and was somewhat greater than that of France. In short, by 1840 the United States was already on a rough par in terms of per-capita and total product with the leading nations of Europe.

These comparisons, it should also be noted, are based on modern concepts of national product that exclude some economic activities that were important in earlier periods of history. In the early U.S. one such activity was the farmer's investment of his own labor and farm materials in constructing farm buildings and in the clearing, fencing, and draining of farm land. Another was the handicraft manufacturing of products in the home largely for the family's own use. Such activities today are not counted in the GNP because they do not involve flows of goods and services through markets. Moreover, they are no longer very important in a quantitative sense. But estimates for 1840 show that they may have had a value equivalent to about 15 percent of the narrower, modern concept of American GNP for that year. Since it is likely that these activities were more important in the United States than in Britain or France, their inclusion in a more comprehensive measure of aggregate national product would make the U.S. level of product and product per capita around 1840 look even larger relative to those of the other two countries.

The finding that the United States as early as 1840 was already among the world's leading nations in terms of product per capita, and that this measure of the American economy's productivity was already growing at a high rate, raises the question of when the process of modern growth began. It seems clear that a per capita product growth rate averaging 1.6 percent per year could not have been present for very many decades before 1840. For such a high rate of growth would imply ridiculously low levels of per capita product in the earlier years. Growing at 1.6 percent per year, real per capita product would double every 45 years. This roughly is what has happened in the U.S. economy since 1840. Had such a rate of growth characterized the American economy during the ninety years before 1840, real per capita product (in 1860 values) would have been only about twenty-four dollars in 1750 and only forty-eight dollars in 1795. On the basis of a variety of other evidence, most American economic historians think that these hypothetical levels are unrealistically low. Accepting this manner of reasoning, one must conclude that the American economy's rate of growth accelerated and reached modern levels sometime during the four to five decades before 1840.

Nothing in the actual historical record of the American economy contradicts such a view. The preceding chapters have reflected and analyzed the economic transformation that took place in the United States before the Civil War. Economic measurement shows that expansion at modern rates of per capita product growth was established by 1840. Combining these insights points to the quarter century before 1840 as the period when economic growth most likely accelerated and began to sustain itself. In that quarter century developments in transportation, agriculture, finance, industry, and commerce began strongly and simultaneously to reinforce one another. Internal markets grew rapidly in these years and as a result the expanding resources of the young American nation began to be combined more effectively. Proceeding as it did on a number of fronts, the acceleration of economic growth after the War of 1812 can be considered more gradual than abrupt, particularly when it is recognized that many of the elements that contributed to it were present earlier in embryonic form. Nonetheless, a new and vibrant economic order emerged in the United States. The emphasis of economic decision making shifted from foreign trade to internal economic development, and a rapidly growing percentage of Americans were drawn into market activity. And all of these developments came during a relatively brief period of the nation's history.

Economic Welfare: Distributing the Gains from Growth

Economic growth refers to how factors such as wealth, income, and production change over time. To measure growth in real terms, adjustments are made to compensate for changes in the value of the measuring rod, normally a monetary unit such as the dollar. And, since a nation with a rapidly growing population will usually have a more rapid growth of total wealth, income, and production than one whose population grows less rapidly, many analysts focus on real changes per capita as the most meaningful indicators of growth performance.

Per-capita measures of real product, income, and wealth, and their rates of growth over time, also tell us something about levels of, and changes in, average economic welfare. Material welfare, for example, is considered greater in nations with higher levels of per-capita product, and is thought to be increasing more rapidly when per-capita product grows at faster rates. But discussions of economic welfare normally move beyond these average measures of the levels and growth rates of production, income, and wealth into a consideration of how these magnitudes are distributed both across the population and by functional groupings. Two nations with equal populations and also with equal amounts of aggregate wealth and production would have the same per capita wealth and product. But they might very well be viewed differently in terms of economic welfare if in one of them the ruler appropriated a large share of the wealth and product for himself and kept the rest of the population at a subsistence level, while in the other nation wealth and production were distributed equally among the people.

Vigorous and sustained economic growth at the high rates characteristic of modern nations, we now know, emerged in the United States between the Revolution and the Civil War. What happened in these years to economic welfare in terms of the distribution of the fruits of economic growth? Information to answer such a question is even more limited than the information that can be used to measure economic growth. This information, moreover, does not lend itself to simple interpretations, although various interpretations are held by different people even when they imply conflicting views of the underlying historical situation.

One long-standing interpretation of the distribution of wealth and income in antebellum America is that of egalitarianism. Numerous foreign observers of American society, such as, the Frenchman Tocqueville, and many native Americans as well, expressed the viewpoint that in both political and economic affairs power and opportunity were much more equally distributed and diffused over the population of free men in the United States than in the old societies of Europe. Later historians adopted this idea and referred to the antebellum period as the era of the common man, an era of relative equality between the more aristocratic colonial and federal periods and the post-Civil War gilded age of industrial expansion with its highly visible inequalities of income and wealth. The egalitarian tradition did not deny that disparities existed in the material welfare of individual free men. Rather it affirmed that in the United States the disparities were relatively narrow compared to Europe's, that more opportunities were open for Americans of modest backgrounds to attain wealth, and that the well-to-do groups of the United States were composed primarily of active and self-made men rather than of idle beneficiaries of inherited wealth.

Another interpretation is offered by revisionist historians, both past and present, who argue in effect that proponents of the egalitarian interpretation were taken in by the rhetoric of equality and the common man in the antebellum era and by their own imaginations. In reality, the revisionists hold, wealth and economic opportunity were very unequally distributed in the early United States, just as they were in Europe. The existence of slavery in the South obviously resulted in marked inequality in the distribution of wealth and income in that section, but neither the egalitarian interpreters nor the revisionists argued their points on that ground. The issue concerns the free population, and the revisionists hold that among free people there were wide economic disparities. Many of the rich, the revisionists argue, derived their positions from inheritance rather than native ability, and well-to-do families tended to preserve their positions of wealth and influence over the decades.

To assess the two positions one would like to have detailed quantitative evidence on wealth and income distributions at various years throughout the antebellum era. Evidence on income distribution does not exist, but for the distribution of wealth some records are available in incomplete form. The Census of 1860, for example, asked Americans to report the value of their personal and real properties, along with their ages, occupations, and places of birth. The original manuscript forms of the 1860 Census are preserved in the National Archives in Washington. They show, for example, that in Springfield, Illinois, lived one Abraham Lincoln, aged 51, a lawyer, born in Kentucky, and the owner of five thousand dollars of personal property and twelve thousand dollars of real property. In Chicago, Cyrus McCormick was fifty years old, occupied in a reaper factory, a native of Virginia, and the owner of $278,000 and $1,750,000 of personal and real property, respectively.

With such detailed information and statistical sampling procedures,

economic statisticians have been able in recent years to estimate with reasonable accuracy the distribution of wealth in the United States and its
constituent parts for 1860. The results of such work indicate a high degree
of inequality in wealth distribution. The richest 1, 5, and 30 percent of all
families in 1860 are estimated to have held 24, 54, and 95 percent, respectively, of the reported wealth. On the other end of the wealth spectrum,
one half of American families in 1860 apparently had no wealth at all.

Variations on the theme of marked inequality of wealth are evident in
subclasses of the manuscript census data. In the United States as a whole,
5.5 percent of free adult males possessed total estates (real and personal
property) greater than $10,000, while 64 percent possessed property of
$1,000 or less. In the South, the proportion of rich men was greater: 9.5
percent of Southern free adult males valued their property—which included slaves—at $10,000 or more, while 62 percent were at or below
$1,000. Lesser, but still substantial, inequality was present in the wealth
distribution of the young northern state of Wisconsin where 1.9 percent of
the adult males had property valued at over $10,000, and 64 percent were
under $1,000. Inequality of wealthholding apparently was greatest in urban
areas. In ten urban counties, all in the North except Washington, D.C.,
4.8 percent of adult males had over ten thousand dollars, but 80 percent
were at levels of one hundred dollars or less, and over 50 percent reported no real or personal wealth at all. By contrast, only 29 percent of
free adult males both in the South and in Wisconsin reported no wealth.*
From the evidence urbanization, a trend of the day, appears to have promoted increased inequality in wealthholdings.

Such findings of substantial inequality in the distribution of American
wealth in 1860 apparently direct a serious challenge to the egalitarian tradition and lend support to the contrary historical interpretations of revisionist scholars. Before turning to this issue, however, it is interesting to pose
the question of whether the wealth distribution was increasing, relatively
constant, or decreasing over the antebellum decades. The notion of a
late eighteenth century aristocratic society and economy, followed by the
era of the common man after 1815, would lead to an expectation of increasing equality over time. On the other hand, recognition of industrial
growth and the urbanization and commercialization of more and more
economic activity would perhaps favor the hypothesis of increased inequality, of increasing differences between the haves and the have-nots.
Or the two trends might have offset each other so that little change in

---

* The data reported in this paragraph come from several studies by Lee Soltow:
"Economic Inequality in the United States in the Period from 1790 to 1860," *Journal
of Economic History*, 31 (December, 1971), 822–839; *Patterns of Wealthholding in
Wisconsin Since 1850* (Madison: University of Wisconsin Press, 1971); and "The
Wealth, Income, and Social Class of Men in Large Northern Cities of the United States
in 1860," in James D. Smith, ed., *The Personal Distribution of Income and Wealth*
(New York: National Bureau of Economic Research, 1975), pp. 233–276.

wealth distributions between early and late antebellum dates would be observed.

Evidence on the trend of wealth distribution from the late eighteenth century to the Civil War is much more restricted than for 1860 alone. But summary statistics computed from distributions of slaves among slaveholders and among families in 1790, 1830, 1850, and 1860 reveal the concentration of this peculiar form of wealth changed little over time. Since in 1860 the inequality of total wealthholdings in the South and in the U.S. as a whole did not differ very much, one might infer from the slave evidence that inequality in the U.S. also changed little over the seven decades. Further information on this point is now becoming available. Comprehensive data on the wealthholdings of Americans in 1790 do not exist, but estimates of the distribution of wealth in the New England and Middle colonies for 1774 have been constructed from information contained in the probate records of the estates of persons who died in that year. These estimates indicate that the richest one fifth of the free adult population in 1774 possessed from 60 to 66 percent of colonial wealth while the bottom half of wealthholders had approximately 8 percent. For 1860 the corresponding estimates are 88 percent and 12 percent.* The estimates of wealth distribution for 1774 and 1860 thus reveal a high degree of inequality at both dates, but also a moderate tendency toward increased inequality over time. However, the underlying wealth data for 1774 are much sketchier than those for 1860. And wealth distributions for the southern colonies, not yet available, will likely show greater inequality than in the still largely rural New England and Middle colonies where slaveholding was of limited significance. Therefore, the hypothesis of a relatively constant and high degree of inequality in the distribution of wealth between the Revolutionary and Civil War eras cannot yet be rejected. But if a change did in fact occur, it was likely in the direction of somewhat increased inequality in wealthholding.

What can be said, then, of the egalitarian interpretation of the era of the common man? Is it all a myth? Surprising as it may seem, given the evidence on widespread inequalities in the distribution of antebellum wealth, there are reasons for doubting that the egalitarian position is altogether mythical. Adults in modern societies tend to move through life in a fairly typical pattern of income and saving, and therefore of wealth accumulation. They tend to have low incomes and low or even negative savings and wealth when they are young; then their incomes, savings, and accumulations grow in the middle adult years before tapering off, and, in the case of savings, becoming negative, in the retirement years.

* On the distribution of slaves, see the above-cited paper by Lee Soltow, "Economic Inequality in the United States in the Period from 1790 to 1860"; and on the wealth distribution for 1774, see Alice Hanson Jones, "Wealth Estimates for the New England Colonies about 1770," *Journal of Economic History*, 32 (March 1972), 98–127.

Now if every individual had exactly the same level and life-cycle pattern of income, saving, and wealth accumulation, it would follow that persons of middle age and older would possess most of the wealth while young adults would have little of it. Moreover, if the young adults were far more numerous than the older adults, a very unequal distribution of wealth would be measured even though each individual's life-cycle pattern of income and accumulation was exactly the same.* In short, a highly egalitarian society when observed at any one point may appear to have a very unequal distribution of wealth.

What does this imply about antebellum America? In 1860 the median age of the American population was only 19.4 years as compared with about 30.2 years in 1950. In other words, only one half the 1860 population consisted of adults. Moreover, the adult group itself was comparatively youthful. Of adult males, over 5 million in 1860 were between ages twenty and thirty-nine, while less than 3 million were aged forty and over; in 1950, by way of contrast, adult males over forty (26.1 million) actually outnumbered those between twenty and forty (22.7 million). In the antebellum era, therefore, a disproportionate number of adults were in the age groups where wealth accumulation would be expected to have been relatively small. This expectation is confirmed in the studies earlier cited, which find a strong and direct relationship between age and wealth in 1860. Consequently, the observed inequality of wealth distribution in 1860—and presumably in earlier years when the American population was even younger—cannot be taken as unqualified evidence against the egalitarian interpretation.

Increasing urbanization of the antebellum American population is another factor bearing on the interpretation of observed inequalities in wealth distribution at given points in time. Inequality appears to have been greater in urban areas; in particular, the proportions of people reporting no wealth or almost no wealth were noticeably larger in urban places than in nonurban areas. Growing immigration to the United States in the late antebellum decades accounts for some of this difference. Immigrants tended disproportionately to settle in urban areas, and the studies of wealth distribution in 1860 indicate, as might be expected, that the foreign born had accumulated less wealth on the average than native Americans. Expanding urban labor markets, moreover, attracted young native-born adults away from alternative rural employment. These Americans, as well as the immigrants, tended to be in the early, minimal-accumulation phases of their life cycle. In increasing numbers they chose to live and work in the seemingly less egalitarian cities because of the economic opportunities and advantages that the cities afforded them.

Geographic and economic mobility thus characterized the American

* This observation comes from Professor Robert E. Gallman of the University of North Carolina at Chapel Hill. See his paper "Professor Pessen on the 'Egalitarian Myth'," *Social Science History* (Winter 1978).

population before the Civil War. In 1860 well over one third of the free population resided in states other than the ones in which they had been born. Such a high degree of mobility was surely a response to economic opportunity, and in this respect it has long played a role in the egalitarian interpretation. Mobility also sheds some light on the revisionist position that inherited wealth and privilege counted for more than ability and hard work in the distribution of wealth. The evidence for the revisionist view comes mostly from examination of who the rich were in the old and large cities of the Atlantic seaboard. These rich tended to come from the old, established families of these cities, and to have substantial amounts of inherited wealth. Evidence from the newer cities of the West and South indicates that the well-to-do were far more likely to have come from other places and to have built their fortunes from their own efforts rather than from inheritance. Throughout history, no doubt, being born into a wealthy family has had its advantages for maintaining a position of wealth during one's lifetime. But the evidence shows that in the expanding American economy of the nineteenth century these advantages hardly precluded other people of initially limited means from attaining wealth. A widespread availability and abundance of resources together with a highly mobile and acquisitive population assured this result. Thus it was perhaps more on a basis of reason and observation than on myth that the United States impressed the egalitarian interpreters who contrasted it with the older societies of Europe.

With regard to the distribution of income in the antebellum economy, such impressionistic evidence and reasoning tends to take on greater weight in historical interpretations because in a quantitative sense much less is known about it than is known about the wealth distribution. It is certain, however, that income was more equally distributed than wealth. In the first place, the distribution of ability to earn income from one's labor was more equal than the distribution of wealth. While the census evidence argues that about one half of all American families had essentially no wealth at all in 1860, it is inconceivable that more than a tiny fraction of these families earned no income by working. Second, estimates of the division of the national income between labor income and property income indicate that labor's share was approximately two thirds of the total. Since labor income was both the largest part of total income and almost certainly more equally distributed than wealth, it is safe to say that the income distribution, if it were actually known for the antebellum years, would show considerably less inequality. Indeed, comparisons of later income and wealth distribution invariably indicate this relationship.

Under the assumption that returns to labor made up about two thirds of the national income in 1860, the average labor income per member of the labor force in that year was about $250 in 1860 values. Although less than one half of the labor force was in the employee category—more than one half of all workers were self-employed—independent estimates of wage levels are broadly consistent with this average annual wage figure. In 1860 farm laborers earned an average of $13 to 14 per month with board, while nonfarm common laborers earned just over $1 a day. Industrial wages on an annual basis ranged from about $200 per year in cotton manufacturing to $350 in iron making. Miners earned from $250 to $350 per year. The antebellum work week was long by present standards. Eleven or twelve hours per day for six days was not uncommon, and labor organizations were still struggling for the ten-hour day in most industries.

By themselves the wage and income data mean little. A better idea of the standard of living in 1860 emerges when they are related to prices of the necessities of life. Rents in the manufacturing towns of the Northeast averaged from $4.50 to $6.00 per month for four- to six-room tenements. In the food category, meats cost ten to fifteen cents per pound and bread seven to eight cents per loaf. Milk was around five cents a quart while a bushel of potatoes could be had for anywhere from twenty cents to a dollar. Men's suits and overcoats ranged upward from $10 and $5 respectively. Detailed budget studies are not available for the period, but a few impressionistic estimates indicate that a typical working-class family of the 1850s spent about one half of its income on food, one fourth on shelter, and most of the remainder on clothing. For the majority of people, then, there was neither much leisure nor, after providing for the basic necessities of life, much money to spend on leisure-time activities.

The standard of living of a typical common man in the U.S., even at the close of the antebellum era, was therefore not very high by modern standards. This conclusion is to be expected. However, the growth process that furnishes us with this expectation was already working at the time. Stanley Lebergott, the distinguished economic historian of American labor, estimates from a wide range of painstakingly gathered evidence that real wages in the United States rose substantially in the decades before the Civil War. After remaining essentially level from 1800 to 1820, real wages, according to Lebergott, rose about 25 percent from 1820 to 1832, another 25 percent from 1832 to 1850, and about 1 percent in the last antebellum decade when immigration increased the competition for jobs. If so, real wages were growing at nearly 1.5 percent per year from 1820 to 1850, and over 1.1 percent per year from 1820 to 1860. The laboring men, women, and children of the antebellum United States were sharing in the fruits of economic growth.

There was, of course, one glaring exception. The basic annual per capita "income" of black slaves—the value of their food, clothing, shelter, and medical care—was an estimated $34 in 1850. This was approximately one third of the American GNP per capita at the time. Adult male slaves had similar "incomes" of $50 to $60 per year, also about one third or less of what they might have earned as free workers. Next to this one great inequality of welfare in the antebellum economy, the others were comparatively insignificant.

Conclusion

Americans of the first half of the nineteenth century lived in an age of transition to economic modernity. In their lifetimes were unleashed the forces that changed the old order of barely perceptible changes in long-run living standards to the new order in which steady increases in the standard of living were taken for granted. Signs of economic progress were everywhere visible—in industry, agriculture, commerce, transportation, and communication. Economic progress was, of course, not an altogether new phenomenon. Earlier periods of history, both in America and elsewhere, had witnessed broad-based economic advances. But in nearly all such periods the elements making for progress had played themselves out or were reversed. The elements of economic progress that emerged in the United States during the early nineteenth century—technological change, specialization of activities, and market growth—were different in that they were capable of being expanded indefinitely. Economic growth, therefore, became self-sustaining, and continuing advances in production and incomes per worker, and per person, were translated into ever-rising standards of material welfare for most people.

Economic modernization was not without its drawbacks. An increasingly specialized and interdependent economic organization produced and distributed goods and services at ever lower real costs in terms of resources, but it also uprooted people from their traditional ways of economic existence and made them more liable to suffer from periodic instabilities of prices, production, and employment. The new economic world made less personal the relationships between employers and employees, between producers and consumers, and, in general, between decision makers and those affected by the decisions. In such ways the economic progress of one generation often led to the problems of the next. Yet so great were the material advantages of the new order that few people in America were in favor of turning back the clock to the simpler economy of the past.

SUGGESTED READINGS

Stuart Bruchey, *The Roots of American Economic Growth 1607–1861: An Essay in Social Causation* (New York: Harper & Row, 1968) is a good introduction to historical issues surrounding the emergence of modern economic growth in the United States. More quantitative and analytic an introduction is the chapter, "The Pace and Pattern of American Economic Growth" in Lance Davis, et al., *American Economic Growth: An Economist's History of the United States* (New York: Harper & Row, 1972), chap. 2. That chapter draws heavily on the basic source of quantitative information on economic growth since the 1830s, namely Robert E. Gallman, "Gross National Product in the United States, 1834–1909," in National Bureau of Economic Research, *Output, Employment, and Productivity in the United States after 1800*, Studies in Income and Wealth, vol. 30 (New York: National Bureau of Economic Research, 1966), pp. 3–76. The pattern of economic growth before the 1830s is a subject of much interest among economic historians for its bearing on the issue of when growth began; it is also rather intractable to the growth statistician. Both points are illustrated in papers by Paul David, "The Growth of Real Product in the United States Before 1840: New Evidence, Controlled Conjectures," *Journal of Economic History*, 27 (June 1967), 151–197; and Robert Gallman, "The Statistical Approach: Fundamental Concepts as Applied to History," in George R. Taylor and Lucas F. Ellsworth, eds., *Approaches to American Economic History* (Charlottesville: University Press of Virginia, 1971), pp. 63–86, which should be read in conjunction.

Economic welfare is a rather nebulous concept subject to many definitions and interpretations. In this chapter we have emphasized aspects that are measurable, such as wealth and income distributions, and trends in wages and living standards. Basic sources of such information include Donald R. Adams, Jr., "Wage Rates in the Early National Period: Philadelphia 1785–1830," *Journal of Economic History*, 28 (September 1968), 404–417; Alice Hanson Jones, "Wealth Estimates for the American Middle Colonies, 1774," *Economic Development and Cultural Change*, 18 (July 1970), part 2; and Alice Hanson Jones, "Wealth Estimates for the New England Colonies About 1770," *Journal of Economic History*, 32 (March 1972), 98–127; Robert E. Gallman, "Trends in the Size Distribution of Wealth in the Nineteenth Century: Some Speculations," in Lee Soltow, ed., *Six Papers on the Size Distribution of Wealth and Income* (New York: National Bureau of Economic Research, 1969), pp. 1–25; Stanley Lebergott, *Manpower in Economic Growth: The United States Record Since 1800* (New York: McGraw-Hill, 1964); Edgar W. Martin, *The Standard of Living in 1860: American Consumption Levels on the Eve of the Civil War* (Chicago: University of Chicago Press, 1942); Lee Soltow, "Economic Inequality in the United States in the Period from 1790 to 1860," *Journal of Economic History*, 31 (December 1971), 822–839; Lee Soltow, *Patterns of Wealthholding in Wisconsin Since 1850* (Madison: University of Wisconsin Press, 1971); Lee Soltow, "The Wealth, Income and Social Class of Men in Large Northern Cities of the United States in 1860," in James D. Smith, ed., *The Personal Distribution of Income and Wealth* (New York: National Bureau of Economic Research, 1975), chap. 9, pp. 233–276; Lee Soltow, *Men and Wealth in the United States, 1850–1870* (New Haven: Yale University Press, 1976); and Peter H. Lindert and Jeffrey G. Williamson, "Three Centuries of American Inequality," *Research in Economic History*, 1 (1976). More interpretative in emphasis are Edward Pessen, *Riches, Class and Power Before the Civil War* (Lexington, Mass.: D. C. Heath, 1973); and Robert Gallman, "Professor Pessen on the 'Egalitarian Myth'," *Social Science History* (Winter 1978).

PART III

THE

TRANSFORMATION

OF THE AMERICAN

ECONOMY

(1860-1914)

INTRODUCTION

The 1860–1914 period opened with a tragic Civil War that ended with the nation intact but badly scarred by the great loss of life and property. Yet the gains were impressive. Slavery was abolished, and the blacks acquired new legal rights that, after bitter setbacks, are the basis for the current thrust toward economic betterment. For the great majority of Americans the preservation of the Union meant both political unity (one nation-state) and all the opportunities that a unified, yet large and diversified, economy afforded: labor and capital had great mobility; national resources could be exploited; and a national market existed for the exchange of goods and services.

Once the ordeal of the Civil War was over, the economic growth of the United States advanced at a dramatic pace. Real GNP per capita grew at an average annual rate of 2 percent and shortly before World War I had reached about three times its 1865 level. An even better record was achieved for total output; real GNP increased at an average annual rate of more than 4 percent—an eightfold advance. In no prior period of American history had economic growth persisted for so many years. Depressions created periodic setbacks, but the secular or long-term trend was upward.

By 1913, the United States had become a predominantly urban industrial economy with the largest manufacturing output of any country in the world. Agriculture had undergone a relative decline in economic importance as urban manufacturing, commerce, and the service industries had increased their share of the national labor force and the national income. This process of economic growth manifested itself in the agricultural sector through the closing of the frontier, an unprecedented expansion of commercial agriculture, and an immense transfer of public land to private ownership.

Basic to all these changes was an increase in the numbers and varied abilities of the American people. Between 1860 and 1920 the population of the United States increased threefold, rising from 31.5 million to 106.5 million. Most of this great population expansion—about 60 percent of it—came from a high rate of natural increase. The other 40 percent came from a gigantic flow of immigrants to the United States. Between 1801 and 1890 some 11.1 million immigrants came, mainly from western Europe. Then from 1890 until 1920 an additional 18.2 million arrived, mostly from southern and eastern Europe.

The tidal wave of immigration was due usually to the pull of economic opportunity in America and the push of adverse economic and social conditions in Europe. From this inflow of immigrants came an increase in the rate of per capita economic growth. This was due in part to the higher percentage of males between the ages of fourteen and forty-four among the immigrants than in the native population. Hence, the American labor force increased at a higher rate than the population, and the level of per capita income rose more than it otherwise would have.

The contribution of immigrants to the American economy included a massive supply of different skills for industry and agriculture, scientific discoveries, and works of art and literature. Since the cost of the immigrants' upbringing and education had been taken care of in their countries of origin, American resources were spared. Thus one great gain for America was in the human capital.

CHAPTER 11

Continental Expansion

and the Modernization

of Agriculture

Between the Civil War and World War I, America's farmers, ranchers, and miners expanded their use of the nation's landed resources on an unprecedented scale. Decision makers at the federal level encouraged this expansion through policies designed to expedite the passing of public lands into individual ownership and use, through grants of land to railroads in order to bring Western resources into the national economy, and through a host of other measures—such as controlling hostile native American Indians—that cleared the way for pioneer settlers from the East. At the same time the vast expansion of land use stimulated inventors and manufacturers to develop and diffuse improved farm implements, machinery, and other equipment and techniques that contributed to spectacular increases in the total output of the primary producing sector and in its productive efficiency.

The consequences were momentous. In just a few decades an enormous amount of land, comparable in size to all of western Europe, was made available to farmers. The frontier—the western line of settlement that had been present from the earliest days of colonization in America—disappeared as a vast area from the Mississippi to the Pacific Ocean became dotted with pioneer communities. Improved transportation facilities, chiefly railroads, bound these communities into national and world markets for agricultural and natural resource products. The result was specialized, commercial production, and the American farmer, as never before, had to concern himself with both the market prices of the commodities he produced and the prices of the productive inputs and consumption goods he purchased.

The rapidity and magnitude of these changes caused major problems of adjustment for American farmers. The tremendous growth of agricultural production would have exerted a depressing effect on farm prices in any case, but when this long-term trend was accentuated by periodic business depressions emanating from outside the agricultural sector, it was easy for the farmers to conclude that they were being deprived unjustly of the fruits of their labor. Remedies for this situation were sought by emerging farmers' organizations and coalitions that sought to use the political process to advance agrarian goals. The goal of higher prices for farm products was sought by calling for various measures to increase the money supply. The goal of lower prices for productive inputs such as credit, transportation, marketing, and processing led to calls for government regulation and other interventions in favor of the farmer. Some of these goals were achieved in the late-nineteenth century. But the golden age of American farming during the two decades before World War I was at least as much the result of a slowing down in the rate of expansion of the agricultural sector relative to other economic sectors as from a partial achievement of the farmers' monetary and regulatory goals.

Land Policy Decisions

During the antebellum years the trend of United States land policy decisions, as shown in chapter 6, was in the direction of making it ever easier for individual Americans to become owners of land. A fundamental reason for this policy was the large quantity of land available in relation to the nation's population. Coupled with internal transportation improvements and the development of wider markets for the products of land, the amount of land in the public domain created irresistible political and social pressure for easier terms of land acquisition by individuals. On the eve of the Civil War one could have predicted with confidence a continuation of this pressure. In the two previous decades the United States had increased its territory almost 70 percent by annexing Texas, by clearing American claims to the Oregon Territory with Great Britain, and by acquiring California and the remainder of the Southwest from Mexico through war and purchase. In 1860 all of these areas were still sparsely populated.

Congress responded in 1862 by passing the Homestead Act and taking an entirely new direction in national land policy. With some exceptions the principle of antebellum land policy had been that public land should be sold to private buyers to provide revenue for the federal government. The Homestead Act embodied a new philosophy, namely, that public land should be given free of charge, subject to certain conditions, to United States citizens. Thus, a person could obtain ownership of 160 acres of the public domain by residing on his claim for five years and cultivating it. Or he could purchase the land after only six months of residence at the prevailing minimum price, usually $1.25 per acre.

Although the Homestead Act embodied the revolutionary concept of free land, historians often have laid stress on certain weaknesses of the act and its amendments. The great bulk of the lands opened up to homesteading lay west of the 99th meridian, from the Great Plains to the Pacific coast. In this semi-arid and arid West a homestead of 160 acres was in general too small a parcel of land to provide an adequate income for a family engaged in dry farming or livestock raising. The Homestead legislation was superimposed, moreover, on a public land system with which it was incongruous in many ways. The federal government continued until 1891 to sell land for cash, and in fact more land was sold this way than was homesteaded. In addition, Congress granted some 130 million acres of public land to railroads, about 140 million to new and old states, and some 175 million acres to Indians for their reservations. Subsequent legislation opened up large tracts of Indian land for sale to settlers.

What this meant was that the great bulk of land put into cultivation after 1865 was in fact bought from the federal and state governments and from the land-grant railroads. Less than one fifth of all the new land was homesteaded. This fact, along with the activities of large-scale land speculators and the use of fraudulent homestead entries made by individuals for the benefit of land, timber, and mining companies, led many scholars to the conclusion that the Homestead Act was in large measure a failure. If by this it is meant that the act precluded individuals from obtaining farms of adequate size given the environmental conditions of the West, there are grounds for disagreements. Congress retained on the statute books the 1841 Pre-emption Act; combined with the Homestead law it made possible farm units of 320 acres. Moreover, in passing the 1873 Timber Culture Act, the 1877 Desert Land Act, and the 1878 Timber and Stone Act, Congress enabled individuals to obtain still larger tracts on favorable terms. All of these land laws together enabled settlers to acquire tracts as large as 1,120 acres in the semi-arid high plains and in the desert and intermountain regions of the West.

These land-policy measures often were poorly drafted from a legal point of view; hence, in the eyes of many observers they could be and were abused by individuals and corporations who obtained large tracts through fraudulent devices and unscrupulous intermediaries. These abuses and the ineptness of public land administration led Congress in 1889–91 to adopt a number of measures to restrict individual acquisition of public land under all laws to 320 acres, to encourage sales to bona fide farmers rather than to speculators, and to introduce a number of additional safeguards to earlier statutes that had been abused.

Despite the limitations of the Homestead Act, the federal land system in the late-nineteenth century appears to have worked very well judging by the progress of owner-operated farms. Outside of the cotton-growing South, where tenancy and sharecropping prevailed after 1865, a great deal of public land was acquired by owner-operators and tenancy was less common. In the public-land states outside the South a total of 1.7 million farms had been created by 1880. Of these, 1.3 million, roughly four fifths, were owner operated. In only four states in the West—California, Oregon, Colorado, and Nevada—did the farms average over 160 acres. Available evidence indicates, further, that much of the land granted to the railroads, given to the states, and purchased in quantity on speculation by absentee owners was eventually divided into single-family farms and sold to settlers. By 1900 the nonsouthern public-land states contained 2.4 million farms; roughly 70 percent were owner operated. Hence, the goal of disposing of the public domain so as to increase the class of small landowners had in good measure been achieved.

The Patterns of Westward Movement

During the later decades of the nineteenth century so many Americans moved into the West that the frontier—a clearly delineated line of settlement—ceased to exist. The population of the trans-Mississippi West increased from 4.5 million in 1860 to 16.4 million in 1900 and to 27.2 million in 1910. The migration of such large numbers of people in so relatively short a time was the result of many changes in the American economy and society. Decisions to transfer great amounts of the public domain to private ownership through the systematic application of old and new public land legislation greatly facilitated the westward movement. But other factors were equally important. One was the great expansion of the nation's population, which nearly tripled from 31.5 million to 92.4 million between 1860 and 1910. Other factors included the great extension of existing technologies, as in the building of transcontinental railroads, and the development of new technologies such as barbed wire, windmills, and farming and mining machinery.

Throughout American history the availability of natural resources had always attracted people to and beyond the westward-moving frontier well in advance of surveyors and public land sales. Hunters and trappers were among the earliest of these people. During the last half of the nineteenth century mineral deposits and grasslands capable of sustaining large-scale livestock production were two additional natural-resource magnets that drew pioneers to the West. More often than not, agricultural production on lands transferred from the public domain to private ownership was the last stage rather than an early stage of western settlement. Mining and cattlemen's frontiers often preceded the farmers' frontier.

Gold was discovered in the California foothills of the Sierra Nevada mountain range in 1848. The gold rush that followed drew thousands and thousands of wealth seekers to the West. The chance of making a fortune was small for any one prospector, but the rewards to the lucky few were high enough to make many persons willing to take the risk of great losses in time and capital.

From the 1850s to the 1890s other discoveries of valuable mineral deposits in the mountains and hills to the east of California led to the development of further mining frontiers. A succession of gold and silver discoveries between 1858 and 1876 caused swarms of miners to seek their fortunes in territories ranging from western Utah, Nevada, and Arizona to Idaho, Montana, the Dakotas, and Missouri. The most famous bonanzas were at Pike's Peak in Colorado, and at the Comstock Lode in western Nevada.

With the 1875–76 Black Hills gold rush the eastward advance of the mining frontier came to an end. At the same time the era of the small-scale placer miner was drawing to a close and the era of the mining capitalist was beginning. With their crude techniques the prospectors had only mined ore close to the surface; they had not been able to touch the far greater quantities of gold and silver contained in quartz lodes beneath the surfaces. After the pioneer miners revealed the potential mineral wealth of the Far West, eastern and British investors decided to invest in the financing of mine-shaft drilling, hydraulic and strip mining, quartz mills, and the numerous tunnels required for bringing the mineral deposits into production. These new sources of capital financed the extraordinary growth of copper, lead, and zinc mining, operations that proved to be more profitable in the long run, after 1875, than the more spectacular gold and silver rushes. By 1881 the center of mining-stock transactions had shifted from San Francisco to New York. Until then more mines had been operated with locally contributed funds on an unincorporated basis, or as closely held incorporations not subject to public sale of stock, than as joint stock companies. But the shift to New York indicated that the future of mining development lay with big corporations and that mining was being integrated into the national economy, on both a financial and a technological basis, rather than remaining a largely isolated western effort on a premodern technological level.

The growing economic importance of the mining industries in the West can be judged by the increase in the value of all metal-mining products from $29 million in 1870 to $131 million in 1890, and $468 million in 1919. Western mineral development had important impacts on economic growth as well as on finance and national politics. The flow of copper, lead, zinc, and other metals from the trans-Mississippi region contributed to developments in manufacturing, transportation, and communication by telephone and telegraph. And the decline in gold production relative to silver production between 1860 and 1894 had significant effects on the composition of the U.S. money supply, and created a major politico-economic movement favoring free coinage of silver from the 1870s to the 1890s (see chapter 15).

Although the various mining bonanzas in the West were picturesque, in most cases they were short-lived. Yet they had longer-term effects on western development because they stimulated an influx of tradesmen, artisans, and professional people—for example, doctors, lawyers, engineers —to provide goods and services needed by the miners. Small farmers and ranchers also were attracted to the bonanzas; they raised crops and livestock in the valleys near the mining settlements and supplied the settlements with foodstuffs, animals, and feed. When the bonanza mines declined many of these communities had reached sufficient size to sustain themselves as viable local economies.

Another natural resource that drew pioneers to the West was abundant grassland. From the Civil War until the 1880s the range-cattle industry expanded from Texas and New Mexico into the central and northern plains. An old gold miner once said of western resources, "There's gold from the grass roots up." Those who saw an element of truth in this remark created the western cattlemen's frontier which became a legendary part of American history.

The emergence of the cattlemen's frontier was facilitated by the removal between 1867 and 1890 of the Indians from their hunting grounds on the Great Plains to the more restricted quarters of government reservations. This drastic change in the way of life of the plains Indians was achieved through the use of military force and by the slaughter of millions of bison, or buffalo, by thousands of hunters. Often encouraged by the military and by land-hungry pioneers, these hunters were unconcerned about the importance of the bison to the Indians as the economic basis of their tribal way of life. The hunters were only anxious to obtain cash for bison hides; stripped of hides, bison carcasses were left to rot on the plains. In this manner, and largely because governments failed to protect the bison or to extend property rights to the Indians, a once vast natural resource of potential value to later generations was virtually extinguished in a few decades. The Indians and their wild cattle gave way to the pioneer cattlemen.

Other conditions and developments also promoted the growth of the range-cattle industry. Among them, on the supply side, were the great extent of the open-range grasslands, stretching from Texas to Montana, and the discovery that Texas cattle, the first to be herded, could withstand being exposed to the severe winters on the northern plains. On the demand side, the late nineteenth century brought an expanding market for meat in the East, especially in the cities, western access to this market through rail connections, and the development of the meat-packing industry, especially in the areas of refrigerated storage and shipping.

Between 1866 and 1885, over five million cattle were driven northward from Texas ranges to cattle markets in Kansas, Missouri, and Nebraska. At an average price of twenty dollars per steer, the sale of these cattle brought roughly one hundred million dollars of gross income to cattlemen. Many of the Texas cattle driven northward were not sold for immediate consumption but were used to stock the northern ranges. Others were fattened on corn and grass before sale. As the range-cattle industry expanded, western meat-packing centers grew up in cities such as Chicago, St. Louis, Kansas City, and Omaha. By moving west meat packers tended to minimize the cost of transporting cattle and meat products from the ranges to the consumers.

By the 1880s the cattle kingdom encompassed the entire plains from the Rio Grande to the Canadian border and from the croplands west of the Mississippi River to the slopes of the Rocky Mountains. The number of cattle on the northern Great Plains increased from 130 thousand in 1860 to 4.5 million in 1880. By the latter date ranching had become a business with efficient methods of operation. Ranchers cooperated with one another, often through the formation of livestock associations that registered different ranchers' brands and enforced each member's right to ranch even though he had simply appropriated a "range right" to public grazing land. As cattle prices and ranchers' profits rose in the early 1880s, capital from the eastern United States and from Europe was invested in the range-cattle industry, leading to the formation of huge ranches. In 1884, some congressmen pointed out that foreigners, mainly from Great Britain, had acquired more than twenty million acres of land, most of it in the range-cattle area. Many of the foreign-owned ranches were held by corporations, and their chief investors came to be known as cattle barons.

The peak of the range-cattle boom was reached in 1884. After that year overstocking of the range and the marketing of cattle at a greater rate than the normal rate of consumption led to depressed cattle prices. Then climatic disasters—a harsh winter of 1885–86 and the great blizzard of January 1887—hit the industry with large cattle losses. These events hastened the decline of open-range ranching. The era of longhorns grazing on the public domain gave way to an era of stocking with improved

European breeds (Herefords, Shorthorns and Anguses), barbed-wire fencing, and winter feeding. Quality of product was increasingly emphasized in the cattle business.

Cattle were not the only livestock herded in the West. During the 1870s many sheep raisers moved from Ohio to California, Colorado, and New Mexico. After achieving success there, they began in the 1880s to move onto the Great Plains. Despite several years of open warfare between cattlemen and shepherds, sheep raising soon became established as an important livestock industry in the West. By 1903 nearly one half of the sixty-four million sheep in the United States were located on the plains and in the Rockies.

After the cattleman and the shepherd came the farmer. During the late 1880s pioneer farmers began to compete with the cattlemen for the land on the Great Plains. Although the farmers were worried by the lack of timber and water on the Plains, they overcame these obstacles through the invention and use of barbed-wire fencing, and by the use of windmills in the pumping of subsurface water for livestock and irrigation. Farm machinery was also utilized to allow mechanical cultivation of the large farms needed to support a family under semi-arid conditions. By 1890 a farmer by himself could plant, take care of, and harvest 135 acres of wheat as against the 7 acres feasible before these inventions.

The new methods of ranching and farming were implemented on a massive scale in the American West. Between 1870 and 1900 millions of farmers occupied hitherto unexploited farm land in Kansas, Nebraska, the Dakotas, Wyoming, Montana and Oklahoma. More land was settled in the last three decades of the nineteenth century than in all of America's past: 407 million acres were occupied and 189 million improved between 1607 and 1870, whereas 430 million acres were settled and 225

TABLE 11-1
Gross and Net Farm Output, Key Years, 1869-1919

Year	Gross Farm Output	Intermediate Products Consumed	Net Farm Output
	(Millions of 1929 dollars)		
1869	3,950	440	3,510
1879	6,180	730	5,450
1889	7,820	1,000	6,820
1899	9,920	1,360	8,560
1909	10,770	1,620	9,150
1919	11,930	2,250	9,680

SOURCE: J. W. Kendrick, Productivity Trends in the United States (Princeton, N.J.: Princeton University Press, 1961), p. 347.

million placed under cultivation between 1870 and 1900. By 1900 this newly occupied western part of the United States raised nearly 50 percent of the cattle, 56 percent of the sheep, about 25 percent of the hogs, and 32 percent of the nation's cereal crop. Fifty-eight percent of the wheat was produced in the western states and territories.

Agricultural expansion continued after the turn of the century but at a much subdued pace. Whereas the number of farms in the United States had more than doubled from 2.7 million to 5.7 million between 1870 and 1900, it increased to only 6.4 million in 1920. Data on real farm output, given in Table 11–1, reveal the change that took place in still clearer terms. From them it can be calculated that gross farm output grew at an annual compound rate of 3.1 percent from 1869 to 1899, and at 0.9 percent from 1899 to 1919. For the same two periods net farm output grew, respectively, at annual rates of 3.0 and 0.6 percent. The early twentieth century deceleration of agricultural growth is quite important to an understanding of why agricultural prosperity followed the late-nineteenth century's agrarian unrest. The disappearance of the frontier implied a reduction in the amount of previously unused land available and suitable for agriculture. Under this new condition American farmers prospered as the growth of demand for their products exceeded the growth of supply.

Agricultural Productivity and Its Sources

As American agriculture expanded in the half century after the Civil War, a number of significant changes took place in the nature of agricultural production. Of these changes by far the most important was mechanization, the substitution of machinery and equipment for labor. The total amount of capital used in agriculture (see Table 11–2) increased at a rate of 2 percent per year between 1869 and 1919, which is virtually the same rate as net farm output (Table 11–1) grew during the same period. Most of the sub-categories of agricultural capital grew at rates not far different from this, but one of the categories, machinery and equipment, grew almost twice as fast, at a rate of 3.9 percent per year over the fifty years.

The significance of mechanization becomes clear when its effects on labor are considered. The agricultural labor force was approximately 6.8 million in 1870 and 10.8 million in 1920. These data imply that the farm labor force grew at 0.9 percent per year, or about 1 percentage point less than the rate of growth of output. In other words, output per worker in agriculture, largely as a result of mechanization, increased at a rate of approximately 1 percent per year. The substitution of capital for labor

TABLE 11-2

Material Capital Stocks in Agriculture, Key Years 1869-1919
(millions of 1929 dollars)

Year	Total	Land	Structures	Machinery and Equipment	Work Stock	Inventories Livestock	Crops
1869	23,145	13,836	4,578	564	623	2,697	847
1879	32,941	19,643	6,367	828	906	3,643	1,554
1889	40,132	23,863	7,006	1,217	1,274	4,698	2,074
1899	48,004	29,107	8,057	1,900	1,504	4,770	2,666
1909	55,295	31,735	11,255	3,012	1,739	4,960	2,594
1919	62,600	34,254	13,671	3,984	1,906	5,745	3,040

SOURCE: John W. Kendrick, Productivity Trends in the United States (Princeton, N.J.: Princeton University Press, 1961), p. 367.

in agriculture had a dramatic effect on the composition of the American labor force. Over one half of American workers labored in agriculture in 1870, whereas by 1920 only about one quarter did so.

The Civil War acted as a catalyst in farm mechanization. Between 1830 and 1860 various machines and implements, notably improved iron and steel plows, seed drills, cultivators, mechanical reapers, and threshing machines, were invented and began to come into use on American farms. When a million farmers were withdrawn from agricultural production to serve in the Union armies, the trend toward mechanization was given a powerful boost. The men and women left on the farms of the North and West turned to the new machinery, especially reapers and threshers, and even succeeded in producing a greater wheat crop than during peacetime.

With mechanization came a general displacement of men by horses as the motive power for agricultural implements. After the war a number of important horse-drawn implements were developed to complement or replace those innovated earlier. These included the Marsh harvester, the twine binder, the sulky, the gang plow, the spring-tooth and disc harrows, the self-binding reaper, and the "combine" reaper-thresher. The new machines created a large demand for horses, and in response to it the number of horses on American farms increased from 7.1 million in 1870 to 16.9 million in 1900. In 1920 there were 19.7 million farm horses, but by that time the horse had begun to be replaced by the gasoline tractor. Introduced in 1905 tractors on American farms increased from 1,000 in 1910 to 246,000 in 1920.

The effect of mechanization on agricultural productivity shows up clearly in studies that have been made of the production of wheat, corn, and oats. Output per farm worker engaged in producing these crops increased between three and four times between 1840 and 1910, or at compound annual rates of 1.5 to 2.0 percent. About 60 percent of the observed increase in productivity is attributed to mechanization. Nearly all of the growth in productivity can be explained by the combined effects of mechanization and the westward expansion of agriculture, two processes that interacted and reinforced one another. The existence of the West meant that great amounts of additional land were available, and the existence of the new machines meant that an individual farmer could plant and harvest many more acres and thresh many more bushels of grain than had previously been possible with hand implements.

Mechanization was much more successful in some types of agriculture, for example, grain production, than in others during the half century before World War I. In this period mechanization had little effect on the production of cotton, tobacco, sugar beets, and garden vegetables, or on the milking of cows. The problems of mechanization in these areas were more complex than they were in grain production. Nonetheless, a failure to mechanize did not prevent some great expansions of output in these areas. Cotton production, for example, increased from 2.5 to 13.4 million bales in the half century after 1869, and cotton for many of these years continued to be the nation's major export product, as it had been in antebellum times. The output of cotton grew because of the abundant supply of unskilled farm labor in the Southeast, the increased use of fertilizer there, and the expansion of the cotton belt to the Southwest. But an inability or a failure to mechanize could and did create large differences in the economic welfare of farmers and regions. In the absence of mechanization, output per farmer remained much lower in the South than in the rest of the country throughout the 1870–1920 period. During the same decades mechanization raised farmer productivity in the Midwest and the Great Plains, which had been well below that of the Northwest and the Far West in 1870, to relatively higher levels.

Regional Specialization in Agriculture

Between the end of the Civil War and the outbreak of World War I, American farmers developed distinct patterns of farming in different regions of the United States which have persisted to the present. A trend to specialization in production, both on individual farms and in particular regions, occurred with an increase in the mechanization of agriculture and striking improvements in transportation and marketing facilities. An increasing number of farmers shifted from the subsistence, diversified farm to the specialized, commercial farm as railroads expanded throughout the country and as markets for farm goods were extended or created by the spread of grain elevators, warehouses, stockyards, packing plants, and transport facilities. Among the important factors determining the location of farm production were the variations in soil and climate from one area to another as well as the distance and transportation cost for specific commodities from the farms to the consuming centers.

Millions of farmers had to engage in decision making about which farm products they wanted to produce in any specific area. Their judgment in any particular case usually depended on applying the principle of comparative advantage. This principle states that an area tends to specialize in the production of those products for which the value of output per unit of input is highest relative to other areas. In other words, a region would tend to specialize in those products for which its cost of production is lowest relative to other areas. That is why the Great Plains came to specialize in wheat production and cattle raising, the corn belt in corn production and livestock feeding, the Lake states and the Northeast in dairy production, and the South in cotton and tobacco production.

Transportation improvements and opportunities for mechanizing production were the major causes of changes in regional specialization to exploit comparative advantages after the Civil War. The shift of wheat production onto the Great Plains provides an instructive illustration of the decision making process. When the railroad reached the Plains, and machinery made it possible for a farmer to plant and harvest large acreages, the center of wheat production moved to the West even though wheat yields per acre were substantially greater in the Midwestern corn belt and the East. This location decision may seem puzzling until one realizes that the opportunity cost of growing wheat in the corn belt or the East would involve the loss of valuable corn and dairy products that otherwise might have been produced. The Plains, in contrast, were not suited for corn and dairy production; therefore, despite relatively low yield per acre the true cost of wheat production was lower than on the more fertile lands to the east.

Agrarian Crises and the Farmers' Welfare

The tremendous increase in land ownership, capital goods, and output in American agriculture between the Civil War and World War I represented an unparalleled advance in the economic well-being of millions of Americans engaged in farming. Measured in terms of the wealth acquired by farmers who had little or no capital at the beginning of their careers, a greater number of poor and tenant farmers became members of the middle class than in any previous period in American history. During periods of prosperity most farmers in the United States seem to have been reasonably content with their lot. But in periods of depression, especially in 1873–79, 1882–85, and 1893–97, the discontent of many farmers, particularly in the Midwest and the South, became intense and inspired them to organize movements to protest against a variety of economic ills.

The first powerful farm pressure group, the Grange, originated in 1867, mainly to fight excessively high railroad and grain elevator rates and to form cooperatives for the purpose of lowering the cost of the commodities the farmers bought and marketing more profitably the farmers' own products. After achieving some notable successes in railroad and elevator rate regulation in the early 1870s, the Grange suffered a sudden decline in popularity in 1876 because of the failure of many of its cooperative enterprises. Many farmers then turned to the Greenback party, a movement that sought a great expansion in the supply of greenbacks in order to counteract the declining price trend and to bring about a rise in the general price level (see chapter 15). When this effort failed after considerable political activity between 1876 and the mid-1880s, many farmers joined together to form new agrarian organizations—farmers' alliances, wheels, unions, and clubs—with widespread support in the cotton-growing South and in the wheatlands of the trans-Mississippi West. Although the original stress in these organizations was on education and self-help through agrarian cooperatives, by 1890 the farmers had turned to politics. In 1892 they helped form the Populist or People's party, which advocated radical reforms of finance, transportation, and other aspects of the economy. Agrarians and others made support of the free coinage of silver the dominant plank of both the Populist and the Democratic party platforms in the presidential election of 1896. Although the Populists (along with the Democrats) were defeated and the Populists disappeared as an effective party, the silver issue put "fire into the belly" of many a champion—and many a critic—of their views. But the question economic historians have to answer today is: How valid were the Grange and Populist complaints in the light of careful statistical and theoretical analysis?

One major protest of American farmers was against the falling price level for farm products from 1867 to 1897. The wholesale price index for farm products fell from 133 in 1867 to 71 in 1890 and to 40 in 1896. Many farmers felt that these falling prices increased the heavy burden of debt repayment on their mortgages, and that this situation hurt their terms of trade when they sold in world competitive markets while buying goods and services in local or national markets, which in certain sections were, and in other sections were thought to be, dominated by monopolies or oligopolies. The farmer often felt that he was caught in a cost-price squeeze. Railroad freight rates were stressed as a specially grievous cost-factor, as was the cost of borrowing money to finance the purchase of such inputs as land and machinery.

What is the verdict of leading scholars today on these charges? Careful analysis of wholesale price indexes for farm and nonfarm products for the period 1867–97 shows that nonfarm prices fell as rapidly as farm prices in many cases, and in some cases fell even more rapidly. Hence, the relative price position of the farmer—of his terms of trade—was not impaired.

On the subject of railroad freight rates, however, the farmers stood on firmer ground. A comparative study of railroad rates and farm prices demonstrates that railroad freight rates fell sharply and steadily from 1867 to 1897, but that farm prices for such major crops as corn, cotton, and wheat fell as much and in some years, for example, the mid-1890s, even more drastically than did railroad rates. Since transport charges constituted a major part of farmers' costs, particularly west of Chicago, many farmers felt that the decrease in railroad rates in the post-Civil War period was not large enough to improve their economic position. In addition, the farmer felt he was a victim of discrimination because rates per ton mile were often much higher from the farm to regional markets than for intercity and interregional shipments. In areas where transport charges were a relatively high percentage of farm cost, the hostility of farmers to the railroads was most intense; considerably less protest came from areas where transport charges were less onerous.

Another important complaint of many farmers centered on the heavy burden of farm mortgages during periods of depression. In 1890 approximately 29 percent of all farms were mortgaged to 35 percent of their value. But in the North Central region, center of the Populist party, almost 39 percent of the farms were mortgaged in 1890. A seeming safeguard against financial injury was the short life span of most mortgages; it ranged from three and one half to five years. Yet when substantial changes occurred in the price level, as in 1873–79 and 1893–97, farmers with mortgage debts based on higher price levels suffered a financial loss.

Meeting the interest payments on their farm mortgages was also difficult for many farmers during periods of depression. In 1880 interest rates on farm mortgages in the Far West were almost twice as high as the corresponding interest rates in the Middle Atlantic region. During the next three decades, as the flow of investment funds from the Northeast to the West increased, this difference in interest rates gradually diminished. Between 1875 and 1900 interest rates dropped sharply in the Great Plains from a high of 16 to 17 percent to a low of 5 to 6 percent. Nevertheless, farmers with a high debt-to-asset ratio encountered great hardships in making their interest payments when the prices of farm products declined. A substantial number of such debtor farmers lost their farms through foreclosures on their mortgages, especially in the North Central states. Western and southern debtor farmers were driven by fear of fore-closure to seeking remedies through the radical programs of the Grangers and the Populists. The farmers' decision to seek political action can be seen as a basically rational response to economic distress, even though one may disagree with some of the remedies proposed.

Many Populists were convinced that strong economic pressures drove a large number of once independent farmers into becoming tenant farm-ers. The U.S. Census statistics show an increase in the percentage of all farms in the United States operated by tenants from 25.6 percent in 1880 to 35.3 percent in 1900 and 38.1 percent in 1920. The basis for concern by the Populists was the fact that the percentage of farm tenancy was highest in the South and Midwest where the impact of debt burden was greatest; on the other hand, the lowest percentage was to be found in New England, the Rocky Mountain states, and the Pacific Coast.

For many American farm tenants, tenancy was a temporary condition, a way of stepping up on the agricultural ladder; young men from the locality and newcomers to the area could start out as farm laborers to gain experience and time before buying land for themselves. But some farmers remained permanently in the status of farm tenants; this was especially true in the South, for both poor whites and poor blacks. Farm tenancy in the South had developed on a large scale after the breakup of the pre-Civil War plantations. Once they had been emancipated, most of the former slaves decided not to work on the plantations as hired labor. They lacked the means to begin farming on their own and were not given any significant economic support by northern Reconstructionists. The freedmen had little choice but to accept small allotments of land (usually forty acres) from landlords, with whom they agreed to share the crop. The landlord and the local country storekeeper provided the tenant with a mule, plow, and means of subsistence and then resorted to crop liens in order to protect their equity. They also helped to have state laws enacted that tied the sharecropper to the land in what came to be called debt peonage. The economic aspects of the sharecropper system were gradually extended to large numbers of poor white farmers, but the percentage of black farmers who were sharecroppers was twice as large in 1900 as that of white farmers: 38 percent versus 19.9 percent. These conditions were intensified by the profound depressions of 1873 and 1893 as well as the lesser depression of 1882.

One major factor in the post-Civil War agrarian unrest was the farm-ers' belief in the contraction of the money supply. Actually, statisticians have demonstrated that the money supply (coin and paper currency plus commercial bank deposits) expanded between 1867 and 1896 at a rate in excess of the growth of population and at about the same rate as that of total production. But price levels fell drastically in the United States and in Europe as well. Hence, although the money supply did not actually contract in the long run, it clearly did not increase rapidly enough to maintain a stable price level. Farmers' organizations and other protest movements were aware both of the widespread demonetization of silver in Europe and America during the 1870s and of a slowing rate of world-wide gold production. This led to calls for more paper greenbacks and the free coinage of silver in the United States.

Since nonfarm prices fell as rapidly as farm prices, the proposed monetary solutions to farm problems probably would not have had much effect. American farmers' problems in the last three decades of the nineteenth century were more the result of nonmonetary developments, in particular the rapid expansion of farm production, the competition of other farmers in new producing areas within and outside of the United States, and the difficulty in agriculture of quickly adjusting production decisions to changes in demand. As we noted earlier, net farm output increased at a rate of more than 3 percent per year between 1869 and 1899. This expansion of production substantially exceeded the growth of population and created supply-demand imbalances at critical phases of the business cycle that caused sharp farm-price fluctuations. When depressions occurred in the 1870s, the 1880s, and the 1890s, employment and income contraction in the manufacturing and service sectors contributed greatly to the hardships of farm producers, particularly those who produced staple crops (for example, wheat, corn, cotton) and livestock. Farmers who went into the production of dairy products, of orchard and citrus fruits, and of garden vegetables were more protected from the bad consequences of business fluctuations because of the rapidly increasing urban demand for their products.

Growing domestic and foreign competition also created difficulties for many farmers. As grain and livestock production expanded in the West, producers of these products in the Midwest and the East faced falling prices and incomes as well as a need to reorient their product mixes. Foreign competition was less directly perceived as a threat by American farmers, but in fact it may have exerted a more powerful influence than domestic competition. On the whole American farmers benefited greatly from world—particularly European—demand for their rising output of agricultural products. The share of U.S. gross farm output absorbed by Europe increased from one eighth to one quarter in the three decades after the Civil War. But the international market could prove fickle in the short run. In the 1880s and 1890s competition in grain production came from newly developed agricultural regions in Canada, Australia, New Zealand, Argentina, and South Africa, as well as from Russia and India. In the 1890s growing competition in cotton came from Egypt and India. As a consequence the American farmer was plagued by uncertainty and fluctuating prices. In some cases, good crops in the United States coincided with bad crops elsewhere, and the American farmer profited. In other cases, bumper crops outside the United States led to falling prices and losses for American farmers. More and more, the farmer found that he was operating in an international market where the prices of agricultural commodities fluctuated widely under changing conditions of world supply and demand.

A third problem faced in greater measure by farmers than by other producers compounded the difficulty of adjusting to the rapid changes in supply and demand that were characteristic of the late-nineteenth century. Agricultural production decisions—the choice of what commodities to produce and how much of each—had to be made many months in advance of the time when the commodities would be ready for marketing. Unlike the nonfarm producers with shorter production cycles, the farmer could not easily vary the flow of material inputs and labor in response to short-run shifts in market conditions. This vulnerability of the farmer to forces over which he had little or no control goes far toward explaining his problems in coping with the dynamics of commercial agriculture in a period of rapid change. Later generations of American farmers sought to enlist still more aid in the form of government programs and regulations in their attempts to deal with their continuing problems of adjustment to change.

The Golden Age of Agriculture

During the period 1897–1915, American agriculture enjoyed the greatest measure of sustained prosperity in its history. What happened was essentially a reversal of the pattern of the three decades before 1897; whereas in this earlier period the supply of farm products increased faster than demand, after 1897 the demand grew faster than the supply.

Real farm output in either gross or net terms, as noted earlier, grew at less than one third of its 1869–99 rate between 1899 and 1919. The slowing of output growth was caused in part by the closing of the frontier, which implied a reduced availability of potential farmland, and in part by a shift of labor in relative terms away from agriculture. In 1900 almost 40 percent of American workers were in agriculture. Fifteen years later the percentage had fallen to less than 30. Workers were attracted to industry rather than agriculture by higher industrial wages and incomes, but the rapidity of the shift during this period resulted in farm workers' wages and farmers' incomes rising relative to those in the nonfarm sector. During the years 1911–15 the average annual net income for persons engaged in agriculture was about $370 compared to $495 per worker engaged in industry. Thus, farm incomes were about three fourths of those in industry, an unusually favorable ratio for the farmers, whose cost of living historically has been lower than that of the urban worker.

While agricultural output growth slowed considerably from earlier rates, domestic and foreign demand for farm products continued to expand at high rates. In the domestic market the factor of crucial significance was the rapid growth of industrial production. By 1915 industrial production was one and one-half times greater than it had been in 1895, whereas agricultural output rose only by one half. Industrial expansion attracted a growing proportion of the population—including large numbers of immigrants—to urban areas where they depended upon the farmer for food instead of competing with him on the land. As a result, the terms of exchange became increasingly favorable to agriculture, and the ratio of prices paid to prices received by farmers remained unusually steady in the years 1910–14, the so-called parity years to which later farm groups would point in seeking government assistance to raise their incomes. These years truly were a golden age, a time when there were more farmers than in any previous or subsequent period of American history, and the relative economic position of these farmers was extremely favorable by historical standards.

Conclusion

From the Civil War to World War I, American agriculture continued in the pattern of absolute expansion but relative decline that had begun in the antebellum period. Agriculture's growth was unusually high during the last three decades of the nineteenth century. Land-policy decisions to continue the rapid transfer of the public domain to private ownership on liberal terms were an important factor in the expansion. The natural resources of the West—minerals, grasslands, and farmlands—acted as magnets to easterners and migrants from overseas. At the same time railroad building on a colossal scale opened up markets for western products and mechanization allowed westerners to increase greatly the amount of land that could be farmed by an individual farmer.

The rapid growth of farm output and the extension of specialization and commercial agriculture to new areas created a number of economic problems for farmers and prompted the emergence of agrarian protest movements during the 1870s, the 1880s, and the 1890s. Even though these movements enjoyed limited success in obtaining their specific objectives, from the experience farmers learned political lessons that were helpful in subsequent decades. The farmer's need for protest organizations and political pressure groups declined rapidly after the end of the century. In the early years of the twentieth century farmers enjoyed a golden age of prosperity, which resulted from a sharp drop in the rate of growth in agricultural output while the demand for farm products continued to expand at high rates as a consequence of rapid industrialization and urban development.

SUGGESTED READINGS

Among the most informative, up-to-date studies on the post-Civil War frontiers and United States land policy are Ray Allen Billington, *Westward Expansion: A History of the American Frontier*, 4th ed. (New York: Macmillan, 1974); Gilbert C. Fite, *The Farmer's Frontier, 1865–1900* (New York: Holt, Rinehart, & Winston, 1966); Paul Gates, *History of Public Land Law Development* (Washington, D.C.: United States Government Printing Office, 1968); Louis Pelzer, *The Cattlemen's Frontier* (Glendale, Cal.: Arthur H. Clark, 1936); and Rodman W. Paul, *Mining Frontiers of the Far West* (New York: Holt, Rinehart, & Winston, 1963); and Walter Prescott Webb, *The Great Plains* (Boston: Ginn, 1931).

For valuable analyses of the economics of mining and cattle raising, see Israel Borenstein, *Capital and Output Trends in Mining Industries, 1870–1948* (Occasional Paper 45, New York: National Bureau of Economic Research, 1954); Orris Herfindahl, "Development of the Major Mining Industries . . . 1839 to 1909," in National Bureau of Economic Research, *Output, Employment and Productivity in the United States After 1800, Studies in Income and Wealth* vol. 30 (New York: Columbia University Press, 1966), pp. 293–346; and Gene M. Gressley, *Bankers and Cattlemen* (New York: Alfred E. Knopf, 1966).

Out of the vast literature on post-Civil War agriculture, the following writings rank high for their illuminating treatment of controversial topics: Harold Barger and Hans Landsberg, *American Agriculture, 1899–1939* (New York: National Bureau of Economic Research, 1942); John W. Kendrick, *Productivity Trends in the United States* (Princeton: Princeton University Press, 1961); Ralph Loomis and Glen Barton, *Productivity of Agriculture . . . 1870–1958* (Washington, D.C.: U.S. Department of Agriculture, Technical Bulletin 1238, 1961); William Parker, "Agriculture," in Lance E. Davis et al., *American Economic Growth* (New York: Harper & Row, 1972), pp. 396–417; Harvey S. Perloff et al., *Regions, Resources, and Economic Growth* (Baltimore: Johns Hopkins Press, 1960); Nathan Rosenberg, *Technology and American Economic Growth* (New York: Harper & Row, Harper Torchbooks, 1972); James H. Shideler, ed., *Agriculture in the Development of the Far West* (Washington, D.C.: Agricultural History Society, 1975); Frederick Strauss and Louis Bean, *Gross Farm Income and Indices of Farm Production and Prices . . . 1869–1937* (Washington, D.C.: U.S. Department of Agriculture, Technical Bulletin 703, 1940); Alvin S. Tostlebe, *Capital in Agriculture . . . since 1870* (Princeton: Princeton University Press, 1957); James W. Whitaker, ed., *Farming in the Midwest, 1840–1900* (Washington, D.C.: Agricultural History Society, 1974); and Vivian Wiser, ed., *Two Centuries of American Agriculture* (Washington, D.C.: Agricultural History Society, 1978); A classic work on agriculture-industry relations, 1896–1914 is *Agriculture in an Unstable Economy* (New York: McGraw-Hill, 1945) by Theodore W. Schultz, a Nobel Laureate in Economics.

On the causes and issues of the Grange and Populist revolts, the following repay careful reading: (pro Populist) Lawrence Goodwyn, *Democratic Promise: The Populist Movement in America* (New York: Oxford University Press, 1976); John D. Hicks, *The Populist Revolt* (Minneapolis: University of Minnesota Press, 1931); Theodore Saloutos, *Farmer Movements in the South, 1865–1933* (Lincoln, Neb.: Bison Books, 1960); and Fred Shannon, *The Farmer's Last Frontier: Agriculture 1865–1897* (New York: Farrar & Rinehart, 1945); (revisionist) Allan Bogue, *From Prairie to Corn Belt* (Chicago: University of Chicago Press, 1963), and *Money at Interest* (Ithaca: Cornell

University Press, 1955); John D. Bowman, "Midwestern Farm Land Values and Farm Land Income 1860 to 1900," *Yale Economic Essays*, 5 (Fall 1965), 317–354; Stephen J. DeCanio, *Agriculture in the Post-Bellum South* (Cambridge, Mass.: M.I.T. Press, 1974); Robert Higgs, *The Transformation of the American Economy, 1865–1914* (New York: John Wiley, 1971); and *Competition and Coercion: Blacks in the American Economy, 1865–1914* (New York: Cambridge University Press, 1977); Anne Mayhew, "A Reappraisal of the Causes of Farm Protest . . . 1870–1900," *Journal of Economic History*, 32 (1972); Roger Ransom and Richard Sutch, *One Kind of Freedom: The Economic Consequences of Emancipation* (Cambridge, Eng.: Cambridge University Press, 1977); and Morton Rothstein, "America in the International Rivalry for the British Wheat Market," *Mississippi Valley Historical Review*, 47 (December 1960).

CHAPTER 12

━━

Mass Production and

the Advent of Big Business

The United States was already a leading industrial nation in 1860. Manufacturing employed almost one seventh of the labor force. Factory production, with coal-burning steam engines to power metal machines, had become typical of a variety of industries. An American System of Manufactures had earned an international reputation for standardization and interchangeable parts, basic elements of mass production. Thus, it is useful to view the Industrial Revolution that took place from 1865 to 1914 as the continuation of a process already well under way and only temporarily slowed by the events of the Tragic Conflict.

From the base established in the decades before the Civil War, manufacturing grew dramatically in the ensuing years. According to Edwin Frickey's widely accepted index, manufacturing production expanded by twelve and one-half times from 1860 to 1914. Similarly, Robert E. Gallman's data (see Table 12–1) on value added by manufacture show a seven and one-quarterfold increase from 1860 just to the end of the century. These figures imply an industrial growth rate of 5 to 7 percent per annum on average. Major advances were recorded in the late 1870s and early 1880s and again from the late 1890s into the early twentieth century.

Industrialization meant not just more production of manufactured goods; it implied a shift in the economic base away from agriculture, the dominant activity of Americans since the beginning of settlement. As rapidly as agriculture was growing in the late nineteenth century, it accounted for a declining share of the nation's economic activity. By the

TABLE 12-1

Value Added in Commodity Output, by Sectors, 1859-99

	(Per cent)			
	Agriculture	Manufacturing	Mining	Construction
1859	56	32	1	11
1869	53	33	2	12
1874	46	39	2	12
1879	49	37	3	11
1884	41	44	3	12
1889	37	48	4	11
1894	32	53	4	11
1899	33	53	5	9

SOURCE: Robert E. Gallman, "Commodity Output, 1839-1899," in Trends in the American Economy in the Nineteenth Century (Princeton: Princeton University Press, 1960), p. 26.

year of America's centennial celebration, farming no longer accounted for even a majority of commodity output. And by the 1880s farmers constituted less than one-half of the country's labor force.

Industrial development did not proceed evenly in all regions of the country. In 1860 it could be said that a manufacturing belt already existed, lying along the Atlantic coast from north of Boston to south of Philadelphia. New England and the Middle Atlantic States then accounted for almost three quarters of the nation's industrial employment. A half century later, the manufacturing belt had extended itself westward to include the Great Lakes region as well; in 1910 establishments in the states east of the Mississippi and north of the Ohio employed 70 percent of U.S. industrial workers. While the Great Lakes made the most impressive gains in industry in the late-nineteenth century, the South and the West also recorded advances.

The economic changes in America were a part of the industrialization that took place in most of the Western nations over the course of the nineteenth century. (Japan was the only non-Western society to experience an Industrial Revolution.) It should be noted that while gains in output in the United States were enormous, so was the increase in population, which more than tripled from 1860 to 1920. This meant that for the United States to maintain the high level of product per capita which it had already attained by 1840 or so, businessmen as the country's major economic decision makers "had to run fast merely to stand still," as Thomas C. Cochran has put it.* Even though the United States was

* Thomas C. Cochran, 200 Years of American Business (New York: Basic Books, 1977), p. 51.

one of the economic leaders during the decades of rapid industrialization, in the rate of per capita increase it lagged behind nations such as Germany and Japan that started from lower levels.

Technology and the Market

Most of the basic raw materials for industrial expansion were at hand: coal, iron ore, and other minerals; lumber and building materials; and cotton and other fibers. However, a growth of manufacturing of the order experienced from 1865 to 1914 rested on a technological revolution. Discoveries in basic science were usually European in origin, but their application was often worked out by Americans who prided themselves on being practical, not theoretical. Most advances in manufacturing were made through empirical, trial-and-error methods. Perhaps the typical inventor of a manufacturing method was a mechanic or an engineer familiar with the problems of his industry. Development of a finished product for consumers was more likely to be the work of amateurs. Only toward the end of the nineteenth century did business begin to organize research laboratories for the systematic pursuit of scientific knowledge and its application to industry. Since the United States patent system encouraged invention by protecting the property rights of the inventor, the number of patents granted serves as a rough measure of the expanding interest in industrial novelty; the number increased from an annual average of twelve thousand in the 1860s to twenty-five thousand in the 1880s and forty thousand in 1914. And studies have revealed a correlation between the number of inventions of capital goods in an industry and the sales volume of capital goods to that industry, suggesting that inventors directed their talents toward areas of the economy in which they perceived growth and profit potential.

Even more important than invention of a new technique, however, was its rapid adoption and diffusion, to minimize the lag or differential between the best practices available (for example, the most efficient machines that had been invented for a particular purpose) and the average level of technique employed in the industry. The idea of progress in nineteenth-century American society encouraged acceptance of new products and ways of doing things. Most industrialists took pride in using "progressive" methods in their factories. Through much of the nineteenth century there was little to discourage or stop innovation. Opposition by workers to the introduction of labor-saving machinery was ineffective; employers had little difficulty in recruiting new workmen on the rare occasions when trouble did develop on this issue. Even a depression might encourage the spread of innovation in an industry as manufacturers sought to reduce their costs to solve the problem of falling prices.

However, businessmen were generally not gamblers. Rather, as W. Paul Strassmann has argued, they approached the possibilities of innovation with "conspicuous caution," seeking ways to reduce the chance of loss that might result from change. But perhaps this caution contributed to a rapid rate of technological change, since there were few spectacular failures to discourage entrepreneurs. Where Americans excelled was in getting inventions into mass production. In contrast to Europe, where emphasis continued to be put on fine craftsmanship, industrialists in the United States were willing to accept products and methods that were imperfect in quality if they reduced costs.

While technology applied to the abundant natural resources of the continent made possible a vast increase in the supply of goods, the American market absorbed the products of an expanding industrial system. Strong demand rested ultimately on population growth and rising income levels. The railroad created for the first time a truly national market. The growth of cities and towns, as well as a greater emphasis on commercial production in agriculture, meant larger numbers of people whose needs and wants could be met only through the market. The middle-income group was particularly important in expanding consumption along lines suggested some years ago by Elizabeth W. Gilboy: "The introduction of new commodities leads people possessed of an economic surplus to try this and that, and finally to include many new articles in their customary standard of life." * The small number of wealthy people could be supplied with expensive handicrafts, while the many poor had little to spend for goods beyond bare necessities of life. It was the middle class that used its purchasing power to incorporate factory-made goods into its consumption patterns. Large flows of goods were marketed vigorously through new channels of distribution, inducing, as J. R. T. Hughes has observed, "an extra margin of consumption from a population increasingly able to absorb the output of the factory system." †

CONSUMER GOODS

The advance of a broad range of consumer-goods industries demonstrates well the influence of strong potential demand in encouraging the

---

* Elizabeth W. Gilboy, "Demand as a Factor in the Industrial Revolution," in *Facts and Factors in Economic History: Articles by Former Students of Edwin Francis Gay* (Cambridge, Mass.: Harvard University Press, 1932), p. 626.
† J. R. T. Hughes, "Summing Up," *Business Enterprise and Economic Change: Essays in Honor of Harold F. Williamson*, Louis P. Cain and Paul J. Uselding, eds., (Kent, Ohio: Kent State University Press, 1973), p. 316.

application of new technology to expand production. In food processing, refrigeration, and particularly the introduction of the refrigerated car, revolutionized meat packing, as did roller grinding for flour milling. Mechanization of processes and advances of scientific knowledge led to the expansion of the canning of food, the bottling of soft and hard drinks, the preparation of dairy products, and the refining of sugar. Even in textiles, America's first factory industry, a large rise in output of cloth accompanied the introduction of new types of spinning and weaving equipment. The knit goods industry, particularly the production of hosiery and underwear, developed rapidly with an expanding market and the invention of equipment to manufacture seamless and then full-fashioned goods.

The application of new technology in many lines made available goods that were better in quality than homemade articles, but lower in price than the products of craftsmen; sometimes the new technology even produced goods that had not existed before. Adaptation of the sewing machine and the development of cloth-cutting machines and other special equipment accelerated the expansion of the ready-made clothing industry; by 1900 "store clothes" accounted for as much as nine tenths of the supply of men's clothing for the nation, providing a wide range of quality for different segments of the market. Adaptation of the sewing machine to leather reduced dramatically the price of boots and shoes. For use in the home, carpets made on power looms replaced handmade rugs, and furniture from Grand Rapids and other locations, however unimaginative in style, appeared superior to homebuilt items and seemed the best possibility for consumers unable to pay for the fine products of skilled craftsmen. Two new industries provided lighting that represented improvement over candles. The principal product of the petroleum industry before 1900 was kerosene for the oil lamp. Electricity replaced manufactured gas for illumination in urban areas by the end of the nineteenth century, although gas had represented an important advance in lighting in the earlier part of the century. New ways of making stoves, ice boxes, and plumbing fixtures reduced their prices, making possible more comfortable living for larger numbers of people. Invention of the linotype coupled with the discovery of processes to make cheap paper brought important changes to printing and publishing—more books, magazines, and newspapers at lower cost. The phonograph, amateur photography, and the movies gave new dimensions to leisure-time activities. The typewriter and other office machines, as well as the telephone, had their principal effects in business during this period. But the possibility of improved personal transportation was eagerly embraced by consumers—first with the bicycle in the late nineteenth century and then with the automobile after the turn of the century. Rubber, which became an adjunct of the automobile industry, was already experiencing significant growth before 1900, with increasing production of rubber footware and bicycle tires.

CAPITAL GOODS

Modern industrialization meant not just an expansion and proliferation of consumer goods. Actually, during this period production of capital goods, or goods used in the production of other goods, increased faster than consumer goods, so that by 1914 capital-goods industries probably accounted for a larger share of total manufacturing output than did consumer-goods industries. This reflected, of course, the continuing substitution of machine for hand labor, not only in manufactures but in other sectors as well. [See table 12–2]. For the economy as a whole the stock of capital increased in size almost fourteen times from 1860 to 1920, while the labor force grew by less than four times. In manufacturing alone, real capital per worker more than tripled from 1879 to 1914. An increasingly intricate nexus of industrial activities was inserting itself between the producer of raw materials and the consumer of final products. It is important that not only was more capital being applied to industrial processes to increase the productivity of labor, but also the capital stock itself was being made more productive as the result of technological and organizational changes. The progress of consumer-goods industries rested on the advances made in the vigorous capital-goods sector. Americans were able to save, or abstain from consuming, a significant portion of current production to invest in capital; this was reflected in the rise in the rate of capital formation to one quarter or more of gross national product in the 1870s and the 1880s from around 15 percent in the 1850s. [See table 12–3.]

METALLURGY

A key characteristic of the Industrial Revolution was the progressive but rapid replacement of wood by metal as the basic material of the economy. Iron was increasingly used in the early nineteenth century by railroads, machinery makers, and manufacturers of other goods. However, what was needed was a stronger and more durable metal that could be produced cheaply. The basic advance was the introduction of the Bessemer process, a technology by which the age of steel began to replace the age of iron in the 1860s. Bessemer steel was not of the same high quality as the expensive steel used in cutlery and hand tools, but it had greater tensile strength and hardness than wrought iron, and it could be produced on a large scale at low cost. The principles embodied in the Bessemer process had been discovered through trial and error by an American and an Englishman working independently. An alternative method, the open hearth process, was developed a little later in Germany. Although initially more expensive to operate, the open hearth process made it possible to control the final product more closely. While each of the two

TABLE 12-2
Net Output of Consumer- and Capital-Goods Industries, 1850-1914

	Consumer-Goods Industries	Capital-Goods Industries
	% of total industrial output*	
1850	43.5	18.2
1870	38.6	23.3
1880	43.8	24.7
1890	35.6	23.6
1900	33.9	28.0
1914	31.1	34.3

*Balance of output was from "excluded indus-
tries" which could not be clearly classified as con-
sumer goods or capital goods.
SOURCE: W. G. Hoffmann, The Growth of
Industrial Economies (Manchester: Manchester
University Press, 1958), p. 96.

TABLE 12-3
Capital in Manufacturing Industries and Capital per Worker, 1879-1914

	Total Capital		
	(1929 prices) ($000,000)	Number of Workers (000)	Real Capital per Worker
1879*	4,821	2,733	1764
1889*	11,157	4,129	2702
1899*	18,626	5,098	3654
1899†	17,452	4,502	3876
1904	23,295	5,182	4495
1909	31,563	6,262	5040
1914	36,737	6,602	5565

SOURCE: U.S. Bureau of the Census, Historical Statistics of
the United States, Colonial Times to 1970 (Washington, D.C.:
United States Government Printing Office, 1975), pp. 666, 685.
*Covers factory and hand and neighborhood industries.
†Covers factory with annual volume of production of $500
or more.

systems had its proponents, the open-hearth technique gained steadily in favor and by 1900 was more widely used than the Bessemer process.

For a time most Bessemer steel went into railroad rails. (Indeed, it was a group of men associated with railroads, like Andrew Carnegie, who initially perceived a profitable use for cheap steel, purchased the patent rights to the new process, and then organized production.) From about 1880, however, more and more mass-produced steel was incorporated into other kinds of products: factory and office machinery, ships, construction and mining equipment, farm implements, cans, wire, bicycles, girders for skyscrapers, and, after 1900, automobiles. Continuing improvements in steelmaking increased the range of applications where high speeds and close tolerances were involved.

Steel production expanded phenomenally, from under 1,250,000 tons in 1880 to over 10,000,000 tons in 1900 and 26,000,000 tons in 1910. By the turn of the century, the United States accounted for over one third of the world's steel production. In this key industry, America clearly had great advantages due to its abundance of iron ore and coal.

THE MACHINE AGE

As the Industrial Revolution metalized the economy, so too did it mechanize more and more manufacturing processes. From the early decades of the nineteenth century, as discussed in chapter 8, American industry held a lead over Europe in the use of specialized machinery. The scope of mechanization then widened considerably in the decades after 1860. As an American engineer observed in 1899:

> In America the tendency is to reduce all production to machine operations. In European countries, the tendency is to employ machinery as an assistant to production, and to rely on skillful hand labor to complete, and in some cases to produce outright, the highest grade of work. The consequence is that we find in America the highest skill and talent devoted to the production of machinery on which the article is made, and in Europe the highest skill devoted to the production of the article itself.*

Thus, attention should focus upon producers as well as users of machinery. Each highly specialized firm not only produced machines and machine tools of the best workmanship and most approved design at the lowest price, but it also developed equipment adapted to the needs of particular sets of customers. The significant point, as Nathan Rosenberg has stressed, is that "the machine tool industry served as the main transmission center" in the diffusion of much of the new technology of mechanized produc-

---

* H. F. L. Orcutt, "Machine Shop Management in Europe and America," *Engineering Magazine*, 16 (1899).

† Nathan Rosenberg, *Technology and American Economic Growth* (New York: Harper & Row, 1972), p. 98.

tion. Producers of specialized machinery acquired skills and techniques in solving the problems of specific customers, and these techniques could then be transferred to other machine-using industries. Experience gained by sewing-machine manufacturers, for example, could be transmitted to bicycle makers; their experience in turn could be applied to the specific problems of automobile producers. Mechanization was applied most extensively to attain low unit costs when two preconditions were present: a large demand for the final product and sufficient standardization to permit use of special-purpose machinery.

POWER ENGINES

Over the period from 1869 to 1914 power employed in American manufacturing increased by more than nine times. Even more significant was the fact that the amount of power per production worker almost tripled.

Water power had been important in the early stages of industrialization, particularly in textile mills in New England. But the latter third of the nineteenth century was to be the age of steam. With the development of anthracite coal mining and the distribution of coal through the northeast, steam power became prevalent in factory industry by the 1850s. Steam had the advantage of freeing industry from having to locate along streams, an area where adequate power sites were becoming scarce. Also, steam raised dramatically the upper limits of power available to an individual establishment. Although steam accounted for just over one half of total horsepower employed in manufacturing in 1869, by the end of the century, at its relative peak, steam supplied four fifths of industrial power.

However, manufacturers in a variety of industries were turning in 1900 to electric power. Initial advantages were savings to be achieved by powering each operation with an individual motor as well as the flexibility which made possible better plant layout and organization of work flows. Furthermore, electricity facilitated the introduction of mechanization into an even wider range of operations. By 1919 purchased electricity accounted for almost one third of the power capacity of the nation's industry.

In the pre-industrial era, wood was a principal source of energy, providing heat and power for industrial purposes as well as domestic use. From the middle of the nineteenth century, coal became closely associated with industrialization. Between 1850 and 1910, coal production nearly doubled almost every decade, coming to account for three quarters of the nation's total energy consumption in the first two decades of the twentieth century. However, by the time of World War I petroleum was already well on the way to becoming an important fuel for industry. [See Table 12–4].

TABLE 12-4
Energy Consumption in the United States,
1860-1910

	Total (trillion BTU)	Coal	Oil	Nat. Gas	Hydro Power	Wood
				%		
1860	3,162	16.4	0.1	—	—	83.5
1870	3,952	26.5	0.3	—	—	73.2
1880	5,001	41.1	1.9	—	—	57.0
1890	7,012	57.9	2.2	3.7	0.3	35.9
1900	9,587	71.4	2.4	2.6	2.6	21.0
1910	16,565	76.8	6.1	3.3	3.3	10.7

SOURCE: Sam H. Schurr and Bruce C. Netschert, Energy in the American Economy, 1850-1975 (Baltimore: Johns Hopkins University Press, 1960), pp. 35-36.

MASS PRODUCTION

Key elements of the system of mass production introduced into the automobile industry by Henry Ford in 1913 included, as he explained, "the planned orderly and continuous progression of the commodity through the shop" and "the delivery of work instead of leaving it to the workman's initiative to find it." * What Ford did was to put together several practices already used in industry. Mass production required standardization and interchangeable parts, developed in the making of firearms a century earlier and employed in a number of industries in Ford's day. Automatic cutting tools built by machinery manufacturers made it possible for one man to operate a battery of drills or other tools. The concept of the moving assembly line could be seen in grain mills dating back to the 1780s, in slaughter houses of the mid-nineteenth century (where it was actually a moving "disassembly line"), and in conveyors used by brewers after 1900 to wash, fill, cap, and label their product with automatic equipment. The scientific management of the late-nineteenth and the early twentieth centuries, led by men like Frederick W. Taylor, put emphasis on organizing the individual worker's labor and on careful scheduling of the flow of materials—necessary prerequisites for a system employing minute division of labor. The productivity gains in Ford's factories were enormous, with a sharp reduction in man-hours required to assemble a car. It is not surprising that mass production methods were soon applied in electrical appliances, farm implements and a variety of other industries.

* Henry Ford, "Mass Production," *Encyclopedia Britannica*, 22nd ed. Quoted in Nathan Rosenberg, *Technology and American Economic Growth* (New York: Harper & Row, 1972), pp. 112–113n.

Government of the Business System:
Issues in Economic Decision Making

Accompanying the sweeping technological changes that brought so many new processes, new products, and even new industries was a revolution in organization that created a new industrial structure. Through the first three quarters of the nineteenth century, growth in America was accomplished through a system of decentralized economic decision making. A multitude of entrepreneurs made decisions about investment, output, and price in relation to their perceptions of the market, an institution in which Americans placed great faith. Most manufacturing firms were small in size, were organized as proprietorships or partnerships of a few men, were managed by their owners, required relatively little capital, performed a single function, produced a single product, and served local markets. Few exceptions were to be found to this pattern except in the cotton-textile industry. By 1914 a new industrial structure was in place. A relative handful of large corporations had become dominant in many key industries. The rise of big business meant not only large size of firm but also the use of the corporation and eventually the separation of ownership and management, applications of large amounts of capital (particularly in machinery and other fixed assets), performance of several functions and manufacture of more than one product, and selling in national and international markets. While the individual was the decision maker in small business, many "organization men" contributed to the making and carrying out of decisions within the bureaucratic hierarchy fashioned by the large corporation.

ORIGINS OF BIG BUSINESS

The businessmen who assumed leadership in organizing large areas of the economy in the late nineteenth century have been seen variously as robber barons or as industrial statesmen. To some they were "semipiratical entrepreneurs who roamed the United States virtually unchecked," but to others what was most important was their constructive achievement.* This generation, born in the 1830s and 1840s, assumed as did most Americans that progress came through competition and the survival of the fittest, and that profit was the most reliable incentive for action. But different

---

* The first evaluation was made by Chester M. Destler "Entreprenuerial Leadership among the 'Robber Barrons': The Trial Balance," *Journal of Economic History*, Supplement 6, 1946, p. 28. Examples of the second approach include Ralph W. Hidy and Muriel E. Hidy, *Pioneering in Big Business, 1882–1911* [History of the Standard Oil Company (N.J.)] (New York: Harper & Bros., 1955) and Allan Nevins, *Study in Power: John D. Rockefeller*, 2 vols. (New York: Charles Scribner's Sons, 1953).

individuals perceived different kinds of opportunities for wealth. Some men, like Jay Gould, Daniel Drew, and Jim Fisk, saw how the increasing use of the corporation, particularly by the railroads, opened the possibility for large profits to be gained through manipulating the value of paper securities (stocks and bonds). Other men, like John D. Rockefeller and Andrew Carnegie, while also believing in no-holds-barred competition, concluded that great wealth could be generated in manufacturing by using new processes, making new products, and devising ways to sell in the national market created by the railroad, utilizing their business talents to build large industrial firms.

POOLS AND TRUSTS

New and improved machines, the use of power, and factory organization made it possible in many lines to produce standardized goods in an almost never-ending stream. Where the new technology yielded economies of scale—a decrease in unit costs accompanying an increase in the number of units produced—there was special incentive for industrialists to expand their production. Reduction of transportation costs increased the market area where each manufacturer could now sell his expanded output, throwing him into competition with other producers whose previous markets, like his own, had been local in nature. Inevitably, in industry after industry, the result was a growth in the supply of even the "most useful and desirable things in excess of any demand at remunerative prices to the producer," * as David Wells recorded in his observations in the 1880s. Since manufacturers had invested in specialized equipment which could be used only for limited purposes, it was impossible for them to withdraw from the market (that is, to transfer capital) without incurring heavy losses. Thus, each manufacturer was led to continue producing as long as the price he received exceeded his direct costs (labor and material). The best that he could hope for by selling at a loss was that his competitors would be driven out of business before he was. But this was not an effective solution; the exit of one competitor through bankruptcy usually resulted in the entry of a new competitor who purchased at a bargain price the equipment of the bankrupt firm. Businessmen described the situation as "ruinous" or "destructive" competition, as they faced, in the words of Alfred S. Eichner, "the prospect of their capital eventually being expropriated by the forces of competition just as Marx had prophesied." * A few of the most efficient firms were able to make money even at low price levels, but most were not.

* David A. Wells, *Recent Economic Changes* (New York: D. Appleton, 1889), p. 71.
* Alfred S. Eichner, "The Megacorp as a Social Innovation and Business History," in Paul Uselding, ed., *Business and Economic History* (Urbana: Bureau of Economic and Business Research, University of Illinois, 1975), p. 56.

To meet the threat posed by falling prices and vanishing profits, industrialists formed national and regional trade associations, and through them they entered into agreements to set minimum prices, limit total output, and/or divide markets. In most European countries such cartel agreements were legally enforced and thereby helped to solve for industry there the same problems of overproduction faced by American manufacturers. However, in the United States these pooling agreements had no standing in courts of law. If a participant broke the agreement by selling at a price below that established by the cartel, he could not be sued, even if the agreement was contained in a written contract. Thus, most pooling agreements lasted only a short period of time, followed by a quick return to price war. To John D. Rockefeller, head of the Petroleum Refiners Association, such groups were no more than "ropes of sand." What happened in copper was typical, as recorded in the comments of one executive after the breakup of a pool:

> We have soon got to go into a fight in which our only weapon will be a lower price than anyone else, and until we inaugurate that it makes but little difference about the feelings of our customers toward us—the lower price will make them all our friends at once.*

The problem was an obvious one: Manufacturers had to devise more permanent forms of combination. A major step was invention of the trust form by John D. Rockefeller and his associates in Standard Oil in 1882. In an adaptation of an old legal device to meet the current needs of business, a board of trustees was empowered to manage the properties of corporations joining the trust on behalf of the stockholders, the legal owners. This arrangement had the advantage of permanence, since the irrevocable deed of trust prevented withdrawal by any participant in the combination. More importantly it put centralized management of the industry in the hands of the trustees, who could make all decisions, including the closing of the least efficient plants. For example, there was a reduction in the number of plants of the Standard Oil trust from fifty-five in 1882 to twenty-two just four years later.

Only eight combinations, operating on a national scale, utilized the trust form in the 1880s, and six of these were successful in controlling their industries—sugar, whiskey, lead, cottonseed oil, and linseed oil, in addition to petroleum. They were pioneers in creating the large industrial enterprise through horizontal combination—the process of joining together a number of firms operating at one level or stage in the productive process. They not only found a legal form for big business, but even more important they began to develop centralized managerial techniques. When the trust form came under legal attack in the early 1890s, soon after New Jersey had changed its incorporation laws to authorize one corporation to

---

* William B. Gates, Jr., *Michigan Copper and Boston Dollars: An Economic History of the Michigan Copper Mining Industry* (Cambridge: Harvard University Press, 1951), p. 76.

own the stock of other corporations, these combinations, as well as others which formed in ensuing years, began to employ the holding company device. Large-scale activity appeared so striking in the 1880s, however, that the term trust continued to be applied to big business long after that legal form had been abandoned.

VERTICAL GROWTH

While some manufacturers seeking to exploit the new technology and to sell in the national market faced pressure on prices from overproduction, other industrialists found their ambitions blocked by the inadequacies of the existing system of wholesalers. Manufacturers producing a large output with continuous-process machinery found that wholesalers could not move their goods quickly enough. Thus, in the 1880s firms making low-priced packaged consumer goods grew into large business units by the process of vertical integration, by assuming marketing functions ordinarily performed by other independent firms. Manufacturers of cigarettes, flour, breakfast cereals, and canned goods set up their own network of sales offices where they employed aggressive marketing tactics. Advertising was a particularly potent weapon; most of the products were new to consumers, and a low unit price made it difficult to stimulate demand by price reductions.

At the same time producers of a variety of new kinds of durable goods, for sale either to consumers or to producers, found the independent wholesaler lacking in ability to perform essential functions, such as demonstration, installation, and repair. Makers of products ranging from sewing machines and agricultural implements to office machinery, electrical equipment, and elevators, created their own national and international marketing organizations; these included franchised retail dealers supported by branch offices, to supply not only a flow of products but also funds (to extend credit for "big-ticket" items), spare parts, and specialized repair service. Producers of perishable goods for the mass market, like meat, beer, and bananas, also found it necessary to build marketing organizations. For example, utilization of the new technology of the refrigerator car in supplying fresh meat to eastern markets required refrigerated warehouses, a facility that local butchers were unwilling to provide.

Many of these firms integrated not only forward into marketing but also backward into purchasing in order to assure supplies for a large volume of production. Manufacturers of durable goods created purchasing organizations and sometimes bought or constructed factories to manufacture parts and materials. Producers of nondurable goods followed similar patterns. Meat packers, for example, bought into stockyards along the cattle frontier, and cigarette makers built their own storing and curing facilities for the tobacco that they purchased directly from farmers.

Few large firms experienced growth along horizontal or vertical lines exclusively. Indeed, the most successful enterprises usually employed both strategies. Standard Oil Trust, for example, represented in 1882 a horizontal combination of kerosene refineries, but the trust then expanded vertically—backward into crude oil production and forward into wholesale and retail marketing—in order to coordinate its large-scale operations more effectively. On the other hand, the American Tobacco Company was formed in 1890 by James B. Duke and four competitors who had already organized their own marketing and purchasing activities; the merger made possible an increase of profits through reducing advertising expenses and other sales costs as well as exercising tighter control of the industry.

PUBLIC POLICY: SHERMAN ANTITRUST ACT

By the end of the 1880s the development of large business combinations had created a great deal of public concern and, in some quarters, alarm. However, the developing movement against the trusts, or big business, was not an attack on business or capitalism. Indeed, some of the strongest critics were businessmen and their spokesmen, particularly small entrepreneurs who had been damaged, or who believed that they had been damaged, by the aggressive behavior of large corporations. They could point to the old sentiment against monopoly, reflecting in turn a widely held belief in America about the virtue of freedom of opportunity. In short, big business appeared to be undermining the traditional business system, one that rested on a wide dispersion of economic decision making and economic power.

There was little doubt about the intensity of public hostility toward the trusts and toward their actions in driving out competitors and injuring consumers by raising prices. Yet people saw some virtue in the combinations because they appeared to be efficient, a value almost as important as competition.

The result of debate about the trusts in and out of Congress was the Sherman Antitrust Act (1890), written in sweeping but somewhat vague terms in declaring illegal "every contract, combination in the form of trust or otherwise, or conspiracy in restraint of trade or commerce among the several states." There ensued over the next decade strenuous efforts to determine what the law really meant or should mean as it related to the evolving economic situation. Some critics blamed the Justice Department for not enforcing the law more strenuously; but it had only eighteen lawyers employed in Washington, and Congress did not appropriate funds to enlarge the staff. Others criticized the conservatism of the courts in interpreting the law in a narrow fashion; but antitrust cases produced volumes of records which had to be evaluated and involved an analysis of economic issues which even professional economists found complex.

Based upon cases brought before the Supreme Court, the meaning of the Sherman Act after a decade seemed to be this: (1) Pooling agreements, or cartels, were clearly illegal; they were contracts made by independent companies to restrain trade. (*U.S.* v. *Addyston Pipe & Steel Company*, 1899). (2) But combinations or mergers of manufacturing companies seemed to escape the Sherman Act, as the Court ruled that a monopoly of manufacture only incidentally and indirectly affected commerce and that it therefore was not subject to a federal statute based on the commerce clause of the Constitution. (*U.S.* v. *E. C. Knight Company*, 1895).

THE GREAT MERGER MOVEMENT, 1897–1903

At the turn of the century there occurred the most important merger movement in American history. In the space of a half-dozen years, over 2,800 business firms entered mergers, including over 1,200 in 1899 alone. Paradoxically, the Sherman Antitrust Act encouraged the formation of large corporations. Businessmen and their lawyers, seeking ways to control their markets, believed that the Supreme Court's decisions in the 1890s implied that consolidation of competing firms was the only legal method to achieve stability. In addition, experience in the depression of the 1890s seemed to show the practical soundness of large combinations; most of them had fared rather well during the hard times.

The finance capitalist, or investment banker, played a leading role in the great merger movement; the development of a market for industrial securities proved to be a decisive factor. In the earlier development of big business, the initiative had been taken by industrialists, who financed acquisitions and internal growth with prior earnings or with bank loans, often arranged through their own banks. Turn-of-the-century mergers, however, often involved far larger capitalization. What particularly sparked the interest of investment bankers in creating combinations was the growing eagerness of investors to buy the stocks of industrial corporations, a type of security that only a few years earlier attracted little market attention. Finance capitalists had already gained experience in financing large corporations through their consolidation and reorganization of railroad companies in the 1880s and 1890s. J. Pierpont Morgan and other leading investment bankers of Wall Street controlled access to capital in large amounts through their ties with brokerage houses; they sold securities to wealthy individuals and institutional investors like life insurance companies and savings banks. Sometimes the investment banker took the initiative in seeking out firms to consolidate and industries to organize, as did Morgan in the founding of the United States Steel Corporation, the first billion-dollar corporation in America. Even when industrialists conceived the idea of consolidating competing firms, they usually turned to Wall Street to arrange the raising of new capital through the issue of securities. The relationship was a continuing one, as investment bankers held positions on the board of directors of the industrial corporation, a practice introduced earlier by Morgan in the railroad field to give him some supervisory power over financial affairs.

BIG BUSINESS AND THE LAW

After Theodore Roosevelt assumed the presidency in 1901, the legality of combination to control the market became less certain. Sensing the strong public concern about big business, Roosevelt pledged strict enforcement of the Sherman Antitrust Act and demanded that large corporations "subserve the public good." In his first action in this area, he ordered prosecution of the Northern Securities Company, a railroad holding company formed by Morgan and other top business leaders, charging that it was an illegal combination. Conviction, upheld by the Supreme Court, lessened the confidence of lawyers that the use of the holding company shielded monopolistic combinations from the provisions of the Sherman Act. Furthermore, Congress in 1903 authorized establishment of a Bureau of Corporations with investigative powers.

President Roosevelt distinguished between "good" trusts, which made for greater efficiency through rationalization, and "bad" trusts, which represented abuse of power. He thus directed his trust busting against the "bad" trusts, those like Standard Oil and American Tobacco which had gained notoriety with their predatory tactics towards competitors. The Justice Department instituted antitrust suits against these two giants, each of which was ordered by the court to be dissolved into several separate corporations. The Supreme Court in upholding these convictions in 1911 set forth the "rule of reason." The Sherman Act had outlawed all restraint of trade, but the Supreme Court now declared that only unreasonable restraint of trade was illegal. In other words, Standard Oil and American Tobacco were guilty not because of their large size but rather because of the ruthless methods that they had used to eliminate competition. But the court did not provide a clear definition of what constituted unreasonableness in business behavior.

Legal problems developed even for the "good" trusts, whose actions Theodore Roosevelt generally approved. For example, with the apparent endorsement of the White House during the Panic of 1907, United States Steel Corporation acquired Tennessee Coal and Iron Company, enabling U.S. Steel to extend dominance over its industry into the southern states. But the Taft Administration later repudiated this understanding, or detente, when it filed an antitrust suit charging that the acquisition was a violation of the Sherman Act.

There continued into the second decade of the twentieth century controversy over an appropriate public policy for big business. Critics of giant corporations argued that the Sherman Antitrust Act was ineffective in dealing with the problem of monopoly. There was a strong sentiment through the country that the power acquired by big business was undermining the foundations of democracy as well as restricting opportunity for small enterprise. In short, critics believed that the antitrust law should be strengthened.

On the other hand, business leaders emphasized not only their own accomplishments in improving production, but also the large area of uncertainty about the scope of governmental authority in determining the boundaries of their decision-making power. With support from political leaders like former President Roosevelt, in 1912 some industrialists advocated establishment of a government commission with power to define how the Sherman Act applied to specific business situations. Such a public agency, it was thought, perhaps could regulate prices, particularly those in heavy industry like steel where price competition was regarded as financially dangerous. Small businessmen and their spokesmen also hoped that a government commission would help their trade associations to stabilize competitive conditions in the sectors where they operated.

In response to the widespread concern about the trusts, Congress passed two statutes in 1914: the Clayton Act as an amendment to the Sherman Act, and the Federal Trade Commission Act. The Clayton Act aimed to spell out the "rule of reason" by defining what constituted unreasonable restraint of trade. Certain practices—such as tying contracts, price discrimination, interlocking directorates, and even mergers—were prohibited, but only "where the effect [of these tactics] may be to substantially lessen competition or tend to create a monopoly." But there was no definition of "substantially." Thus the power of the Clayton Act to police business relationships would depend on administration by the executive branch and interpretation by the judiciary. Nevertheless, some held the hope that the law was a sleeping giant that might some day arise to do battle with giant business.

The Federal Trade Commission Act established a commission; members were to be appointed by the president, and would have the power to investigate and to issue cease and desist orders, subject to judicial review. The law forcefully stated that "unfair methods of competition in commerce are hereby declared unlawful," reflecting a widespread assumption that giant corporations had gained their economic power through ruthless competition. But Congress did not define what constituted unfair competition, on the grounds that "there is no limit to human inventiveness in this field." * It would be the task of the newly established Federal Trade Commission (FTC) to interpret the general rule.

During the first decade and one half of the twentieth century, the basis of a new relationship between business and government was developed. In the view of nineteenth-century businessmen, government had no meaningful function in economic life unless called upon by business to support specific efforts of the private sector. During that era the work-

---

* Quoted in William Letwin, *Law and Economic Policy in America* (New York: Random House, 1965), p. 277.

ing of the competitive market protected society, to some extent at least, against the "fallout" from unrestrained economic individualism. When the structure of much of industry was altered from the competitive system of an earlier era, government regulation attempted to establish an element of social control over the economy. By 1914 businessmen had to adjust to a new reality: government would apply the antitrust laws not only to punish business for transgressions of what was regarded as the "public interest," but also to prevent business abuses. As Robert Wiebe has put it, executives of large corporations now had to accept "the government as a superior power with unquestioned rights to regulate business." *

TRANSITION TO OLIGOPOLY

At the turn of the century, when the monopolistic combination of members of an industry appeared to be legal, many businessmen regarded merger as a panacea to prevent expropriation of their property by the forces of competition. Industrialists often justified combinations as a device to achieve economies of scale, appealing to the national belief in the virtue of efficiency, even as they raised prices to increase the level of profits.

But not all combinations resulted in the cherished goal of high profits through elimination of competition. Some failed financially, especially when promoters had "watered the stock," or set an unreasonably high capitalization for the new corporation. In other cases, the unanticipated happened: the collapse of the market for the combination's products. For example, the American Bicycle Company was formed in 1899, and controlled about two thirds of its industry. Bicycles constituted a great growth industry in the 1890s, but shortly after the combination's formation sales dropped abruptly as the market had become saturated.

On the other hand, unusual success and high profit margins, stemming from control of an industry, sometimes attracted the competition of newcomers. The changing political and legal environment after 1900 made it impossible for the large combination to destroy its competitors and to "mop up" an industry, as Standard Oil and others had done in the 1880s and 1890s. The concern of the public and the response by government in effect imposed an upper limit, however ill-defined, on the share of the market that any firm could control.

Successful challengers usually copied the leader's pattern of vertical integration, thereby realizing the economies to be derived from coordination of successive stages of production and marketing. Significantly, newcomers could concentrate their efforts on the most rapidly growing segments of an industry. For example, Standard Oil, with large investments in kerosene refineries, found its share of the petroleum industry declining,

* Robert H. Wiebe, "The House of Morgan and the Executive, 1905–1913," *American Historical Review*, 65 (October 1959), p. 60.

even before its dissolution in 1911; other firms bypassed the industry's "age of illumination" and moved directly into gasoline and industrial fuels. (Standard's control of United States refining capacity declined from 82 percent in 1899 to 64 percent on the eve of dissolution.)

What had emerged in mass production industries by 1914 was an industrial structure now familiar to us as oligopoly. Successful "new" firms in these areas in the early twentieth century were themselves large, they were vertically integrated, and they were few in number relative to the total business population. Where one firm had apparently established monopoly control of its market at some point during the combination movement, it usually found its dominance challenged. But this did not mean a return in these industries to the nineteenth-century pattern of many firms competing largely on a price basis. Developments in steel illustrate the kind of change taking place in mass-production sectors. At the time that the United States Steel Corporation (Big Steel) was formed, it controlled 44 percent of the nation's ingot capacity, this share rising slightly in the ensuing years. As a result of its policy of stable prices and high profit margins, Big Steel in effect held an umbrella over the industry, allowing less efficient companies to remain in business and to expand their operations through acquisitions or internal growth. Top management believed that U.S. Steel had to build a reputation for good behavior toward competitors in order to avoid an antitrust suit. But not all members of the industry benefited equally from Big Steel's "cooperative competition," or avoidance of price cuts that would have driven some competitors out of business. Note that the eleven largest steelmakers, which were or became vertically integrated, increased their share of the industry's capacity from 55 percent in 1904 to 63 percent in 1920, while U.S. Steel's share declined to 40 percent. Most notable was the rapid growth of Bethlehem, accomplished by exploiting new processes, new products, and new sources of materials under aggressive entrepreneurial leadership.

Clearly, entry was not easy into industries characterized by mass production and mass distribution. The most important set of considerations centered around the substantial barriers to entry into oligopolistic sectors. Sometimes, the oligopolists controlled essential raw materials. In other cases, large manufacturers used patent controls and copyrights to police their industries. But even where these factors were not significant in controlling entrance, newcomers would have to create not only large-scale manufacturing facilities but also distribution systems and purchasing organizations in order to compete effectively with established firms. An important oligopolistic tactic came to be product differentiation—the effort by a seller to use brand names, trademarks, and advertising to instill in consumers a preference for his product over nearly identical products offered by other sellers. One point is clear: In the new economic and political environment of the twentieth century, oligopoly, by discouraging the entry of new firms, proved to be far more effective in stabilizing prices in mass production industries than the old style ruthless practices employed in driving competitors to the wall.

MANAGERIAL ENTERPRISE

The corporate revolution implied not only new industrial structures and changing relationships between business and government but also innovations in the machinery of decision making within the firm. Where ownership and management were separated, as they came to be in large enterprise, honesty and efficiency could no longer be assumed. In the early history of the modern corporation, managers with little ownership interest saw nothing wrong in taking advantage of their positions as insiders to make private gains as, for example, in selling supplies from companies they owned to companies they managed. Unscrupulous operators worked out ways to transfer corporate assets into their own pockets. During the last half of the nineteenth century, rules of conduct were worked out for managers of other people's property, stimulated by the growing awareness that an improvement in ethics contributed to the ability to attract capital to corporate enterprise, a practical application of Benjamin Franklin's dictum that "honesty is the best policy." While cooperation to advance the welfare of the company was expected of managers, competition for promotion within the hierarchy, on the basis of ability and merit, was assumed to stimulate the exercise of initiative, thereby overcoming the lack of direct economic incentives. For many men accustomed to the freedom of action in independent business, it was not easy to accept the discipline inherent in group effort and accountability to an organization.

In contrast to the one-man management and informal relationship characteristic of the small family firm, participation of many individuals in the making and carrying out of decisions in the large corporation ultimately required formalization of channels of communication and lines of authority. The problem was to find an appropriate structure that could be applied to the large manufacturing company. The pattern of organization earlier developed by the railroads was not especially well-suited to the operation of the large industrial corporation with its greater variety of activities carried on over a larger geographical area. While early combinations had improvised ways to delegate authority and share power, their successful functioning usually depended on personal leadership exerted by an unusually able entrepreneur rather than on the formally coordinated efforts of professional managers. The problem was complicated by the fact that former owners of independent firms conceived of the large corporation, of which they were now officers, as a legalized cartel, with its components to be operated along the same lines as prior to the merger.

Over the course of the first decade and a half of the twentieth century, large corporations were developing a unified structure of management, by which they could coordinate operations and determine the allocation of resources. One task was to reorganize the facilities inherited from predecessor companies into departments, with each department to manufacture a different type of product or perform a specific function such as sales, purchasing, development, legal, or financial. At the same time, an executive committee composed of the president and the heads of major departments became the company's ruling body, with the job of appraising the performance of the departments, coordinating the flow of materials through the corporation's plants and warehouses, and planning the lines of future growth. Special attention was directed to improving accounting procedures to provide the information on which to base decisions. This centralized plan, however, proved to be but one stage in the evolution of modern managerial structures, as by the 1920s the continuing growth of giant enterprises made apparent the need for greater decentralization.

THE BUSINESS SYSTEM

The emergence of the "megacorp," the growth of "managerial enterprise," or the "corporate revolution," as various writers have termed the rise of large-scale enterprise, was the most significant change in the organization of economic decision making since the development of market orientation and capitalist institutions in the Middle Ages. Within the short space of a quarter century, large business corporations had come to dominate a number of key manufacturing industries, generally those that were capital-intensive, used continuous or large-batch production technology, and produced for the mass market. In contrast to the early combinations, whose affairs were guided by unusually gifted and aggressive entrepreneurs, by 1914 evolution of rational bureaucratic structures made it possible for more ordinary executives working in groups to manage the giant enterprise. In the large corporation, as Alfred D. Chandler, Jr., has observed, "the visible hand of management replaced the invisible hand of market mechanisms in administering and coordinating day-to-day production and distribution." *

The sudden appearance of big business caused widespread concern in the early years of the century. However, the large enterprise appeared to be gaining ever increasing acceptance in American society. Some intellectuals pictured the corporation as the "model of reform and a microcosmic blueprint for the good of society," by the time of World War I, as large scale business seemed to them to represent the move away from the

---

* Alfred D. Chandler, Jr., *The Visible Hand: The Managerial Revolution in American Business* (Cambridge: Harvard University Press, 1977), p. 286.

old order of individualism toward a new era of collectivism.† More and more middle class people, convinced that the antitrust laws had imposed restraints on corporate power, were accommodating themselves to big business; they "found new things to praise and found much less to criticize," * especially as the growth of the bureaucratic corporation expanded career opportunities in various types of white collar occupations.

Yet the rise of big business did not mean the extinction of the small firm. Generally, as Thomas C. Cochran has observed, the large-scale sectors "were those in which small business either had never existed or had been superceded at an early stage." † There still existed a structure of small and medium-sized firms over which a layer of several hundred large corporations had become superimposed. In spite of the prophesies of doom pronounced upon small-scale enterprise, the nonfarm business population, comprising mainly small firms, actually grew in the early years of the century at a slightly faster rate than the total population of the nation. New kinds of opportunities developed in trade and service. Even in manufacturing, alert entrepreneurs could find "niches" where a small firm could produce efficiently and did not compete directly with giant enterprise. Although many observers stressed the importance of economic integration and large-scale production, some economists then and since, like Allyn A. Young in the 1920s, argued that "industrial differentiation has been and remains the type of change characteristically associated with the growth of production" and pointed to "the increase in the diversification of intermediate products and of industries manufacturing special products or groups of products." ‡ More capital was necessary for entry into many lines of business than had been the case in the mid-nineteenth century, but increased savings were available to finance the entry of entrepreneurs. In the same economic environment that encouraged the growth of the giant enterprise, small enterprises multiplied in numbers.

Summary

The process of industrialization, the central element of modern economic growth, involved the widespread application of technology as well as the increased use of capital, with an expanding market absorbing the

† James Gilbert, *Designing the Industrial State: The Intellectual Pursuit of Collectivism in America, 1880–1940* (Chicago: Quadrangle Books, 1972), p. 29.

* Louis Galambos, *The Public Image of Big Business in America, 1880–1940* (Baltimore: Johns Hopkins Press, 1975), p. 258.

† Thomas C. Cochran, *American Business in the Twentieth Century* (Cambridge: Harvard University Press, 1972), p. 56.

‡ Allyn A. Young, "Increasing Returns and Economic Progress," *Economic Journal*, 38 (December 1928) p. 537.

ever-increasing output of consumer goods. The age of wood gave way to the age of iron, and then, with the invention of the Bessemer process, to the age of steel. Machinery came into use in more and more manufacturing processes, with machine tools playing a key role in the transmission of the technology of mass production. The latter part of the nineteenth century was the age of steam generated by coal, although use of electric power spread rapidly through industry in the early decades of the twentieth century. Key elements of mass production—standardization, interchangeable parts, automatic cutting tools, and the moving assembly line—were incorporated by Henry Ford into a system to make automobiles and then applied to other major industries.

Accompanying the revolution in production was a revolution in organization—the rise of Big Business. One route to becoming a large-sized firm was horizontal combination, a method used by manufacturers in several prominent industries as they sought to stabilize prices and profits by monopoly control. Another method was vertical growth (or vertical integration), a way for industrial firms to expand backward toward sources of materials and/or forward to create marketing channels. Most giant corporations grew both horizontally and vertically. By 1914 a new relationship between business and government had emerged, with the principle of government regulation of corporate behavior firmly established even though public policy, as embodied in the antitrust laws, had not drawn the precise boundaries of legally permissable action by the large corporation. The structure that emerged from the experience of business fitted neither of the long familiar models of competition and monopoly. Rather, oligopoly had come to characterize a number of key industries—dominance of a set of economic activities by a relatively few large corporations, with most of them vertically integrated. Large size also required development of new methods of decision making within the firm, as bureaucratic organizations came to replace the captains of industry who had created the giant enterprises. Yet there still existed a structure of small and medium-sized firms, as the total nonfarm business population continued to grow by capitalizing on new opportunities in trade, service, and manufacturing.

SUGGESTED READINGS

Victor S. Clark, *History of Manufactures in the United States*, Volume II, 1860–1893, and Volume III, 1893–1928, 1929 ed. (New York: Peter Smith, 1949) is still the most comprehensive historical account of major industries in the United States. However, useful summaries of industrial growth in the nineteenth and the early twentieth centuries are contained in Lance E. Davis et al., *American Economic Growth: An*

Economist's History of the United States (New York: Harper & Row, 1972), Chapter 12, "Manufacturing"; and in Harold F. Williamson, ed., *The Growth of the American Economy*, 2d ed. (Englewood Cliffs, N.J.: Prentice-Hall, 1951), Chapters 22, "Processing of Agricultural Products After 1860"; 23, "Products of the Earth, 1866–1918"; 24, "The Heavy Industries"; and 25, "Light Manufactures". Nathan Rosenberg, *Technology and American Economic Growth*, (New York: Harper & Row, 1972) is the starting point for reading on technology, while Paul Uselding, "Studies of Technology in Economic History," *Research in Economic History*, Supplement 1 (1977) reviews the extensive body of literature dealing with the development and application of technology to industry. Allan R. Pred, *The Spatial Dynamics of U.S. Urban-Industrial Growth, 1800–1914*, (Cambridge, Mass.: M.I.T. Press, 1966) examines the link between industrialization and urbanization, and Albert W. Niemi, *State and Regional Patterns in American Manufacturing, 1860–1900* (Westport, Conn.: Greenwood Press, 1974) gives a statistical account of changes in the regional distribution of industrial activity. The following works present case studies of the growth of individual industries, demonstrating the changing relationships of technology, the market, and industrial structure: Harold F. Williamson and Arnold R. Daum, *The American Petroleum Industry: The Age of Illumination, 1859–1899* (Evanston: Northwestern University Press, 1959); Harold F. Williamson et al., *The American Petroleum Industry: The Age of Energy, 1899–1959* (Evanston: Northwestern University Press, 1963); Peter Temin, *Iron and Steel in Nineteenth-Century America: An Economic Inquiry* (Cambridge, Mass.: M.I.T. Press, 1964); Gertrude G. Schroeder, *The Growth of Major Steel Companies, 1900–1950* (Baltimore: Johns Hopkins Press, 1953); and Paul F. McGouldrick, *New England Textiles in the Nineteenth Century: Profits and Investment* (Cambridge, Mass.: Harvard University Press, 1968). Stuart Bruchey, *Growth of the Modern American Economy* (New York: Dodd, Mead, & Company, 1975) serves as a concise and readable summary of the recent scholarship dealing with industrialization and economic growth in the United States.

The most comprehensive history of the big business sector in America is Alfred D. Chandler, Jr., *The Visible Hand: The Managerial Revolution in American Business* (Cambridge, Mass.: Harvard University Press, 1977). Thomas C. Cochran, *American Business in the Twentieth Century* (Cambridge, Mass.: Harvard University Press, 1972) places the development of large-scale enterprise in the context of an evolving business system. Glenn Porter, *The Rise of Big Business, 1860–1910* (New York: Thomas Y. Crowell, 1973) serves as an excellent guide to the literature of the early history of the modern corporation. Matthew Josephson, *The Robber Barons: The Great American Capitalists, 1861–1901* (New York: Harcourt, Brace, 1934) is a colorful account whose title implies its bias. On the other hand, Ralph W. Hidy and Muriel E. Hidy, *Pioneering in Big Business, 1882–1911* [*History of Standard Oil Company (New Jersey)*] (New York: Harper & Brothers, 1955) emphasizes the constructive achievements of Rockefeller and his associates, as do Joseph F. Wall, *Andrew Carnegie* (New York: Oxford University Press, 1970), Harold C. Livesay, *Andrew Carnegie and the Rise of Big Business* (Boston: Little, Brown & Company, 1975), Robert N. Hessen, *Steel Titan: The Life of Charles W. Schwab* (New York, Oxford University Press, 1975) for their subjects. Alfred S. Eichner, *The Emergence of Oligopoly: Sugar Refining as a Case Study* (Baltimore: Johns Hopkins Press, 1969) and Reese V. Jenkins, *Images and Enterprise: Technology and the American Photographic Industry, 1839 to 1925* (Baltimore: Johns Hopkins Press, 1975) focus on competitive behavior and changing industrial structures. Glenn Porter and Harold C. Livesay, *Merchants and Manufactures: Studies in the Changing Structure of 19th Century Marketing* (Baltimore: Johns Hopkins University Press, 1971) discusses the role of marketing in the growth of large manufacturing firms. Ralph L. Nelson, *Merger Movements in American Industry, 1895–1956* (Princeton: Princeton University Press, 1959) supplies an analysis of the great merger movement at the turn of the century. Arthur S. Dewing, *Corporate Promotions and Reorganizations* (Cambridge, Mass.: Harvard University Press, 1914) contains useful case studies of a number of unsuccessful combinations. Louis Galambos, *The Public Image of Big Business in America, 1880–1940: A Quantitative Study in Social Change* (Baltimore: Johns Hopkins University Press, 1975) and James Gilbert, *Designing the Industrial State: The Intellectual Pursuit of Collectivism in America, 1880–1940* (Chicago: Quadrangle Books, 1972) attempt to determine, in different ways, the

CHAPTER 13

——

Labor in the Industrial

Society

As the United States developed into the leading industrial nation of the world between the mid-nineteenth and early twentieth centuries, the American labor force became caught up in many of the stresses and strains as well as the benefits of economic modernization. In size, the labor force nearly quadrupled between 1860 and 1920, growing even more rapidly than the nation's population. In terms of functional composition, the important change was a relative shift away from agriculture and toward manufacturing. This change implied a locational shift of work (again, in relative terms) from the countryside and small towns to urban, industrial centers.

Both the growing size and the changing composition of the labor force in these decades were responses to employment opportunities created by industrialization. And a high degree of labor mobility made it possible for workers to take advantage of these opportunities. As new resources, industries, and markets were opened up by the driving forces of technological change and improved transportation, emerging wage and income differentials attracted workers away from less remunerative occupations and locations. Workers decided to move not only within the United States but also from other countries, as relatively more attractive job opportunities in the United States prompted millions of foreign workers to emigrate there. American wage levels and living standards were not only higher than anywhere else in the world; they also were increasing more rapidly than in most other countries.

But if the rapidity of change in the American economy created new

opportunities, it also led to many new problems for the working population. At the heart of most of these problems were fundamental changes
in the nature of work. In 1860 the United States was predominantly a
nation of farmers and self-employed workers whose work habits, life
styles, and decisions were marked by a high degree of independence. By
1914 it had become a highly industrialized, urbanized nation in which the
majority of individual workers were employees who depended upon their
employers—often large, impersonal businesses and corporations—for their
livelihoods. Such workers had far less control over the types of job available and the conditions of work—wages, hours, security, safety, and so
on—than workers of earlier generations had enjoyed.

To cope with these new problems and to increase their bargaining
power, workers began to join organizations that would advance their
interests. These organizations, adopted a wide range of approaches and
tactics which in turn were met by a wide range of responses—some favorable to labor and others unfavorable—from business and government.
Greater recognition of organized labor's rights and responsibilities took
decades, but by the time of World War I national labor organizations
were an accepted part of American economic life.

Immigration and the Size of the Labor Force

Between the Civil War and World War I the American economy expanded at a faster rate than in any other period of comparable length in
its entire history. This growth was, of course, based on many things—in
particular, on abundant quantities of land and other natural resources and
on technological breakthroughs across a wide range of productive activities;
but it was also helped by the rapid growth of the nation's labor force. Between 1860 and 1920 the population of the United States grew at a compound rate of 2.0 percent per year, while the labor force grew still more
rapidly at a rate of 2.2 percent per year (see table 13-1). Thus, for the
population as a whole, the labor force participation rate—the percentage
of all Americans who were in the labor force—rose over the entire period,
with an especially marked expansion between 1870 and 1910.

Through most of American history increases in population and the
labor force have come primarily from natural increase—that is, from the
excess of births over deaths of people living in the United States. And
this was also true for the period 1860 to 1920, in every decade of which,
except 1901–10, natural increases accounted for 60 to 72 percent of the
population increases. But during these decades there was also another
factor at work: immigration. The flow of foreign-born immigrants to the

TABLE 13-1
Population, Labor Force, and
Participation Rate, 1860-1920

Year	Population (millions)	Labor Force (millions)	Participation Rate (percent)
1860	31.5	11.1	35
1870	39.9	12.9	32
1880	50.3	17.4	35
1890	63.1	23.3	37
1900	76.1	29.1	38
1910	92.4	37.5	41
1920	106.5	41.6	39

SOURCES: Population: U.S. Bureau of the Census, Historical Statistics of the United States, Colonial Times to 1957
(Washington, D.C., 1960), Series A2, p. 7; Labor Force: Stanley Lebergott, "Labor Force and Employment, 1800-1960,"
in National Bureau of Economic Research, Output, Employment, and Productivity in the United States After 1800 (New
York: National Bureau of Economic Research, 1966), Table 1,
p. 118; Participation Rate: Labor Force divided by Population.

United States assumed massive proportions during this period and had
both immediate and long-run impacts on the nation's economy. Between
1861 and 1890 some 11.3 million immigrants arrived, mainly from the
United Kingdom, Germany, and the Scandinavian countries. Then from
1890 until 1920 another 18.2 million came, mostly from southern and eastern European countries such as Italy, Austria-Hungary, and Russia.

Decisions by foreigners to emigrate to the United States were based
upon economic conditions both in this country and in the lands of their
birth. The pull of economic opportunities in the United States is evident
in the time pattern of immigrant arrivals which tended to increase during
periods of United States prosperity and decrease during and after depressions. But foreign economic conditions also influenced the flow of migration. As the industrial revolution spread across Europe during the nineteenth century, it was accompanied by large increases in European
populations. But in many European countries the initially high rates of
industrial growth were not sustained and the resulting shortage of jobs
and economic hardships prompted many Europeans to embark for America, the land of opportunity. Modern-day scholars believe that this sequence of events largely accounts for the changing origins of immigrants
arriving in America during this period. Northern and western Europeans
were predominant among immigrants before about 1890, whereas Southern and Eastern European nationality groups predominated after that date.

Although about one-third of the 29.5 million immigrants who came to the United States between 1860 and 1920 eventually returned to Europe, the 20 million who remained constituted over one-fourth of the total increase in the American population during this period. Whether one considers the gross number of immigrants who came or the net number who stayed, such large accretions to the American population from overseas had important economic effects. Thus, it is highly probable that immigration made a positive contribution to the rate of economic growth per capita if for no other reason than that the structure of the immigrant population was very different from that of the native population. More than half of the immigrants were males between the ages of fourteen and forty-four—a prime working-age group. On the other hand, the very young, the very old, and females—all groups that were less likely to work—were underrepresented among immigrants in comparison with the native population. Hence, the rise in immigration during this period was probably an important reason for the rise in labor force participation rates already noted (see table 13-1). And, of course, an increase in labor force participation would tend to raise both the level and the growth of per capita income.

Another related aspect of the immigrant contribution to the American economy has come in for attention in recent years. Insofar as the immigrants were raised and trained or educated in their countries of origin, immigration made a net addition to the stock of human capital in the United States. To put it another way: If Americans had sought to have the same population without allowing immigration, then they would have had to devote vast additional American resources to child rearing and education.

Immigrants came from, and entered into, all walks of life, from farming to the professions and from highly skilled industrial work to domestic service. They furnished a large and continuous flow of workers, especially for the rapidly growing heavy industries as well as for textiles, clothing, mining, meat packing, and construction. Various ethnic groups were quite important in the labor forces of particular industries; for example, the Irish were leaders in heavy construction, the Italians in the building trades, and the Jews in the clothing industry. In agriculture certain groups, notably the Italians and the Japanese, drew on their experience to teach intensive farming methods to Americans. Individual immigrant inventors also made economically important contributions to major industries. In electricity, for example, Charles Steinmetz, a German, was awarded some two hundred patents for electromagnetic ideas and devices; Nikola Tesla, a Croatian, developed the use of alternating current; and Michael Pupin, a Serbian, invented among other things devices that made possible the long-distance telephone. All of these men of genius came to America between the ages of fourteen and twenty-eight.

Many historians have argued that the economic position of immigrants in America between 1860 and 1920 was substantially inferior to that of native workers; some have gone so far as to maintain that immigrants—particularly the "new" immigrants from southern and eastern Europe between 1890 and 1920—were grievously exploited both as workers and as consumers. More recent research, however, has demonstrated that although each new immigrant group tended to come in at the bottom of the economic ladder, as they acquired literacy, fluency in English, and other skills, their earnings rose and were not out of line with those of native-born and "old" immigrants from northern and western Europe. This does not mean that the "new" immigrants did not experience great hardships in finding employment and in locating places to live or that they did not face discrimination in employment opportunities and job security. What it does mean is that we must discard the old stereotype of the immigrant living on subsistence wages and with no opportunity to escape poverty. Immigrants and immigrant groups not only differed in social origin and economic background; they were also quite mobile, economically and socially, after they reached this country.

Despite the undeniable contributions of immigrants to the American economy and to the enrichment of American life, they encountered much resentment from native-born and "older" immigrant workers who, fearing the effect of cheap, abundant immigrant labor on their own wages, opposed unlimited immigration. The Chinese were the first target of the movement to limit immigration. Congress in 1882 passed the Chinese Exclusion Act prohibiting the immigration of Chinese for ten years, and in 1902 this prohibition was made permanent. Then in 1885 the Knights of Labor (a labor organization we shall discuss in more detail later) got Congress to prohibit the importation of workers under contract, a practice that had been legalized as an emergency measure during the Civil War. Later, in an effort to stem the flow of Japanese labor to the United States that had begun in the 1890s, the United States and Japan in 1907-8 reached an accord whereby Japan agreed to stop the emigration of some of its unskilled workers. Finally, in 1917 opponents of the "new" immigration succeeded in getting Congress to pass, over Woodrow Wilson's veto, an act requiring a literacy test for every immigrant admitted to the United States. A few years later quota laws ended the free flow of immigrants which for a century had been regarded as one of the strengths of the American democratic and economic system.

Labor Mobility within the United States

The same economic forces that led overseas immigrants to America—greater job opportunities in this country than at home—caused many workers to move into different occupations and geographic areas. Between

TABLE 13-2
Percentage Distribution of the Labor Force
by Industry, 1860-1920

Year	Agri-culture	Manu-facturing	Trade	Trans-portation	Other*	Total
1860	53	14	8	2	23	100
1880	51	19	11	3	16	100
1900	40	20	14	4	22	100
1920	26	27	14	6	27	100

*Includes workers in fishing, mining, construction, professions, and domestic and other services.
SOURCE: Stanley Lebergott, "Labor Force and Employment, 1800-1960," in National Bureau of Economic Research, Output, Employment, and Productivity in the United States after 1800 (New York: National Bureau of Economic Research, 1966), Table 2, p. 119.

1860 and 1920 the biggest source of new jobs was the rapidly growing manufacturing sector. As Table 13–2 demonstrates, in 1860 there were almost four workers in agriculture for every one in manufacturing, and as late as 1900 agricultural workers still outnumbered workers in manufacturing by a ratio of two to one. By 1920, however, manufacturing had surpassed agriculture as the largest employment sector. It is also important to note that during this same period of 1860 to 1920 the trade and transportation sectors doubled their combined share of the labor force.

Since the centers of American manufacturing and trade were in the cities of the northeast and the Great Lakes, these were the magnets that attracted labor. Immigrants and domestic migrants settled in these centers in such numbers that the urban proportion of the total population increased from 20 percent in 1860 to 51 percent in 1920.

One aspect of domestic labor mobility during this period, which was to become even more significant after 1920, was the migration of black labor out of the South. At the outbreak of the Civil War, 92 percent of the black population, most of them slaves, lived in the South, primarily on plantations and small farms, and by 1900 the proportion was still 90 percent. But by 1920 the beginnings of outward migration were evident, as the proportion of blacks in the South dropped to 85 percent. (Fifty years later, in 1970, the black population of the United States was about evenly divided between the South and the rest of the country.)

Blacks left the South for many reasons, among which were low pay for farm labor, dissatisfaction with the sharecropping system, and discrimination against their race in education, housing, voting rights, and justice. In this respect black migration was similar to overseas migration: Both were inspired in part by unsatisfactory economic and social conditions at home. But the attraction of job opportunities outside the South was probably more important for blacks. Prior to 1910 most black migration had been to the West and the Southwest: Agriculture was expanding in these newer regions, and racial discrimination was far less prevalent than in the older parts of the South. The North attracted relatively few black migrants from the South before 1910—that is, as long as the flow of unskilled immigrants was sufficient to satisfy the demand for low-skilled employment. In the decade 1910–20 this situation changed. World War I and then legal restrictions on immigration cut down on the flow of unskilled, foreign-born workers to the United States; at the same time demands for new industrial workers increased because of the war. To take advantage of these new opportunities, black workers began to migrate from the South to the North.

As a result the number of black wage earners in industry increased sharply. In 1900 about 87 percent of the blacks gainfully employed were in agriculture and domestic and personal service; by 1920 this proportion had declined to 67 percent, and 31 percent of the blacks gainfully employed —about 1,506,000—were in manufacturing, mechanical industries, trade, and transportation. Most black workers went into the lower-paying unskilled and semiskilled jobs. In manufacturing, for example, they worked in automobile plants, foundries, meatpacking houses, and steel mills. Others labored in road building and construction or went into transportation as Pullman porters. The percentage of black females employed in agriculture also decreased. Many black women shifted into domestic and personal service and manufacturing. But black workers—both male and female— continued to suffer from inadequate training in many cases and also from the refusal of most established trade unions to admit them to membership.

Although the centers of industry that attracted these new immigrants from overseas and from the rest of the country were for the most part in the northeastern quadrant of the United States, the South also began to be industrialized during the late nineteenth and early twentieth centuries. Southern industrial development was often characterized by the establishment of a paternalistic system of mill villages—reminiscent of the early textile industry in New England—where poor southern white farmers settled as a permanent working class. After 1900, however, a number of predominantly industrial cities—for example, in Alabama, Birmingham, (iron and steel), in South Carolina, Greenville (textiles), and in North Carolina, Gastonia, (textiles), and Durham and Winston-Salem, (tobacco) —attracted large numbers of migrants from the countryside. But racism limited the opportunities for blacks in southern industry, and the presence of many low-skilled white workers in the South tended to discourage foreign-born immigrants from locating there.

Expanding employment opportunities in industry, trade, and services brought more women into the labor force. For the most part women tended to work in low-paying industrial jobs, domestic service, and the clerical and sales fields. During the half-century before 1920 the proportion of female workers in domestic and personal service declined, while that in clerical occupations and professional service increased. Another important activity of women in these years—although not one that is usually recognized in definitions of the labor force—was taking in roomers and boarders. There was much demand for these services in urban areas, because many migrants from the countryside and from overseas were unmarried males. In the cities married women often supplemented their family incomes by providing rooms and meals for such men.

Changing Conditions of Employment

The American economy's increased emphasis on manufacturing and the declining importance of agriculture between 1860 and 1920 was accompanied by far-reaching changes in the conditions of labor. Most American farmers were independent businessmen who engaged in a wide range of decision-making activities. Although guided by market demands and the productive resources at his disposal, the individual farmer could still decide what commodities to produce, how to produce them, the amount of effort to devote to various farm activities, and so on. In contrast, the typical worker in manufacturing and also increasingly in the trade, transportation, and service sectors was an employee whose boss told him what to do, how to do it, how long to work, and how much he would be paid for his labor. The employee's loss of control over many of the key decisions regarding his or her work is undoubtedly one of the major reasons for the growing worker discontent that has invariably manifested itself during economic modernization.

WAGES AND HOURS

Yet despite these real difficulties, the statistical evidence contradicts the Marxian view that the American working class was doomed to increasing misery and lower living standards. Both daily wages and annual earnings in manufacturing increased about 50 percent between 1860 and 1890, one of the highest percentage increases in American history. Typical daily wages increased from $1.00 to $1.50, and real annual earnings increased from just under $300 in 1860 to just over $425 in 1890. During this same period the average workday was shortened by 7 percent to ten hours in 1890, and the normal work week was cut to six days. At least one-fifth of the increase in real wages and earnings was due to the relative shift of workers from soft goods industries like cotton and woolen textiles where wages were low to hard goods industries like iron and steel where wages were high. Wage differences functioned to improve the allocation of labor within manufacturing, just as they were drawing workers from agriculture to industry.

Until recently it was believed that real wages did not rise after 1890 but stagnated from that year to 1914. Albert Rees, however, has shown that the real earnings of manufacturing workers rose 37 percent in this time span, at an annual compound rate of 1.3 percent as against 1.6 percent compounded annually for the period 1860–90. By 1914 real earnings had increased to around $580, and the workweek had fallen to 50 to 55 hours. But it is true that the rate of growth for real wages in manufacturing was less rapid than the increase in output per man-hour. The reason was that the cost of using more capital per unit of output had to be covered before real wages could rise if the flow of capital investment was to be sustained.

WORKING CONDITIONS

Between 1860 and 1914 employment in manufacturing and construction tripled, and the physical output of manufacturing rose six times. This great industrial expansion was accompanied by mechanization that in many cases destroyed the need for the special skills of handicraftsmen or artisans and in fact increased the importance of less skilled workers. In some cases, as in the clothing industry, managers subdivided a complex process that had been the responsibility of one skilled artisan into simple operations that were carried out by groups of unskilled workers. But in most instances, as in the iron and steel industry, the highly skilled worker was replaced by new machines that permitted a greater utilization of unskilled and semiskilled workers and thus enabled employers to pay comparatively lower wages while securing them a larger labor supply. For the workers, however, the shift to less skilled labor meant that they were more dependent upon their employers and could more easily be replaced.

Among the consequences of this greater use of machines and simplification of tasks was an increase in the routine and the tedium of factory work as well as in the number and the percentage of industrial accidents. Between 1905 and 1920 at least 2,000 fatal work-related injuries occurred every year in the coal mines, the worst record for any important coal-mining country. The next most dangerous occupation was railroading. Overall, there were 25,000 fatal industrial accidents in 1913 and 23,000 in 1919. Moreover, the financial burdens of these industrial deaths and injuries fell upon the workers affected rather than upon their employers. In the latter part of the nineteenth century the courts had invoked the common law assumption that when a person agreed to work for an employer, he took full responsibility for all the ordinary dangers in his work, all the unusual hazards if he were in a position to know them, and all the consequences flowing from the ignorance, the carelessness, or the incompetence of his fellow workers.

JOB SECURITY

In addition to long hours of work and the very real danger of injury and hardship from industrial accidents, job insecurity was a constant threat to working life. Depressions and recessions ushered in cyclical unemployment; changes in weather and style brought seasonal unemployment; novel machine practices rendered handicraft skills obsolete and caused structural unemployment.

The depressions that afflicted the United States in 1873–78, 1883–85, and 1893–97 were particularly serious for the workers. In 1897 the country embarked on a period of long-term business expansion. Nevertheless, workers suffered from widespread unemployment during a brief depression in 1908–9 and a relatively severe depression in 1913–14 that ended only when the demands of World War I brought about a restoration of prosperity. The percentage of unemployed workers varied from 6 to 18 percent during the worst depression years.

Cyclical unemployment threatened economic security, but at least only temporarily. More serious perhaps were the problems of the many who were unable to work or were unable to earn enough when they did work. According to surveys by sociologists and social workers, many workers in key industrial cities such as New York and Pittsburgh, as well as miners in West Virginia and Kentucky and migratory workers in California, earned wages considerably below the minimal health and decency budgets drawn up by government and private social workers. Studies such as Robert Hunter's *Poverty* * in 1904 suggested that in the industrial states of the United States over one-fifth of the American people, or more than six million, lived in poverty as a result of unemployment, old age, illness, dependent youth, and other types of dependency.

INDUSTRIAL DISCIPLINE AND LABOR RELATIONS

The spread of the factory system and the development of great corporations altered drastically the close relationships that had previously existed between employers and their workers. Where once a few workers had labored in a shop under the direct supervision of an employer, by the late nineteenth century the labor forces of many enterprises numbered in the hundreds. In the 1879–99 period the average labor force in single steelworks and rolling mills rose from 220 to 412; and by the late 1880s individual railroad companies had labor forces numbering in the tens of

* Robert Hunter, *Poverty* (New York: Macmillan, 1904).

thousands. Large factories and plants tended to have an impersonal hierarchical structure ranging from the factory and plant superintendents or managers and "overseers" of departments down to foremen and the workers they supervised at the machines. The control of time on the job, the flow of materials, the use of machines, and the transmission of orders became systematized. Punctuality, following orders, and efficiency at work were highly valued, and violations of these requirements were penalized.

In some cases, owners or managers and workers continued to maintain close personal relations. (In the industrial South the cotton mill owners or their agents assumed the responsibility for building mill villages, with houses, schools, and churches.) But regardless of how the problem of status and equality was resolved within an industrial plant, outside the plant most employers and managers did not have close relations with their workers. Class divisions developed in terms of housing, schools, clubs, and churches. The growing distinction between employers and employees, both on and off the job, contributed to class consciousness among workers and increased their interest in organizing to promote working-class interests.

The Emergence of National Unions, 1850–78

American labor unions developed in a situation of change—change in technology, in market structures, in business organization, and in dominant social values. As far back as the 1850s local unions in more than a dozen trades organized national craft unions in order to increase their bargaining power with individual employers and employers' associations. However, the depression that lasted from 1857 to 1861 brought about the collapse of the weakened national unions and many of the locals. Still, three national unions now in existence—those of the printers, the molders, and the machinists—managed to survive.

At the outbreak of the Civil War, fewer than 2 percent of the American labor force were union members; and these were mainly confined to trades outside the factories, since the labor force in the mills consisted for the most part of women, children, and recent immigrants. By 1862, however, rising living costs and labor shortages provided a powerful stimulus for labor organizations. Inflation, a product of wartime financing, caused real wages to fall by one third between 1860 and 1865. Numerous strikes were called by workers in order to maintain their standard of living. In 1864 total union membership had risen to 200,000.

During the 1860s and early 1870s many local unions were formed throughout the industrial areas of the country. A score or more of national craft unions were also organized; among them were locomotive engineers, cigar makers, tailors, carpenters, and bricklayers. A forerunner of the modern industrial union was the Knights of St. Crispin, a shoe workers' union founded in 1867 to protect the skilled workers against the introduction of new machinery and the influx of unskilled hands. By 1870 it was the largest national union in the country, but within a decade it disintegrated owing to drastic wage cuts and the failure of the producers' cooperatives which the union organized to counteract the new machinery. Two other unions powerful in the late 1860s—the iron molders and the anthracite coal miners, each at its peak claiming a membership of over 300,000—were weakened in the early 1870s.

In the 1860s the successful formation of city central offices of all local unions, and the national organization of all locals of a given craft, inspired an attempt to establish a national body that would include all the national unions and the trade assemblies. In 1866, the National Labor Union (NLU) was formed with both national unions and city trade assemblies represented, along with farmers' societies and other reform political groups. This body concentrated its attention upon the eight-hour day, producers' cooperatives, currency and land reform, and alien contract labor. In 1868 the NLU persuaded Congress to pass a law limiting the hours of Federal employees (laborers and mechanics) to eight a day; but in 1872, after an unsuccessful effort to form a National Labor Reform party, the organization dissolved.

During the prolonged depression of 1873–79 many national trade unions disappeared. The whole movement was weakened by unemployment, lack of funds, the resort by employers to the blacklist and lockout, and their refusal to negotiate. As a result, labor organizations often became more or less secret societies. Many bitter strikes were called to protest against successive wage cuts, the introduction of labor saving machinery, and other innovations that took away jobs or depressed working conditions. The railroad strikes of July 1877 against successive wage reductions led to nationwide rioting and bloodshed and the destruction of millions of dollars of railroad property; state and federal troops were called in to quell these disorders and thereby to break the strikes.

THE KNIGHTS OF LABOR

The depression of the 1870s convinced many workers of the necessity for a united labor organization. The Noble Order of the Knights of Labor, founded in 1869, was the first important attempt in the United States to unite the workers of all industries and occupations in one big general union, and it admitted to membership any person who worked or had worked for wages. At first the Knights were a small and secret organization, but under the leadership of Terrence V. Powderly it developed into a spectacular mass movement. Its members included workers of all trades and degrees of skill, of both sexes, and of all races. The Knights aimed at the ultimate substitution of a cooperative society for the existing wage system. But the order also emphasized such trade-union demands as the eight-hour day, the prohibition of child labor, compulsory arbitration, health and safety laws, and a mechanics' lien law. The Knights were also interested in monetary reform, antimonopoly legislation, and land reform.

The structure of the Knights of Labor consisted of local assemblies, organized along either craft or mixed lines; these were combined into district assemblies with sole authority within their respective jurisdictions; and finally, the General Assembly had full and final jurisdiction. The local assemblies bargained with employers and conducted strikes, often calling out workers in various trades to aid strikers within a particular trade or plant.

The membership of the Knights of Labor grew slowly at first, but the depression and wage cutting of 1884 began a rapid expansion. In 1885 spectacularly successful strikes against railroads controlled by Jay Gould and the occurrence of almost two hundred boycotts stimulated a sevenfold membership increase within one year. By the fall of 1886 there were over 700,000 members, almost 10 percent of the existing industrial wage earners.

But it could not last. Many of the new members were unskilled and semiskilled workers, small-town merchants and mechanics, and farmers with little interest in the problems of urban wage earners. The result was disunity of purpose, internal conflict, and a decrease in effectiveness. A series of railroad strikes in 1886 almost completely eliminated the Knights from the western railroads and exposed serious weaknesses in their organizational structure. A mass movement for the eight-hour day led to a general strike in May 1886 which, after a few limited victories, ended essentially in failure.

The power of the Knights was further diminished by the general public's horrified reaction to the bombing and rioting in Haymarket Square in Chicago in May 1886. Although the Knights were not responsible, their reputation as a labor organization suffered greatly from unwarranted charges made against them. The greatest threat to the organization, however, came from the dissatisfaction of many skilled workers who were leaving it to form craft unions. The membership of the Knights fell to 100,000 in 1890; and by 1900 they had practically ceased to exist as a national movement.

The fate of the Knights of Labor demonstrated the difficulty of establishing in nineteenth-century America a strong, stable, nationwide labor organization for economic and political action. Skilled workers were persuaded only for a time to subordinate their craft interests to a program for helping the mass of unskilled workers. Nevertheless, the Knights of

Labor remains important in American labor history as a trailblazer for the idea of industrial unionism, which decades later was to find some realization in the CIO.

The American Federation of Labor

As early as 1881 the Federation of Organized Trades and Labor Unions of the United States and Canada had been formed by a group of national trade-union leaders, disaffected craft union groups from the Knights of Labor, and Socialists. But the new Federation could not compete effectively against the expanding Knights of Labor. In 1886 the hostile attitude of the Knights toward craft unions induced those favoring them to found the American Federation of Labor (AFL), which then united with the Federation of Organized Trades and Labor Unions. Samuel Gompers of the Cigar Makers' Union became the first president of the AFL and continued in that office, except for one year, until his death in 1924.

The basic units of the AFL were the national or the international (North American) craft unions, each of which had complete autonomy. The new union philosophy put a high value on businesslike methods and centralization of authority, stressed trade organization, the control of jobs, and the negotiating of written agreements with employers. The AFL leaders, unlike those of the Knights of Labor, minimized or disparaged direct participation in political organizations and programs of radical and social reform. Instead, they concentrated on furthering the special interests and economic strength of each craft.

During its first decade the AFL had to face and surmount some difficult circumstances. Although the national unions affiliated with the AFL grew in number, most of them were small and in a weak financial condition. The total membership of the AFL unions grew slowly until after the 1893–97 depression; then it rose at increasingly faster rates. The changes in membership were as follows:

1886	140,000
1898	278,000
1904	1,676,000
1914	2,020,000
1920	4,078,000

During the early 1890s the AFL revived the strike for an eight-hour day and won some victories for the building and printing unions. One major setback, however, was the failure of the Homestead iron and steel strike in 1892. A comparable big business resistance brought defeat to the American Railway Union in the Pullman strike of 1894.

The period from 1898 to 1904 was one of rising prices, prosperity, and comparative industrial peace. The AFL unions received wide recognition from employers and increased their membership considerably. They were aided by such business-dominated or middle-class organizations as the National Civic Federation, the National Consumers' League, and the National Child Labor Committee. Collective bargaining became more widely accepted. During the anthracite coal strike of 1902, President Theodore Roosevelt pressured the employers into accepting arbitration by a presidential commission. Thereafter, the United Mine Workers (UMW) expanded into a large and well organized affiliate of the AFL. During this period a score of new national unions chartered by the AFL were established; among them perhaps the most notable was the International Ladies' Garment Workers' Union (ILGWU), organized in 1900.

The very success of business unionism caused a stiffening of employer resistance to the AFL's organizing activities, with the result that total union membership remained almost stationary between 1904 and 1910. In the early 1900s antiunion employers started a campaign of propaganda against the closed shop and unionism in general, with considerable success, particularly in small towns.

Then about 1910 there was a renewed burst of activity among some unions, especially those in the coal-mining, building, clothing, and railroad industries. One successful strike of coal miners occurred in 1910, and another in 1912, each of which strengthened the bargaining power of the miners. In the women's clothing industry two major strikes in New York City in the 1900s increased the size and power of the International Ladies' Garment Workers' Union. On the other hand, in the men's clothing industry, a group within the active United Garment Workers' Union revolted against the AFL leadership and established a new industrial union, the Amalgamated Clothing Workers (ACW), which was independent of the AFL. Each of these unions was vigorous and grew in membership at a rapid rate.

The Industrial Workers of the World

The AFL's failure to organize semiskilled and unskilled workers was criticized by many groups. The most stringent attacks came from labor radicals who in 1905 founded the Industrial Workers of the World, the IWW or "Wobblies." The IWW was "one big union" made up of such

diverse groups as the Western Federation of Miners and previously unorganized migratory workers in northwestern wheat fields and lumber
camps. It appealed to all workers irrespective of skill level, nationality,
race, or sex; and it attempted to organize the workers in different industries into large industrial unions. The philosophy and rhetoric of the IWW
were those of revolutionary industrial unionism: the ultimate goal was to
replace capitalistic society with an industrial democracy in which the
unions would own and operate all industries. The major efforts of the
IWW, however, were directed toward winning improvements in wages,
hours, and working conditions for the hitherto unorganized workers. In
this respect the IWW and the AFL shared a common objective, even
though they differed on the craft versus the industrial union method of
organization, on militant versus peaceful tactics, and on whether capitalism should be retained or supplanted by a workers' democracy.

In the West the IWW organized the unskilled metal miners and
migratory shipping and farm laborers. In the East the "Wobblies" provided leadership for immigrant workers, especially those in the textile
factories. The IWW's greatest strike success was at Lawrence, Massachusetts, in 1912. The membership of the IWW was very unstable and
perhaps never exceeded sixty or seventy thousand paid members at its
height before World War. I. Yet between 1909 and 1918 some two to
three million workers passed through its ranks, and millions more were
influenced by its teachings and activities.

With the entry of the United States into World War I, which the
leaders of the "Wobblies" had strongly opposed, the IWW went into a
fatal decline. But this did not diminish the importance of the IWW as
a protest against the AFL's claim to represent a working class that from
1890 to 1914 consisted to an increasing extent of unskilled workers, native
and immigrant. The IWW proved that migratory, casual, and unskilled
workers with varied languages, customs, religions, and antipathies could
be organized. In addition, the Wobbly campaigns and strikes awakened
various progressive and reform leaders of the 1900–1917 era to industry's
domination of many local and state governments and to its use of government against strikers without regard to civil rights or to the deplorable
living conditions of many working families. Thus, the IWW had a significant impact upon the progressive movement and future social legislation.

Industrial Conflict, the Courts, and Labor Legislation

Workers in different trades established labor unions as their decision-
making agencies in dealing with employers on such vital subjects as wages,
hours, and working conditions. In some cases management and labor were

able to negotiate mutually satisfactory agreements, but in others unions decided to use the strike as a means of settling disputes. Some strikes were notorious. Among the disastrous labor conflicts of the post-Civil War period were the July 1877 national railroad strike, the May 1886 strikes and Haymarket riot in Chicago, the 1892 Homestead, Pennsylvania, iron and steel strike, and the 1894 Pullman strike in Chicago. The number of strikes rose from an annual average of 530 for the years 1881–95 to a high of 3,100 for the years 1911–15. Between 1881 and 1903, in over 50 percent of the strikes the workers were successful, but between 1904 and 1915 the success rate was only 36 percent. The record shows that whereas strikes by unorganized workers almost always failed, unionized workers won from one-third to two-thirds of theirs. The score of union successes was much higher in prosperity than in depression phases of the business cycle.

The struggles of workers for improvements in wages, hours, and working conditions were often hindered by decisions of state and federal courts. In the late 1870s various judges opposed railroad strikes through skillful use of their contempt powers. Employers often were able to persuade judges to issue injunctions against labor strikes, picketing, and boycotts, and the courts were hostile to boycott actions by organized labor. The U.S. Supreme Court applied the Sherman Act to unions in the Danbury Hatters' case in 1908 and in the Bucks Stove case in 1911. In the first case the United Hatters' Union (AFL) was held liable for triple damages because of a nationwide boycott against hats produced by a nonunion firm in Danbury, Connecticut. In the second case three AFL officers, including Samuel Gompers, were held guilty of contempt of court and sentenced to jail for instituting a boycott against the Bucks Stove Company. AFL officers then tried to curb the powers of the court through the Clayton Act of 1914, but later court decisions proved this act ineffective.

When Congress and the state legislatures passed laws to prevent employers from discriminating against unions, the Supreme Court often intervened on the side of the employers. In 1908 the Court, in *Adair* v. *United States*, declared unconstitutional Congress's prohibition of discrimination against employees because of membership in a labor organization. A few years later, in the *Coppage* v. *Kansas* case, the Court nullified a state law outlawing antiunion contracts. Before the 1930s the balance of judicial power in cases involving labor law and industrial relations usually favored employers over organized labor.

Other types of legislation affecting unorganized as well as organized labor also faced judicial prejudice. The movement for protective labor legislation, especially for children and women, had begun in the United States before the Civil War. Children were the first workers protected by legislation in various states. Congress in 1916 made it unlawful to ship in interstate commerce any product produced in violation of specified standards on the labor of children. The Supreme Court, however, declared this law unconstitutional in 1918, and did likewise with a similar one in 1922. Legislation regulating the employment of women was passed after the Civil War to protect the health of working women who often were mothers as well as wage earners. About 1913, after the Supreme Court in *Muller* v. *Oregon* (1908) sustained the right of the state to enact a ten-hour law for women, the movement for such legislation reached its peak.

The most controversial labor legislation of the early twentieth century involved maximum hours for men. In 1898 the Supreme Court upheld the constitutionality of such a law applying to miners in the case of *Holden* v. *Hardy*. But in 1905 the Court ruled in *Lochner* v. *New York* that legislation regulating hours of bakers was unconstitutional. The pressure of public opinion gradually affected the Court, and in 1917 it upheld held an Oregon law regulating hours of work in *Bunting* v. *Oregon*.

Conclusion

In the late nineteenth and early twentieth centuries the American labor force expanded more rapidly than did the nation's population, in part owing to millions of immigrants from overseas. As the main source of employment shifted from agriculture to manufacturing and trade, workers were able to take advantage of the other opportunities afforded by the high rate of growth and changing sectors of production. Like the immigrants, blacks and woman were drawn into the paid labor force by industrial and commercial expansion and the growth of cities. But the drastically changed nature of work under conditions of mass production and the changed relationships between workers and employers created much discontent.

Industrial wage earners after the Civil War benefited greatly from the rise of real wages and of the standard of living. Nevertheless, workers were acutely concerned about improving their wages, hours, and working conditions and experimented with different types of trade unions, some socially idealistic, others narrowly self-interested. They secured some improvements, especially for workers in the craft unions. But for decades organized labor encountered strong opposition on many issues from state and federal courts, and thus was not to emerge as a powerful political force on the national level until the 1930s.

SUGGESTED READINGS

For informative studies on trends in United States population, immigration, and internal migration, see Richard A. Easterlin, "The American Population," in Lance Davis et al., *American Economic Growth* (New York: Harper & Row, 1972); Oscar Handlin, ed., *The Positive Contribution by Immigrants* (Paris: UNESCO, 1955); Peter J. Hill, *The Economic Impact of Immigration in the United States* (New York: Arno Press, 1975); Conrad and Irene B. Taeuber, *The Changing Population of the United States* (New York: John Wiley, 1958); Philip Taylor, *The Distant Magnet: European Migration to the U.S.A.* (New York: Harper & Row, 1971); and Brinley Thomas, *Migration and Economic Growth*, 2d ed. (New York: Cambridge University Press, 1973).

On changes in the economic position of industrial workers, the latest findings are given by Stanley Lebergott, *Manpower in Economic Growth* (New York: McGraw-Hill, 1964) and *The American Economy* (Princeton: Princeton University Press, 1976); Clarence D. Long, *Wages and Earnings in the United States 1860–1890* (Princeton: Princeton University Press, 1960); Albert Rees, *Real Wages in Manufacturing, 1890–1914* (Princeton: Princeton University Press, 1961); and W. S. Woytinsky et al., *Employment and Wages in the United States* (New York: Twentieth Century Fund, 1953).

The social life of industrial workers has been explored by Melvyn Dubofsky, *Industrialism and the American Worker, 1865–1920* (New York: Crowell, 1975); and Herbert C. Gutman, *Work, Culture and Society in Industrializing America* (New York: Knopf, 1976). The problems of black and women workers are forcibly presented by Robert Higgs, *Competition and Coercion: Blacks in the American Economy, 1865–1914* (New York: Cambridge University Press, 1977); Sterling D. Spero and Abram L. Harris, *The Black Worker* (New York: Atheneum, 1968); and Robert W. Smuts, *Women and Work in America* (New York: Schocken Books, 1971).

Among the interesting yet scholarly books on the varied developments in trade union history and labor law are John R. Commons et al., *History of Labour in the United States*, vols. 2–4 (New York: Macmillan, 1918–35); Archibald Cox, *Cases on Labor Law* (Brooklyn, N.Y.: Foundation Press, 1948); Melvyn Dubofsky, *We Shall Be All: A History of the Industrial Workers of the World* (New York: Quadrangle Books, 1969); Lawrence W. Friedman, *A History of American Law* (New York: Simon & Schuster, 1973); Gerald Grob, *Workers and Utopia . . . 1865–1900* (New York: Quadrangle Books, 1969); Joseph Rayback, *A History of American Labor* (New York: Free Press, 1966); Lloyd Ulman, *The Rise of the National Trade Union* (Cambridge, Mass.: Harvard University Press, 1955); and Norman Ware, *The Labor Movement in the United States, 1860–1895* (New York: Vintage Books, 1964).

CHAPTER 14

―――

Building National Railroad

and Communication Networks

The revolutionary developments in transportation and communication that began in the quarter century after 1815 reached full flower in the decades following the Civil War. To the railroads in transportation and to the telegraph and, later, to the telephone in communication fell the Herculean labor of unifying America economically and making it into one great market place. These technologies were equal to the task. By the first years of this century the products of the land and the factory as well as people themselves moved quickly and freely throughout the continental United States over a vast network of steel rails. Information flowed even faster as messages were carried instantaneously over millions of miles of telegraph and telephone wire. The railroads especially, but also the wire communication enterprises, were great industries in their own right; the demands they generated as they grew stimulated expansion in numerous other activities. Their true significance, however, lay in the fact that the services they provided were critical inputs into virtually all types of economic activity and processes of decision making. Amazing as it may seem, many people living in 1900 could remember when neither railroads nor telegraphs nor telephones existed. In a sense, such people were older than the American economy, a phrase that had seldom been used at the time they were born because it lacked content when economies were local and regional in nature.

The expansion of the key technologies of transportation and communications during the late nineteenth century was stupendous. Although the thirty thousand miles of railroad operated in the United States in 1860 represented about one half of the mileage in the entire world at that date, this achievement pales in the light of subsequent growth. Main track mileage of American railroads nearly quadrupled in the two decades after the Civil War and then doubled between the mid-1880s and 1914 when 289,000 miles were in operation. In the case of the telegraph, in 1866 some two thousand offices transmitted roughly five million messages over seventy-six thousand miles of wire. By 1912 the number of telegraph offices had increased to thirty-one thousand, and these offices handled 109 million messages sent over 1.8 million miles of wire. Railway mileage grew at a continuously compounded rate of 4.3 percent per year over the period 1865–1914, and at 6.5 percent per year between 1865 and 1885. Mileage of telegraph wire operated grew even faster, at 6.9 percent per year compounded from 1866 to 1912. Neither the railroad nor the telegraph were new in the 1860s. By that time they had already passed through the very rapid growth stages characteristic of infants. Yet they remained important growth industries for decades. In the case of the telephone, which was not patented until 1876, growth was phenomenal. After a rather subdued beginning during the initial seventeen years of patent monopoly, the number of telephones in the United States grew at a rate of 17 percent per year between 1893 and 1914. In the latter year, over ten million telephones were in operation, one for every ten Americans, and calls averaged forty million per day in local exchanges and a million per day in toll service.

Such data alone tell us little about the decision-making processes that gave form to transportation and communication expansion. Nor do they say much about the impact of such expansion on the economy, the polity, and the society. These subjects are worth further investigation as a way of understanding the past. But they are also important for understanding the present. In the railroad and the telegraph we see for the first time in history the emergence of gigantic business enterprises. The huge capital investment requirements and the scale of operation of these enterprises gave rise to new forms of business management and organizational structures. And the nature of the technologies utilized dictated that there would be only one, or at most a few, suppliers of their services in any given market area; competition for sales among suppliers was therefore much more limited than in most markets. Moreover, the operations of these enterprises did not stop at local or state boundaries. As national transportation and communication networks were formed in the context of monopolistic or oligopolistic market structures (one or few sellers) problems of intrastate and interstate commerce arose that called forth state and federal regulatory institutions. This marked the beginning of a very significant long-term development in the American political economy.

Railway Expansion under Corporate Organization

American railroads were private enterprises organized as corporations under governmental charters. As such they differed from earlier modes of transportation. The great canals of the early nineteenth century were developed and owned primarily by state governments while the steamboats that revolutionized internal waterway transportation were for the most part individual proprietorships and partnerships. Unlike canals and steamboats, the railroads had two functions: they both built their roadways and then moved the traffic of freight and passengers. These functions required building complex organizations, gaining access to large amounts of capital, and continuing administrative coordination and decision making on a great many levels. Neither the limited governments nor the small-scale family and partnership enterprises, which were the characteristic forms respectively of public and private economic organization for much of the nineteenth century, were suitable to the performance of these tasks.

But governments could help. The corporate charters they conferred enlisted the right of eminent domain to secure routes for the corporations and brought them the limited liability so useful in attracting private capital funds to finance investment. Governments, moreover, could also use their own resources to subsidize railway development in instances where they perceived the social returns from improved transport as exceeding the private returns that railroad corporations themselves could capture through their charges.

The corporate form of organization and decision making proved to be a remarkably flexible and dynamic method for linking together a continent's resources, producers, and consumers in a network of rails in the half century from 1865 to 1914. Figure 14–1 gives a summary outline of the expansion that occurred before, during, and after these years in terms of main-track mileage. The rate of expansion was very high in the 1850s, but at the end of that decade most of the mileage was still in the northeastern quarter of the United States. The Civil War years, as might be expected, markedly slowed the expansion. With the war ended the work of covering the entire nation with a network of dependable rail facilities began in earnest. Mileage doubled between 1865 and 1873; the highlight of this boom came when the first transcontinental route was completed with the driving into the ground of the famed golden spike near Ogden, Utah, in 1869. After the deep and widespread business depression of the mid-1870s two more booms in railway building followed in close succession during the years 1878–83 and 1885–93. These carried the main tracks to 181 thousand miles, a sixfold increase over 1860. By the early 1890s the national network was virtually complete. The substantial additions from

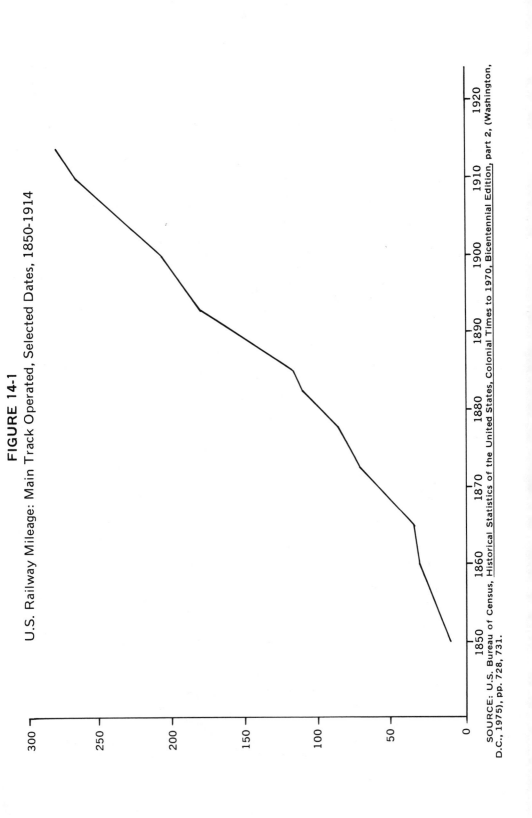

FIGURE 14-1

U.S. Railway Mileage: Main Track Operated, Selected Dates, 1850-1914

SOURCE: U.S. Bureau of Census, *Historical Statistics of the United States, Colonial Times to 1970*, Bicentennial Edition, part 2, (Washington, D.C., 1975), pp. 728, 731.

1900 to 1914 represented the filling out and further equipping of an American rail system whose outline had already been set.

While the tremendous post-Civil War expansion of railroading was taking place the strategies of railroad leaders and their companies, as well as the scale of their operations, were transformed in dramatic ways. Antebellum railroad corporations were large enterprises in their time, but even the larger ones owned tracks of but a few hundred miles in length; in their limited extent they were like the earlier great canals with which they had competed and then made obsolete. Just after the Civil War, for example, the Pennsylvania Railroad—considered to be one of the largest and best-managed of all American roads—operated slightly fewer than five hundred miles of track or, in other terms, less than 2 percent of the nation's total track at that time. There were hundreds of smaller roads but few that were larger. By the early 1870s, however, the Pennsylvania led the way into the future as far as American railroads were concerned by growing into a line that owned or controlled through leases nearly six thousand miles of track, some 8 percent of the national total, and a corporation with assets of nearly 400 million dollars, which was just under 13 percent of all U.S. railroad investment. This was at a time when nonrailroad enterprises with assets of one million dollars were considered large.

What had happened to cause the decision makers of a railroad such as the Pennsylvania to transform their already large corporation into a gigantic one? Essentially it was competition, a phenomenon that presented special problems for enterprises with large amounts of capital investment. Competition had not been much of a problem for antebellum railroads. Where it had been present in the form of wagons on the roads and boats on the canals and rivers, competition had worked to the railroads' advantage because they were both faster and more flexible and reliable than their competitors. But in most cases the numerous, small lines of the early railroad era did not face much competition. They were built to facilitate trade between established population centers along their routes. Neither the corporate charters offered by governments nor the economic incentives offered by private sources were very favorable to the construction of directly competing lines. When in time the volume of interregional and intersectional trade in the United States became relatively more important, however, the threat of competition became more evident and loomed as potentially damaging to the small, regional railroads. The threat could arise when, for example, an eastern road, negotiated agreements with, or otherwise gained control over, roads farther west in order to divert western traffic from other eastern roads to its own line.

The situation just described is roughly what confronted the Pennsylvania Railroad in the late 1860s and the Baltimore and Ohio and the New York Central a little later, after the noted (some would say notorious) financier Jay Gould gained control of the Erie Railroad in 1868. In order to increase the traffic and hence the earnings and securities values of the

Erie, Gould moved quickly in an attempt to gain control of midwestern lines that could connect the Erie with Chicago, St. Louis, and other midwestern centers. In the end Gould failed in this effort—perhaps because his attentions were diverted to other nonrailroad speculations such as trying to corner the American gold market in 1869—but his threatening actions toward the other big eastern roads forced them to expand their regional lines into interregional and intersectional systems. Leaders of the larger eastern railroads knew, of course, that a steady, high volume of through traffic was essential to the operating and financial health of their capital-intensive companies. Jay Gould had demonstrated to them that with competition they could not take such a volume of traffic for granted. Their responses took the form of decisions to increase the scale of their companies many times over either by buying or leasing existing roads or by constructing new lines to round out the system.

The irrepressible Jay Gould, having taught his competitive lessons in the northeast, next turned to instructing the newer western roads. The Union Pacific Railroad, one of two lines that had formed the first transcontinental, had been rocked by both scandal (see below) and the general business depression that began in 1873. Gould bought enough of its stock at low prices to gain control by 1874. The Union Pacific tracks extended westward from Omaha so that traffic between Omaha and cities in the east used other railroads. Gould attempted to assure favorable eastern connections through agreements with these roads—the Northwestern, Rock Island, and Burlington—but they resisted his overtures. Gould therefore embarked on a campaign to build his own system by using his considerable stock-market skills to gain control of other companies. By 1881, Gould's roads comprised nearly sixteen thousand miles of track, some 15 percent of the nation's total, and reached from Boston and New York in the east to New Orleans, El Paso, Denver, and Omaha in the south and west. Other western roads as well as eastern holdouts got the message from Gould's actions. Either they had to build extensive interterritorial systems of their own, or they ran the risk of losing traffic to other systems and perhaps of being absorbed by them. Thus, by the early 1890s gigantic railroad systems had come to dominate a transportation arena that earlier had been made up of numerous small companies. In 1893 the thirty-three railroad corporations with at least $100 million of assets operated nearly 70 percent of total United States rail mileage; by 1900 the percentage had risen to 80.

Building large systems did not guarantee profitable operations. The rush to systems that was generated by competition resulted in some overbuilding during the 1880s, and once the systems had been built they in turn competed with one another. These problems came to a head in the depression of the mid-1890s when many roads, including some systems, could not cover their bond interest charges. Track miles numbering in the tens of thousands passed into the hands of receivers. These defaults and the ensuing bankruptcies of large rail corporations brought investment bankers such as J. P. Morgan into the railroad reorganization and management picture. The bankers at first attempted to reduce the riskiness of railroading in two ways. They increased the ratio of equity to debt in the railroads' capital structures to reduce the risk of bankruptcy, and they negotiated cartel arrangements between competing roads with a view to sharing traffic and revenues in "orderly" ways. The financial strategy bore some fruit but the gentlemen's agreements proved less effective. Cartels tend to be unstable because of the incentives to individual members as well as to outsiders to increase profits by undercutting the cartel price and taking business away from those who stick to the cartel agreement. American railroad cartels exposed this Achilles heel with great frequency.

The final resolution of these competitive problems came shortly after the turn of the century. Bankers and railway managers further consolidated existing systems and developed communities of interest by having competitive systems invest in the stock of their competitors. These enlarged systems and communities of interest acted to discourage both rate cutting and the competitive construction activities of earlier years. At about the same time federal regulation, as we shall see below, was strengthened to the point where tendencies toward "destructive" competition were curbed by law. Hence, by the first decade of this century just seven groups or coordinated communities of interest exercised control of two thirds of America's rail mileage. The age of railroad expansion and competition was over.

Railroad Investment and Finance

The construction and equipping of railroads devoured capital funds available for investment after the Civil War. The net capital stock of the United States railroads, amounting to about $1.06 billion on the eve of the Civil War, rose to $10.5 billion by 1909. These figures are comparable since they both represent track and equipment valued in 1909 dollars. Gross investment, which does not adjust for the depreciation or wearing out of track and equipment, was, of course, much larger. Estimates show the gross investment, again in 1909 dollars, was nearly $1 billion in the 1860s, $2 billion in the 1870s, $4 billion in the 1880s, $2.5 billion in the 1890s, and almost $5 billion in the first decade of this century. To put these figures in perspective, we have made some rough calculations of the ratio of railroad gross investment to all gross investment. They indicate that railroads accounted for 12 to 16 percent of all investment in the 1870s and 1880s, and 7 to 8 percent of all investment in the 1890s and 1900s.

These are impressive ratios for but one component of the economy's transportation sector, and they came, moreover, in an era when the proportion of all investment (all plant, equipment, and residential construction) to GNP was rising to record heights in United States history.

The flow of funds into railroad investment between 1860 and 1910 is estimated in the range of $9 to $16 billion. These figures are of the same order of magnitude as the total of the gross investment figures cited above but there are important conceptual differences. The flow of funds figures are in terms of dollars that varied in purchasing power over time rather than in 1909 dollars. Also, in many cases, the prices at which securities were actually sold to initial investors by railroad companies differed from their nominal or stated values. Bonds, for example, were often sold at discounts from the stated par value; the advantage to newly projected railroads was a reduced current interest cost, to be made up later when the bonds matured, and the bondholders were paid off at par from the income of a going concern. And stock was sometimes, in the terminology of the times, "watered." This meant that the par or market value, or both, of the shares was in excess of the funds actually raised by the railroad company when it issued the stock. While some stock-watering practices were questionable, the phenomenon itself is not as mysterious or unethical as contemporaries assumed it to be. Equity shares tend to obtain their market value from the prospective future earnings and the dividends of the assets they represent, not from the historical cost of these assets to the shareholders who first financed railroad investment by purchasing them. When the earnings prospects of a railroad were viewed optimistically its shares tended to rise in market value. Shareholders reaped this benefit, but they might reap even greater benefits through the publicity gained from having management declare a stock dividend, that is, an increase in the number of shares. In many cases that was what stock watering amounted to, but in the nineteenth century's new world of security capitalism the practice appeared suspect to many people. A century later such practices are everyday occurrences, neither glorified nor vilified with terms like stock watering.

Who furnished the billions of dollars of funds that built America's railroads? For the most part the funds were raised from private investors, although government aid in a variety of forms was instrumental in the financing of a number of roads. The nature of government involvement as well as other significant features of finance in the railroad age are highlighted by the experience of the first transcontinental road, the Union Pacific—Central Pacific link completed in 1869. The notion of a railroad to the Pacific Coast had been suggested to Congress as early as 1845, but local and sectional bickering over the proposed route delayed passage of the Pacific Railroad Act until 1862, with revisions coming in 1864. These acts authorized private enterprise to build the road with government aid, on the ground that unaided private enterprise would not risk such a huge project through largely empty terrain. Aid came in two forms. One was a loan of federal government bonds in amounts from $16,000 to $48,000 per mile constructed, depending on the terrain. Once some mileage had been built the company could collect the bonds due from the government and sell them on the market to raise funds for further construction. In this manner the first transcontinental was lent some $65 million of U.S. bonds.

A second form of aid to the Union Pacific—Central Pacific project came in the form of grants of public land. For every mile of track laid, the railroad company was to receive twenty sections or square miles of public land—every other section in a forty mile-wide strip of land centered on the railroad. Because of the way the public lands were surveyed, this meant that the forty mile strip took the form of a checkerboard with, if you like, the federal government retaining the black squares and the railroad being granted the reds. There were several motives behind this decision. One was that the land grants would give the railroad companies an asset base that would induce private investors more readily to invest in their securities. Another was that the railroad itself would make the land more valuable so that it could be sold at a higher price to raise funds. Finally, the government would benefit to the extent that the railroad increased the value of the alternate sections of land the government retained for itself.

Despite the promise of government loans and land grants, the promoters of the Union Pacific Railroad had considerable difficulty in raising enough cash from private investors to commence construction. The solution to this problem, later adopted by other railroads, took the form of a company, the Credit Mobilier, created and controlled by the Union Pacific's private promoters to act as a general contractor for the road's construction. The construction company supplied limited amounts of its owners' funds to the railroad, and it received from the railroad large amounts of bonds and stocks at a discount, which it then either retained, used as collateral for loans, or resold at a profit to other investors. Some, but not all, of the proceeds were spent on building the railroad. In the end, the Union Pacific issued some $93.5 million of securities to finance a road on which only $57 million was actually expended. Its promoters, through the Credit Mobilier, owned most of the stock of the road even though they had put up very little cash. Their profit has been estimated at from $13 to $16.5 million on their own investment of $3.9 million.

Considering the risks perceived by private investors, as evident in their reluctance to buy the Union Pacific's securities except at substantial discounts from their nominal par values, modern scholars have argued that the profit reaped by the promoters was not far out of line with what was reasonably justified. In the early 1870s, however, the company had difficulty earning enough from operations to pay the interest charges on its large bonded debt. Government officials and others then seized upon exaggerated calculations of the promoters' profits to argue that both the railroad and the public had been robbed by a small group of profiteers. This turn of events—the so-called Credit Mobilier scandal—was instrumental in causing the federal government to cease its policy of land grants and financial aid for railroad construction. It also depressed the value of Union Pacific stock to the point where Jay Gould, as noted earlier, was able to move in and gain control of the company.

Between 1862 and 1871, however, the federal government did grant 200 million acres of public land to railroads; failures to meet construction time limitations imposed along with these grants reduced the total actually claimed to 131 million acres. Some states also made grants of land as well as cash subsidies. But even with generous valuations of the public lands donated, it seems clear that public aid financed less than 10 percent of the total investment in U.S. railroads between 1860 and 1910. Most of the resources used to build America's railroads were financed by private investors.

A significant portion of the private investment came from abroad. Foreigners made their decisions to invest in the United States by comparing the yields they could obtain on American securities with those available at home. Because the American economy was growing more rapidly than the economies of Europe and because wealth had not accumulated to the same extent in the United States as in Europe, the yield differential was in favor of the United States. This had been true for decades and had in fact led to a flow of federal, state, local, and private securities to Europe. After the Civil War, however, both economic interests and developments in technology and institutions combined to increase dramatically the flow of European funds into American railroads. Railroads moved the cheap foodstuffs of the American heartlands to tidewater for export to an industrializing Europe. At the same time the information flows necessary for efficient decision making in the context of international markets for basic commodities and investments were greatly improved by the laying of underseas cables to carry telegraphic messages. And investment banking houses, often with branches in both Europe and the United States, perfected techniques for marketing large issues of American securities to Europeans.

Estimates of the flow of European funds into American railroad investment are imprecise but they suggest that some $2.5 to $3.0 billion migrated across the Atlantic between 1865 and the turn of the century. If these figures are accurate, they imply that European investors supplied over one third of the financing for American railroad building in these years. The British undoubtedly accounted for the major portion. An 1898 estimate, derived from British tax records, of the value of British investment in American railways places the total at four hundred million pounds, or nearly $2 billion at the prevailing rate of exchange between the pound sterling and the dollar.

The decision of foreigners to invest on such a scale in the railroads of the United States was more than a mere investment decision on the part of passive rentiers. Some foreign investors had entrepreneurial ambitions to exploit America's undeveloped resources and to open up new markets. These looked after their investments by gaining control of the roads and becoming involved in their management. The United States benefitted from such activities because they involved a transfer of European expertise in technology, finance, and management to America. For example, British engineers came over to inspect and offer technical advice to roads in which their countrymen had invested, and their firms undertook various types of construction, such as tunneling, in which the British had expertise. Through their interest in railroads, the British also introduced to the United States types of financial instruments, for example, convertible securities, as well as advanced accounting practices.

The contributions of foreign investors and American governments were important but the majority of funds for railroad building were raised from American private investors. Some of these were persons of wealth who had accumulated or inherited their assets from earlier ventures in other lines of economic activity. The capitalists of Boston, for example, had accumulated fortunes in foreign commerce in the eighteenth and early-nineteenth centuries; after the Civil War they became heavily involved in western railroad development and management. Cornelius Vanderbilt's stake had come in shipping before he and his son parlayed it into a fortune while building the New York Central system. But it is doubtful that the level of investment would have reached the heights that it did without the participation of hundreds of thousands of smaller investors. These persons had learned of the nature of bond investments during Jay Cooke's mass marketings of federal securities in the Civil War years. Improvements in communication kept them aware of developments in the emerging national capital market. With the economic benefits of rail transportation a matter of everyday observation and with techniques of financial investment increasingly understood, the stage was set for the widespread involvement of ordinary Americans in the myriad investment decisions that financed railroads.

Railroad Productivity and Its Sources

What persuaded Americans of the enormous economic benefit of rail transportation were the twin factors of cost and convenience. We may infer something about the latter from the sheer size of the national railway system as it developed in the decades before World War I when it approached its all-time peak mileage. American railroads in 1859 carried 2.6

billion ton-miles of freight and 1.9 billion passenger miles. In 1910 the corresponding figures are 255 billion ton-miles and 32.5 billion passenger miles. Thus, freight output increased nearly one-hundredfold and passenger output over sixteenfold.

This rapidly growing volume of transportation services was supplied at falling costs. The average passenger-mile rate in 1859 was 2.44 cents; in 1910 it was 1.94 cents. Freight rates fell even more rapidly. In 1859 the average rate to carry one ton one mile was 2.58 cents; in 1910 it was .75 cents, or less than one third of the charge fifty years earlier. These cost reductions, large as they are, fail to do complete justice to the gains of consumers in rail service. For 1910 service was much more reliable and speedier than it had been on the eve of the Civil War.

Competition among railroads had much to do with the falling prices and improved service to consumers. Competition for control of railroads and for the traffic they carried was intense and was carried on from Main Street to Wall Street. Perhaps the best testimony to the strength of competition were the efforts devoted by the railroads to circumventing it. These ranged from pooling of traffic and earnings to the building of large, interterritorial systems under unified control, and ultimately to support of government regulation, the erstwhile enemy of "destructive" and "disorderly" competition.

Competition itself, of course, will not lead to reduced prices unless more fundamental technological and organizational changes are acting to bring about cost reductions. Where such changes are possible, competition will serve to secure their rapid implementation. In the case of railroads, consider the substitution of steel for iron rails. Cheap steel first became available with the development of the Bessemer process in Britain at the end of the 1850s. In 1862 steel rails were introduced on the Pennsylvania Railroad; the head of the railroad, J. Edgar Thomson, had viewed them abroad. By 1880 nearly 30 percent of U.S. track mileage consisted of steel rails, and just ten years later the percentage had increased to 80. (Andrew Carnegie, who as a young man worked for the Pennsylvania Railroad and was a disciple of Thomson, soon became a leader in American steel production; Carnegie honored his mentor by calling his great mill at Pittsburgh the J. Edgar Thomson works.)

What was behind the decision of railroad leaders to switch to steel? Two technical factors were at the forefront. First, steel rails were much more durable than iron rails and thus had to be replaced less frequently. Second, steel rails could support much heavier loads. The latter factor meant that heavier, more powerful locomotives could be used to pull longer trains made up of larger capacity cars at higher rates of speed. Lesser but related technological changes went along with steel's important impetus to increased railroad efficiency. Among them were block or interval-distance signaling equipment to coordinate traffic movement with greater safety, automatic coupling devices to facilitate the making up and breaking down of long trains, and air brakes which allowed such trains to run at greater speeds with safety. It has been estimated that if the railroads of 1870, which were mostly without these technological improvements, had been asked to carry the actual traffic of 1910, the incremental cost would have been approximately $1.3 billion greater than the actual cost in 1910. Freight and passenger charges, therefore, would have been correspondingly greater. It is doubtful that these savings would have been as large or as rapid without the intense competitive pressures of late nineteenth-century railroading.

Cooperation among railroads also aided in the advance of productivity. Cooperation is sometimes regarded as the antithesis of competition, and people often split into two camps, each being for one and opposed to the other. Practically there is little to be said for the essential goodness or badness of either concept of economic organization and decision making. Competition, as we have just argued, may in some cases promote a high rate of technological progress. But it may also have negative aspects, such as was seen in railroading when competitive bluffs led to the costly and wasteful construction of parallel lines that threatened the financial stability of some roads. Similarly, cooperation among railroads had negative effects when its intent was to stifle competition through such devices as pools and cartels that were designed to keep up prices to consumers of transportation services. But cooperation, like competition, also had its positive sides. A steady flow of traffic was important to the operating and financial health of such heavily capital-intensive enterprises. Yet, at the start of the great postbellum surge of railroad growth, there were major barriers to the smooth flow of traffic. Most of the roads were small, regional operations. This created a problem of transshipment for the interregional and intersectional movement of traffic. Either because track guages and other equipment had not been standardized or because the operating problems of sharing equipment and revenues had not been worked out, freight and passengers often had to be transferred from one line's equipment and track to another's when moving over long distances. Realizing that this raised costs and otherwise impeded attainment of the goal of maximum traffic flow, the railroads began to cooperate to standardize equipment and guages, and to work out the business arrangements for sharing equipment and revenue equitably. By the late 1880s and the early 1890s, these problems had been solved through railroad cooperation.

Another aspect of late nineteenth-century railroad cooperation deserves mention. In a large country like the United States the coordination of interterritorial railroad traffic movements ran into a real obstacle: timing. Before the advent of such movements, scattered communities dotting the American landscape maintained their own local methods of reckoning time. This posed a problem for making up railroad schedules and for ensuring that trains operating under different methods of time reckoning did not bump into one another. In the 1880s the solution was found in standard time with its 24 zones of 15 degrees longitude, starting from the Greenwich Observatory in London, England. American railroad leaders, almost of necessity, were among the prime movers for this world-wide system of time reckoning.

Both the competitive and the cooperative aspects of railroad decision making in the late-nineteenth century were carried out by a new breed of men. American railroads were the progenitors of modern large-scale, multi-division enterprise. By 1890, when the Pennsylvania Railroad alone employed 110,000 workers, the giant railroad systems of the United States were the largest business enterprises in the world. Large-scale operations led to efficiency but also created tremendous problems of administrative coordination. To cope with these problems, the railroads had to develop new and complex management structures and staff them with professional managers. Under one organization, functions such as finance, operations, and traffic were recognized as separate specialities. In many railroad corporations separate accounting, treasury, legal, purchasing, and freight (akin to marketing) departments emerged. The railroads' large-scale, capital-intensive technology and their massive volume of output meant that professional managers within the enterprise assumed more and more of the coordinating functions that external markets had performed in the earlier era of small-scale enterprise. As the noted business historian Alfred D. Chandler, Jr., has so aptly phrased this transition, "the visible hand" of administrative coordination by managers was replacing (or supplementing) Adam Smith's "invisible hand" of market coordination by prices.

The Social Savings of Railroads

Development of steam-powered railway transportation was a most prominent feature of American economic life in the last half of the nineteenth century. The achievements, the antics, and the failures of American railway promoters were watched closely by most Americans and indeed by many throughout the world because individual livelihoods were influenced in perceivable ways by railroad developments in the United States. The European farmer was no less affected than his counterpart in America, for example, and the same could be said of bond and stock investors in the two continents. The romance of the rails, moreover, was captivating: generations of children and their parents would ride real trains and play with toy models of them.

That being the case, it is hardly surprising that many observers, both past and present, have seriously espoused the notion that the railroad was indispensable to the growth of the American economy. If such a notion is taken to mean that the railroad had a profound impact on the course of American economic life as it actually unfolded in the railroad age, few would find it exceptionable. But if it is taken to mean that the American economy without railroads would have grown at a much slower rate and would have attained levels of total and per capita income substantially lower than the ones that actually prevailed with railroads, there are some grounds for doubt. The discipline of economics teaches us that among the more powerful and controlling influences on the demand for and supply of any good or service is the availability of substitutes. And economic history usually teaches us that the range of available substitutes is wide indeed.

Economists define the social savings of an innovation as the difference between the actual cost of performing the work done by the innovation and the higher cost of doing the job that would have been entailed with available alternative technologies. In the case of nineteenth-century railroads the alternative would have been a combination of water and wagon transportation. Calculations of the social savings of American railroads in 1859 and 1890 (see the suggested readings at the end of this chapter) indicate that in each of these years the savings were on the order of 5 percent of GNP. In other words, had the railroad not existed, about 5 percent of the resources that the American economy had in fact been able to devote to other productive purposes would have had to be diverted to the transportation sector in order to carry railroad traffic by other, nonrail means. The 1890 estimate is too low because it ignored passenger services, and it has also been criticized for failing to take into account dynamic impacts of a greatly enlarged railroad sector on the rest of the economy. Nevertheless, whether the social savings in 1890 was 5 or 10 percent of GNP, the implication of such calculations is that American economic growth would not have suffered greatly had the railroads not been present.

This finding of cliometrics (that is, analytic and quantitative history) is significant. No innovation did more to shape the contours of the modern American economy than the nineteenth-century railroad. Its impacts on the location of economic activities, on the mobility of goods and persons, on business organization, on capital markets, and on political and social institutions were so pervasive as to render suspect any quick summary and evaluation. Yet a modern economy, it now appears evident, is such a complex organization of resources and decision making that no single innovation or industry is critical to economic progress.

The basic reason why the railroad does not appear to have been the indispensable ingredient of nineteenth-century growth that many considered it to be is, of course, that other possibilities in transportation existed. This was not the case everywhere in the world but it was in the United States. Great improvements in river and canal transportation antedated the railroad age and did much to reduce transport costs to levels where water transport was nearly competitive with rail transport. Moreover, had the railroad not come along when it did, water transportation would undoubtedly have been improved and extended. Those who thought the railroads indispensable as far as economic growth was concerned probably meant that cheap transportation, with which they associated the railroad—for good historical reasons—was indispensable. There were in the United States other means of cheap transportation. These means were not quite as efficient as the railroad but neither were they vastly inferior to it. Indeed, to this day on many routes and for many commodities, water transportation remains competitive with rail and other land-based modes of transport.

Railroads and the Political Economy of Regulation

Despite the fact that late nineteenth-century railroads were carrying increasing amounts of traffic at falling charges to consumers of their services, large numbers of the consumers and, for different but related reasons, railroad leaders themselves were unhappy with the existing situation. The basic problem stemmed from variations in the degree of competition faced by the railroads. On the long hauls between major cities in different regions competition for traffic was intense, whereas on short hauls between cities and their surrounding countrysides, competition was virtually nonexistent. The strategy of railroad-pricing decisions therefore called for low freight rates on the long hauls and high rates on the short hauls. But this strategy did not sit well with farmers and small-town merchants who had to pay the high short-haul rates. They complained in ever more voluble tones of discrimination, and when to this evident discrimination by place was added the revelation that certain large users of rail services, notably Rockefeller's Standard Oil Company, were favored with low personal rates through hidden rebates, the complaints of discrimination became deafening. Railroad leaders resented the charges that they possessed an evil intent to charge the small shipper all that the traffic would bear while giving bargains to the big intercity shippers. Although they did not say so in public, they wanted to charge *all* shippers what the traffic would bear. To that end they were continually attempting through pools, cartels, and other forms of gentlemen's agreements to maintain rates at monopolistically high levels. But on the long hauls where a number of separately managed routes, both rail and nonrail, were available, the railroads found that such gentlemen's agreements were exceedingly difficult to maintain.

By the early 1870s, in reaction to charges of railroad rate discrimination, several midwestern states passed so-called Granger laws, after the farmers' organizations that had promoted the legislation. These laws created state commissions empowered to regulate the rates and charges of railroads and other middlemen with whom the farmers dealt in their purchasing and marketing. Enterprises so regulated protested to the courts that some features of regulation amounted to illegal confiscation of their property. In 1877, however, the Supreme Court in *Munn* v. *Illinois*, a case dealing with a grain elevator but extended to railroad cases as well, held that the states had a right to regulate private enterprises vital to the public interest. This right, strictly speaking, applied only to intrastate shipments because the Constitution reserved to Congress the right to regulate commerce between the states. When the Illinois regulators transgressed this boundary of federalism by attempting to set rates on interstate shipments, the Wabash Railway protested and was sustained by the Supreme Court in an 1886 decision.

The Wabash case helped pave the way for passage by Congress of the Interstate Commerce Act of 1887, which marked the beginning of federal regulation by commission. The newly created Interstate Commerce Commission (ICC) was to see that railroad rates were reasonable and just, and to prohibit personal and locational rate discrimination as well as agreements for the pooling of traffic and revenues. Railroads themselves were by no means opposed to all features of the regulatory act. They had long sought ways to bring more order to their competitive struggles. And, in fact, in its *Second Annual Report* the ICC went on record as opposing unreasonably low rates as being unfair to investors and a threat to good service. Hence, it is not too surprising that federal regulation allowed the railroads to raise their rates on the previously competitive long-haul routes while mollifying the public through less discriminatory rate structures and relative declines in short-haul rates.

Nonetheless, when an individual railroad thought that regulatory decisions went against its particular interest it instituted actions in the courts. And the railroads were often successful in overturning authority the ICC had thought it possessed. In the Maximum Freight Rates decision of 1897, the Supreme Court ruled that the ICC had only the power to declare existing rates reasonable or unreasonable and not the power to prescribe future rates; that power remained with the railroads. In the same year, in *Interstate Commerce Commission* v. *Alabama Midland Railway Company*, the Court, citing some ambiguous language in the 1887 Interstate Commerce Act, overturned the ICC's power to prevent short-haul rates from exceeding long-haul rates on the same railroad. Thus, although the genie of federal regulation had been loosed from its bottle, it was far from vigorous in solving the problems perceived from their different vantage points by the railroads and the public.

Since regulation had initially proved to be a weak method for solving their competitive problems, the railroads continued their earlier efforts to envelop competition by means of giant, consolidated systems. The movement for more regulation was, however, far from dead. When some of the railroads' interests and the public's interest appeared to coincide, stronger regulatory laws were forthcoming. Thus, the Elkins Act of 1903 was designed to end the practice of rebates to large shippers; the public resented rebates as discrimination in favor of large corporations whereas the railroads resented the surreptitious competition that rebates fostered. But it required strong presidential and congressional leadership to restore to the ICC the regulatory powers it had assumed it had before the Supreme Court decisions of the 1890s proved otherwise. With the support of President Theodore Roosevelt, Congress in 1906 passed the Hepburn Act, which gave the ICC the power to prescribe maximum railroad rates. Four years later the Mann-Elkins Act undid the Alabama Midland decision of 1897 by granting the ICC clear authority over long- and short-haul rate differences. The power of the ICC to regulate railroad rates was thus firmly established. By that time, however, the condition of intense competition on some routes coupled with monopoly on others (monopoly had provided the initial impetus to regulation), had been altered by the railroads themselves through consolidations. The people were nonetheless satisfied that their government, through the ICC, was looking after the public interest. In time, as new modes of transportation were developed, the railroads would find that the ICC would look after their interests as well.

Even a cursory glance at the origins of regulation through supposedly independent government commissions is sufficient to suggest that decisions to regulate were the outcome of complex crosscurrents of economic, social, and political forces rather than that they were taken to protect consumers from the ill effects of monopoly, as is held in the simplistic traditional view. Problems of competition as perceived by railroad leaders stood along with problems of monopoly as perceived by consumers in the early drive for government regulation. This finding, documented extensively by modern historical scholarship, is important for a fair understanding of the past. But it also lends valuable perspective on the present day when disaffection with the effects of vastly expanded government regulation has become widespread.

Advances in Communication

Modern economies require a huge volume and rapid flow of information for efficient decision making. Advanced technologies of large-scale production in concentrated areas, for example, would be less feasible without a continued flow of up-to-date information on resource prices and market demands in distant places. Seen in this light, the railroad represented an enormous advance in rapid communication and in the spread of information. It moved both people and informational goods, such as newspapers, at faster speeds than previously had been possible, and through all kinds of weather. The railroad also played a large role in the formation of the modern postal system. In 1847 railroads accounted for some 11 percent of the miles that mail was transported by the federal postal service. Just ten years later the figure had risen to 33 percent. The efficiency of railroads in carrying mail was reflected in price as well as in volume and speed. In 1850 it cost five cents to send an ounce of mail up to three hundred miles and ten cents beyond that distance. Five years later the standard rate was three cents per ounce for any distance. The rising efficiency of service and the rising volume of mail transported by rail led to the adoption of new methods for making the posting of a letter more convenient while at the same time saving on post-office labor. It was not a coincidence, for example, that the printed postage stamp made its first appearance and passed into general use at the time when railroads were revolutionizing mail service. In earlier days one took one's letters to the post office during the hours when it was open and personally paid a clerk for postage charges.

Great as were the gains of railways in the speedy movement of people, goods, and mail, they did not suffice for all purposes. Railway managers, for example, could hardly coordinate the simultaneous movement of a number of trains over their roads with messages sent by train because the trains might crash before the messages designed to prevent such crashes could be delivered. Here the electromagnetic telegraph furnished a better solution by providing near instantaneous communication between widely separated points. Its first practical demonstration came in the mid-1840s when, with the aid of a federal subsidy, the inventor Samuel F. B. Morse and his associates built a line between Washington and Baltimore. In 1851 the Erie Railroad introduced the telegraph to control train movements, thus commencing a long and fruitful relationship between the two technologies. The railroad supplied an already existing right-of-way for telegraph wires, and the telegraph supplied the quick communications needed to manage efficiently a complex and far-flung enterprise.

With telegraphic technology the advantages of administrative coordination within a single large enterprise over the coordination of many competing firms through markets were early demonstrated. By 1866 the Western Union Company had absorbed its rivals and it became in effect the telegraphic system of the United States. Its near monopoly of telegraphic communication, however, produced no major outcry on the part of the public, in part because the mails offered a viable alternative in many cases and also because the threat of potential competition in telegraphy itself was real. When Jay Gould, the Mephistopheles of Wall Street who had done so much to convince other railroad leaders of the advantage, if not the necessity, of building large systems, was putting together his own rail system during the 1870s, he initiated a threat to Western Union by creating a telegraph system to go along with his rail empire. Whether Gould actually wanted his own telegraph company or from the beginning planned to sell out at a profit to a worried Western Union is unclear, but he did take the latter action in 1878. It was a rewarding tactic for the clever and well-heeled financier, and he soon decided to repeat it by forming a second telegraphy company. Word of Gould's new project was sufficient to depress the price of Western Union's stock to the point where even Jay Gould thought it a good buy! By his influence in the decision-making councils of Western Union secured by his purchase of its stock, Gould encountered few problems in selling his second independent company to the giant of telegraphy.

Although the railroad and the telegraph brought about significant improvements in the flow of information required for better decision making in a growing and increasingly complex economic organization, the problem of instantaneous voice communication between individuals separated by various distances remained. It was, in principle, solved when Alexander Graham Bell in 1876 invented and patented a working prototype of the telephone, an instrument that transmitted the sound of a human voice through vibrations produced by an electric current passing through a wire. The development of American telephony over the ensuing four decades furnishes an interesting case study of decision making under both monopoly and competition. It also provides a further insight into the mix of motives underlying the historical emergence and early behavior of modern regulatory institutions.

Within a decade of Bell's initial patent the organizational structure of the Bell System, the dominant enterprise in American telephony ever since, had emerged. Alexander Graham Bell assigned his patents to a company organized by his backers; after several name changes it became in 1880 the American Bell Telephone Company. In 1882 the Western Electric Company was acquired to manufacture and supply equipment for the system, and in 1885 the American Telephone and Telegraph Company was organized as a subsidiary to provide long lines, or long-distance phone service. During these years a number of subsidiary regional companies were formed to lease Bell equipment to local subscribers and to operate local service. Theodore N. Vail, a man experienced in telegraph operations, was brought in as the Bell Company's general manager in 1878; it was his policy to maintain Bell control of the telephone business through large-scale expansion. Vail vacated his position when the company's board of directors, cognizant of their monopoly, opted instead for a policy of limited expansion and a high rate of profit. As we shall see, Vail was to return—vindicated—at a later date.

Seventeen years (1876–1893) of telephone development under the

Bell patent monopoly ended with 266,000 Bell phones in service in the United States. The monopolistic prices charged by Bell had restricted development mainly to the business centers of large urban areas. Many communities on the fringes of these central business areas, as well as smaller towns and rural areas, were largely without telephone service. After 1893, when the first Bell patents expired, such places became prime targets for invasion by independent telephone companies that were organized to compete with Bell. The emergence of independent telephone companies after 1893 is a most interesting phenomenon in light of the common view that the business of telephony is, from the nature of its technology, a natural monopoly, that is, a business in which one producer in principle can supply a market more efficiently than a group of competitive producers. Telephone service may very well be a natural monopoly, at least on the local level. But the emergence of competition in American telephony after 1893 demonstrates a further and perhaps more subtle point: the right to provide telephone service can be opened up to competitive bidding even if the provision of service is best left to one supplier. The independent telephone movement caught on after 1893 when the new companies undercut Bell's monopoly rates and secured franchises to provide service in areas that Bell had ignored.

The effects of competition in telephony were striking. Between 1893 and 1907, when the independent movement reached its peak in relative terms, the number of phones in the U.S. increased from 266,000 to 6.1 million. Of these 3 million were independent and 3.1 million were Bell phones; Bell's market share had fallen from 100 percent to 51 percent. Although its market share had been cut nearly in half, Bell did react vigorously to the new competition by cutting its charges to subscribers and by adding more than ten times as many phones during 1893–1907 as it had put into service in the era of its monopoly from 1876 to 1893. But the old monopoly, called American Telephone and Telegraph Company (AT&T) after 1900, was not exactly enthusiastic about competition, which had cut its rate of return on investment from over 40 percent under the patent monopoly to only 8 percent over the years 1900–06. It began to propagandize against competition and against particular competitors. Bell also attempted to weaken its competitors by refusing either to sell them equipment or to allow them to connect into Bell's established long-distance network. The former tactic had little effect because several independent telephone-equipment manufacturers filled the void, but Bell's refusal to interconnect with the independents was a more powerful weapon in the competitive struggle.

After 1907, Bell System policies were altered and the company appeared to become more conciliatory toward independent competition. The impetus for this change came from bankers who had observed AT&T investing greater and greater amounts of capital in the effort to keep pace with its competitors, while at the same time suffering a falling rate of return on its investments. A New York banking group headed by George F. Baker and J. P. Morgan took control of the Bell System in 1907 and brought Theodore Vail back as president. Vail changed the emphasis of the Bell System's struggle against competition from private concern for its own financial interests to a "public" concern over the wastefulness and duplication of competition. In terms of tactics, with the independents stymied by Bell's refusal to interconnect, Bell under Vail began to offer them a solution to their problem by acquiring them. It even reversed the ban on equipment sales both because the independents had grown to a size where they constituted an attractive equipment market and because growth through acquisition was easier if the independents were already using Bell equipment. Vail's policies were effective in turning around the System's trend of market share. By absorption and expansion Bell added some 2 million phones between 1907 and 1912, while the independents collectively grew by only 0.6 million.

The cornerstone of Bell's post–1907 corporate policy to reverse its relative decline involved an about-face with respect to regulation. During its thirty years of operation under both patent monopoly and relatively free competition the Bell System generally had opposed government regulation. In 1907, under Vail, the System became more accommodating. Vail and the bankers had observed the stabilizing effects of the ICC on railroad markets and price structures, and they concluded that telephony might benefit from similar arrangements. One of the first practical results of Bell's policy shift came in 1910 when the Mann-Elkins Act, already cited in connection with railroad regulation, bestowed upon the ICC the authority to regulate telephone and telegraph companies. Both the Bell System and the independent telephone industry approved of this extension of federal regulatory power; they were less and less enamored of the competitive struggle. From then on the Bell System began to invest considerable resources in shaping the new regulatory climate at both the federal and state levels. With the decline of competition and the growth of regulation, Bell's market share increased for several decades and then stabilized at about five sixths of all U.S. phones. And AT&T became, in terms of such measures as tangible assets and profits, the largest private corporation in the world.

Conclusion

The railroad, the telegraph, and the telephone were the transportation and communication links that by the beginning of this century bound the far-flung regions of the United States into a unified economy of un-

precedented dimensions in world history. These nineteenth-century innovations had, as we have seen, many impacts, but their greatest achievement was in giving operational meaning to the idea of a national economy.
The size of the free-trade area within the borders of the United States
in itself became a source of growth and development because of the
stimulus it gave to the development of new resources, to the implementing of large-scale technologies of production, and to continual increases
in specialization and in the division of labor. People in other regions of
the world of similar size might possess resources and technical knowledge
equal to that available to Americans, but no people had the opportunity
to exploit a marketplace of comparable size. From the time of the
signing of the Constitution, the American political and economic environment favored the development of a national economy. A century later
transportation and communication technologies, which were unknown in
1787, made it possible.

SUGGESTED READINGS

For concise historical surveys of transportation and other economic developments
in this period, see Edward C. Kirkland, Industry Comes of Age: Business, Labor and
Public Policy, 1860–1897 (New York: Holt, Rinehart and Winston, 1961) and Harold
U. Faulkner, The Decline of Laissez-Faire, 1897–1917 (New York: Holt, Rinehart and
Winston, 1951). These two studies are especially helpful on the emergence of railroad
regulation. A more analytical economic survey is given in Lance Davis, et al., American
Economic Growth: An Economist's History of the United States (New York: Harper &
Row, 1972), Chapter 13, "Internal Transportation." That chapter, among other things,
summarizes the estimates of railroad social savings in 1859 and 1890; the details of social
savings calculations and penetrating analyses of economic issues in railroad development
may be found in Albert Fishlow, American Railroads and the Transformation of the
Antebellum Economy (Cambridge: Harvard University Press, 1965), and Robert W.
Fogel, Railroads and American Economic Growth (Baltimore: Johns Hopkins Press,
1964). Passenger social savings are the subject of J. Hayden Boyd and Gary M. Walton,
"The Social Savings from Nineteenth Century Rail Passenger Services," Explorations
in Economic History, 9 (Spring 1972), whereas the detailed and sometimes controversial
debate that arose over interpreting the social-savings findings is dealt with at considerable
length by Robert W. Fogel, "Notes on the Social Savings Controversy," Journal of
Economic History, 39 (March 1979).

The multi-prize winning book of Alfred D. Chandler, Jr., The Visible Hand: The
Managerial Revolution in American Business (Cambridge: Harvard University Press,
1977) analyzes the pioneering contributions of railroads to modern economic organization. Chandler deals to some extent with individual railroad leaders, but for a more
personal view Matthew Josephson's The Robber Barons: The Great American Capitalists
1861–1901 (New York: Harcourt, Brace and World, 1962) is fascinating reading. For
aspects of railroad finance, see Dorothy R. Adler, British Investment in American Railways, 1834–1898 (Charlottesville: The University Press of Virginia, 1970); Stanley L.
Engerman, "Some Economic Issues Relating to Railroad Subsidies and the Evaluation
of Land Grants," The Journal of Economic History, 33 (June 1972); and Robert W.

Fogel, *The Union Pacific Railroad: A Case in Premature Enterprise* (Baltimore: The Johns Hopkins Press, 1960). The best study of the growth of railroad productivity and its causes is Albert Fishlow, "Productivity and Technological Change in the Railroad Sector, 1840–1910," in National Bureau of Economic Research, *Output, Employment and Productivity in the United States after 1800, Studies in Income and Wealth,* vol. 30 (New York: National Bureau of Economic Research, 1966). Challenging analyses of the early regulatory movement are Gabriel Kolko, *Railroads and Regulation, 1877–1916* (Princeton: Princeton University Press, 1965); Paul MacAvoy, *The Economic Effects of Regulation* (Cambridge, Mass.: M.I.T. Press, 1965); and Albro Martin, *Enterprise Denied: Origins of the Decline of American Railroads, 1897–1917* (New York: Columbia University Press, 1971), a vigorous critique of Kolko's book.

Alfred Chandler's *The Visible Hand,* cited above, gives some attention to the communications industries. On early telephony, see Richard Gabel, "The Early Competitive Era in Telephone Communication, 1893–1920," *Law and Contemporary Problems,* 34 (Spring 1969), and J. Warren Stehman, *The Financial History of the American Telephone and Telegraph Company* (New York: Augustus M. Kelley, 1967).

CHAPTER 15

The Financial System

Under Stress

The Civil War, like all major wars in the nation's history, placed great strains on the American financial system. The war created a new financial situation, and from that time forward in the United States decision making at the federal level came to predominate. In the period of creative political economy under the Federalist management of Alexander Hamilton in the 1790s, the basic outlines of American arrangements in money, banking, and government finance emerged. Later antebellum decades were marked by backing and filling—in short, marginal adjustments—at the federal level. The more important financial developments of this era emerged from considerable experimentation with new institutional forms and regulatory arrangements, primarily in banking, among private and state governmental decision makers.

As a result of these antebellum experiments, when the Civil War made it necessary for national leaders to make major financial decisions there was a wealth of financial experience, both good and bad, upon which they could draw. The choices they made had wide and lasting ramifications for their own and for later generations of Americans. Indeed, most of the financial developments of historical significance during the next half century in the United States were rooted in the decisions of 1861–65.

Legacies of Civil War Finance

The major financial problem faced by governments in wartime is how to divert economic resources from peacetime uses to the war effort. In peacetime, economic resources—labor, capital, and land (or natural resources)—are used to produce the consumer and capital goods and services, including governmental goods and services, that satisfy peoples' present and future wants. In wartime, when the survival of a society is often threatened, ways must be found to reduce the satisfaction of normal private and collective wants in order to win the war.

Three financial methods that a government can use to achieve the necessary diversion of resources to war objectives are taxation, borrowing, and money creation. Each in a different way removes purchasing power from individuals and private organizations and places it at the disposal of the government. In most modern, large-scale wars a combination of the three methods has been employed. The American Civil War was not an exception to this historical generalization.

TAXATION

Of the three methods of government finance, taxation is the least complicated and most direct. Taxes embody the idea of compulsory payments to the government that imposes them and enforces their collection. There has always been a clash between different economic groups over raising revenue by taxation as against borrowing and money creation. When the Civil War began there was reluctance by a few federal officials to rely on tax finance. But patriotism made the American people accept more taxation every year. As a result, by 1865 taxes paid for as much as one fifth of the federal government's total wartime expenditures. This precedent made it possible for taxes to pay for about two fifths of the U.S. government's expenditures during World War I and three fifths during World War II.

Although the federal government's tax effort during the Civil War was relatively small in comparison with later great wars, it was much more extensive than that of earlier wars. During the War of Independence the power of the national government to enact formal taxes was essentially nonexistent, while during the War of 1812 the power to raise taxation was understood but the will to do so developed only late in the war and then without substantial effect. During the Civil War there was neither a lack of power nor of will nor of imagination on the part of federal decision makers. Indeed, virtually every kind of tax that had ever been put into effect by any level of government in the United States was adopted by Congress, and some new ones were added to the list. In the former category, tariffs were increased and direct taxes on real property, as well as excises, license taxes, and stamp duties based on earlier federal precedents were revived and extended. All manufactured articles were taxed at either specific or ad valorem rates, and gross receipts taxes were placed on the sale of a variety of services such as transportation and advertising. In the new-tax category were an income tax and an inheritance tax. The ratio of tax revenues to total federal expenditures increased from 10 percent in 1862 to 25 percent in 1865. This large but insufficient increase can be explained by the magnitude of the war effort, which was far greater than had been anticipated at the outset, and by the relatively low rates of the taxes and the problems that arose in administering and enforcing them.

With the end of the war in 1865, federal expenditures fell off sharply. The first of many consecutive years of federal budget surpluses appeared in fiscal year 1866, creating a favorable climate for tax reduction. But decisions had to be made regarding which taxes to reduce or eliminate. The choice was often cast in terms of tariffs and internal taxes. And when cast in such terms the choice seemed obvious. Tariffs on imports had been a mainstay of federal finance from the very beginning of the government under the Constitution. Unlike the internal taxes, the customs duties—they had increased markedly during the War—had a large, organized, and influential body of supporters in the producers who were protected in varying degrees from foreign competition by taxes on imports of their products. The internal taxes, in contrast, had no such long precedent or constituency. Most of them were instead viewed as temporary, as nuisances, or as tending to check development. Farm and labor groups supported the income tax, but manufacturing and banker pressure groups against the tax proved more powerful until the tide turned in 1913.

And so, in the late 1860s and early 1870s, nearly all of the internal taxes imposed during the Civil War were reduced and then eliminated. Of the main revenue producing taxes, the manufacturers' excises and gross receipts taxes were repealed in 1867 and 1868, and the income tax in 1872. After the latter date the only high-yielding internal taxes retained were those on liquor and tobacco products, two items of consumption almost unique in their capacity to generate both a steady tax revenue and a popular feeling that they deserve to be taxed.

In terms of taxation, then, the significant aspect of wartime financial decisions for later economic developments was a return—a return that persisted for several decades—to high tariffs on imports as the mainstay of federal finance. Average tariff rates, measured by the ratio of customs duties to the value of taxed imports, had fallen from over 50 percent in the late 1820s to approximately 20 percent in 1860. During the Civil War the average tariff rate rose to between 40 and 50 percent and remained at such levels until 1913. To a great extent the late nineteenth-century tariffs taxed consumer goods, as did, more obviously, the federal government's two important domestic taxes, those on liquor and tobacco. When the nation's economy expanded at high rates in the postwar decades, the consumption of imports, liquor, and tobacco—and consequently federal revenues—all increased. But federal spending did not increase to the same extent. Post-Civil War administrations were faced, therefore, with a financial problem—one rather alien to their successors a century later—namely, what to do about budget surpluses. As luck would have it, the use during the Civil War of another method of diverting resources from private hands to the government furnished a solution.

BORROWING

The federal government's reluctance to tax during the Civil War meant that borrowing became the primary technique of government finance. It took on two forms. In one, the traditional form, the government swapped its promises to pay given sums of money at some specified time in the future for current purchasing power and paid stipulated interest on the debt thus created. In the other form, the government issued what was termed a "non-interest-bearing debt" that usually did not have a specific redemption date but only the implicit promise or understanding that the paper would be redeemed. This latter form of debt was essentially the printing by the government of fiat paper money. It is treated below under Money Creation.

During the war years the issue and sale of interest-bearing debt was unprecedented. This form of federal debt rose from $90 million in 1861 to $2,322 million in 1866. In current dollar terms (that is, dollars unadjusted for inflation), the government borrowed in a few years a sum roughly twice as large as what had been expended by investors on the construction of antebellum railroads in three decades. Under the stimulus of this massive government borrowing, both financial technologies and financial institutions underwent widespread changes that modernized the American capital market.

In the area of financial technology, the huge volume of federal securities marketed during the war required a vastly different system of distribution from the ones developed before its outbreak. Before the war most federal and state securities and some private securities were sold through a loan-contracting process in which the issuer would advertise the amount and terms of the loan and invite bids from interested investors. The highest bids were accepted, and the winning contractors disposed of the securities through their private channels of distribution. This system worked fairly well for small and infrequent issues, but the Civil War loans were of a different magnitude.

After older methods were tried and found wanting, the Treasury turned over its bond-selling business to the agency of Jay Cooke, a private banker of Philadelphia. Cooke devised new methods of security distribution with great success. From October 1862 to January 1864, Cooke's organization sold $362 million of a $510 million issue of the so-called five–twenties (6 percent bonds callable after five years, and maturing in twenty years) at par, and other sales were stimulated by his methods. In January 1865, Cooke was again called upon by the Treasury to act as general agent in its bond sales, and his organization succeeded in selling most of an $830 million issue of so-called seven–thirties (7.3 percent notes maturing in 3 years) in several months. By then Jay Cooke's name had become a household word and he was admired as one of the great architects of the Union victory.

Cooke's methods were relatively simple but their implementation depended crucially on a large volume of sales; this is why they had not appeared earlier in the United States. For a payment of only a fraction of 1 percent of the proceeds of the loans, he was able to employ an army of agents and subagents who canvassed the country, selling bonds in denominations as low as fifty dollars to people in all walks of life, including federal troops, and at all levels of income and wealth. The agents numbered some two thousand five hundred in the five–twenty campaign and four to five thousand in the sale of the seven–thirties. They included most of the country's banks and bankers who not only retailed the bonds but also bought them for their own accounts and financed sales by lending money to nonbank purchasers.

After the extensive agency system, the next distributional innovation of importance in the success of Jay Cooke's bond campaigns was the extensive use of advertising. Newspapers all over the nation carried Cooke's ads and stories written by Cooke and his aides to explain the features of the federal loans and to tell of the great successes already achieved in their distribution. These and the numerous handbills circulated by the agents appealed to the patriotism of small investors as well as to their economic self-interest. Larger investors were told that the bonds constituted a first mortgage on all the wealth and income of the country.

Jay Cooke's innovations in security distribution were quite naturally pressed into the service of promoting a second great change in financial technology and institutions resulting from the war—the National Banking System established in 1863. More on this system will follow in this chapter (see Banking Problems below). For now it suffices to note that the banking bills before Congress in 1862 and 1863 required the proposed national banks to become heavy buyers of federal bonds. Jay Cooke realized that the existence of such banks would aid his bond-selling campaign. But opposition to federally chartered banks was strong, especially on the part of the state banks. Cooke therefore decided to urge his agents and the newspapers from whom he bought advertising space to tout the advantages of the proposed system over the old state banks. He saw to it, moreover, that congressmen received word of the public opinion thus properly informed. After the bill allowing national banks became law, Cooke helped organize several of the new banks, including the first to receive a charter, and he wrote a pamphlet, distributed in part through his agents, telling others how to form the new banks.

Methods of large-scale security distribution and a system of national banks holding significant amounts of the federal debt were enduring consequences of the federal government's debt financing during the Civil War. Numerous individuals and enterprises were introduced to investments in paper wealth. The nation's banks through the national banking system were drawn into a close relationship with federal finances. A single, national capital market began to emerge out of the heterogeneous and loosely related markets of earlier decades. At the center of this capital market was the market for government securities. Here the financial mechanisms created in the war years were kept active after the war as the government first funded a variety of its short-term obligations into long-term bonds, and then refunded large portions of the debt into bonds carrying lower interest rates when market yields dropped. While these operations were being carried out during the late 1860s to the early 1870s, and also for many subsequent years, the federal government helped to spread the new techniques of high finance to other sectors of the capital market through its policy of debt retirement. Perhaps the word "policy" is misleading in this context, for debt retirement was less a conscious policy decision than a course of action thrust upon postbellum administrations by growing tax revenue coupled with relatively stable expenditures. The annual surpluses generated by tax and expenditure policies were disposed of by retiring outstanding government bonds. In this process, many of the investors who sold their bonds to the government for cash then sought new investment outlets. Through the increasingly organized and efficient capital market, the nations growth sectors—transportation, manufacturing, and state and local public works—provided more than an ample supply of new securities to replace the retired government bonds.

MONEY CREATION

Inadequate tax finance and problems connected with borrowing early in the Civil War forced the Lincoln administration to turn to still a third method of commandeering resources away from private hands: printing and spending paper money. In July 1861, the Congress as a part of a $250 million loan package had authorized the issue of up to $50 million of noninterest-bearing notes redeemable on demand in specie. These so-called demand notes were made acceptable for payments to the government and for some payments by the government such as government employees' salaries. But with the redeemability feature they were still a debt instrument. When at the end of 1861 the banks of the country and the government itself were forced to suspend specie redemption of paper liabilities, the financial emergency that paralleled the military crisis created a situation of desperation for government finance. The result was the Legal Tender Act of February 1862. This law authorized the Treasury to print up and spend $150 million of U.S. notes, which were not specifically redeemable at any future date or in any monetary metal. The greenbacks were declared by law to be full legal tender for almost all public and private debts, and thus they became the first fiat paper money issue of the U.S. government. The exceptions to full legal tender were that greenbacks were not accepted by the government for payment of customs duties nor could they be used by the government to pay interest on the federal debt. Specie payments continued to be required in these transactions throughout the seventeen-year period (1862–1878) when the United States was off a specie standard.

The first issue of greenbacks in the spring of 1862 did little to alleviate the Treasury's financial position. War expenditures were draining off funds as fast as they came in, prompting renewed trips to the printing press. In mid–1862 and again in early 1863, additional $150 million issues of greenbacks were authorized, making the total authorization $450 million.

The result of this massive infusion of fiat paper money along with other government debt issues and bank-created money was a rapid rise in prices. Demand for economic resources simply exceeded supply at given price levels, and price inflation was the mechanism through which markets were cleared. The extent of the Civil War inflation can be grasped in a number of ways. At their peak in January 1865, wholesale prices were about 2.3 times their level at the outbreak of the war in April 1861; this represents a rate of inflation of 25 percent per year. Estimates of the cost of living indicate an approximate doubling of consumer prices during the war. A third measure is the premium on gold. When, as before the war, paper dollars were convertible into gold dollars, there was no premium. Before the first greenbacks were issued in 1862, but after the banks and the government had suspended convertibility of paper liabilities into gold at fixed rates, it took $1.02 in paper to buy a gold dollar. In mid–1864, at the peak of the paper dollar's depreciation, $2.62 in paper bought a gold dollar. But by mid–1865 when the war was over, a gold dollar could be purchased for $1.43 in paper. A major objective of postwar financial policy, as we shall see below, was the elimination of this discrepancy between the value of the gold dollar and that of the greenback dollar.

In summary, the financing of the Civil War by the federal government brought about tremendous changes in the American financial system. At the war's end large problems remained and decisions had to be taken to resolve them. Increases in old taxes and the imposition of many new ones had resulted in a tax contribution of about one fifth of the government's total war expenditures, but these taxes were far more than adequate to finance the greatly reduced levels of federal expenditures after the war. The solution of postwar governments was to eliminate internal taxes, with the exception of the sumptuary excises on liquor and tobacco products, but to maintain for decades the large increases in customs duties enacted during the war. Even with tax reductions the federal budget was in surplus for over a quarter of a century after 1865. But a huge war debt had been incurred, and these surpluses were used to reduce it by transferring money from taxpayers to bondholders. A new system of national banks had been created to aid war finance, but in 1865 whether the new system would play a major or minor role in American finance was still far from decided. Finally, as a result of a number of unprecedented monetary schemes adopted during the war, of which the fiat greenback issues were the outstanding example, the nation's money supply was greatly enlarged, price levels had doubled, and the paper dollars most people used were worth substantially less than the interconvertible gold, silver, and paper dollars of antebellum decades. The agenda of postwar monetary and banking problems, to which we now turn, was a large one indeed.

Money and Prices

The story of money and prices in the United States during the half-century following the Civil War is an extremely interesting one for students of economic history. If one considers the period as a whole, the story might seem to represent a continuation of broad trends established earlier. In chapter 7 we saw that during the four decades prior to the Civil War the nation's money supply grew at a rate of about 5 percent per year while the overall trend of prices was stable or perhaps very mildly downward. From 1867 to 1914 the money stock, defined as coin and paper currency plus commercial bank deposits owned by the public, grew at a trend rate of about 5.3 percent per year while wholesale prices *declined* at a trend rate of 1.3 percent per year. As before the Civil War, there were notable fluctuations in monetary growth and price movements about these trends during the postbellum decades. Indeed, most of the attention of both contemporaries and later analysts was devoted to aspects of these shorter-term fluctuations, and we shall take them up here as well.

But before doing so, let us reflect for a moment on the long-term trends not only because they are interesting in themselves but also because they are helpful to an understanding of the shorter-term financial problems.

In the United States and elsewhere in the Western World the monetary and price history of the nineteenth century appears to have differed markedly from that of our own and earlier centuries. The main difference lies in the divergent behavior of long-term monetary and price trends. In the nineteenth century considerable innovations in monetary arrangements, including both the explicit addition of governmental fiat elements to the older metallic bases of monetary systems and a persistent spread of banking institutions that added increasing amounts of bank money to metallic and fiat paper currencies, led to substantial growth of money supplies. American evidence, for example, indicates that the money supply trended upward at an annual rate of over 5.5 percent from 1820 to 1914. Another way of viewing this monetary expansion and putting it in perspective is to note that the U.S. money supply in 1914 was 190 times its level in 1820 whereas population increased only 10.3 times in the same period. Thus money per capita was $163 in 1914 but only about $9 in 1820. Yet in spite of such high absolute and relative rates of monetary expansion, which both before and after the nineteenth century have usually been associated with rising price levels, the long-term trend of nineteenth-century prices was mildly downward.

Why in this one century did units of money such as the United States dollar and the British pound sterling become more valuable in terms of their ability to purchase goods despite enormous increases in their supply? The answer of economists must surely be that the demand for money over this century increased even more rapidly than the supply of money, and why did this happen? No doubt increases in population and the growth of per capita production through technological improvements, capital accumulation, and the augmentation of all kinds of economic resources account for much of the growth of monetary demand. Neither population nor total economic output, however, grew anywhere near as fast as the supply of money, and so they cannot by themselves account for the excess demand for money that was eliminated by falling price levels for goods. A complete accounting would therefore have to include other factors. Among the more important of these factors was the increase in market-oriented economic activity relative to nonmarket activity over the course of the nineteenth century.

The effect of an increase in market activity on the demand for money is easily illustrated. Consider the typical American family—which would be a farm family—of the early nineteenth century in comparison with its counterpart a century later. The farm family produced most of what it consumed at home and traded for much of the rest of its needs with neighbors in the local community. It accumulated wealth mostly in the form of real assets such as land, buildings, and livestock—and lifetime economic security was provided by intergenerational transfers within the family unit. A century later the typical family—now as likely to be urban as rural—specialized in production and sold its resources (for example, labor) and products in markets for cash, using the proceeds to purchase consumer goods and capital assets. Wealth accumulation was by then as much a matter of purchasing financial assets—money, savings accounts, life insurance policies, and perhaps even stocks and bonds—as of buying real assets, for example, farms and houses. A part of the motivation for new forms of asset accumulation came from the erosion of older intrafamily forms of lifetime economic security by growing specialization, increased mobility, and a wider range of economic opportunities. Market exchanges penetrated virtually all areas of economic activity where a century earlier they had been far less pervasive. This resulted in an increased demand for the medium of exchange, or money, that was greater than the increase of economic activity itself.

While the demand for money was thus increasing, the supply of money, despite its rapid growth, could not quite keep up with the demand in the sense of growing fast enough to maintain stable long-term price levels. A basic constraint on the growth of nineteenth-century money supplies was a quaint and widespread belief not only that the real and true money was that made of some precious metal, usually gold, but also that a true monetary unit, for example, the dollar, had to be a fixed quantity of that metal. Practical people would not let such a belief stand in the way of creating and using vastly increased quantities of substitutes for the "true" money, but the belief, enshrined in laws and institutions, nonetheless remained. And it asserted itself ever so often in the form of conscious economic policies, deflationary trends that provoked protest movements, and financial upheavals that ultimately led to reform of the whole system of monetary institutions and beliefs. These points are illustrated by the major issues of financial history in the half century following the Civil War.

The Economics of Resumption

At the end of 1861, American banks and the federal government were forced to suspend convertibility of their paper monetary liabilities in specie. They simply did not possess enough metallic money to meet the demands of holders of paper liabilities. Paper money issued by the government, most notably the legal tender greenbacks or United States notes, replaced gold as the monetary base of the nation. For seventeen years starting in 1862, when a holder of bank money desired to convert it into

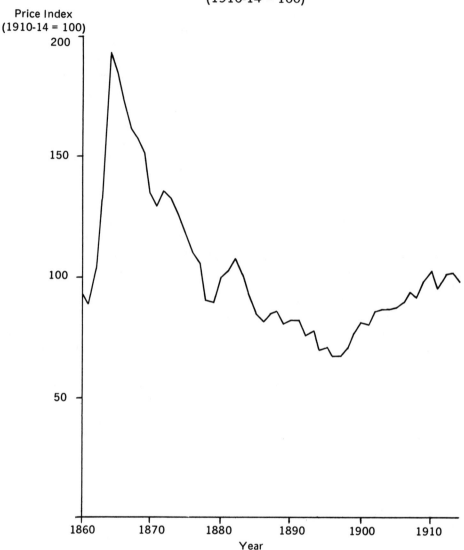

FIGURE 15-1
Wholesale Price Index, 1860-1914
(1910-14 = 100)

SOURCE: George F. Warren and Frank A. Pearson, <u>Prices</u> (New York: John Wiley, 1933), Table 1, pp. 11-12.

"lawful money," he received—much as he does today—paper obligations of the government rather than specie. Under the pressures of war finance the monetary base of paper, and along with it the money supply, was greatly enlarged. As a result the general price level and the price of gold dollars or equivalent bullion in terms of paper dollars had roughly doubled during the war.

Virtually all of the nation's leading economic and political decision makers in 1865 were in agreement that the monetary and financial consequences of the war, however necessary they might have been to preserve the Union, were abnormal, and that measures had to be taken to return to prewar conditions in which paper monetary liabilities were convertible into specie, dollar for dollar. At the time the gold dollar sold at a premium of approximately 50 percent over the paper dollar. Hugh McCulloch, the Secretary of the Treasury, therefore proposed in 1865 to eliminate the premium on gold through a policy of retiring the greenbacks with budget surpluses and funding short-term "near" monies that the government had issued during the war into long-term bonds. Congress in 1866 authorized McCulloch to implement this policy of monetary contraction. Its economic basis was to reduce the supply of paper money and thus raise its value in terms of both goods and gold. Since paper money was the monetary standard, this meant that the market prices of goods and of gold in terms of paper dollars would have to fall.

And fall prices did. This can be seen in Figure 15–1 which charts the course of wholesale prices in the United States from 1860 to 1914. The fall of prices from the wartime peak in 1864 to 1868 can be attributed largely to policies associated with monetary contraction. But the decision to make paper dollars more valuable turned out to be much less popular when businessmen and farmers, many of whom had contracted debts at inflated prices, discovered that in practice it meant that the prices of the products they sold, from the proceeds of which debts would have to be repaid, were falling. Congress in 1868 therefore repealed the policy of contracting the outstanding supply of greenbacks. As our chart indicates, however, ending the contraction of the paper currency did not end the price decline which, in fact, continued almost without interruption until 1879. In the latter year, prices had fallen to pre-Civil War levels. The price decline included the price of gold and the gold dollar; on January 2, 1879, in accordance with the Resumption Act passed by Congress in 1875, the United States government and the banks of the country once again offered to exchange gold dollars for their paper dollar liabilities. To the surprise of many, there were few takers. Paper dollars were equal in value to gold dollars and somewhat more convenient to use for most monetary purposes.

How was resumption of paper dollar–gold dollar convertibility accomplished in the decade after policies of explicit paper money contraction were abandoned in 1868? It was done essentially by a very limited expansion of the nation's money supply coupled with a large expansion in the output of goods and services. Figure 15–2 plots the behavior of both the United States money supply and the monetary base (specie and paper money liabilities of the federal government) from 1867 to 1914. The monetary base exhibited no growth at all from 1867 to 1879. And the money supply in the same period grew very slowly at a trend rate of just over 1 percent per year, the result of small increases in the ratios of bank deposits to bank reserves and of the public's holdings of bank money to its holdings of coin and paper currency. At the same time prices declined very rapidly; the wholesale price index, for example, fell at a rate of about 5 percent per year from the end of the Civil War to the accomplishment of resumption. Slight increases in the money supply coupled with rapidly falling prices imply either that the income velocity of money fell or that the real output of the economy expanded, or a combination of the two. Detailed evidence on total output of the economy for the postwar deflationary period is sketchy but warrants the conclusion that most of the price decline resulted from an expansion of production.

Thus, resumption of gold dollar–paper dollar interconvertibility in 1879 resulted from replacing the initial postwar policy of explicit and absolute monetary contraction with a policy of implicit and relative contraction—relative in the sense that monetary growth was kept well below the rate of growth of the economy. The price the nation paid for this heavy dose of deflation, in terms of perceived business depression, social unrest, and—as we soon will see—fundamental divisions among groups of Americans regarding proper monetary arrangements, was not inconsiderable. But the deflation, rather than preventing a high rate of real economic growth, seems to have been in large measure the result of a considerable expansion of production.

Most people, economists included, consider a stable general price level or, what is the same thing, a stable value of money, to be desirable. Much of the utility of money as a social contrivance arises from the economy and convenience of information concerning relative values of goods, services, and productive resources when these values are expressed in terms of a single monetary unit. A changing value of the monetary unit unnecessarily introduces additional uncertainty into economic decision making, and it also tends to distort relative values from what they would be under stable price levels.

These considerations suggest that it is not at all obvious why a course of fairly drastic price deflation was deliberately chosen after the Civil War. The guiding idea of the time was that the gold dollar remained the true standard of value and that the market premium of gold over paper dollars represented a temporary aberration that had to be eliminated. Such a view was reinforced by the use throughout the greenback era of gold dollars in payment of customs duties and interest on the federal debt. The dominant gold-standard view came under increasing attack as price

FIGURE 15-2
U.S. Money Supply and Monetary Base, 1867-1913
(billions of dollars, ratio scale)

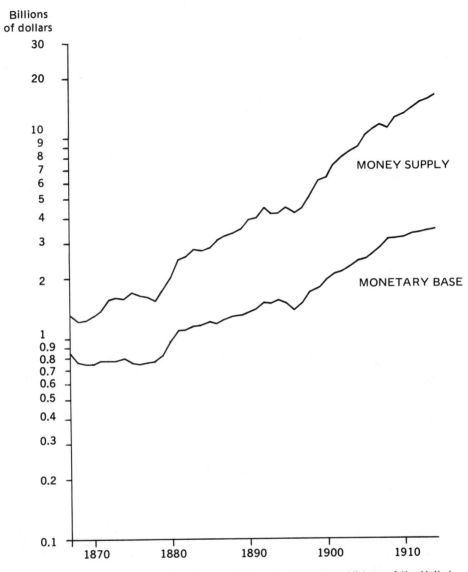

SOURCE: Milton Friedman and Anna J. Schwartz, A Monetary History of the United States 1867-1960 (Princeton: Princeton University Press, 1963), Tables A-1, pp. 704-708 and B-3, pp. 799-801.

deflation continued, but it managed to hold its ground and remain orthodoxy.

An alternative policy that would have avoided the need for deflation while at the same time preserving much of the gold-standard orthodoxy would have been for the United States to devalue the gold dollar in 1865. Law, it should be noted, defined the gold dollar as 23.22 grains of gold. In 1865 that weight of gold could be purchased on the market for about $1.50 in paper money. Had the law then been changed to redefine the gold dollar as 14.81 grains, two thirds of its former weight, a paper dollar would immediately have become equivalent to a gold dollar. Such a decision, which would have avoided the rapid deflation of 1865–79, seemed so arbitrary that it was not given any consideration. It would not, however, have been unprecedented. In 1834 Congress reduced the weight of the gold dollar from 24.75 to 23.2 grains in order to encourage the minting and circulation of gold coins. That devaluation achieved its objective. Three decades later the thinking of monetary policy makers was less flexible. A long period of deflation and monetary agitation were among the consequences.

Greenbackism and Free Silver

Currency contraction and deflation began to polarize the monetary thinking of various economic groups in the United States during the late 1860s. Foreign traders, eastern bankers, and some manufacturers favored contraction as a means of achieving early resumption of gold–paper interconvertibility at the prewar parity. But farmers, labor groups, western businessmen and bankers, and other manufacturers wanted to reverse policies of contraction in order to stem the depression of prices and the consequent increase of debt burdens. The result was an uneasy compromise in which the federal government did little either to expand or contract the currency. Economic growth increased the demand for money, and prices continued to fall.

Resistance to continued deflation strengthened in the depression following the financial panic of 1873. In 1874 both houses of Congress passed a bill to expand the issue of greenbacks, but President Grant, who advocated resumption, vetoed this so-called Inflation Bill. Deflation continued. In 1875 various of its opponents organized the Greenback party, which had currency expansion as a major objective. In 1876 its presidential candidate got less than 1 percent of the vote, but in the 1878 Congressional elections the party garnered 10 percent of the vote and won fourteen Congressional seats. Resumption was accomplished before this Congress took office, however, and by 1880 the party was no longer much of a political force. By then it was calling for unlimited coinage of silver, a position that remained live even after the Greenback party had disappeared.

Although at the start of the Civil War the United States in a legal sense was still on a bimetallic monetary standard, full-weight silver coins (371.25 grains to the dollar) had not been in circulation since the 1830s. The reason was that 371.25 grains of silver were worth more than one dollar in the market so that it did not pay a silver owner to take his metal to the U.S. mint for coinage. In the 1850s a shortage of small coins led to the establishment of a subsidiary silver coinage, that is, coins containing less silver than their face value. But the standard silver dollar remained in theory if not in practice a recognized coin. Then in 1873 Congress, without much debate, brought theory into line with practice in an amendment to the coinage laws that discontinued the coinage of standard silver dollars.

Soon thereafter the supply of silver from the opening of new mines in the United States began to increase. At the same time world-wide demand fell because a number of European countries abandoned silver or bimetallic monetary standards in favor of a monometallic gold standard. The price of silver fell to the point where, by 1875, American silver producers would have found it profitable to bring their metal to the mint for coinage had not the 1873 amendment foreclosed that possibility. Reactions were predictable. Silver producers branded the discontinuance of silver dollar coinage the "Crime of 1873," and they were joined by opponents of deflation such as Greenbackers in calling for monetary expansion through a return to free coinage of standard silver dollars, or, as it was often termed, free silver.

The free silver movement won two partial but significant legislative victories in the two decades (1876–1896) when it flourished. The first was the Bland-Allison Act of 1878. Originally a free-coinage measure when it passed the House in 1877, the bill was amended in the Senate to limit the amount of silver the federal government would purchase. President Hayes, like Grant a "sound" money president, vetoed the bill but was overriden by Congress. Under the act's provisions, $2 million to $4 million worth of silver were to be purchased at market prices each month and coined into silver dollars. Despite the legal tender status of these silver dollars the Treasury often had difficulty keeping them in circulation, in part because of the tendency of gold monometallists and others to pay taxes in silver or silver certificates rather than in gold obligations.

The second legislative triumph of the free silver forces came in 1890. In return for supporting the protectionist McKinley Tariff bill that year the silverites gained sufficient protectionist support to secure passage of the Sherman Silver Purchase Act. This act provided that the Treasury purchase 4.5 million ounces of silver per month at the market price. This represented an increase in silver purchases as compared with actual amounts purchased under the Bland-Allison Act, which the Sherman Act repealed. The silver was purchased with a new paper currency issue, the Treasury notes of 1890. These notes were made full legal tender and were redeemable in either gold or silver, although in practice the Treasury redeemed them in gold.

The two major legislative victories of silver adherents were largely in vain. Additions of silver to the U.S. money supply created monetary confusion both within America and abroad, and far from preventing price deflation they actually contributed to it by braking the growth of or causing declines in United States gold reserves. Within the United States such problems as, for example, those of the Treasury in keeping silver and silver certificates in circulation were not, as the silver forces alleged, part of a plot to prevent monetary expansion but rather a reaction to the relative values of gold and silver. No matter how much an American might have desired monetary expansion, as long as he knew that the silver in a silver dollar was worth less than a dollar on the market while the gold dollar was worth a dollar, uncertainty about the monetary standard would lead him to prefer to hold monetary assets in gold or gold equivalents and to make payments in silver. Foreigners were in a similar situation. They were reluctant in the period of silver agitation to invest in the United States because the gold or gold equivalents they would give up to acquire dollar assets might have to be repatriated in silver with consequent capital losses. If foreigners already held dollar assets they would be tempted to sell them for gold whenever the silver threat to the gold standard grew in the United States. Thus the incentives of both Americans and foreigners were such, given the silver situation in the U.S., as to promote decisions to exchange silver and paper money for gold. Those decisions tended to reduce the Treasury's gold stock and thus threaten the ability of the government to maintain dollar–gold interconvertibility.

These monetary problems, ever present since 1878, came to a head in 1893 when the Treasury's gold reserve fell below $100 million for the first time since resumption in 1879. In May of 1893, financial panic broke out as both Americans and foreigners, fearing that gold payments could not be maintained by the government, liquidated assets in an attempt to get gold or currency still convertible into gold. Bank credit and prices fell rapidly while unemployment and interest rates rose. President Cleveland summoned a special session of Congress to repeal the Silver Purchase Act, which it did in the fall of 1893.

Silver purchases ceased in 1893, but the political movement for free silver continued with even greater fervor as a result of this legislative setback and the continuance of the business depression that followed the financial panic. This created great problems for the federal government. The silver agitation and doubts about the strength of our economy prompted foreigners to withdraw gold in great amounts. And the depression reduced government revenues by reducing imports and customs collections. Committed to the maintenance of gold payments, for political as well as economic reasons, the government had little choice but to borrow gold, often on unfavorable terms.* During the years 1894–96, the Treasury sold some $262 million of new bonds to cover its deficits and to replenish its gold reserves. This amounted to an increase of 45 percent in the interest-bearing federal debt in less than three years, an uncommon experience for the United States in times of peace. Both the monetary crisis and the silver agitation ended in 1896 when the great spokesman for free silver, William Jennings Bryan, was defeated for the presidency by William McKinley, a conservative, sound-money man. In 1900 the United States officially adopted the gold standard which, with great difficulties, it had more or less maintained in fact for the two previous decades.

Banking Problems

By 1860 the business of commercial banking was a very important one in the United States. Well over two thousand banks were operating. See Figure 15–3. The majority were banking corporations chartered by state governments but there were also significant numbers of unincorporated proprietorship and partnership banks. The latter, the "private" banks, were generally smaller and less noteworthy than the chartered banks; they also avoided the political problems of chartering and government regulation that impinged upon the chartered banks. The liabilities—deposits and notes—of chartered and private banks made up the larger part of the American money supply, with gold and small amounts of silver coins making up the rest.

During the subsequent half century commercial banking continued to be a growth sector of the economy. As Figure 15–3 indicates, the number of banks grew ninefold while deposit liabilities increased some twenty-three times. The implied rates of expansion far exceeded those of either population or national product between 1860 and 1910. Yet despite its robust growth and definite contributions to economic expansion, the American banking system was plagued by serious problems in these years. Two in particular were pervasive. First, how was the banking system to be organized and how were its component parts to fit together? And,

* Milton Friedman and Anna J. Schwartz in *A Monetary History of the United States, 1867–1960* (Princeton: Princeton University Press, 1963), p. 111 assert that abandonment of the gold standard was not "economically undesirable," but "politically unacceptable."

FIGURE 15-3

Number and Deposits of Commercial Banks in the U.S., 1860-1910

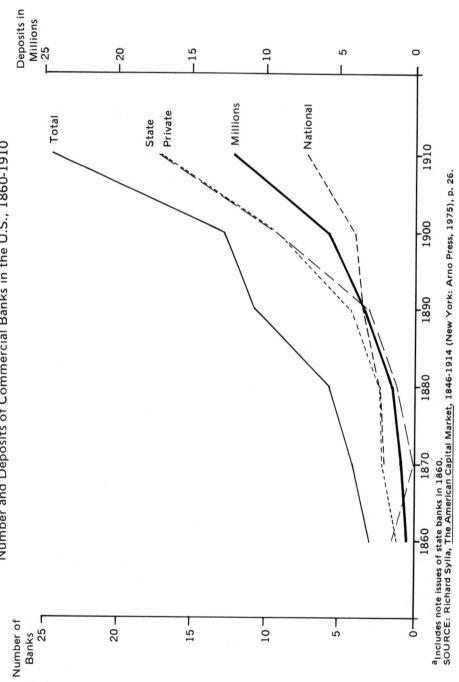

ᵃIncludes note issues of state banks in 1860.
SOURCE: Richard Sylla, The American Capital Market, 1846-1914 (New York: Arno Press, 1975), p. 26.

second, how could the system overcome its periodic tendency to produce or contribute to general financial panics that spread out from the financial sector to weaken the whole economy? Policy decisions gave rise to both problems, and new policy decisions would attempt to overcome them.

The Civil War contributed to both of these problems through one of its major legislative consequences, the federal laws of 1863 and 1864 that established the National Banking System. The intent of these laws was twofold. One objective, a pressing one in 1863–64, was to provide a captive market for federal wartime loans by requiring the new national banks to purchase federal bonds. The other major objective, one that antedated the Civil War, was to furnish the nation with a uniform paper currency to replace the variegated note issues of some one thousand six hundred state chartered banks. National bank notes were to be uniform in design and backed by federal bonds that the banks would buy and deposit with a newly created Treasury Department office, that of Comptroller of the Currency, in return for the notes. Then, should a national bank fail, the bonds could be liquidated and the noteholders compensated without loss.

It was a good idea, with precedents in earlier state banking laws, but its time had not quite come. Federal officials had contemplated that all of the nation's note issuing banks would give up their state charters and join the National System but many were reluctant. The problem was that the new legislation contained provisions that were more restrictive than the ones existing banks had been operating under. Among these were the bond purchase requirements, a limitation on the amount of notes any one national bank could issue to 90 percent of the par or market value of the bonds deposited with the Comptroller, whichever was less, and a ceiling on the total national bank note issue for the whole country. Still other provisions of the law set minimum capital requirements for national banks that were too high to make national banking both feasible and competitive in smaller towns and cities, and prohibited loans extended on the basis of real estate collateral, a definite drawback to national banking in a still largely agricultural nation, with land as the major asset possessed by many people. Faced with these potential restrictions on their business, many existing banks chose to keep their state charters rather than join the new national system.

The recalcitrance of bankers in pursuing their private interests did not sit well in Washington. Political muscle was used. In March, 1865, Congress enacted a 10 percent tax, effective in 1866, on any state bank note paid out by any bank. This effectively killed the note issuing business of most state banks by destroying its profitability. Many took out national charters but some two to three hundred, primarily in cities where deposit banking had eclipsed note issue in importance, remained state banks. And, of course, private banks, which normally had not issued notes, remained and even flourished, unhampered by either federal or state regulation.

Thus was created the so-called "dual banking system" which has lasted to our own day. From 1864 on most American banks have operated under either federal or state charter, with different rules and regulations. By the early part of the present century most private banks had been absorbed into one or the other of the two chartering arrangements. The Civil War objective of making all banks national banks was not achieved. There were important economic effects related to this policy failure in the late-nineteenth century. The national banks with their restrictive provisions were ill-suited to the small town and agricultural expansion of the newer parts of the country, and as a result they remained heavily concentrated in the northeastern part of the nation. State banking was nearly destroyed by the note-issue tax. It recovered rather slowly as deposit banking habits spread and the states gradually liberalized their laws to make state charters more attractive to would-be bankers. Restrictive provisions on national banking were also gradually relaxed, most notably in 1900 when minimum capital requirements were lowered. Nonetheless, for some two to three decades after the Civil War there were definitely inadequate banking facilities over large parts of the United States. Is it any wonder that the greenback and free-silver movements flourished, or that bankers were unpopular and widely varying interest rates were widely deplored? Decisions taken regarding the organization and expansion of the banking system were the fundamental problem but, as so often happens, symptoms came to be confused with causes.

A second major problem that plagued American banking before 1914 was the susceptibility of the banking system to financial panic. Fractional reserve banking of the kind practiced then and now is based on the notion that not every depositor will attempt to convert his deposit into base money—be it gold or government-backed paper currency—at the same time. This allows banks to lend out most of their resources while keeping a fractional reserve of base money just in case day-to-day withdrawals exceed day-to-day deposits. Normally—that is to say, usually—this arrangement presented no problems. The public found it convenient to make payments in bank money by writing checks against deposits and also to take out loans in the form of bank deposit credits. Since bank deposits were normally convertible into base money the public showed no marked tendency to make such conversions, except for day-to-day transactions where cash—coins and paper money—was more convenient than checks.

Two cycles of economic activity served to complicate the normal situation. One was the business cycle, the ebb-and-flow sequence of economic activity that typically occurred over a period of three to four years. The other was a seasonal variation in the demand for cash and bank credit that was related to agriculture; in the spring of the year and again in the late summer and autumn this demand would increase in the agricultural regions of the country as farmers first borrowed to plant their crops and later as middlemen borrowed to finance marketing of them. When this seasonal demand arose, country banks would draw on the deposits they had made in city banks during times of low seasonal demand for loans in rural areas. The National Banking System encouraged this practice of interbank lending through its reserve system. All national banks were required to hold reserves against their deposit liabilities but for most national banks half or more of legally required reserves could take the form of deposit balances in city banks. Since the city banks paid interest on these bankers' balances, they were an attractive and liquid investment for banks with excess funds. New York City as the nation's financial capital was the magnet toward which great amounts of these funds were drawn. The large national banks of New York were able to pay interest on bankers' balances from all over the United States because they in turn could relend the funds to their customers, most notably to individuals and firms that dealt in New York's bond and stock markets.

When peaks of business cycle activity, which were usually accompanied by both heavy commercial loan demand and extensive speculation in the securities markets, coincided with peaks in seasonal credit demands from the countryside, the banks of New York and other large cities sometimes found themselves in a bind. They could meet the country withdrawals of cash and deposits only by contracting their own lending. This caused problems for their loan customers. At its worst, the shortage of loanable funds would lead to business failures and securities market liquidation. With the people and enterprises to whom the banks had lent in trouble, depositors in banks would become fearful that their own funds were in danger and would rush to convert their deposits into base money. This in essence was financial panic. Once started, it fed on itself. Demands to convert deposits to cash caused further credit contraction, business failures, and securities market declines. Sometimes the banks were forced to suspend conversion of deposits into cash. Panics ended quickly but the damage inflicted caused business to be depressed for a longer period. This was true of the panics of 1873, 1884, 1893, and 1907.

How to prevent panics from happening became, toward the end of the century, a major concern of financial decision makers. The problem they faced was commonly described as one of inelasticity of the money supply. By this some analysts meant that the money supply did not conform to "the needs of trade." For example, at business cycle peaks credit demand was strong but the money supply, based as it was on relatively stable stocks of gold and government-backed paper currency, could not expand sufficiently to accommodate all borrowers or to prevent rising interest rates. In depressions on the other hand, conditions were said to be such that more money existed than was needed. This interpretation of the inelasticity problem was very popular but its foundation in economic reasoning was and is weak. To impart elasticity by creating more and more money when business was booming and both interest rates and prices were rising would have been to run the risk of protracted inflation. And to contract the money supply during depressions would have hindered economic recovery by promoting price declines and preventing interest rates from falling to the point where increased borrowing for investment purposes would have been encouraged. Making the money supply elastic in these senses would have been the opposite of a wise policy decision.

More perceptive analysts realized that the basic problem during panics was that the supply of currency—coin and paper money—was inelastic. Panics occurred when a large number of depositors doubted that their bank deposits could be converted into currency; in testing their doubts the depositors acted to confirm them. What was needed was some way to expand the volume of currency during incipient panic situations in order to allay rather than confirm the doubts of deposit holders. After the panic of 1907, the federal government acted to deal with this fundamental problem of monetary inelasticity in a systematic way. The first result was the Aldrich-Vreeland Act of 1908, which provided both a temporary solution and an impetus to long-term reform. The temporary solution came in the form of an authorization to groups of banks threatened by depositor panic to issue an emergency currency backed by certain types of their loan and investment assets, with a progressively rising tax on such emergency issues in order to ensure that they would be retired after the emergency had disappeared. The Aldrich-Vreeland Act's impetus to reform came with its provision for a National Monetary Commission, composed of senators and representatives, which was authorized to make extensive studies of monetary and banking systems and to recommend appropriate changes in American arrangements. The work of the National Monetary Commission during the next few years led to passage of the Federal Reserve Act in 1913, and the establishment of the Federal Reserve System, the central bank of the United States, in 1914. This was a momentous change in American institutions. Its intents and results are taken up in chapter 22.

The Financial Sector and Capital Formation Trends

A major function of the financial sector in any modern economy is to transfer in an efficient manner the surplus funds of savers into the hands of investors. This is one of the ways—and one that increases in relative terms with higher levels of economic development—that capital formation is financed. Primitive economies do not have much need for a financial sector. To the extent that capital formation occurs in them it is usually through self finance, as for example, when a farmer decides to sacrifice leisure and current consumption in order to clear his land of trees and perhaps to make split rail fences for his fields from the fallen timbers. A more advanced economy will feature direct finance, which is the activity of savers directly lending their funds to investors or buying equity shares in enterprises. The division of labor in finance can be, and customarily is, carried even further, giving rise to indirect finance. Savers, instead of lending to enterprises or directly investing in them, place their surplus funds in financial intermediaries such as banks, investment companies, life insurance companies, and pension funds. The intermediaries attract funds by selling savers desirable products such as bank deposits, investment diversification, life insurance, or retirement incomes. And the intermediaries in turn invest the pooled resources of savers, with economies of scale and advantages of specialization and diversification, in the debt and equity instruments offered by productive enterprises whose demand for funds exceeds what they themselves can generate from current income.

As the American economy grew in size and complexity during the late-nineteenth century, the number of financial intermediaries increased at a rapid rate and they became ubiquitous features of the economic institutional landscape. In what ways did they affect the performance of the economy? Insofar as they offered savers more attractive products, in terms both of the type of product and of increased investment yields through the economies and the efficiencies in specialized investment, the intermediaries acted to raise the attractiveness of saving and investment and hence its volume. And insofar as their larger scale enabled them both to gather more information on potential investments and to reduce risks through investment diversification, the intermediaries acted to reduce barriers to capital mobility and to promote efficient use of savings by tending to equalize the interregional and the interindustry costs of funds to users of financial capital.

There is evidence that intermediaries had both of these effects. Studies of commercial bank-lending rates, for example, show that interest rates to bank borrowers were very different in different regions of the United States during the 1860s and the 1870s, but that by the first decade of this century many of the interregional differences had been eliminated. The rapid growth in numbers and competitiveness of bank and nonbank intermediaries during the period played a large role in this fashioning of a more unified national capital market.

The other expected effect of financial intermediation—an increase in the volume of saving and investment—is also evident in the historical record of the post-Civil War decades. An increase in relative levels of saving and investment during these decades is in fact one of the more striking characteristics of that period documented by recent economic-historical research. Figure 15–4 presents data on the share of aggregate capital formation in total economic product and also on one of its key components, the tools, machinery, and equipment represented by "manufactured producer-durables."

FIGURE 15-4

Percentage Shares of Gross Capital Formation and Producer-Durable Capital Formation in GNP, Overlapping Decade Averages, 1839-48 Through 1899-1908 (measured in constant prices of 1860)

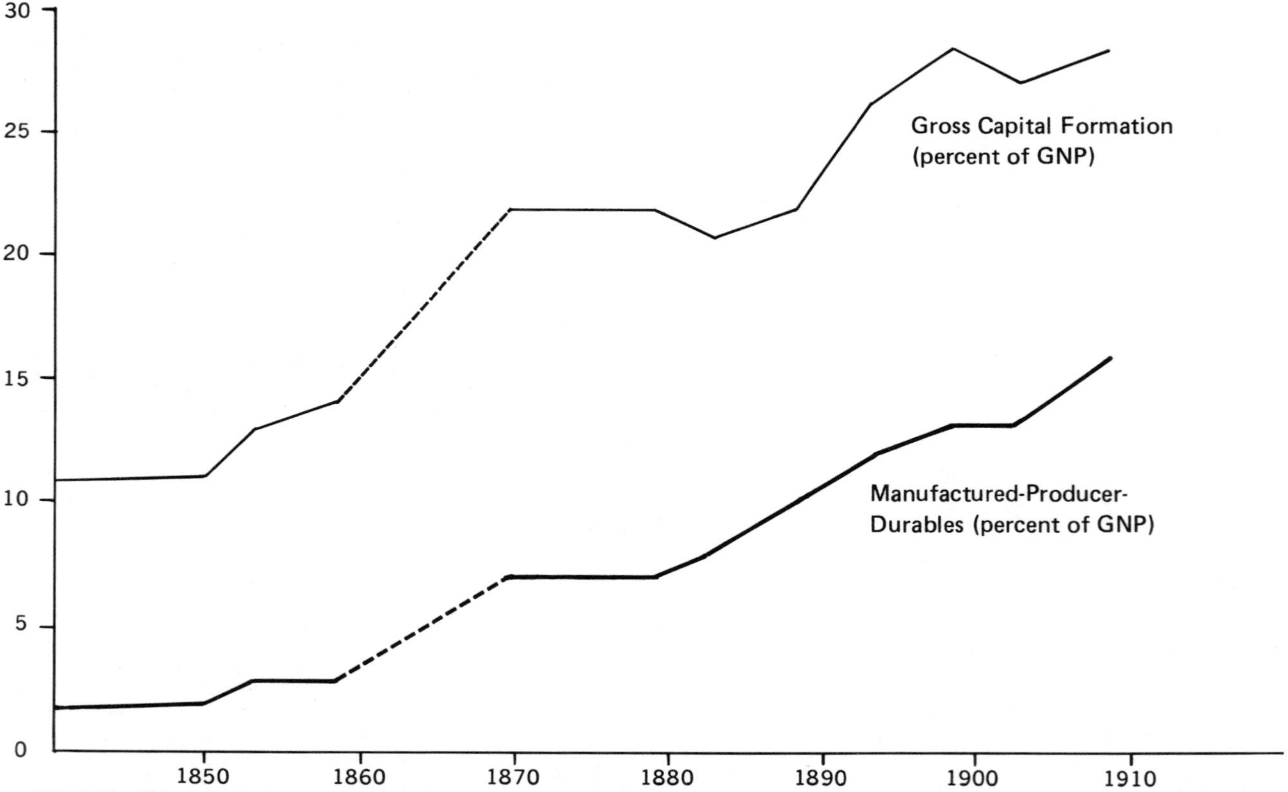

Gross Capital Formation (percent of GNP)

Manufactured-Producer-Durables (percent of GNP)

SOURCE: Robert E. Gallman, "Gross National Product in the United States, 1834-1909," in National Bureau of Economic Research, Output Employment and Productivity in the United States after 1800. Studies in Income and Wealth, vol. 30 (New York: Columbia University Press, 1966), Table 3, page 11; Table A-1, page 26; and Table A-3, page 34. Data are not available for 1859-68.

What is striking about the capital formation rates exhibited in Figure 15-4 is not their rising trend over the decades—this is not an unusual characteristic of developing economies—but rather the magnitude of the overall rise, and especially the jump between the pre- and post-Civil War eras. Rates of capital formation, which were rising during the prewar decades, doubled between the 1840s and the 1870s and between the 1850s and the 1890s. Increases in the producer-durable goods component of capital formation are even greater.

Although financial intermediaries undoubtedly contributed to rising rates of capital formation by making savings and investment more attractive, it is unlikely that their development by itself can explain all, or even most, of the increase. The intermediaries continued to develop in the twentieth century but rates of capital formation did not maintain the upward momentum of the late-nineteenth century. Other and more specifically historical forces of the period must have aided the rising rate of capital formation, which in its magnitude is most unusual for an economy where decision making by individuals and by individual enterprises determines savings and investment behavior.

Financial policies of late nineteenth-century federal decision makers, although perhaps not intended to stimulate capital formation, may in fact have had that result. One such policy, covered earlier in this chapter, concerned the public debt. As can be seen in Figure 15-5, the federal interest-bearing debt rose to unprecedented levels during the Civil War years. Then, for more than a quarter of a century after the war, the federal government took in more money in tax revenues than it spent and used the resulting surpluses to redeem government bonds for cash. (The only significant exception to this pattern came in the late 1870s when the Treasury floated bonds in order to purchase gold to resume specie payments.) When the Treasury redeemed bonds, it transformed budget surpluses into funds available to private investors. This increased capital funds and depressed market interest rates and other capital costs. The actual impact of debt retirement on private capital formation was much greater than the nominal amount of debt retired. When the debt was growing during the Civil War the federal government borrowed inflated greenback dollars, but when after the war it paid interest on its debts and redeemed them with surplus cash, it did so in dollars that had increased in value as a result of falling price levels. Thus, the purchasing power the Treasury returned to private investors was much greater than what investors had given up when they bought government's bonds during wartime.

A fuller understanding of why the federal debt policies very likely increased capital formation can be gained by considering the sources of surplus federal revenues. There were two main sources. One was customs duties on imported goods; the duties appear to have raised the costs of consumer-goods imports more than the costs of capital-goods imports. The other main source of federal revenue was excise taxes on tobacco products

FIGURE 15-5

Public Debt (Interest Bearing) of the Federal Government, 1860-1914

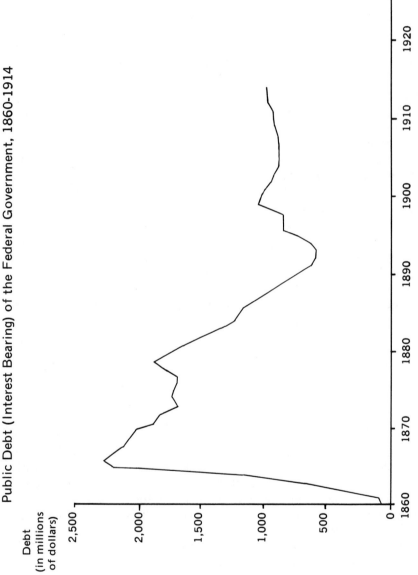

Debt
(in millions
of dollars)

SOURCE: U.S. Bureau of Census, Historical Statistics of the United States, Part II (Washington, D.C.: 1975), p. 1118.

and alcoholic beverages, popular consumer goods. So the net effect of post-Civil War federal debt, tariff, and tax policies was to transfer purchasing power from consumers to investors. These policies almost certainly promoted higher rates of capital formation and economic growth after the Civil War.

Conclusion

Civil War finance brought about innovations in taxation, borrowing, paper money, and banking. Financial policy decisions of 1861–65 helped to solve some of the federal government's pressing problems, but at the same time they sowed the seeds of later financial difficulties and discontents. Disagreements over tariff, tax, and debt questions, over the organization and operation of the banking system, and over the foundation or base of the money supply became staples of American political economy in the late-nineteenth century. Widespread perceptions of the inadequacies of existing financial arrangements led to experimentation with other approaches but these, too, as in the case of silver policies, appeared to cause at least as many problems as they had been designed to solve.

Yet the American financial system matured considerably in the decades after 1860. Banks and other financial intermediaries ultimately spread throughout the nation and promoted economic efficiency in the mobilization and distribution of capital. The federal government's tax and debt policies, perhaps inadvertantly but nonetheless effectively, stimulated high and ever-rising levels of capital formation. During these decades the United States exhibited the highest rates of tangible capital formation and also the highest rates of economic growth in its history. In attempting to understand the intricacies of financial problems in this era, one should not lose sight of the financial sector's achievements; they were substantial.

SUGGESTED READINGS

Two works that discuss impacts of the Civil War on the American economy are David T. Gilchrist and W. David Lewis, eds., *Economic Change in the Civil War Era* (Greenville, Delaware: Eleutherian Mills Hagley Foundation, 1965) and Stanley L. Engerman, "The Economic Impact of the Civil War," *Explorations in Entrepreneurial History*, 2nd Series, 3 (Spring/Summer 1966), 176–199. Wartime financing problems at the federal level are treated by Bray Hammond, *Sovereignty and an Empty Purse* (Princeton: Princeton University Press, 1970). For a detailed discussion of taxation issues before, during, and after the Civil War, see Sidney Ratner, *Taxation and Democracy in America* (New York: W. W. Norton, 1942, Science Editions rev. ed., 1967). Ratner's *The Tariff in American History* (New York: Van Nostrand, 1972) is an incisive introduction to the tariff history of the period. On debt policy Henrietta M. Larson's study, *Jay Cooke, Private Banker* (Cambridge, Mass.: Harvard University Press, 1936) is valuable, as is Robert T. Patterson, *Federal Debt-Management Policies, 1865–1897* (Durham: Duke University Press, 1954).

For the general financial history of this and other eras of American history a helpful work is Paul Studenski and Herman Krooss, *Financial History of the United States*, 2nd ed. (New York: McGraw-Hill, 1963). The classic work on the monetary history of this and subsequent periods is Milton Friedman and Anna J. Schwartz, *A Monetary History of the United States, 1867–1960* (Princeton: Princeton University Press, 1963). An excellent economic analysis of issues involved in the resumption of specie payments after the Civil War is James K. Kindahl, "Economic Factors in Specie Resumption: The United States, 1865–79," *Journal of Political Economy*, 59 (February 1961), 30–48.

Banking problems and the evolution of the banking system in these (and earlier) years is the subject of Fritz Redlich's encyclopedic study, *The Molding of American Banking* (New York: Johnson Reprint Corporation, 1968). For more economic analysis of these subjects see Richard Sylla, *The American Capital Market, 1846–1914* (New York: Arno Press, 1975), a work that also analyzes the impact of federal debt management on the economy, and John A. James, *Money and Capital Markets in Postbellum America* (Princeton: Princeton University Press, 1978). Richard H. Timberlake, *The Origins of Central Banking in the United States* (Cambridge, Mass.: Harvard University Press, 1978) treats a wide range of monetary, banking, and financial issues in addition to central banking.

The emergence of an efficient national capital market is a major theme of the Sylla and James works cited above. Both were inspired by the pathbreaking study of Lance Davis, "The Investment Market, 1870–1914: The Evolution of a National Market," *Journal of Economic History*, 25 (September 1965), 355–399, which is worth consulting both for its analysis and its extensive data on interregional interest rates, 1870–1914.

The essential findings on economic growth and capital formation trends are set forth by Robert E. Gallman, "Gross National Product in the United States, 1834–1909," in National Bureau of Economic Research, *Output, Employment and Productivity in the United States after 1800, Studies in Income and Wealth*, vol. 30 (New York: Columbia University Press, 1966). Finally, for a provocative, highly technical economic analysis of financial and other economic issues of the post-Civil War era, see Jeffrey G. Williamson, *Late Nineteenth Century American Development* (Cambridge, Eng.: Cambridge University Press, 1975).

CHAPTER 16

———

National and World Markets

for Mass Production

The years between 1860 and 1914 witnessed major changes in the marketing of both manufactured goods and agricultural commodities, changes that were comparable to those taking place in the methods of production. Indeed, the two were related, for technological innovations and entrepreneurial decisions that led to mass production were paralleled by those that created mass marketing. Specialization in marketing at both the wholesale and the retail levels had already emerged before the Civil War and had begun to erode the position of unspecialized merchants who combined such functions as shipping, importing, wholesaling, and retailing in their mercantile enterprises. After the Civil War, marketing specialization continued, particularly in the mass distribution of agricultural commodities at the wholesale level. But the distinctive marketing developments of the postbellum decades were in two other areas. At the retail level, mass marketing appeared in the widespread proliferation and expansion of the department store and in two innovations: the chain store and the mail-order house. The other key development occurred when mass manufacturers bypassed independent wholesale distribution channels by creating their own purchasing and marketing organizations.

Marketing innovations such as these were based to an important extent on urban growth and on the emergence of nationwide transportation networks that could move mass-produced goods quickly and cheaply from industrial centers to buyers; both the concentration of population in cities and the spread of railways helped to reduce distribution costs. Mass communication fostered another development, namely, the increased use of advertising to promote the demand for particular products. Despite the advantages of new marketing institutions in terms of the variety of goods and services available, some critics charged that distribution costs were too high, and that much advertising was misleading and wasteful. Others resisted the newer forms of distribution because they represented a threat to established commercial interests, and judicial decisions were necessary to resolve the conflicts.

In foreign trade two significant changes reflected the maturing of the American economy. The first was a shift from an unfavorable to a favorable balance of trade. Up to the mid-1870s the United States usually spent more on imports than it received for exports; after that time, the situation was reversed. The second important change had to do with the composition of exports. In the quarter century before World War I exports of American manufactures increased dramatically relative to exports of the traditional agricultural commodities that had long been the staples of American trade with other parts of the world.

Important changes also took place in the nation's commercial policies toward the rest of the world. First, the level of tariff protection increased markedly. Whereas tariffs on imports of foreign goods had been declining during the three decades before the Civil War, during that war they were raised to substantially higher levels where they remained for five decades. As a result, tariff policies became among the most heated issues debated by national decision makers in these years. Finally, the growth of American commercial and strategic interests around the world led to territorial acquisitions and, more important, to the beginnings of dollar diplomacy, that is, the use of governmental powers to support American commercial and financial interests in other lands.

The Creation of a Nationwide Marketing System

By the middle decades of the nineteenth century, the United States from the Atlantic Coast to the Great Plains had become an integrated market area for many of the products of agriculture and industry. After mid-century, continued population growth and the extension and improvement of transportation and communication technologies continued to expand the size of the nation's market area. Growing concentrations of population in urban areas provided an additional stimulus to trade by reducing costs of wholesale and retail trade. As the percentage of the American population engaged in farming declined, the urban population (defined as those people living in places with 2,500 or more inhabitants) increased from 20 percent of the total population in 1860 to 51 percent in 1920. In 1860 only nine cities had more than one hundred thousand inhabitants, but by 1920 sixty-eight places could claim this distinction. At the time of World War I the cities of New York, Chicago, and Philadelphia each surpassed the one and a half million mark. (See Table 16–1.)

TABLE 16-1
Growth of Urban Population
and Cities, 1860-1920

Year	Percentage of Total Population	Number of Cities	
		Over 2,500	Over 100,000
	(1)	(2)	(3)
1860	20	392	9
1870	26	663	14
1880	28	939	20
1890	35	1,348	28
1900	40	1,737	38
1910	46	2,262	49
1920	51	2,722	68

SOURCE: For column 1, 1960 Census of Population, Final Report PC (1)-1A, United States Summary, Tables 4, 5b; for columns 2 and 3, U.S. Bureau of the Census, The Statistical History of the United States (New York: Basic Books, 1976), p. 11, Series A 43-56.

Transportation improvements and urban growth led an increasing proportion of the American labor force to become engaged in the distribution of goods as contrasted with their production. The resulting increase in economic specialization led to a greater dependence by individuals, households, and businesses on goods and services sold through markets. The effect of these forces of specialization on the demand for marketing activities is evident in the doubling of the proportion of American workers engaged in trade and transportation from 10 percent in 1860 to 20 percent in 1920.

SPECIALIZATION AND INTEGRATION IN DISTRIBUTION

In the years between 1840 and 1890, a new specialized marketing system developed that met the demands of both the intermediate and the ultimate consumers of goods. The general merchant in the pre-1840 period had combined the functions of the importer, wholesaler, and retailer. But the rising volume of trade brought firms that specialized in one or several functions of the earlier general merchant. Domestic wholesalers became distinct from importers, and dry-goods wholesalers came to specialize in one or several types of goods such as millinery, sheetings, or dress goods. As a result, commission houses and jobbers developed on a wide scale. By 1861 independent wholesalers were in control of the distribution of more than 95 percent of all manufactured products sold in the United States. (An exception was the railroad supply industry, where railroads developed their own contacts with the manufacturers.)

THE WHOLESALER AND MASS DISTRIBUTION

From the 1850s to the early 1880s these increasingly specialized wholesalers dominated the American distribution system. They created large purchasing networks through which they bought directly from manufacturers at home and abroad, and they developed extensive marketing organization for selling to general country stores and to specialized urban retailers. Until 1850 wholesalers had been concentrated on the eastern seaboard of the United States; western storekeepers and southern factors came east to get their supplies. With the continental expansion of the railroad and the telegraph, wholesalers moved west to cities like Cincinnati, Chicago, and St. Louis, although wholesalers from New York, Philadelphia, and Baltimore continued to compete for the orders of country merchants in the midwest. Wholesalers from the midwest and from Baltimore and Louisiana concentrated on supplying the numerous country stores that grew up in the South after the Civil War.

Specialization occurred as early as the 1850s and the 1860s in the marketing and distribution of agricultural products. The distribution of grain and cotton was dramatically changed by the expansion of the railroad and telegraph and the growth of related enterprises like grain elevators, cotton presses, warehouses, and an important new institution—the organized commodity exchange. These exchanges, based on telegraphic communication, made it possible for cotton, grain, and other commodities to be bought and sold while in transit, or even before they had been harvested. The merchants who decided to standardize and systematize the marketing procedures of the commodity exchanges changed drastically the methods of financing agricultural commodities and also reduced their transportation costs.

The first such reforms emerged in the marketing and financing of the grain trade and led to the establishment in 1848 of the Chicago Board of Trade. Similar institutions were founded in St. Louis, Buffalo, New York, Philadelphia, and other cities. In the post-Civil War period, dealers and brokers on these commodity exchanges distributed and marketed crops such as wheat, barley, corn, oats, and rye.

Similarly, once Southern railroad and telegraph networks had been rebuilt after the Civil War, the marketing of cotton changed. Instead of depending upon the services of the cotton factor, the dominant middleman of the antebellum cotton economy, cotton dealers were able to buy directly from planters, small farmers, and general storekeepers. Cotton exchanges were created in New York in 1870 and in New Orleans in 1871.

The administrative networks created by the commodity dealers often were global enterprises, but they did not necessitate more than a small investment in capital facilities and needed only a few managers. These organizations lowered the cost of credit for crop movements and enabled a closer integration of supply and demand through improved information and scheduling. As a result, both farmers and buyers of agricultural products had better information on which to base their decisions. In the period from 1860 to 1914, when agricultural exports were extremely important to American economic growth, the development of large commodity dealers and commodity exchanges increased the efficiency of the marketing of agricultural commodities.

Many of these commodity organizations of the 1860s and 1870s have continued to function in the twentieth century. The independent middleman has retained his role as the link between the manufacturer and the retailer in the grocery, drug, hardware, dry-goods, and jewelry trades. But after 1880, wholesalers in other lines began to be challenged, and eventually even replaced, by two developments: mass retailing and the integration of production and marketing.

INNOVATIONS IN RETAILING

During the last half of the nineteenth century a movement toward integration of functions occurred in retail marketing through the establishment of department stores, chain stores, and mail-order houses. Department stores developed in the 1860s as the growing cities provided a wide middle-class market for the constantly expanding quantity and diversity of mass-produced consumer goods. The department store has been defined as a retail establishment carrying many lines of merchandise, ranging from apparel and accessories for women and children to small wares, usually dry goods, and home furnishings, with each of these lines in a separate department, but all under one roof and one central management. Among the earliest and most important pioneers in this field were Macy's in New York, Marshall Field in Chicago, and John Wanamaker of Philadelphia and New York. The most rapid expansion of the department stores was during the late 1890s and the early 1900s. Among the practices introduced by the large department stores were selling at a fixed price, buying for cash, and purchasing directly from domestic and foreign manufacturers.

Chain stores represented another way of integrating retail marketing and thereby attaining economies of scale through volume buying and selling. The term chain stores applied to several retail establishments combined and operated under one ownership and management. Through their specialization in a few chosen lines, the chain stores developed expert management quite rapidly and exercised a growing influence over the producers and distributors of consumer goods. Since each store remained relatively small and did not try to compete with the department stores in offering customer services, the cost of sales and overhead were held to a minimum. The first of the modern retail chain store systems was the Great Atlantic & Pacific Tea Company, established in New York in 1859. Its success stimulated many imitators. By 1900 about 60 chains offering a variety of goods had emerged. By 1910 the number had grown to 257 and by 1920 to 808.

F. W. Woolworth's five-and-ten-cent store chain was perhaps the most successful to begin operations in the 1870–1900 period. The key ingredients of Woolworth's success were selling a variety of goods on a cash basis in small as well as large cities and buying in volume from manufacturers to permit volume selling at low prices. The rapid expansion of other chain stores was facilitated by the low capital-output ratio of retail enterprise. Although a major problem of the chain store was finding and retaining reliable store managers and clerks, the gains outweighed the losses. F. W. Woolworth's ideas and practices eventually had a global influence.

While department stores and chain stores integrated retail marketing in an urban environment, mail-order houses performed the same integration for the rural market. During the late 1860s and the early 1870s a number of concerns engaged in mail-order selling of such specialized items as books, novelties, and pictures. The first general merchandise mail-order concern was established in Chicago in 1872 by A. Montgomery Ward. He succeeded in developing direct mail-order transactions with farmers and small-town people throughout the United States and for many years carried on the largest retail mail-order business in the country. His success was based on offering goods at the lowest possible prices through cash sales, backed by a warranty for all items and the right of return if the customer was not satisfied. Ward's chief competitor was Sears, Roebuck and Company, formed in 1893 by Richard W. Sears and a former employee. With the aid of such able administrators as Julius Rosenwald, Sears eventually established his firm as first in the mail-order business, a lead Sears, Roebuck has retained until this day.

The expansion of the mail-order business in the United States was aided by the national government's establishment of rural free delivery in 1896 and parcel-post service in 1912; both systems greatly helped with the distribution of mail-order catalogues and goods. As a result, the pre-Civil War local monopoly of rural markets by general stores was eroded between 1895 and 1914 by the massive growth of mail-order firms. Among other reasons for the increase in sales were the opening of branch distributing centers that resembled private wholesale houses and the gradual extension of installment selling. By 1900, Sears was selling pianos, furniture, and other durable goods on credit, and added automobiles in 1910. After World War I the expansion of the urban population and the widespread use of automobiles induced the two giant general mail-order houses to open retail stores in various cities. This change created management difficulties that eventually were solved by the creation of a large degree of autonomy for those in charge of the retail stores.

INTEGRATION OF PRODUCTION AND MARKETING

The trends discussed thus far stemmed from the coordination of manufacturing and marketing activities by means of specialized markets. Hence, another distinctive business development of the late-nineteenth century might run counter to expectations: the integration of mass production and mass marketing within a single enterprise or corporation. This process developed when the nature of the mass produced goods shifted the marketing advantage away from independent specialists and toward marketing specialists within a firm. The resulting integration of economic functions within one giant enterprise was not actually an exception to the rule that specialization has advantages, for in a real sense an organization such as a corporate marketing department, which specialized in the distribution of one firm's products, was even more specialized than an independent distributor who carried the products of a number of producers.

Among the manufacturers who made the decision to go into marketing were the makers of consumer goods whose products posed special marketing problems. Some manufacturers had to use refrigeration or another temperature-controlling process to distribute their products; for example, the producers of meat, beer, bananas, cigarettes, and photographic negatives. Among the entrepreneurs in these five fields were meat packers like Armour and Swift of Chicago; brewers like Schlitz, Pabst, and Blatz of Milwaukee; Andrew Preston, the founder of the United Fruit Company; James B. Duke, a pioneer in cigarette mass manufacture and distribution; and George Eastman, notable for his role in the development and sale of photographic negatives.

Other manufacturers who elected to handle their own marketing were those who made mass-produced consumer durables that required demonstrations, consumer credit, and special maintenance services. In this group were the makers of sewing machines, cash registers, typewriters, harvesters, and other farm equipment. Two such companies, the Singer Sewing Machine Company and the McCormick Harvesting Machine Company, pioneered as early as the 1850s. Emulators of their methods from the 1880s on included the Remington Company and other typewriter firms; John H. Patterson and other makers of cash registers; Colonel Albert Pope and other bicycle manufacturers; and John Deere, his successors, and other makers of agricultural equipment.

A third group of manufacturers who were in marketing were those who produced for other enterprises products or machinery requiring expert installation and servicing, such as electrical equipment, explosives, and streetcar systems. Among the major innovators in this group were the two leading electrical manufacturing companies, Westinghouse and General Electric. Still another group of manufacturers were able to market their volume output of fairly standardized commodities at lower cost than could be done by small independent distributors. Among these business firms were the makers of Bessemer steel and the manufacturers of such metals as copper and other producer goods.

Still another marketing technique by which the manufacturer controlled the retailing developed in the automobile industry in the early twentieth century. During the 1900s the automobile manufacturers sent their cars to wholesalers, who sold the cars to retailers in the urban areas around them. In the 1910s the large companies dispensed with wholesalers in the major urban markets by having their factory branches supply retail dealers directly. About 1915, Ford established regional assembly plants and eliminated all wholesalers.

This practice of dealing directly with retailers was followed by many other manufacturers in the 1920s and created a revolution in mass distribution. In 1929 a census survey revealed that independent wholesalers handled less than one third of the flow of manufactured goods from American factories. Manufacturers sold the other two thirds of their goods directly to industrial and home consumers, to the manufacturers' own wholesale and retail outlets, and to independent retailers.

OVERCOMING BARRIERS TO NATIONWIDE COMMERCE

Innovators of mass marketing methods in the post-Civil War years faced hostility from vested interests on the local and state levels. The Constitution of the United States had given Congress the power to regulate commerce between states, but for a century Congress did little to assert its power. As a result, state and local laws and regulations controlled commerce except in the few instances when appeals to the Supreme Court of the United States had resulted in decisions overturning them. Thus, when mass manufacturers decided to create their own mass distribution organizations, they often ran afoul of established state and local interests that used their legislative and judicial systems to protect themselves from outside competition.

The Singer Sewing Machine Company decided to create its own distributing organization, largely because it found that independent distributors were unable to provide the credit, make the demonstrations, and furnish the repair service the company needed to market its machines on a mass basis. Local interests, to protect their markets, invoked peddler licensing and tax laws which discriminated against out-of-state products and against the traveling salesmen the company employed. Singer stood to gain greatly if such statutes could be overturned, and possessed the financial resources to fight protracted legal battles. Singer therefore appealed convictions of its agents under the protective state laws all the way to the United States Supreme Court. The Court ruled in favor of Singer in 1876 and 1880. Peddler licensing laws were found to be in fact discriminatory taxes on out-of-state products. The Court also reasoned that unless such state laws were voided, the nation could easily slip backwards into tariff wars between states such as had existed in the 1780s prior to the adoption of the Constitution.

Mass producers and marketers of fresh meat also found themselves the targets of local interests. The innovation of refrigerated rail transportation allowed the big packers to achieve economies of scale in processing meat at central locations like Chicago and then shipping it hundreds of miles for sale at prices below what local butchers were charging. With their market eroding, local butchers raised the red flag of monopoly and induced a number of states to pass inspection laws; their enforcement was meant to eliminate competition from the Chicago packers. When an agent of Armour, one of the big meat packers, was convicted under a Minnesota statute, the case was appealed to the United States Supreme Court. In 1890, the Court found for the defendent, reasoning that under the guise of such inspection laws the states could keep virtually any product of out-of-state manufacture from being sold within their borders.

As the foregoing examples demonstrate, the formation of a nationwide market was not an automatic result of mass production and cheap transportation. Although American consumers generally benefited from mass marketing, the new competition often threatened the interests of local manufacturers, processors, and distributors. Overcoming these parochial interests often required lengthy, expensive legal battles. Big business had the incentives and the financial ability to fight these battles, and the United States Supreme Court showed an understanding of the larger economic issues involved in them. But the victories in the late-nineteenth century were not total. Vested interests continued to enlist the licensing, taxing, and regulatory powers of state and local government to protect themselves from competition in the marketplace.

ADVERTISING AND THE CONSUMER

The new methods of marketing also generated new techniques for attracting customers. Before the Civil War advertising in newspapers by merchants consisted mainly of the communication of information about the arrival of goods and their prices at some store or dealer. In the post-Civil War period, with the expansion of national markets by railroads and the new developments in newspaper typesetting and popular magazines, advertising shifted from communicating information to making deeply emotional appeals. In effect, two types of advertising prevailed. One, directed primarily to businessmen through trade media was mainly factual and informative. The second, directed to consumers, sometimes resorted to fraudulent claims and the questionable use of authority or other status symbols in an attempt to increase sales.

Advertising enabled manufacturers and other producers to acquaint customers in the national market with their products. Consumers, it was hoped, would then ask retailers to carry the product, and wholesalers would be induced to handle it. The pioneers in this technique of evoking consumer pressure upon retailers were the makers of patent medicines—Castoria, Purina, and Lydia Pinkham. This group was joined by the soap makers (for example, Pears soap) the food producers (Baker's Cocoa and Royal Baking Powder) and the manufacturers of such new products as the sewing machine, the typewriter, and the bicycle.

In 1865 media revenues from advertising were estimated at only $7.5 million. By 1919 advertising expenditures had risen to over $2 billion. The ratio of such expenditures to the GNP rose from 0.7 percent in 1867 to 3.2 percent in 1904. Contributing to this great expansion in advertising spending was the notable increase in daily newspaper and magazine publishing between 1890 and 1910. The popularity of magazines like the *Ladies' Home Journal* and the *Saturday Evening Post* caused monthly magazine circulation to quadruple between 1890 and 1905 and to increase still more in subsequent years. In addition to advertisements in the mass media, advertisers exploited the possibilities for advertising in trolleys, subways, suburban trains, roadside billboards, and illuminated electric signs in major cities.

Between the Civil War and World War I the lead in advertising expenditures was taken by companies that sold consumer goods in such extremely competitive lines as soaps and cosmetics (for example, Proctor and Gamble), meat packing (Swift and Cudahy), and automobiles (General Motors and Packard). Among the other high advertising spenders were manufacturers of household goods such as mattresses, and of food products such as packaged cereals. In many cases, the differences between the products advertised were rather slight and existed mainly in packaging and other minor characteristics. But the differentiation between products that advertising helped to create was an important factor in some companies achieving leadership in sales over their rivals who were less skillful in advertising. Advertising thus joined such characteristics as price and quality as an element of competition between firms for sales of their products to consumers.

Although in the nineteenth century businessmen showed little concern about the issue of truth in advertising, by the early 1900s newspapers and magazines began to realize that advertisements offensive to their readers' standards of accuracy created consumer incredulity. Scrupulous and intelligent firms like Wanamaker's and Macy's were among the pioneers in eliminating dishonesty from advertising copy. Groups concerned about enforcing truth in advertising achieved unity by 1911, forming vigilance committees and lobbying for truth-in-advertising statutes. This movement concentrated on eliminating factual misstatements in order to protect the reputable advertisers. It did not go into deeper ethical questions concerning the value of "conspicuous consumption," and "ostentatious display" raised by critics of business like Thorstein Veblen.

Despite the critics, many would argue that advertising, when its excesses were curbed, encouraged economic growth and helped consumers by bringing information about possible choices to the largest possible audience of potential buyers. In an age that stressed frugality, the virtue of saving against spending, and puritanism in consumption, advertising became the one American social institution that stressed the virtues of constantly increasing one's standard of living and enjoying consumer products. Where to draw the line between abstinence and indulgence required wisdom and knowledge on the part of the consumer; increased consumer education, consumer research, and the setting of standards of purity and quality could help to create those qualities.

THE COST OF DISTRIBUTION

The revolution in mass distribution by manufacturers, wholesalers, and retailers brought numerous advantages to the general public. But many people, especially farmers and factory workers, became convinced that wholesale and retail distribution costs were excessive. The price spread between what the producer received for his goods and what the consumer had to pay seemed too high, probably because of unnecessary waste or excessive distributive profits, or both. The best statistical study on distribution costs in the United States in the post-Civil War period showed a small but steady rise in the cost of wholesale and retail charges to the consumer (when measured as a percentage of the retail value of all commodities sold on the retail market) from about 33 percent of retail value in 1869 to about 37 percent in 1909. These figures omitted the cost of national advertising by manufacturers of consumer goods and the merchandising activities of producers or distributors of unfinished goods. Including these costs would raise the figures for distribution costs between 1869 and 1909 by at least 10 percent and perhaps as much as 17 percent. Such a revision would mean that the distribution costs ranged from about 48 percent of retail prices in 1869 to over 50 percent in 1909.

Did distribution cost too much? Although the increase in the proportion of retail costs attributable to distribution between 1869 and 1909 was not great, the overall magnitudes proved disturbing to many people. Some contended that the evolving distribution process resulted in unnecessary duplication of sales efforts, a multiplicity of sales outlets, excessive customer services, too many brands of essentially similar products, and wasteful advertising. The phenomena thus referred to might, however, be viewed in a different light. Thus, it could be argued that the distribution system gave consumers greater varieties of goods and of retail outlets, greater convenience of shopping, more personal services in the stores, other services such as home delivery and the privilege of returning goods, and more information to aid in purchasing decisions. The critics of distribution costs might consider whether, if American consumers had preferred lower prices at the cost of forgoing these conveniences and service, entrepreneurs would not have taken advantage of that preference.

The United States in a Growing World Economy

From 1860 to 1914, we have seen, the United States was building up a great nationwide distribution network that allowed the free movement of goods and services over an area as large as Europe. But during this same period the United States in its commerce with other countries frequently erected barriers to free international trade by imposing tariffs on imports. Nevertheless, so rapid was the development of the American economy that even highly protective policy decisions could not prevent the United States from becoming an increasingly important factor in world commerce.

The rise of the United States in the world economy was not the result of a slow growth in world trade. Quite the contrary. The advantages of an international division of labor were so great that during the nineteenth century the network of international trade grew in size and activity to levels never before reached. The ratio of world trade (exports and imports combined) to world production is estimated to have risen from about 3 percent in 1801 to 16 percent in 1860 and to 33 percent in 1914. In 1867–68 the total value of world trade came to about $10.5 billion; by 1913 it had increased to about $40.6 billion, implying a rate of growth of over 30 percent per decade. The share of combined American exports and imports in these world values was roughly 6 percent in 1867–68 and 11 percent in 1913.

As world trade grew relative to world production, most of the major industrial countries of western Europe and Japan also experienced an increase in their own foreign trade–production ratios. The United States, however, did not. The American ratio was about 15 percent in the early 1870s and only 11 percent in 1913. The size and diversity of the United States in terms of its natural and human resources was so great that the possibilities for internal specialization and exchange were much more extensive than they were for other nations. It may seem something of a paradox that the United States was becoming relatively more important in the world economy at the same time that the world economy was becoming relatively less important to the United States.

The paradox is resolved by the fact that economic growth was more rapid in the United States than elsewhere. In the setting of world trade and production between the American Civil War and World War I, the United States developed into the most powerful industrial nation while at the same time maintaining and even increasing its importance as a major supplier of foodstuffs and raw materials to western Europe and other parts of the world. American industrial growth was the key factor in its rise to economic pre-eminence. In 1870, the United States' share in world manufacturing output was 23.3 percent, second to that of Great Britain. But by 1913, the United States share rose to 35.8 percent and greatly outdistanced the shares of Britain, Germany, and France, its major rivals in manufacturing. (See Table 16–2.)

TABLE 16-2

The Growing United States Share in World Manufacturing Output
(World = 100 percent)

Period	U.S.A.	United Kingdom	Germany	France	Russia	Others
1870	23.3	31.8	13.2	10.3	3.7	17.7
1881-1885	28.6	26.6	13.9	8.6	3.4	18.9
1896-1900	30.1	19.5	16.6	7.1	5.0	21.7
1906-1910	35.3	14.7	15.9	6.4	5.6	22.7
1913	35.8	14.0	15.7	6.4	5.3	22.6

SOURCE: Folke Hilgerdt, Industrialization and Foreign Trade (Geneva: League of Nations, 1945), p. 13.

TRENDS IN FOREIGN TRADE AND PAYMENTS

Between 1860 and 1914 a dramatic increase in the value of United States merchandise exports and imports occurred. Exports rose from about $340 million to a figure six times as large, or $2.4 billion; meanwhile, imports grew from $360 million to $1.9 billion, a fourfold increase. From 1860 to 1873, with the one exception of 1862, American imports exceeded exports. But in 1874 a permanent revolution in American foreign trade began. From then until 1914 American exports exceeded American imports in value, with the exception of three years: 1875, 1888, and 1893. Yet spectacular as these increases in exports and imports were, they represented, as noted earlier, a relatively small and declining percentage of the gross national product. Exports, for instance, reached a high of 9 percent of the GNP in 1879 but then slowly sank to 6 percent in 1914; during the same period imports reached a peak of 7.1 percent in 1869 and gradually declined to 5.3 percent in 1914.

The maturing of the American economy was evident in the dramatic changes that occurred in the composition of American trade between the 1870s and the 1910s. In the 1870s, over four fifths of American exports consisted of raw materials and foodstuffs whereas less than one fifth was nonfood manufactures. By the 1910s the share of nonfood manufactures rose to about one half. On the import side the changes were not quite so marked, but the share of imported manufactures declined somewhat, whereas that of raw materials increased quite rapidly. In short, between the Civil War and World War I the nature of the United States' comparative advantage in the world economy shifted away from agriculture and toward manufacturing.

The export of American manufactured goods to Europe and other parts of the world from 1890 to 1914 was considered so great that some writers described it as an American "commercial invasion" of Europe. The most important manufactured exports in terms of value were iron and steel manufactures, refined petroleum, copper, cotton goods, leather and leather products, and agricultural implements. Among the specific articles listed under the heading of iron and steel manufactures were electrical machinery, sewing machines, typewriters, locomotives, cash registers, and shoe machinery. These manufactured exports reflected the industrialization of the American economy and the increasing ability of various American manufacturers to compete in foreign markets with leading European industrial powers such as Great Britain and Germany. At the same time imports of crude materials other than foodstuffs became relatively more important to the American economy, reflecting the growing economic relations between the United States and various supply-source areas in Asia, Oceania, the Middle East, Canada, and Latin America. (See Table 16–3.)

From 1860 to 1914 Europe was America's greatest market and also its chief source of imports. In 1870 that continent, including the United

TABLE 16-3

The Expansion of United States Foreign Trade 1861-1915

Period	Merchandise in Millions of Dollars		Excess of Exports (+) or Imports (−)	Value per Capita	
	Exports	Imports		Exports	Imports
1861-1870	320	351	−30	6.73	8.94
1871-1880	650	566	+85	12.86	11.87
1881-1890	817	741	+76	13.31	12.12
1896-1900	1,138	845	+292	14.41	10.81
1906-1910	1,741	1,271	+469	18.54	13.29
1911-1915	2,515	1,837	+678	23.98	17.46

SOURCE: Statistical Abstract of the United States, 1957, pp. 888-889.

Kingdom as a leading customer, took 80 percent of American exports; gradually the figure fell, but in 1914 it was still 64 percent. As for imports, 55 percent came from Europe in 1870; by 1914 its share dropped to 46 percent. As American trade with Europe declined, Asia—especially Japan, the Philippines, and Indonesia—grew in importance as a supplier of products for the American market and as an absorber of American exports. Next to Asia in economic importance were America's commercial relations with Canada and Latin America. American trade with Africa and Oceania increased rather rapidly in the pre–1914 era, but the amounts involved were still very small.

Changes in the United States's balance of payments with the rest of the world in the late-nineteenth century showed the maturing of the American economy. In earlier decades, imports of goods and services typically exceeded exports, and the United States financed its deficit on current account by means of loans from foreigners eager to earn the high returns on capital invested in America. Payments deficits on current account thus were balanced by surpluses, or net credits, on capital account. During the 1870s the balance of commodity trade shifted from deficit to surplus, but for some two decades the whole current account remained in deficit because trade surpluses were more than offset by payments to foreigners in the form of interest and dividends, tourist expenditures overseas, transportation charges, and remittances from immigrants who sent a portion of their earnings in the United States to relatives and friends in their native lands.

The continuing deficits on current account from the 1870s to the 1890s were offset, as they had been earlier, by credits arising from the flow of foreign capital to the United States and also from small exports of specie. In these decades the capital coming to America from overseas—mostly from Europe—went into the development of American railroads and cattle, land, and mining enterprises. But during the 1890s there were signs that the centuries-old pattern of Americans importing capital was beginning to change. The current account of the balance of payments followed one of its components, the commodity trade account, into surplus, and America's net current earnings from international commerce were used to finance investments in other countries. The United States had transformed itself from a capital-poor to a capital-rich economy. Since 1914 the United States typically has lent overseas more than it has borrowed from abroad. (See Table 16–4.)

THE PROTECTIVE TARIFF

The increase in American exports from 1860 to 1914 was higher than that of imports by a ratio of three to two. A major reason for this disparity was the use of the protective tariff by the Republican party to "protect" various American industries by excluding or limiting the flow of

TABLE 16-4

U.S. International Balance of Payments 1869-1913, Five-Year Totals
(millions of dollars)

Period[1]	Merchandise, Net (1)	Services: Income on Investments, Net (2)	Other Services (3)	Net Unilateral Transfers (4)	Current Account Balance (5)	U.S. Capital[3] (6)	Foreign Capital[2] (7)	Capital Account Balance (8)	Net Change in Monetary Gold Stock[3] (9)	Errors and Omissions (10)
1869-1873	−553	−418	+170	+16	−785	0	0	+786	0	+1
1874-1878	+488	−459	+151	−60	+120	0	0	−48	−71	−1
1879-1883	+820	−418	−16	−52	+334	0	0	−10	−324	0
1884-1888	+278	−474	−311	−137	−644	0	0	+794	−150	0
1889-1893	+290	−659	−176	−237	−782	0	0	+719	+63	0
1894-1898	+1316	−621	−114	−243	+338	0	0	−191	−148	1
1899-1903	+2612	−463	−179	−487	+1483	0	0	−848	−424	−211
1904-1908	+2500	−339	−565	−786	+810	−454	+454	0	−465	−345
1909-1913	+2265	−351	−937	−1034	−57	−699	+1171	+472	−249	−166

[1] Fiscal years through 1900; thereafter, calendar years.
[2] An outflow of funds is shown as negative.
[3] An increase is shown as negative.

NOTE: From 1869 to 1898 the capital account balance functions in effect in the same way as the errors and omissions item does from 1899 to 1913. From 1881 through 1899 the figures for net change in the monetary gold stock are also included in the totals for the capital account balance.

SOURCE: U.S. Census Bureau, Statistical History of the United States from Colonial Times to the Present (New York: Basic Books, 1976), Series U 1-25, pp. 864-68; Harold G. Vatter, The Drive to Industrial Maturity (Westport, Conn.: Greenwood Press, 1975), p. 310.

competing products from abroad, particularly those from the United Kingdom and Germany. Because changes in tariff rates could either increase or decrease competition from foreign producers, they had important effects, at least in the short run, on the profits of particular industries and the economic welfare of all connected with those industries. Policy decisions on the tariff thus became the subject of intense lobbying and pressure politics as various producing groups tried to use governmental powers and processes to further their private economic interests. Considerations of consumer welfare were not very important in the policy debates and decisions. Because there were many more consumers than producers and because the interest of any individual consumer in a decision usually was not very great, it was difficult to organize effective consumer opposition to highly protective duties. Tariff policies, therefore, affected economic welfare by redistributing income from consumers to producers, and also among various groups of producers. Whether the protective tariff had much effect on the nation's economic growth is much less certain.

During the three decades before the Civil War the average ad valorem duties on imports moved downward from 49 to 20 percent and reversed in large measure the protectionist trend that had developed between 1816 and 1832. But the secession of eleven southern states enabled organized northern industrial groups, with their free-soil farming allies in the Republican party, to gain control of Congress. They then enacted high protective tariff legislation, partly to get revenue for waging the Civil War, and partly to aid American manufacturers in meeting foreign competition while burdened by heavy internal taxes during the war. Three minor tariff acts were passed between 2 March and 24 December 1861. As the war progressed and the need for revenue constantly increased, Congress was induced by different pressure groups, led by iron, cotton, and woolen manufacturers, to change the tariff again and again. Two major tariff statutes were enacted in July 1862 and June 1864. The average ad valorem rates on dutiable commodities were increased from 37.3 percent under the 1862 act to 49 percent.

At the end of the Civil War, federal revenues exceeded the needs of the national government. By 1872 most of the internal taxes, including the income tax, had been abolished in response to strong pressures for relief from the heavy Civil War taxes. But no similar drastic action was taken towards the reduction of import duties. The 1864 Morrill Tariff Act, although an emergency war measure, remained virtually unchanged for over twenty years. Although most Democrats and some Republicans favored a tariff for revenue, the Republicans, who controlled Congress for most of the period between 1865 and 1912, were able to retain or increase most Civil War tariff duties.

After 1880 the large Treasury surpluses created public pressure for reduction of high protective tariff duties, but no effective reduction was achieved for decades. In 1890 the Republicans achieved a drastic extension of high protection through the McKinley Tariff Act. Average customs rates on dutiable items came to 49 percent. One concession to consumers was the putting of raw sugar on the free list, but a bounty was given for the production of sugar within the United States.

Four years later the Democrats made a gallant effort to reduce the protective duties on manufactured goods. But protectionist Republicans and Democrats in the Senate prevented tariff reform and made the Wilson-Gorman Tariff Act of 1894 into a statute with only slightly moderated protective intent. The average ad valorem rate on dutiable goods was 41 percent. A duty was again imposed upon raw sugar; this benefited the sugar growers of Louisiana, but harmed Cuban sugar interests.

The 1896 election was waged primarily on the free silver issue, but the victorious Republicans acted as if they had received a mandate for a high protective tariff. The next year they pushed through Congress the Dingley Tariff Act with the second highest average rate on dutiable goods in American history—52 percent. During the twelve years that the Dingley Tariff Act was enforced a strong public opinion developed in favor of downward revision of the tariff. The Payne-Aldrich Tariff Act of 1909, however, preserved the extremely high rate structure and the hostile attitude toward foreign trade of the earlier 1890 and 1897 tariff measures. Nevertheless, the average ad valorem duty on dutiable goods went downward to about 42 percent. For the first time in decades the extreme champions of protection were on the defensive.

In the election of 1912, Woodrow Wilson came to power on a reform program directed against high protective tariffs and monopolistic big business. The next year he succeeded in getting Congress to pass the Underwood-Simmons Tariff Act, in defiance of powerful lobbying by industrial interests. The new law greatly expanded the "free list" of articles excepted from tariff duties. Yet moderate protection was given to "legitimate" domestic industries; hence, the average ad valorem rate on dutiable goods fell only to 36 percent during the first year the new tariff was in effect. With the return to moderate protection went a provision for an income tax, which had been made possible by enactment of the Sixteenth Amendment to the Constitution. As a result the burden of taxation was shifted from the low-income to the high-income classes, and there was a reduction in the cost of living for consumers.

Most discussions of the protective tariff have stressed the nominal rates imposed on specific commodities and have given the average ad valorem rate as a measure of the protection given to domestic industries. But recently economists have discovered that the effective rates of protection were often much higher than the nominal rates. This occurred when, for example, finished goods like woolen and cotton textiles and steel rails were made from raw materials and components taxed at lower rates. In the case of cotton textiles, if the value of cotton produced domestically or imported free of duty made up half the value of the final product, then the effective tariff duty on cloth was twice the nominal duty, say 20 percent rather than 10 percent. The implication of these new analyses for tariff history is that the profits made by industrialists and the costs imposed upon consumers were much greater than past opponents of the protective tariff realized.

Although tariffs redistributed income from consumers to producers and between various groups of producers that were protected to different degrees, economists disagree about their effects on the nation's economic growth. The judgment of most economists is that tariffs are barriers to trade that hinder economic growth by interfering with international specialization and the exploitation of comparative advantages. In the United States, however, rates of economic growth during the period of high tariffs from the Civil War to World War I were as high as at any other time in the nation's history. Protectionist economists argue that the potentially adverse effects of tariffs on economic growth may have been offset in part by the absence of restrictions on the flow of labor and capital to the United States from abroad and by the increased capital investment in, and efficiency of, some, if not all, of the protected industries.

Another consideration that these economists invoke relates to government finance. Tariff duties furnished a large part of federal revenue. To have maintained the same revenue in the absence of protection would have required other forms of taxation, with other effects on economic efficiency and growth. To have reduced revenues through lower customs duties would have meant reduced budget surpluses or increased federal deficits. These, too, would have necessitated other policy changes affecting growth and welfare. For example, reduced budget surpluses would have meant less federal debt retirement in the late nineteenth century. As we saw in chapter 15, debt retirement may have stimulated capital formation and economic growth. Considerations such as the foregoing illustrate the problems that arise in attempting to reach sound conclusions about the effects of tariffs on growth and welfare.

TERRITORIAL AND ECONOMIC EXPANSION OVERSEAS

The late-nineteenth century emergence of the United States as the world's pre-eminent industrial power kindled the interest of various private and governmental decision-making groups in markets and territories overseas. Products ranging from those that embodied advanced technologies to those that were simple but cheap attracted the attention of foreign buyers, and America's mass manufacturers were ready to supply them. At the same time, the rapid growth of American industry created a demand for raw materials from abroad, and the rising incomes of Americans increased their demands for imported consumer goods. Behind these developments was an international diplomatic-economic system in which many of the industrial nations of the world were seeking to expand their colonial possessions and spheres of influence around the world.

American territorial expansion in the nineteenth century was relatively limited. In 1867, the United States, for strategic rather than economic reasons, purchased Alaska from Russia for $7.2 million. Later in the century, largely as a result of the Spanish-American War in 1898, the United States acquired Puerto Rico, Guam, and the Philippine Islands as outright colonies, and in 1901 Cuba was made a self-governing protectorate of the United States. The motivations for these decisions for territorial expansion were partly strategic and partly economic. Another result of the 1898 war with Spain was that the United States annexed Hawaii, ostensibly for strategic reasons. However, Hawaii had fallen under the control of American sugar planters in 1893, and annexation made Hawaiian sugar a domestic American product with duty-free entry to the mainland.

Except for the Alaskan and the Spanish-American War episodes, American expansion, or imperialism, involved no acquisition of foreign territory, but rather "dollar diplomacy," that is, intervention in the affairs of neighboring countries in support of previous American financial or commercial penetrations. In the early twentieth century this activity was focused on the Caribbean, where fear of European imperialist designs and strategic concern for the Panama Canal were dominant factors in American policy. American military interventions, followed by the establishment of protectorates, occurred in Panama in 1903, in the Dominican Republic in 1905 and 1916, in Nicaragua in 1912, and in Haiti in 1915. The Panama incident arose out of American strategic interests and gave to the United States a seemingly perpetual lease of the Canal Zone. In Nicaragua, the American government gained the right to build a canal and a naval base while American bankers won control over Nicaragua's finances, banking, and railways. As a result of all these American actions from 1898 on, and the purchase of the Virgin Islands in 1917, the Caribbean came to be considered an "American lake."

American interests were also involved in Mexico where a series of revolutions occurred between 1910 and 1920. American business interests had huge investments in Mexican mines, oilfields, railroads, and rubber plantations. President Wilson refused to recognize the first revolutionary government, a conservative one established by force under General Huerta. Wilson did recognize the leader of the popular party, Carranza, as Mexican president in 1914. Yet this American support for the new government did not prevent the Mexican constitution of 1917 from vesting all subsoil rights in the Mexican people and thereby furnishing the legal basis for Mexico's expropriation in 1938 of all foreign oil holdings.

In China the United States also attempted to gain influence, although with less success than in Latin America. After the defeat of China by Japan in 1895, England, France, Germany, and Russia had obtained naval bases, ports, and spheres of influence from the weak Chinese government. American businessmen feared that China would be closed to American trade, and missionaries argued that they needed government protection to operate in the Far East. The result was that in 1899 and 1900 the United States asked the European powers to accept an Open Door Policy in China which would mean the granting of free trading opportunities to all nations. When all the powers involved except Russia agreed, John Hay, the secretary of state, announced the Open Door Policy to be in operation. During the Taft administration (1909–13), the American State Department tried to get American bankers to join European bankers in making investments in Chinese railroads. But the outbreak of revolution in China in 1911 threatened the success of this enterprise, and in 1913 President Wilson withdrew American support from the venture. He feared that it impinged upon China's sovereignty and might invite foreign intervention.

Conclusions

Between 1840 and 1890 a nationwide marketing system emerged in the United States as the country became integrated through railroad and water transportation, and as many individuals and families became less self-sufficient and more dependent upon the wholesale and retail merchants for the exchange of goods and services. The growth of cities and mass production industries led to the integration of urban retail marketing through department stores and chain stores. Meanwhile mail-order houses carried out the same function of integration for the rural market. All these developments helped the consumer obtain a greater variety of goods, often at lower prices and with greater convenience than had been possible before.

From the 1850s to the early 1880s wholesalers dominated the American distribution system. They performed many valuable services as middlemen between domestic and foreign manufacturers on the one hand, and between general country stores and urban retailers on the other. But a revolution in mass distribution occurred when manufacturing companies increasingly eliminated the wholesaler by dealing directly with retailers and the ultimate consumers. Independent wholesalers continued to play an important part in some sectors of the distribution system, but they handled a declining percentage of the total volume of manufactured goods flowing from American factories.

As the United States rose to industrial pre-eminence, the nation's long established patterns of economic relations with the rest of the world were altered. The balance of foreign trade became favorable, with merchandise exports exceeding imports, and by the early twentieth century the United States became a net exporter of capital. Although traditional exports of agricultural commodities continued to increase, exports of American manufactures increased much more rapidly. The United States was developing the largest free trade area in world history at home, but its stance toward the rest of the world during and after the Civil War became highly protectionist. Well organized manufacturing interests secured economic gains at the expense of consumers and foreign producers through steep tariffs on imported goods.

Decisions to erect barriers to the flow of foreign products into the United States did not reflect a policy of isolation. On the contrary, the United States—like other industrial powers—became caught up in the scramble for overseas territories and spheres of influence. The purchase of Alaska, the annexation of Hawaii, and the acquisition of territories resulting from the brief war with Spain were motivated more by strategic and political than by economic considerations. But the United States government then developed in Latin America and the Far East a "dollar diplomacy" based upon the interests of American businessmen and bankers. Champions of "dollar diplomacy" contended that the standard of living of the people in Latin America and the Far East was raised and that the American consumer benefited from the products exported from these areas to the United States. Moreover, the United States by such actions often prevented European intervention in Latin America. Yet the dislike for the United States that "dollar diplomacy" created in areas such as Central and South America was to make later generations of Americans conscious of the need to fashion more enlightened diplomatic and commercial policies to promote the nation's international interests.

SUGGESTED READINGS

Two superb books on the history of the revolution in mass distribution are: Alfred Chandler, The Visible Hand: The Managerial Revolution in American Business (Cambridge, Mass.: Harvard University Press, 1977); and Thomas C. Cochran, 200 Years of American Business (New York: Basic Books, 1977). Some excellent supplementary studies are Lewis Atherton, Main Street on the Middle Border (Bloomington: Indiana University Press, 1954); Harold Barger, Distribution's Place in the American Economy Since 1869 (Princeton: Princeton University Press, 1950); Paul J. Stewart and J. Frederic Dewhurst, Does Distribution Cost Too Much? (New York: Twentieth Century Fund, 1939); Glenn Porter and Harold C. Livesay, Merchants and Manufacturers (Baltimore: Johns Hopkins University Press, 1971), and Harvey S. Perloff et al., Regions, Resources and Economic Growth (Baltimore: Johns Hopkins University Press,

1960). For a penetrating study of the role of large corporations and the courts in overcoming state and local barriers to nationwide marketing, see Charles W. McCurdy, "American Law and the Marketing Structure of the Large Corporation, 1875–1890," *The Journal of Economic History,* 38 (September 1978), 631–649.

The importance of American foreign commerce is brought out in Robert E. Lipsey, *Price and Quantity Trends in the Foreign Trade of the United States* (Princeton: Princeton University Press, 1963); that of the protective tariff in Sidney Ratner, *The Tariff in American History* (New York: D. Van Nostrand, 1972). The role of business and banking interests in American territorial and commercial expansion has elicited sharply conflicting interpretations. Objective accounts of salient facts are to be found in Cleona Lewis, *America's Stake in International Investments* (Washington, D.C.: Brookings Institution, 1938); and Mira Wilkins, *The Emergence of Multinational Enterprise: American Business Abroad from the Colonial Era to 1914* (Cambridge, Mass.: Harvard University Press, 1970). Stringent criticism of American diplomacy and pressures from business interests is given in Walter LaFeber, *The New Empire . . . American Expansion, 1860–1898* (Ithaca: Cornell University Press, 1963); and other volumes by William A. Williams and his followers. Studies that challenge the theories, facts, and conclusions of the "Williams school" include James A. Field, Jr., et al., "American Imperialism," *American Historical Review,* 83 (June 1978), 644–683; Paul S. Holbo, "Economics, Emotion, and Expansion," in H. Wayne Morgan, ed., *The Gilded Age,* rev. ed. (Syracuse: Syracuse University Press, 1970); John A. S. Grenville and George B. Young, *Politics, Strategy, and American Diplomacy . . . 1893–1917* (New Haven: Yale University Press, 1966); and Marilyn B. Young, *The Rhetoric of Empire: American China Policy, 1895–1901* (Cambridge, Mass.: Harvard University Press, 1968). D. K. Fieldhouse, *Economics and Empire, 1830–1914* (Ithaca: Cornell University Press, 1973); and W. Arthur Lewis, *Growth and Fluctuations, 1871–1914* (London: Allen & Unwin, 1978) are valuable for penetrating analyses and balanced perspectives on the world scene.

PART IV

THE

SUPERINDUSTRIAL

ECONOMY

(1914-1979)

INTRODUCTION

Since 1914 the United States has been the foremost industrial nation of the world. Great advances in science and technology promoted a tremendous increase in the production of a wide variety of goods. New industries emerged, like synthetic fabrics and aircraft. New power sources, such as electricity, and new forms of transport, like the automobile, changed the American way of life. Meanwhile, a technological revolution transformed agriculture and increased productivity so much that the percentage of those engaged in farming dropped from about 30 percent of the labor force in 1914 to about 2 percent in 1979.

Parallel scientific and technological developments affected transportation. The dominance of railroads ended in the 1930s, to be succeeded by that of the automobile. Since the 1940s and 1950s, where high-velocity mobility is involved, the airplane has reigned supreme. Inland water transport in the last two decades has gradually taken a more important place in the national economy, but our foreign merchant marine has declined greatly, except in wartime, and has survived mainly through subsidies.

The long-run rise in the U.S. GNP, although interrupted by several recessions and the Great Depression, was accompanied by a corresponding trend in consumer income, standards of living, and volume of consumer expenditures. This made possible the high level of mass consumption that at the same time absorbed and stimulated the mass production of goods. The largest portion of consumers' incomes was spent on domestic goods, but increasing amounts of American dollars have gone for foreign imports, especially in recent decades.

Since 1914, while American industry, transportation and commerce have been expanding dramatically, the labor force made remarkable progress. Real income has risen, hours of work decreased, and Social Security was instituted. The rise in the general wage level was achieved through increases in labor productivity, due to capital investment in machinery and the improved education and skill of workers. Nevertheless, workers suffered extensive unemployment in the depression and there was hard-core unemployment in periods of prosperity.

Small and medium-sized businessmen worried about the competition and power of giant corporations; small farmers, tenant farmers, and farm workers have been concerned about their economic survival and welfare.

Unprofitable railroad companies and overseas merchant ship companies expressed anxiety about domestic and foreign competition. Industrial workers have complained about job insecurity, low wages, and other grievances against employers. All these groups have turned to the government for help either through government regulation or subsidy. As a result, the responsibilities and the exercise of power by the government, particularly in Washington, have mounted gigantically since World War I and particularly since the Great Depression.

During the last six decades numerous reasons led government to play an important economic role in different situations or movements. One such situation has been war and the government controls war has evoked over production, the allocation of resources, taxation, prices, the use and consumption of scarce commodities, and manpower. Another has been economic crisis—a recession, or deep depression when pressure for expansionary fiscal and monetary policies has often been overwhelming. A third situation has involved the effort to limit glaring inequalities of wealth and income through estate and income taxation. A fourth has centered on pollution and environmental problems; a fifth, on health and safety of workers in dangerous occupations, and of consumers endangered by unhealthy or injurious articles. A sixth has revolved around the persistent problem of unemployment and has made the government attempt to achieve high-level employment. A seventh has had businessmen and corporations seeking tariff protection against foreign competition and asking for financial aid when faced by bankruptcy.

All these demands by different pressure groups made the government into a wielder of tremendous power. Although some eloquent theorists and business groups have appealed for a return to the limited government prevalent in Thomas Jefferson's day, it seems reasonable to believe that some form of strong government will continue to exist. The problem rather is one of judging what is the proper measure of power that the government should have, not whether it should have any power at all, or only the minimum power of a century ago.

CHAPTER 17

―――

Science-Based Industries and
New Corporate Structures

For over six decades from 1914 to the 1970s, in times of peace and of war, the United States has been the superindustrial power of the world. None of the other great powers, no matter how powerful militarily, or how large in territory or population, approaches the magnitude of the United States in economic strength. As early as 1913 the United States produced 36 percent of the world's manufactured goods as against 16 percent for Germany and 14 percent for the United Kingdom. During the following sixty years America's share in world industrial output has been, with some variations, close to 40 percent. This relative and absolute superiority in manufacturing production has been decisive in the United States' ability to help its allies win two world wars. It has also been the basis for the United States occupying a pivotal place in the peacetime world economy through its foreign trade, its investments abroad, and its power to attract foreign capital to the United States.

The Importance of American Industry

During World War I the demand for American industrial products increased as never before. The main expansion occurred in the metal, chemical, and machine industries that produced the weapons of war, but

huge orders also went to such industries as flour milling, canning, and
wool manufacturing. Between 1914 and 1919 the value added by manufacture rose from $10 billion to $25 billion in current dollars. At the end
of the war American industrial capacity was greatly in excess of the peacetime demand.

Although in the early 1920s both the United States and Great Britain
suffered a brief, yet severe, economic depression, the middle and later
years of that decade were marked by continual growth of industrial pro-
suffered a brief, yet severe, economic depression, the middle and later
duction throughout the world. A peak in world industrial production of
nearly 48 percent above the 1913 level was achieved in 1929. (The figure
excludes Soviet Russia.) Prosperity in the United States was based upon a
widespread boom which carried to greater lengths the economic advances
of World War I, particularly in new industries with a promising future like
automobiles, rubber, and electricity. In the next three years, however, the
Great Depression, especially in the United States and Germany, wiped out
all the production gains and by 1932 brought down the world's output to
below the 1913 level. The New Deal did much to counteract the worst effects of the Depression, but the Roosevelt administration was not able to
bring about a steady recovery in production to match the 1929 peak.

The outbreak of World War II in Europe in 1939 and the entrance of the United States into the war in 1941 definitely ended the Depression and led to a phenomenal increase in the industrial production of
the United States. Between 1939 and 1944 the gross national product of
the United States (the total output of goods and services), measured in
current dollars, increased by almost 125 percent. The volume of manufactured goods, moreover, far outpaced the general rise; it nearly tripled in
these five years as American plants succeeded in pouring out planes and
guns, ships and shells, tools and tanks, plus civilian goods in massive
volumes. Meanwhile the output of raw materials increased by 60 percent.
By 1944 the United States had indeed become the "arsenal of democracy." It outproduced the Axis in combat munitions by more than 50
percent and accounted for nearly 45 percent of the combined armament
output of all belligerent nations.

This achievement was made possible by the expansion of manufacturing facilities in the United States through the construction of a vast
number of new plants. Between 1939 and 1944, manufacturing concerns
spent over $13 billion on new plants and new equipment, while the fed-
eral government spent approximately the same amount for the same purpose. Most of this investment went into the manufacture of aircraft, synthetic rubber, chemicals, and other important wartime products.

As World War II came to a close many economists and businessmen
were worried about the possibility of a great postwar depression and a
drop in the level of prosperity and employment to one far below that of
World War II. But these apprehensions proved to be unwarranted. Al-

though recessions occurred between 1945 and the mid-1970s, most of them lasted only about a year or less, and none of them approached the severity of the Great Depression of 1929–1933. During these three decades American manufacturing output increased steadily, with only minor setbacks. According to the Federal Reserve Board's index, manufacturing production doubled between 1945 and 1965 and tripled between 1945 and 1976.

LABOR PRODUCTIVITY IN MANUFACTURING

Manufacturing has been recognized by economists and the general public as the largest single sector of the American economy. Between 1869 and 1969 the share of manufacturing in the national income rose from 15 percent to 30 percent, with a slight decline to 25 percent in the 1970s. Meanwhile, the share of manufacturing in the national labor force rose from 17.6 percent in 1869 to about 26 percent in the 1960s and the 1970s. Since the 1960s the growth of the service and information-processing industries has increasingly challenged the dominance of the manufacturing industries. Nevertheless, they always will be important as an indispensable source of supply in peace and war for consumer and capital goods as well as defense weapons.

A notable feature of American manufacturing has been the impressive increase in its labor productivity. In the half century between 1860 and 1910 labor productivity in manufacturing, measured by the value added per worker, had doubled, and in the half-century from 1910 to 1960 labor productivity quadrupled. Since the amount of capital invested in industry had not grown sufficiently to explain this acceleration, many economists have concluded that technological innovation and improvements in the conditions of industrial production have been major sources for this advance in labor productivity. But other factors undoubtedly have to be considered, such as economies of scale within individual industries, efficient interindustry resource allocation within the manufacturing sector, and the quality and availability of natural and human resources within and outside the boundaries of the United States. Still another factor that enhanced the productivity of industry is the volume of public services such as transportation facilities, education, and public health and safety.

Between 1966 and 1978, however, a sharp decrease in productivity occurred both in the American economy as a whole and in the manufacturing sector. Output per man-hour in manufacturing since 1965 increased much less in the United States than in eleven other advanced countries. Between 1965 and 1970 the average United States annual rate of increase was 2.0 percent as against 6.7 percent for the other eleven countries. The differential was considerably less after 1970, and wage-rate increases abroad exceeded productivity by a larger margin than in the United States. Although American trends in unit labor costs and prices were favorable, these international comparisons nevertheless aroused concern over the recent United States productivity record and may help to explain the reason for the excess of imports over exports in the United States in recent years.

TECHNOLOGY AND INDUSTRIAL CHANGE

One important reason for the spurt in labor productivity since the Civil War was the remarkable advance in technology. In the nineteenth century innovations sprang in large part from predominantly empirical inventive activity and owed little to abstract scientific principles or organized knowledge. Twentieth-century technology, on the other hand, according to the researches of Nathan Rosenberg, saw a shift in inventive activity away from the empirically-based toward the newer science-based industries. Instead of the crude empiricism and trial-and-error methods of previous generations, this new technology was based upon the mastery of systematic, complex bodies of knowledge.

An unusual number of important technological breakthroughs created new products and in certain cases new industries. New types of steel came from advances in ferrous metallurgy. The chemical industries used discoveries in molecular chemistry for the creation of a variety of organic polymers, ranging from plastics, synthetic fibers, packaging materials, synthetic rubber, light-weight thermal insulation, and water-repellent coatings to high-strength adhesives. Those same industries exploited the achievement of chemists in the transformation of materials through changes in atomic or molecular structure to obtain the refinement of fuels like petroleum, natural gases and coal, and of basic raw materials needed for the production of cement, rubber, and glass.

In the field of physics, progress in quantum mechanics and semiconductor technology laid the basis for the invention of the transistor, its supplanting of the vacuum tube, and the development of electronic data processing. The growth of the computer industry in America was based upon these advances. The development of modern genetics and biochemistry had equally revolutionary results in plant and animal breeding, and in the utilization of herbicides, insecticides, and commercial fertilizers, especially synthetic nitrogenous fertilizers. Here again a whole sector of the American economy, agriculture, became transformed through these discoveries.

Competition between industries was stimulated through the discovery and the use of new materials substitutes, for example, aluminum instead of steel, structural concrete instead of steel, plastics as a substitute for natural fibers, wood, rubber, leather, glass, and many metals. Substitutes for standard products of the past were also made possible through the use of synthetic materials such as rayon instead of natural fibers like cotton and silk.

In the field of energy, two innovations involved the development of the steam turbine and the electric motor as means of transmitting "fractionalized" electric power on a low-cost, mass-production basis. The related area, research on the atom bomb, led not only to the production of nuclear weapons on a larger scale than those of World War II, but also to the emergence of nuclear power plants for peacetime energy uses.

New dimensions in the transportation sector of the economy were opened up by the invention of the airplane in the early 1900s and of rockets and outer space vehicles in the World War II and post-World War II periods. Of comparable importance in the health field were discoveries in basic medical research, from the 1920s to the 1970s, resulting in such practical achievements as antibiotics, heart pacers, laser beams, and new methods of cataract surgery.

The impact of these technological innovations upon the American economy was so great that one may be justified in saying that they have caused a second industrial revolution. Industrial production processes in the last four decades challenged the dominance of mechanization in industry and made chemistry, electronics, biology, and nuclear physics into recognized foundations of contemporary American industry. In addition to new producer goods, this new technology made available to the American public an unprecedented variety of novel and improved consumer products. New types of food, clothing, household furnishings, housing materials, transportation facilities, and entertainment became so abundant as to transform the everyday life of the average American and to create in some cases a communication gap between generations.

Important as basic scientific and technological research is to the advancement of industry, this beneficial connection was not apparent to big business corporations until the end of the nineteenth century. Among the earliest firms to establish laboratories were Edison, Kodak, Goodrich, General Electric, DuPont, and the Bell Telephone System. The industrial research and development (R & D) laboratory was an important departure from the past practice of relying upon the inventions of independent individuals like Eli Whitney, Samuel Morse, and Cyrus McCormick. Since World War I, R & D expenditures by private business and government have increased at a considerably higher rate than that of the net national product. At first, private industry was the main source of support, but during and after World War II the federal government became increasingly involved, until now it finances almost two thirds of all R & D.

The lion's share of these expenditures (66 to 70 percent in the latter half of the 1960s) went to development rather than to basic scientific research. Indeed, private business often focused on such modest objectives as the annual design changes of consumer durables. And the federal government concentrated most of its spending on defense and space technology. Thus, while the great increase in research and development generated much economic growth, a disproportionate percentage of the R & D expenditures probably went to military and political objectives rather than to ones that might have brought the social welfare of the American people to a still higher level.

Changes in American Industry

The history of American industry after World War I reveals a changing pattern as individual industries varied in their rates of growth. Some gave way to new industries or to expanding old ones, while some remained fairly stable. Others made great advances and provided the conditions for the development of new corporate structures.

Among those industries suffering setbacks owing to competition from new industries or expanding old ones were: coal, as against petroleum, natural gas, and hydroelectric energy; cotton textiles, as against rayon, nylon, and other synthetic fibers; lumber, as against concrete, metals, and plastics; and gas and kerosene lamps, as against electric lighting. Industries in which, except in wartime, there was stability or a decrease in rate of growth, included leather, iron and steel, and the older nonferrous metals. Among those experiencing a tremendous growth, the most spectacular example was perhaps the automobile industry, both in terms of its unusually fast expansion and its impact upon such related industries as steel, rubber, glass, and petroleum. Research and development in industrial chemistry resulted in a transformation of the petroleum refining, rubber, and paper industries, and led to the emergence of new industries involved in the manufacture of such products as light metals, plastics, and synthetic fibers.

Dramatic confirmation of the shifting picture is provided by United States government data on manufactures. Of the ten largest industries (measured by value added by manufacture) listed in 1960, only two had appeared in a similar 1910 list. Examination of four of the growth pacesetters—motor vehicles, synthetic chemicals, aircraft, and machine tools—adds depth to our understanding of the dynamics of the American economy.

AUTOMOBILES AND MASS PRODUCTION

The progressive assembly-line, mass-production system introduced by Henry Ford in 1913–14 constituted epoch-making innovations in business management and in the integration of industrial operations. These changes progressively reduced the cost and sales price of cars so that by the mid-1920s mass personal ownership of automobiles became a reality. By that time automobile manufacturing ranked first in value of product and third in value of exports among American industries. From that time on the automobile industry was the life blood of the petroleum industry, one of the main customers of the steel industry, and the largest consumer of numerous other industrial products, especially plate glass, rubber, and lacquers.

The first great period of rapid growth for the automobile industry ended with Great Depression of the 1930s. The low point was 1932 with the sale of only 1.3 million cars, but gradually sales picked up, especially after World War II. Between 1919 and 1949 the number of cars and trucks produced each year increased more than two and one-half times, but from 1949 to 1971 United States car and truck production grew by less than three quarters. By the 1960s the automobile had come to be regarded as a major social problem especially in relation to environmental pollution, urban sprawl, the increasing cost of living, and the large number of accidental deaths and injuries. In the 1970s the Arab oil embargo and dramatic increases in the cost of oil caused many American car owners to shift to the purchase of small cars, many of them from Europe and Japan.

Since the 1960s, U.S. automobile corporations have been losing their international advantage in productivity and sales. As a result of this situation and of the problems caused by the energy crisis, automobile manufacturers, their customers, and the national government will have to make hard decisions concerning the future role of automobiles in American society and its economy. Shall American manufacturers concentrate on the production of small cars? Should there be a major shift to mass transit? Should the government intervene in the producer-consumer decision-making process by using rewards and penalties to support a new national transportation policy? Whatever the answers to these questions, it is unlikely that the giant automobile companies will fade away. If mass transportation were adopted on a large scale, it seems probable that General Motors and Ford would make their main business the designing of modular transportation systems for metropolitan areas. In that case, the American automobile industry would continue to be prosperous and powerful through diversification of products.

THE NEW CHEMISTRY

Although chemistry and chemical processes in American industry underwent considerable development between 1880 and 1914, the military demands of World War I more than doubled the output of chemical products. In the 1920s chemical firms turned to the peacetime manufacture of carbon, nitrogen compounds, sodium, and other basic chemicals. The manufacture of synthetic dyes utilized German patents seized during the war and distributed to American manufacturers.

Perhaps a major contribution of twentieth century chemistry was the reduction of man's dependence upon specific natural resources through the production of synthetic products. From the 1930s on DuPont and other American companies succeeded in producing synthetic fibers like rayon and nylon that became widely used in clothing, carpets, and upholstery. Another spectacular breakthrough was the development of plastics; they proved of great utility in the electrical industry. In World War II these turned out to be a timely substitute for wood and various metals. Among other World War II achievements in chemistry were the production of synthetic rubber and synthetic gasoline. Also, the postwar production of various rare metals proved indispensable in the development of rockets and space vehicles, which require materials able to withstand severe climactic conditions unknown on earth.

THE AIRCRAFT INDUSTRY

The aircraft industry received its initial impetus from government orders in World War I. Despite Post Office subsidies to airlines during the 1920s and the 1930s, the industry remained small as compared to others in the economy. The massive demands of the U.S. Armed Forces during World War II, the Korean War, and the Vietnam War made aircraft one of the major industries of the United States. The connection of the aircraft, electronics, and munitions industries with the military establishment has led to their often being described, criticized, and defended as "the military-industrial complex."

The success of the aircraft industry was dependent upon the continued technological development of lightweight, high-strength airframe structures and of lightweight, high-power engines. The interdependent development of new materials and new engines produced aircraft with greater speed, range, payload, reliability, and safety. One product of this research was the jet airplane which became a crucial factor in the increase of American airpower, military and civilian, after World War II.

MACHINE TOOLS

Machine tools (power-driven, metalworking machines) played a strategic role in the industrial development of the United States from World War I to the 1970s. Machine tools constituted the primary means employed in the precision shaping of large quantities of metal products at progressively lower and lower costs. An increase in the durability, speed, and cutting power of such tools was achieved by the use of new metals, especially molybdenum, tantalum, and tungsten-steel, and by the introduction of carbide alloys. By 1940 cutting tools made from the new nonferrous materials were nine to fourteen times as productive as the pre-1914 machine tools.

With the introduction of the electric motor, machine-tool operations acquired greater flexibility; portable hand tools contributed to the speed and ease of assembly. Large special-purpose tools, consisting of several units linked into a series, were constructed for mass production on a successive process basis. A dramatic development in the machine tool industry after 1949 was the invention of NC machine tools (machine tools controlled by means of numerical instructions expressed in coded form, usually on cards or tapes). Started by the United States Air Force for the benefit of the aircraft industry, by 1972 NC represented over 21 percent of the value of shipments of all metal-cutting machine tools.

Shifts in Energy Sources for Industry

The strategic importance of power in the development of modern industry, especially in mass production, has been apparent for a half century. Twentieth-century American industry grew rapidly through utilizing tremendous quantities of mineral-derived energy in the production and transportation of commodities. Energy consumption from mineral, hydropower, and fuel wood sources in the United States increased more than fourfold between 1900 and 1955. During this time a profound shift occurred in the importance of different sources of energy. In the early 1920s coal's share of the total energy consumption stood close to three quarters, and oil and natural gas together at not much more than 15 percent, with hydropower and fuel wood making up the remainder. By the mid 1940s, however, coal accounted for about one half the nation's total energy consumption, oil for about one third, and natural gas for not much more than one tenth. But by 1958, 45 percent of total consumption was supplied by oil (and natural gas liquids or NGL), somewhat more than 25 percent by natural gas, slightly less than 25 percent by coal, and just under 5 percent by hydro-power. In the last five decades, the shift from dependence on coal as the major energy source for industry to oil and natural gas was justified so long as the latter were easily available at low prices, without danger of their foreign supply sources being cut off. Since 1973, the international situation makes imperative America's return to a much higher reliance upon coal and a drastic cutback in its reliance upon oil and natural gas.

THE AGE OF ELECTRICITY

Electrification was superimposed upon the changing composition and expansion of the primary energy sources, coal, oil and natural gas. Although most electricity was generated by water or steam power, with nuclear power a relatively recent source, the convenience and ease of transmission of electricity to factories and homes were so great as in many ways to make the twentieth century the age of electricity. By the 1950s electrical machinery and appliances of all sizes were being utilized to produce heat, light, and motion.

Although electrification began in the 1890s, it had its first great development only after the steam turbine had been made sufficiently efficient for the establishment of thermal power stations and highly centralized electric-power generation. Quantitatively, electric power production rose from 43.4 billion kilowatt hours in 1917 to 114.6 billion in 1930 and 397.7 billion in 1975. This expansion in electrification strengthened the trend toward mass-production technology in large energy-using industries, particularly those producing aluminum, magnesium, other nonferrous metals, steel, paper, and various chemical products.

The rapid electrification of American industry is demonstrated by statistics showing that electric motors constituted only 5 percent of total manufacturing power in 1899, but rose to 25 percent in 1909, 55 percent in 1919, and about 90 percent in 1939. The widespread availability of electric power at low cost enabled businessmen to change the location and design of their plants because they no longer had to consider the availability of coal as a crucial determinant of location. Moreover, small enterprises were able to compete with larger firms by taking advantage of the efficient, small-scale use of electric power and of truck deliveries for small shipments of goods. While the largest corporations were utilizing mass-production economies to center their resources on a few standardized models, small specialty shops had greater opportunities for producing the variety their customers wanted at a somewhat higher price.

The developments we have surveyed in the automobile, aircraft, chemical, and machine-tool industries are representative of the intricate interplay of factors that produced the phenomenal upswing of American industry during the past six decades. The resulting increase in both the quantity and variety of consumer and producer goods had a highly visible impact on the daily lives of Americans. The quality and pace of life, especially in the cities, were both positively and negatively affected by the explosive growth of automobile and air transportation. For some, pollution and related costs threatened to outweigh the gains in travel and suburban living that greater mobility made possible for many. The new synthetic materials and fuels made the chemical industries essential to the progress of the clothing, construction, and automobile-aircraft service industries, yet these gains were at the expense of those engaged in such fields as the growing and manufacture of cotton and woolens. Typical of this era of change was the extent to which scientific discoveries, inventions, or new manufacturing methods in one industry led to successive repercussions on other industries. Prime examples of this were the advances in the machine-tool industry, which led to tremendous expansion in the number and types of machines, fostering growth in agriculture, manufacturing, and transportation, which in turn stimulated change in other sectors.

Industrial Concentration and Economic Growth

The spectacular changes in the methods and scale of manufacturing in the twentieth century have involved significant changes in the structure of business enterprises. At the present time, a high concentration of corporate control over markets exists in many American industries, the result of three waves of business mergers.

MERGERS AND GIANT CORPORATIONS

The first great merger movement, as indicated in chapter 12, occurred between 1895 and 1903. Leading bankers, industrialists, and lawyers used the corporate merger to create giant firms that could obtain near-monopoly control in certain markets. During the next two decades, mergers were made at a relatively slow rate. A second wave of mergers developed between 1925 and 1931, when entrepreneurs made decisions resulting in 5,846 mergers, with a peak of 1,245 in 1929. The major effect was that the share of total manufacturing assets held by the one hundred largest industrial firms rose from 35.6 percent in 1925 to 43.9 percent in 1931.

Another consequence was that various industries became transformed from the status of near-monopoly to oligopoly (a situation in which a few firms dominate a market). This process was advanced by the new mergers being undertaken, not by the largest firm in an industry, but by those in the second rank. Examples can be found in cement, cans, petroleum, automobiles, agricultural implements, glass, and steel. In the steel industry, the chief firms backing mergers were Little Steel—Bethlehem and Republic—not Big Steel—U.S. Steel. In the food industry, considerable merger activity took place, with National Dairy, Borden, General Foods, and General Mills as the leaders. On the whole such mergers led to local oligopoly in the primary products, e.g. fluid milk, bread, and to national oligopoly in lesser products such as cheese.

After a lull until the mid-1950s, merger activities increased and stayed at a high level until the mid-1970s. According to the Federal Trade Commission, the number of manufacturing and mining firms acquired during the 1955–1973 period was 20,084. From 1960 to 1970, 118 industrial firms in the very large class ($100 million and over) were acquired, with assets of $31.7 billion. The disappearance of these large independent decision-making units in an economy with an existing highly concentrated industrial structure distressed the champions of small and medium-sized business enterprises. The question raised for American decision makers on several levels is whether the potential gains from mergers, in the form of technological and economic efficiency, outweigh the potential losses in the form of reduced competition and greater corporate control of input and product markets.

CORPORATE DIVERSIFICATION

Reinforcing the trend toward larger corporations was the decision by big manufacturing firms to diversify by expanding into new products for new markets. This became an explicit strategy of growth. Top managers started to search for new products and new markets. The aim was to promote the long-term health of an enterprise by more profitably using its managers, facilities, and specific technological resources. Thus, in the 1920s chemical companies like DuPont and electrical manufacturers like General Electric expanded into new industries. During the 1930s, automobile companies began to manufacture and sell diesel locomotives, appliances, tractors, and airplanes. The metal and rubber industries offer similar examples.

During World War II, diversification was further stimulated by demands for new, technologically complex products like synthetic rubber, high-octane gasoline, radar, and electronic antisubmarine devices. This led large corporations to pool scientific and technological knowledge and to undertake major expansion. In this way, manufacturers involved with petroleum, rubber, and metals, and some food companies developed the capacity to produce a wide new range of chemicals and synthetic materials. Electrical and radio companies acquired the facilities for the manufacture of a variety of electronic products.

In the post-World War II era of rapid growth, the top managers of more and more integrated industrial enterprises resorted to the strategy of diversification. Moreover, firms that had already diversified were encouraged to move into still other product lines. By the 1960s almost all the leading firms in chemicals, rubber, glass, paper, electrical machinery, transportation devices, and food processing were making products in ten or more different specific industries. A majority of the large metal, oil, and machinery companies operated in from three to ten such industries.

The massive needs of the Department of Defense for different weapon systems were met by the large industrial companies adding separate divisions or groups of divisions for atomic energy, weapons, or government business in general.

Another mode of expansion, through foreign investment, contributed to the growth of multinational corporations. During the 1920s a small number of oil, chemical, rubber, and automobile companies made direct investments in subsidiaries in foreign countries, but this movement slowed down during the 1930s. In the 1950s and early 1960s, however, many American industrial concerns began an intensive drive for foreign markets. Direct American investments in Europe alone rose from $1.7 billion in 1950 to $24.5 billion in 1970. Two hundred firms were responsible for more than half of these sums. These concerns were located in the capital-intensive, technologically-advanced industries in the United States that had integrated, diversified, and then adopted the multidivisional form of organization. Their large overseas investments from the 1950s on made many of them into multinational corporations.

The increase in size and in number of large corporations led some to portray American industry as completely dominated by giant monopolies. Others, advocates of competitive capitalism, see the economy as still predominantly competitive. Rigorous analysis reveals diversity in the present and in the past seven decades. The various manufacturing industries exhibit a range from powerful oligopoly (for example, automobiles, aluminum, light bulbs, and cigarettes) to highly competitive enterprises (for example, apparel, lumber, furniture, and cotton fabrics). The distinction between competition and oligopoly is usually determined by whether the top four firms in an industry control one half or more of the sales in that market. Industries where the top four companies control no more than one quarter of the market are generally considered competitive. Heavy manufacturing—metals, machinery, chemicals, aircraft, and automobiles— is universally characterized as strongly oligopolistic. Light manufacturing— clothing, textiles, furniture, beverages, and food—varies from weak or moderate oligopoly to atomistic competition. On the whole, about half of American manufacturing falls into the oligopoly side of the spectrum and the other half into the competitive side.

In sectors of the economy other than manufacturing, high market concentration is prevalent in public utilities, communication, large-scale contract construction, metal mining, and rail and air transportation. Highly competitive industries include: coal mining, housebuilding, forestry, fisheries, wholesale and retail trade, real estate, the parts of agriculture that are unregulated, and most of the service industries. In such fields as medicine and construction, professional associations or unions limit competition. The role of the government is decisive in the control of entry, output, and/or price in regulated agriculture, oil production, communication, public utilities, and transportation. Finally, the national, state, and local governments including the armed services, the schools, the post office, and power projects, account for one-eighth of the gross national product. Hence about one-quarter of the economy falls under the category of oligopoly; another quarter is government-operated or regulated; and about one-half is effectively competitive.

PROS AND CONS OF MARKET CONCENTRATION

Many small businessmen, farmers, and economists have regarded monopoly and oligopoly as undesirable economically, politically, and socially. Some important economists, for example, Joseph Schumpeter and John K. Galbraith, have argued that, on the contrary, large firms with great market power have an advantage over small business in improving products through research and development and in lowering costs. Whatever higher prices an oligopolist may charge at any one time would, in their judgment, be counterbalanced by a greater decline in costs and prices than would have occurred under pure competition. Industrial research and development have been regarded as especially important to the progress of large corporations and are prime justifications for their existence.

These theses have been questioned by various scholars, for example, Edwin Mansfield, and F. M. Scherer. So far as R & D is concerned, they have demonstrated that despite the large amount of industrial research conducted in corporate laboratories, the independent individual inventor has been responsible for more than half of sixty-one important twentieth-century inventions. Since World War II, three quarters of the notable inventions came from individual inventors, small firms, universities, and government. On the crucial question of corporate magnitude, it was discovered that the largest firms in an industry do not spend proportionately more on R & D than medium-sized firms. Nor are there great economies of scale in R & D for the largest as against the medium-sized firms. There is little evidence that industrial giants are needed in all, or even most, industries to insure rapid technological change and rapid utilization of new techniques.

On the subject of the relations between sales prices and production costs, many authorities agree that over any prolonged period of time either monopoly or oligopoly results in a larger price-cost difference, larger profits, and lower output than does atomistic competition. In fact, Harvey Leibenstein has convinced many economists that operation below full efficiency is the normal situation in industry. This seems especially true for oligopolies because of the absence of the stimulus of competition. Moreover, except when confronted with a major drop in profits, most managers in oligopolies do not seem especially concerned with reducing costs.

Opinion has not always favored unfettered competition, however. The Robinson-Patman Act of 1936, for example, was an effort to restrict it in order to prevent small retail stores from being driven out of business by the large chain stores. The Miller-Tydings Act of 1937 limited the antitrust laws by permitting manufacturers of branded items to set the retail price through contracts with retailers. Patent laws are another restriction on competition because they grant the inventor temporary monopoly over the use of his invention for a given time.

Public Policy and Antitrust

The present industrial situation is the result of a multiplicity of decisions by large and small entrepreneurs concerning what products would be most useful or most profitable to manufacture, what manufacturing processes to adopt, whether to invest in R & D, how to allocate financial, physical, and human resources, and how to structure their enterprises. Interacting with these entrepreneurial decisions have been not only changing domestic and international conditions, but also the decisions of farmers and consumers about their needs and economic interests. Many citizens have been concerned about the impact of large corporations not only on the economy but also on the vitality of the democratic system. They have often distrusted the influence of powerful business interests on governmental officials, legislators, and policies. Hence Congress, the courts, and the Executive branch have been faced with the recurrent necessity for decisions about ways to restrict the power of big business. The dual aims have been to preserve the advantages of large-scale industrial plants and at the same time to curb the growth of giant corporations.

The major instrument for limiting the power of giant corporations has been antitrust legislation. Chapter 12 discussed the Sherman Antitrust Act, the Clayton Act, and the creation of the Federal Trade Commission as attempts to preserve competition by declaring illegal agreements by competitors to fix prices or control production. Monopolizing—actions undertaken by one or several firms to exclude competitors from an industry—was also prohibited. Enforcement of the antitrust laws depended, however, upon interpretation of the laws by the courts. In 1911 the Supreme Court proclaimed as the guiding principle the "rule of reason," that is, that the Sherman Act did not outlaw all trusts, but only unreasonable combinations in restraint of trade. In 1920 this rule was invoked by the U.S. Supreme Court to declare that U.S. Steel's large size and potential monopoly power were not legally relevant because "the law did not make mere size an offense or the existence of unexerted power an offense." This interpretation in regard to monopolies and near-monopolies remained the law of the land for the next two decades. When cases were brought against Eastman Kodak and International Harvester for controlling very large shares of their market, the court applied the rule of reason and found them free of guilt because they had not used overt coercion or predatory practices.

A major change resulted in 1945 from a decision by a U.S. court that the Aluminum Corporation of America (Alcoa) had violated the Sherman Act by monopolizing the manufacture of newly refined aluminum. The court held that Alcoa, because it controlled practically all the industry's output (90 percent), violated the antitrust laws. For the first time, the court used market structure rather than overt market conduct as a test of legality. The Truman administration went beyond the court's decision and took constructive action by selling its wartime aluminum plants to two competitors of Alcoa.

In 1948 the Justice Department won one of its greatest antitrust victories when the United States Supreme Court ruled that the Cement Institute had to abandon its basing-point pricing system, a method of reducing price competition. This decision obliged some twenty-five other industries, among them steel, also to give up their basing-point systems. Nevertheless, the gigantic size of the largest corporations continued to cause anxiety to the general public. In 1950 Congress passed the Celler-Kefauver Anti-Merger Act which prohibited a company from acquiring all or part of the assets of another if the consequence would be to reduce competition. Numerous mergers, as we have seen, took place despite this law. But when the Brown Shoe Company, controlling 4 percent of the market, acquired the Kinney Shoe Company, controlling 1.5 percent of the market, the United States Supreme Court in 1962 ordered divestiture on the ground that in some lines of shoes or in some cities, a dangerous horizontal concentration of power would result.

One of the most important cases in the history of antitrust occurred in 1961, when the General Electric Company, the Westinghouse Electric Corporation, and twenty-seven other electrical equipment manufacturers were convicted of using a secret code to fix the prices of their products, share the market, and eliminate competition. Seven company officials were given jail sentences, and the firms had to pay large amounts to customers in order to compensate them for overcharges.

During the 1960s many mergers were organized as conglomerates; firms in seemingly unrelated businesses and industries were joined together under unified management. The Justice Department at first thought this type of merger could not be shown to lessen competition. But in the last decade the Justice Department succeeded in blocking several of the largest attempted conglomerate mergers.

Actually, since the 1890s the American public has been divided on the proper policy to be adopted toward giant corporations and oligopolies. Hence there has been an alternating rhythm of action against and action favorable to big business. These fluctuations, it has been maintained, have hampered the effectiveness of the antitrust laws. Edward Mason and other authorities present evidence indicating that the statutes have nevertheless had an important impact on corporate behavior and markets. Sometimes the influence has been as a deterrent, since top officers of large companies have had to take into account possible violations of antitrust as they decided on various courses of action. The current cases against International Business Machines (IBM) and AT&T attest to the continuing vitality of the antitrust movement, although the government has until recently been more successful in preventing proposed mergers than in breaking up existing giants.

Epilogue on Lagging Productivity

Although we commented earlier on some of the problems of lagging productivity, we can now see more clearly how our policies on technology, energy, market structure, regulation and antitrust bear on the crucial issue of productivity. Everyone recognizes the productivity slowdown since 1973 in most major American industries outside agriculture, notably in mining, construction, utilities, wholesale trade, the service industries, and government. The causes have not all been definitively analyzed. Yet there is considerable agreement on some of the reasons for this situation. Two important factors have been a decrease in the volume of capital investment and changes in the age–sex composition of the labor supply leading to a pool of less-experienced workers. Another factor has been the decline in the intensity of scientific and technological research and development in the United States.

Some economists have suggested that the oil embargo of 1973–74 and the subsequent quadrupling of oil prices had an adverse impact on productivity and growth. Others have considered increased economic and social regulation of industry as having adverse effects on productivity, although bringing highly desirable environmental, health, and safety benefits. Those concerned about the problems of competition and oligopoly in industry believe that increased competition through vigorous enforcement of antitrust and other measures would help to increase the productivity of our economy. In any case, speedy remedial action is needed if American industry is to move forward at the same high rate of growth as it has enjoyed in the past.

Conclusion

Since 1914, the United States has been the foremost industrial nation of the world. Crucial advances in science and technology fostered a massive increase in the amount and variety of goods produced. The productivity of labor was multiplied, responding both to technological aids and to the higher level of public services, such as education. New industries emerged, ranging from synthetic fabrics to aircraft. New power sources, such as electricity, and new modes of transport, such as the automobile, contributed to the transformation of the American way of life.

As manufacturing changed, so did the forms of business enterprise. The number and size of giant corporations increased, often through mergers. In both the producer and the consumer goods industries, oligopolies were formed. From the 1920s on, big manufacturing firms began to diversify on a large scale by expanding into new products for new markets. Another form of expansion, through foreign investments, generated the multinational corporation.

Defenders of big business stress its lower costs and support of R & D; others present evidence that the giant corporations do not in the long run have an advantage over medium-sized firms in these respects. The public, Congress, and the courts have tended to fluctuate between support of big business and efforts to curb it. The antitrust laws have, with varying success, continued to be the chief means of breaking up or preventing excessive concentrations of market power. Important decisions lie ahead for citizens and government concerning the best ways of preserving the advantages of large-scale plants without sacrificing the benefits of competition.

SUGGESTED READINGS

Excellent introductions to the structure and development of American industry are Walter Adams, ed., *The Structure of American Industry*, 4th ed. (New York: Macmillan, 1971); U.S. Commerce Dept., *Industrial Outlook, 1977* (Washington, D.C.: United States Government Printing Office, 1977); and Leonard W. Weiss, *Case Studies in American Industry* 2nd ed., (New York: John Wiley, 1971). Much light on industrial management and organization is given by these insightful studies: Alfred Chandler, *The Visible Hand* (Cambridge, Mass.: Harvard University Press, 1977); Thomas C. Cochran, *200 Years of American Business* (New York: Basic Books, 1977); and F. M. Scherer, *Industrial Market Structure* and *Economic Performance* (Chicago: Rand McNally, 1973).

Superb guides to the power sources of American industry and to technology are supplied by Sam Schurr and Bruce C. Netschert, *Energy in the American Economy,*

1850–1975 (Baltimore: Johns Hopkins University Press, 1960); and Nathan Rosenberg, *Technology and American Economic Growth* (New York: Harper & Row, 1972). On mergers, oligopolies, and antitrust, valuable analyses of trends and issues are to be found in Ralph L. Nelson, *Merger Movements in American Industry—1895–1956* (Princeton: Princeton University Press, 1959); Samuel R. Reid, *The New Industrial Order* (New York: McGraw-Hill, 1976); Clair Wilcox and William G. Shepherd, *Public Policies Toward Business*, 5th ed. (Homewood, Ill.: Richard D. Irwin, 1975).

The student interested in recent economic analyses of the corporation and industry will find rewarding Harvey J. Goldschnid et al., eds., *Industrial Concentrations: The New Learning* (Boston: Little, Brown, 1974), John McDonald, *The Game of Business* (Garden City, N.Y.: Doubleday, 1975); and Robin Marris and Adrian Wood, eds., *The Corporate Economy* (Cambridge, Mass.: Harvard University Press, 1971). Indispensable studies on industrial capital and productivity are Daniel Creamer et al., *Capital in Manufacturing and Mining* (Princeton: Princeton University Press, 1960); and John W. Kendrick, *Productivity Trends in the United States* (New York: National Bureau of Economic Research, 1961) and *Postwar Productivity Trends in the United States, 1948–1969* (New York: National Bureau of Economic Research, 1973). The most recent study on productivity is Edward F. Denison, *Accounting for Slower Economic Growth: The United States in the 1970s* (Washington, D.C.: Brookings Institution, 1979). This supplements and supplants Denison's *Accounting for United States Economic Growth, 1929–1969* (Washington, D.C.: Brookings Institution, 1974).

—

CHAPTER 18

Toward a Second

Agricultural Revolution

The mounting manufacturing productivity of the past sixty years has been paralleled by greatly increased agricultural productivity. The advances in each sector fostered growth in the other and in the rest of the economy. In the context of changing conditions of demand and supply, the four major factors in agricultural productivity have been land, labor, management, and capital. Capital investment in land, buildings, machinery, and livestock has in recent decades come to play a far greater role than in the past; agriculture has become highly capital intensive. The resulting increased efficiency of the individual farm owner reduced the need for farm workers and tenant farmers; their exodus provided needed labor for other sectors of the economy, but ultimately created vast welfare problems. (See Table 18–1.)

An imbalance between the high growth rate of agricultural productivity and low elasticity of consumer demand has created long-term problems. As farm production rose, the peacetime demand for food did not keep pace. The high income of consumers in periods of prosperity resulted in only a relatively small increase in demand for agricultural products as against nonagricultural goods. Relatively large increases in supply and relatively small increases in demand tended over the years to reduce prices and incomes in agriculture. The main exceptions to this trend have occurred during the United States' involvement in four wars between 1914 and 1972, and during those peacetime periods when food production crises elsewhere in the world led to abnormal demands for American farm products.

TABLE 18-1
The Revolution in U.S. Agriculture, 1910-70

	Number of Farms (millions)	Farm Employment		Index of Output per Farm Worker
		Million	% of Total	
1910	6.4	13.6	31	147
1920	6.5	13.4	27	166
1930	6.3	12.5	22	202
1940	5.8	11.0	17	254
1950	5.2	9.9	12	352
1960	4.1	7.1	9	592
1970	2.9	4.5	4	1077

SOURCE: Population and employment percentage based on U.S. Bureau of the Census, Historical Statistics of the United States (Washington, D.C., 1976), Series A57-72, K174-183, pp. 11-12, 468; and Statistical Abstract of the United States, 1977, pp. 15, 674. Other series derived from: Changes in Farm Production and Efficiency, 1964 and 1971, U.S. Department of Agriculture Statistical Bulletin 233; Walter W. Wilcox et al., Economics of Agriculture, 3d ed., (Englewood Cliffs, N.J.: Prentice-Hall, 1974), p. 5. The index of output per farm worker has 100 for the year 1870 as its base.

American farmers depended mainly upon the free-market system for disposal of their products, until the Depression of 1929 led them to demand government aid and support. From the New Deal to the present, there has been a striking shift from decentralized decision making by individual farmers to increasingly centralized decision making by governmental authorities and farm organizations.

Rising Production and Fluctuating Demand

THE IMPACT OF WORLD WAR I

World War I (1914–18) was immeasurably tragic in its human and material costs, but acted as a stimulus to agriculture and industry throughout the world. The combined foreign and domestic demand for American food products put great pressure on the United States for increased farm production during the war years. By 1919 agricultural production was 10 percent higher than in 1913. The failure of agriculture to expand beyond this peak figure stemmed from several factors present at the outbreak of the war: there was little slack in farm resources; important innovations in farm technology were not yet available; massive additions to the land stock through an expansion of the frontier was no longer feasible. Yet this 10 percent increase in production was sufficient to save Great Britain, France, and Italy from critical food shortages. The United States insured an adequate flow of food exports, especially wheat, hogs, and sugar, to its allies by a partial embargo on food shipped to neutral countries and by inducing the American public to cut out the 15 to 20 percent of its food consumption in excess of what was necessary to maintain public health. By 1919 farm-commodity exports amounted to nearly 20 percent of the total American farm production.

A precedent for later government intervention was the creation in 1917 of the Food Administration, directed by Herbert Hoover. This new organization increased the production of wheat by guaranteeing a minimum price on wheat through the centralization of allied purchasing in the Food Administration and through the purchases and sales of grain by the United States Grain Corporation. Similarly, in 1918 Hoover helped to create a Sugar Equalization Board that arranged to purchase raw sugar from different producing regions, within and outside the United States, at the price necessary for each region. In order to raise the production of hogs to the level needed by the United States and its allies, the Food Administration fixed the price of hogs at a high level in relation to the price of corn and led the farmers to concentrate on the raising of hogs.

During World War I the great majority of the farmers made important gains in real income. Their numbers did not increase, but the prices paid for their products did, and their total output was sustained. The prices of raw farm products grew steadily after 1913, reaching 106 percent above that year in 1918. The purchasing power of the realized income (that is, the net income available for spending after paying income taxes) of all those obtaining income from agriculture was 25 percent higher in 1918 than in 1915, with the major part of the gain going to the farm owners, rather than to the farm workers.

The total net income of farmers, measured in current dollars, more than doubled between 1914 and 1918, rising from $4 billion to $10 billion. In that same period the value of farm property, including farm land, buildings, machinery, and all livestock, rose from $47.4 billion to $61.5 billion. These increases in income and capital value induced many farmers to invest their savings in more farm land, often supplementing their own capital with mortgage loans. At the time this seemed like a sound investment, but the future proved it to be unwise speculation.

POSTWAR IMBALANCE OF SUPPLY AND DEMAND

Within eighteen months after the end of World War I, American farm prices suffered a drastic reduction. Between 1919 and 1921 the prices received by farmers declined by almost 40 percent. The economic distress of farmers, especially those in the spring wheat region and the corn belt, was intensified by the legacy of the wartime speculative rise in the prices of farm land and the heavy increase in farm-mortgage debt, which led to many foreclosures of farm property during the mid-1920s. The rest of the American economy soon recovered from the downturn in the business cycle, and by 1921 the prosperity of the 1920s seemed firmly established. Yet agriculture did not share proportionately in this upward trend.

A number of factors combined to keep American agriculture depressed. One was that agriculture in the war-devastated areas of Europe and elsewhere recovered rapidly from the effects of the war and expanded through progress in technology. Another was that, since the United States insisted on the repayment of war loans and enacted high protective tariffs, foreign countries had reduced means for buying American food exports and were forced to cut their imports. Hence, the European nations encouraged increased production at home and made foreign purchases from those countries that accepted industrial goods in payment.

Nevertheless, since domestic consumption rose enough to counterbalance the decline in foreign demand, income in agriculture recovered by the mid-1920s and stayed on something of a plateau from 1925 until 1929. Technological advances, however, continued to increase farm output considerably. The use of tractors, trucks, and automobiles grew rapidly, and the "all-purpose" tractor prompted a movement toward large-scale farming. Although the productivity of agriculture in this period rose less rapidly than that of industry, the number of persons supplied by one farm worker rose from about eight in 1917–20 to almost ten in 1930. But the domestic demand was too inelastic to absorb a constantly increasing supply. Not only did the population increase less rapidly than before the war, but, even more important, most American consumers decided to use their higher incomes to buy new products of industry such as automobiles and refrigerators rather than more food. This imbalance kept farm prices and incomes from rising to levels considered adequate by the farmers.

Governmental Decisions and Controls

These adverse conditions initiated a trend toward increasing centralization of decision making for agriculture. Farmers formed a new organization, the American Farm Bureau Federation, which joined with the older National Grange and the Farmers' Union to create a bipartisan farm bloc in Congress that worked for agrarian legislation. Congress responded in 1921 by reviving the War Finance Corporation as a lending agency to finance the export of farm surpluses, and passed a Futures Trading Act that curbed speculation in grain prices. In 1922 a Co-operative Act exempted agricultural cooperatives from the antitrust laws, and the next year an Intermediate Credits Act established a system of twelve intermediate credit banks. These aided farmers in the more orderly marketing of their products and also enabled them to borrow against crops in storage in order to hold them for hoped-for higher prices on the market.

The slogan, "Equality for Agriculture," inspired the farm bloc to get through Congress the McNary-Haugen Bill which provided for a two-price plan highly favorable to the farmers. But President Coolidge vetoed the measure in both 1927 and 1928. The farm bloc succeeded, however, in its push for enactment of the Agricultural Marketing Act of 1929, which created the Federal Farm Board to promote cooperative marketing agencies for farm commodities. The Board was equipped with a revolving fund of five hundred million dollars to enable producers to achieve a high degree of price control. The experiment failed because of lack of measures for production control and the bad effects of the 1929 Depression on consumer demand for food products.

In addition to these appeals for government intervention, American farmers in the late 1920s also established large national cooperatives in the hope of expanding consumer demand through quality control and of raising farm prices through market management. But these attempts at self-help proved unsuccessful because there was no effective control of production. Hence, most farmers came to look to the government for mechanisms that would overcome the deficiencies of voluntary organizations.

THE NEW DEAL

Despite these private and public efforts, the plight of the farmer worsened. Between 1929 and 1932 the realized gross income of farm operators fell 54 percent. Because the cost of production did not decrease proportionately, their net income fell nearly 70 percent. This situation was due in large part to a sharp decline in domestic and foreign demand for farm products while total farm output not only failed to decline, but in 1931 and 1932 increased slightly above the 1929 level. Moreover, the farm problem was intensified by the fact that the farm population, which had declined almost 1.4 million between 1920 and 1929, grew by more than 1 million between 1929 and 1933. Paradoxically, instead of people leaving agriculture as farm prices declined, they stayed and other people migrated back to the farm impelled by the scarcity of employment opportunities in the nonfarm sectors of the economy.

With such great distress in agriculture, Franklin D. Roosevelt and the Democrats were able to win the support of most farmers in the 1932 elections. They then launched a bold, innovative program for recovery in agriculture as well as in industry. Given the apparent failure of the farmers' previous reliance on the competitive market system and on the commodity cooperatives, the decision makers in the national government chose to eliminate highly competitive markets and to replace them by a cartel form of organization in agriculture; sharp reductions in production and price fixing became the preferred means of bringing higher income to farmers.

An alternative procedure would have been for the government to stake the farmers' welfare on a Keynesian fiscal policy: spending on a massive scale so as to restore adequate purchasing power to the consumers, whose purchases of food would then revive agriculture. But this proposal was never seriously considered; it was too revolutionary in theory and seemed less practical and politically expedient than the path chosen by Roosevelt and Congress. Their new approach focused on farm prices as the main objective of farm policy. This program reflected pressures from the agricultural hierarchy dominated by prosperous farmers, the American Farm Bureau, and various agricultural economists concerned more with the efficiency of large-scale farming than with the welfare of small farmers, tenant farmers, and farm workers.

The first major New Deal farm legislation was the Agricultural Adjustment Act (AAA) of 12 May 1933. This measure aimed at a drastic reduction in production of certain basic farm commodities, especially corn, wheat, cotton, tobacco, and hogs. Cash payments to producers participating in these programs were funded by new taxes imposed on the sale of these products to processors. The Commodity Credit Corporation (CCC) was established to keep products temporarily off the market when necessary. The program ended, however, in January 1936, when the United States Supreme Court ruled the AAA unconstitutional.

The next month Congress passed the Soil Conservation and Domestic Allotment Act. This attempted to reduce the production of future surplus crops through payments to farmers from federal funds for improved land use and conservation practices. Whereas the 1933 AAA had tried to restore the prewar 1909–1914 price level, the 1936 legislation made its goal income parity. This was defined as the ratio of purchasing power of the net income per person on farms to that of the income per person not on farms that had prevailed during the period from August 1909 to July 1914. The decline in farm prices that followed large crops in 1937 soon brought pressure for a new farm program. The Agricultural Adjustment Act of 1938 authorized comprehensive supply adjustment programs for each of the major crops. Provisions were made for (1) mandatory price-support loans at 52 to 75 percent of parity on corn, wheat, and cotton; (2) necessary marketing quotas that were geared to acreage allotments on tobacco, corn, wheat, cotton, and rice; and (3) permissive supports for other commodities.

Although subsequently amended in various ways, this act established the basic framework for all the major farm programs since that date. The Commodity Credit Corporation continued under this act as the principal price-supporting agency of the government. When it could not support prices through loans or purchase agreements, the CCC bought farm commodities outright and disposed of them in ways that would not disrupt the farm price levels. Between 1937 and 1941 the CCC accumulated 10 million bales of cotton, 419 million bushels of wheat, and 403 million bushels of corn.

ECONOMIC AND SOCIAL EFFECTS

To evaluate the New Deal's agricultural programs in a balanced way is difficult. But a statistical analysis shows that both farm income and farm prices rose markedly from the low levels reached in 1932. By 1937 net income of persons on farms from farming (including the wages paid to farm workers living on farms) had increased more than two and one-half times.

In the 1937–38 recession, net farm income fell from the high 1937 level, but was still twice as high as the 1932 low. A substantial part of the improvement in farm net income came from the general rise of national income, which in turn increased the demands for farm products. Another favorable influence came from the recurrent and severe droughts of the mid-1930s. A third factor was the granting of subsidy payments to the farmers for their reductions in acreage of certain major crops through what were called CCC nonrecourse loans to farmers on the difference between current market prices and the parity prices set by the government.

On the negative side, it can be asserted that the acreage reduction program of the 1933 AAA did not lead in general to a reduction in the production of the major farm products. Moreover, the 1933 price supports encouraged farmers to devote their resources to certain products, irrespective of current demand and varying rates of technological improvements in different areas of agriculture. The 1938 AAA, an improvement upon the 1933 action—introduced the principle of the ever-normal granary. The application of this principle by the CCC led to the accumulation of large stocks of wheat, corn, cotton, and tobacco which later were sold at a profit when the United States became involved in World War II. If it had not been for the war, this practice by the CCC would have been criticized for establishing minimum prices that falsely inflated the farmers' price expectations.

The New Deal contributed much to agriculture in terms of improved efficiency. The use of machines was encouraged. Measures were developed for reducing soil erosion. Farmers were taught methods of contour plowing and dry farming. Programs were set up for conservation and land rehabilitation.

However, New Deal price supports and production controls encouraged American agriculture to overproduce and to overvalue farm resources. Owing to a rise in land values based upon the expectation of profits due to government programs, the use of land increased during this period, although farm employment decreased by 1.5 million. In the same period, farmers also increased their investment in most types of durables and expendables. The controls that might be considered justifiable temporary measures produced situations that were economically questionable in the long run.

The New Deal in agriculture was least successful from the human point of view. The 1933 AAA did not benefit the tenant farmers, especially the Southern share croppers, most of whom were blacks. Many of them were evicted by their landlords. The major benefits went to the wealthier farmer. The larger the size of the farm, the higher were the subsidies from the government. The New Deal led to a heavy labor outflow from agriculture into manufacturing and the service industries, and into the cities. Many who could not find employment swelled the ranks of those on relief. Although farm wage rates increased, they dropped relative to nonfarm wage rates.

Pressure politics, as exerted by the farm bloc, prevented the exploration of other possible remedies for the farmer such as the one of increasing the purchasing power of the urban consumers. A noted economist, Theodore W. Schultz, suggested that the farm problem of the 1930s was due in large part to the low expansion of industrial output between 1930 and 1939. With 1920 industrial production as a base, the index of industrial production between 1920 and 1939 rose almost 50 percent, and between 1930 and 1939 only 24 percent. In short, the low rate of industrial expansion and the deterioration of foreign trade in the 1930s were among the primary causes of "the farm problem" that the New Deal planners found so formidable until the needs of World War II provided a solution.

The Second Agricultural Revolution

WORLD WAR II

World War II triggered the second American agricultural revolution by initiating a series of major changes in farm land use, policies, output, management, and way of life. Between 1939 and 1941, however, most American farmers thought that the advent of a world war would only increase the severe agricultural problems of the 1930s. Since the New Deal agricultural programs had been centered on the reduction of farm output, it required Pearl Harbor and a revolution in the decision-making processes of farmers, Congress, and the Executive before the United States translated the "Food for Freedom" program into increased agricultural production goals for 1942.

The great foreign demand for American food, especially from Great Britain, Soviet Russia, and China, induced Roosevelt to join Churchill in establishing the Combined Food Board to allocate foodstuffs among the allies. Meanwhile the domestic demand for American food products also increased because of the great expansion of the United States armed forces, the growing nonfarm income, and the increasing restrictions placed upon nonessential consumer expenditures. Hence, an urgent need developed for an accelerated growth rate in American agricultural production.

The consequent possibility of achieving prosperity through a free market system did not, however, lessen the trend toward centralization. Various farm organizations, led by the American Farm Bureau, pressed for a continuation during the war of government support for farm prices. Early in 1941 Congress raised support prices on the basic commodities (wheat, corn, cotton, tobacco, rice, and peanuts) to 85 percent of parity. Later that year the Steagall Amendment was passed, requiring the secretary of agriculture to support the price of any commodity for which an increase in production was required at a level of not less than 85 percent of parity. This mandatory level was raised to 90 percent of parity in 1942, with support to be continued at this level for two years after the end of the war. The Steagall Amendment was in effect until December 1948; subsequent legislation continued this degree of support on most commodities through 1949 and 1950.

Roosevelt established the War Food Administration in 1943 to provide more centralized control over the handling of war-food problems. Nearly all production controls on the crops were removed by 1944. After price ceilings came into existence in 1942, they were applied to farm products, but at generally high levels. Price controls proved to be more effective in holding down prices of articles farmers bought than in holding down prices of articles they sold.

American agriculture succeeded in raising total farm output by 25 percent between 1939 and 1944. This was due in large part to a long run of unusually favorable weather, favorable government price policies, the greatly increased use of fertilizer, more intensive land cultivation, and the rapid expansion of farm mechanization, especially the use of "all-purpose" gasoline tractors. As a result, there was an increase of more than one third in output per farm worker between 1939 and 1944, and of one sixth in average crop yields per harvested acre.

During World War II the proportion of the nation's labor force engaged in agriculture dropped from about 20 to 15 percent. Millions of workers decided to migrate from the farms to the cities, and many others, while maintaining their residence in rural areas, gave up farm work to take up other employment, often in factories. Many rural women and children joined the farm labor force to take the place of men who had left for military service. On the other hand, draft deferments encouraged a high rate of entry into farming from the young age bracket. This increased the commitment of many young men to agriculture and enabled the necessary farm output expansion to take place.

Although land use increased by only 1.7 percent between 1942 and 1947, the earnings of land and the value of land rose considerably during this period. Throughout World War II farm incomes increased greatly. The net income for farm producers rose from $5.3 billion in 1939 to $13.6 billion in 1944. Despite the marked increase in marketing costs, this probably gave the farmer a larger percentage of the consumer's dollar than he had ever previously received. With the aid given by the Farm Security and Credit Administration, and with high farm prices, an unusually large number of farm tenants were able to achieve farm ownership during the war. The percentage of farm tenancy dropped from 42.4 in 1930 to 31.7 in 1945. The wages of hired farm workers, though less than one third of those of industrial workers in 1939, almost tripled by 1945 and came to about 40 percent of the industrial workers' wage level.

During the war, civilian food consumption reached the highest level in American history, even though almost one fourth of U.S. total food output went to the armed forces and to American allies through lend-lease. The civilian per capita consumption in 1944 was 9 percent above the 1935–39 average. The nutritive quality of the national diet also improved, especially for low-income people.

Despite these great achievements, some policy decisions and practices of the United States in World War II were open to severe criticism. Livestock production was unquestionably overstimulated. Too large a percentage of cereal crops went into feed for livestock rather than into food for people in starvation areas abroad. Dairy products as compared with meat products were not given adequate support. The use of price supports for farm products when there was a high demand for food seemed unwise to champions of Keynesian and free-market economics. The over-extension of tillage, along with a reduction in soil-building and protective crops, intensified the possibilities of soil erosion.

POST-WORLD WAR II DEVELOPMENTS

Wartime markets for farm products, domestic and foreign, lasted for three years after the end of the war in 1945. Although several recessions occurred in the following three decades, the American economy experienced a long-term expansion and prosperity that few economists had fully anticipated. Nor had they realized that the technological revolution, which had begun after World War I, was going to accelerate in the post-World War II period. The problem of adjusting the constantly increasing supply of agricultural products to the changing domestic and foreign demand was to challenge the best brains in Congress, in the various farm organizations, and in the economics profession.

In any case, Congress, fearful of bad times for farmers, extended the price supports which had proved unnecessary in World War II. One result was an excessive accumulation of stocks in 1948–49. In 1949, Charles Brannan, Truman's secretary of agriculture, proposed a plan to let the free market determine prices for certain farm products, and have the government pay the farmer if the market price was below a modernized parity price. But Congress rejected this attempt to avoid surpluses and production controls. Again, the outbreak of a war dissolved a problem. The Korean War, which began in June 1950, produced an increased domestic and foreign demand for agricultural products. As a consequence, the general level of prices received by farmers began an upward movement. The surplus stocks of 1948–49 became absorbed through domestic or export use.

At the end of the Korean War surpluses became important once more. Between June 1952 and June 1954 the Commodity Credit Corporation inventories rose from $1.3 billion to $5.8 billion. Farm output during the years 1950 to 1959 increased 20 percent, and farm prices correspondingly declined 20 percent between 1951 and 1960. Strong efforts to support agricultural prices through buildups in surplus stocks and large price-support expenditures proved of no avail.

The mounting surpluses and increased cost of government programs led the Eisenhower Administration and Congress to enact a flexible price-support program. The objective of the Agricultural Act of 1954 was to decrease price-support levels when surpluses were large and to reduce the production of surplus commodities. Despite the lower price supports, farm production increased, and surpluses continued to rise. Several years had to pass before the policy makers in government recognized that the sustained impact of new technology on farm output was a new factor in the supply-demand situation and required new policies. In the interim a number of makeshift, semi-emergency programs were formulated to deal with specific commodities.

During the 1950s two other programs were adopted in an effort to improve the condition of agriculture. Public Law 480, formally known as the Agricultural Trade Development and Assistance Act of 1954, provided for the sale of farm products abroad against payments in foreign currency. Large amounts of agricultural products were shipped abroad. But the consequences were not always beneficial. Some countries, for example, India, became so dependent on food imports from the United States as sometimes to create artificial shortages for American consumers. This was not good for domestic price stability or the United States balance of payments.

The other program passed during this period was the Soil Bank, established by the Agricultural Act of 1956. Farmers were given payments for shifting land away from farming by placing their farm land under either the acreage reserve or the conservation reserve. Between 1957 and 1962 about twenty-five million acres were diverted from farming by the Soil Bank. This reduction in land use was good, but was achieved at a high cost. Moreover, an increasing use of fertilizers and supplemental irrigation on remaining land offset a considerable part of the benefits that came from the land retirement under the Soil Bank. Congress ended the acreage reserve program in 1959, and the conservation reserve program in 1965, when a new land-retirement policy was adopted.

Kennedy's Secretary of Agriculture, Orville Freeman, attempted in vain to win Congress to a policy of "supply management," a deliberate restriction of farm supplies for the purpose of raising farm prices and farm incomes. Hence, Kennedy's farm policy was one of the least successful ventures of his career. On the other hand, his full employment policy, by increasing effective domestic demand, helped to raise farm income. Another contribution of the Kennedy administration was the Food-Stamp Plan of 1961. Families taking part in the program purchased food coupons according to the size of the family and its income. After the program proved its efficiency in expanding farm markets and improving the nutrition of needy families, the Food Stamp plan became a law in 1964. By the end of 1974, 17.1 million people were taking part in the program throughout the country.

In 1965 Lyndon Johnson proposed to Congress a reduction of market farm prices to internationally competitive levels. Such a reduction had been achieved in wheat as early as May 1963, but much had to be done for other farm products, especially cotton. President Johnson succeeded in getting Congress to approve a four year Food and Agriculture Act that established government price-supporting loans at or near world price levels, instead of at the higher percentage-of-parity levels of earlier years. Government payments were made to voluntary cooperators who agreed to acreage planting allotments for wheat and cotton. The Act recognized chronic excess capacity as a persistent problem in agriculture and authorized the secretary to reduce excessive stocks to desirable reserve levels.

Critics pointed out that although the 1965 Act reduced the farm-subsidy cost to the government, the amount of direct government payments to cooperating farmers still was enormous. It had increased from $702 million in 1960 to $3.7 billion in 1970. Moreover, the average size of farms receiving payments, especially those in cotton, had risen greatly. By 1970, the government was paying several large-scale cotton farmers over $1 million a year for their share in the voluntary cotton and other adjustment programs.

In 1969 the Nixon administration decided upon a farm program aimed at bringing about the maximum use of market prices and vigorous promotion of export markets. But various farm pressure groups opposed these objectives. The result was a compromise measure, the Agricultural Act of 1970. The new law required that, in order to qualify for price-support loans, farmers had to keep out of production a specified part of their allotment of land for wheat, cotton, and feed grains. A limit of fifty-five thousand dollars per crop was set on individual producer payments, yet a single farmer could obtain the maximum subsidy on each of three crops. The results of the first two years of the set-aside programs, 1971–72, were disappointing. Farmers liked the additional freedom given to them, and government payments to farmers in 1972 set a new record; nevertheless, acreage adjustments obtained in feed grains and wheat were smaller than desired.

TURNING POINTS IN THE 1970S

From the mid-1950s until 1973 production continued to exceed consumption substantially and to create chronic surpluses. Prices, we have seen, had not been allowed to fall and clear the markets. After 1972, however, the agricultural situation underwent a dramatic change. A sharply increased demand for American farm products developed from a variety of sources. In western Europe, Japan, and other parts of the world, a rapid increase in income and population created an increased demand for U.S. food and fiber. Moreover, a shift in consumer dietary preferences in western Europe and Japan resulted in increased consumption of red meat and poultry and hence a greater demand for feed grains. Also, the devaluation of the dollar in 1971 and 1973 made American farm products cheaper for foreigners to purchase. Other factors affecting the supply-demand balance for United States food included the poor crop harvest in various countries and the opening of Soviet Russian, Communist Chinese, and Eastern European markets to American farm products. For example, the widely debated sale of over one billion dollars of American grain to the Soviet Union occurred in 1972.

A consequence of these developments was a sharp reduction in domestic food supplies and a spectacular rise in retail food prices. This led to the passage in 1973 of a radically new farm program. The Agriculture and Consumer Protection Act, effective for four years, ended the long-established system of acreage restrictions and government purchases to support prices. A new system of target prices was established for the key crops of corn, wheat, and cotton. These were guaranteed minimum prices on basic agricultural products, considerably below the 1973 high price level but above the support prices of previous laws. If market prices remained above the target prices, no government payments were to be made. If market prices fell below the targets, the government would make up the difference to the farmer. Government payments of any kind were limited to twenty thousand dollars per individual farmer for all commodity programs combined. This was an improvement on the 1970 limit of fifty-five thousand dollars per crop. The goal of the legislation was to increase the production of food to meet world-wide demands.

Under the new policy of market orientation and expanded output, American agriculture enjoyed unusually high prosperity from 1973 to 1975, with record quantities of exports pushing commodity prices to new heights. But some disturbing events cast a shadow over the scene. In October 1973 the Arab–Israeli war led to sharp price increases on Arab oil and to an Arab embargo against the United States for one year. Finally, a strong cartel of petroleum-exporting countries (OPEC), united in holding oil prices at triple preembargo levels. This greatly increased fuel costs for agriculture and, as a result, food prices throughout the United States. Concern about the situation led the United States to impose export embargoes on food that strained long-standing trading relations between the United States and other countries, especially Japan.

In 1975 huge Soviet purchases of American grains caused the U.S. government to negotiate an agreement with the USSR that freed U.S. markets from the erratic fluctuations that had resulted from past Soviet purchases. Soviet Russia agreed to buy six to eight million tons of corn and wheat in each of the next five years. The same year the United States also established informal understandings on grain purchases with Japan and a few other countries. The importing nations expressed their purchase intentions, and the United States indicated that under normal conditions the grain would be available. These understandings were efforts to make amends for the rather arbitrary embargoes on the export of foods that the United States had imposed in the past.

The importance of large farm exports to the American international balance of payments became dramatically apparent: a record high in food exports in mid-1975 produced an overall trade surplus for the United States. The U.S. agricultural surplus, formerly a problem, had become a major American and world asset. It strengthened our balance of payments position at a time of expensive and increasingly large oil imports. The United States had emerged as the world's bread basket. It was both the world's major exporter of wheat and feed grains and also the leading exporter of rice and soybeans. The United States and Canada together controlled a larger share of the world's exportable surplus of grains than the Middle East did of the current world oil exports.

This favorable situation did not last. Between 1975 and 1977 American farm conditions and policies underwent a drastic change. OPEC's high oil prices and huge increases in the cost of fertilizer and machinery caught many farmers in a cost-price squeeze. While American cereal farmers continued to produce bumper crops, good harvests in Soviet Russia and other grain-importing nations greatly decreased U.S. grain exports. When the Carter administration came into office in 1977, it had to confront a powerful lobby of wheat farmers and wheat-state congressional spokesmen. This group succeeded in winning support for the potentially high-cost Food and Agricultural Act of 1977. The act set price supports at levels designed to give income protection to farmers, yet low enough to ensure that United States commodities remain competitive in world markets. If in the future United States farm production exceeds demand, and food prices fall, the rise in direct payments to producers will considerably increase the cost of commodity programs. On the other hand, if consumer demand outpaces supply and market prices rise, the cost of the commodity programs will decrease.

Government decision makers had hoped that the anticipated high government outlays under the new statute would stabilize food prices and help to insure low inflation rates. This did not happen, because decisions taken by the farmers altered the picture considerably. The 1977 Food and Agriculture Act placed under the control of the farmers a massive reserve of food and feed grains. The government gave loans for three years on crops withheld from the market, and subsidies to wheat and corn farmers for reducing their acreage 10 to 20 percent. This lessened pressure on farmers to sell their crops. Late in 1978, grain and soybean prices were higher than the year before, because farmers were selling only when market prices met their demands. A new situation has arisen in which government aid to the farmer has altered the traditional supply-demand interaction in competitive farm commodity markets.

What the future holds for the American farmer depends in part on the increasing need for food for the world's rapidly expanding population; in part on the reserves of American farm products and the willingness of American farmers, without government subsidy, to sell in world markets at prices that the rest of the world can afford to pay. If the bumper crops of the mid-1970s are repeated, there is the danger that the pre-1972 supply-demand imbalance will return.

INEQUALITIES IN ASSETS AND INCOME

The technological changes behind agricultural productivity and the government legislation of the past four decades have transformed the structure of agriculture. Decisions in the national government and in private farm enterprise, as well as the new technologies, encouraged the trend toward larger and fewer farms. The number of farms in the United States attained a peak of 6.8 million in 1935, and then steadily decreased to a low of 2.8 million in 1976, a decline of 55 percent. Meanwhile, the average farm size rose from 138 acres in 1910 to 390 in 1976. This development reflects the consolidation of small, less efficient units into units where modern technologies became profitable. The value of privately-owned tangible assets used in farm production rose from about $40 billion in 1910 to $310 billion in 1970 (in current dollars).

A source of concern was the increase in the number of farms of 500 acres and over from 6 percent of the total number of farms in the United States in 1950 to 13 percent in 1969. A related development was the movement of corporations and conglomerates into the farming business. Some writers feared that the family farm was going to lose out to corporate farming. But a recent study showed that in 1970 66 percent of all corporate farms were family-owned, another 14 percent were individually owned, and the remaining 20 percent were owned by a group larger than the family. The total number of corporations directly engaged in farming and ranching was probably about 1 percent of all commercial farms, operating about 7 percent of the land in farms, and accounting for possibly 8 to 9 percent of the sales of all farm products. These statistics disproved the theory about the take-over of farm production by large corporations. The problem was rather that the largest corporate farms received some of the biggest subsidies from the government, until Congress placed some limits on subsidies.

The debate on the social implications of the changing size of the average American farm has long been tied in with the major "farm problem" of the substantially lower level of farm income compared to nonfarm income. In 1934 per capita farm income was about 33 percent of per capita nonfarm income. During the 1950s it was still in the 50 to 60 percent range and just before the 1972 surge in export demand little more than 70 percent, with a large part of the gain coming from government payments. Then the record farm prices of 1973 raised per capita farm income above nonfarm levels, with government payments only a relatively minor portion of the total. Since 1973 the farm income level has been between 92 and 82 percent of the nonfarm income levels. (See Table 18–2.)

The disparity between farm and nonfarm incomes explains why about

TABLE 18-2
Per Capita Disposable Personal Income, Farm and Nonfarm Population, Selected Years 1934-1975

Year	Per Capita Income from All Sources		Farm as Percentage of Nonfarm (percent)
	Farm Population (dollars)	Nonfarm Population (dollars)	
1934	163	500	32.6
1940	245	671	36.5
1950	840	1,447	58.1
1960	1,086	2,014	53.9
1970	2,510	3,390	74.0
1972	2,710	3,629	74.7
1972	3,223	3,866	83.4
1973	4,665	4,267	109.3
1974	4,313	4,654	92.7
1975	4,553	5,081	89.6

SOURCE: U.S. Department of Agriculture, *Farm Income Statistics,* July 1976 Statistical Bull. 557, p. 42.

41 percent of the almost 34 million Americans classified as poor in 1965 lived in rural areas, about one fourth on farms. This pov erty group repre- sented almost 30 percent of the total farm population, a larger proportion than is found in urban areas. Yet it would be an error to infer that all farmers have been, or are, poor. There has always been a great disparity in income among farmers. Table 18–3 indicates a large number of very low-income farmers (52 percent of all farmers) along with a smaller num- ber of medium-income ones (44 percent), and a few with relatively high incomes (4 percent). In 1975 this 4 percent of all the farms in the United States accounted for 47 percent of the total farm output. At the other ex- treme, the lowest three income classes, selling less than $10,000 worth of farm products a year, constituted 52 percent of all commercial farms but produced only 5 percent of the marketed farm output. The gap between the few most affluent and the large number of very low-income farmers explains the concern among economists and the general public. (See Table 18–3.)

TABLE 18-3
Distribution of Commercial Farms
by Size of Sales, 1975

Value of Farm Products Sold	Percent of Total Farms	Percent of Total Output
$100,000 or more	4	47
$40,000-$99,999	12	24
$20,000-$39,999	20	19
$10,000-$19,999	12	5
$5,000-$9,999	9	2
$2,500-$4,999	17	2
Less than $2,500	26	1
Total	100	100

SOURCE: U.S. Department of Agriculture, Farm Income Statistics July 1, 1976, Statistical Bull. 557, p. 58.

The number of poor farmers has been reduced over the past six dec- ades by an amazingly large migration of low-income farm owners, tenants, and workers to the cities of the northeast and northwest. The percentage of the civilian labor force employed mainly in agriculture fell from 31 per- cent in 1910 to 4.2 percent in 1975. Those who could not find jobs in the manufacturing and service industries in the cities went on welfare. Among the consequences have been the tremendous problems of welfare costs, the flight of the middle class to the suburbs, and the decay of the inner cities.

A development that has not received as much attention as it deserves is that, in the last decade, one half or more of the incomes of farm people have come from nonfarm jobs. Of the total increase in the income of the farm population from 1960 to 1970, 62 percent came from nonfarm sources. In the formulation of farm commodity policies, government decision makers and the taxpaying public should consider the fact that only 36 percent of farms are at present operated by families deriving more than one half their income directly from the farm. These families are the only ones that will realize any substantial benefit from government farm subsidies.

Conclusion

The twentieth century has seen what amounts to a second agricultural revolution. This has been characterized by rising productivity based upon technological advances and massive capital investment. Integral to these developments, especially after 1940, was the substitution of capital goods for labor in the agricultural input mix. In 1910 each farm worker produced enough food and fiber to support seven persons; in 1975, each worker produced enough to support over fifty.

After World War I, the increasing productivity of agriculture and a highly inelastic consumer demand in peacetime created a long-term problem. When the free market system was relied on, the supply-demand imbalance was not resolved, owing in large part to the relatively fixed character of human and property resources, and the pressures for speedy relief measures in the 1929 crisis. From the New Deal on, the national decision makers focused on limiting farm output and stabilizing farm prices at a higher level than the free market would have brought in most years. The success of the government's extensive scientific research programs accentuated the supply-demand imbalance. The reliance on farm price supports, based on the parity principle, did not prevent cumulative farm surpluses year after year. The government experimented, with varying success, with costly programs designed to reduce the supply of farm products and to increase the demand for them. Many economists have criticized the public decision makers for not having tried to counteract the misallocation of resources, and for giving the largest subsidies to the largest and politically most influential farm owners, and the least help to those in the lowest farm income and property classes. The resulting great exodus of displaced farmers and farm workers to the cities has not eliminated the problem of agricultural poverty, while in large part contributing to the urban welfare problem.

Complicating the picture have been the fluctuations in foreign demand for American food products. In the early 1970s a rise in foreign demand produced higher income for farmers, rising food prices for consumers, and a favorable trade balance for the United States. After 1975 a drop in foreign demand for U.S. grains and steadily rising production costs threatened the farmers' high profits and worsened the international balance of payments position of the United States. The future of American agriculture depends both on the long-term world demand for U.S. food and fiber and on the wisdom of our decisions on domestic farm policies.

SELECTED READINGS

The most comprehensive history of American agriculture, 1914–50, is Murray R. Benedict, *Farm Policies of the United States 1790–1950* (New York: Twentieth Century Fund, 1953). An illuminating documentary history of the periods 1914–40 and 1941–73 is to be found in Wayne D. Rasmussen, ed., *Agriculture in the United States*, vols. 3, 4 (New York: Random House, 1975). A useful guide to agricultural technology is John T. Schlebecker, *Whereby We Thrive, A History of American Farming, 1607–1972* (Ames, Iowa: Iowa State University Press, 1975). Excellent introductions to recent economic problems are Dale E. Hathaway, *Problems of Progress in the Agricultural Economy* (Chicago: Scott, Foresman, 1964); Earl A. Heady, *A Primer on Food, Agriculture and Public Policy* (New York: Random House, 1967); and Vernon W. Ruttan et al., *Agricultural Policy in an Affluent Society* (New York: W. W. Norton, 1969).

For detailed economic analysis and policy discussion the reader will profit from Rueben C. Buse and Daniel W. Bromley, *Applied Economics, Resource Allocation in Rural America* (Ames, Iowa: Iowa State University Press, 1975); Willard W. Cochrane and Mary E. Ryan, *American Farm Policy, 1948–73* (Minneapolis: University of Minnesota Press, 1976); Glenn L. Johnson and C. Leroy Quance, eds., *The Overproduction Trap in U.S. Agriculture* (Baltimore: Johns Hopkins University Press, 1972); Theodore W. Schultz, *Agriculture in an Unstable Economy* (New York: McGraw-Hill, 1945); Alvin S. Tostlebe, *Capital in Agriculture* (Princeton: Princeton University Press, 1957); and Walter W. Wilcox et al., *Economics of American Agriculture*, 3d ed. (Englewood Cliffs, N.J.: Prentice-Hall, 1974). Different views on current problems and policies are given in *Food and Agricultural Policy* (Washington, D.C.: American Enterprise Institute, 1977); *Economic Report of the President* and *Annual Report of the Council of Economic Advisers* (Washington, D.C.: United States Government Printing Office, 1978); and *International Economic Report of the President* (Washington, D.C.: United States Government Printing Office, 1973–77).

On the impact of recent American agricultural technology on the environment and the importance of American agriculture to the underdeveloped world, three provocative studies are Lester R. Brown, *By Bread Alone* (New York: Praeger, 1974); Michael Perelman, *Farming for Profit in a Hungry World* (Montclair, N.J.: Allanheld, Osmun, 1977); and Sterling Wortman and Ralph W. Cummins, Jr., *To Feed This World* (Baltimore: Johns Hopkins University Press, 1978).

CHAPTER 19

Innovation and Obsolescence

in Transportation

The history of the United States in the twentieth century could be told in terms of the successive introduction of new modes of transportation. Each in part supplants the older forms and in part develops new and expanded patterns of the movement of goods and people. In 1920, the railroads' near-monopoly of freight and passenger traffic still prevailed. By 1930, motor vehicles—passenger cars, trucks, and buses—had come to dominate traffic on land. By the 1940s and the 1950s airplanes had become an integral part of modern transportation. Underground, thousands of miles of pipelines were laid to move massive quantities of oil and natural gas. Finally, a whole new area of transportation was initiated with the creation of space vehicles which have taken man and his products around the earth and to the moon and back. These revolutionary developments flowed from the interplay of decisions made by the providers and users of varied transportation facilities and services, and by the agencies of the national, state, and local governments.

Such profound changes in the modes of transportation had repercussions throughout the entire American economy. Utilizing both old and new forms of transportation, each region of the country was able to specialize in the goods and services it could produce with maximum benefit in exchange for the goods and services of other regions. Industrial entrepreneurs were able to determine the cheapest methods of transporting raw

TABLE 19-1
Volume of Passenger and Freight Traffic, by Type of Transport, 1930-1970

Agency	Percent of Total Passenger-Miles					Percent of Total Ton-Miles				
	1930	1940	1950	1960	1970	1930	1940	1950	1960	1970
Railroads	10.7	8.7	6.4	2.8	0.9	74.3	63.2	57.4	44.7	39.8
Highways	88.7	91.4	89.6	92.6	88.7	3.9	9.5	15.8	21.5	21.3
Inland Waterways	0.6	0.5	0.2	0.3	0.3	16.5	18.1	14.2	16.6	16.5
Pipelines (oil)						5.3	9.1	11.8	17.2	22.3
Airways		0.4	2.0	4.3	10.0			0.03	0.1	0.2

SOURCE: Interstate Commerce Commission, U.S. Bureau of the Census, The Statistical History of the United States (New York: Basic Books, 1976), Series Q 1-11, 12-22, p. 707.

materials or semi-manufactured goods and to ascertain the most easily accessible markets for their products. Thus, the increase in efficient and cheap transportation encouraged both mass production and mass consumption throughout the country. Beyond that, these new forms of transportation—along with the new mass communication technologies—greatly increased the mobility of the American people, diminishing sectional differences and regional provincialism, and promoting political, economic, social, and cultural unity.

Today, in the most advanced industrial countries, transportation services, excluding expenditures on private automobiles, account for between 5 and 10 percent of gross national product—and that figure would be considerably larger, especially in the United States, if we were to add the amount spent on private automobiles. In 1975 the American people spent $141 billion on the movement of freight and $177 billion on the movement of passengers, with the total transportation bill, including the purchase of cars, aircraft, and other vehicles, accounting for 21 percent of the nation's GNP.

The pervasive role of transportation in all areas of the nation's economic life can also be gauged by other indicators. Thus, in 1976 transportation and related activities, such as transportation equipment manufacturing, accounted for 11 percent of total employment in the United States. Transportation and related industries also contributed about 15 percent of the federal taxes, and 26 percent of the state taxes collected in 1975. And, on the other side of the ledger, in 1976 national and state governments jointly expended over $34 billion to provide such domestic transportation facilities as highways and airports.

The proportion of the total traffic carried by each mode of transport underwent a striking change over a period of four decades. As Table 19–1 shows, between 1930 and 1970 the share of the total ton-miles of railway freight fell from 74 to 40 percent. Meanwhile, motor transport, which accounted for only 4 percent of the total ton-miles in 1930, had quintupled by 1970. The proportion of intercity railway passenger-miles fell from nearly 9 percent of the total movement in 1940 to .9 percent in 1970. In the same period, the airways' share of passenger traffic increased from .4 percent to 10 percent. The more recent modes of transport grew partly by taking traffic away from the older types and partly by creating new traffic and new types of construction.

An important factor in the development of American transportation has been the economic regulation of the different transport industries by government agencies. For several decades, many regarded as desirable government restriction of competition within any one transport industry and between different forms of transport. In recent years, however, many economists have urged abandoning or modifying these restrictions and taking advantage of unsubsidized free market competition.

The Railroads

GROWTH AND DECLINE

Historically, the United States has been the biggest railway builder in the world. But the great period of railroad construction was followed by a period of steady decline: The total of first main railway track reached its peak of 254,000 miles in 1916, and gradually fell to below 205,000 by 1970. Mileage of all tracks reached a maximum of 430,000 miles in 1930, and decreased to 390,000 by 1970. This decrease in mileage was the result of many factors: the exhaustion of the mines, forests, and other natural resources which had justified the construction of many branch lines; intensified highway, water, and airway competition; and the process of coordinating and consolidating numerous railway corporations into larger systems.

During World War I the numerous railroad companies were unable to coordinate their work in meeting the increased transportation demands arising from the war effort. In December 1917 President Wilson ordered the U.S. Railroad Administration to take over the operation of the railroads. This governmental innovation proved successful in meeting the war's transportation needs. But from a financial point of view, the takeover resulted in losses owing to increased wages and prices not covered by corresponding increases in rates and fares.

After the war, despite labor union pressure for government ownership, the Transportation Act of 1920 returned the railroads to private ownership. A government plan for consolidating all the existing railroads into a limited number of large ones was never realized. Instead, different large railroads purchased the stock of strategic connecting lines. Stock prices rose to extraordinary heights, but with the Great Depression, rail revenue decreased drastically. The Reconstruction Finance Corporation aided some railroads but could not prevent the operators of one-third of the nation's railroad mileage from going into bankruptcy and receivership by 1937. Most of these receiverships were eliminated through the financial reorganization of the railroads in the late 1930s and the prosperity created by their increased earnings arising from the great need for railroad services during World War II.

WORLD WAR II AND AFTER

In spite of their problems, even during the hard times of the 1930s, there were numerous innovations in railroad plants, equipment, and methods which increased greatly both railroad capacity and efficiency. Hence, in World War II the railroads, although remaining under private management, met all the challenges of the war-transportation demands. With one-fourth fewer cars, one-third fewer locomotives, and nearly one-third fewer men than in World War I, they were able to handle twice the traffic of the first war, without delay or congestion.

During World War II railway rates and fares remained the same in spite of increases in wages and the prices of materials and supplies. After the war in the period of 1945 through 1960, the level of railroad wages and the prices paid for materials and supplies more than doubled. As a result the railroads increased their average freight charge for carrying a one ton cargo a mile about 50 percent and their average charge for carrying a passenger per mile about the same. These higher rates as well as increased competition from airplanes, trucks, and inland-water carriers reduced the level of railroad earnings during this period.

Throughout the post-World War II years the railroads initiated a massive program of capital improvements, with annual expenditures for such purposes averaging more than $1 billion. It is estimated that during the 1940s alone capital investment was as great as the entire net sum invested during the years 1870 through 1890, when railway expansion was at its peak. Perhaps the most important changes were the displacement of the steam locomotive by the diesel-electric; the introduction of container or trailer-on-flat-car service, popularly called piggy-backing; and the development of the automatic terminal with electronic controls, or the push-button yard.

These capital investments occurred in the face of decreased net earnings after 1947, especially in the industrial heartland of the nation—east of Chicago and north of the Potomac and Ohio Rivers. As a result, a large number of railroads went into bankruptcy. The average rate of return on net railroad investment fell from 4.25 percent for the 1940s to 2.46 percent for the 1960s and 1970s. Since 1955, the rate of return has exceeded 3 percent in only six out of sixteen years, the most recent being 1966.

The financial problems of the railroads renewed the trend toward consolidation. Most of the decline in the number of railroad companies between 1920 and 1957 was due to total abandonment of short roads rather than to mergers of big companies. But between 1957 and 1973, mergers reduced the number of Class I railroads from 116 to about 60. Three particularly notable mergers were the Seaboard Coast Line, the Penn Central, and the Burlington Northern System.

Great operational savings were anticipated and claimed for nearly every proposed railroad merger, and when the consolidation was well planned and orderly, such economies were in fact often realized. The merger problems confronting the Penn Central, however, were so difficult that the railroad was forced into bankruptcy in 1970, after only two years of corporate existence. This incident led some economists to question the wisdom of railroads like the Penn Central organizing holding companies which, in addition to acquiring all or most of the stock of the railroad company, also acquired a controlling interest in a variety of noncarrier enterprises.

The Interstate Commerce Commission also discovered that some of the railroad conglomerates carried on practices which were positively detrimental to the controlled railroad such as paying special dividends to the holding company; transferring the railroad's nonrailroad property to the holding company at less than its market value; and having the holding company make loans to the railroad company so as to enable it to pay it dividends. Such transactions led to the suspicion that the holding companies were, in some cases, taking grossly improper advantage of the railroad companies.

The failure of private rail enterprise to stem the sharp decrease in rail passenger service in the 1960s led to government intervention. In 1971 most of the nation's rail-passenger service on the privately owned railroads became the responsibility of the federally operated National Railroad Passenger Corporation, later known as Amtrak. Amtrak managed to provide a generally improved passenger service, but at the cost of cumulative deficits of almost $1.5 billion for the period 1971 through 1976. If the energy shortage since 1973 leads to an increase in Amtrak's traffic, Amtrak may succeed financially in its operations; otherwise complete government ownership seems a likely alternative.

A parallel development was the creation by Congress of USRA (United States Railway Association) to plan the restructuring of the northeastern railroad network in seventeen states and to make loans of up to $1.5 billion for that purpose. Congress also created ConRail (Consolidated Railroad Corporation) to operate the railroad company that was to emerge from the restructuring of the bankrupt lines.

The final plan of the USRA for the restructuring of the Northeast Railroad System went into effect in April, 1976. On that date ConRail took over about seventeen thousand miles of line and was prepared to expend $2.1 billion for rehabilitation, improvement, and equipment during the first five years and $7 billion over ten years. How successful this reorganization program will be, only the future will tell. But there is little doubt that the national government had to act in 1973 to avert a financial collapse of a major part of the nation's railroad service.

CAPITAL INVESTMENT AND PRODUCTIVITY

The financial problems of the railroads in the past few decades have discouraged new outside capital from investing in railroads. Prior to 1900 railroads had secured nearly all of their capital needs from external sources: the capital markets with stocks and bonds or other railroad securities. By

World War I American railroads had come to rely on internal sources for more than 40 percent of all their financial requirements. About two-thirds of this came from retained profits, the rest from depreciation charges. Net new issues of long-term securities provided nearly all the remaining funds. But from 1921 on, 95 percent of the funds were generated internally. Stocks and bonds were issued as supplementary sources of funds, but this financing was offset almost entirely by the liquidation of current liabilities.

The railroad managers were usually successful in persuading their stockholders to permit them to withhold a portion of the earnings for reinvestment in the property, but continuation of this support in the future will depend on their ability to earn sufficient revenues. And the decrease in net earnings since 1947, noted above, has made it difficult to obtain outside capital. Dramatic changes in current economic trends and in the structure of the industry are required if the railroads are to be transformed into efficient, competitive, and profitable enterprises.

Although the role of railroad output has steadily declined in national economic importance—since 1916 when it accounted for 9 percent of the gross national product to 5.1 percent of GNP in 1950 and less than 1 percent of GNP by 1975—the relative efficiency of the railroad industry as against other sectors of the economy remained high. Over the long period, 1899 to 1953, the average annual rate of increase in combined capital and labor productivity (known as total factor productivity) in railroad transportation was 2.6 percent, as compared with 1.1 percent in farming and 2 percent in mining and manufacturing. (In both World War I and World War II the railroads did even better, showing average rates of productivity increase of around 3.5 percent a year. Even since 1948, the average annual rate of productivity gain has remained around 2.7 percent. A careful analysis of the relative contributions of labor and capital to total factor productivity for the period 1899–1953 reveals greater labor productivity than capital productivity. The average annual rate of change in the contribution of capital was 1.0 percent during this period, that for labor was 2.8 percent.

One consequence of this increase in labor productivity was a considerable increase in railroad wages and salaries over the past few decades, as well as a decrease in the total number of rail workers. Another consequence was greatly improved service for shippers of freight, especially coal, lumber, agricultural products, and motor vehicles, although shortages of freight cars have become increasingly common as many carriers diverted their investments into nonrail activities. Passenger service, on the other hand, declined sharply during the same period. The general public, however, was impressed by the increases in the price of rail services combined, in many areas, with a decline in the extent and quality of those services. The lack of maintenance of track and equipment in many cases caused serious safety problems, leading to thousands of derailments annually.

GOVERNMENT REGULATION

National and state regulation of railroads has focused on the rates they charged (usually so as to preclude monopoly profits) and on the quality and safety of the services they provided. National and state railway commissions also controlled entry into the railroad industry, financial practices, and accounting methods.

Back in 1920 Congress directed the Interstate Commerce Commission to set railway rates at a level that would permit the roads to earn an average return of 5.5 percent; this was regarded as a fair return on the value of their properties. When this objective was not achieved, Congress in 1933 directed the ICC to consider the effect of rates on the movement of traffic. In other words, it called for returns that would enable the railroads to attract new capital. Congress thus recognized that in the competition with other modes of transport, the desired level of earnings in rail transport might best be obtained by lowering, rather than raising, rates.

The Motor Carrier Act of 1935 and the Transportation Act of 1940 made the ICC the regulator of both the railroads and their competitors, the trucks, buses, and inland water carriers. The ICC ordered rates that allowed both railroads and trucks to share in most of the traffic. Keeping truck and rail rates close to parity meant that the lower-cost carrier was not able to reduce rates to obtain all the traffic for which it had a cost advantage. As a result each form of transportation carried traffic for which its competitor had a cost advantage. But since trucking, unlike the railroad, could provide flexible door-to-door service, a policy of rate equality in effect encouraged the growth of trucking at the expense of the railroads. Since the railroad rate structure is based on the principle that the higher the value or selling price of a commodity, the higher the rail rates, trucks have tended to take over the high-valued commodities, while the low-valued ones have continued in the main to be carried by the railroads.

Such policies resulted in the continual decline of the railroads. The impending bankruptcy of some major railroads spurred Congress to pass the Transportation Act of 1958, which directed the ICC to give greater consideration to competitive cost factors in determining the legality of railroad rates. But disregarding the act, the ICC in 1965 actually prevented the railroads from lowering rates to compete with other carriers in those instances when these new rates were below their fully distributed costs.

Hence, despite the Transportation Act of 1958, many railroad managers continue to believe that their industry is overregulated. Nor have they felt any important improvement as a result of the establishment in 1966 of a new Department of Transportation. Throughout the early 1970s the continued low rate of return on railroad investment, the heightened concern over railroad safety, and the danger of bankruptcy for various

Eastern railroad lines increased the sense of crisis for many within and outside the railroad industry. In any case, it seems clear that the ICC, by acting as a court rather than as an economic planner, has failed to work out a national transportation policy that would place greater reliance on competition. A wholesale abandonment of regulation in transportation might recreate the chaotic competition that once inspired regulation. Nevertheless, a combination of competition and minimum government controls would enable the railroads to allocate their resources so as to eliminate the economic inefficiencies that have developed in the regulated railroad industry.

A turning point in the fortunes of the railroad industry may be at hand. The decline of railroad transportation and the tremendous upsurge of automobile and airplane transportation was based on the widespread belief that America had unlimited energy supplies, especially in petroleum, to burn in the foreseeable future at relatively low cost to consumers. The Middle East oil shortages since 1973 have brought home to many Americans the necessity for a drastic reevaluation of our transportation policies.

Motor Transport

SURFACED HIGHWAYS

During the latter half of the nineteenth century the great expansion of the American railroad system led to a prolonged lull in good road building. Then, as more and more of the general public became users first of bicycles in the 1890s, then of automobiles in the 1900s, the national government once more became interested in roads as a means of meeting these new demands and of reducing the farmer's isolation. In 1916 Congress passed the Federal Aid Road Act which initiated a national policy designed to secure a nationwide system of roads backed by the national government. This new policy was strictly an aid policy, however. While the national government assisted state and local governments with funds and in the planning of a national highway network, the actual construction and maintenance were left to the states and localities.

As the American automobile industry created a revolution through mass production of automobiles for mass consumption, total annual highway expenditures by all levels of government increased from about $1 billion in 1921 to $3.8 billion in 1950, and $16.7 billion in 1970. During the past half century, over $300 billion were expended on the provision of highways. At first, the national government's share was small—only 6 percent in 1921; but by 1958 it had reached about 25 percent of the total, and it was to continue around that figure into the mid-1970s.

During the 1930s the national government extended aid to urban as well as to rural portions of the highway network. A sharp drop in highway construction and maintenance during World War II required postwar construction for the greatly expanded number of motor vehicles. In 1944 Congress planned a national system of interstate and defense highways for which the 1956 Highway Act authorized spending $42 billion over thirteen years. Although the construction was slower than anticipated and the cost higher than planned, a system of nationwide superhighways came into being. These multiple-lane, limited-access roadways were adapted to the more powerful postwar vehicles and promoted high-speed, long-distance driving.

But with the passage of time not even the most modern highway designs were able to eliminate or prevent congestion. Moreover, the social costs of vehicle air pollution raised doubts about the wisdom of increasing either highway construction or automobile production. Nevertheless, for better or for worse, for the majority of Americans who own automobiles there is a network of over three million miles of surfaced highway, much of it in first class condition. And governmental decision makers do not seem to have the courage, at least in peacetime, to interfere with the nation's love affair with the automobile, in spite of its contribution to problems of energy and ecology.

MOTOR CARRIERS

Only after World War I did motor-truck transportation begin to have an impact on the national economy. Postwar improvements in truck design, the invention of large pneumatic tires, and the improvement of the highway system led to a steadily increasing use of motor trucks in agriculture, construction, wholesale and retail trade, public utilities, and personal transportation. During the 1920s intercity and interstate trucking developed at a steady rate. Although motor freighting suffered some setbacks in the depressed years of the early 1930s and during World War II, the trucking industry resumed rapid and steady growth after the war. The number of registered trucks in the United States grew from 99,000 in 1914 to 4.8 million in 1940, and 17.6 million in 1970. In that year trucks moved 596 million tons of intercity freight, gave employment to over one million persons and were responsible for over 21 percent of total U.S. ton-miles.

Several factors accounted for this increase. First, there was the economic advantage of trucks against railroads for short hauls and small shipments. Another was that motor trucks offered certain services that the railroads could not match, such as relatively flexible schedules and complete door-to-door service. A third was that trucking rates could be lower because the required plant investment was far less proportionately than that of the railroads, and the costs of going over the highways, despite user charges and gasoline taxes, was less than the costs for the construction and maintenance of railbeds and rail track. Finally, as we have seen, there was the Interstate Commerce Commission's protection of the motor trucking industry from the railroad competition.

The profit opportunities in motor trucking attracted many individuals and small firms to the industry, especially during the depression years of the 1930s. As a result, the large trucking firms, fearful of excessive competition, pressured a majority of the states to institute some form of control over common and contract carriers of property and persons. In 1935 Congress passed the Motor Carrier Act, which gave the ICC the power to control maximum and minimum rates for common carriers and minimum rates for contract carriers as well as to set the conditions for entry into the industry.

Four decades of federal regulation of motor transport have made economists increasingly critical of both the theoretical basis and the practical consequences of ICC policy. Motor transport does not have the monopolistic characteristics of railroads and should not be forced into the same mold. Since there is effective competition among firms, there seems to be no need for regulation of rates.

As we have seen, moreover, the ICC has also been criticized for creating a rate structure for the railroads that has turned out to be in favor of the trucking industry. The ICC seems to have encouraged the trucking industry to adopt a "value of service" rate structure similar to the railroads, and thus provided an incentive to business and other shippers to avoid the higher rates on high-valued commodities by using their own trucks. Consequently, private trucking expanded from the 1950s on, not because it was inherently more economical, but because of the special transportation pricing system that the trucking industry had adopted. Since this practice has resulted in the cutting down of business for common carriers in the trucking industry, the economic rationale of decisions of both the ICC and the dominant truck firms is open to serious question.

Air Transport

Although air transport began with the first controlled flight by the Wright brothers in 1903, it emerged as a commercial enterprise only after World War I. The war stimulated aircraft development and trained some ten thousand men to fly; many of them became the entrepreneurial reserve for the airlines founded in the late 1920s and early 1930s. The first regular commercial passenger air service was established between

Florida and Cuba in 1920; the first domestic scheduled passenger service in 1925; and the first domestic freight service in 1925.

The take off of commercial aviation was the result of a series of government decisions favorable to private enterprise. In 1919 the Post Office had established regular government (Army) air mail service on a transcontinental basis. But in 1925 Congress authorized the Post Office to begin letting contracts to commercial airlines on the basis of competitive bids, a move that stimulated the development of commercial aviation since the carriers were required to transport passengers as well as mail. A second advance occurred when the national government assumed responsibility for aids to navigation, safety regulations, and the development of the airways. This was achieved through the Air Commerce Act of 1926, which established what is today the Federal Aviation Agency now in the Department of Transportation. Finally, the Civil Aeronautics Act of 1938 established what was later known as the Civil Aeronautics Board (CAB) with the power to regulate the conditions of routes, fares, and of entry and exit in the air transport industry; it also created a regulatory shelter for established carriers.

One consequence of all these measures was a division of activities: government ownership and operation of the airways and private ownership and operation of the commercial airlines, subject to control by the CAB. Another consequence was the way these acts promoted the economic progress of commercial aviation in several directions. The airlines' share of domestic intercity commercial (common carrier) passenger miles rose from less than 1 percent in 1930 to 14.4 percent in 1950 and over 77 percent in 1974. Their share of the passengers traveling between overseas countries and the United States went from a small fraction of the total in the late 1930s to less than half in the late 1940s and 94 percent in 1974. (Indeed United States airlines have held over 50 percent of the world's overseas air market.) In addition to passengers, air freight (cargo, mail, and express) has rapidly become an increasingly important proportion of the airline business. Air freight revenues in 1974 came to over $1.2 billion; this amounted to approximately 9 percent of all airline revenues and over 1 percent of the freight revenues of all modes of transport.

The growth of commercial aviation has been phenomenal: The airline's revenues in 1974, it has been calculated, came to 4 times those of 1960, 12 times those of 1950, and almost 150 times those of 1940 ($150 million). Can this amazing growth be expected to continue? Can the United States maintain its competitive advantages in an increasingly competitive international market? Part of the answer lies with the decision makers in the air transport industry; part with the American managers of the energy crisis. But part also lies with the Civil Aeronautics Board.

There is no doubt that the Civil Aeronautics Board has attempted to build up the air transport industry by favoring rates and subsidies that will enable all the companies to survive and to prosper. Yet despite the progress of the commercial airlines, economists criticize both Congress and the CAB for various inadequacies. Congress erred in presuming that the air transport industry needed the type of control developed for rail carriers in a monopolistic industry, while at the same time stressing the need for competition and the prevention of monopoly. For these inconsistencies the CAB cannot be faulted. But, it can be taken to task for not having decided conclusively whether air transport should be treated as a regulated monopoly or controlled as a competitive industry.

A new era of competition in the airline industry was opened by the Airline Deregulation Act of 1978 which in effect ended forty years of federal protection. The powers of the Civil Aeronautics Board to regulate fares and routes will end completely by 1983, and the agency will go out of existence in 1985. Meanwhile, the CAB is pledged to carry further recently instituted policies actively favoring competition. Other enunciated aims are: the establishment of air service to small and isolated communities, the development of an antitrust policy, and the expansion of consumer protection. An early result of deregulation has been a marked increase in business as the airlines lowered fares, with a sometimes bewildering array of options for the traveler.

Water Transport

DOMESTIC WATERWAYS AND SHIPPING

After the Civil War, when the railroads became the dominant mode of transportation in the United States, shipping on the inland waterways seemed doomed to extinction by the end of the nineteenth century. But early in the twentieth century there was a revival of public interest in domestic waterways. One reason was public concern about the conservation of our natural resources. Another was the widespread belief that waterways provided a cheaper means of transport than railroads. Finally, many felt that competition from water transport would bring about a lowering of railroad rates and provide a means for measuring their reasonableness.

The 1908 report of the Inland Waterways Commission prompted the federal government to start various large canal and river canalization projects. In 1924 the Inland Waterways Corporation was established to operate a barge line on the Mississippi. Combined with technological advances that increased the efficiency of diesel-powered tugboats, special-purpose barges, and tankers, these developments brought about a significant return of traffic to the inland waterways.

The opening of the Panama Canal in 1914, although an international enterprise, provided an effective water route for domestic trade between the three seacoasts of the United States. Another major step in the development of inland waterways came with the opening of the St. Lawrence Seaway in 1959. This project was a joint Canadian-American affair that connected the Great Lakes with the St. Lawrence River and benefited the commerce of both nations.

Today, the United States has a notable system of inland waterways, comprising more than twenty-seven thousand miles of navigable rivers and canals, but by definition excluding the Great Lakes and the coastal shipping lanes. In 1973 the system carried over 358 billion ton-miles of freight, an increase of 75 percent over the 1961 level. This constituted about 15 percent of the total intercity freight movements in the country.

Domestic water transport differs from other forms of transport in that it is based on the individual boat as the operating unit. This may range all the way from small motor launches and ferries to great iron ore freighters on the Great Lakes, cargo-passenger ships, or a huge towboat on the Mississippi which can handle forty thousand tons of freight at a time. The ownership of the units varies from the owner of a small vessel to the owner or owners of relatively large fleets.

The waterways for this traffic are public highways, and the investment in them for navigational improvements has historically been supplied by public funds. Terminal facilities, such as harbors and docks, have been financed from public and private sources, with waterway improvements in the harbor and navigational aids coming from public funds. On the other hand, the vessels which furnish transport service to domestic trade have in the main been privately owned. They have served as carriers for hire or as private carriers; the carriers for hire have been common carriers or contract carriers. It has been established that about 93 percent of domestic water transport has not been regulated.

For the first forty years of the twentieth century the regulation of domestic water transportation was carried out in a limited way by different agencies under a variety of laws. Thus, the Interstate Commerce Commission had the authority to establish routes for joint rail-water services, and it had the power to fix maximum joint rates. In 1916 the United States Shipping Board was given the authority to regulate vessels operating regular routes in coastal or intercoastal trade as well as common carriers on the Great Lakes. Although the Board could not fix minimum or actual rates, it had to be notified about maximum rates, fares, and charges. In 1938 the Federal Maritime Commission, which had superseded the Shipping Board, was given the authority to set minimum rates for domestic deep-water common carriers, except for those operating on the Great Lakes.

During the period between the two wars Congress became increasingly concerned about the severe competition and declining earnings that prevailed in the domestic shipping industry, and decided that further regulation was necessary to cure these troubles. The Transportation Act of 1940, which placed domestic water carriers under the jurisdiction of the Interstate Commerce Commission rather than the Maritime Commission, was supposed to protect domestic water transport from destructive competition among water carriers. The law recognized two types of water carriers as subject to regulation, common carriers and contract carriers, and in general applied the same control provisions that the ICC had worked out for motor vehicles.

The experience of three decades of regulation under the act, however, has little to commend it. The legislation did not resolve the difficulties that have troubled domestic shipping. Common and contract carriage have not been preserved by efforts to limit competition because so much of inland water transport has been exempted from any rate regulation. Maximum-rates cases were never important under the 1940 statute, few charges of discrimination were filed by shippers, and the water carriers were rarely charged with abusing their privileges. It seems clear that inland water transportation was controlled because of its competitive effect on other forms of transportation, especially the railroads.

THE MERCHANT MARINE

From colonial times down to the outbreak of the Civil War the American merchant marine flourished. Then there followed a long depressed period during which the United States fell behind England in large part because of the English advantage in the building of iron or steel ships. As a result United States tonnage registered for foreign trade decreased two-thirds between 1860 and 1910. While the value of foreign commerce in that half century quadrupled, the share carried in American bottoms dropped precipitously from 66 percent to 8 percent. These declines were in sharp contrast to those for shipping in the protected domestic trade, which in 1910 were 6.7 million tons, almost nine times the amount of the American foreign-trade shipping.

Then World War I transformed the merchant marine. Concerned that roughly 92 percent of the nation's foreign commerce was carried by European ships, Congress in 1916 established the United States Shipping Board. By 1921 its ambitious shipbuilding program had resulted in the United States displacing Great Britain from first place among the world's merchant fleets.

After that, however, American tonnage engaged in foreign trade again dropped from 11 million tons in 1921 to a low of 3 million tons in 1941. Congress attempted to turn the tide in 1929 by an act that provided generous grants through mail payments to those lines that were willing to build new ships. But this measure could not prevail against the cheaper costs of foreign operation and construction.

To remedy this situation, Congress in 1936 established the Maritime Commission, which was authorized to grant operating-differential and construction-differential subsidies to overcome the difference between American and foreign costs in the building and operation of vessels. The operating subsidies were given only to lines approved for specific "essential trade routes." In effect roughly three quarters of the operating subsidies compensated for the difference between the pay of American and foreign officers and crews. Militant maritime union action from 1936 on pushed American wages so much ahead of foreign wages, however, that many unsubsidized American vessels found it more profitable to operate under foreign flags of convenience, especially those of Panama and Liberia.

The construction-differential subsidies, designed to keep American shipyards active, absorbed up to one-half the cost of construction in foreign yards. When World War II came, the subsidized merchant marine proved its worth through its fine ships, trained mariners, and operational skill. Once more the national government embarked on a gigantic emergency building program, producing 5,777 vessels, one-half of which were the large but slow Liberty ships. After World War II those American lines engaged in essential foreign trade routes continued to be rather successful. Some of the other shipping profited from the congressional stipulation that at least one-half of the cargo shipped abroad in the various foreign aid programs of the United States had to be carried in American-flag vessels.

In this postwar period, a sharp decline occurred in that part of the American merchant marine engaged in coastal and intercoastal shipping. Part of this decrease was credited by the shipping industry to the "railroad minded" Interstate Commerce Commission. Other difficulties stemmed from the still-mounting wages of mariners and longshoremen and from the competition of trucks. On the other hand, barge traffic on inland waterways and traffic on the Great Lakes flourished.

American shipping engaged in foreign trade after World War II steadily decreased in volume from 29.7 million gross tons in 1946 to 14.7 million in 1960. To counteract this continuing trend Congress passed the Merchant Marine Act of 1970, extending and liberalizing the terms of the 1936 act. The almost-monopoly control over the subsidy benefits was taken away from the lines on the specific "essential trade routes." The construction-differential subsidies were increased so as to produce thirty ships per year for the next ten years. Bulk-cargo ships became likely beneficiaries owing to the increasing need for oil and gas from overseas. The legislation had a speedy quickening effect on merchant shipping, although some of the initial enthusiasm was lost after President Nixon's 1973 budget reduced the funding of the program from $455 million to $275 million.

Whatever changes may affect the United States merchant marine in the future, there is no doubt that shipping underwent more drastic changes in the 1970s than in any period since the Civil War. The increased speed in travel resulting from jet airplanes had a devastating effect upon regular ocean passenger service. Many passenger liners were laid up, sold, or became involved in the fast-growing development of pleasure cruises. As America's pre-World War II petroleum, gas, and mineral self-sufficiency was replaced by an increasing need for seaborne cargoes, the size of oil tankers expanded more than tenfold, special ships were designed for natural gas, and many bulk carriers were built to bring iron and other essential minerals for American industry from overseas.

Conclusion

In twentieth-century America, the great network of diverse modes of transportation has been the cornerstone of a complex continental economy with far-flung global connections. As consumers' incomes rose, the demands for transportation services not only grew at a fantastic rate, more than doubling between 1950 and 1970, but they changed in character. The railroads increasingly shrank in importance from the 1930s on, losing part of their traffic to trucks, buses, and airplanes, and part to water carriers and pipelines. Mass transit decreased and individual ownership of automobiles multiplied, to the point that ours has been called "a car culture." Only the airlines had a more rapid growth; their success in overseas travel forced most passenger liners into retirement.

These developments and others were shaped, on the one hand, by innumerable individual decisions on alternative means of transportation, and, on the other hand, by the stimuli and constraints of government policies. Government regulation followed from the fact that any individual decision in this field would inevitably have public consequences; the problem throughout has been to mediate between these realms of interest. The private automobile, for example, diminished public transit, facilitated the weakening of the inner cities, and raised the levels of accidents and air pollution. Unfortunately, no clear consensus on national transportation goals has evolved to guide decisions concerning such conflicts between individual satisfactions and public interest, or between economic growth and environmental protection.

An important means of translating public transport policy into action has been the economic regulation of the varied transport industries through government agencies such as the Interstate Commerce Commission and the Civil Aeronautics Board. Economists now criticize as unwise various economic regulations that focused on restricting competition either within a particular transport industry or between different modes of transport. The tendency now is to place more stress on the advantages of unsubsidized free market competition. Thus commercial airlines benefited from recent moves in the direction of deregulation. Similar measures, along with financial aid, may improve the competitive position of the railroads and may lessen the opposition of other transport interests to this type of reform.

The implications of the energy crisis for the future of American transportation have not been adequately understood and acted upon by our decision makers in government and in private industry. A realistic appraisal of American energy needs and world resources could generate a comprehensive energy conservation program. One likely result, for example, might be a revitalization of the railroad industry, since railroads carry freight and passengers at a fraction of the cost in energy consumption of airplanes, trucks, buses, and passenger cars. When national, state, and local governments and the average citizen face realistically the energy problem as it applies to transportation and reorder their priorities, they will have to cut back drastically the use of automobiles and airplanes, expand mass transit, and persuade more of the population to shift from the suburbs to the cities. By reducing America's dependence on oil through massive reductions in oil consumption and greater exploitation of other energy sources, the American economy will be strengthened both domestically and internationally.

SUGGESTED READINGS

An excellent quantitative study of the changing modes of transport is Harold Barger, *The Transportation Industries 1889–1946* (New York: National Bureau of Economic Research, 1951). The best one-volume history of railroads is John F. Stover, *The Life and Decline of the American Railroad* (New York: Oxford University Press, 1970). The problem of railroad regulation by the Interstate Commerce Commission has aroused great controversy. The view that the railroads wanted regulation and dominated the ICC is presented by Gabriel Kolko, *Railroads and Regulation, 1877–1916* (Princeton, N.J.: Princeton University Press, 1965) and is vigorously attacked by Albro Martin, *Enterprise Denied: Origins of the Decline of American Railroads, 1897–1917* (New York: Columbia University Press, 1971). An incisive, balanced critique of the ICC is Ari and Olive Hoogenboom, *A History of the ICC: From Panacea to Palliative* (New York: W. W. Norton, 1976). On the trends in capital formation by the railroads, the best analysis for the period after 1914 is Melville J. Ulmer, *Capital in Transportation, Communications, and Public Utilities* (Princeton, N.J.: Princeton University Press, 1960).

Lively and scholarly books on the automobile, its use, and manufacture are John B. Rae, *The American Automobile* (Chicago: University of Chicago Press, 1965) and *The Road and the Car in American Life* (Cambridge, Mass.: M.I.T. Press, 1971); Emma Rothschild, *Paradise Lost: The Decline of the Auto-Industrial Age* (New York: Random House, 1973); and Lawrence J. White, *The Automobile Industry Since 1945* (Cambridge, Mass.: Harvard University Press, 1971).

A brilliant study on the airline industry is Richard Caves, *Air Transport and its Regulators* (Cambridge, Mass.: Harvard University Press, 1962); an excellent history is R. E. A. G. Davies, *Airlines of the United States Since 1914* (London: Putnam, 1972).

Attractive, informative books on domestic water transportation and the overseas merchant marine are Charles W. Howe et al., *Inland Waterway Transportation* (Washington, D.C.: Resources for the Future, 1969); Samuel A. Lawrence, *United States Merchant Shipping Policies and Politics* (Washington, D.C.: Brookings Institution, 1966); and Carleen O'Loughlin, *Economics of Sea Transport* (London: Pergamon Press, 1967). The standard work on pipelines is Arthur M. Johnson, *Petroleum Pipelines and Public Policy* (Cambridge, Mass.: Harvard University Press, 1967).

Transport economics and policies are admirably analyzed and presented in Donald V. Harper, *Transportation in America: Users, Carriers, Government* (Englewood Cliffs, N.J.: Prentice-Hall, 1978); John L. Hazard, *Transportation: Management, Economics, Policy* (Cambridge, Md.: Cornell Maritime Press, 1977); James T. Kneafsey, *Transportation Analysis* (Lexington, Mass.: D. C. Heath, 1975); Herman Martins, Jr., *National Transportation Policy in Transition* (Lexington, Mass.: D. C. Heath, 1972); and John R. Meyer et al., *The Economics of Competition in the Transportation Industries* (Cambridge, Mass.: Harvard University Press, 1959).

Fresh approaches to present and current problems are explored in the 1977 World Conference on Transport Research symposium, Evert J. Visser, ed., *Transport Decisions in an Age of Uncertainty* (The Hague, Netherlands and Boston, Mass.: Martinus Nijhof, 1977).

CHAPTER 20

——

Domestic and Foreign Markets

in the Era of

Mass Consumption

Mass consumption today rivals mass production as a major economic phenomenon in the United States and the rest of the industrialized world. All western-oriented industrialized countries have been enjoying unprecedentedly high standards of living and their high per capita incomes are matched by a seemingly insatiable demand for goods and services. In chapter 17 we discussed how new methods of mass production created the possibility of satisfying this ever-increasing demand at home and abroad. In this chapter we shall see how the distribution of these mass-produced goods to the multitude of American consumers was accomplished after World War I by the phenomenally rapid development of new types of wholesale and retail marketing. As a result, consumers were faced with more, and more-varied, decisions on how to allocate their incomes among the constantly widening array of available domestic and foreign products and services. At the same time foreign consumers in the advanced industrial economies were experiencing a similar expansion of choices. United States exports abroad contributed to this, and were in part compensated by large imports from overseas.

Until the end of World War II, America's foreign commerce was carried on under the aegis of a high or modified tariff protectionism.

Then the United States shifted to advocacy of tariff reduction and free trade around the world. In the 1940s, as in the 1920s, the United States became the chief exporter of the monetary and physical capital required to restore the economic health of war-devastated countries. By the 1950s this economic reconstruction had initiated a rapid expansion of world income and world trade. A major consequence was that by 1970 the world's gross annual product achieved the unprecedented level of some $3.2 trillion. World trade was five times higher than in 1950.

During this period of enormous change in the structure of the world economy, the gap between the United States and the rest of the developed world has been narrowing. At the same time, the traditional pattern of Americans exporting more goods than they imported has gradually been reversed. For some years after World War II, the large American foreign investments brought in sufficient income to sustain a limited negative balance of trade. In the 1970s, however, the energy crisis and a prolonged deterioration in the exchange rate for the United States dollar have created serious balance of payment problems. These still await an adequate solution. Nevertheless, the phenomenon of mass consumption at home and abroad evidences signs of continuing vitality and future growth. Domestic and foreign commerce, whatever temporary recessions may occur, seem destined to continue to grow in the foreseeable future.

Mass Distribution and Social Change

MASS MARKETERS

Prior to 1919 wholesalers and manufacturers played the leading role in directing the production and marketing of consumer goods in the United States. But after World War I retailers came to assume an increasingly important role in this area. Large-scale retailers not only began to introduce their own brands of merchandise but actively sought to create consumer loyalty to themselves as against the manufacturers. The manufacturers, however, managed to retain a special place in the market through advertising and other devices.

Retail enterprises grew by adding new lines and, to an even greater extent, by adding new outlets or stores. The chain store, especially the established ones, such as the A&P and Woolworth, developed into the fastest growing channel of distribution, growing faster than new department stores or mail-order houses. Between 1918 and 1929 the number of chain store units increased over fivefold, expanding into the drug, grocery, and other trades previously dominated by the wholesaler and the small retailer. But the crash of 1929 reduced the number of chain-store units and concentrated their ownership in fewer hands. Mail-order houses, like Sears Roebuck and Montgomery Ward, found their rural markets declining in the 1920s and built chains of retail department stores to gain sales in urban and suburban markets. The supermarket began its career in retailing during the 1930s and became central to the shopping centers that developed in the suburbs after World War II. Their success led many chain stores to adopt various supermarket practices.

For most of the interim period department stores were able to maintain their position in the retail distribution structure. But from the early 1930s on it was the low-price department store chains that began to account for an increasing share of total department store sales. In order to survive the Great Depression many of the higher-price department stores became units in chains. Relatively few continued as independent, locally owned businesses.

Since World War II some retailers have moved successfully into operating discount houses. Beginning with hard goods such as appliances, cameras, jewelry, and furniture at substantial price cuts, the system of discount sales spread to soft goods and foods. The development of these new types of stores, many in abandoned factories, at first appealed primarily to low-income groups. Gradually, however, they also won acceptance among middle-income groups. By 1960 about 2,500 discount stores had sales amounting to $3 billion, about one-fourth of the business done by department stores.

Although there is no doubt that in most of the interim period independent wholesalers of many consumer goods lost ground to department stores, mail-order houses, chain stores, and manufacturers, since 1939 wholesale trade has grown more rapidly than any other private sector of the economy except construction. By 1967 there were more firms in wholesale trade than in manufacturing, and their sales exceeded those of retailers buying directly from manufacturers' outlets.

One factor in this growth of wholesale selling was the increasing specialization resulting from the spectacular increase in the variety of manufactured consumer goods. Wholesalers of electrical goods, for example, developed a special type of wholesaling. Other wholesalers concentrated on such new or rapidly expanding markets as amusement and sporting goods, industrial chemicals, iron and steel products, commercial machinery and equipment, and construction machinery. Other factors contributing to the prosperity of the wholesalers were their proved operating methods and controls and their closer cooperation with retailers. Wholesalers came to recognize that their own strength depended on having strong retailers, and this led them to help the retailers become effective merchants in their own right.

Changes in Population Distribution and Life Styles

The rapid growth of mass wholesale and retail trade since World War I reflected an adjustment to major changes in the numbers, distribution, and purchasing habits of the American people as well as in the availability of a vastly increased quantity and variety of goods. In the sixty years between 1910 and 1970 the United States population more than doubled. Equally important was the continuing migration from rural to urban areas which greatly increased the demand for finished goods and the concentration and growth of large-scale wholesale and retail trade. By 1970 only 5 percent of the population was living in rural areas.

After World War II the trend to suburban living that had begun in the 1920s increased to the point where by 1970 more people were living in the suburbs than in the central cities. As families moved to the suburbs many, but not all, retail and service businesses followed, and suburban shopping centers increased in number and size. The movement out of the cities by middle-income people was countered, however, by the movement into the cities of lower-income consumers, often with different ethnic backgrounds and consumer tastes. While some relatively affluent families have been returning to the central cities, the general trend to the suburbs has continued despite the increase in gasoline prices since the conclusion of the 1973 Arab-Israeli War.

During World War I and the 1920s many American consumers significantly changed their buying habits. They acquired a liking for new products and improvements in familiar products. Decade after decade technology and industry made available an ever-increasing supply of new products: automobiles, refrigerators, washing machines, electric vacuum cleaners, radios, and television sets.

From 1920 to the present, style became an increasingly important factor in the buying of many consumer goods with all social groups throughout the country, not just among the elite. This style consciousness of consumers, fostered by advertising, gradually extended to decisions in the purchase of such durable goods as electrical appliances, home furnishings, and such perishables as food, beverages, and cosmetics.

THE CONSUMER AS DECISION MAKER

In general the level and pattern of consumer expenditures exerted a major impact upon the growth of the American economy during this period. In 1929 total consumer expenditures accounted for about three-quarters of the gross national product; from World War II to the 1970s the percentage was, on the average, about two-thirds of the GNP. When aggregate demand increased at a rapid rate, the American economy usually expanded, sometimes creating a boom that led to inflation. When aggregate demand decreased markedly, a recession was likely to occur.

Over most of the past six decades consumers have spent the largest share of their personal disposable income on nondurable goods such as food, clothing, and household supplies, about triple what they spent on durables like household appliances, automobiles, and furniture. Nevertheless, as personal incomes went up after World War II, more people had enough discretionary control over their income to spend larger percentages of their incomes for expensive durable goods, and correspondingly, smaller percentages for food and clothing. There has also been an increase of expenditures on consumer services such as medical care, transportation, recreation, and education. Shortly after World War II, Americans spent thirty-one cents out of every dollar of disposable income for such services; by the early 1970s, this figure was up to forty-five cents. These changes in their spending reflected the decisions made by consumers, as members of households and as individuals, about the kinds of satisfactions they preferred.

CONSUMER SPENDING AND INCOME DISTRIBUTION

Of course, in the past, as in the present, consumers have also been influenced by the size of their money income and the level of commodity and service prices. The lowest income groups (in a 1960–61 study) spent on the average 20 percent more on consumer goods than they earned as income. As income rose, the proportion of income devoted to consumption expenditures tended to decrease. In the highest bracket, those with income of twenty-five thousand dollars and more, the average amount spent on consumer goods fell to about two-thirds of the income available.

The growth in the magnitude of personal consumer expenditures in the United States during the last five decades has been spectacular: from $77.3 billion in 1929 to $1.2 trillion in 1977 or about fifteen-fold, while per capita consumer expenditures rose from $675 to $5,665 or about eight-fold. Such statistics, however, do not reveal the great differences between various income groups or classes. The share of income of the top 5 percent declined slightly during the depression years of the 1930s, and then underwent a sharp reduction during World War II, as income tax rates were raised drastically. Since 1947 the evidence indicates a slight downward trend in the share received by the highest income class.

Changes in income distribution for all income classes, and not just the top groups, have been measured by the national government only since 1929. The evidence is overwhelming that since the early 1940s a majority of the American people have experienced a rise in income that led to a widespread movement of families to higher levels in the income scale. Various groups did not benefit as much as the majority, for example, the unskilled, the uneducated, and the aged, yet many in these groups did become better off than they had been in previous decades.

There has been a long-term increase in the income available for personal consumption expenditures. Between 1914 and 1970 the population increased from 99.1 million to 204.9 million; meanwhile GNP (in current dollars) increased from $38.9 billion to $977.1 billion. The growth in disposable personal income (most important for consumer expenditures) in this period ranged from $33.3 billion to $691.7 billion. The increased power to buy the widening variety of goods and services raised the standard of living. In a study of the average annual family expenditures by different family income groups around 1960, it was found that the higher the income of any family group, the larger the size of its consumer expenditures. The difference between the highest and the lowest income groups in this respect was enormous.

A trend towards a sharp increase in income inequality existed in the United States economy from 1820 to World War I. Although income inequality fell noticeably between 1929 and the early years after World War II, there has been little change since. As a result the upper income groups have been responsible for a large part of the total income expended on goods and services. For example, the families receiving over $7,500 a year in the early 1960s formed only 30 percent of the population, but accounted for almost one-half of the expenditures. Those families with incomes under $7,500 composed almost 70 percent of the population, but accounted for only 52 percent of the expenditures. These disparities in income level notwithstanding, the overall purchasing power of the American people was sufficient to sustain the highest mass consumption level of any large country in the world. It continues to provide an expanding market for domestic products and for large imports from abroad. These, in turn, have been made possible in large part by earnings from America economic investments abroad and United States agricultural and industrial exports.

The United States in the World Economy, 1914–79

The great expansion in American domestic trade and consumption during the past six decades was matched by an equally great expansion in American foreign trade. This trade was based in part on the war needs of the United States and its allies in four wars. In even larger part, the expansion reflected the constantly increasing consumer demand in the United States and in other parts of the world for foreign goods that supplemented or, in certain cases served as substitutes for, domestic products. World War I accelerated the emergence of the United States as a major creditor nation and as a leading world power, displacing Great Britain. One important factor in this shift of power was the increase in America's share of world manufactures, from 23 percent in 1870 to over 42 percent in 1926–29. Except for a brief decline during the Depression the United States share in the world's manufacturing output has equalled or exceeded 42 percent ever since.

The relation between United States output and the magnitude of United States exports was also in the United States' favor. In the 1920s the United States became the world's first exporter and chief investor, yet remained second to Great Britain as an importer. By 1970 the United States accounted for about 17 percent of the world's total commodity imports and 20 percent of total world exports.

Thus the economic policies and strength of the United States were of the greatest importance to its foreign suppliers, customers, and debtors. Easy access to American markets, stability in United States employment and income, and a continuous stream of American loans were vital concerns of the United States' trading partners. Abrupt changes in the United States tariff, ill-considered shifts in its foreign lending policy, or severe contractions in its business cycle could disrupt the economic balance in most countries of the world. America's position of leadership, achieved in the 1920s, brought responsibilities that the country was not yet ready to assume.

FOREIGN MARKETS AND UNITED STATES TRADE

From the outbreak of World War I to the 1970s the United States enjoyed a mainly positive or favorable balance of trade. Negative foreign trade balances occurred during the depression years 1934–40, and again during the 1970s. (See Table 20–1.) Ordinarily, as a mature creditor nation, the United States was able to balance trade deficits with net earnings from foreign investments. After the Arab oil embargo of 1973 and the subsequent increases in oil prices by OPEC, however, American trade deficits grew so large as to weaken foreign confidence in the stability of the American economy.

But up to 1973, continuous increase in the industrial strength of the United States during the twentieth century was reflected in the composition of American exports. The leading exports of the United States from 1914 to the 1970s were finished manufactures; next in magnitude of value were crude materials and semi-manufactures. The share of finished manufactured goods, excluding foodstuffs, rose from almost 31 percent in 1911–15 to 63 percent in 1951–55 and has fluctuated around that point in the succeeding years. By the 1960s the United States export of

TABLE 20-1
Balance of Merchandise Trade of
the United States
1909-1976

Period	Annual Average Millions of Dollars
1909-1918	+1,332
1919-1929	+1,380
1929-1938	+462
1939-1948	+5,394
1944-1953	+5,527
1954-1963	+4,040
1964-1968	+4,039
1969-1976	−9,730

SOURCE: U.S. Census Bureau, Statistical History of the United States (New York: Basic Books, 1976), p. 884. Series U 187-200; Economic Report of the President . . . January 1976 (Washington, D.C.: United States Government Printing Office, 1978), pp. 368-369; Robert Lipsky in Lance Davis et al., American Economic Growth (New York: Harper & Row, 1972), p. 578.

machinery and motor vehicles represented nearly 40 percent of the total value of exported goods.

The economic importance of American exports can be judged not only from the percentage of our output in different commodities that went into exports but also from the estimated employment in 1960 attributable to exports. This was calculated to be 3.1 million persons out of a total of 52.9 million employed persons. Of these 3.1 million, 1.5 million worked in industries producing directly for export or were indirectly involved in exporting their goods; 1.6 million were employed in industries supporting the production, transportation, or marketing of exported goods.

Of all the foreign markets for American products, Europe, taken as a whole, has always been the most important. But Europe's share in the total value of United States exports declined sharply from about 64 percent in 1911–20 to 33.5 percent in 1961–70. Meanwhile Canada's share in American foreign trade grew almost twofold from about 13 percent for the 1911–20 period and 21 percent for the 1961–70 period. At the same time Asia's share in the purchase of United States exports rose threefold, from 7.1 percent in 1911–20 to 22 percent in 1961–70.

The kinds of United States imports have undergone dramatic changes. Since 1914 American businessmen have shifted the highest percentage of their imports from finished goods and manufactured foodstuffs to crude materials like rubber, copper, and raw silk, and crude foodstuffs like coffee and sugar. After World War II American imports moved away from preponderantly agricultural products toward metal products, especially machinery and vehicles. One relatively unimportant import up to World War II that has gained tremendous strategic as well as economic importance is petroleum and its products. In 1945 the United States spent $152 million on importing petroleum; by 1955 this amount had risen to over $1 billion, by 1970 to $2.8 billion, and by 1978 to $33.1 billion.

Prior to 1914 Europe had been the chief source of America's imports. Between 1911–20 and 1941–50 Europe's share of United States imports fell from 33.5 percent to 11.7 percent, but then rose to 29.2 percent in 1961–70. During these same six decades America's reliance upon the crude rubber supplies of southeast Asia and the raw silk supplies of Japan grew greatly. After 1950 America also became a large importer of Japanese automobiles, cameras, and electronic equipment.

Foreign Economic Policy and Balance of Payments

Before World War I the United States was a net debtor nation; in 1914, United States assets abroad came to $3.5 billion, as against some $7.2 billion in European investments in this country. During World War I the great demand by the allied powers of Europe for American goods and services was financed in part by the liquidation of foreign-owned American securities, the shipping of gold to the United States, and, in largest part, by American loans. The consequence was that the United States became a net creditor nation; by 1919 private American assets abroad amounted to some $6.9 billion as against foreign assets in the United States of some $3.9 billion. During the 1920s Europe's demand for American goods continued, but American tariffs, passed in 1921, 1922, and 1930, prevented Europe from paying for its imports from the United States through an adequate amount of exports to the United States. The American political and business decision makers chose to maintain high protective tariffs. In order to encourage Europeans to buy American goods, they made successive loans to European nations as well as large capital investments abroad.

The 1930s were a period of massive international movements of capital to the United States. In the 1930s American foreign investments decreased from $17.2 billion to $11.5 billion. Meanwhile various economic and political crises in Europe and the Far East caused a flight of an estimated $8 to $11 billion in capital from Europe and elsewhere to the United States. In the same period these conditions caused almost $15 billion of gold to flow into the United States.

The impact of World War II on the United States' balance of payments and its position as a mature creditor nation was of unparalleled magnitude. During the years 1941–45, American unilateral transactions under the lend-lease program brought about a transfer of American goods and services of about $48 billion; three-fifths to the United Kingdom, one-fifth to Soviet Russia, and the remainder to France, China, and other countries. (See Table 20–2.) In part this outward flow of goods was covered by the transfer of foreign gold to the United States during and after the war, and by the liquidation of American debts in Europe. Additional coverage was provided by reverse lend-lease transactions, the financial obligations of the United States government for military purchases and expenditures for American troops abroad.

TABLE 20-2
United States Balance of Payments by Periods, 1914-45
(In Billions of Dollars)

Period	Goods and Services Net	Income on Investment Net	Capital Trans- actions	Unilateral Transfers	Gold	Errors and Omissions
914-1919	+14.7	+1.0	−14.1	−1.5	−0.8	−0.7
920-1933	+7.8	+8.5	−7.0	−5.1	−1.4	−2.8
934-1946	+2.8	+2.3	+7.4	−1.3	−14.9	+3.7
941-1945	+36.7	+1.8	+0.8	−41.6	+1.9	+0.4

SOURCE: Based on U.S. Bureau of the Census, Historical Statistics of the United States, 1789-1945
Washington, D.C.: United States Government Printing Office, 1949), pp. 242-43, and statistical analysis by Harry Gideonse in Harold Williamson, ed., The Growth of the American Economy, 2d ed. Englewood Cliffs, N.J.: Prentice-Hall, 1951), pp. 541, 789.

Even before the military defeat of Nazi Germany and Japan, the United States had to anticipate how it would deal with the tremendous destruction of industrial plants and transportation facilities in Europe and the Far East. There was danger of widespread suffering from economic want and political turmoil. The expansion of Soviet Russia into Eastern Europe also had to be faced. The top American political and economic decision makers used various measures to aid the war-devastated countries in different parts of the world. The United Nations Relief and Rehabilitation Administration (UNRRA) was one important means of meeting the immediate postwar relief problems; by 1947 UNRRA had distributed supplies valued at nearly $4 billion; 70 percent of that amount was contributed by the United States.

A new expansionist era in American foreign economic policy began with the Marshall Plan. In March 1947 President Truman, inspired by Soviet pressure against Greece and Turkey, offered direct aid to nations resisting direct or indirect subjugation by foreign dictatorships. This led

Secretary of State Marshall in June 1947 to propose that all European countries draw up a coordinated program designed to place Europe on its feet economically. Soviet Russia refused to allow its satellites to take part in the program. Nevertheless, the Marshall Plan, or European Recovery Program (ERP), was put into operation in early 1948. By the end of 1949 the United States had spent more than $30 billion in postwar aid to foreign countries through outright government grants and loans. Japan also received assistance, but on a smaller scale than western Europe. After the ERP came to an end in December 1951, the United States shifted its aid toward grants to the North Atlantic Treaty Organization (NATO) and other military alliances.

During World War II the political and economic leaders of the United States and western Europe had started planning for the liberalization of foreign trade and the creation of a stable world economy. The United Nations governments, without the participation of Soviet Russia, created two new financial institutions, the International Monetary Fund (IMF) and the International Bank for Reconstruction and Development (IBRD). The long-run goal of the IMF was to encourage relative stability of exchange rates and ultimately the free convertibility of national currencies. The IMF discouraged the resort to devaluation as a means of promoting the welfare of one nation at the expense of others; free convertibility was based on the expectation that an increasing number of nations would move in the direction of a free international economy. The World Bank was geared to the promotion of international investment as a means of fostering recovery and economic development, especially in underdeveloped countries. It sought to guarantee and supplement private international investment throughout the world.

The United Nations governments, without the cooperation of the communist bloc, also attempted to reduce tariff barriers, first by the International Trade Organization (ITO) and then through various bilateral understandings that were combined to form the General Agreement on Tariffs and Trade (GATT), generally referred to as the Geneva Agreement of 1947. This became the basis for a series of important tariff reductions over the next three decades. The so-called Kennedy Round (1964–67) was the sixth in the series of major bargaining rounds that GATT, as a forum for trade negotiations, had promoted. The 1967 agreement reduced tariff duties an average of about 35 percent on some sixty thousand items representing an estimated $40 billion in world trade. Further rounds for the later-1970s were agreed to by GATT in a 1973 Tokyo conference.

By the end of 1949 the Marshall Plan and other aid programs had helped Japan, Western Germany, Holland, France, and Italy to achieve a remarkable period of productivity growth that has continued into the 1970s. This increased the competitiveness of foreign economies with the American economy. The United States also had to bear the tremendous burden of military programs such as the Korean War (June 1950–July

1953), the Vietnam War (August 1964–January 1973), and the North Atlantic Treaty Organization (NATO) alliance, as well as civilian foreign-aid programs. As a consequence of all these factors plus a great increase in United States corporate foreign investments, the world's dollar shortage of the 1950s became transformed into the dollar glut of the 1960s and 1970s. Although this shift drained dollar reserves and gold from the United States, it had no serious consequences for the United States balance of international payments position until 1965 when the Vietnam War escalated, and the United States failed to finance the increased government expenditures in a noninflationary way.

Despite foreign aid tied to purchases in the United States and government controls over United States private foreign investment, the deficit in the United States balance of payments (defined to cover imports and exports, tourism, military expenditures, investment income, and long-term capital flows), increased sharply in 1969 and 1970 to an annual level of $3 billion. In the first half of 1971 a further sharp deterioration increased the deficit to an annual rate $9 billion. One important factor in this situation was a drastic drop in our merchandise trade balance. Another was a series of massive short-term outflows of dollars, attracted by the prospect of an upward revaluation of European currency, or a devaluation of the dollar.

A drastic countermove to these developments was President Nixon's new iternational economic program of 15 August 1971. He stunned the United States' trading partners by suspending the convertibility of the dollar into gold and other reserve assets, by imposing a temporary 10 percent surcharge on imports, and by proposing other measures designed to cut down on United States foreign aid and defense spending.

By suspending the gold convertibility of the dollar, Nixon's new economic policy brought to an end the effort by the Bretton Woods system to work with stabilized exchange rates. Fundamentally this effort was wrecked by the impossibility of pegging exchange rates in a world where electorates in the welfare capitalistic economies were not willing to deflate and to tolerate stagnation even though balance of payments deficits under a pegged parity rate called for such heroic remedies.

Attempts in the 1970s by leading IMF countries to devise a system to replace Bretton Woods did not succeed. Yet, without any master plan as a basis, the world developed a partially managed floating exchange rate system. A step in this direction was the December 1971 Smithsonian Accord by the major trading nations of the world. The United States agreed to devalue the dollar by about 8 percent and to remove the 10 percent surcharge on imports. Gold was not to be used to settle international indebtedness arising from the accumulation of dollars by foreign monetary authorities until a new basic payments system was worked out, and the currencies of some surplus countries were to be revalued upward. As a result, the Dutch guilder, the Belgium franc, the German mark, the Swiss franc, and the Japanese yen were raised in value by amounts ranging up to 17 percent.

Although the Smithsonian Accord achieved a major realignment of exchange rates, it did not set up a new monetary system. It did, however, retain the Special Drawing Rights (SDRs) which had been created by the International Monetary Fund in 1970, a new type of international money designed to give each member of the IMF an account to draw on up to a specified quota. This "paper gold" was to be a supplement to gold and the American dollar.

Nevertheless, from the Smithsonian Accord until late 1978, the world was effectively operating on a de facto dollar standard. As the dollar was not convertible into gold, its ultimate value was given by the American goods and services that dollars could be used to buy. But one crucial problem with such a dollar system was that the kind of American inflation that upset the Bretton Woods system was no less upsetting to a dollar system, particularly when the purchasing power of the world's dollar reserves was being constantly eroded.

As the inflation of the United States throughout the 1970s continued unchecked, the United States balance of payments never regained the relatively satisfactory position it had held in the 1960s. In October 1973 the United States officially raised the dollar price of gold by 10 percent. As most industrialized countries maintained the value of their currencies in terms of gold and SDRs, this action decreased the exchange value of the dollar by 10 percent.

Since 1973 the economies of the United States and most industrial countries have been extremely hard hit by the series of sharp and ever-larger increases in oil prices imposed by the Organization of Petroleum Exporting Countries (OPEC). The problem of "recycling" the billions of dollars received each year by the Persian Gulf countries threatened both world prosperity and the multilateral balance of payments equilibrium. Although the OPEC countries have made huge investments in the United States, the net burden on the United States' balance of payments since 1973 has been tremendous.

Since 1977, the Carter administration has attempted to follow a somewhat conservative fiscal-monetary policy, but the pressures for high-level employment and a higher economic growth rate have led to expenditures and a tax cut that have increased the national debt. The result has been an increasing lack of foreign business and government confidence in the American dollar and the stability of the American economy. This reaction has been questioned by some noted economists, who assert that an analysis of the United States balance of international indebtedness (which includes *all* United States assets and liabilities), demonstrates that the United States' net long-term claims on foreigners far exceed United States net liquid liabilities to foreigners. Hence, the United States has been a net international creditor. The average businessman and many officials do not realize that the balance of payments measures not wealth, but solvency. Just as it is possible for a firm with substantial net long-term assets to run into financial problems for lack of cash on hand, so it has been possible for the United States to be in a similar position in the international economy. (See Table 20–3.)

TABLE 20-3
United States International Investment Position, 1960 to 1975, and by Selected Area, 1975
(in billions of dollars)

Type of Investment	1960	1971	1975			
			Total[1]	Western Europe	Canada	Latin American Republics[2]
U.S. net international investment position	45.0	56.1	93.6	−41.0	46.6	41.1
U.S. assets abroad	85.7	179.5	225.2	79.1	59.3	61.2
U.S. official reserve assets	22.3	12.2	16.2	.1	(z)	—
U.S. private assets	49.4	133.1	246.1	70.2	59.0	52.0
Foreign assets in the U.S.	40.7	123.3	210.5	120.2	12.9	20.1
Foreign official assets in the U.S.	11.9	52.5	87.0	49.0	1.1	4.7
Other foreign assets in the U.S.	38.8	70.9	123.6	71.1	11.8	15.4

[1] Includes other countries, international organizations, and unallocated, now shown separately.
[2] Includes other Western Hemisphere.
SOURCE: U.S. Bureau of the Census, Statistical Abstract of the U.S., 1977 (Washington, D.C.: 1977), pp. 854.

In the next few years, the American decision makers in politics and economics face the task of devising a policy that will both protect the export and employment positions of American industry and labor and at the same time not disturb the economies of allies of the United States in western Europe, the Middle East, and the Far East. Some experts place their hopes on a twofold solution of this problem: first, the United States should encourage Germany and Japan to grow faster economically, and second, Congress and the American people should be persuaded to adopt a vigorous energy program that will limit United States oil imports. In that happy but unlikely eventuality, the United States dollar might float upward.

FOREIGN AID

A major concern of American foreign policy has been the granting of aid to allies and to underdeveloped countries. The total sum expended on such aid between 1945 and 1974 was less than 10 percent of the United States GNP in the single year, 1974. Moreover, United States foreign aid has been decreasing over the years, if measured as a percentage of GNP and adjusted for changes in the purchasing power of the dollar. Yet this American foreign-aid expenditure is very important to the recipients, who include the two billion people who live in the underdeveloped countries of the world.

Over the past few decades, the focus of United States foreign aid shifted considerably. Western Europe received the lion's share between 1945 and 1950. In 1949, President Truman initiated his Point Four program of technical assistance to underdeveloped countries. In the 1950s the main concern for economic development was directed toward Asia and the Middle East, but by 1961 the increase in the number of newly independent states in Africa and the growth of anti-Americanism in Latin America forced the American government decision makers to broaden the scope of their aid program. Under President Kennedy this program was expanded to include two new projects: the Peace Corps, which involved sending young American volunteers to underdeveloped parts of the world to furnish technical aid; and the Alliance for Progress, a plan to spend $20 billion over a ten-year period for economic development in Latin America. Although the Peace Corps won much good will throughout the world, the Alliance for Progress failed to achieve its goals.

An important part of American foreign aid has been military assistance that has been available since 1949 to members of the North Atlantic Treaty Organization. In addition, military grants have been given from the 1950s to the 1970s to the French in Indochina, to the Nationalist Chinese, to South Korea, and to South Vietnam. Military assistance has also been given to Israel and to various friendly governments in Latin America. After the late 1940s the military percentage of foreign aid has increased greatly, yet has represented a declining percentage of the United States budget and GNP, a fact masked by inflated prices of military equipment.

New measures by the highly industrialized countries of the world will be necessary to narrow substantially the gap between rich and poor countries of the world. Valuable as even the limited aid to Asia, Africa, and Latin America has been, the less-developed countries need a great deal of aid in building up their human capital as well as their agricultural, transportation, and industrial capital. Unfortunately, the OPEC countries that have acquired so much wealth since 1973 have been more concerned with reaping profits through investments in western Europe and the United States than in giving the massive aid needed by the other underdeveloped countries of the world.

Conclusion

The long-run rise in the United States GNP, although interrupted by several recessions and the Great Depression, was accompanied by a corresponding rise in consumer income, standard of living, and volume of expenditure. The iconoclastic economist, Thorstein Veblen, satirized the "conspicuous consumption" of the idle rich. For the vast majority of the working and middle classes, however, the luxuries of the wealthy were socially objectionable only if restricted to a favored few. Mass production and the development of new methods of mass marketing, such as chain stores and discount houses, made possible satisfaction of this demand for consumer goods. Still, despite the indisputable rise in the general standard of living, a considerable number of low-income Americans lacked many satisfactions taken for granted by the great middle-class majority.

In the arena of international commerce and finance, the United States has towered above its rivals in the size of its exports, imports, overseas investments and foreign aid. Whatever the protectionist errors in foreign economic policy committed prior to World War II, the United States since then has been committed to a policy of reducing tariff barriers and stimulating free trade around the world. The explicit aims have been to enable the United States and other economies to benefit from the most efficient allocation of world resources and to direct United States resources into sectors of comparative advantage. Some critics of our trade policy regard it as benefiting mainly the exporting industries of the United States. However, Japan, Western Europe, and many other countries seem to have felt that the United States approximation of a free trade policy has been distinctly better than any likely protectionist alternative.

The breakdown of the international monetary system in 1973 created still-unsolved problems in American monetary, fiscal, and trade policy. It has not been possible to reconcile conflicting views both here and abroad concerning such matters as the importance of curbing inflation, government spending for full employment, and maintaining substantial international reserves. Most developing countries favor an expansion of American foreign aid combined with stabilized commodity prices, free access to American technology, and control over multinational corporations. But no general agreement on these matters has been worked out with the United States and the other highly industrialized countries.

The domestic and foreign commerce of the United States, despite threatening recessions, seems assured of long-term future expansion. American consumers provide a continuing strong market for both domestic and foreign goods. The growth in world population and the thrust toward an improved standard of living in other parts of the world will generate increased demand for the products of American industry and agriculture. Two dangers, however, have to be adverted: One is the increasing power of OPEC to raise oil prices and injure the economic stability of the United States and other large oil-importing countries; the other is the threat of increased Soviet armed forces and Soviet expansion in Africa, the Middle East, and the Far West. Wise statesmanship and decisive action will be required to solve these problems.

SUGGESTED READINGS

Penetrating studies of the post-1914 changes in wholesale and retail distribution are presented by Alfred D. Chandler, Jr., *The Visible Hand: The Managerial Revolution in American Business* (Cambridge: Harvard University Press, 1977); Thomas C. Cochran, *200 Years of American Business* (New York: Basic Books, 1977); Reavis Cox, *Distribution in a High-Level Economy* (Englewood Cliffs, N.J.: Prentice-Hall, 1965); and E. Jerome McCarthy, *Basic Marketing* (Homewood, Ill.: Richard D. Irwin, 1977). Two expert analyses by economists are Harold Barger, *Distribution's Place in the American Economy Since 1869* (Princeton: Princeton University Press, 1955); and Victor R. Fuchs, *The Service Economy* (New York: National Bureau of Economic Research, 1968). The role of the consumer is dissected skillfully by Executive Office of the President, Office of Management and Budget, *Social Indicators, 1973* (Washington, D.C.: United States Government Printing Office, 1973); Stanley Lebergott, *The American Economy* (Princeton: Princeton University Press, 1976); and Herman P. Miller, *Rich Man, Poor Man* (New York: T. Y. Crowell, 1971). A classic work on American urbanization is Jean Gottmann, *Megalopolis* (New York: Twentieth Century Fund, 1971). Two valuable essays are Peter H. Lindert and Jeffrey G. Williamson, "Three Centuries of American Inequality," *Research in Economic History* 1 (1976), 69–123; and Paul A. David and Peter Solar, "A Bicentenary Contribution to the History of the Cost of Living in America," *Research in Economic History*, 2 (1977), 1–80.

Lucid treatments of the world trade background are given by William Ashworth, *A Short History of the International Economy Since 1850*, 2nd ed. (London: Longman, 1965); Alfred Maizels, *Growth and Trade* (Cambridge, Eng.: Cambridge University Press, 1970); and W. S. Woytinsky and E. S. Woytinsky, *World Commerce and Governments* (New York: Twentieth Century Fund, 1955). Important studies on the level and structure of world foreign trade are Simon Kuznets's essays, "Quantitative Aspects of the Economic Growth of Nations," *Economic Development and Cultural Change*, 13, no. 1 (October 1964) and 15, no. 2 (January 1967). New insights on American foreign trade can be found in Charles P. Kindleberger, *Foreign Trade and the National Economy* (New Haven: Yale University Press, 1962) and Robert E. Lipsey, *Price and Quantity Trends in the Foreign Trade of the United States* (New York: National Bureau of Economic Research, 1963). The most recent official figures and analysis are given in the *Economic Report of the President, January, 1979*, and *Annual Report of the Council of Economic Advisors* (Washington, D.C.: United States Government Printing Office, 1979). The history of the U.S. tariff and reciprocal trade agreements is presented in Sidney Ratner, *The Tariff in American History* (New York: D. Van Nostrand, 1972).

The problems of the U.S. balance of payments and the foreign exchange market are perhaps best approached by the layman and student through Peter Kenen and Raymond Lubitz, *International Economics*, 3rd ed. (Englewood Cliffs, N.J.: Prentice-Hall, 1971) and Gerald M. Meier, *Problems of a World Monetary Order* (New York: Oxford University Press, 1974). On U.S. business and investments abroad, some highly informative books are Robert Gilpin, *U.S. Power and the Multinational Corporations* (New York: Basic Books, 1975); Cleona Lewis, *America's Stake in International Investments* (Washington, D.C.: Brookings, 1938); Raymond Vernon, *Storm over the Multinationals* (Cambridge, Mass.: Harvard University Press, 1977); and Mira Wilkins, *The Maturing of the Multinational Enterprise . . . 1914 to 1970* (Cambridge, Mass: Harvard University Press, 1974).

Among the most helpful books on special areas, periods, and problems of United States foreign trade and finance are Robert Z. Aliber, *The International Money Game*, 2nd ed. (New York: Basic Books, 1976); Bela Balassa, *Changing Patterns in Foreign Trade and Payments* (New York: W. W. Norton, 1978); Fred L. Block, *The Origins of International Economic Disorder* (Berkeley: University of California Press, 1977); James L. Clayton, ed., *The Economic Impact of the Cold War* (New York: Harcourt Brace Jovanovich, 1970); Richard Cooper, *A Reordered World* (Washington, D.C.: Potomac Associates, 1973); William Diebold, Jr., *The United States and the Industrial World . . . in the 1970's* (New York: Praeger, 1972); Klaus Friedrich, *International Economics* (New York: McGraw-Hill, 1974); Gerald M. Meier, *Problems of Trade Policy* (New York: Oxford University Press, 1973); Andrew Shonfield et al., *International Economic Relations of the Western World—1959–1971*, 2 vols. (London: Oxford University Press, 1976); and Brian Tew, *The Evolution of the International Monetary System, 1945–1977* (New York: Halsted Press, 1977).

CHAPTER 21

___

Labor in a Maturing
Industrial Economy

___

The American labor movement made more economic and political gains during the years between 1914 and 1970 than in any previous period. Despite continuing setbacks, especially in depressions, real incomes increased, and there was greater protection against the hazards of unemployment and coercion by employers.

This increase in organized labor's economic and political power was considered revolutionary by many capitalists in the 1930s and the 1940s when Big Labor competed with Big Business and Big Agriculture in making decisions concerning the development of the American economy. After World War II, the American middle class acted to reduce what it considered the excessive power that organized labor had acquired during the New Deal. However, swings in public opinion favorable to organized labor occurred, especially under Democratic Congresses and Presidents. This chapter will treat the development of industrial unions and will explore the reasons for the fluctuations in their power and prestige.

Changes in the Labor Force

SIZE AND COMPOSITION OF THE WORK FORCE

The increase in the size and skills of the American labor force contributed significantly to the economic growth of the past six decades. As the population of the United States grew at an average annual rate of about 1.4 percent, the number of Americans increased from some 92.4 million in 1910 to 215.3 million in 1976. What the relation of this changing population was to the labor force (those gainfully employed) during these years is shown in Table 21–1. There has been a tendency for the labor force to grow slightly more rapidly than the population.

Most of the growth in the American population and the labor force for the period 1910–70 came from natural increase, the excess of births over deaths. But during those years some 17.2 million immigrants came to the United States; two-thirds of them stayed permanently and made important contributions to the quality as well as to the quantity of the American labor force. Restrictive legislation, passed in 1921 and 1924, ended open immigration, however, and limited the contribution of immigrants to the population growth of the United States.

TABLE 21-1
Population and Labor Force

Year	Population (millions)	Labor Force (millions)
	(1)	(2)
1910	92	37
1920	106	42
1930	123	49
1940	132	56
1950	151	65
1960	179	74
1970	203	86

SOURCE: Col. 1, U.S. Bureau of the Census, Statistical History of the United States (New York: Basic Books, 1976), p. 8, series A 6-8; Col. 2 ibid., p. 139, series D 167-1. Figures for 1970 from U.S. Bureau of the Census, Pocket Data Book, USA 1973 (Washington, D.C.: United States Government Printing Office, 1973), pp. 37, 130. Figures for Labor Force, 1970, are adjusted to conform with criteria for previous census years.

One major result of the drastic restriction on European immigration was that American industry and agriculture came to depend to an increasing extent upon a flow of unskilled laborers from Puerto Rico and immigrants from Canada and Mexico. Another important consequence was that American businessmen and industrialists began to employ to a greater extent black workers who migrated from the South to the North. The percentage of blacks in the United States residing in the South dropped from about 90 percent in 1919 to 53 percent by 1970.

This new phase in black labor history achieved its most important

FIGURE 21-1

Employment By Sector, 1920-1970

(percent)

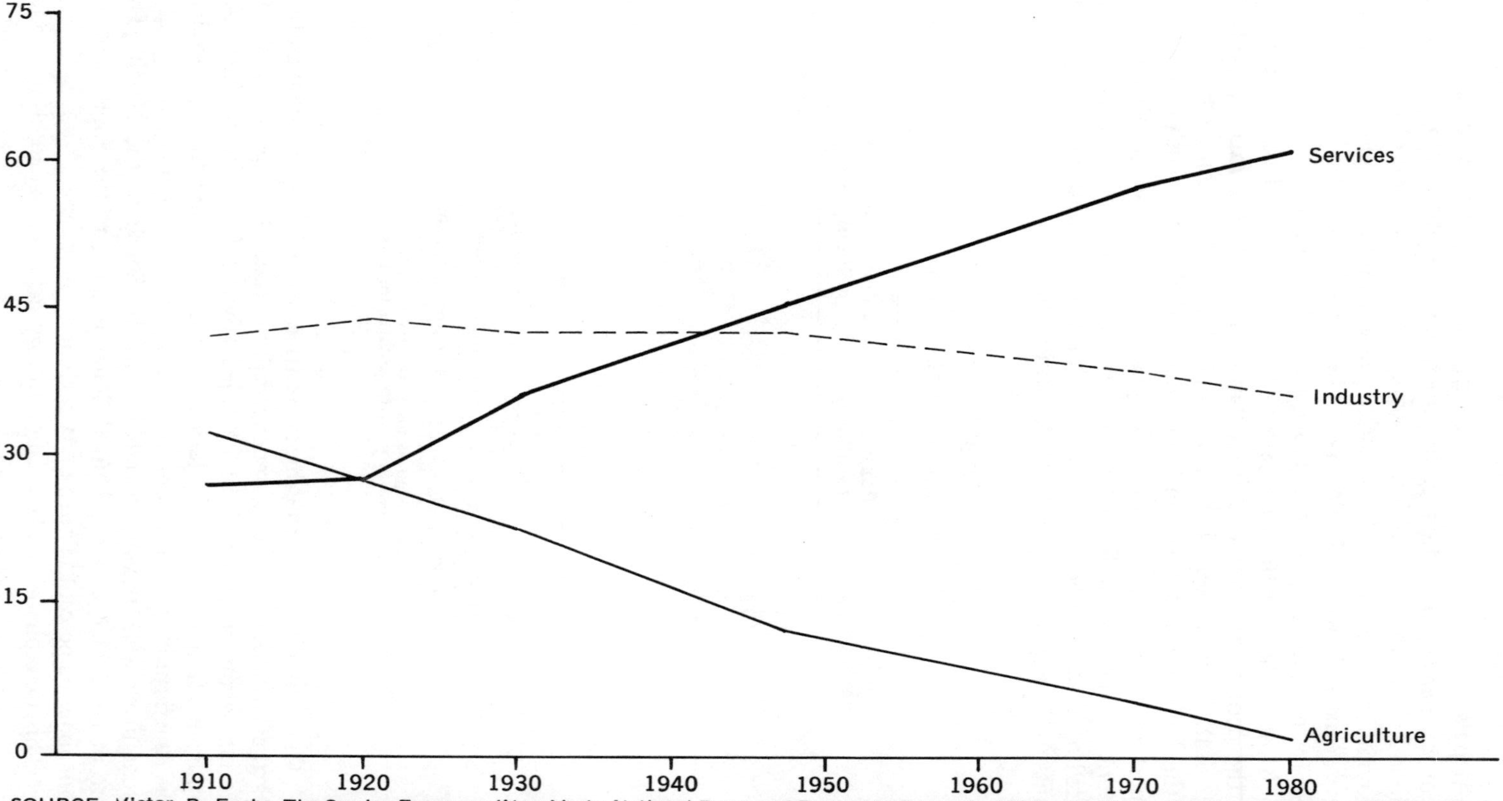

SOURCE: Victor R. Fuchs, The Service Economy (New York: National Bureau of Economic Research, 1968), pp. 19-24; Manpower Report of the President (Washington, D.C.: U.S. Government Printing Office, 1973), p. 225. The industry sector includes mining, construction, manufacturing, transportation, communication, public utilities, and government enterprise. The service sector includes wholesale and retail trade, finance, insurance, and professional, personal, business, and repair services.

development with the industrial boom that extended from World War II into the 1970s. During World War II blacks acquired a foothold in industrial unions in the steel industry, in the fabricating of new metals, and in the automobile industry. This position was strengthened by federal Fair Employment Practices regulations, first issued in 1941 and then extended by fair employment legislation on the state and municipal level and by action within the AFL-CIO.

Between World War I and the 1970s various changes in the American economic structure affected the composition of the working class. One major change was the decline in the number of those employed in agriculture; it went down from 25.6 percent of the labor force in 1920 to 4.7 percent in 1970. Meanwhile the industrial sector, broadly defined, which had increased in relative importance from 40.9 percent in 1910 to 44.8 percent in 1920, sank slightly to 37.6 percent in 1970.

But the biggest change occurred in the service sector of the economy. In 1920 less than 30 percent of the labor force was employed in service industries; in 1970 the proportion was nearing 60 percent and was still rising. Indeed, since 1947, *net* increases in employment have been concentrated almost entirely in the service sector, as against the goods-producing industries. And within the service sector, the most rapidly growing areas have been government service and professional, personal, and repair services; in the 1970s these two areas employed almost 30 percent of the labor force. This increase reflected both relative increase in demand for services and the lower productivity of the service sector.

In contrast to the larger and more impersonal production units in industry, the service economy involves relatively small-sized plants. Moreover, many service activities require high-level skill and training, involve personal contact with the consumer, and allow a wide gamut of satisfying work activity. By employing a higher proportion of white-collar workers, of women workers (almost 50 percent), and of part-time workers (more than one-quarter), service industries have been reshaping the composition of the labor force and changing the character of labor markets. In the 1970s fewer than 10 percent of workers in the service sector were unionized, compared with more than 40 percent in the goods-producing sector. Hence, unless unions succeed in spreading through the service industries, they will be a declining power in the economy. Even if they do succeed, the nature of the union movement will be altered considerably.

Since World War I, the economically active population has included smaller (and declining) proportions of the very young and the very old, larger (and growing) proportions of women, and relatively constant proportions of adult men. Under the impact of child-labor and compulsory school attendance laws the full-time employment of children under sixteen had declined from about one-fifth of the boys and one-tenth of the girls in 1910 to less than 2 percent of those under sixteen in 1940.

At the same time there was a decline in the work-force participation of those sixty-five and over, from 32 percent in 1920 to 21 percent in 1970. This decline in employment for senior citizens was mainly due to systematic retirement-income arrangements, especially Social Security. But a decline in self-employment opportunities, particularly on the farm, was also a contributing factor.

This curtailment in labor-force participation by the young and the old was more than offset by the increased participation of women, especially married women, in work outside their homes. The percentage of women gainfully employed rose from 23 percent in 1920 to 38 percent in 1970.

While the proportion of employed men remained relatively constant, employment opportunities for nonwhite men were much less than for white men. Indeed, as the educational and occupational requirements for jobs at different age levels rose, and as nonwhites increasingly moved from rural areas to the cities, labor force participation rates for nonwhite men have actually declined, at least since 1940. The reverse has been the case for women. From 1920 to the 1970s, the labor participation rates for nonwhite women have been consistently higher than for white women and nonwhite men.

In World War I, World War II, the Korean War, and the Vietnam War, wartime needs greatly affected total labor-force participation rates for women, including participation in the military services. After each war, in general, these rates dropped sharply for both military and civilian sectors. Then the long-term upward trend in the female participation rate became prominent, except during a severe depression, as in the 1930s.

TABLE 21-2

Labor Force Composition by Sex, 1900-70
(Percentage of persons 16 and over in Labor
Force, except prior to 1974, 14 years and over)

	Male	Female
1910	82	18
1920	80	20
1930	78	22
1940	75	25
1950	71	29
1960	68	32
1970	63	37

SOURCE: U.S. Census Bureau, Statistical History of the United States (New York: Basic Books, 1976) Series D 29-41, p. 132. The figures for 1910 are calculated by interpolation from the figures for 1900 and 1920.

RISE IN REAL WAGES

There is no doubt that many American workers have had to struggle against bad working conditions, low pay, and periods of prolonged unemployment, especially during depressions. But careful statistical analysis has established that the compensation of employees in the United States has increased from about 54 percent of the national income in 1910 to about 73 percent in 1970. Although real wages fluctuated during these six decades, the overall trend was upward. Thus the considerable gains in real wages during World War I and the 1920s were greatly reduced during the prolonged depression of the 1930s. But from 1940 to 1970 advances in real wages were greater than those made in the preceding half-century.

From 1910 to 1970 the average real annual earnings of nonfarm workers rose more than threefold from $607 to $1,980. In current dollars (uncorrected for price level changes), the average hourly wage of workers in manufacturing rose from 20 cents in 1910 to $3.36 in 1970, while the average weekly wage increased from $10 to $133.73 in the same period. Meanwhile, the average weekly hours of workers in manufacturing declined from a peak of 51 hours in 1910 to a low of 39.8 hours in 1970. The facts on the advance in real wages and the reduction in hours of work destroy the basis for pessimism about the possibility of progress for the American working class.

The question remains: What explains the upward movement of real wages? Clearly several factors are involved. One important element is the increase in the demand for labor relative to the supply of workers, due to the increasing consumer demand for goods and services, which we discussed in the preceding chapter.

Another factor has been a marked increase in the value of physical capital in manufacturing from $2,164 per worker in 1900 to $8,700 in 1968. Progress in technology on a wide front, for example, electronics, petrochemicals, the computer, enhanced the quality of capital. This improvement in factory equipment furthered a steady increase in the productivity of labor. The ratio of fixed capital to output in manufacturing decreased gradually from 1904 to 1929, and then sharply from 1929 to 1948. From the 1920s on it took fewer dollars of capital to produce a dollar of output. Manufacturing workers benefited also from vastly increased supplies of nonhuman energy. With electrical, nuclear, and other sources of energy, the amount of nonhuman energy per worker in 1970 was about nine and one half times that available in 1900.

The sharp upward shift in the educational background of the American labor force from World War I to the 1970s also contributed by upgrading the skills and versatility of labor and thus fostering the rise in real wages and productivity. Indeed, an estimated 25 to 45 percent of the long-term growth in real income has been due to increased education.

Still another factor in the upward trend of real income was the improved reallocation of resources as workers were attracted to capital-intensive manufacturing industries and moved away from low-productivity sectors of agriculture, especially after the 1930s. It has been estimated that the movement of labor from low- to high-productivity industries since World War I accounts for about one-sixth of the increased real-wage and product per worker.

Along with these gains were those that came from the achievement of larger markets and economies of scale as small units of production in industry were replaced by larger units. Between 1900 and 1960 the efficiency of labor in the American economy outside the government sector increased by roughly 54 percent more than the efficiency of capital.

Unemployment and Workers' Protection

PERSISTENT UNEMPLOYMENT

Still, while the statistical record with respect to increased real wages and reduced working hours has been impressive, historians cannot disregard the persistent problem of unemployment. Large-scale unemployment has hit workers where it hurts the most—at their job security and a steady income.

The fluctuations in unemployment levels suggest that an element of insecurity is present even during good times. Unemployment for the civilian labor force in the period 1914–33 rose in depressions to over 8 percent in 1915, nearly 12 percent in 1921, and almost 25 percent in 1933. In World War I and the 1920s unemployment fell to 1.4 percent in 1918 and just over 2 percent in 1923–24 and 1928.

The diversified relief, recovery and reform programs of the New Deal undoubtedly helped to relieve the distress of unemployed workers and have been credited by some economists with reducing the unemployment rate to about 14 percent in 1937. Roosevelt's attempt to balance the budget brought about the recession of 1937–38 and raised the unemployment figure to 19 percent in 1938 and 17 percent in 1939. By the end of the 1930s, a great deal of excess industrial capacity had been liquidated, residential construction was displaying signs of revival, and a creative technology was opening up new investment opportunities. If Germany and Japan could have been restrained from unleashing World War II, private investment in the United States might possibly have increased to such an extent that full employment would have been feasible without major government intervention. In any case, after Pearl Harbor the American economy was under the pressure of meeting war production goals, and unemployment dropped to the unusually low figure of 1.2 percent in 1944.

The fluctuations in employment levels in the postwar years raise the question of whether or not the ideal of full employment is realistic. From 1946 to 1956 unemployment was kept down to about 4 percent in periods of prosperity and to 3 percent in the Korean War. But following the recession of 1957 the rate of unemployment rose to a high of 6.8 percent in 1958 and then stayed at an annual average unemployment rate above 5 percent from 1959 through 1964. This led to a national debate on the increasing importance of hard-core structural unemployment—the unemployment of the old, the less-educated, and the less-skilled workers as a result of technological advances in manufacturing, agriculture, and the service industries.

EFFORTS TO CURB UNEMPLOYMENT

At the end of World War II both Democrats and Republicans agreed that another Great Depression could not be allowed and this broad consensus produced the Employment Act of 1946. The Truman administration was fortunate enough to boast of a relatively low level of unemployment. The Eisenhower administration that followed from 1953 to 1960 regarded economic growth and particularly price stability as more important goals than a high target for employment. When the Kennedy administration came into power in January 1961, however, it envisioned a more vigorous role for fiscal policy and greater efforts to achieve the goal of full employment.

Kennedy's successors have not been able to fulfill these goals. The 1964 tax cut and such factors as the demands of the Vietnam War reduced unemployment to 3.5 percent by 1969. Yet under the Nixon administration's restrained monetary-fiscal policies, the unemployment rate rose to almost 6 percent by 1971, and neither Nixon, who resigned as President in August 1974, nor Gerald Ford, his successor, could prevent the unemployment rate from rising to over 8 percent in 1975. After the election of Jimmy Carter as President in 1976, the unemployment rate began to decline although action on radical new approaches to reducing unemployment has been hindered by fear of persistent inflation.

INCIDENCE OF UNEMPLOYMENT

The impact of unemployment has been very uneven for different groups within the American labor force. Thus laborers have experienced much more unemployment than skilled manual workers, and skilled manual workers have experienced considerably higher rates of unemployment than clerical workers. Nonwhite (especially black) workers endured substantially more unemployment than white workers, often, because they were in the lower occupational groups. Teenagers and the elderly have had much higher unemployment rates than workers aged twenty-four to fifty-five.

The year 1969 can serve to illustrate the differences in employment opportunities for various kinds of workers. Thus in June 1969 average male unemployment varied from 2.2 percent for white-collar workers, craftsmen, and foremen to 3.4 percent for operatives and 6.6 percent for unskilled workers. By age level, the unemployment rate was 1.6 percent for workers over twenty-five; 5.1 percent for those twenty to twenty-four; and 11 percent for those under twenty. Different levels of education led to an unemployment rate of 1.9 percent for those with some college education, 3.7 percent for workers with only twelve years of formal schooling, and 5.9 percent for those with fewer than twelve years. The unemployment rate in 1969 was 3.1 percent for whites and 6.4 percent for nonwhites.

Beginning in late 1969, however, the American economy suffered from a relative stagnation that lasted until the middle of 1975. In 1975, blacks made up about 11 percent of the civilian labor force, but over 18 percent of total unemployment. And the unemployment rate among black teenagers was almost 40 percent, compared to roughly 18 percent among their white counterparts.

As the share of the labor force composed of young men and women has increased, the unemployment rates for these groups have become considerably higher than those for adult males. Hence, the problem of structural unemployment, since it does not respond easily to an increase in aggregate demand, has become increasingly troubling. In other words, with prevailing wage rates, the supply of labor is excessive relative to demand in specific age-sex groups.

The higher unemployment rates for the unskilled and least educated in urban ghettoes and depressed rural areas led the Kennedy-Johnson administrations to expand greatly manpower training programs in the 1960s and to improve the placement and counseling activities of the national-state employment service.

But these efforts had relatively little impact and the Nixon-Ford administrations cut back federal manpower programs while seeking to shift much of the responsibility to state and local governments. With the Carter administration some have suggested that the goal of full employment should be reformulated in structural, as well as in aggregate demand terms, with employment targets set up for particular sectors of the labor force classified by age, sex, and race or ethnic group. Realizing such specific targets would call for enlarged and improved manpower training programs combined with incentives for private firms to hire and train the disadvantaged. There would also be a need for programs of public-service employment with the government empowered to serve as the employer of last resort. These are controversial proposals, popular with various minority groups, but not as yet supported by a wide public.

SAFETY AND HEALTH

An important problem that many workers in America have had to face has been the danger of death, permanent injury, or partial disability as a result of work-related accidents and injuries. There were over twenty thousand deaths from industrial accidents and 2 million industrial injuries of varying severity a year in the early 1920s. The number of injuries causing death and permanent total disability has declined since World War II. Nevertheless, recent statistics still can be shocking. For example, in 1968, over 14,000 people died in industrial accidents, 90,000 workers suffered permanent impairment from industrial accidents, and 2.1 million suffered total, but temporary, disability.

Public measures to protect workers from industrial injuries in the past half century have encompassed safety laws and other state regulations aimed at preventing work-related injuries and diseases, and a system of workmen's compensation and rehabilitation laws designed to ameliorate such injuries by providing for medical care and cash compensation. In 1969 workmen's compensation covered almost 85 percent of the labor force, and paid out $2.5 billion—$1.5 billion for disability, $875 million for medical benefits, and $185 million for survivors benefits. Employers paid about $3 billion in insurance premiums and bore a part of the burden of social disutilities of hazardous employment, but this represented only a small portion of the total costs to the nation.

In general, while the decline in the rate of accidents in the manufacturing industries was not impressive, it is most likely that without these state safety laws and the efforts of individual employers and private insurance companies, the accident rate, far from declining, would have multiplied.

American Trade Unions

EXPANSION OF UNIONS

Between 1910 and 1970 trade union membership grew from about 2 million to over 19 million, or from 5.6 to 22.6 percent of the labor force. The major increases in union membership occurred in three periods: 1917–20, 1933–37, 1941–45.

During World War I the unusually high demand for and short supply of workers, and the conciliatory attitude of employers and the national government, led to an unprecedented growth in union membership from

2.7 million in 1916 to 5 million in 1920. The support of the American Federation of Labor (AFL) for the war effort was rewarded by the appointment of AFL officers to most of the war boards organized by the government. Special labor adjustment boards were set up for shipbuilding, railroads, and the maritime industry. For other war industries a National War Labor Board was established in order to mediate disputes. The board encouraged employers to recognize the workers' right to organize and to engage in union activities.

But after the Armistice in 1918, the government, employers, and the public acquired a fear of and hostility to the American labor movement, a fear generated in part by the Bolshevik Revolution in Russia. This affected public attitudes towards the numerous strikes that broke out in 1919 involving over 4 million wage earners. The important AFL strike in 1919 against the U.S. Steel Corporation failed when the company refused to negotiate and broke the strike by using scare propaganda and black strikebreakers.

During the 1920s the courts resorted to various anti-union devices, for example, the use of injunctions to prevent unions from inducing breaches of yellow-dog (anti-union) contracts. Although efforts were made by some states and by the federal government to remove some of these legal restrictions, the United States Supreme Court greatly limited the ability of the unions to operate by upholding their liability to injunctions and by assessing triple damages for violation of the antitrust laws. Hence, the "prosperous" 1920s, while good for big business, were a period of rapid decline for organized labor. By 1929 trade union membership had fallen to 3.4 million, and by 1933 the Great Depression had reduced union membership still further, to 2.8 million, or just about the 1916 level.

Under the impact of the Great Depression all this began to change. The AFL in 1932 began advocating a compulsory system of unemployment insurance as well as large-scale public work projects while at the same time attempting to prevent a reduction in wages. That year Congress passed the Norris-LaGuardia Act, which made it extremely difficult for federal courts to issue injunctions against unions conducting peaceful strikes and made anti-union employment contracts unenforceable in federal courts.

The presidency of Franklin D. Roosevelt brought federal legislation favorable to union organization and a recovery in economic conditions, especially between 1933 and 1937. Trade union membership increased by almost 3.6 million members between 1933 and 1939 or from 5.4 to 11.5 percent of the labor force.

One major factor in the success of the trade union organization drive was the creation in 1935 of the Committee for Industrial Organization (CIO), known after 1938 as the Congress of Industrial Organizations, with John L. Lewis as chairman. Rejecting the craft unionism of the

American Federation of Labor, the CIO aimed at promoting unionization in the mass-production industries. This objective was realized in the steel, automobile, rubber, metal mining, marine transportation, packing, and textile industries as well as in longshoring. The ensuing rivalry between the AFL and the CIO led the former to charter industrial unions, and the latter to set up craft unions. As a consequence, total union membership in 1941 rose to three times what it had been in 1933, with 5.2 million in the AFL and 2.7 million in the CIO.

During these years, the New Deal further transformed the position of labor in America through the national government's intervention in relations between employers and workers. The codes for industrial self-regulation established under the National Industrial Recovery Act (NIRA) of 1933 prescribed minimum wages and maximum hours and eliminated child labor. Section 7A of the NIRA made it possible for workers to organize and bargain collectively without employer interference. Although the Supreme Court declared the NIRA unconstitutional in 1935, Congress later that year enacted the National Labor Relations (Wagner) Act which strengthened and extended the union guarantees of Section 7A of NIRA. The statute made anti-union activities by management unfair labor practices.

The Wagner Act created a new three-man National Labor Relations Board (NLRB) with the power to supervise representation elections, to designate appropriate bargaining agents, and to hold hearings on unfair employer practices. The Board was also empowered to issue cease-and-desist orders, which were enforceable through the federal circuit courts of appeal. Another statute that aided labor was the 1938 Fair Labor Standards Act. It established minimum wages and maximum hours, and abolished child labor for all businesses engaged in interstate commerce. Finally, the Social Security Act of 1935 created a joint federal-state system of unemployment insurance, financed by a tax on employers' payrolls, as well as a system of old-age and survivors' insurance financed by a payroll tax on both employers and employees.

During World War II labor relations were subject to federal controls. The War Labor Board (WLB) with representatives from labor, management, and the public, practically imposed compulsory arbitration even though the courts ruled that the "directive orders" of the War Labor Board were only "advisory." The Board tried to stabilize wage rates after January 1941 by tying wage increases to rises in the cost of living. When this ruling aroused great discontent among union members, the WLB began approving "fringe benefits" rather generously. It also ruled that women deserved equal pay for equal work.

Nevertheless, various strikes and short work stoppages in 1943–45 caused Congress to pass the Smith-Connally War Labor Disputes Act over the President's veto. This Act authorized the President to take over plants closed by labor disputes and provided for a government-conducted strike vote prior to any work stoppage, a provision that turned out to be completely ineffective.

The high demand for labor made it difficult to control wages; it also made an expansion of the labor force during the war imperative. This need was met in part by the increased use of women workers and the creation of new opportunities for black workers. To curb discriminatory employment, an Executive Order in June 1941 established the Fair Employment Practice Committee (FEPC), and in May 1943 the government required nondiscrimination clauses in all war contracts. The war also initiated further union growth, an expansion that was to continue through the 1950s.

With the conclusion of hostilities in August 1945, war controls over prices and wages soon ended, prices rose, and unions asked for large wage increases. The result was a great wave of strikes in 1945 and 1946. The combined effect of the strikes—rising prices and shortages of goods—led to a Republican victory in the 1946 Congressional elections and the passage in June 1947 of the Taft-Hartley Labor-Management Relations Act over President Truman's veto. The Act imposed important restrictions and obligations upon the unions. They were required to present financial reports to their members; union officials had to take an oath that they were not members of the Communist party; featherbedding was declared illegal; unions were made liable for the acts of their officials; and the closed shop was prohibited.

Although union leaders attacked the new law as a slave labor act in congressional and presidential elections from 1948 on, they were unsuccessful in their efforts to have the law repealed. Many states adopted right-to-work laws, which outlawed both union shops and closed shops, but union political activity managed to confine these laws almost exclusively to nonindustrial states in the South and Midwest.

Another factor hindering union expansion was the internal friction in the CIO on the communist issue. Finally, in 1949 and 1950 the CIO purged itself of eleven communist unions, even though they represented perhaps a million members. Five years later, the AFL and CIO effected a merger.

The new federation of the AFL-CIO then felt strong enough to face another major problem, the elimination of corrupt elements from the labor movement. In 1957 the AFL-CIO expelled three unions for malpractices and misuse of union funds. Further revelations by a Senate committee of improper practices in certain trade unions resulted in the enactment by Congress of the Landrum-Griffin Labor Management Reporting and Disclosure Act of 1959. The new measure required regular elections of officers and the disclosure of union finances. It also prohibited extortion picketing (but not other forms of picketing) and almost all forms of secondary boycott.

By 1953, union membership reached an all-time high of 25.7 percent of the civilian labor force. But since the late 1950s, there has been a stagnation in union membership. In 1962 the membership dropped to a low of 14.9 million, but then increased to 20.5 million in 1974. Nevertheless, union membership had declined relative to total nonagricultural employment, a reflection of the fact that the total United States work force was growing faster than union membership. This leveling off of union membership was due in large part to the increasing resistance that unions met as they tried to penetrate white-collar employment, smaller establishments, smaller cities and towns, and heavily agricultural regions.

An additional block to union expansion has been a decided shift in public attitudes towards unions. Some critics have argued that the labor movement has grown bureaucratic, complacent, and slack in its drive for expansion. For its part, organized labor made a strong effort during the Kennedy-Johnson administrations to stem the tide of opposition. With the Carter administration, the AFL-CIO leaders have tried to exert pressure for legislation favorable to the unions, but have not met with success.

Nevertheless, organized labor has continued its activities and broadened its scope as in the organization of public employees. During the 1960s, public-sector employment grew dramatically as a result of new federal, state, and municipal programs. The public-sector work force included both relatively secure civil servants and numerous unskilled and semiskilled service workers, many of whom were black and underpaid when compared with their counterparts in the private-sector of the economy. In January 1962 federal employees were given the right to organize and bargain collectively when President John F. Kennedy issued Executive Order No. 10988. Similar rights were received by state and municipal employees when state legislatures enacted public employee labor relations statutes, for example, Wisconsin in 1959, Michigan in 1965, New York in 1967, Minnesota in 1971. By 1975 more than one-half of the states had enacted such laws. As a result of these governmental actions, by 1970 over one-half of the federal employees were organized, and although unions were not as strong in state and local government employment, government employee union membership more than doubled between 1950 and 1968.

After World War II, Britain, the Netherlands, and the Scandinavian countries experimented with direct pressure on wages and prices in an effort to maintain high employment and at the same time moderate the advance of wage incomes, profit incomes, and the price level. They relied mainly on exhortation, publicity, and voluntary cooperation, but on occasion used legal controls. The United States did not move in this direction until in 1962 President Kennedy's Council of Economic Advisers advanced the idea of guidelines for wage and price behavior. Enforcement was accomplished by occasional presidential intervention in wage and price decisions; this "jawboning" often brought about modification or rescinding of private decisions and may have lessened the rate of wage-price increase from 1962 to 1966.

A continuing problem has been the relation between inflation and the United States government's efforts to secure high-level employment. Since the mid-1970s inflation has threatened the standard of living of organized and unorganized labor as well as the middle classes. (Chapter 22 on government finance deals with this problem in more detail.) From 1967 to 1977 the annual inflation rate had averaged 6.5 percent, and by the fall of 1978 had risen to 9.5 percent. Meanwhile nonfarm workers in private enterprise had succeeded in getting an annual average rise of 6.9 percent in their average hourly earnings. Some economists feared that these wage increases acted as cost-push factors in the inflationary spiral; but other economists stressed other factors, such as increases in the money supply. In any case, President Nixon resorted to wage-price controls from August 1971 to April 1974, with debatable success in 1971–72, but with greatly increased inflation once controls were lifted. In 1978 President Carter set forth proposals for holding down wage-price increases, mainly by voluntary business-labor cooperation. The top leadership of the AFL-CIO has been critical of any voluntary program of wage-price control, and the alarming increase in inflation in late 1978 and 1979 makes the success of Carter's program in the future highly questionable.

Undoubtedly full or high-level employment has been the greatest problem facing the labor movement. In 1946 Congress established full employment as a national goal, but it became an increasingly difficult objective in the mid-1970s. Unemployment hit a high of 8.5 percent in 1975 and remained at about 6 percent in 1978. Therefore, businessmen, economists, and politicians tended to change their definitions of "acceptable" unemployment levels upward. To many, inflation became more important than unemployment as the central concern of the national government. But with six to eight million people unemployed in the late 1970s, there were strong calls for government action. The response in Congress was passage of the Humphrey-Hawkins Full Employment and Balanced Growth Act of October 1978. This called for reduction in the overall unemployment rate to 4 percent and a reduction in the inflation rate to 3 percent, both goals to be achieved by 1983. The bill's labor champions had been forced to accept the anti-inflation target to win congressional approval of the unemployment goal. The bill's supporters were successful, however, in getting the national government designated as the employer of last resort, that is, government work projects would guarantee jobs for those who could not find employment in the private sector. A realistic appraisal of this measure indicates that it may enable the national government to provide from 2.5 to 3 million jobs for those unemployed because of cyclical or structural economic reasons. It would be unwise, however, to expect that the national government can take care of all potential job seekers since their number might exceed 20 million. The private sector of the economy will have to be relied on to provide jobs for any number larger than the 3 million mentioned.

Conclusion

Labor has made remarkable progress during the past six decades. Real income has risen and hours of work have decreased; social security has been instituted; working conditions have been made safer and healthier. Trade unions and government have played an important role in this process of improvement. Nevertheless, many American workers have suffered from large-scale unemployment during depressions and hard-core unemployment even in periods of prosperity. Hence, full or high-level employment has been a persistent goal of the trade union movement.

An important recent development has been the opening of new job opportunities to blacks, Hispanics, other ethnic minorities, and women. They rightly charge that the trade union movement has been insufficiently concerned about their rights. Their increasing entrance into the labor force has required many adjustments and difficult decisions and will entail more in the future. One such problem involves numerical quotas for minorities in different occupations.

A problem that has worried both the craft unions and the industrial unions involves their future membership growth. Since 1957, union membership has failed to keep pace with the expansion of the labor force, owing largely to resistance by white-collar workers in the service industries.

Another persistent problem that organized labor has had to grapple with is the public's view of the rights of management against the claims of the trade unions. Consumers' interests are involved in terms of the effects on price, quantity, and quality of goods and services.

As early as 1946, Congress affirmed the ideal of national responsibility for high-level employment. This objective has been a persistent concern of the trade union movement which worked for the passage in 1978 of the Humphrey-Hawkins Full Employment and Balanced Growth Act, aimed at reducing unemployment to 4 percent by 1983. One of the major decisions involved in meeting this goal will be the allocation of public as against private employment. There is general sympathy for many of labor's goals, but important decisions will also be required concerning the relationship between wage increases and growth in productivity, within the context of the still unsolved problem of inflation.

The future of labor-management relations undoubtedly will involve questions concerning the right of labor to intervene in management decisions on working conditions that create a feeling of alienation on the part of workers and on environmental dangers from pollution that come from such sources as the production of coal, oil, and nuclear energy. The problem of balancing business profits from high output against the workers' need for diversity of work experience, leisure, and cultural enrichment is extremely difficult, but is beginning to be raised and discussed. American labor and management have been changing the rules of the game so much that their relations under welfare capitalism may yet defy past and current stereotypes.

SUGGESTED READINGS

On changes in population, immigration, and the labor force, three valuable books are Gertrude Bancroft, *The American Labor Force* (New York: John Wiley, 1958); Richard A. Easterlin, *Population, Labor Force, and Long Swings in Economic Growth* (New York: National Bureau of Economic Research, 1968); and Irene B. and Conrad Taeuber, *The People of the United States in the 20th Century*, A 1960 Census Monograph (Washington, D.C.: United States Government Printing Office, 1973). Works that explore the changing composition of the American labor force in terms of occupation, nationality, race, and sex include Victor R. Fuchs, *The Service Economy* (New York: National Bureau of Economic Research, 1968); Daniel O. Price, *Changing Characteristics of the Negro Population*, A 1960 Census Monograph (Washington, D.C.: GPO, 1969); Arthur M. Ross and Herbert Hill, eds., *Employment, Race, and Poverty* (New York: Harcourt, Brace, 1967); and Robert W. Smuts, *Women and Work in America* (New York: Schocken Books, 1971). The importance of older workers in the economy has only recently been recognized. Discussions of major issues are to be found in Juanita M. Kreps et al., *Employment, Income, and Retirement Problems of the Aged* (Durham, N.C.: Duke University Press, 1963).

Questions concerning the real income, hours, and working conditions of American laborers have always aroused keen debate. Scholarly and well-written analyses can be found in Richard B. Freeman, *Labor Economics* (Englewood Cliffs, N.J.: Prentice-Hall, 1972); Sar Levitan et al., *Human Resources and Labor Markets*, 2d ed. (New York: Harper & Row, 1975); F. Ray Marshall, Allan M. Carter and Allan G. King, *Labor Economics*, 3d ed. (Homewood, Ill.: Richard D. Irwin, 1976); Lloyd G. Reynolds, *Labor Economics and Labor Relations*, 6th ed. (Englewood Cliffs, N.J.: Prentice-Hall, 1974); and W. S. Woytinsky et al., *Employment and Wages in the United States* (New York: Arno Press, 1976).

The exciting and varied history of the American trade union movement has been captured in such works as Irving Bernstein, *The Lean Years . . . The American Worker 1920–1933* (Baltimore, Md.: Penguin Books, 1970) and *Turbulent Years . . . the American Workers 1933–1941* (Boston: Houghton Mifflin, 1971); M. Derber and E. Young, eds., *Labor and the New Deal* (Madison: University of Wisconsin Press, 1957); Melvyn Dubofsky, ed., *American Labor Since the New Deal* (New York: Quadrangle, 1971); Walter Galenson, *The CIO Challenge to the AFL* (Cambridge, Mass.: Harvard University Press, 1960); Clarence D. Long, *The Labor Force Under Changing Income and Employment* (Princeton, N.J.: Princeton University Press, 1958); Joel Seidman, *American Labor from Defense to Reconversion* (Chicago: University of Chicago Press, 1976); Philip Taft, *Organized Labor in American History* (New York: Harper & Row, 1964); and Leo Troy, *Trade Union Membership, 1897–1962*, Occasional Paper 92 (New York: National Bureau of Economic Research, 1965).

On inflation and wage-price controls three valuable studies are Craufurd D. Goodwin, ed., *Exhortation and Controls: The Search for a Wage-Price Policy, 1945–1971* (Washington, D.C.: Brookings, 1975); Arnold R. Weber and Daniel J. B. Mitchell, *The Pay Board's Progress: Wage Controls in Phase II* (Washington, D.C.: Brookings, 1978); and John T. Dunlop et al., eds., *The Lessons of Wage and Price Controls—The Food Sector* (Cambridge, Mass.: Harvard University Press, 1978). A good book on labor, the courts, and Congress is A. Howard Myers et al., *Labor Law and Legislation*, 5th ed. (Cincinnati: South-Western Publishing Co., 1975). On the Humphrey-Hawkins bills, see the article by H. H. Humphrey in *Challenge* (May-June 1976); the articles by M. J. Piore et al. in *Challenge* (May-June 1978); and Eli Ginzberg, "The Pursuit of Equity: Mirage or Reality?" *Columbia* [University Magazine] (Fall 1978). A challenging reappraisal of "stagflation" and employment problems is given by Melville J. Ulmer, "Old and New Fashions in Employment and Inflation Theory," *Journal of Economic Issues* (March 1979).

CHAPTER 22

———

Expanding Economic
Responsibilities of Government

The twentieth century has brought a greatly expanded scope of governmental decision making in the economic affairs of the United States. Future historians may well regard the enlarged role of government as the most significant feature of American economic history in this century, just as industrialization and the revolution in internal transportation are today viewed as the outstanding economic features of the nineteenth century. In addition, after decades of expansion of government's claims on economic output and of its role in economic decision making, many Americans today are questioning and reassessing the results. It is doubly fitting, therefore, that we conclude our study of the history of the American economy with an analysis of the changing economic role of government. Why has governmental decision making increased so markedly? What have been the effects of this epochal change?

To give focus to our inquiry we shall examine in detail three broad areas of expanding governmental economic responsibilities. The first is the search for more rational banking and monetary arrangements. Besides providing a continuation of earlier discussions in chapters 7 and 15, this subject offers a case study of the more general trend toward increased economic regulation and control that has characterized the twentieth-century expansion of government. The second trend we shall examine is that of an increased proportion of governmental expenditures and income. Finally, we shall consider the increased recognition by both public and private decision makers that government has a major responsibility to promote economic stability and growth as a means of enhancing the economic welfare of Americans.

Central Banking and Monetary Policy:
The Economics of Regulation and Control

In discussing banking in the post-Civil War era toward the end of chapter 15, we noted that two problems were pervasive. One was the question of how the banking system was to be organized and how its components would be fitted together. The other problem was how to overcome the tendency of the system to produce, or contribute to, the general financial panics that periodically undermined the stability of the economy.

By the turn of the century a part of the organizational pattern that was to persist in the future had become clear. A dual system of national and state banks had emerged. The restrictive laws and regulations that had hampered the spread of banking during the late-nineteenth century had given way to a more lenient legal and regulatory climate at both the national and state levels. As a result the number of independent commercial banks in the United States roughly doubled from twelve thousand to twenty-four thousand between 1900 and 1910; there was a further increase to over thirty thousand, of which eight thousand banks were national and twenty-two thousand were state, in 1920. On this last date independent banking development in the nation was close to the all-time peak. After the early 1920s the increased mobility of people associated with the diffusion of automobiles decreased the need for so many small banks. Consequently, an increase in bank mergers and the emergence of branch banking acted to reduce the number of independent banks in the United States. But it is fair to say that most Americans, as befits an enterprising people, have not been far from the services of a bank during the twentieth century.

A giant step in the direction of solving the recurring problem of bank panics came with the establishment of the Federal Reserve System in 1914. With the creation of the Fed, as it is often called, the United States somewhat belatedly followed the example of other leading nations in establishing a central bank, a bank that would act as a bankers' bank, as the government's bank and fiscal agent, and as a means of promoting economic stability through centralized control of the nation's supplies of money and credit.

ORGANIZATION OF THE FED

Americans have always had a pronounced—many would say healthy—fear of the concentration of economic and political power. Those who created the Fed in 1913–14 were not exceptions. Through extensive studies under the National Monetary Commission of 1908–12, they had familiarized themselves with the structure and operations of banking systems in other countries. But rather than establishing a single central bank on the pattern of the Bank of England and other European central banks, they divided the United States into twelve districts with a Federal Reserve Bank in each. All national banks were required to become members of the Federal Reserve System by purchasing capital stock in the Reserve Banks of their respective districts and by holding their reserves as deposits in the Reserve Banks. State banks were given the option of becoming members on the same terms. Ownership of the Fed, however, was divorced from control; the member banks who owned the capital stock of the system were granted 6 percent dividends but control lay elsewhere. At the head of the system was the Federal Reserve Board in Washington, D.C., consisting of seven members: the secretary of the treasury, the comptroller of the currency, both ex officio, and five others appointed by the President. Each of the twelve district Reserve Banks had nine directors, three appointed by the Board and six—of whom only three could be bankers—elected by the member banks of the district.

Thus checks and balances were in the structure of the Fed as well as in its vaults and ledgers. It was a typically American institution, rather like the national and state governments under the Articles of Confederation, and with time it, too, evolved toward more centralized control. For nearly two decades after 1914 the individual Reserve Banks exercised considerable autonomy. Their boards elected governors to serve as operating heads. The governors, individually and as a group, exercised considerable policy power within the Federal Reserve System. This was especially true of the New York Reserve Bank, located at the center of American finance, and of its governor, Benjamin Strong. Until his death in 1928, Strong was actually the dominant figure in the Fed. The Federal Reserve Board in Washington attempted to coordinate system policies and actions but considerable Reserve Bank autonomy characterized the early years of the Fed. Then, with the monetary, banking, and general economic debacles of the 1930s (about which more will be said below) centralized authority was clearly established. The Banking Acts of 1933 and 1935 gave the Federal Reserve Board control of the system's main policy tool—its purchases and sales of government securities (open market operations)—renamed the Board the "Board of Governors" and removed the two ex officio members from it, and changed the title of the operating head of a district Reserve

Bank from governor to president. From that time on control of the policies of the Federal Reserve System rested with the Board of Governors in Washington.

FUNCTIONS AND TOOLS OF THE FED

Central banks everywhere perform a number of routine service functions for individual banks and the government; their more important functions lie in the ability to control the supply of money and credit throughout the economy. These control functions are directed toward economic stabilization.

The impetus for establishing the Fed, it will be recalled, came from the periodic financial panics in the decades prior to 1914. In those decades the banks of the nation held their reserves of base money—coin and government-backed paper currency—as cash in their own vaults or in the form of deposits at other banks. There was no central pool of reserves, although the large national banks of New York City came close to being one. Reserves were necessary because the banks had a contract with their depositors to pay them base money on demand—in short, to cash their checks. The flaw in this system which produced the panics was that the total supply of base-money reserves in the nation was much less than the total amount of deposits that holders might wish to cash. Normally, the flaw was not apparent. People preferred the convenience of holding most of their money in the form of bank deposits subject to withdrawal by check rather than in coins and paper currency in normal times—that is, times when people did not doubt the ability of banks to cash their checks. When people started having doubts and these became widespread, panics occurred because many people tried to cash checks at the same time. There simply was not enough cash for the banks to cash all the checks and pay off the depositors at one time.

What was needed to prevent panics was a method of expanding the supply of reserves of base money during incipient panic situations in order to allay the fears of depositors. The Fed, in fact, embodied several such methods. Member banks of the Federal Reserve System were required from the start to hold some percentage of all their deposits in a reserve account at the Fed. These required reserves were not so much a pool of funds upon which the member banks might draw when cash was needed as a method of controlling the nation's total supply of money and bank credit. But by becoming members of the Fed, individual banks gained the privilege of borrowing from the Fed, using some of their own assets as collateral for their loans. In this way bank loans could be rediscounted or converted into cash at the Fed, which charged the banks an interest or discount rate that it could vary down or up depending on whether it wished to encourage or discourage the borrowing of the member banks.

Under this method there was no reason for a general financial panic to occur. A solvent but illiquid bank—one basically sound but short of cash reserves—could convert some of its illiquid assets into cash by rediscounting them at the Fed, the bankers' bank. Knowing this, the depositors of any properly managed bank would have no reason to doubt that their deposits would be converted into cash on demand, and so they would have no reason to demand cash en masse.

The Fed, in short, had the power to create additional bank reserves when it deemed them to be needed. The monetary base of the country no longer consisted simply of the sum of the coins, bullion, and paper currency that happened to be in the bank vaults at a given moment; now the monetary base could be expanded or contracted by the Fed almost at will. "Almost," because some restraints were placed on the Fed's power to create reserves. One was a qualitative restraint: only certain types of the assets of the member banks were eligible for rediscount at the Fed. The other was a quantitative restriction; just as member banks were required to hold reserves equal to some percentage of their deposit liabilities, so too the Fed was required to hold gold reserves equal to a percentage of its liabilities of Federal Reserve notes—a new form of paper currency in the United States in 1914—and similar fractional gold reserves against its own deposit liabilities that were the reserves of member banks. This seemed to base the revamped monetary and banking systems upon a foundation of gold, but in reality the flexibility of the Fed's powers marked another step away from a metallic-based system.

The rediscounting mechanism described above was initially regarded as the main method by which the Fed would control supplies of money and credit in the United States and eliminate the threat of financial panic. But controlling bank reserves through the rediscount mechanism relied on the willingness and ability of the member banks to take an active role; if the banks had adequate reserves from their own point of view they might refuse to borrow from the Fed even if the Fed thought more reserves and money were needed to achieve some broader economic objectives. The Fed by the 1920s had learned that it could *directly* control the quantity of bank reserves in existence by purchases and sales of open market securities, usually U.S. government securities. Open market purchases of securities by the Fed added to bank reserves as the private sellers deposited the Fed's checks in their own commercial banks. Similarly, the Fed's open market sales destroyed bank reserves as the purchasers drew down their commercial bank balances to pay the Fed. Control of total bank reserves through open market operations, although it appears to have been discovered as a by-product of other Fed activities, quickly became the chief method of implementing Fed policy. Appropriate open market policy is decided by the Federal Open Market Committee which, since 1935, has consisted of the seven members of the Board of Governors plus five of the twelve district bank presidents, always including the president of the Federal Reserve Bank of New York because of its strategic position in American finance.

In addition to the rediscounting and open-market mechanisms, the Fed since the 1930s has had one more general method of altering the money supply and credit conditions. This is its power to vary the percentage reserve requirements of member banks. Beginning in 1914 member banks were required to hold reserves of 7 to 13 percent of their demand deposits, the applicable rate for any individual being fixed and dependent on its classification as a central-reserve-city, reserve city, or country bank, and all member banks were required to hold reserves of 3 percent against time deposits. The Banking Act of 1935 gave the Fed the power to vary reserve requirements between these initial ratios and ratios twice as high, for example, 6 percent against time deposits. Changing reserve requirements does not affect the total of member banks reserves but it does affect the amount of reserves available to support new bank lending and so can have a pronounced impact on the money supply and credit conditions.

Because changes in reserve requirements have such pervasive impacts on all member banks they in general have been changed infrequently and then only by small amounts. Rediscounting was important in the early years of the Fed, but because it relies on member banks rather than the Fed to play the active role, it has declined in importance since the 1930s. As a result, open market operations, chiefly in the market for United States government securities, have since the 1930s been the primary method of Federal Reserve control over money and credit.

THE RECORD OF THE FED, 1914–50

The original objective of the Fed, as stated in the 1913 legislation creating it, was "to furnish an elastic currency." Some interpreted this to mean a currency that would expand when the economy was expanding and decline when the economy was contracting. Today this position of calling for the money supply to expand and contract according to the alleged "needs of trade" is rather discredited since it would serve to increase rather than reduce economic instability. But another interpretation of "elastic currency" made more sense. Financial panics occurred because one component of the money supply, the public's holdings of bank deposits, could not be exchanged on a large scale for the base money of currency and coins that had been created by the government. Through its powers of rediscounting member bank assets and purchasing open market securities the Fed could make the supply of base money elastic, thereby eliminating the major cause of panics. In situations leading up to panics prices were usually rising and unemployment was low, while during and after panics prices fell and unemployment soared. Hence,

FIGURE 22-1
Wholesale Price Index, 1914-78
(1967 = 100)

Price
Index
(1967 = 100)

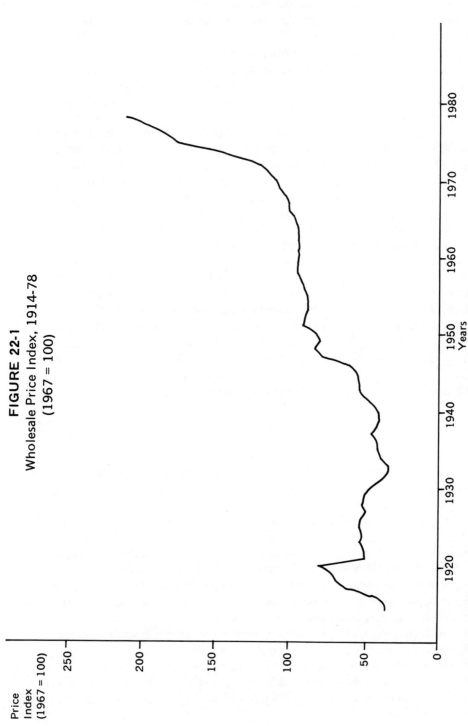

SOURCES: 1914-1970: U.S. Bureau of Census, Historical Statistics of the United States (1975), p. 199; 1971-78: Economic Report of the President (1978), p. 319.

the power of the Fed to prevent panics implied a power to make both the general level of prices and the level of unemployment more stable than they otherwise would have been. In time the stabilizing powers of the Fed were increasingly understood, and today it is widely recognized that the Fed has a responsibility to promote price stability and full employment.

The historical record of the Fed may therefore be explored by considering the stability of price levels and unemployment since 1914. Figures 22–1 and 22–2 show, respectively, the government's Wholesale Price Index and annual estimates of the percentage of the labor force unemployed. They show that the price level and the rate of unemployment have not been very stable in the years since 1914, although each of the two variables has had periods of relative stability.

Let us first examine the broad outlines of price level behavior. Three extended periods of rapidly rising prices are evident. In each of these periods the price level roughly doubled. The periods are 1915–20, 1939–48, and 1964–77; as this is written (1979) the last period of price inflation continues so that 1978, unlike 1920 and 1948, cannot be considered a terminal date. As was the case with pre-1914 periods of sharp price inflation in the United States, each of the post-1914 inflationary periods is associated with efforts on the part of the federal government to divert economic resources on a large scale from peacetime civilian uses to war-related activities. This happened during World War I (1914–18), during World War II (1939–45), and again during the Vietnam War from the mid-1960s to the early 1970s. A fourth period of price inflation, short but sharp, occurred between 1949 and 1951 and was related to the Korean War buildup. The last period of extended price inflation, which continues in the late 1970s, differs from the earlier ones in failing to come to a stop within three years of the cessation of formal hostilities.

Two periods of relatively stable prices are also evident from Figure 22–1. They are 1921–29 and 1951–64. The only extended period of price deflation since 1914 came during the Great Depression, 1929–33. A short but extremely steep decline in prices occurred during 1920–21, and the recovery of prices from their Depression lows in 1932–33 was interrupted by renewed deflation from 1937–39.

The unemployment situation in the United States since 1914 appears from Figure 22–2 to exhibit considerable instability. On a year-to-year basis this is certainly the case. However, it is well to keep in mind two points when examining this particular historical record. The first is that the outstanding feature of the unemployment record since 1914 is the very high rate of unemployment in all the years between 1929 and 1942, in other words between the onset of the Great Depression and the active involvement of United States forces in World War II. The second point to remember is that "full employment" in a mobile society, in which at any given time many workers are moving into and out of the labor force and from one job to another, is normally defined by economists as some

FIGURE 22-2

Unemployment as Percentage of Civilian Labor Force, 1914-78

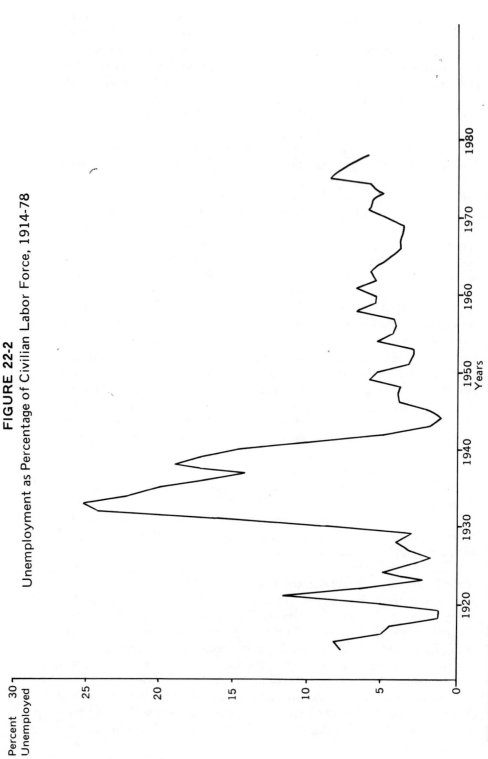

SOURCES: 1914-70: Bureau of Census, _Historical Statistics of United States_ (1975), pp. 126, 135; 1971-78: _Economic Report of the President_ (January 1979), p. 217.

positive level or range of measured unemployment. This accepted or normal level or range may vary over time and also from observer to observer at a given time. Today various economists (but perhaps few workers) take 4 to 5 percent unemployment as representing a reasonable approximation to full employment, a situation where the unemployed represent those in the movement between jobs. If we broaden this range to 3–6 percent, it follows that over much of the period from 1914 to the late 1970s, especially for most of the period since World War II, the American economy has not been far from full employment. The years 1930–41 are the outstanding exception, with protracted deviations from reasonably full employment; the other years when the unemployment rate exceeded 6 percent were 1914–15, 1921–22, 1961, and 1975–79. Unemployment actually fell below the 3 percent lower bound of our range in three wartime periods (1918–19, 1943–45, 1952–53) and one peacetime year (1926).

To what extent have decision makers at the Federal Reserve contributed to the observed record of economic stability (and instability) of prices and unemployment? And to what extent may the decision makers and their institution be praised or faulted for their performance by the economic historian? These are complex questions. The Fed began its work with the responsibility of furnishing an elastic currency in order to prevent financial panics, and in time it assumed responsibilities in the areas of price stability and employment. Evaluation of the Fed's record must be tempered by recognition of its changing responsibilities and its changing understanding of its mission. Such evaluation must also be tempered by a realization that the Fed is not the only institution with responsibilities in the areas of economic stability, and by a recognition that the course of human events, for example, a war, may have caused the Fed to sacrifice its normal economic objectives in order to solve what seemed to be more pressing problems.

With these points in mind, let us examine the record of the Fed from its inception through 1950, reserving study of its more recent history for a later point in the chapter. How the Fed may best use its powers to promote economic stability is still a matter of some dispute among scholars of monetary policy. Some argue that the Fed should use its instruments of control—primarily open market operations that create and destroy bank reserves—to vary interest rates and other credit market conditions that have an impact on short-run production, employment, and pricing decisions in the economy. Others emphasize the numerous lags between the time an instability problem develops and the time any responding change in monetary policy has its effects on the economy. These scholars are skeptical of the Fed's ability to promote economic stability through short-term policy changes. Taking a longer view, they contend that the Fed should act to promote a steady expansion of the money supply at a rate consistent with high employment, price stability, and the nation's long-term rate of economic growth. The two views of how the Fed should

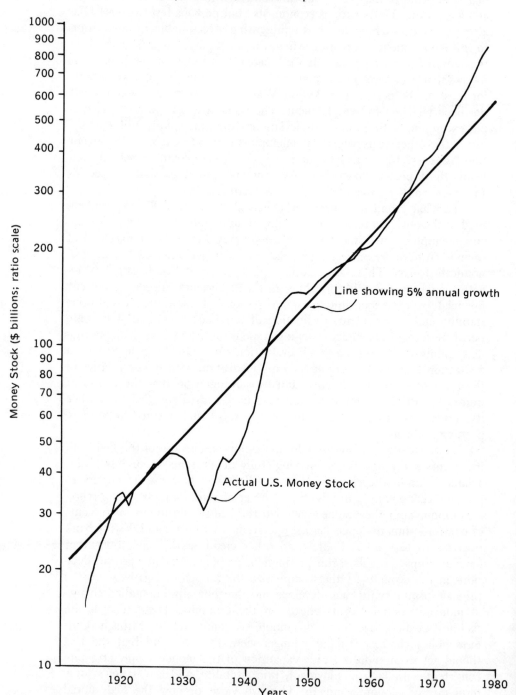

FIGURE 22-3
Money Stock, 1914-1978
($ billions; ratio scale)

Money Stock ($ billions; ratio scale)

Line showing 5% annual growth

Actual U.S. Money Stock

Years

SOURCES: Data are for M₂ (currency and all commercial bank deposit holdings of the public) in December of each year. 1914-60: Milton Friedman and Anna J. Schwartz, <u>A Monetary History of the United States</u> (Princeton, 1963), pp. 708-722; 1961-78: <u>Economic Report of the President</u> (1979), p. 251.

make monetary policy decisions are not necessarily as opposed as they might seem; an actively changing monetary policy attempting to overcome short-run destabilizing forces in the economy could very well be consistent with steady monetary growth over a period of years or decades.

No one knows with any exactitude what the optimal long-run trend of monetary growth should be. Nor is it likely that the optimal rate would be constant over time. Yet one can gain some insight into the Fed's role in the nation's price and unemployment histories since 1914 by comparing actual monetary growth trends with an assumed constant rate of expansion. Data for such an endeavor are graphed in Figure 22–3, which presents the actual behavior of the American money supply since 1914 along with a trend line representing a constant rate of expansion of 5 percent per year. Five percent is selected both because it approximates the trend of the actual monetary series since 1914 and because it is close to the actual behavior of the monetary series during two periods which, as we have already seen, were characterized by a fair degree of price-level stability and reasonably full employment, namely the periods 1921–29 and 1951–64.

The two periods of rapid and protracted price inflation between 1914 and 1950 were associated with World Wars I and II. From 1914 to 1920 wholesale prices rose at an annual rate of 15 percent, and from 1939 to 1948 they rose at an annual rate of 9 percent. In each period the price level roughly doubled. In each case the inflation was supported by Federal Reserve management of the United States money stock; it increased at an annual rate of 13 percent during the World War I episode and by 12 percent during the era of World War II. The cumulative impact of these rapid rates of monetary expansion on the growth of the money supply can be seen and compared with our assumed standard of 5 percent per year in Figure 22–3.

The mechanisms through which the money supply expanded were similar in the two great wars. Before the United States entered actively into the hostilities, in 1917 and in late 1941, respectively, the primary impetus to monetary expansion came from gold flows into the United States, mostly from Europe, to finance purchases of war materiel. The Fed in effect created dollars to purchase the gold, and this added to the nation's monetary base. Once the United States entered the wars, huge deficits in the federal government's budget were financed by Fed-created dollars which underwrote the government's bond sales to the public, to the banking system, and to the Fed itself.

The Fed's decisions in these war periods were undoubtedly such as to cause monetary expansion and price inflation. But the Fed did not really have much latitude in its decision making during these national emergencies. The goal of moderate monetary expansion consistent with price stability was compounded by abnormal gold inflows and ultimately sacrificed in favor of the more pressing and immediate goal of financing successful war efforts. Greatly enlarged government spending in the two wars, accompanied by accommodating money creation by the Fed, did have beneficial effects on the rate of unemployment. Unemployment, high when each of the war periods began (see Figure 22-2), was rapidly reduced by government spending and monetary expansion. However, for the same reasons that it would be wrong to be unduly critical of federal budgetary and monetary policies in causing inflation during the war eras, so it would be wrong to give them major credit for promoting full employment in these years. The policies were motivated more by major overseas political events impinging directly on the national security of the United States than by the conscious efforts of the decision makers in the Fed to promote national economic goals.

In the two decades of peace, 1919–39, the Fed's record in promoting economic stability in the United States was rather erratic. Moderate and stable monetary expansion marked the years from 1921 to 1929, and in these years, which have been termed "the high tide of the Reserve System," the price level was also stable and unemployment was low. Both before and after these years, however, major instabilities plagued the American economy, and the Fed had a large role in them. During 1919, after World War I had ended, the Fed took no effective action to stem the continuing inflation; instead, perhaps to aid Treasury financial goals by maintaining low yields and high prices on government securities, the Fed maintained its discount rate at below-market levels and thus encouraged the nation's banks to make more loans based on Fed-created dollars. Inflation accelerated. Sensing this, rather belatedly, the Fed moved abruptly against inflation. The rediscount rate—then the Fed's major policy weapon —had been held at 4 percent in New York from April 1918 to November 1919. Between then and June 1920, it was raised in a series of abrupt steps to 7 percent where it remained for nearly a year. There were signs that the economy was already weakening as the Fed took these actions. Their effect was to turn a decline into a rout. The money supply exhibited one of its very rare declines on a year-to-year basis, falling some 9 percent from 1920 to 1921. Unemployment soared from 4 percent to nearly 12 percent in the same period, and wholesale prices in 1921 on average were nearly 40 percent below their 1920 levels (See Figures 22–1, 22–2, and 22–3). The price collapse of 1920–21 was perhaps the sharpest in United States history.

A greater disaster, largely because it was much more protracted, began to unfold at the end of the decade of the 1920s. Between 1929 and 1933, the real product, the wholesale price level, and the money supply of the American economy all fell to approximately two-thirds of their 1929 levels, and unemployment rose from just over 3 percent to 25 percent. This was the Great Depression. Recovery from it was not fully completed in terms of full employment and a return to price levels of the 1920s until the United States entered World War II. It appears from an analysis of the record that the Federal Reserve System played a large role in bringing on the Depression, in making it as severe as it was, and, finally, in delaying the recovery.

The stock market crash of October 1929 is widely associated with the onset of the Great Depression. While the direct effects of the crash on the economy's subsequent performance are often exaggerated, its indirect effects through the negative impact it had on the confidence of businessmen, consumers, and investors were of some importance. And it is evident that the Federal Reserve played a role in the Wall Street collapse. In 1927 the Fed, worried over signs of emerging weakness in the economies of the United States and Europe, adopted a policy of monetary ease by lowering discount rates and engaging in open market purchases. These measures, however, came at a time when the volume of credit created for speculation in stocks was rising, and it served to stimulate even more of that speculation. By 1928 the economy had recovered from its pause, so that the continuing securities speculation on credit became a major concern of the Fed. Discount rates were raised (in New York) to 5 percent in July 1928, their highest level since 1921. The speculation continued into 1929, despite the fact that the economy again showed signs of weakness. Concentrating on the speculation, the Fed again raised its discount rate to 6 percent in August 1929. By then the nation's monetary base had been more or less constant for two years, and the expansion of the money supply had slowed from its rates of growth in the mid-1920s. Two months later came the crash on Wall Street.

There followed a year or so of continued securities liquidation, contraction of both money and prices, and rising unemployment. While matters were not yet out of hand, the Fed did next to nothing to reverse these developments. The monetary base was in fact allowed to decline somewhat in 1930. The Fed's inactivity in this period seems to have followed from its interpreting declining market interest rates as a sign of monetary ease, even though the supply of money was falling. During this first year of the Depression, economic and psychological factors were reducing the demand for money; rather than letting the supply of money decline in response to these factors (in line with the perverse notion of elastic currency), the Fed should have maintained or increased the money supply and eased credit costs in the process. Such a policy decision might have mitigated or even reversed the initial economic decline.

Instead, the money and banking situation turned from bad to worse. In the fall of 1930 began the first of three great waves of bank failures that culminated in the proclamation of the nationwide bank "holiday" by President Roosevelt in March 1933, when all United States banks were ordered closed for about a week. Bank failures had been frequent during the 1920s, but there were major differences between these failures and the failures of 1930–33. There were many more bank failures per year during the latter period and, more important, unlike the failures of the 1920s, the 1930s failures were accompanied by sizeable declines in the money supply. The number of bank suspensions during the early 1930s was as follows: 1930—1,350; 1931—2,293; 1932—1,453; and 1933—4,000. Not all suspending banks failed, but the majority never reopened.

The bank failures of the early 1930s played a major role in causing the Depression to become Great because they caused much of the severe monetary contraction. Failures had this effect primarily because of their impact on the behavior of the nation's banks and the public. Witnessing other banks failing, remaining banks became very cautious in their lending policies and attempted to hold more reserves per dollar of their deposit liabilities. In fact the ratio of deposits to reserves at commercial banks fell from over thirteen in 1929 to less than eight in 1933. Even more severe were the effects of bank failures on the nonbank public. Americans held more than eleven dollars of commercial bank deposits per dollar of coins and paper currency in 1929; by 1933, reflecting the growing distrust of banks, this proportion had fallen to about five dollars.

The Fed might have prevented, or at least counteracted, these contractive effects of bank and public behavior on the money supply through sufficient increases in the monetary base of currency and bank reserves, but it did not. In short, the Fed did not do in the 1930s what it had been designed to do in 1913, namely, to prevent banking panics and failures by making the monetary base elastic in times of incipient banking panic. The reasons why the Fed failed to discharge this duty are far from clear. Some have argued that the Fed's attention was focused on international considerations such as the United States gold position; this could explain why the Fed acted to tighten credit conditions in late 1931, in the midst of the Depression, when gold began to leave the United States due to European fears about maintenance of the international gold standard. If so, the Fed's priorities were misdirected. Others argue that the Fed did not move to stem bank failures because it thought they were attributable to bank mismanagement, as for example in the form of questionable loans both at home and abroad during the economic euphoria of the 1920s. To some extent, some banks may have been mismanaged. But during the deflation of the early 1930s even the soundest bank loans could become questionable since lenders and borrowers could not have fully anticipated the drop in prices, production, and demand. In the end, it must be concluded that the Fed was negligent in allowing the Depression to become as Great as it did.

A final episode from the troubled interwar era once again illustrates that creation of an institution with broad powers to promote economic stability carries with it an ability to contribute as well as to instability. The episode is the sharp recession of 1937–38, which shows up very clearly in historical charts of the money supply, price levels, and unemployment rates. Recovery from the depths of the Great Depression in 1933 was exceedingly rapid during the subsequent four years. In this recovery, the money supply, wholesale prices, and total output of the economy in real terms all increased at annual rates of 10 to 12 percent. While unemployment was still distressingly high at over 14 percent of the labor force in 1937, the rate of unemployment had fallen by over 10 percent from the 1933 level.

The Fed was essentially passive during the recovery of 1933–37. Increases in the money supply emanated from two other sources. One was the increase in the United States gold stock resulting in part from devaluation of the dollar in 1934 (which made the then nationalized gold stock worth more dollars) and in part from gold imports from 1934 to 1937. When during 1933 and early 1934, the Treasury purchased virtually all of the monetary gold held by Americans and then purchased gold flowing in from abroad in 1934–36, it did so in effect by printing the money and increasing the monetary base. The second source of monetary growth was a rise in the proportion of its money holdings that the public held in the form of bank deposits. When the public lost confidence—with good reason —in the banking system during 1929–33, its ratio of deposits to currency fell sharply and accentuated the collapse of the money stock. But after the bank "holiday" of 1933, the ratio began to rise; it went from less than 5 in that year to more than 7 by 1936. An important reason for the public's renewed confidence in bank money was federal insurance of bank deposits. The Banking Act of 1933 authorized creation of the Federal Deposit Insurance Corporation (FDIC), which began to insure deposits on 1 January 1934. Few if any of the innovations in American governmental economic policies induced during the 1930s by the Great Depression have had a more lasting and beneficial impact on economic stability than the FDIC.

The confidence of the nation's bankers, however, did not return so quickly after the debacle. Instead of creating more deposits per dollar of bank reserves held, after 1933 they continued to increase the ratio of reserves to deposits. In doing so, the bankers conformed to a pattern characteristic of the aftermath of earlier banking panics. But the rise of bank reserves in relation to deposits continued until 1940, an uncharacteristically long time. In any case, by the middle of the 1930s, the Fed, noticing the recovery of prices and production, began to worry that the excess reserves of bankers carried a potential threat of runaway inflation. At the same time, the Fed received enlarged powers; the Banking Act of 1935 gave the Fed the power to vary the reserve requirements of member banks between the percentages that had been fixed in 1917 and twice those percentages.

The Fed did not wait long to employ its new powers in attacking the source of its worry. Between August 1936 and May 1937, bank reserve requirements were doubled in three steps. These policy decisions in effect wiped out a large part of the bank's desired excess reserves; in an effort to rebuild them the banks contracted their lending. As a result the money supply contracted, prices fell, and unemployment rose, from 14 percent in 1937 to 19 percent in 1938. From that time forward the Fed was more cautious in changing reserve requirements.

Federal Reserve monetary policy was the primary method of economic stabilization used by governmental decision makers from 1914 into the early 1930s. The persistence of the Great Depression then caused many to doubt whether monetary policy could by itself give rise to an effective stabilization program. This view was exaggerated. But when it grew out of an examination of what the Fed had actually done rather than what it might, and probably should, have done, the view contained an element of validity. In any case the Depression era marked the beginning of experimentation with other types of stabilization policies. These were in the fiscal area. They consisted of varying governmental expenditures and taxation with a view to promoting stabilization goals. The framework of modern fiscal policies rests on the foundation of a greatly enlarged share of government spending and revenues in the American economy and so we shall now examine how that foundation itself has emerged in the twentieth century.

Expanding Economic Roles of Government

In 1913, just before the outbreak of World War I in Europe, all levels of government—federal, state, and local—in the United States absorbed about 7 percent of the GNP in purchases of goods and services. In 1976, on the two hundredth anniversary of independence, that share had more than tripled to almost 22 percent. In other words, government has grown considerably faster than the economy as a whole.

However dramatic this fundamental change in the nature of the American economy may seem, it understates if anything the magnitude of the expanded role of government. For in discharging their economic functions governments do more than purchase goods and services. They also transfer purchasing power from some individuals and groups to others. The most important of these transfer payments today fall under the rubric of social security and social welfare; workers and their employers, for example, pay payroll taxes to government; it then uses the funds to pay pension and health benefits to the elderly and retired, and other benefits to the disabled and unemployed. Another important category of transfer payments is interest on governmental debt; here funds are transferred from taxpayers to holders of the debt. Governments also transfer large sums between themselves; federal revenue sharing with, and other grants-in-aid to, state and local governments are examples. Intergovernmental transfers ought properly to be netted out if we are to get a true picture of the relative growth of total government spending—purchases of goods and services plus transfer payments—in this century. If we do so, the results indicate (see Table 22–1) that total government spending increased from roughly 8 percent of GNP in 1913 to almost 34 percent of GNP in 1976. In this comparison the share of government quadruples, which implies that total governmental spending has grown still faster than governmental spending on goods and services alone.

TABLE 22-1
Total Government Spending on Goods and Services and Transfer Payments as Percentage of GNP, Selected Years, 1913-76

Year	Purchases of Goods and Services (%)	Transfer Payments[1] (%)	Total Government Spending (%)
1913	7.1	0.5	7.6
1929	8.5	1.4	9.9
1939	14.9	4.7	19.6
1949	14.9	8.1	23.0
1959	20.0	6.9	26.9
1969	22.2	8.3	30.5
1976	21.6	12.3	33.9

[1]Excludes intergovernmental transfer payments; includes transfer payments to individuals and foreigners, net interest paid on government debt, and net subsidies of government enterprises.

SOURCES: Calculated from data in U.S. Bureau of Census, Historical Statistics of the United States, Colonial Times to 1970, Bicentennial Edition, parts 1 and 2 (Washington, D.C., 1975), and Economic Report of the President (Washington, D.C., 1976 and 1977).

The share of total government spending in GNP has increased steadily since 1913. But the largest relative increase came during the 1930s, the decade of the Great Depression. In that one decade of minimal economic growth the share of total goods and services purchased by government nearly doubled, while the share of governmental transfer payments more than tripled.

Another significant aspect of the growth of government in relation to the economy concerns the relative role of government on the federal, state, and local levels. Some pertinent data are shown in Table 22–2. The federal government has grown by far the fastest. Its total spending was only about 2 percent of GNP in 1913, and approximately 20 percent in 1976. However, in terms of purchases of goods and services the myriad state and local governmental units absorbed much more of the GNP

TABLE 22-2
Federal and State and Local Government Spending by Category, as Percentage of GNP, Selected Years, 1913-76

| | Federal Government | | | State and Local Governments | | |
| | Purchases of Goods and Services (%) | | | | | |
Year	Total	National Defense	Transfer Payments[1] (%)	Purchases of Goods and Services (%)	Transfer Payments (%)	Total
1913	1.8	0.8	0.1	5.3	0.5	5.8
1929	1.4	0.7	1.1	7.1	0.4	7.5
1939	5.7	1.3	3.0	9.1	1.8	10.9
1949	7.9	5.1	7.2	7.0	0.8	7.8
1959	11.1	9.4	6.2	9.0	0.7	9.7
1969	10.4	8.2	7.5	11.8	0.8	12.6
1976	7.9	5.2	11.5	13.7	0.8	14.5

[1]Excludes federal grants-in-aid to state and local governments since these are included in state and local governmental spending.
   SOURCES: Calculated from data in U.S. Bureau of Census, Historical Statistics of the United States, Colonial Times to 1970, Bicentennial Edition, parts 1 and 2 (Washington, D.C.: 1975) and Economic Report of the President (Washington, D.C.: 1976 and 1977).

in 1913 than did the federal government, and that is also the case in the 1970s. During the 1950s and 1960s the cold war and the hot wars in Korea and Vietnam swelled federal defense spending in relation to GNP (as, of course, did World Wars I and II, whose effects on spending are not indicated in Table 22–2), but in the 1970s the share of GNP devoted to national defense has fallen back to post-World War II levels. The relative decline of defense spending has been more than offset by rapidly rising transfer payments (especially in the area of old-age assistance) in recent years, so that the share of total federal spending in GNP has continued to increase. Many economists have argued on the basis of the historical trends that with the exception of national defense, state and local governments have an advantage over the federal government in purchasing most goods and services needed to provide Americans with what they desire from the public sector, while the federal government has an advantage in operating the transfer payment mechanisms connected with broad social welfare programs.

WHY HAS GOVERNMENT GROWN?

This is a question that puzzles many young people and disturbs more than a few Americans when they confront evidence of the rapid expansion of government in this century. Historical analysis sheds much light on the question. The growth of government in the twentieth century represents a relative expansion in the domain of collective or social decision making as compared with private decision making in the economic life of the nation. We may, therefore, approach an understanding of the growth of government if we examine when and in what areas government has expanded and see why these areas involve collective as opposed to private decision making.

Broadly speaking, the largest areas of government spending today are social welfare, defense, education, and economic development including transportation. In this last area, one important reason for the growth of government spending during the early part of this century was the spread of the automobile and other motor vehicles. These popular innovations created a demand on the part of Americans for more and better streets, roads, and highways. The demand was met through collective decision making because in most respects that was the efficient solution. Once a road is built the social cost of having one more automobile on it is negligible (unless the road is congested), and so it would in general be economically inefficient to charge tolls. However, unless private decision makers could charge tolls they could not hope to recoup the costs of building the road. Similar arguments apply to a wide range of governmental activities that are worth doing but would not be done, or would be done to a less-than-efficient extent, through private decision making.

Education is another area of greatly enlarged government spending. Americans have demanded more and better education in this century. Governmental spending on education has increased steadily from a little over 1 percent of GNP in the early part of the century to roughly 6 percent in the 1970s. And during these decades the average educational attainments of adult Americans, in terms of years of schooling completed, have about doubled from six to twelve years. The usual argument for collective decision making in the area of education is that the social benefits of education exceed its private benefits to individuals; given that assumption, individuals considering only their own private benefits and costs will not decide to buy as much education as they ought to from the social standpoint. Hence, society, through government, collectively decides to produce and subsidize education.

The provision of transportation facilities such as streets, roads, and highways as well as the provision of most formal education in the United States is primarily an activity of state and local governments. Together the two cover a good part of the increase in the share of GNP accounted for by these levels of government in the twentieth century.

Spending on national defense, as the data in Table 22–2 indicate, has made up the largest part of the federal government's purchases of goods and services in recent decades. Increased spending for defense therefore accounts for a good part of the increase in government's share of GNP in this century. Defense against foreign aggression is the classic example of a public good, one provided through collective decision making. Efforts to defend one citizen's person and property from external threats almost necessarily defend the person and property of other citizens as well; the latter cannot be excluded from the benefits of defense. That being the case, individual decision makers, in looking after their own personal interests, might well be tempted to purchase very little defense. They would like to be defended but they can easily reason that others' defense expenditures would defend them as well, so they might just as well become free riders. Since all might reason in this fashion, the result could very well be less defense than anyone wanted. Hence, defense becomes recognized as a public good and its proper amount is determined through collective decision making.

The twentieth century has been plagued by war. That fact in itself has caused large increases in defense spending on a number of occasions. To understand the longer-term rise, however, it is necessary to recognize that the United States, as a result of its relative economic position, has assumed a leading role in the defense planning of a large part of the world. Also, improved technologies of war and peace have decreased the traditional space and time barriers between nations, while at the same time ideological and other differences between nations have given rise to a series of continuing threats to peace. Given these geopolitical and economic factors, an increase in U.S. defense spending in relation to GNP becomes understandable. The relative increase, however, topped out in the 1950s; as a fraction of GNP, defense spending has dropped rather sharply since that time. But the defense share remains well above its pre-World War II levels, and given the international tensions in Europe, the Middle East, and the Far East, it is likely to remain there for the foreseeable future.

Finally, we consider the broad area of social welfare spending by government. This is the area of government activity that has increased most rapidly in the twentieth century, especially in recent decades. Earlier data on the rising share of governmental transfer payments in relation both to total governmental spending and to GNP reflect this trend. By far the largest transfer activity, and also the largest single category of federal government spending today, is that of income security, of which the Social Security program of old-age, survivors, and disability insurance (OASDI) comprises the major part. Federal budget outlays on income security, financed largely by payroll taxes on today's workers and employers, rose from $37 billion to $137 billion between 1969 and 1977, and are projected to rise to $160 billion by 1979. Thus, federal spending for income security will more than quadruple in the 1970s in current dollars. After income security, the next largest category of federal spending in the area of social welfare is health. Health spending will also more than quadruple during the 1970s; it rose from $12 billion in 1969 to $39 billion in 1977, and is projected at $50 billion in 1979. Today federal spending for income security and health makes up more than 40 percent of all federal budget outlays and approximates 10 percent of the nation's GNP.

Half a century ago most federal programs in the areas of income security and health did not exist, and for those that did exist spending was negligible in relation either to the federal budget or to GNP. Thus, their growth during the past half century furnishes a problem of interpretation of the first magnitude. Programs such as Social Security were born during the Great Depression, in the "relief, recovery, and reform" activities of President Roosevelt's New Deal. It is not difficult to understand why Americans became more concerned with income security at that time; unemployment was high and the wealth of many citizens had been greatly reduced by the economic disaster. Still, longer-term forces were at work. A century of economic development had changed the United States from an agricultural and commercial society to an industrial, highly mobile, and technologically oriented society with substantially higher average incomes. In such a society old-age security could not so easily be internalized within the family or community as it had been on the family farm. At the same time improvements in health technologies combined with declining population growth were giving rise to relative increases in the ranks of the elderly.

These longer-term trends, which were as visible in the 1930s as they are today, have created a growing demand for programs of income security and health-care delivery. But they do not necessarily call for relative increases in government spending and collective decision making. Private decision making acting through markets can and long has delivered programs of insurance for income security and a variety of health services. Experience shows, however, that not everyone would, or in certain cases could, buy these products voluntarily. Powerful social groups, acting through political rather than market forms of decision making, appear to have decided that all who are capable should buy these products and that those who are not capable should receive them through governmental assistance. The unprecedented increases in governmental spending on social welfare in the past half century must then reflect a fundamental political and social change. This change is in the direction of increased governmental intervention and increased pressures for mandatory redistribution of income between individuals and groups of Americans; these pressures seem large to upper income groups, but are moderate in the eyes of most western Europeans.

CHANGING METHODS OF GOVERNMENT FINANCE

The growth of government spending in this century has been accompanied by substantial changes in public finance. Taxes normally finance 90 percent or more of American government spending (the remainder is financed from borrowing and from specific charges), and it is in taxation that the greatest changes have occurred. It will be recalled from chapter 7 that during the years 1789–93, the first federal administration under the Constitution enacted a tax program consisting of customs duties on imports and internal excise taxes. More than a century later, with these two types of taxes yielding more than 90 percent of revenue, the federal tax structure, despite the radical changes of the Civil War, was little changed. In 1913 customs duties supplied 47 percent of federal tax revenue while 46 percent came from excises, chiefly on alcoholic beverages and tobacco products. By way of contrast, in 1976 these mainstays of nineteenth-century federal finance furnished only about 7 percent of federal tax revenue, customs duties yielding a little over 1 percent and excises not quite 6 percent.

The fundamental change in taxation that has taken place since 1913 may be described compactly as a shift away from indirect taxation and toward direct taxation. All taxes are, of course, ultimately paid by people, not by alcohol, tobacco, imports, or even corporations. But when these latter products and institutions are taxed, people pay the taxes indirectly. When taxes are levied on incomes, wealth, or payrolls, individuals are taxed directly. Direct taxation in the United States received a major boost at the beginning of the period we are now studying. This came in the form of the Sixteenth Amendment to the Constitution, which in 1913 explicitly granted Congress the power to levy income taxes without apportionment among the states according to population. Article 1, section 9, of the Constitution had stated that "no capitation or other direct tax shall be laid, unless in proportion to the census. . . ." Before 1895 federal income taxes were considered constitutional. But from 1895 to 1913 a conservative Supreme Court made these taxes unconstitutional. The mild 1 percent tax on the net income above $5,000 of every corporation organized for profit enacted in 1909 illustrates the problems faced in income taxation before 1913. This tax was actually a measure pushed by conservatives in order to stave off growing pressure for taxation on individual incomes, but since in law the corporation is a legal person, opponents of the 1909 tax claimed that it violated the Constitution. The United States Supreme Court sustained the corporation tax but only by declaring that it was an excise rather than a direct tax.

An individual income tax with progressive rates of up to 7 percent was enacted in 1913 to go along with the corporation income tax. The advantages and flexibility of these relatively new forms of taxation were quickly demonstrated during World War I. Tax rates were raised to unprecedented heights—as high as 77 percent in the case of individual incomes over $1 million—and by the end of the war the two taxes were bringing in well over one half of all federal tax revenue. Tax rates were reduced after the war along with government spending, but the income taxes continued to provide the major part of federal revenue until the Great Depression so drastically reduced incomes. Of the two, the corporation tax was the larger yielder until World War II. Before that war the individual income tax, with exemptions that were high in relation to average incomes, was largely a tax on the well to do rather than a mass tax paid by nearly all income recipients. During World War II, as in World War I, tax rates were raised to unprecedented levels—as high as 94 percent on individual incomes over 200,000 dollars. More important, the income tax exemption was reduced to 500 dollars per person, and the tax collections were changed from a deferred basis, under which all income tax due for one year was paid at a single time during the following year, to a current or withholding basis. As a result of these changes and of rising incomes, the number of persons paying income tax rose from only 4 million in 1939 to 43 million in 1945. And much of the pain of having to pay income taxes was alleviated by withholding.

During the 1930s another form of direct taxation began to assume importance in federal finance. In 1935 the Social Security Act established federal old-age and unemployment insurance for many workers with financing provided by payroll taxes on the workers and their employers. By 1940 payroll taxes accounted for some 14 percent of federal revenue. This percentage was about the same two decades later, even though the payroll tax base had increased greatly, because rising individual and corporate income tax collections were the main supports of enlarged federal spending in these years. Since 1960 the revenue situation has altered. The share of federal tax revenues coming from payroll taxes has risen from 14 percent in 1960 to 22 percent in 1970 to 32 percent in 1977. Moreover, in 1977 Congress enacted large increases in payroll taxes to take effect in 1979 and subsequent years, while individual and corporate taxes (which respectively furnished 45 percent and 14 percent of federal tax revenue in 1977) were reduced in 1977 and 1978. Hence payroll taxes, having passed the corporate income tax in importance during the 1960s, seem to be on their way to becoming the leader in tax revenue production at the federal level in the 1980s.

Changes in the nature of state and local taxation since 1913 have not been as dramatic as at the federal level. During the nineteenth and early twentieth centuries general property taxes were the chief supports of state and local finance. This remains true at the local government level where the property tax furnishes about 80 percent of tax revenue, down little from its 90 percent share in 1913. The main tax change at the state level in this century has been a shift from property taxation to general sales, excise, income, and payroll taxes. Property taxes accounted for about half of state tax revenue early in the century, a position occupied by sales and excise taxes from the 1930s to the present. And, cognizant of the federal example, many states and some local governments have adopted income taxes.

Considering all levels of government together, the twentieth century decision to change the emphasis of taxation is clear. In 1913, income and payroll taxes provided American governments with less than 2 percent of their tax revenues. In the late 1970s these taxes add up to approximately 70 percent of total tax revenues. This fundamental alteration in the emphasis of American taxation is part and parcel of changing concerns about growth and welfare. Economic growth, with its continuing increases in specialization and hence interdependence of economic and social relations, has created a correspondingly great increase in the demand for public services and collective solutions to problems. At the same time growth enlarges the base of money incomes and the technologies for governments to tax that base with a high level of efficiency. Given the growth of demand for public services the shift to income and payroll taxes was inevitable. Today's levels of federal tax revenue could not be raised through customs duties and domestic excise taxes on products such as alcohol and tobacco. If such taxes were tried the rates would have to be increased many times over and to do this would so reduce the demand for the products that the result could easily be less rather than more revenue. The gain from the changed emphasis of taxation has promoted economic equity and security, but may have reduced the rate of economic growth. High income and payroll taxes can affect the supply of and demand for labor, impair executive mobility, and affect the supply of investable funds and the patterns of personal investment. Recent tax laws have tried to counteract some of these adverse effects by granting liberal depreciation allowances and a credit for investment outlays on equipment.

Most economists recognize that many of the public goods and services financed mainly by taxation are of substantial value and contribute to, as well as reflect, economic growth. They also realize that a part (perhaps an increasing part) of the motivation for the changed stress of taxation has been to attempt to increase economic welfare by redistributing income between groups and generations of Americans, for example, between the high-income groups and the low-income groups, and between the employed and the unemployed or the retired population groups. If our tax system were based on the benefit principle, taxpayers would receive from the government only the goods and services for which they would pay in taxes. But the increased redistributional emphasis of taxation, seen perhaps most clearly in the unusually large growth of transfer payments on the expenditure side of government ledgers, demonstrates that many Americans believe taxation should be based on the ability to pay principle and on raising the relative welfare levels of low income and low property groups. As a result statesmen and citizens today have the problem of reducing the conflict between the two goals of economic growth and increased welfare that long have gone together instead of conflicted in American economic history.

Fiscal and Monetary Policies Since the 1930s

Fiscal policy may be described as governmental decision making regarding the levels and types of public expenditures and taxes and, as a consequence, the balance of the government budget. Although economists and public officials were long aware that increased public spending had beneficial effects on employment and business conditions when and where the funds were expended, significant use of this insight to attack an economy-wide problem did not come until the Great Depression of the 1930s. Then it came in response to the magnitude of the disaster and was also motivated by the seeming inability of Federal Reserve monetary policy, discussed earlier in this chapter, to bring about the recovery of employment and production. It took the form of a host of federal spending programs that were part of President Roosevelt's New Deal program of relief and recovery.

At the same time that the New Deal was searching for fiscal solutions to unprecedented economic problems, a conceptual and theoretical rationale for its fiscal activities came forth from the pen of the eminent British economist, John Maynard Keynes. Keynes's 1936 book, *The General Theory of Employment, Interest and Money*, demonstrated in theory that an economy could become stuck in an equilibrium of less than full employment, and also that attempts to raise employment through increases in the supply of money could prove ineffective if the new money were in some sense hoarded rather than spent. In the United States, the persistence of high levels of unemployment throughout the 1930s, as well as the tendency of banks to hold large excess reserves rather than engage in more lending, appeared to be explained by Keynes's theories. From a theoretical explanation of the fact of depression, Keynes proceeded to a theory of how it might be alleviated or even ended. The problem, as he saw it, was a level of spending or aggregate demand on the part of consumers, investors, and government that was insufficient to employ all of the economy's resources, and the solution was for government to eliminate the deficiency of demand by its own increased spending or by tax reductions to stimulate consumer and investor spending. The government budget would have to be deliberately unbalanced—expenditures would have to exceed tax revenues—at least until resources were fully employed.

Keynes's novel ideas had a limited impact on United States fiscal policy in the 1930s. The New Deal spending measures before 1938 were based more on pragmatic experimentation than on a new conceptual framework of economic theory. But by the end of World War II, the idea that massive government budget deficits could end a depression and restore full employment appeared to have been demonstrated. The Keynesian framework of thinking was by then widely accepted, and economists and public decision makers were prepared to refine and adapt it to problems of maintaining economic stability.

NEW DEAL FISCAL POLICY IN DEPRESSION AND WAR

Despite large increases in federal spending and federal budgetary deficits under the New Deal of the 1930s, recovery from the Depression was painfully slow. The strong expansion of 1933–1937 came to an end in the severe recession of 1937–1938. Hence, in 1939 the unemployment rate still was 17.2 percent of the labor force and the real GNP (adjusted for price level changes) was about the same as it had been a decade earlier despite an increased population and labor force. Those who favored limited government and balanced budgets while distrusting both Roosevelt and Keynesian ideas could point to this record in support of their view that deficit spending was ineffective or counterproductive or both. Supporters of the New Deal, however, could argue that the deficit spending policies had substantially improved the economic situation following the trough of the Depression in 1933.

We know today that both these views are open to correction. The budget deficits of the 1930s, both before and after the New Deal, were largely the result of the Depression rather than a means of recovery from it. The collapse of incomes during the early years of the Depression led to declining tax revenues for all levels of government taken together, and this revenue decline, more than expenditure increases, produced the deficits of those years. In response to the revenue fall-off, taxes at both the federal and state-local levels were actually increased during the Depression. The Federal Revenue Act of 1932, for example, coming in the depths of the Depression, constituted a substantial tax increase. Later, New Deal deficits tended mainly to offset the demand-reducing effects of this and other tax increases, so that the stimulating effects of government fiscal policies on the economy, while considerable up to 1937, were not as high as they could have been.

A useful way to evaluate the stimulus of fiscal policies, some economists have argued, is to see what they imply about the balance of the government budget at a full-employment level of national income rather than at actually existing levels. Since tax collections depend to a large extent on income, they tend to increase as the economy expands from lower income or output levels with unemployment toward higher levels of production consistent with full employment of resources. It was from this point of view that New Deal fiscal policies were deficient; the actual budget deficits of the 1930s would, with unchanged levels of government spending, have turned into substantially lower deficits or perhaps even surpluses had the economy been at or near full employment. In effect,

American governments counteracted with increases in tax rates much but not all of what they were attempting to do with increased spending, and this is part of the explanation of why recovery from the Great Depression was good from the contemporary point of view up to 1937 and in 1939–40, but not adequate from the point of view of many present-day economists.

World War II fundamentally altered the climate of governmental decision making and provided, under rather unusual conditions, a demonstration of what an active fiscal policy might accomplish. While tax revenues swelled through increases in tax rates and the imposition of new taxes, government spending increased much more rapidly, giving rise to unprecedented budget deficits. The Federal Reserve was effectively taken out of the economic policy decision-making framework by being assigned the rather mechanical task of creating enough money to keep interest rates on government securities issued to finance the deficits at low levels. At the same time, resources were diverted from civilian consumption and investment to war purposes through a system of rationing and price controls. The effects of these policies of spending and regimentation on economic recovery are clearly revealed in the labor unemployment record. As of 1940, unemployment had not been below a rate of 14 percent since 1930 (see Figure 22–2). In 1942 it fell to less than 5 percent and in 1944 to less than 2 percent. To be sure, the wartime policy mix was directed by considerations other than economic recovery. But viewed as an experiment in large-scale fiscal stimulation, it contained rather clear lessons for economists, policy makers, and indeed the public at large.

EVOLUTION OF STABILIZATION POLICY, 1946–61

The fiscal lessons of depression and war were not wasted. Soon after World War II, the Employment Act of 1946 committed the federal government to the promotion of economic stability. The act stated that "it is the continuing policy and responsibility of the Federal Government to use all practical means . . . to promote maximum employment, production, and purchasing power." Although the specified goals were subject to different interpretations, they were widely thought to mean full employment, healthy economic growth, and stability of the general price level. To aid federal decision makers in formulating policies to achieve these goals, the act established the President's Council of Economic Advisers and a congressional Joint Economic Committee composed of members of the Senate and House of Representatives.

A view of many Americans at the end of World War II was that the depressed economic conditions of the 1930s would return once heavy wartime spending was phased out. Government spending on goods and services did in fact contract sharply, from an annual rate of almost $100 billion in early 1945 to only $35 billion a year later. But only a brief and mild recession resulted, and in 1946, as wartime price controls began to be dismantled, the economy recovered very rapidly. The driving force of the expansion was pent-up demand on the part of consumers who had accumulated large amounts of liquid assets—money, near monies, and government securities—during the war while at the same time stinting on consumption. With the war over, consumers went on a buying spree. Prices rose rapidly from 1945 to 1948, and unemployment remained below 4 percent.

The business cycle was, however, not a thing of the past. In 1948–49, as again in 1953–54, 1957–58, and 1960–61, the economy slipped into recessions characterized by rising rates of unemployment and unutilized productive capacity. The important point to be made here is that these post-World War II recessions were much milder in terms of price and unemployment changes than were the pre-war downturns of 1920–21, 1929–33, and 1937–38 (see the earlier Figures 22–1 and 22–2). A good part of the credit for the greater economic stability in the two decades after World War II can be given to the expanded economic role of government, including its explicit commitment to promote stability. But one must be careful not to exaggerate the role of the government's commitment to economic stability; in the two postwar decades this commitment may have had more effect on the confidence of consumers, investors, workers, and businessmen than on some government policy decisions taken to promote stability when it appeared to be threatened.

To understand why this was likely the case in these decades, we must distinguish between automatic and discretionary stabilization policies. In the fiscal area much of the credit for greater postwar stability must be given to the so-called automatic fiscal stabilizers rather than to discretionary policy actions. Expenditure stabilizers include such payments as unemployment compensation, which go up when unemployment rises in recessions and then down as the economy improves. Tax stabilizers move in the opposite direction; individual and corporate income tax receipts as well as payroll and excise tax collections fall off with declining incomes during economic downturns and then rise as the economy recovers and moves toward full employment. The result is that fluctuations in the balance of the government's budget automatically stabilize private incomes relative to fluctuations in the GNP. With the relative growth of government in the economy since the 1930s, these automatic fiscal stabilizers have played a large role in stabilizing the economy.

Discretionary fiscal policy actions—conscious decisions to vary government spending or taxes for purposes of promoting economic stability—were generally less important than the automatic budgetary changes up to the 1960s except for the high taxes levied during the Korean War and the important increases in social security taxes imposed in the 1950s. When discretionary changes occurred, they were often motivated by considerations other than economic stability. Thus, the 1948 income tax cut, which helped stabilize the economy during the 1948–49 recession, was based more on a general public desire for lower taxes than on the impending recession, and was in fact passed over the veto of President Harry S. Truman who worried about the inflation, still a fact in 1948, and the need to finance cold-war defense expenditures. And tax cuts during the 1953–54 recession had been previously scheduled and probably would have taken place without the recession; the recession itself, many scholars believe, was caused by rapid reductions in federal spending at the end of the Korean War. In the 1957–58 and 1960–61 recessions and subsequent recoveries, Eisenhower's concern over inflation led to rather tight fiscal and monetary policies.

While the theory of discretionary fiscal policy for economic stabilization was increasingly understood by economists and policy makers in these years, practical political and economic constraints severely limited its application. Concern over balanced budgets was one of these constraints. Even when budget deficits were the result of a weak economy, many considered them to represent profligacy on the part of government and called for reduced expenditures or higher taxes. Those measures, of course, were the direct opposites of what stabilizing fiscal policy called for. Then there were the real and inescapable lags in policy implementation: the need for action had first to be recognized, then appropriate action had to be decided upon and implemented, and finally, with a still further lag, would come the economic effects of the action. Such constraints and such lags limited the ability of discretionary fiscal decisions to reduce the duration or severity of the postwar recessions. Fortunately, the automatic stabilizers were not so limited.

An independent monetary policy in the postwar era was not possible until 1951, when the Federal Reserve was released from its obligation, entered into during World War II, to peg interest rates on government securities at low levels. After 1951 monetary policy attempted to promote economic stability by "leaning against the wind." In practice this meant that the Fed attempted to restrain an expanding economy from becoming overheated in the inflationary sense, and to counteract recessions through low-interest, easy-money policies. The main concern of the Fed during the 1950s was inflation, and in retrospect, it did a creditable job on this front. Toward the end of the decade, however, the Fed's image became a bit tarnished as it contributed to the 1957–58 recession by failing to ease monetary and credit conditions until after the downturn had occurred, and then contributed to the 1960–61 recession by an excessively restrictive policy in 1959, before recovery from the previous recession was complete. These short-term policy mishaps led many economists to conclude that the Fed was slowing down the nation's economic growth through too much restraint on monetary expansion.

THE TRIUMPH OF THE NEW ECONOMICS, 1961–66

The recessions of 1957–58 and 1960–61, coming so close together, furnished important political issues during the presidential campaigns of 1960. When John F. Kennedy won a narrow victory after a campaign in which he promised "to get the country moving again," he brought with him to Washington economic advisers who believed more strongly than their predecessors in active fiscal and monetary policies to promote stability and economic growth. Increases in defense spending aided the recovery from recession in 1961, and in 1962 a tax credit and liberalized depreciation rules were implemented in order to encourage business investment. In 1963, when unemployment was still over 5.5 percent, the Kennedy administration proposed a major cut in individual and corporate income taxes. Coming at a time of substantial deficit in the federal budget, this was a startling proposal to many observers. But the case for the tax cut was carefully explained by administration economists, and the measure became law under Lyndon Johnson, Kennedy's successor, in early 1964. The effect was salutary. Between 1963 and 1966 the economy grew at rates of 5 to 6 percent per year, prices were relatively stable, and unemployment declined from 5.7 to 3.8 percent. Monetary policy cooperated with fiscal policy during the long expansion of the early 1960s; rather than leaning against the wind as it had in the 1950s, the Fed allowed the money supply to expand at moderately higher rates in these years.

The new economists were justifiably proud of their economic management by the mid-1960s. They could point out to those few who remained unpersuaded that despite the tax cuts (or rather because of the tax cuts!) the federal deficits of fiscal 1965 and 1966 were substantially reduced from 1962–64 levels. Rising income more than offset the decline in income tax rates as far as federal revenue was concerned. The new economists held out the promise of an even better future. Because tax revenue would continue to rise with an expanding economy, they argued that it would be possible and even necessary for the government again and again to cut tax rates or expand government spending without increasing taxes. These fiscal dividends would have to be paid in order to prevent the federal budget from becoming a drag on economic expansion.

A TIME OF TROUBLES, 1966–75

The glowing prospects held out by the new economists were not soon to be realized. By the end of 1965 increased military expenditures accompanying growing American involvement in the Vietnam conflict threatened to overstimulate an economy already working at full capacity. The rate of price-level inflation began to accelerate. In these circumstances fiscal policy should have been reversed, with tax increases or with reductions in nonmilitary spending. But such policy measures were not forth-coming in 1966, nor even recommended by the administration until 1967. Hence, the Federal Reserve took the lead in fighting inflation with tight money policies in 1966. The so-called credit crunch of that year, marked by rapidly rising interest rates and low monetary growth, did slow down the economy by early 1967, but increases in military spending and in spending on President Lyndon Johnson's Great Society programs quickly restored the inflationary expansion. Congress considered the administration's proposal to enact a temporary tax surcharge in 1967, but the economic slowdown early in that year delayed passage of the measure until mid-1968. Many economists predicted that since the tax surcharge of 1968 was billed as temporary, it would have little effect on private spending. The economists were right. Unfortunately, the Federal Reserve was not persuaded by their prediction, and it was anxious to avoid another credit crunch such as that of 1966. So in 1967 and 1968 the money supply was allowed to grow at very high rates compared to earlier years. Inflation accelerated, and since full employment continued, the fight against inflation became the main goal of economic policy for the new Nixon administration in 1969.

The major policy decision of 1969 was to reduce inflation gradually, so as not to increase unemployment, through limited monetary and fiscal restraint, including the Tax Reform Act of 1969. This decision did not prove effective in restraining inflation, but it did serve to cause a recession with rising unemployment in 1970–71. The conjunction of inflation and rising unemployment, called "stagflation," proved very disturbing to economists and policy makers because it seemed inconsistent with accepted theories and, indeed, with most experience in how the economy worked. The introduction of ideas of inflationary expectations appeared to reconcile the conjunction of inflation and rising unemployment, in theory. The policy need thus become how to reduce or eliminate inflationary expectations. In August 1971, the Nixon administration decided upon the extreme policy of a temporary wage-and-price freeze to be followed by several phases of more or less flexible wage and price controls lasting until 1974. This policy seemed to have some success in 1972, as unemployment declined and the rate of inflation was somewhat reduced from 1968–70 levels. (In 1972 Nixon also tried to hold down the budget and increase the taxation.) The decline in unemployment proved to be very limited and this led the Federal Reserve to pursue a policy of rapid monetary expansion from 1972 to early 1974. This action by the Federal Reserve by itself would likely have accelerated price inflation in these years within the actual loose framework of price controls. But the inflation rates of 1973–74, the highest in over a quarter century, were aided by the external shocks of crop failures abroad and markedly higher petroleum prices as a result of the behavior of the OPEC cartel.

Once again, as in 1969–70, attempts to restrain inflation with mone-

FIGURE 22-4

Public Debt (Interest-Bearing) of the Federal Government, 1914-1979
(in billions of dollars)

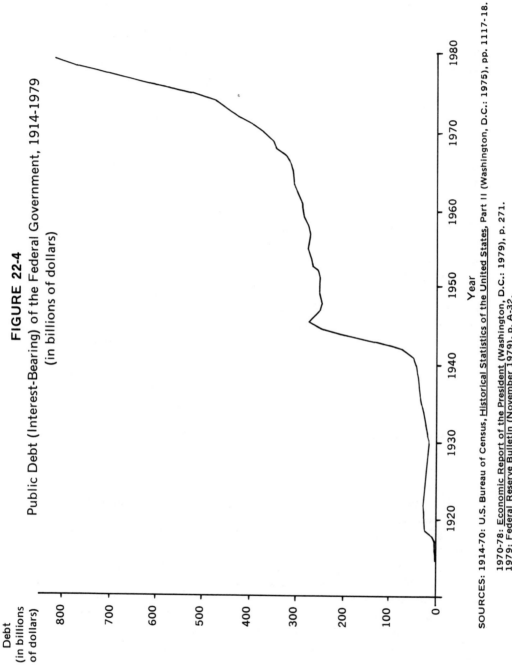

SOURCES: 1914-70: U.S. Bureau of Census, <u>Historical Statistics of the United States</u>, Part II (Washington, D.C.: 1975), pp. 1117-18.

1970-78: <u>Economic Report of the President</u> (Washington, D.C.: 1979), p. 271.
1979: <u>Federal Reserve Bulletin</u> (November 1979), p. A-32.

tary and fiscal policies produced instead a recession marked by rising unemployment and continued price increases. The recession of 1974–75, was, in fact, the worst since the 1930s, with negative real growth in the two years and unemployment averaging 8.5 percent in 1975. A timely tax cut in 1975 coupled with a return to the high rates of monetary expansion of 1972–73 helped to end the recession after mid-1975, but the ensuing recovery during 1975–78 was again marked by continued inflation, only moderate declines in unemployment, and a continued explosion of the national debt as huge federal deficits were financed by borrowing (see Figure 22–4).

Two developments during 1978, each rooted in past failures of governmental economic policies, appeared to signal to some the beginning of a return to policy approaches that were common in the United States before the twentieth century's expansion of government in economic affairs. One was a popular movement, termed by some a "taxpayers' revolt," to limit government spending and tax revenues. Prompted by some successes of this movement in state and local referenda, some national political leaders began to jump on the bandwagon of economy in government and to push proposals that would limit federal employment, spending, and taxes. The second development resulted from the battering of the United States dollar in foreign exchange markets as holders of dollars sold them in large amounts because they feared that American economic policies would continue to cause "stagflation," the conjoining of rapid inflation with high unemployment, weak capital formation, and limited real economic growth. In response the Fed moved to support the dollar through monetary stringency and the Carter administration promulgated a wide-ranging program that included voluntary guidelines for wage and price increases, further measures to support the dollar's international value, and a renewed pledge to hold down government employment and spending in the hope of reducing drastically the large federal deficits of the previous decade. These developments reflected a growing belief among some national leaders and many middle-class Americans that government policies of ever larger spending programs, deficit finance, and money creation to ease the interest-rate pressures that the deficits would otherwise generate in financial markets were more a cause of the stagflation problem than a solution to it. But doubts remained as to whether the new policies would be effective, and, given the record of the previous decade and the lack of action to limit the huge oil imports, whether they would even be carried out if, as many feared, they contributed to a recession in 1979 or 1980.

Thus, as we end our survey of experience with economic stabilization policies up to the late 1970s, there exists a notable lack of confidence on the part of most governmental decision makers concerning their ability to achieve simultaneously acceptable levels of unemployment and inflation. The confidence of many, but not all, of the new economists of the early 1960s that such a goal was attainable by known means accompanied by political willpower seems to have been shattered.* But throughout the time of troubles the obligation of government to achieve overall economic stability was not seriously questioned and remained as one of the more important changes of twentieth-century American economic history.

Conclusion

A greatly expanded economic role of government has been a dominating characteristic of American economic history in this century. In terms of the absorption of resources and products, the allocation of resources, and the distribution of income, public decision-making processes have increased relative to private ones. In this chapter we have explored some of the reasons for this epochal change. We have also noted that sometimes the results of governmental economic decisions have not been what was hoped for or expected. It is too early to tell whether the developments of the late 1970s—the "taxpayers" revolt by middle- and high-income groups, the moves to deregulate areas of economic life previously regulated, the renewed calls for economy in government and for a reversal of fiscal and monetary policies that have contributed to inflation—represent a relative resurgence of private decision making as happened during the early part of the nineteenth century, the post-Civil War period, and the 1920s. Some current signs point in such a direction, but counter-movements by labor unions and groups dependent on welfare should not be discounted. Moreover, the energy crisis, as it becomes more acute, will lead the national government to increasingly massive programs of energy development and control that will require more taxes, government spending, and government regulations.

One thing does seem certain. The twentieth-century rise of governmental economic decision making is not a new phenomenon in American history. Our study has analyzed the crucial role of public economic decisions at many times in the American past. And, as J. R. T. Hughes has argued in a recent and perceptive book, government interference in private market activity is as old as settlement by Europeans on these shores.† The real question facing Americans is not whether government should intervene in private economic affairs—it always has and always will —nor even what is the proper mix of private and public decision making. Rather, the important question is what kinds of public and private decisions will be made. American economic history demonstrates that, for

---

* James Tobin, The New Economics One Decade Older (Princeton, N.J.: Princeton University Press, 1974) is a powerful defense of the new economics.
† Jonathan R. T. Hughes, The Governmental Habit: Economic Controls from Colonial Times to the Present (New York: Basic Books, 1977).

the most part, private decisions guided by market information have been conducive to economic efficiency, economic growth, unprecedented profits for the enterpreneurial classes, and great gains in material welfare for the majority of the population. Government has played a positive role in public education, health, justice, defense, land distribution, transportation, public finance, and care for the aged and the unemployed. Sometimes governmental decisions—especially in the twentieth century—have worked in opposition to market decisions. Hughes argues that what public decision makers wanted to achieve was an interference with market outcomes that they, or at least large groups of their constituents, deemed undesirable. Hughes uses this insight to explain how many, but not all, public economic interventions have grown up in a patchwork fashion and have often worked at cross-purposes to one another as well as to whatever market forces were dominant at a given time. Given the complexity of the economy and the pressure of powerful business, farm, and labor groups, certain public decisions to intervene in the market economy have become increasingly ineffective.

Further insight into the decision-making problems of the modern economy can be gained from the pathbreaking research of Herbert Simon, the 1978 Nobel laureate in Economics. In his noted book, *Administrative Behavior*, Simon described the functions of social organization as follows:

> 1. Organizations and institutions permit stable expectations to be formed by each member of the group as to the behavior of the other members under specified conditions. Such stable expectations are an essential precondition to rational consideration of the consequences of action in a social group.
> 2. Organizations and institutions provide the general stimuli and attention-directors that channelize the behaviors of the members of the group, and that provide those members with the intermediate objectives that stimulate action.*

Both the economy and the government (or federal, state, and local governments), even though huge in size, can be considered organizations in Simon's sense. Private economic decisions within certain limits and areas, seem to be rather effectively guided by market stimuli; the regularities of economic behavior, moreover, make for relatively stable expectations concerning the results of economic decisions for the individual or group decision makers. Governmental decisions, in contrast with competitive, but not oligopolistic markets, exercise economic control by contravening market processes. In the words of Hughes, "What was controlled traditionally were four crucial points in the flow of economic transactions: (1) number of participants in a given economic activity, (2) conditions of participation, (3) prices charged by participants either for products or services,

---

* Herbert A. Simon, *Administrative Behavior: A Study of Decision-Making Processes in Administrative Organization*, 2nd ed. (New York: Macmillan, 1959), pp. 100–101.

and (4) quality of products or services." * In addition certain governmental decisions to control have arisen, and have been administered, on an irregular *ad hoc* basis not usually conducive to the formation of stable expectations by the private sector. Unlike private economic decisions in highly competitive markets, but like those in markets dominated by strong farm, business, or labor oligopolies, public decisions have the greatest impact on individuals and groups other than the decision makers. In some such cases governmental interventions may impede, and in certain areas have impeded, efficiency and growth.

This need not be the case. As Charles Schultze, Chairman of President Carter's Council of Economic Advisers, has pointed out in a poignantly titled book, *The Public Use of Private Interest*, the emphasis of government economic policies could be changed so as not to work at cross purposes with market-guided behavior.† Instead of attempting to command and control the activities of private decision makers in ways that are inimical to their economic interests, government policy makers could make decisions that would accomplish the desired objectives by giving private decision makers economic incentives to behave in socially desired ways. As our study of the evolution of the American economy has shown at numerous points, public decisions usually were most successful when they provided the nation's private decision makers with economic incentives for the promotion of growth and welfare. But our study also shows that public decisions in crises of war and depression and in matters affecting the general welfare, such as public education, unemployment, and pollution, require collective decision making. The test of wisdom lies in the proper mix and quality of private and public decision-making mechanisms.

SUGGESTED READINGS

A concise introduction to twentieth-century economic policy problems is Robert Aaron Gordon's *Economic Instability and Growth—The American Record* (New York: W. W. Norton, 1977). The formation and subsequent record of the Federal Reserve System are treated at great length in Milton Friedman and Anna J. Schwartz, *A Monetary History of the United States, 1867–1960* (Princeton: Princeton University Press, 1963); a compact yet illuminating discussion of the Fed's record is given in a chapter of Douglas Fisher's *Money and Banking* (Homewood, Illinois: Richard D. Irwin, 1971). For a discussion of alternative interpretations of monetary policy at the time of the Depression of 1929–33, see Peter Temin, *Did Monetary Forces Cause the Great Depression?* (New York: W. W. Norton, 1976).

The expansion of government spending and taxation is described in Sidney Ratner, *Taxation and Democracy in America* (New York: John Wiley, 1967) and in consider-

* Hughes, *The Governmental Habit*, p. 9.
† Charles L. Schultze, *The Public Use of Private Interest* (Washington, D.C.: Brookings Institution, 1977).

able detail by Paul Studenski and Herman Krooss, *Financial History of the United States*, 2nd ed. (New York: McGraw-Hill, 1963), but for greater analysis of the long-term issues, see Richard A. Musgrave and Peggy B. Musgrave, *Public Finance in Theory and Practice*, 2nd ed. (New York: McGraw-Hill, 1976), and Joseph A. Pechman, *Federal Tax Policy*, 3rd ed. (Washington, D.C.: Brookings Institution, 1977).

On the theory, practice, and results of stabilization policies, the following works are of value for general and specific insights: E. Cary Brown, "Fiscal Policy in the Thirties: A Reappraisal," *The American Economic Review* 46 (December 1956), 857–879; Rudiger Dornbisch and Stanley Fischer, *Macro Economics* (New York: McGraw-Hill, 1978); Walter W. Heller, *New Dimensions in Political Economy* (Cambridge: Harvard University Press, 1964); Wilfred Lewis, Jr., *Fiscal Policy in the Postwar Recessions* (Washington, D.C.: The Brookings Institution, 1963); Arthur M. Okun, *The Political Economy of Prosperity* (New York: W. W. Norton, 1969); David J. Ott and Arthur F. Ott, *Federal Budget Policy*, 3rd ed. (Washington, D.C.: Brookings Institution, 1977); and Herbert Stein, *The Fiscal Revolution in America* (Chicago: University of Chicago Press, 1969).

The questions regarding past, present, and future governmental economic decisions raised in the conclusion of this chapter may be explored in more detail by reading John K. Galbraith, *The Affluent Society* (Boston: Houghton Mifflin, 1958); Jonathan R. T. Hughes, *The Governmental Habit: Economic Controls from Colonial Times to the Present* (New York: Basic Books, 1977); Abba P. Lerner, *The Economics of Control* (New York: Macmillan, 1944); Charles L. Schultze, *The Public Use of Private Interest* (Washington, D.C.: Brookings Institution, 1977); James Tobin, *National Economic Policy* (New Haven: Yale University Press, 1966); and Lowdon Wingo and Alan Evans, eds., *Public Economics and the Quality of Life* (Baltimore: Johns Hopkins University Press, 1977).

Every economic historian will benefit from the new insights in Herbert Simon's Nobel Prize lecture, "Rational Decision Making in Business Organizations," *American Economic Review* 69 (September 1979).

INDEX